Zero Lower Bound Term Structure Modeling

Applied Quantitative Finance series

Applied Quantitative Finance is a new series developed to bring readers the very latest market tested tools, techniques and developments in quantitative finance. Written for practitioners who need to understand how things work "on the floor," the series will deliver the most cutting-edge applications in areas such as asset pricing, risk management and financial derivatives. Although written with practitioners in mind, this series will also appeal to researchers and students who want to see how quantitative finance is applied in practice.

Also available

Chris Kenyon, Roland Stamm
DISCOUNTING, LIBOR, CVA AND FUNDING
Interest Rate and Credit Pricing

Marc Henrard
INTEREST RATE MODELLING IN THE MULTI-CURVE FRAMEWORK
Foundations, Evolution and Implementation

Adil Reghai
QUANTITATIVE FINANCE
Back to Basic Principles

Ignacio Ruiz
XVA DESKS: A NEW ERA FOR RISWK MANAGEMENT
Understanding, Building and Managing Counterparty and Funding Risk

Leo Krippner
ZERO LOWER BOUND TERM STRUCTURE MODELING
A Practitioner's Guide

Zero Lower Bound Term Structure Modeling

A Practitioner's Guide

Leo Krippner

ZERO LOWER BOUND TERM STRUCTURE MODELING

Copyright © Leo Krippner, 2015.

All right reserved.

First published in 2015 by
PALGRAVE MACMILLAN®
in the United States—a division of St. Martins Press LLC,
175 Fifth Avenue, New York, NY 10010.

Where this book is distributed in the UK, Europe and the rest of the world,
this is by Palgrave Macmillan, a division of Macmillan Publishers Limited,
registered in England, company number 785998, of Houndmills,
Basingstoke, Hampshire RG21 6XS.

Palgrave Macmillan is the global academic imprint of the above companies
and has companies and representatives throughout the world.

Palgrave® and Macmillan® are registered trademarks in the United States,
the United Kingdom, Europe and other countries.

ISBN: 978–1–137–40832–7

Library of Congress Cataloging-in-Publication Data

Krippner, Leo.
    Zero lower bound term structure modeling : a practitioner's
    guide / Leo Krippner.
        pages cm.—(Applied quantitative finance)
    Includes bibliographical references and index.
    ISBN 978–1–137–40832–7 (hardback)—
    ISBN 1–137–40832–4
    1. Finance–Mathematical models. 2. Structural equation modeling.
    3. Economics, Mathematical. I. Title.

HG176.5.K75 2015
339.5'30151953–dc23   2014027511

A catalogue record of the book is available from the British Library.

Design by Newgen Knowledge Works (P) Ltd., Chennai, India.

First edition: January 2015

10 9 8 7 6 5 4 3 2 1

Printed in the United States of America.

To my parents, Jim and Teresa Krippner, and my partner, Iris Claus.

Contents

Figures

Tables

Preface

Around early 2011, I was considering undertaking some work relating the risk premiums obtained from yield curve models to currency movements, in particular for the New Zealand dollar versus the US dollar. The problem was that the yield curve models I had available were Gaussian, and were therefore not appropriate to apply to US yield curve data constrained by the zero lower bound (ZLB). I mentioned to my manager that I had a simple idea to fix the problem, using bond options, which had occured to me previously when undertaking my Ph.D. thesis. His reply was something like, "You had better work quickly on that, because US interest rates might not remain at zero much longer." Similarly, after developing my initial shadow/ZLB yield curve framework, a US economist mentioned something like the following to me in conversation: "We hope that interest rates will remain briefly at zero, and then we can continue to use standard Gaussian models with an appropriate footnote for the exceptional period."

Four years later, and the United States along with most other major economies still have their policy interest rates effectively at zero. Furthermore, expectations from yield curve data and market surveys are for interest rates to remain at or close to zero at least well into next year, and longer for some economies. While fortunate from the perspective of my research (and providing yet another anecdote on the forecasting prowess of economists), the fundamental challenges of reconsidering the traditional frameworks for financial markets and operating monetary policy effectively based on unconstrained interest rates remains an open topic.

In this book, I outline shadow/ZLB yield curve models as one convenient perspective for undertaking those reconsiderations. As I explain, my shadow/ZLB yield curve framework is relatively easy to apply and interpret, it maintains the theoretical basis of Gaussian yield curve models with a ZLB adjustment, and it has already been used to resolve practical issues faced by users of Gaussian models at the ZLB. However, as I also discuss, there are a number of questions that remain to be further investigated. For example, what is the best shadow/ZLB yield curve model specification in principle and/or for practical applications, either overall or for particular topics? Also, how should one best obtain and use the information from shadow/ZLB yield curve models?

By giving readers the background and the details on how to develop and apply shadow/ZLB yield curve modeling, my hope from this book is that the answers to these and related questions can be added more quickly to the now steadily expanding ZLB yield curve literature. The ultimate aim is to deliver general, practical, and robust frameworks that can be applied to the real-world challenges faced by central bankers and financial market participants in the current ZLB environment. And even after the present period of ZLB constraint does eventually pass, there is no telling when they might be required again in the future.

Acknowledgments

I thank the Reserve Bank of New Zealand, and Christie Smith and John McDermott in particular, for allowing me to undertake this book project, and for providing me with flexible working arrangements that made it possible. I also thank my colleagues in the Economics and Financial Market Departments of the Reserve Bank of New Zealand, both for their general support and encouragement during the project and for their comments and suggestions on earlier drafts of chapters. In particular, I offer special thanks to Nick Sanders, who provided many insightful comments on the draft material and its exposition that greatly improved the final manuscript. Michelle Lewis, Christie Smith, Roger Perry, Michael Reddell, Ben Wong, and Jason Wong also provided welcome feedback during internal discussion and presentations.

I also thank those who have commented on my articles, papers, and presentations that form a large part of the book. Hopefully without any serious omissions, and subject to my disclaimer further below, the list includes Tobias Adrian, David Andolfatto, Ray Atrill, Michael Bauer, Luca Benzoni, Martin Berka, Carl Chiarella, Jens Christensen, Edda Claus, Stefania D'Amico, Toby Daglish, Kris Dawsey, Frank Diebold, Michael Dotsey, Greg Duffee, Craig Ebert, Sandra Eickmeier, Richard Finlay, Ippei Fujiwara, Pedro Gomis, Arne Halberstadt, Danica Hampton, Hibiki Ichuie, Laura Jackson, Ben Jacobsen, Mike Jones, Edward Kane, Daniel Kaufman, Don Kim, Martin Lalley, Ahn Le, Wolfgang Lemke, Canlin Li, Hai Lin, Mico Loretan, Kim Martin, Antonio Moreno, Emanuel Moench, Chris Neely, Maurice Obstfeld, Aaron Pancost, Monica Piazzesi, Peter Phillips, Marcel Priebsch, Jean-Paul Renne, Roberto Rigobon, Glenn Rudebusch, Eric Schlogl, Ken Singleton, Helena Stapf, Jari Stehn, Lars Svensson, Dan Thornton, Kozo Ueda, Yoichi Ueno, Julia von Borstel, Chris Waller, Martin Weale, Min Wei, Tomasz Wieladek, John Williams, Jonathan Wright, Cynthia Wu, Feng Zu. To that list, I add the participants at the following presentations: the 2011 Reserve Bank of New Zealand conference, the 2012 New Zealand Finance Colloquium, the 2012 New Zealand Econometrics Study Group meeting, the 2012 Australasian Finance and Banking Conference, the 2012 Auckland Finance Meeting, the 2013 mid-Western Finance Association meeting, the 2013 New Zealand Association of Economists conference, the 2013 National Australia Bank Superannuation FX Conference, the 2014 NBER East Asian Seminar on Economics (2014), and seminars at the Bundesbank (2011), the University of Waikato (2012), the Federal Reserve Bank of St. Louis (2012), the Federal Reserve Board (2012), the University of Pennsylvania (2012), the Federal Reserve Bank San Francisco (2012), the Bank of New Zealand (2012), the Federal Reserve Bank of

Chicago (2013), the Federal Reserve Bank of New York (2013), Goldman Sachs (2013), the Bank of Japan (2013), the Reserve Bank of Australia (2013), the Sydney Financial Mathematics Workshop (2013), Stanford University (2013), and the Hong Kong Monetary Authority (2014).

I especially thank James Bullard for his early and ongoing encouragement on the topic, and Scott Richard for both his early observations that ultimately led me to the greatly simplified derivation of my shadow/ZLB yield curve framework in chapter 4, and also for his welcome comments on the manuscript.

My biggest thanks go to my partner, Iris Claus, who read the entire draft manuscript and offered suggestions from many perspectives, including editing, technical, and exposition. Her support and encouragement was also invaluable during the entire project.

Finally, I thank the production team at Palgrave Macmillan, particularly Brian Foster who initiated the project, and Sarah Lawrence, Bradley Showalter, Alexis Nelson, Kristy Lilas, and Laurie Harting. They have all helped greatly to make the task of writing this book less daunting than it might have been otherwise.

As usual, I offer the disclaimer that the opinions and any errors in the book are my own, and they should not be attributed to anyone I have mentioned above.

Selected List of Notation

I have listed the notation by chapter largely in the order in which it is introduced, and I have also provided subheadings to put the notation in context.

This is not an exhaustive list of the notation used in book; it is list I have selected based on the criterion that the notation is commonly used between different models and/or in multiple chapters. For example, the GATSM notation for specification and estimation carries over to K-AGM and B-AGM models. Other notation used in the book is generally self-contained within each chapter.

Chapter 2

Gaussian affine term structure models (GATSMs):

- t, time.
- τ time to maturity in the context of interest rates and forward rates, and horizon in the context of future short rates.
- $r(t)$, short rate at time t.
- $r(t+\tau)$, future short rate (at time $t+\tau$ as a function of horizon τ).
- $R(t,\tau)$, interest rates (at time t and as a function of time to maturity τ).

Shadow/ZLB-GATSMs:

- $r(t)$, shadow short rate.
- $r(t+\tau)$, future shadow short rate.
- $\underline{r}(t)$, ZLB short rate.
- $\underline{r}(t+\tau)$, future ZLB short rate.
- $R(t,\tau)$, shadow interest rates.
- $Z(t,\tau)$, physical currency option effect on interest rates.
- $\underline{R}(t,\tau)$, ZLB interest rates.

Chapter 3

GATSM specification and derivation:

- $\mathbb{P}$, denotes the physical probability measure.
- $\mathbb{Q}$, denotes the risk-adjusted probability measure.
- N, number of state variables.
- a_0, constant.

- b_0, constant $N \times 1$ vector containing the weights for each state variable $x_n(t)$.
- $x_n(t)$, state variable n.
- $x(t)$, $N \times 1$ vector containing the N state variables $x_n(t)$.
- θ, constant $N \times 1$ long-run level vector under the $\mathbb{P}$ measure.
- κ, constant $N \times N$ mean-reversion matrix under the $\mathbb{P}$ measure.
- σ, constant $N \times N$ standard deviation matrix.
- $N(0,1)$, unit normal distribution.
- $\tilde{\theta}$, constant $N \times 1$ long-run level vector under the $\mathbb{Q}$ measure.
- $\tilde{\kappa}$, constant $N \times N$ mean-reversion matrix under the $\mathbb{Q}$ measure.
- $\exp(-\tilde{\kappa}\tau)$, matrix exponential of the $N \times N$ matrix $-\tilde{\kappa}\tau$. The result $\exp(-\tilde{\kappa}\tau)$ is itself an $N \times N$ matrix.
- $\sigma\sigma'$, $N \times N$ covariance matrix for innovations to $x(t)$.
- $\tilde{\mathbb{E}}_t[r(t+\tau)|x(t)]$, expected path of the short rate conditional on $x(t)$, under the $\mathbb{Q}$ measure
- $\omega(\tau)$, standard deviation of the future short rate distribution under the $\mathbb{Q}$ measure.
- $VE(\tau)$, volatility effect.
- $f(t,\tau)$, GATSM forward rate at time t as a function of time to maturity τ.
- $R(t,\tau)$, GATSM interest rate.
- $a(\tau)$, time invariant component of $R(t,\tau)$.
- $b(\tau)$, $N \times 1$ vector of interest rate factor loadings.
- $P(t,\tau)$, GATSM bond price.

GATSM estimation using the Kalman filter:

- Δt, time increment between yield curve data observations.
- t as a subscript indicates an index for time from 0 to T in integer steps. Each integer step represents a time increment Δt.
- K, the number of interest rates of different times to maturity τ_1 to τ_K used to represent the observed yield curve at each time increment t.
- x_t, $N \times 1$ vector of state variables at time index t.
- R_t, $K \times 1$ vector representing the yield curve data at time index t. R_t contains the values $R_t(\tau_k)$ for $k = 1$ to K.
- x_t^-, $N \times 1$ vector for the prior estimate of x_t.
- P_t^-, $N \times N$ matrix for the prior estimate of the covariance matrix for x_t.
- x_t^+, $N \times 1$ vector for the posterior estimate of x_t.
- P_t^+, $N \times N$ matrix for the posterior estimate of the covariance matrix for x_t^+.

ANSM(2) example:

- ϕ, rate of exponential decay for the forward rate Slope factor loading.
- $x_1(t)$, Level state variable.
- $x_2(t)$, Slope state variable.

- $G(\phi, \tau) = \frac{1}{\phi}\left[1 - \exp(-\phi\tau)\right]$, convenient notation for a reoccuring integration result in ANSMs.

ANSM(3) example (notation additional to ANSM(2) only):

- $x_3(t)$, Bow state variable.
- ϕ, repeated eigenvalue of ANSM(3) mean-reversion matrix $\tilde{\kappa}$. ϕ determines the rate of exponential decay for the forward rate Slope factor loading, and governs the persistence of forward rate Bow factor loading by time to maturity τ.
- $F(\phi, \tau) = G(\phi, \tau) - \tau \exp(-\phi\tau)$, convenient notation for a reoccuring integration result in the ANSM(3).

Chapter 4

All of the state variables, parameters, and derived quantities are as defined in chapter 3, but they apply to the shadow term structure of the Krippner shadow/ZLB-GATSM framework. The additional notation relative to the GATSM notation is:

- r_L, potentially non-zero lower bound value for the ZLB term structure.
- $\underline{r}(t)$, ZLB short rate.
- $r(t)$, shadow short rate.
- $\max\{-r(t), 0\}$, short rate option.
- $\underline{f}(t, \tau)$, ZLB forward rate from the Krippner framework.
- $z(t, \tau)$, forward rate option effect from the Krippner framework.
- $\underline{R}(t, \tau)$, ZLB interest rate from the Krippner framework.
- $Z(t, \tau)$, interest rate option effect from the Krippner framework.
- $\underline{P}(t, \tau)$, ZLB bond price from the Krippner framework.
- $Z_P(t, \tau)$, bond price option effect from the Krippner framework.
- $N\{\cdot, \cdot\}$, normal distribution as a function of a given mean and variance.
- $\phi[\cdot]$, probability density function for the unit normal distribution.
- $\Phi[\cdot]$, cumulative probability density function for the unit normal distribution.
- $\Delta\tau$, the constant time-to-maturity increment for numerically integrating $\underline{f}(t, \tau)$ to obtain $\underline{R}(t, \tau)$.

Chapter 5

All of the state variables, parameters, and derived quantities are as defined in chapter 3, but they apply to the shadow term structure of the Black shadow/ZLB-GATSM framework. The additional notation relative to the GATSM and chapter 4 notation is:

- $\underline{f}^B(t, \tau)$, ZLB forward rate from the Black framework.
- $z^B(t, \tau)$, forward rate option effect from the Black framework.

- $\underline{R}^{B}(t,\tau)$, ZLB interest rate from the Black framework.
- $Z^{B}(t,\tau)$, interest rate option effect from the Black framework.
- $\underline{P}^{B}(t,\tau)$, ZLB bond price from the Black framework.
- $Z_{P}^{B}(t,\tau)$, bond price option effect from the Black framework.
- δ, time-to-maturity increment for term structure derivations.
- $\underline{P}^{B}(t,\tau,\delta)$, Black ZLB forward bond at time τ, expiring at time $t+\tau$, with a time to maturity of δ on expiry.
- $\underline{P}(t,\tau,\delta)$, Krippner ZLB forward bond at time τ, expiring at time $t+\tau$, with a time to maturity of δ on expiry.

Chapter 6

- $L(t)$, Level state variable.
- $S(t)$, Slope state variable.
- $B(t)$, Bow state variable.

Classification and Abbreviations for Term Structure Models

This list of abbreviations for the term structure models introduced in the book is organized by class, then subclass, and then the names of particular models within each subclass. I also provide a brief description at each level of the classification. Note that the Krippner and Black affine Gaussian models are shadow/ZLB-GATSMs, which are ZLB term structure models based on a GATSM shadow term structure model. Note also that, for convenience, I have deliberately designed the abbreviations to read as two-syllable words. For example, GATSM may be spoken as "gats-em", ANSM as "ans-em", K-AGM as "kag-em", K-ANSM as "kans-em", K-NSM as kins-em, etc. (all subject, of course, to local preferences for vowel pronunciations).

GATSM, Gaussian affine term structure model.
- Stationary GATSM. All state variables follow mean-reverting processes under the risk-adjusted $\mathbb{Q}$ measure.
  - GATSM(2), GATSM with two state variables.
  - GATSM(3), GATSM with three state variables.
  - GATSM(N), GATSM with N state variables.
- ANSM, arbitrage-free Nelson and Siegel (1987) model. Subclass of GATSMs in which the Level state variable follows a random walk process under the risk-adjusted $\mathbb{Q}$ measure.
  - ANSM(2), ANSM with two state variables (Level and Slope).
  - ANSM(3), ANSM three state variables (Level, Slope, and Bow).
  - ANSM(N), ANSM with N state variables.
  - NSM, Nelson and Siegel (1987) model, which is a subclass of ANSMs with the standard deviation parameters set to zero.

K-AGM, Krippner affine Gaussian model.
- Stationary K-AGM. Krippner framework with a stationary GATSM to represent the shadow term structure.
  - K-AGM(3), K-AGM with three state variables.
  - K-AGM(N), K-AGM with N state variables.
- K-ANSM, Krippner framework with an ANSM to represent the shadow term structure.
  - K-ANSM(2), ANSM with two state variables (Level and Slope).
  - K-ANSM(3), ANSM with three state variables (Level, Slope, and Bow).
  - K-ANSM(N), ANSM with N state variables.
  - K-NSM, K-ANSM with the standard deviation parameters set to zero.

B-AGM, Black affine Gaussian model.

- Stationary B-AGM. Black framework with a stationary GATSM to represent the shadow term structure.
  - B-AGM(1), B-AGM with one state variable.
  - B-AGM(3), B-AGM with three state variables.
  - B-AGM(N), B-AGM with N state variables.
- B-ANSM, Black framework with ANSM to represent shadow term structure.
  - B-ANSM(2), B-ANSM with two state variables (Level and Slope).
  - B-ANSM(3), B-ANSM with three state variables (Level, Slope, and Bow).
  - B-ANSM(N), ANSM with N state variables.
  - B-NSM, Black framework with NSM to represent represent shadow term structure.

1 | Introduction

The purpose of this book is to introduce practical term structure frameworks and associated monetary policy measures that are explicitly designed to accommodate near-zero nominal interest rates. It is motivated by the prevailing global situation in which interest rates in the world's six largest economies, except China, and many other economies have now essentially been at zero for five years since late 2008/early 2009. Furthermore, guidance from central banks and different measures of market expectations indicate that interest rates are likely to remain at or near zero in some economies for several more years.

Interest rates near zero, or more specifically nominal interest rates that are constrained by the zero lower bound (ZLB), are unprecedented historically, apart from in Japan a decade ago. Therefore, the behavior of interest rates and their relationships with the macroeconomy in a ZLB environment are likely to be unfamiliar to central bankers. Similarly, financial market participants are likely to be uncertain how term structure models or related frameworks that are not designed to respect the ZLB constraint will perform in a ZLB environment. Term structure modelers will already be aware of the theoretical deficiencies in standard Gaussian term structure models, but may not be aware of relatively straightforward solutions that are available for such models.

In short, new term structure frameworks are required for the new environment, and that is what I have written this book to deliver. I have designed the book to appeal to several distinct groups of potential readers:

- **General monetary policy readers.** I envisage that this first group will include people such as central bank practitioners and applied economists with a general interest in the topic, but more specifically in using the output from the models for applications related to monetary policy. For example, the shadow short rates and/or the Effective Monetary Stimulus results from the ZLB term structure models may be used for monitoring the stance of monetary policy and as data for related analysis.
- **General financial market readers.** I envisage that this second group will be people such as financial market practitioners and applied financial researchers with a general interest in the topic, but more specifically using the output from the

models for applications related to financial markets. For example, the estimated state variables and parameters for the ZLB term structure models can be used for a risk framework in fixed interest portfolios, and the parameters for the estimated models can be used to value options on bonds.

- **Term structure modelers.** The third group will be those interested in learning about the specifics of term structure modeling and its extension into ZLB environments, so they can develop and apply their own ZLB term structure models. I expect this group will include people such as central bank researchers, financial market quantitative analysts, academic researchers, and students.

In the following section I provide an overview of the remaining eight chapters of the book, and then in section 1.2, I provide my reading suggestions for the three different groups. Sections 1.3 to 1.5 provide some further preliminaries that help to put the book in context.

1.1 Chapter overview

The following list provides a brief overview of the chapters in this book:

- **Chapter 2: A new framework for a new environment.** I provide background and motivation appropriate to the book by introducing some basic principles about monetary policy and term structure modeling, and the complications introduced by the ZLB. As a solution to those complications, I introduce the shadow/ZLB class of term structure models, which will be the predominant focus of the remaining chapters.
- **Chapter 3: Gaussian affine term structure models.** I outline the Gaussian affine term structure model (GATSM) framework, including the popular and parsimonious subclass of arbitrage-free Nelson and Siegel (1987) models (ANSMs). The outline first serves to establish the present standard for term structure modeling, and I also use GATSMs to represent the shadow term structure in the shadow/ZLB-GATSMs in the remainder of the book. Related to that point, I can then present the shadow/ZLB-GATSM framework and its estimation in chapter 4 as a relatively tractable modification to the GATSM class.
- **Chapter 4: Krippner framework for ZLB term structure modeling.** I develop the Krippner (2011, 2012b,c, 2013d,e) shadow/ZLB framework based on GATSMs outlined in chapter 3. I begin with the Krippner shadow/ZLB-GATSM, or K-AGM, framework because it is relatively tractable compared to the Black (1995) framework that I will discuss in chapter 5. In particular, the K-AGM is designed to use many of the standard results directly from the GATSM literature.
- **Chapter 5: Black framework for ZLB term structure modeling.** I provide an exposition of the shadow/ZLB-GATSM framework based on the approach first

suggested in Black (1995) and using a GATSM to represent the shadow term structure. The Black shadow/ZLB-GATSM, or B-AGM, framework is seen by many as the benchmark for shadow/ZLB-GATSMs, but I argue that there is a strong case for using the K-AGM framework as an alternative, at least from a practical perspective and potentially also on theoretical grounds. Providing readers with a complete overview of the B-AGM framework and an explicit comparison to the K-AGM framework will best enable them to make an informed choice of which framework to use.

- **Chapter 6: K-ANSM foundations and "Effective Monetary Stimulus."** I outline a generic economic foundation, based on well-accepted principles from the term structure literature, for ANSMs. There are several motivations for providing this ANSM economic foundation:

  - It provides a justification for using ANSMs generally as a parsimonious and realistic representation of the shadow term structure.
  - It provides a theoretical perspective for considering the pricing foundations of the K-ANSM and the B-ANSM frameworks.
  - It helps justify the "Effective Monetary Stimulus" or EMS summary measure for the stance of monetary policy.

- **Chapter 7: Monetary policy applications.** I discuss some of the practical applications of shadow/ZLB-GATSMs to various aspects of monetary policy. In particular, chapter 7 will discuss how several outputs from shadow/ZLB-GATSMs can be used to indicate the stance of monetary policy or as data for related analysis.
- **Chapter 8: Financial market applications.** I discuss the practical application of shadow/ZLB-GATSMs within financial markets. In particular, I have selected two topics for which applying standard methods and GATSMs suitable for a non-ZLB environment would be very unsuitable in a ZLB environment, and for which shadow/ZLB-GATSMs can be used to bridge the gap. The first topic is the quantification of mark-to-market risk in fixed interest portfolios, and the second topic is the pricing of options on bonds in a ZLB environment.
- **Chapter 9: Conclusion and future research directions.** I provide a brief summary of the key points from each of the main chapters, and then give an overview of the case for using K-ANSMs as a standard term structure model that will accommodate both non-ZLB and ZLB environments. I conclude with a list of future research that remains to be undertaken for K-ANSMs.

1.2 Suggested reading

In the following subsection I provide suggested reading from the perspective of the three groups mentioned earlier.

1.2.1 Group 1: General monetary policy readers

I suggest that members of this group begin in chapter 2 where I provide the key intuition of non-ZLB and ZLB term structure modeling without resorting to the somewhat specialized mathematics that typically, and necessarily, accompanies the term structure literature. With the intuition from reading chapter 2, readers can turn directly to chapter 7 for an overview of the ZLB term structure models that I develop and estimate, and the applications of the output from those models to issues associated with monetary policy. The summary in chapter 9 will be useful to obtain an overview of the key results from other chapters. Note that both chapter 7 and chapter 9 include cross-references to intervening chapters and sections, so it is easy for readers to follow up on particular topics in more detail if they wish.

1.2.2 Group 2: General financial market readers

I suggest that members of this group also begin in chapter 2 to obtain the intuition of the topic, and then read at least section 7.1 from chapter 7 to obtain the overview of the shadow/ZLB term structure models that I develop and estimate. With the intuition from chapter 2 and the overview from chapter 7, readers can turn to chapter 8 for practical applications of shadow/ZLB term structure models to topics more specifically related to financial markets. The cross-references to the intervening chapters and sections that I have included in chapters 8 and 9 allow readers to easily seek out further details on particular topics if they wish.

1.2.3 Group 3: Term structure modelers

Those interested in learning more about developing and estimating shadow/ZLB term structure models will be able to work through all the chapters, and particularly the details on term structure models contained in chapters 3 to 6. The applications in chapters 7 and 8 provide illustrations on how the output from those models can be applied to various topics, and chapter 9 gives a summary, including a list of topics for future research.

Within chapters 3 to 6, I make few assumptions about the background knowledge of readers or their proficiency with the theory and practice of term structure modeling. Those with more proficiency can obviously skip through the familiar material more quickly. For example, those already familiar with GATSMs and their estimation need only read sections 3.1 and 3.2 to familiarize themselves with the notation I carry through to the remainder of the book.

I have included a very detailed focus on the estimation of all the models I present, for two reasons. First, a theoretical model is of no particular use in practice if it hasn't been parametrized to adequately represent the actual data that are of relevance to the practitioner. Second, a practitioner is less likely to proceed to an estimation if the connection from a specified term structure model to a form that can be estimated is not clearly established or if it is left implicit. I prefer to have the book self-contained, so the reader can follow the development of the expressions for the term structure models and also see explicitly how those expressions are converted into a form for estimation.

Readers of chapters 3 to 6 should already be comfortable with symbolic scalar, vector, and matrix notation, or be prepared to become so. This notation is essential to make the expressions tidy, concise, unambiguous, and amenable to convenient manipulation and programming. In appendix A, I have provided an overview of the matrix notation and operations that I will use in the book, including the associated algebraic and calculus manipulation. I have also included a section to indicate the equivalence of matrix and index/summation notation, given that some readers may be more familiar with the later.

I have been very pendantic with my introduction and discussion of notation. The reason is again to keep the book self-contained and notationally consistent across the different perspectives of the models and their estimation. I have always found that very helpful as a reader, so it is only natural to offer it as a writer. Inevitably there will be notational errors, but they should hopefully be apparent from the context and easily allowed for. Nevertheless, I apologize in advance and ask that readers please point them out to me (email: leo.krippner@rbnz.govt.nz) so I can note and correct them appropriately.

1.3 Data

I predominately use the US experience and data to make my points in the book. That helps ensure consistency throughout the chapters, and of course the United States is of interest in its own right as the world's largest economy. I provide some results for other economies in chapter 7, in the context of relative monetary policy and currency movements.

Most of the data I use is publicly available and online:

- The macroeconomic and monetary data I use is sourced from FRED, the Federal Reserve Economic Database available from the Federal Reserve Bank of St. Louis. The web address is http://research.stlouisfed.org/fred2/. The Federal Funds Rate, Federal Funds Target Rate, Treasury bill rates, and currency rates are also from FRED.
- The survey data I use is sourced from the Survey of Professional Forecasters, which is maintained by the Federal Reserve Bank of Philadelphia. The web address is http://www.phil.frb.org/research-and-data/real-time-center/survey-of-professional-forecasters/.
- The US government bond yield curve data I use is described in Gürkaynak, Sack, and Wright (2007) and is available from the Federal Reserve Board. The web address is http://www.federalreserve.gov/pubs/feds/2006/200628/200628abs.html.

- The US overnight indexed swap data that I splice to the Gürkaynak, Sack, and Wright (2007) data set are from Bloomberg (code S0042Z). These data are not publicly available.
- The euro-area overnight indexed swap data and the government bond data that I use in chapter 7 are from Bloomberg (codes are F082 for the United States, I082 for the United Kingdom, I018 for Japan, F910 for Germany, and EUSWE for the euro area). These data are also not publicly available.

The cut-off point for all of the data I use was end-March 2014. Because it is available in real time, the interest rate and exchange rate data is therefore up to March 2014. However, the macroeconomic and survey data was that available at the cut-off time.

1.4 Availability of results and code

All of the results from my estimations in this book are available online at the Reserve Bank of New Zealand website. I have also included the publicly available yield curve data and supplementary data used in this book, as noted in the previous section. I intend to provide regular updates of my estimations, although the historical data will be subject to change as I note with regard to program updates below. The yield curve data is available at a daily frequency, so I will also provide daily and weekly estimates of the different monetary policy measures discussed in chapter 7, although not necessarily updated at those frequencies. The higher-frequency results will be useful for event-study analysis, for example, investigating market reactions to monetary policy events as in Claus, Claus, and Krippner (2014a,b).

I also intend to make the MatLab code I have created to estimate the models and generate the data available on the website, and to compile stand-alone executable files (if possible) for those without access to MatLab. However, the code will be subject to change as it is tidied and updated, and so the results it produces will therefore also be subject to change.

1.5 References to the literature

The literature on shadow/ZLB term structure modeling has been expanding steadily over the past few years, but is still very much work in progress. To provide an approximate timeline on recent developments, my references therefore often include multiple entries to working papers where the original work has been updated and/or released in a different source. Obviously, the last version will generally be the most relevant for readers wanting to follow up on any details mentioned in the book. I have also included references to preliminary work by many authors, which I expect will be soon be forthcoming as working papers. Indeed, I have found many of the preliminary versions available on the internet.

One further comment on my references to the literature is that, following the theme of the book, they are largely confined to term structure modeling and its overlap with monetary policy. There is, of course, a much wider field of general research on monetary policy at the ZLB. The references in subsection 2.1.2 provide some links to that wider research.

1.6 Other preliminaries

I have adopted the terminology "ZLB" throughout this book because it is convenient and standard in the related literature. However, that terminology should not be taken to imply a strict lower bound of zero for interest rates. A non-zero lower bound, either slightly positive or negative, may be appropriate in practice to accommodate institutional frictions (e.g., see Jarrow [2013] for further discussion) and/or central bank policy rate preferences. On the latter, many countries have adopted a slightly positive policy rate (e.g., the US 0 to 0.25% or the UK 0.50% targets), but the Danish and Swedish central banks, and the European Central Bank are three examples where slightly negative policy rates have been set (i.e., a rate for bank deposits with the central bank as low as -0.20%, -0.25%, and -0.10% respectively, although the settings of central bank lending rates have not been lower than zero). Examples of slightly negative interest rates on securities traded in financial markets are Switzerland in the 1970s, Japan in the early 2000s, and those countries plus the United States, and Germany in the period following the Global Financial Crisis (GFC). Non-zero lower bounds can be incorporated readily into the shadow/ZLB term structure models as I discuss in the book.

2 | A New Framework for a New Environment

In this chapter, I provide the background and motivation to the book by introducing some basic principles about monetary policy and term structure modeling.

I begin in section 2.1 with an overview of the conventional operation of monetary policy prior to the Global Financial Crisis (GFC). I then provide an initial indication of the complications introduced by the ZLB for nominal interest rates.

In section 2.2, I introduce a class of standard term structure models that has proven very popular for many applications. However, I also show that models of that class are no longer appropriate to use in a ZLB environment.

As a resolution to the deficiencies of those standard term structure models, I introduce the class of shadow/ZLB term structure models in section 2.3, which will be the predominant focus of the remaining chapters. In section 2.4, I briefly return to the topic of monetary policy to show how the output from shadow/ZLB term structure models, such as the "Shadow Short Rate" or particularly the "Effective Monetary Stimulus," can be used to monitor and quantify the stance of monetary policy in ZLB environments.

The final section, 2.5, briefly discusses alternative ZLB models. This section is not necessary for those specifically interested in shadow/ZLB-GATSMs and their application, but it is useful to explain why alternative ZLB models do not necessarily provide a satisfactory solution to modeling the term structure in ZLB environments.

2.1 Monetary policy

2.1.1 Pre-GFC

Operating and monitoring monetary policy with a policy interest rate used to be relatively simple before the GFC, in principle at least. In non-ZLB environments, policymakers in central banks would first gauge the state of the real economy and inflation relative to their objectives. They would then freely set the policy rate above or below their judgment of a neutral interest rate, which I will discuss further below, to efficiently achieve the macroeconomic objectives over an appropriate horizon.

For example, consider a central bank facing inflation below its target rate due to economic output (the level of gross domestic product, or GDP) being below potential output (the noninflationary level of output). The central bank would seek to bring inflation back to target by lowering the policy interest rate and perhaps offering indications of likely future settings. Participants in financial markets would observe the current policy rate and indications of future settings, and would appropriately incorporate those into wider financial markets, such as equity prices, currency rates, and the many different categories of interest rates in the economy (e.g., government bond markets, interbank interest rates, household and business lending rates, etc.). In this particular example, the resultant higher equity prices, lower exchange rate, and lower interest rates would help stimulate economic activity, thereby leading to faster output growth. Hence the level of output would rise relative to potential output, which would in turn help bring inflation back to target. That relationship is typically summarized by a Phillip's curve, which relates inflation to the output gap (i.e., output as measured by real GDP relative to potential output).

Of course, as is typically the case in economics and finance, the in-principle simplicity above is subject to many practical caveats and complexities in practice. Even the causation I have implied is readily subject to more nuanced interpretations. For example, equity prices should rise partly due to the expectations of faster output growth anticipated in response to the lower policy rate. For the purposes of this introduction, I simply give several broad examples of the practical issues and note that numerous journal articles and entire textbooks are filled with material on aspects relating to each of the individual items and their subcategories.[1]

- **Central bank objectives may vary over time.** Even if the single objective is an inflation target, that target or the horizon for achieving it can change. More generally, central banks may have explicit or implicit multiple objectives/responsibilities (e.g., employment, macroeconomic stabilization, macroprudential oversight, etc.), and so the policy rate setting may emphasize different objectives at different points in time.
- **The current states of the real economy and inflation are uncertain.** First, macroeconomic data are published after the period to which they relate and are often revised, so the current values of the relevant data must be estimated by the central bank.[2] Second, concepts such as output relative to potential output (or unemployment-based proxies) are quantities that are unobservable. Hence, they must also be estimated, which also needs to allow for time variation (because potential output growth varies with changes to labor productivity, population, capital investment, etc.).
- **The appropriate policy rate setting given the (changeable) objectives and the (uncertain) macroeconomic environment is somewhat subjective.** First, the neutral interest rate is a conceptual and unobservable quantity that is essentially a policy setting that would keep output at its potential and inflation at its target.

It must be estimated, and changes to inflation, potential growth, and so forth will lead the neutral rate to vary over time. Second, the transmission of the policy rate settings is uncertain, initially into financial markets (as discussed in the points immediately below), then into the components of output growth such as consumption, investment, and so on, and ultimately into output growth, the output gap, and inflation.

- **Market participants may disagree with the central bank on its indications of future policy settings.** First, market participants may be uncertain about the objectives of the central bank and/or how it will set the policy rate given the likely evolution of the data. Second, market participants may anticipate different evolutions of macroeconomic data and therefore different future policy settings than the central bank's indications. Third, financial markets may also have different views of longer-term fundamentals, such as potential output growth and the neutral interest rate.

- **Aspects other than monetary policy settings can influence prices in financial markets.** In particular, financial markets need to allow for many different types of risk in asset prices and interest rates, such as mark-to-market risk, default risk, and liquidity risk. These can be in turn be related to the macroeconomic and macrofinancial environment, and also to the confidence markets have that the central bank will adhere to its objectives in the long run (e.g., central bank credibility on a given inflation target). Finally, speculation unrelated to macroeconomic fundamentals can also influence market prices.

While bearing those practical issues in mind, I provide an illustration in Figure 2.1 of the in-principle monetary policy process using US data. Panel 1 plots the macroeconomic data, in this case the output gap based on real GDP and the US Congressional Budget Office real potential output series, and year-on-year inflation calculated from the Personal Consumption Expenditure deflator. I have also indicated the National Bureau of Economic Research (NBER) recessions with the shaded areas, which I will include without an associated legend in most time series plots throughout this book.

Panel 2 plots two examples of prescriptive policy rates based on two well-known "Taylor rules." Taylor rules are simple mechanical relationships that suggest a policy rate setting based on the output gap, inflation, targets for both of those series, and an assumed neutral interest rate. Therefore, Taylor rules conveniently summarize how a policy rate setting might arise from the relevant macroeconomic data, the central bank's policy objectives (implied targets of a zero output gap and 2% inflation given the parameters below), and a neutral interest rate assumption (an implied value of $\pi(t) + 2\%$ given the parameters below). Taylor rules have been found to provide a reasonable approximation to central bank policy rate settings in practice. However, all of the practical issues discussed earlier still apply, and so Taylor rules are obviously an oversimplification of how policy rates would be set in practice.

Macroeconomic data

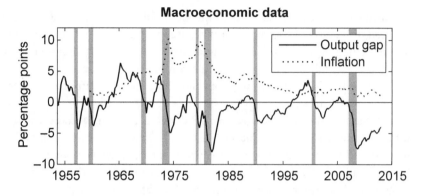

Prescriptive and actual policy rates

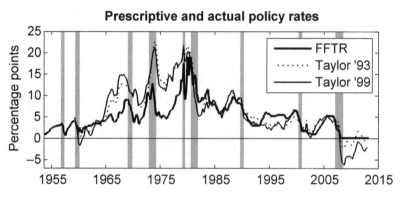

Market interest rates and spread

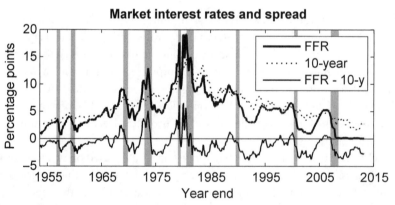

Figure 2.1 The operation of monetary policy with a policy interest rate. The central bank observes prevailing macroeconomic data (panel 1), sets the policy rate to achieve its objectives (panel 2), and financial markets set interest rates in the economy (panel 3) according to the policy rate setting and expectations of future settings.

The Taylor 1993 series is based on the Taylor (1993) specification that takes the form

$$r^{T}(t) = \pi(t) + \alpha Y_{G}(t) + \beta\left[\pi(t) - \pi^{*}\right] + r^{*} \qquad (2.1)$$

where $r^T(t)$ is the prescriptive policy rate at time t, $\pi(t)$ is inflation, $Y_G(t)$ is the output gap (i.e., $Y_G(t) = \log Y(t) - \log Y^*(t)$, where $Y(t)$ and $Y^*(t)$ are respectively actual and potential output and log is the natural logarithm), $\pi^* = 2\%$ is the inflation target, $r^* = 2\%$ is the real neutral interest rate, and $\alpha = 0.5$ and $\beta = 0.5$ are the respective weights on the output gap and deviations of inflation from target. The Taylor 1999 series is based on the same specification, but with the value $\alpha = 1$ noted on Taylor (1999) p. 325, in reference to a related paper by Federal Reserve Board authors at the time. More recently, Rudebusch (2009) also obtains similar figures to the Taylor 1999 specification, including for the ZLB environment that I will discuss in section 2.1.2.

Panel 2 also plots a series that represents actual policy rate settings. The series is composed of the Federal Funds Target Rate (FFTR), the Federal Reserve's policy lever from November 1982. Here and subsequently I have represented the 0-25% range for the FFTR that has applied since December 2008 with the mid-point of 0.125%. Before November 1982 I have plotted the actual Federal Funds Rate (FFR). This is to reflect the settings of monetary policy under the different monetary policy regimes that prevailed prior to November 1982.

Panel 3 plots two interest rates that trade in financial markets. The first is the FFR, at which designated depository institutions trade reserve balances held at the Federal Reserve. The FFR is highly influenced by the policy rate setting, because the Federal Reserve undertakes open market operations (buying and selling securities to inject and withdraw reserve balances) designed to achieve a FFR close to the FFTR. The FFR is in turn a highly relevant benchmark for short-maturity lending and borrowing in the wider economy, because depository institutions can substitute borrowing and lending with the wider economy for the trading of reserve balances between themselves.

The second interest rate is the yield on the 10-year Treasury note, which is an interest rate for government borrowing and a key benchmark rate for longer-maturity lending and borrowing in the economy. The 10-year interest rate follows the policy cycles somewhat, but less so than the FFR because longer-maturity interest rates are also influenced more by expectations of the path of the FFR and the other financial market influences discussed earlier.

For the purposes of this introduction, the 10-year interest rate is also of a long enough maturity to provide a proxy (albeit imperfect) for the neutral interest rate assumed by the market. That is, the 10-year interest rate embeds market expectations of short-maturity interest rates beyond the monetary policy cycle prevailing at any point in time, so it should roughly reflect the market's expectation of where short-maturity interest rates will revert to in the future.

Therefore, prior to the onset of the GFC (which I will discuss in the following section), the FFR/10-year spread in Figure 2.1 provides an indication of the stance of monetary policy in terms of the policy rate relative to a rough measure of the neutral rate as perceived by the market. Based on that measure, the monetary policy tightening and easing cycles are evident respectively from the increases and decreases in the FFR/10-year spread over the time.

The clearest example in Figure 2.1 of all the principles discussed above working in practice is the disinflation period of the late 1970s/early 1980s. During that period, the Federal Reserve under Chairman Volcker sought to lower the high rate of inflation at the time by sharply tightening monetary policy, leading to high market interest rates and an economic recession. That recession turned the output gap negative and therefore reduced inflation. From the perspective of monitoring monetary policy, the central bank and financial markets could infer a very tight stance of policy during the disinflation period from the high FFR/10-year spread at the time (which has turned out to be the widest in the entire sample). Examples of policy easings are the early 1990s and early 2000s recessions, where lowering the policy rate helped restore the output gap to zero while inflation remained contained.

2.1.2 Post-GFC

I now turn to the situation during and following the GFC, in which the policy rate was set to zero. Reaching the ZLB brings yet another practical complication to operating and monitoring monetary policy. From the perspective of central banks, even if the macroeconomic data suggested that a lower policy rate would be appropriate, there would no longer be the freedom to lower it. More specifically, if the central bank tried to set the rate for lending in the economy below zero (i.e., so lenders paid interest to borrowers), then lenders would prefer the alternative investment of calling in their loans and holding physical currency at an effective interest rate of zero. Or, more directly, banks would seek to borrow from the central bank, and hold physical currency.

As an example of the ZLB constraint in practice, consider panel 2 of Figure 2.1 and the zoomed version in panel 1 of Figure 2.2. These panels show that the output gap and inflation since the time of the GFC in 2008 suggested that a negative policy rate setting would have been appropriate, as low as 6% for the Taylor 1999 specification and still materially negative with the macroeconomic data at the time of writing. However, the FFTR has been set to a range of 0 to 0.25%, or effectively zero, because the Federal Reserve can not lower the policy rate below zero to provide further monetary stimulus. Similarly, near-zero policy interest rates have been maintained in Japan since the 1990s, in the United Kingdom since late 2008/early 2009, and in the euro area and non-euro European economies over recent years, even though central banks in all of those economies have expressed a desire for easier monetary policy to stimulate their economic growth.

Hence, central banks in ZLB environments have resorted to unconventional monetary policy actions to provide further monetary stimulus beyond a near-zero policy rate setting. I use the US experience to briefly provide specific examples of the two main mechanisms employed (and other actions), but many of the economies mentioned earlier have also implemented some form of the mechanisms described below.

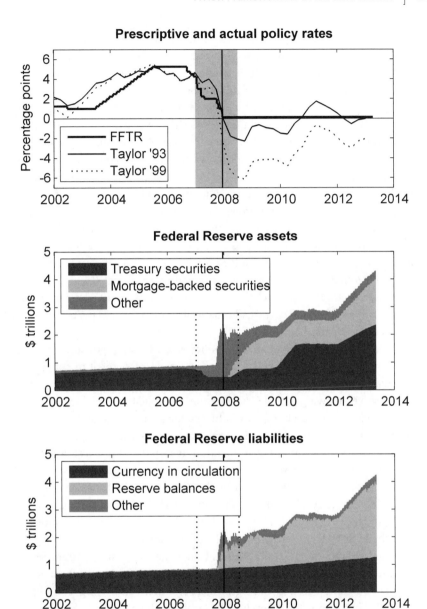

Figure 2.2 The ZLB constraint and unconventional monetary policy. Negative rates are not possible even if the prevailing macroeconomic data suggests that would be appropriate (panel 1). Quantitative easing is one way to further ease policy; the central bank purchases assets from the market (panel 2), and thereby increases the quantities of money available in the economy (panel 3).

- **Quantitative easing (QE) and targeted asset purchases.** Panel 2 of Figure 2.2 shows that the asset side of the Federal Reserve's balance sheet has increased markedly since the GFC, reflecting the Federal Reserve's purchases of mainly government bonds and mortgage-backed securities from the market. In particular, the profile of panel 2 indicates the onset and completion of QE1 from November 2008 to March 2010, QE2 from November 2010 to June 2011, and QE3 from September 2012, which is being wound down at the time of writing. I will provide further details on those programs in chapter 7, but the important point here is that such asset purchases result in a corresponding increase to the liability side of the Federal Reserve's balance sheet, as indicated in panel 3 of Figure 2.2. Specifically, the Federal Reserve's asset purchases have predominantly increased the reserve balance accounts of depository institutions, although currency in circulation has also risen slightly. Those rapid increases in the monetary base represent easier monetary policy via QE, which should in principle stimulate output growth and inflation. In addition, if the central bank targets particular assets for purchase, such as mortgage-backed securities, it can create a so-called portfolio balance effect in which private-sector investors reallocate the central bank funds they receive to other asset classes. That effect can reduce interest rates or the cost of capital on the targeted assets and other assets classes and therefore help stimulate output growth and inflation. Sections 2 and 3 of Woodford (2012) provide an excellent discussion of the principles and practice of these mechanisms.

- **Long-horizon forward guidance on policy rates.** Forward guidance from central banks on likely future policy setting is a standard element of conventional monetary policy, as noted in section 2.1.1. However, the guidance from the Federal Reserve following the GFC has been more explicit and for longer horizons than previously in an attempt to influence longer-maturity interest rates. For example, when the 0-0.25% policy rate range was set in December 2008, the Federal Reserve also indicated an intention to keep the FFR "exceptionally low" for "some time," which was changed to "an extended period" in March 2009. The quotes are from Federal Open Market Committee (FOMC) statements. As I will detail in chapter 7, the FOMC subsequently adopted more specific forward guidance in August 2011 with a calendar-based conditional commitment to keep the FFR at exceptionally low levels "at least through mid-2013," which was extended in January 2012 to "at least through late 2014," and again in September 2012 to "at least through mid-2015." In December 2012, the Federal Reserve adopted outcome-based forward guidance, essentially indicating it would keep the FFR at exceptionally low levels while the unemployment rate remained above 6.5%, conditional on expected inflation remaining below 2.5 percent. Section 1 of Woodford (2012) again provides an excellent discussion of the principles and practice of forward guidance.

- **Other policy measures.** These examples do not fall neatly into the two categories above, but they have similar effects. For example, the Federal Reserve's maturity-lengthening program in late 2011 (the so-called "Operation Twist"; see Swanson (2011) for a detailed discussion) was similar to QE except that long-maturity bonds were bought with the proceeds from selling short-maturity bonds to the market rather than issuing currency or reserve balances. Liquidity measures, like the Term Auction Facility to provide longer-term liquidity to banks and swap lines with other central banks to provide US dollar liquidity to non-US banks, were important around the GFC. These measures had mainly a targeted asset purchase effect to reduce risk premiums in interbank markets. However, panel 2 of Figure 2.2 shows they were a significant component of the initial increase in the size of the Federal Reserve's balance sheet, so they would also have had some QE effect.

While the examples for the United States above show that unconventional monetary policy measures can be used to operate monetary policy with a ZLB constraint, obtaining a consistent measure of the stance of monetary policy or the degree of monetary stimulus in such environments becomes more challenging. In particular, the FFR and the FFR/10-year spread mentioned earlier no longer contain any useful information about the stance of policy. Indeed, panel 3 of Figure 2.1 shows the ambiguous interpretations that could arise from naively following either one of those indicators. That is, since late 2008 the FFR has remained static, suggesting a steady stance of policy, while the FFR/10-year spread has risen, suggesting a tighter stance of policy. In reality, a zero policy rate in conjunction with unconventional measures provided further stimulus and therefore represented an easier stance of policy than a zero policy rate alone.

This measurement issue is relevant for even casually monitoring the stance of monetary policy over time. Specifically, gauging whether current monetary policy is relatively stimulatory or restrictive compared to a year ago, three years ago, or to some point within the conventional policy period requires a metric for monetary stimulus. More generally, quantifying the stance of monetary policy in a standardized and consistent manner over conventional and unconventional policy periods is crucial for any research and analysis associated with monetary policy. In turn, that research and analysis is necessary to help central banks assess the likely influence of monetary policy settings, and therefore meet their ultimate policy objectives.

Two summary measures that could potentially be used to quantify the stance of monetary policy over conventional and unconventional policy periods without a policy rate are the following:

- **Money statistics.** The money supply and/or money growth are standard data that are already available, and Figure 2.2 shows that the Federal Reserve's QE and targeted asset purchase programs clearly increased the money supply dramatically as they were implemented. And, in principle at least, money measures should also correlate with output growth and inflation. However, there are two practical issues. First, history has shown that the relationships between money measures and macroeconomic data have not been reliable in the past, which was one reason that central banks began working in terms of interest rates. Second, any historical relationships may now be quite different and variable in the post-GFC period. For example, the fact that currency in circulation has not risen much but reserve balance accounts have in response to Federal Reserve asset purchases indicates that the typical channels for transmission into wider money measures and economic activity may not be working as before.

- **A longer-maturity interest rate.** QE and forward guidance are designed to influence longer-term expectations and longer-maturity interest rates, and such rates are far enough away from the ZLB to move freely in response to unconventional monetary policy events. Indeed, there is already a large empirical literature relating QE events to movements in 10-year rates; see Williams (2011) and Kozicki, Santor, and Surchnek (2011) for extensive summaries. Regarding forward guidance, 10-year rates dropped steadily to their cycle lows in July 2012 following the first forward guidance announcement in August 2011 and its extension in January 2012. However, aside from monetary policy influences, movements in 10-year rates will also reflect changes to neutral real interest rates, inflation expectations, and risk premiums, in both conventional and unconventional monetary policy environments. Therefore, the 10-year rate is likely to be a somewhat noisy measure of the stance of monetary policy, and perhaps inconsistent between conventional and unconventional monetary policy depending on the key drivers of its movement in each period.

Hence, while either or both of the measures above could be used, neither is particularly satisfactory. An alternative is to use information estimated from a yield curve model, that is, a model designed to represent the interest rates of different maturities along the yield curve at a given point in time and to represent how all of those interest rates can evolve over time. The level and shape of the yield curve should in principle reflect the market's assessment of the current settings of monetary policy and expectations of how the policy rate and interest rates in general will evolve over time. In particular, whether or not monetary policy settings are being delivered through policy rate changes, asset purchases, forward guidance, or any combination of the three, the influence of those policy actions should be reflected in the market's settings of interest rates of different maturities along the yield curve.

Therefore, using a term structure model to distill the information from the interest rates of different maturities should be useful for inferring, at each point in time, the market's view of the stance of monetary policy and expectations of how it will evolve over time. In turn, monitoring how those views and expectations extracted from the yield curve change with each new observation of yield curve data therefore offers a means of monitoring the stance of monetary policy and consistently quantifying it as a time series for further analysis.

2.2 Term structure modeling

While I introduced term structure modeling at the end of the previous section from the perspective of monitoring the stance of monetary policy, term structure models are of course applied to a diverse range of topics spanning monetary policy, macroe-conomics, and financial markets. From that perspective, I summarize in section 2.2.1 the key features of a very popular class of term structure models and provide examples of applications prior to the GFC. In section 2.2.2, I discuss how models of that class are no longer appropriate to apply in a ZLB environment.

2.2.1 Pre-GFC

Term structure modeling also used to be straightforward in the non-ZLB envi-ronments that prevailed before the GFC. In short, Gaussian affine term structure models (hereafter GATSMs), including the popular subclass of arbitrage-free Nel-son and Siegel (1987) models (hereafter ANSMs), were widely favored by many academics, researchers, central bankers, and private-sector practitioners, as I will discuss further below. In section 2.5, I will mention some other term structure mod-els often used for pricing interest-rate-related options. However, it is sufficient to say here that the relative complexity, specialized nature, and performance of those models compared to GATSMs have limited their widespread application.

I will provide full notation and details for GATSMs in chapter 3. The essential point for the discussion in this chapter is that GATSMs are based on a short rate that is assumed to follow a Gaussian diffusion. The short rate may be regarded as a very short-maturity interest rate (like a policy rate), and a Gaussian diffusion means that it is specified to evolve randomly into future times with a Gaussian (i.e., normal) distribution from its current value. I represent current time by t and future times as $t + \tau$, where τ is the horizon from time t. Hence, potential future values of the short rate $r(t + \tau)$ will evolve with a Gaussian distribution from the current short rate $r(t)$. Note that the horizon τ will also be synonymous with the time to maturity for interest rates, as I will explain shortly below, but I will continue to refer to horizon in the context of expected short rates.

Panel 1 of Figure 2.3 illustrates a Gaussian diffusion by plotting some potential paths of the short rate that I have generated for one of the GATSMs I estimate in chapter 3. Gaussian diffusions for GATSMs are specified with an allowance for mean reversion, so all short rate paths tend to evolve toward a fixed long-horizon value at all times, in this case upward from the starting value of 2.11%. Panel 2 illustrates the distribution of the potential short rates at given horizons. These distributions are Gaussian, and I have plotted ± three standard deviations around the expected value (i.e., the mean value) of the short rate distribution at each horizon. The mean reversion property for GATSMs corresponds with the center of the distribution con-verging to a given value for long horizons (i.e., the expected value of the distribution mean reverts to the given value). However, the width of the distribution increases as a function of the horizon because there is a higher probability of the short rate paths reaching more extreme values relative to the mean as the random innovations to individual paths aggregate over longer periods of time.

The term structure of interest rates, or the yield curve, produced by a GATSM is the expected return from a compounded investment in the short rates up to each

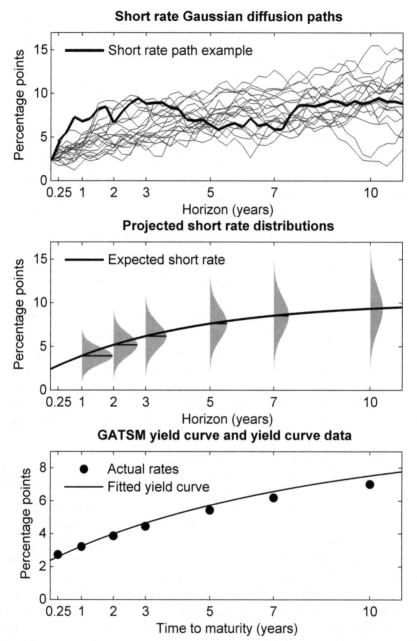

Figure 2.3 A Gaussian diffusion for the short rate (panel 1) produces projected distributions of future short rates (panel 2) and interest rates as the expected return on the short rates up to each future horizon/time to maturity τ (panel 3).

future horizon τ. I denote GATSM interest rates as $R(t, \tau)$, where t is current time and τ is the time to maturity (hence, $t + \tau$ is the time of maturity). $R(t, \tau)$ is essentially the average of the path of the mean or expected short rate for the GATSM up to each given horizon. However, the precise relationship, which I will define in chapter 3, uses an intermediate step involving a forward rate expression that allows for the effect that the variance of the short rate distributions has on expected compounded returns.

Panel 3 plots the GATSM yield curve for my particular example, which is actually a model representation of the US yield curve data for September 1995. I have also plotted the yield curve data at that time to show that the GATSM fits the data quite well in this case.

The Gaussian diffusion foundation makes GATSMs very tractable, or easy to estimate and apply in practice, relative to other term structure models. Specifically, regardless of how they are specified, estimating GATSMs only involves standard Gaussian distributions, and GATSMs also produce standard closed-form analytic solutions for pricing standard interest rate securities, for example, bonds and options on bonds. (This comment is only strictly correct when the GATSM is specified in continuous time, which is a concept I will introduce in chapter 3. GATSMs specified in discrete time require the iteration of difference equations, but that is also very straightforward.)

The tractability of GATSMs, even with quite general specifications, has led them to be applied to a wide variety of yield-curve-related topics spanning monetary policy, macroeconomics, and financial markets. As such, Hamilton and Wu (2012) introduces GATSMs as "the basic workhorse in macroeconomics and finance" and notes 14 recent examples of their application. Diebold and Rudebusch (2013) provides an overview of many forecasting, finance, and macrofinance applications of arbitrage-free Nelson and Siegel (1987) models, which are a subclass of GATSMs. I have briefly listed below some of the topics to which GATSM (in which I include the ANSM subclass) have been applied, along with selected examples:

- **Gauging expectations of monetary policy rates.** The current shape of the yield curve should reflect expectations of future policy rates. Hence, Dahlquist and Svensson (1996) originally proposed using the Nelson and Siegel (1987) model (and later the Svensson [1994] variant) to fit yield curve data as a means of gauging market expectations of central bank policy rates. GATSMs in general are routinely used for this purpose in central banks.
- **Yield curve forecasting.** The current shape of the yield curve should contain information about how it will evolve in the future. Applying GATSMs provides a convenient way of extracting and using that information at each point in time. For example, Krippner (2006) and Christensen, Diebold, and Rudebusch (2011) use ANSMs to forecast the yield curve (out of sample) and obtain results better than the standard benchmark of assuming unchanged yields.
- **Quantifying risk premiums.** Interest rates observed in financial markets should be composed of policy rate expectations and risk premiums. Applying GATSMs to yield curve data allows those two components to be quantified in a model-consistent way. Kim and Orphanides (2007) provides an excellent overview of the topic, including estimated results and related discussion.

- **Macrofinance.** This field is essentially about establishing relationships between macroeconomic data (e.g., output growth and inflation) and financial market data, particularly interest rates. Both data sets should be inherently interconnected, and so jointly modeling them potentially offers greater insights about the economy as a whole rather than modeling each separately. GATSMs provide a convenient framework for representing the interest rate data in conjunction with the macroeconomic data. For example, see Ang and Piazzesi (2003), Hördahl, Tristani, and Vestin (2008), and Krippner (2008). Rudebusch (2010) provides a survey of applications within this topic, and Veronesi (2010), pp. 635–44 provides a simplified but intuitive model that relates the yield curve and macroeconomy.
- **Inflation expectations.** Applying GATSMs jointly to nominal and inflation-indexed yield curve data allows expectations about real interest rates and inflation to be extracted, along with estimates of the risks associated with those expectations. Hence, yield curve data can be used to provide implied market expectations of inflation and inflation risks in real time, which is of use to central banks and financial market participants. Christensen, Lopez, and Rudebusch (2010) is an example of applying an ANSM to this topic.
- **Fixed interest portfolio management.** GATSMs generally describe interest rates of different maturities and their typical changes well, with factor loadings similar to principal components. Therefore, such models can be used from several perspectives for fixed interest portfolio management:
  - *Gauging and hedging the financial risks.* Changes to the value of portfolios of fixed interest securities from unanticipated changes in interest rates can be summarized well by several factor loadings. For example, Diebold, Ji, and Li (2006) develops such a framework based on Nelson and Siegel (1987) models, and Krippner (2005) develops a framework for ANSMs. Veronesi (2010, chapter 4) provides a related framework based on principle components, which is common practice in industry. I mention the pitfalls of such a framework from a ZLB perspective in section 2.2.2, and I will provide details in chapter 8.
  - *Identifying relative value trades.* If a GATSM is assumed to offer an indication of the "fair value" of interest rates along the yield curve, then interest rates for particular securities that deviate from a GATSM may suggest an opportunity to buy cheap securities or sell expensive securities. Veronesi (2010), pp. 570–71, provides an example of how a GATSM could be used in that manner to add value to a portfolio, and many banks and investment banks use fair-value yield curves and/or publish them for clients for that purpose. Ioannides (2003), Sercu and Wu (1997), and Krippner (2005) are examples that formally test whether relative value trades add value, and whether the results are positive even when trading costs are included.

Notwithstanding their popularity and widespread use, GATSMs have one well-acknowledged downside, but this was small enough pre-GFC to ignore relative to their benefits. The downside is that GATSMs technically admit arbitrage opportunities when applied to the "real world." That is, specifying a Gaussian diffusion process for the short rate implicitly specifies Gaussian diffusions for the interest rates of all maturities (because interest rates are the average of expected short rates). Therefore, GATSM interest rates themselves follow a Gaussian diffusion. That inherent property mathematically implies non-zero probabilities of any interest rate for any maturity evolving to negative values. Negative interest rates would be inconsistent with observed history, and such values would also be theoretically inconsistent in the "real world" where physical currency is available as an alternative investment. If negative interest rates did occur, then one could realize an arbitrage profit by borrowing funds (therefore receiving the absolute interest rate) and holding those funds as physical currency (with a known return of zero). Alternatively, one could sell bond options based on the non-zero probabilities of negative interest rates in GATSMs, but with no probability of an out-of-the-money expiry in practice.

Nevertheless, GATSMs were applied with the assumption that the inherent probabilities of negative interest rates were sufficiently small to make such models immaterially different to a "real world" model subject to the ZLB. For example, see Piazzesi (2010, p. 716) or Filopovic (2009, p. 86), although the assumption is typically left implicit. Figure 2.4 shows that such an assumption was perfectly valid even up to slightly before the FFR reached the ZLB. Panel 1 shows the model fit to the data for August 2008, and panel 2 shows that the projected distributions of future short rates had an immaterially small component of negative values. These projected short rate distributions are like those illustrated in panel 2 of Figure 2.3, but I have generated them directly by using the August 2008 estimated yield curve and its parameters to calculate the future expected value (i.e., the mean) of the short rate distribution and its standard deviation.

Panel 3 shows the one year projected distribution for interest rates on the yield curve, that is, the distributions for each of those interest rates in one year's time from August 2008. Again, I have generated these projected distributions directly by calculating the future expected value and the associated standard deviations for each interest rate. The important point is that the distributions show essentially zero probabilities of being at negative values.

Therefore, applying a GATSM would be an acceptable representation of the observed yield curve data even up to August 2008 when relatively low interest rates prevailed. Unfortunately, by December 2008 the FFR was essentially set to zero and, as I will now proceed to discuss, GATSMs can no longer provide an acceptable representation to observed yield curve data in such an environment.

2.2.2 Post-GFC

Assuming negligible probabilities of interest rates evolving to negative levels in a GATSM becomes untenable when interest rates approach the ZLB. To illustrate this

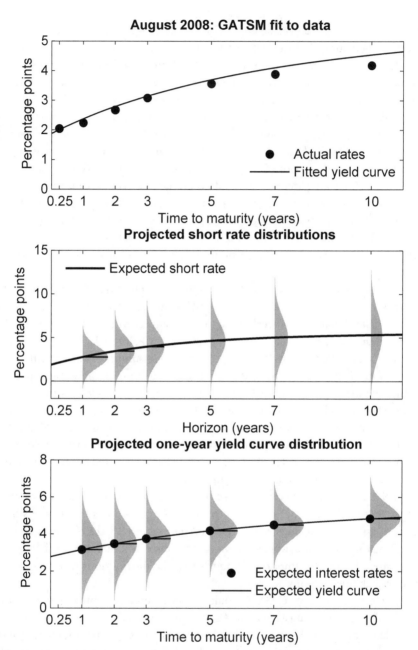

Figure 2.4 A GATSM estimated from data observed in a non-ZLB environment (panel 1) implies practically immaterial projected probabilities of future negative short rates (panel 2) and projected probabilities of future negative interest rates (panel 3).

point, Figure 2.5 repeats the yield curve perspectives in Figure 2.4, but for July 2012. Panel 1 shows that the yield curve data at this time was very constrained by the ZLB, as evidenced by all interest rates out to three years being close to zero. The model fit to the data is no longer very close or even a natural match in shape, although I will return to this point below.

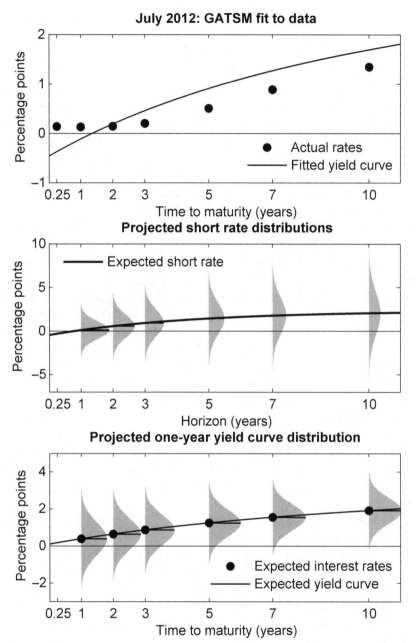

Figure 2.5 A GATSM estimated from data observed in a ZLB environment (panel 1) implies very material projected probabilities of future negative short rates (panel 2) and projected probabilities of future negative interest rates (panel 3).

The key point in Figure 2.5 is in panel 2, where the projected short rate distributions have very material probabilities of being negative, even out to the 10-year horizon. In turn, panel 3 shows the one-year projected interest rate distributions for many maturities have very material probabilities of being at negative levels. Even for the 5- and 7-year interest rates, the probabilities of negative interest rates are noticeably greater than zero.

Those probabilities of negative interest rates from the GATSM imply a severe misspecification relative to the observed data that the model is trying to represent. In essence, the GATSM is implicitly assuming that short rates and interest rates can freely evolve to negative values, but in reality the observed data is constrained by the ZLB from evolving to negative values. Therefore, the estimated GATSM cannot provide a valid and realistic representation of the term structure and its dynamics. However, shadow/ZLB-GATSMs can, as I will explain in the next section.

The results I have presented in panels 2 and 3 are a general feature that would apply to any GATSM used to represent the data. Specifically, while the fit of the model to the data in panel 1 could be improved by applying a more flexible GATSM, the issue of material probabilities of negative projected future short rates and interest rates would remain.

Figure 2.6 provides another perspective on how GATSMs are inconsistent with the yield curve data from a ZLB environment. There I have plotted the interest rate volatilities (annualized standard deviations of interest rate changes, in this case monthly changes) for different maturities calculated over three different sample periods. The first period is my entire sample of yield curve data from November 1985 to March 2014, the second period is the data prior to December 2008 (which I call the non-ZLB environment), and the third period is the data from December 2008 (which I call the ZLB environment). Note that I will describe the data set completely in chapter 3 and summarize it in chapter 7.

The key point in Figure 2.6 is that there is a distinct change in the volatilities of all interest rates between the non-ZLB and ZLB periods, and particularly when comparing the volatilities for the shorter-maturity interest rates. GATSMs imply that the interest rates of a given maturity should have the same volatility at each point in time. Therefore, a GATSM will not be able to accommodate the change in volatility apparent in Figure 2.6.

As a related aside of relevance to the next section, the distinctly lower volatilities for shorter-maturity interest rates in the ZLB periods occur because short-maturity interest rates are "sticky" in a ZLB environment, that is, they tend to stay approximately static around zero for an extended period of time. This stickiness property is apparent in the time series plots of the FFTR in Figures 2.1 and 2.2, and it is translated to all shorter-maturity interest rates in a ZLB environment. GATSMs cannot accommodate that stickiness property, but shadow/ZLB-GATSMs can, as I will explain in the following section.

In summary, GATSMs will not provide a valid representation of the term structure when any interest rates on the yield curve is close enough to zero to be materially constrained by the ZLB. As discussed in section 2.1.2, that is unfortunately the case for many developed economies at the time of writing. The issue is not just theoretical; in a ZLB environment, all of the applications of GATSMs mentioned in section 2.2.1 will be invalid and their output misleading, potentially quite seriously.

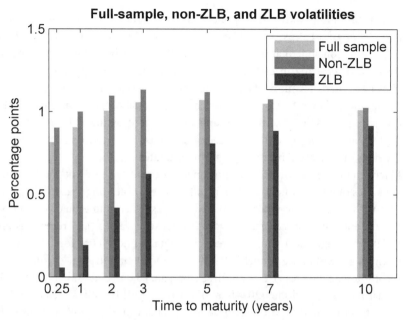

Figure 2.6 The changing volatility pattern of interest rate data between non-ZLB and ZLB environments, and within ZLB environments, cannot be matched by GATSMs.

To make the latter point clear, I provide relevant comments for each of the applications previously mentioned. I also mention in brackets where shadow/ZLB term structure models, which I will discuss in the next section, have already been applied to resolve the issues that arise when using GATSMs in a ZLB environment.

- **Gauging expectations of monetary policy rates.** Fitting yield curve data in a ZLB environment with a GATSM will overstate market expectations of when the policy rate will be increased. In essence, this occurs because GATSMs cannot accommodate the stickiness property of short rates at the ZLB, and will always strongly mean revert back to their long-horizon value. Bauer and Rudebusch (2013) and Richard (2013) provide related analysis and discussion on this point (and demonstrate how shadow/ZLB term structure models provide more plausible implied market expectations).
- **Yield curve forecasting.** Similar to the discussion in the previous point, GATSMs will tend to predict a normalization of the yield curve to its typical historical shape more quickly than the stickiness property of short-maturity interest rates in a ZLB environment would suggest. Bauer and Rudebusch (2013) and Christensen and Rudebusch (2014) provide such evidence for GATSMs (and demonstrate improved forecasting performance using a shadow/ZLB term structure model).
- **Quantifying risk premiums.** Because GATSMs do not allow for a ZLB, they will tend to ascribe movements in longer-maturity interest rates to movements

in risk premiums rather than policy rate expectations. For example, Adrian and Fleming (2013) used results from the Adrian, Moench, and Crump (2014) GATSM to conclude that the sharp rise in US 10-year bond rates following the mention of tapering in early 2013 was entirely due to risk premium changes. However, market commentary at the time suggested at least some role for changes to policy rate expectations. Carriero, Mouabbi, and Vangelista (2014) discusses how GATSM term premiums are distorted by the ZLB (and demonstrate that allowing for the ZLB using a shadow/ZLB term structure model provides more reasonable term premium estimates).

- **Macrofinance.** If a GATSM can no longer adequately represent the level and dynamics of interest rate data, then it will likely be misleading to use in conjunction with macroeconomic data. Indeed, the issues are quite nuanced: output growth and inflation can freely evolve to negative values (i.e., recessions and deflationary episodes) while interest rate data cannot. Therefore, a GATSM within a macrofinance model will have a difficult time trying to consistently accommodate the properties of both sets of data. (Bauer and Rudebusch [2013], Richard [2013], Jackson [2014], and Priebsch [2014] estimate shadow/ZLB term structure models with macroeconomic data, which generally improves the shadow/ZLB term structure estimates. Wu and Xia [2013, 2014], Lombardi and Zhu [2014], and Francis, Jackson and Owyang [2014] estimate macroeconomic models using pre-estimated shadow short rates as the policy variable and obtain better results in the non-ZLB environment than using the FFR.[3])

- **Inflation expectations.** If a GATSM can no longer adequately represent the level and dynamics of nominal interest rates, then using it to compare to inflation-indexed yield curve data will provide a misleading gauge of inflation expectations and associated risks. Related to the discussion in the previous two bullet points, the issues are again quite nuanced. First, the real and inflation components of interest rates are individually free to evolve to negative values (e.g., inflation-indexed yield curve data has often been observed at negative values), but the nominal interest rate data that combines those real and inflation components are not. Second, the risk premium ascribed to long-horizon inflation expectations will be distorted by not allowing for the ZLB in the nominal interest rate data. Carriero, Mouabbi, and Vangelista (2014) provides further discussion on these issues (and how using a shadow/ZLB term structure model resolves those issues).

- **Fixed interest portfolio management.** If a GATSM can no longer usefully describe interest rates of different maturities and their typical changes, then they will not be valid to apply to fixed interest portfolio management. Specifically:

  - *Gauging and hedging the financial risks.* GATSM or principal component risk measures are implicitly based on the assumption that unanticipated changes to the yield curve will be similar to those observed over history, that is, of similar magnitude and symmetric. In a ZLB environment, shorter-maturity interest rates will have much lower volatilities due to the stickiness property mentioned earlier (and apparent in Figure 2.6). The lower volatility also transmits to some extent into longer-maturity interest rates, but not completely, so the shapes of potential changes to the yield curve will also change. Finally, the potential yield curve changes in a ZLB environment will be asymmetric, because the ZLB constraint means that interest rates have lower probabilities of downward movements than upward movements. In combination, these three issues mean that assuming the standard framework (GATSMs or principal components) for risk measurement and hedging in fixed interest portfolios could be highly flawed. Richard (2013) discusses these issues (and notes how a shadow/ZLB term structure model provides a better framework).

- *Identifying relative value trades.* If a GATSM cannot describe the level of interest rates and their relationship by time to maturity well, then it can no longer be relied on to provide an indication of fair value that can be used to identify cheap and expensive securities. Note that a more flexible model could always be used to mechanically provide a closer fit to the data, but it would still be inadvisable to use it as a fair-value model because the extra flexibility would simply be masking fundamental deficiencies in the GATSM relative to the data.

2.3 Shadow/ZLB term structure models

Shadow/ZLB-GATSMs offer solutions to the issues that arise with monetary policy and GATSMs in ZLB environments. Shadow/ZLB-GATSMs use a GATSM to represent the shadow term structure,[4] which is essentially the term structure that would exist if physical currency were not available. This section provides an overview of the key points regarding shadow/ZLB-GATSMs from the perspective of the previous two sections. I will provide the complete details in subsequent chapters.

2.3.1 ZLB mechanism

The fundamental building blocks for shadow/ZLB-GATSMs are ZLB short rates $\underline{r}(t)$ that are constrained to be non-negative via the following mechanism from Black (1995):[5]

$$\underline{r}(t) = \max\{0, r(t)\} \tag{2.2}$$

where $r(t)$ is the shadow short rate from a GATSM specification. The ZLB mechanism represents the real-life choice available to investors at any point in time, which is to hold surplus funds as physical currency with a nominal return of zero or to invest the surplus funds at the shadow short rate $r(t)$. When the shadow short rate is negative, investors will prefer to hold physical currency with a return of zero rather than accept a negative return from investing at the shadow short rate.

The ZLB mechanism means that a Gaussian diffusion for the shadow short rates can freely adopt negative values, or even begin at negative values, while the ZLB short rate diffusion will remain bounded below by zero. Those properties respectively carry over to shadow interest rates $R(t, \tau)$ and ZLB interest rates $\underline{R}(t, \tau)$, as I will illustrate shortly. First, I will note that I use the underscore "_" here and in all notation following to indicate quantities that are subject to a lower bound, and I omit the underscore for shadow quantities. Also note that the using non-zero value in equation 2.2, that is, $\underline{r}(t) = \max\{r_L, r(t)\}$, would provide the mechanism for a non-zero lower bound. I will use zero as the lower bound throughout this chapter for clarity, but it is easy to relax that assumption, as I will show in chapter 4.

To illustrate the foundation and intuition of shadow/ZLB-GATSMs, I use two figures based on one of the shadow/ZLB-GATSMs I estimate later in the book. Figure 2.7 contains the shadow yield curve, and Figure 2.8 contains the associated ZLB yield curve generated by applying the ZLB mechanism.

In Figure 2.7 I have first plotted a Gaussian diffusion for the shadow short rate by generating some paths for $r(t + \tau)$. These paths are free to start at and evolve to negative values. Panel 2 shows the projected distribution of shadow short rates for different horizons τ. These distributions have substantial probabilities of negative values, which is consistent with the many negative values for $r(t + \tau)$ in the simulated paths. Note that $r(t + \tau)$ has the same mean reversion and distribution properties previously discussed for the GATSM in Figure 2.3, because the shadow term structure is defined as a GATSM. Panel 3 contains the shadow yield curve $R(t, \tau)$, which is essentially the mean of the expected shadow short rates up to each horizon τ. The shadow yield curve can adopt negative values.

Figure 2.8 shows the ZLB term structure perspectives associated with each of the shadow term structure perspectives in Figure 2.7. Hence, panel 1 contains the ZLB short rate diffusions obtained using $\underline{r}(t + \tau) = \max\{0, r(t + \tau)\}$, where $r(t + \tau)$ is obtained from the paths in panel 1 of Figure 2.7. By construction, no paths of $\underline{r}(t + \tau)$ will contain negative values. Panel 2 contains the projected distributions of ZLB short rates. These may be seen as the projected shadow short rate distributions in panel 2 of Figure 2.7 with negative values set to zero. The mean or expected value of the ZLB short rates at each horizon will therefore always be positive, because it is the mean of zero and positive values from the distribution of $\underline{r}(t + \tau)$. Note that the expected values (or mean values) of the ZLB short rates will always be higher than the expected shadow short rates in Figure 2.7, because the latter includes negative values, but those are set to zero before calculating the mean of ZLB short rates.

Panel 3 contains the ZLB yield curve, which is essentially the mean of the expected values of the ZLB short rates up to each given horizon. I provide the precise relationship in chapter 4, which again uses an intermediate step involving a forward rate expression. Panel 3 also contains the observed yield curve data, which is for July 2012. The fit of the shadow/ZLB-GATSM to the data is now very good compared to the fit of the GATSM to the same data in Figure 2.5. The improvement is simply due to adding in the ZLB mechanism; I have not changed anything else in

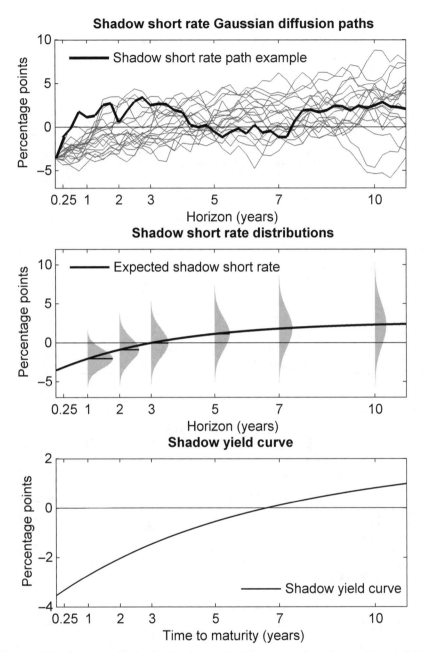

Figure 2.7 A Gaussian diffusion for the shadow short rate (panel 1) produces projected distributions of future shadow short rates (panel 2) and shadow interest rates as the expected return on the shadow short rates up to each future horizon/time to maturity τ (panel 3).

the model specification. More importantly, the yield curve data and the ZLB yield curve from the shadow/ZLB-GATSM are now both subject to the ZLB constraint, unlike the GATSM, so there is no longer a misspecification of the model relative to the data being modeled.

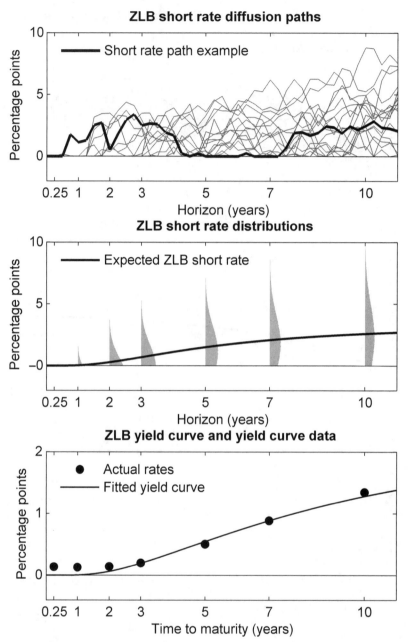

Figure 2.8 The zero-truncated Gaussian diffusion for the shadow short rate (panel 1) produces projected distributions of future ZLB short rates (panel 2) and ZLB interest rates as the expected return on the ZLB short rates up to each future horizon/time to maturity τ (panel 3).

Figure 2.9 illustrates that the shadow/ZLB-GATSM can also accommodate the volatility pattern by the maturity of interest rate data in ZLB environments, which was illustrated in Figure 2.6. Panels 1 and 2 respectively show the shadow and ZLB yield curves for July 2012 from Figures 2.7 and 2.8, and then the one-year

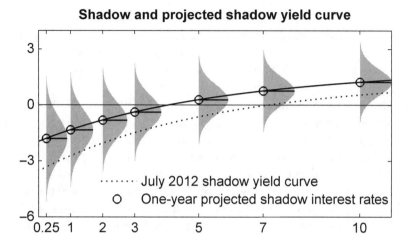

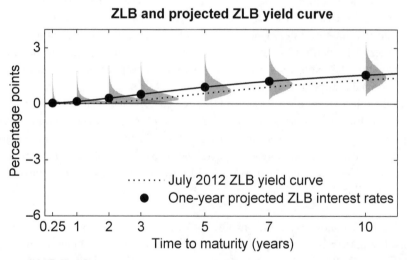

Figure 2.9 ZLB environment example of the shadow/ZLB-GATSM. The shadow yield curve and its projected shadow interest rate distributions can freely adopt negative values (panel 1), while the associated ZLB yield curve and its projected ZLB interest rate distributions are constrained by the ZLB mechanism to be non-negative (panel 2).

projected shadow and the ZLB yield curves along with the projected distributions of selected interest rates. There are several points of note from the two panels:

- The shadow yield curve has Gaussian dynamics, consistent with its GATSM specification. Hence, the projected shadow yield curve relative to the prevailing shadow yield curve can evolve freely, and the projected distributions of interest rates around the central projections are Gaussian and therefore symmetric.

- The shadow/ZLB-GATSM can represent a current and expected shape of the yield curve consistent with an ongoing ZLB constraint. In particular, the projected 0.25- and 1-year interest rates in this example essentially remain at zero. Hence, the shadow/ZLB-GATSM can represent the stickiness property of interest rates in a ZLB environment.
- The stickiness property of ZLB interest rates is directly related to the probability of shadow interest rates evolving to positive values over a given passage of time (e.g., one year in Figure 2.9). That probability is in turn dictated by the probabilities that shadow short rates will be positive over the given passage of time and the remaining time to maturity of each interest rate, as indicated in Figures 2.7 and 2.8. For example, the low probabilities of positive shadow short rates over 1.25- and two-year horizons means that the one-year projections of 0.25- and 1-year interest rates in figure 2.9 are still very close to zero. The interest rates for longer times to maturity are less sticky, which is consistent with the larger probabilities of positive shadow short rates over those longer horizons.
- The projected rises in longer-maturity interest rates are larger than for short-maturity interest rates. Hence, the shadow/ZLB-GATSM can represent the pattern of volatility for interest rates by time to maturity already presented in Figure 2.6. Note that annualized volatility is proportional to the one-year projected changes I have presented.
- The projected distributions around the projected ZLB yield curve are very asymmetric for shorter-maturity interest rates. This correctly reflects that downward surprises to interest rates cannot lead to lower interest rates at shorter maturities because they are already constrained below by the ZLB. The asymmetry becomes less for longer-maturity interest rates because they are less constrained by the ZLB.

Figure 2.10 shows that the shadow/ZLB-GATSM can also accommodate the volatility pattern by maturity of interest rate data in a non-ZLB environment, so the shadow/ZLB-GATSM is equally applicable to non-ZLB environments. The panels are analogous to those from Figure 2.9, but the results are obtained from the shadow/ZLB-GATSM for August 2008 (which is within the non-ZLB environment). The August 2008 shadow yield curve therefore displays exactly the same GATSM dynamics as Figure 2.9, but the entire shadow yield curve is at a higher level than the shadow yield curve in Figure 2.9. That higher level means there is an immaterial constraint from the ZLB, and so the shadow/ZLB-GATSM allows more of the Gaussian dynamics from the shadow yield curve to be transmitted into the ZLB yield curve. In turn, ZLB interest rates have one-year projected distributions very similar to the projections for the shadow interest rate and their distributions. In other words, the ZLB interest rates in this example are not sticky and they display one-year changes and hence the pattern of volatility consistent with the non-ZLB pattern of volatilities in Figure 2.6.

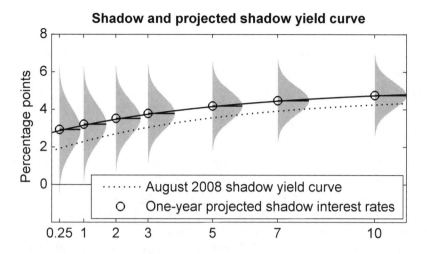

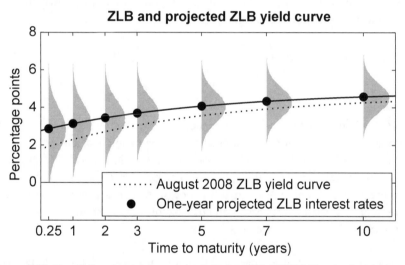

Figure 2.10 Non-ZLB environment example of shadow/ZLB-GATSM. The shadow yield curve and its projected shadow interest rate distributions (panel 1) are similar to the associated ZLB yield curve and its projected ZLB interest rate distributions (panel 2).

Comparing panel 2 from Figures 2.9 and 2.10 shows that the shadow/ZLB-GATSM can represent the overall reduction in the volatility of observed interest rates from the non-ZLB environment to a ZLB environment, which is a notable feature in Figure 2.6. Specifically, the shadow/ZLB-GATSM allows freer movement of all ZLB interest rates in the non-ZLB environment, as shown by the larger change in the one-year projection, compared to the ZLB environment in which the projected changes are much less.

2.3.2 Options to hold physical currency

An alternative and more intuitive expression of the Black (1995) ZLB mechanism in equation 2.2 is to rearrange it explicitly into a shadow short rate component and a physical currency option component. Specifically:

$$\underline{r}(t) = r(t) + \max\{-r(t), 0\} \tag{2.3}$$

where $\max\{-r(t), 0\}$ represents the payoff from the option to hold physical currency at time t. Under this arrangement, investors are now willing to always invest surplus funds at the shadow short rate, whether it is negative or positive, so long as they are also given options to insure against the possibility of receiving a negative shadow short rate should such a realization occur.

With that decomposition, the ZLB short rate diffusion for $r(t + \tau)$ and hence the ZLB yield curve $\underline{R}(t, \tau)$ at time t as a function of time-to-maturity τ may therefore be envisaged as the sum of two components, that is,

$$\underline{R}(t, \tau) = R(t, \tau) + Z(t, \tau) \tag{2.4}$$

where:

- $R(t, \tau)$ is the shadow yield curve generated from the expected value of the shadow rate $r(t + \tau)$ for all instants between time t and $t + \tau$, and
- $Z(t, \tau)$ is what I will call the "physical currency option effect." $Z(t, \tau)$ cumulates the expected value of the option payoffs $\max\{-r(t + \tau), 0\}$ for all instants between time t and $t + \tau$. In other words, $Z(t, \tau)$ is a portfolio of European options that insures each potential shadow rate outcome $r(t + \tau)$ against negative values between time t and $t + \tau$.

Essentially, any ZLB yield curve can therefore be envisaged as a shadow interest rate $R(t, \tau)$ that would prevail in the absence of physical currency and a ZLB, and an option effect $Z(t, \tau)$ that exists because the availability of physical currency establishes the ZLB. More specifically, $Z(t, \tau)$ represents expected payoffs to holding physical currency (at an effective nominal interest rate of zero) against the alternative of being obliged to invest at the shadow short rate when it is negative. The shadow short rate is the instantaneous rate on the fitted yield curve, which is $R(t, \tau)$ evaluated with a time to maturity $\tau = 0$; i.e. $r(t) = R(t, 0)$.

Figure 2.11 illustrates the decomposition of ZLB yield curves (and selected fitted interest rates) into their shadow yield curve and option effect components. I have selected three dates to show how the shadow short rate and the associated yield curve components change depending on whether the ZLB constraint is negligible, material, or large. Hence, panel 1 of Figure 2.9 shows that when all interest rates are far enough from the ZLB, then the shadow short rate is positive and the

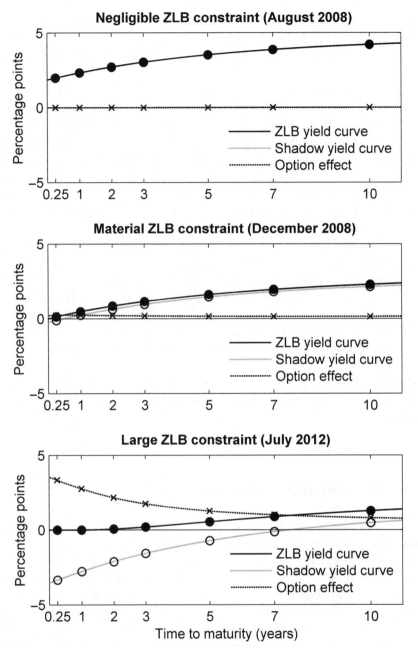

Figure 2.11 Examples of the ZLB yield curve decomposed into a shadow yield curve and option effect component for three different degrees of the ZLB constraint on the yield curve data.

option effect is small for all maturities. In other words, the expected value of the option to hold physical currency is small, which in turn follows from the small probabilities that shadow short rates could evolve to negative levels within ten years (and the relatively small payoffs if they did, i.e., from Figure 2.10, the values of the projected distribution below zero are very small). The shadow short rate in this example is $r(t) = R(t,0) = 1.87\%$. The option effect $\max\{-r(t),0\}$ is therefore zero, and so the ZLB short rate equals the shadow short rate, that is, $\underline{r}(t) = R(t,0) = 1.87\%$.

Panel 2 shows that when some interest rates are close to the ZLB, then the shadow short rate can become negative, and the option effect becomes noticeable for all maturities. That is, $r(t) = R(t,0) = -0.22\%$, and there are now apparent differences between all points on the ZLB yield curve and the shadow yield curve. The option effects are larger than in panel 1 because the probabilities of a payoff to the option to hold physical currency at any of the points in time over the next ten years are larger, as are the potential payoffs themselves. For example, the option effect for the $\tau = 0$ maturity is the option payoff $\max\{-r(t),0\} = \max\{-(-0.22\%),0\} = 0.22\%$. The ZLB short rate is $\underline{r}(t) = -0.22\% + 0.22\% = 0\%$.

Panel 3 shows that with many interest rates close to the ZLB, which indicates a large constraint from the ZLB, the shadow short rate can take on very negative values. In this example, $r(t) = R(t,0) = -3.54\%$. The option effect also becomes large for all maturities, and particularly so for shorter maturities. The large values for short-maturity interest rates reflect the high probabilities that shadow short rates will remain negative. Specifically, referring to panel 2 of Figure 2.9, even after three years there is a 50% probability of the investor exercising the option to hold physical currency. The option effect for the $\tau = 0$ maturity is $\max\{-r(t),0\} = -3.54\%$, which gives a ZLB short rate of $\underline{r}(t) = 0\%$. The option effect declines for longer maturities as the probability and payoff from the option to hold physical currency reduces.

2.4 Monetary policy revisited

The shadow short rate (SSR) is one output from shadow/ZLB-GATSMs that suggests itself as a means quantifying the stance of monetary policy in ZLB environments. The SSR is analogous to the FFR, because the SSR is the shortest-maturity interest rate on the shadow yield curve in both non-ZLB and ZLB environments, but it can take on negative values rather than being constrained at zero. Therefore, on the face of it, using the FFR as a policy rate in conventional monetary policy periods, combined with the SSR in unconventional policy periods, suggests itself as a consistent measure of the stance of monetary policy over non-ZLB and ZLB environments.

Using SSRs in this manner has been advocated in Krippner (2011, 2012a,b,c, 2013c) as cited by Bullard (2012, 2013), and Wu and Xia (2013, 2014) as cited by Hamilton (2013), Higgins and Meyer (2013), and Zumbrun (2014). To this end, Figure 2.12 plots the times series of the FFTR, when it is positive (i.e., up to November 2008), and an estimated SSR from December 2008 onward (i.e., after the FFTR

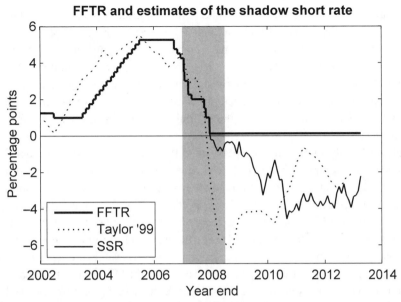

Figure 2.12 Potential use of an estimated shadow short rate (SSR) as a proxy for the FFTR, and therefore as an indicator of monetary policy, during a ZLB environment.

was set to a range of 0 to 0.25%). I have also plotted the Taylor 1999 policy rate prescription as a comparison.

There are two issues related to using estimates of the SSR to indicate the stance of monetary policy. I will briefly mention them here and will follow up with more details in chapter 7. The first is practical. That is, SSRs can be very sensitive to the model and data used to estimate them. The second issue is theoretical. That is, how should one consider the potential influence of an estimated negative SSR on the economy, given that the actual policy rate and related interest rates in the economy remain subject to the ZLB? In particular, borrowers and lenders in the economy do not transact at negative interest rates (where lenders would pay borrowers the absolute interest rate), but at a minimum of zero interest rate with appropriate margins. Therefore the potential stimulus from lowering a negative SSR cannot be as great as lowering a positive FFR.

Due to these issues, one should be cautious about interpreting either the level or changes in estimated SSRs in the same way as levels and changes in the FFR or FFTR. As one example, Taylor policy rules suggest a level of the FFTR given the output gap and inflation. However, if the levels and changes of negative SSRs are not theoretically equivalent to the FFTR, then Taylor rules will not necessarily provide a suitable prescription for the SSR. Moreover, the sensitivity of estimated SSRs means that one could not be confident that a particular level of the SSR had actually been obtained.

All that said, if SSRs from a range of models show similar profiles, then one should at least be able to use them as an ordinal measure of monetary policy.

That is, upward movements would indicate more restrictive policy and downward movements indicate more stimulatory policy. I will revisit this in chapter 7.

A more robust and theoretically appealing measure of the monetary policy stance is the "Effective Monetary Stimulus." The Effective Monetary Stimulus (EMS) is also estimated from shadow/ZLB term structure models, but it aggregates the current and expected component of actual policy rates (i.e., zero or positive), and it does so relative to an estimate of the neutral rate that is also obtained from the shadow/ZLB-GATSM.

Figure 2.13 illustrates the concept of the EMS at two selected points in time; it is essentially the total area between the estimated neutral rate and the expected path of the SSR, truncated at zero if required to leave just the "effective" or economically relevant component of the SSR and its expectations. For the August 2008 example in Figure 2.13, the SSR and its expected path are all positive, so no truncation at zero is required to calculate the EMS. For the July 2011 example, the SSR and its expected path are initially negative, and so those negative values are set to zero. The zero settings represent that only the positive part of the SSR relative to the neutral rate is effective for monetary stimulus, because the actual interest rates faced by economic agents cannot fall below zero.

Figure 2.14 illustrates the time series of the EMS. Higher values indicate larger amounts of monetary stimulus. In practice, as I will detail in chapter 7, EMS measures are more robust than SSRs with respect to the model and data used to estimate them.

2.5 Alternative ZLB models

This section is not necessary for those specifically interested in shadow/ZLB-GATSMs and their application. However, it will be useful for readers who may have something like the following question in mind: why not just use one of the alternative ZLB models that have long been available in the literature instead of shadow/ZLB-GATSMs?

The initial answer from the perspective of jointly addressing monetary policy and term structure modeling is that alternative ZLB models do not produce the potential information provided by a shadow term structure. Specifically, the advantage of shadow/ZLB-GATSMs is that the shadow term structure provides shadow short rate and interest rates, and other information that can continue to be used to indicate the stance of monetary policy.

Furthermore, even from the narrower perspective of term structure modeling in its own right, alternative ZLB term structure models have several issues that limit their widespread application in non-ZLB and ZLB environments. One issue is that these models often have implausible model-implied dynamics compared to the dynamics of observed interest rates, particularly near the ZLB. Alternative ZLB

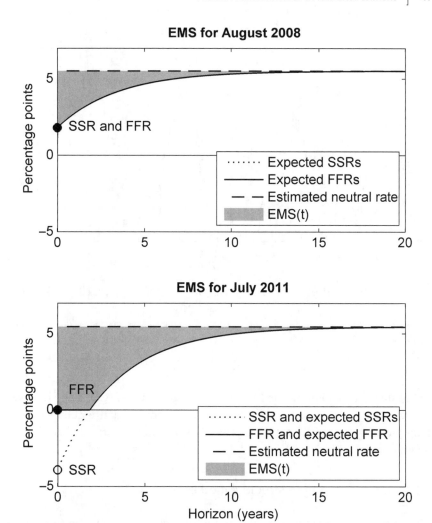

Figure 2.13 Examples of the "Effective Monetary Stimulus" for a non-ZLB environment (panel 1) and a ZLB environment (panel 2).

models are also generally less tractable than K-AGMs, particularly for general specifications in which the short rate diffusions introduced in section 2.3 are a function of several so-called state variables, which themselves undergo a diffusion process. A lack of general tractability therefore obliges the user to trade off the flexibility of the model specification against the practical challenges of estimating the model from the data. Conversely, Krippner (2011, 2012b,c, 2013d,e) shadow/ZLB-GATSMs, like GATSMs themselves, are guaranteed to retain a high degree of tractability regardless of their specification, and will therefore be always be straightforward to apply to the observed data.

I will discuss just the three standard classes of ZLB models in subsections 2.5.1 to 2.5.3 to make the points noted above. An excellent reference for further discussion

EMS estimates

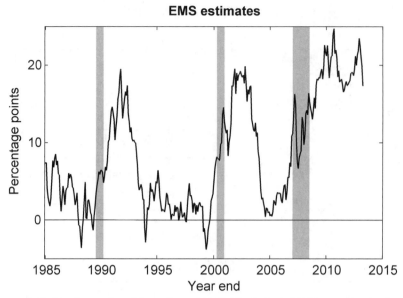

Figure 2.14 The time series of the estimated EMS. The indicated EMS areas for the August 2008 and July 2011 examples in Figure 2.13 each provide a single data point for this EMS time series.

on the three models is James and Webber (2000) pp. 226-335, which also discusses several other positive interest rate models. Three recent alternative ZLB models are Filipović, Larsson, and Trolle (2013), Renne (2013), and Monfort, Pegoraro, Renne, and Roussellet (2014).

2.5.1 Square-root term structure models

The original single state variable square-root model was presented in Cox, Ingersoll, and Ross (1985b), and so I will use the terminology CIR dynamics hereafter. The state variable is the short rate $r(t)$ itself and CIR dynamics means that the volatility of $r(t)$ is specified to be proportional to $\sqrt{r(t)}$ rather than constant as in GATSMs, that is respectively $\sigma\sqrt{r(t)}$ versus σ. Therefore, the volatility of $r(t)$ becomes smaller as $r(t)$ approaches zero, and such dynamics eliminate the probability of $r(t)$ evolving through zero. The CIR model also produces closed-form analytic solutions for bond prices and options, along with the relatively simple noncentral chi-square distribution that is used for estimations.

However, the attenuation of volatility for low values of $r(t)$ is also one of the pitfalls of the CIR model. Because $r(t)$ is the single state variable, the volatilities of all interest rates across the entire yield curve in the CIR model will also be proportional to $\sqrt{r(t)}$. Therefore, the volatilities of all interest rates in the CIR model will approach zero as $r(t)$ approaches zero. Obviously that property is counter to empirical evidence. For example, Figure 2.6 has already illustrated that longer maturity interest rates retain volatilities in a ZLB environment that are similar to the non-zero environment.

Specifications of CIR models with more than one state variable have more flexibility to cope with the interest rate volatility issue noted above. However, Singleton (2006) p. 327 notes that the results from such models are still empirically unsatisfactory with respect to the covariances of the state variables and adequately representing the market prices of risk.

CIR models with more than one state variable are also not generally tractable. Closed-form analytic solutions for interest rate securities and estimation distributions are available for special cases in which the covariances between the state variables are set to zero, although they involve the relatively complex evaluation of the product of noncentral chi-square distributions (e.g., see Chen and Scott [1992] for the case with two state variables, and the general comment in Piazzesi [2010] p. 727). Closed-form analytic solutions and estimation distributions are no longer available with non-zero covariances. A final issue regarding CIR models is that they require constraints on their parameters to prevent the variance of the short rate from becoming negative. Therefore, estimation is more complex than for GATSMs and shadow/ZLB-GATSMs.

2.5.2 Log-normal term structure models

Log-normal term structure models include the Black, Derman, and Toy (1990) and Black and Karasinki (1991) models with one state variable, which are well known in financial markets. The short rate $r(t)$ in those models is the exponential of the Gaussian diffusion process for the state variable (or potentially a linear combination of more than one state variable could be used). Taking the exponential of the Gaussian diffusion process therefore ensures that $r(t)$ remains positive.

One can also view log-normal models directly from the perspective of the process for the short rate $r(t)$. The volatility of the short rate turns out to be proportional to $r(t)$ for low values of $r(t)$. Therefore, like the original CIR model, log-normal models also have the property that the volatilities of yields along the yield curve will approach zero as $r(t)$ approaches zero. Regarding tractability, log-normal models do not have a closed-form analytic solution for bonds. Therefore, estimation from yield curve data must be undertaken using relatively time-consuming numerical methods (e.g., an interest rate tree, which is a method I will briefly discuss in subsection 5.2.3).

2.5.3 Quadratic Gaussian term structure models

Quadratic Gaussian term structure models use a short rate $r(t)$ that is a quadratic function of the Gaussian diffusion process for the state variables, rather than the linear function used for GATSMs. With appropriate restrictions on the parameters for the quadratic function, the short rate can be guaranteed to remain positive.

However, the dynamics produced by quadratic Gaussian models include reflections from the ZLB, that is, a negative innovation to one or more state variables when r(t) is near the ZLB will result in r(t) rising. Such behavior would be counter to the stickiness property of short-maturity interest rates. Regarding tractability, closed-form analytic solutions are available for some specifications, although the solution is relatively complex even for models with one state variable.

Aside from the in-principle issues already presented above, Andreasen and Meldrum (2013) finds that shadow/ZLB-GATSMs provide a better representation of yield curve data in a ZLB environment than quadratic Gaussian models. Kim and Singleton (2012) find that shadow/ZLB-GATSMs perform well compared to quadratic Gaussian models.

2.6 Summary

- Nominal interest rates in nearly all major economies effectively reached the zero lower bound (ZLB) in late 2008/early 2009, and have remained there since. In such environments, it is no longer possible for central banks to lower their policy interest rates to provide monetary stimulus to the economy. Unconventional policies, such as asset purchases and forward policy guidance, have been employed to provide further stimulus, and the policy rate alone is therefore no longer a useful metric for monitoring the stance of monetary policy and its effect on the economy.

- Gaussian affine term structure models (GATSMs) used for many financial market applications are deficient when interest rates are near the ZLB. The key issue is that GATSMs implicitly assume that interest rates can evolve below the ZLB, but that is inconsistent with observed history and because economic agents would opt to hold physical currency with an effective return of zero rather than accept a negative interest rate.

- The shadow/ZLB-GATSM class of term structure models resolves the issue of negative GATSM interest rates. A GATSM is used to represent the shadow term structure, and the shadow/ZLB framework provides an appropriate adjustment to ensure that actual, or ZLB, interest rates are constrained to be non-negative. The adjustment is effectively the optionality from the availability of physical currency as an alternative to negative interest rates. The option effect is large near the ZLB and fades to essentially zero when the ZLB is no longer materially constraining.

- The shadow yield curve from the shadow/ZLB-GATSM also provides information useful for operating and monitoring monetary policy in ZLB environments. Alternative ZLB models do not provide such information.

- In this chapter, I have presented a non-technical overview of the key concept of term structure modeling in non-ZLB and ZLB environments. Chapters 3 to 6 provide the full details on their specification, derivation, and estimation.

3 | Gaussian Affine Term Structure Models

In this chapter, I outline the GATSM framework, explain how GATSMs may be estimated from yield curve data, and use estimation results to detail the practical pitfalls of applying them in ZLB environments. The outline first serves to establish the present standard for term structure modeling, given that GATSMs are used extensively by researchers and practitioners, as already discussed in chapter 2. I also use GATSMs to represent the shadow term structure in the shadow/ZLB-GATSMs in the remainder of the book, so it is important to establish the precise notation and estimation methods for GATSMs that will carry over to those shadow/ZLB-GATSMs. Related to that point, I can then present the shadow/ZLB-GATSM framework and its estimation in chapter 4 as a relatively tractable modification to the GATSM class.

I begin with an exposition of GATSMs in section 3.1, including their specification, associated dynamics, and the resulting term structure expressions. In section 3.2, I provide an overview of how GATSMs are estimated using the Kalman filter.

In section 3.3, I provide an extensive fully worked example that shows how the material in sections 3.1 and 3.2 is applied in practice. I will carry that example forward to related fully worked examples of specifying, estimating, and applying shadow/ZLB-GATSM in chapters 4 and 5.

Section 3.4 provides a summary of key analytic results for many different GATSM specifications. These results also carry through to shadow/ZLB-GATSMs and their applications later in the book. In section 3.5, I provide some empirical results from estimating GATSMs that I will use to illustrate why it is not valid to apply GATSMs to yield curve data in ZLB environments. Section 3.6 briefly discusses alternative methods for estimating GATSMs.

For readers wanting more background on GATSMs and their estimation, there are many textbooks available that discuss GATSMs at varying levels. I have found that Piazzesi (2010) provides an excellent overview, and Singleton (2006) is a very comprehensive textbook that includes GATSMs and their estimation within the wider context of dynamic asset pricing models. Diebold and Rudebusch (2013) is an excellent reference for the specification and estimation of the arbitrage-free Nelson and Siegel (1987) class of models, which are a subclass of GATSMs that I will use throughout this book. More specifically on estimation techniques, there are many textbooks available on the Kalman filter and its application to maximum likelihood estimation. I have found that Hamilton (1994) provides an excellent overview, and Durbin and Koopman (2012) is a very comprehensive textbook. Simon (2006) and Grewal and Andrews (2008) are two comprehensive textbooks specifically on the Kalman filter that I will also refer to in this and subsequent chapters.

3.1 GATSMs

I will adopt the generic GATSM specification from Dai and Singleton (2002) pp. 437-38 in this section and for the remainder of the book. Dai and Singleton (2002) is a standard reference in the literature, it uses matrix notation that is very convenient for general specifications of GATSMs, and it already contains closed-form analytic term structure expressions for standard GATSM specifications. I refer readers that want an introduction or refresher on matrix notation to Appendix A.

The Dai and Singleton (2002) GATSM specification is also in continuous time, which naturally relates to the continuous-time shadow/ZLB-GATSMs that I will develop. The main advantages of continuous-time specifications are that they are more amenable to mathematical manipulation, and they lead to closed-form analytic solutions for all representations of the term structure, that is, forward rates, interest rates, and bond prices. Standard interest rate securities such as options on bonds also have closed-form analytic solutions.

Note that GATSMs can also be specified and estimated in discrete time, where interest rates evolve over small increments of time rather than as a continuous Gaussian diffusion. The associated term structure expressions take an iterative form based on difference equations. See Backus, Foresi, and Telmer (2010), Singleton (2006), and Piazzesi (2010) for details and further discussion. Joslin, Singleton, and Zhu (2011), Hamilton and Wu (2012), and Adrian, Moench, and Crump (2014) provide efficient methods for estimating discrete-time GATSMs. However, for small time increments, discrete-time GATSMs are completely analogous to continuous-time GATSMs.

3.1.1 GATSM specification

The short rate $r(t)$ at time t is a linear function of the state variables $x(t)$ at time t:

$$r(t) = a_0 + b_0' x(t) \tag{3.1}$$

where $r(t)$ is a scalar (i.e., dimensions of 1×1), a_0 is a constant scalar, b_0 is a constant $N \times 1$ vector containing the weights for the N state variables $x_n(t)$, and $x(t)$ is an $N \times 1$ vector containing the N state variables $x_n(t)$. Under the physical $\mathbb{P}$

measure, which I discuss shortly below, $x(t)$ evolves as a correlated vector Ornstein-Uhlenbeck process:

$$dx(t) = \kappa \left[\theta - x(t)\right] dt + \sigma dW(t) \tag{3.2}$$

where θ is a constant $N \times 1$ vector representing the long-run level of $x(t)$, κ is a constant $N \times N$ matrix that governs the deterministic mean reversion of $x(t)$ to θ, σ is a constant $N \times N$ matrix representing the potentially correlated variance of innovations to $x(t)$, and $dW(t)$ is an $N \times 1$ vector with independent Wiener components $dW_n(t) \sim N(0,1)\sqrt{dt}$, where $N(0,1)$ is the unit normal distribution.

The future evolution of the short rate under the $\mathbb{P}$ measure is therefore determined by the $\mathbb{P}$ measure process for $x(t)$. Note that the $\mathbb{P}$ measure is also known as the objective measure, and it refers to the actual expectations, and distributions around those expectations, that economic agents have about the future values of the state variables and short rates.

Securities in financial markets are priced under the risk-adjusted $\mathbb{Q}$ measure. The $\mathbb{Q}$ measure is also known as the risk-neutral measure, and the expected returns for all assets under this measure are equal to the risk-adjusted short rate. Hence, the $\mathbb{P}$ measure process for $x(t)$ and $r(t)$ must be adjusted for risk before it can be used to represent the observed term structure.

In GATSMs, the market prices of risk are typically specified as a linear function of the state variables, which allows the market prices of risk to vary over time:[1]

$$\Pi(t) = \sigma^{-1}\left[\gamma + \Gamma x(t)\right] \tag{3.3}$$

where $\Pi(t)$ is an $N \times 1$ vector containing the market prices of risk for each state variable, γ is a constant $N \times 1$ vector containing the constant component of the market prices of risk, and Γ is a constant $N \times N$ matrix that specifies how the market prices of risk vary with the state variables.

Under the risk-adjusted $\mathbb{Q}$ measure, $x(t)$ also evolves as a correlated vector Ornstein-Uhlenbeck process:

$$dx(t) = \tilde{\kappa}\left[\tilde{\theta} - x(t)\right] dt + \sigma d\tilde{W}(t) \tag{3.4}$$

where $\tilde{\kappa} = \kappa + \Gamma$, $\tilde{\theta} = \tilde{\kappa}^{-1}(\kappa\theta - \gamma)$, and $d\tilde{W}(t) = dW(t) + \Pi(t)dt$. The future evolution of the short rate under the $\mathbb{Q}$ measure is therefore determined by the $\mathbb{Q}$ measure process for $x(t)$. As a related aside, risk premiums in the term structure may be gauged by the difference between expectations for the future evolution of the short rate under the $\mathbb{P}$ measure, and expectations adjusted for risk under the $\mathbb{Q}$ measure. Risk premiums are a combination of the quantities of risk, provided by the standard deviation matrix σ, and the market prices for those risks, $\Pi(t)$.

As I will show in the following two subsections, the GATSM state variables in conjunction with the GATSM parameters provide a complete description of the current yield curve and its evolution into future times. In particular, the yield curve that arises from the GATSM specification will be represented by factor loadings multiplied by their associated state variables. The factor loadings are simple functions of time to maturity. For example, the arbitrage-free Nelson and Siegel (1987) model (ANSM) specification with three state variables that I will introduce in section 3.3.1 produces Level, Slope, and Bow factor loadings, which correspond to the components typically observed in yield curve data.

3.1.2 GATSM dynamics and related calculations

The dynamics for the state variable vector $x(t)$ under the $\mathbb{P}$ measure are given by the solution to the stochastic differential equation in equation 3.2. From Meucci (2010) p. 3.

$$x(t+\tau) = \theta + \exp(-\kappa\tau)[x(t) - \theta] + \int_t^{t+\tau} \exp(-\kappa[\tau - u])\sigma\,dW(u) \quad (3.5)$$

where τ is the future horizon from time t and $\exp(-\kappa\tau)$ is a matrix exponential. Note that equation 3.5 is essentially a first-order vector-autoregression, but in continuous time.

For the analytic manipulations required in this book, the matrix exponential $\exp(-\kappa\tau)$ may be expressed in terms of scalar exponentials via an eigensystem decomposition of κ. Hence, the eigensystem decomposition of κ is

$$\kappa = V\kappa_D V^{-1} \quad (3.6)$$

where V is a constant $N \times N$ matrix containing the eigenvectors in columns and κ_D is a constant $N \times N$ diagonal matrix of eigenvalues, $\kappa_D = \mathrm{diag}[\kappa_1,\ldots,\kappa_n,\ldots,\kappa_N]$. Note that the eigenvectors and eigenvalues can be complex, unless restrictions are imposed to preclude that result in practice, in which case entries will appear in pairs of complex conjugates. The matrix exponential $\exp(-\kappa\tau)$ is then

$$\exp(-\kappa\tau) = \exp\left(-V\kappa_D V^{-1}\tau\right)$$
$$= V\exp(-\kappa_D\tau)V^{-1}$$
$$= V\,\mathrm{diag}\left[\exp(-\kappa_1\tau),\ldots,\exp(-\kappa_N\tau)\right]V^{-1} \quad (3.7)$$

where the entries in the diagonal matrix are now the scalar exponentials $\exp(-\kappa_n\tau)$. Appendix A provides further details on the matrix exponential and its eigensystem decomposition.

To generate expressions relevant for the GATSM state equation in section 3.1.4, I apply the expectation and variance operators conditional on $x(t)$ to equation 3.5. Note that I use the subscript t and no tildes on $\mathbb{E}_t$ and var_t to denote that those operators are under the $\mathbb{P}$ measure and are applied at time t.

The respective results are[2]

$$\mathbb{E}_t \left[x(t+\tau) | x(t) \right] = \theta + \exp(-\kappa\tau) \left[x(t) - \theta \right] \tag{3.8}$$

and

$$\text{var}_t \left[x(t+\tau) | x(t) \right] = \int_0^\tau \exp(-\kappa u) \sigma\sigma' \exp\left(-\kappa' u\right) du$$
$$= V\Theta(\tau) V' \tag{3.9}$$

where $\Theta(\tau)$ contains the entries (by row i and column j)

$$[\Theta(\tau)]_{ij} = \Sigma_{ij} \frac{1}{\kappa_i + \kappa_j} \left[1 - \exp\left(-\{\kappa_i + \kappa_j\}\tau\right) \right] \tag{3.10}$$

and

$$\Sigma = V^{-1}\sigma\sigma' V'^{-1} \tag{3.11}$$

The dynamics for $x(t)$ under the $\mathbb{Q}$ measure are analogous to those for the $\mathbb{P}$ measure:

$$x(t+\tau) = \tilde{\theta} + \exp(-\tilde{\kappa}\tau) \left[x(t) - \tilde{\theta} \right] + \int_t^{t+\tau} \exp(-\tilde{\kappa}[\tau - u]) \sigma dW(u) \tag{3.12}$$

To generate expressions relevant for the GATSM term structure, I apply the expectations and variance operators conditional on the prevailing state variable vector $x(t)$ to obtain the respective results:

$$\tilde{\mathbb{E}}_t \left[x(t+\tau) | x(t) \right] = \tilde{\theta} + \exp(-\tilde{\kappa}\tau) \left[x(t) - \tilde{\theta} \right] \tag{3.13}$$

$$\widetilde{\text{var}}_t \left[x(t+\tau) | x(t) \right] = \int_0^\tau \exp(-\kappa u) \sigma\sigma' \exp\left(-\kappa' u\right) du \tag{3.14}$$

where the tildes on $\tilde{\mathbb{E}}_t$ and $\widetilde{\text{var}}_t$ denote that those operators are applied under the $\mathbb{Q}$ measure.

The expression for $\tilde{\mathbb{E}}_t \left[x(t+\tau) | x(t) \right]$ provides the conditional expectation of the short rate under the $\mathbb{Q}$ measure, $\tilde{\mathbb{E}}_t \left[r(t+\tau) | x(t) \right]$:

$$\tilde{\mathbb{E}}_t \left[r(t+\tau) | x(t) \right] = a_0 + b_0' \tilde{\mathbb{E}}_t \left[x(t+\tau) | x(t) \right]$$
$$= a_0 + b_0' \left\{ \tilde{\theta} + \exp(-\tilde{\kappa}\tau) \left[x(t) - \tilde{\theta} \right] \right\} \tag{3.15}$$

and the expression for $\widetilde{\text{var}}_t[x(t+\tau)|x(t)]$ provides the conditional variance $[\omega(\tau)]^2$ of the short rate under the $\mathbb{Q}$ measure:

$$
\begin{aligned}
[\omega(\tau)]^2 &= \widetilde{\text{var}}_t[r(t+\tau)|x(t)] \\
&= b_0'\,\widetilde{\text{var}}_t[x(t+\tau)|x(t)]\,b_0 \\
&= \int_0^\tau b_0'\exp(-\kappa u)\sigma\sigma'\exp(-\kappa'u)\,b_0\,du \qquad (3.16)
\end{aligned}
$$

The final required calculation related to GATSM dynamics is what I refer to as the volatility effect. The volatility effect, which I denote as $\text{VE}(\tau)$, captures the influence that volatility in the short rate has on expected returns due to Jensen's inequality. Specifically, the expected compounded return from investing in a volatile short rate over time t to $t+\tau$ is less than the compounded return from investing in the expected short rate over the same period.[3] The required calculation is the double integral:

$$
\text{VE}(\tau) = \int_0^\tau b_0'\exp(-\tilde{\kappa}[\tau-s])\sigma\left[\sigma'\int_s^\tau \exp(-\tilde{\kappa}'[u-s])\,b_0\,du\right]ds \qquad (3.17)
$$

Heath, Jarrow, and Morton (1992) provides this expression along with examples based on diagonal $\tilde{\kappa}$ and σ matrices (i.e., independent state variables). Tchuindjo (2008, 2009) extends the Heath, Jarrow, and Morton (1992) examples to arbitrary $\tilde{\kappa}$ and σ matrices, which therefore explicitly allow for dependence between the state variables.

As an aside on volatility effect calculations, $\text{VE}(\tau)$ for GATSMs can alternatively be obtained as the matrix product of single integrals rather than the double integral:

$$
\text{VE}(\tau) = \frac{1}{2}\left[\int_0^\tau b_0'\exp(-\tilde{\kappa}u)\,du\right]\sigma\sigma'\left[\int_0^\tau \exp(-\tilde{\kappa}'u)\,b_0\,du\right] \qquad (3.18)
$$

Appendix I of Krippner (2013d,e) demonstrates this result for the three GATSM specifications in that article. I have further confirmed that the result holds for all of the GATSMs that I introduce in sections 3.2 and 3.3, including those with more than three state variables, and I also have the sketch of a general proof. Hence, using the more straightforward matrix product of single integrals should facilitate the development of GATSMs with an arbitrary number of state variables. As I will note later in the book, that will provide further flexibility that is likely to be required to adequately represent the observed term structure for some financial market applications.

Finally for this section, to remove any doubt about the dimensions of the expressions, I note that $\mathbb{E}_t[x(t+\tau)|x(t)]$ and $\tilde{\mathbb{E}}_t[x(t+\tau)|x(t)]$ are $N \times 1$ vectors, $\exp(-\kappa\tau)$, $\exp(-\tilde{\kappa}\tau)$, $\text{var}_t[x(t+\tau)|x(t)]$ and $\widetilde{\text{var}}_t[x(t+\tau)|x(t)]$ are $N \times N$ matrices, and $\tilde{\mathbb{E}}_t[r(t+\tau)|x(t)]$, $[\omega(\tau)]^2$, and $\text{VE}(\tau)$ are scalars.

3.1.3 GATSM term structure

GATSM forward rates have the following expression:

$$f(t,\tau) = \tilde{\mathbb{E}}_t \left[r(t+\tau) | x(t) \right] - VE(\tau) \tag{3.19}$$

where $\tilde{\mathbb{E}}_t \left[r(t+\tau) | x(t) \right]$ is the expected path of the short rate under the risk-adjusted $\mathbb{Q}$ measure and $VE(\tau)$ is the volatility effect, both from the previous section.

The expression for GATSM interest rates $R(t,\tau)$ is obtained using the standard continuous-time term structure relationship:

$$
\begin{aligned}
R(t,\tau) &= \frac{1}{\tau} \int_0^\tau f(t,u)\, du \\
&= -\frac{1}{\tau} \int_0^\tau VE(\tau) + \frac{1}{\tau} \int_0^\tau \tilde{\mathbb{E}}_t \left[r(t+u) | x(t) \right] du \\
&= a(\tau) + [b(\tau)]' x(t) \tag{3.20}
\end{aligned}
$$

where I have used u as a dummy variable for τ to evaluate the integral. Note that references for this standard term structure relationship and others I use subsequently in the book are, for example, Filipović (2009) p. 7 or James and Webber (2000) chapter 3.

Closed-form analytic expressions for $a(\tau)$ and $b(\tau)$ are available from Dai and Singleton (2002) for the case where $\tilde{\kappa}$ has distinct and non-zero eigenvalues. The examples in sections 3.3 and 3.4 will illustrate how to obtain closed-form analytic expressions for $a(\tau)$ and $b(\tau)$ in more general cases where $\tilde{\kappa}$ includes zero and/or repeated eigenvalues. The important point to note at this stage is that GATSM interest rates are always an affine (i.e., linear) function of the state variables $x(t)$. That property means that the Kalman filter algorithm may be used to estimate GATSM, as I will outline in the following section.

GATSM bond prices take an exponential affine form:

$$
\begin{aligned}
P(t,\tau) &= \exp \left[-\tau R(t,\tau) \right] \\
&= \exp \left[-A(\tau) - [B(\tau)]' x(t) \right] \tag{3.21}
\end{aligned}
$$

where $A(\tau) = \tau a(\tau)$ and $B(\tau) = \tau b(\tau)$.

Again to remove any doubt about dimensions, I note that $f(t,\tau)$, $R(t,\tau)$, $P(t,\tau)$, $a(\tau)$, and $A(\tau)$ are all scalars, while $b(\tau)$ and $B(\tau)$ are $N \times 1$ vectors.

3.2 GATSM estimation

If a GATSM is to be applied as a useful representation of the observable yield curve data, it first needs to be estimated from that data itself. From this point onward, I will make an important distinction between what I will call a full GATSM estimation and a partial GATSM estimation, and these will carry over analogously to the shadow/ZLB-GATSMs in subsequent chapters. Hence:

- A full GATSM estimation estimates the parameters for the specified GATSM, and the state variables associated with those parameters are also an output of the estimation. The advantage of a full estimation is that the estimated parameters and associated state variables will provide the best representation of the data that the GATSM specification can deliver, and the diagnostics of the estimation results can also be used to assess whether the representation is adequate. The disadvantage is that a full estimation requires repeated applications of the Kalman filter algorithm, which I will introduce shortly below, within an optimization algorithm.
- A partial GATSM estimation estimates just the state variables for the data given a suitable set of parameter for the specified GATSM. The advantage is that only a single application of the Kalman filter algorithm is required, but the disadvantage is that the parameters and state variables will not be optimal for the given data set. Nevertheless, if the parameters are already closely related to the given data set, for example, available from a related full estimation over a historical period (like the parameters provided in this book) or from an occasionally updated full estimation, then the state variables will be entirely suitable for practical use.

Both full and partial GATSM estimations are implemented using the Kalman filter algorithm. Therefore, I proceed in section 3.2.1 with a description of the Kalman filter and its related parameters from the perspective of estimating GATSMs. In section 3.2.2, I provide an overview of how a single application of the Kalman filter algorithm obtains a partial GATSM estimation from the yield curve data and a suitable set of parameters. Explaining that single application of the Kalman filter algorithm leads naturally into section 3.2.3, where repeated applications are required for a full GATSM estimation via maximum likelihood.

Note that the maximum likelihood process I will outline is standard for estimating GATSMs, and the Kalman filter is itself a common technique for many applications including GATSMs. However, the Kalman filter literature and its application to GATSMs contains a vast range of terminologies and notations, which is why I take some time to establish the appropriate background and notation relevant to this book. I will follow this up with a fully worked example in section 3.3 to precisely explain the individual steps of applying the Kalman filter to a GATSM in practice. Both of these expositions will be useful in chapters 4 and 5, where I will show precisely how estimating shadow/ZLB-GATSMs differs from estimating GATSMs.

3.2.1 Kalman filter equations and related parameters

The Kalman filter is based on a state equation, which specifies how the state variables evolve over time, and a measurement equation, which specifies how the state variables explain the observed data at each point in time. For GATSMs, the state variables are in the vector $x(t)$, the measurement equation is the GATSM yield curve expression as a function of $x(t)$, and the data is the observed yield curve data at each point in time.

I have specified how the GATSM state variable vector $x(t)$ evolves in continuous time, but the yield curve data used for estimating any given GATSM will of course be observed at discrete intervals of time (e.g., daily, weekly, monthly, etc.). I denote the discrete time interval as Δt, which is a parameter determined by the data set. The GATSM state equation to use within the Kalman filter will therefore be a discrete-time expression, and its form is derived explicitly from the continuous-time GATSM expressions and the parameter Δt.

Specifically, the GATSM state equation arises from the dynamics for the state variable vector $x(t)$ under the $\mathbb{P}$ measure in equations 3.5 evaluated with the discrete time interval Δt:

$$x(t+\Delta t) = \mathbb{E}_t\left[x(t+\Delta t)\,|\,x(t)\right] + \int_t^{t+\Delta t} \exp\left(-\kappa\left[\Delta t - u\right]\right)\sigma\,\mathrm{d}W(u)$$

$$= \theta + \exp\left(-\kappa\tau\right)\left[x(t) - \theta\right] + \varepsilon\left(t+\Delta t\right) \tag{3.22}$$

Equation 3.22 may be equivalently expressed as a first-order vector autoregression by subscripting the state variable vectors with an integer index t to represent the progression of time in steps of Δt:

$$x_t = \theta + \exp\left(-\kappa\Delta t\right)\left(x_{t-1} - \theta\right) + \varepsilon_t$$

$$= \theta + F\left(x_{t-1} - \theta\right) + \varepsilon_t \tag{3.23}$$

where $F = \exp\left(-\kappa\Delta t\right) = V\exp\left(-\kappa_D\Delta t\right)V^{-1}$, and ε_t is the $N \times 1$ vector of innovations to the state variables. The variance of ε_t is also required for applying the Kalman filter to GATSMs, and it is obtained by substituting Δt for τ in equation 3.9:

$$\mathrm{var}\left[\varepsilon_t\right] = \mathrm{var}_t\left[x(t+\Delta t)\,|\,x(t)\right] = V\Theta\left(\Delta t\right)V' \tag{3.24}$$

where $\Theta\left(\Delta t\right)$ is defined as

$$\left[\Theta\left(\Delta t\right)\right]_{ij} = \Sigma_{ij}\frac{1}{\kappa_i + \kappa_j}\left[1 - \exp\left(-\left\{\kappa_i + \kappa_j\right\}\Delta t\right)\right] \tag{3.25}$$

with $\Sigma = V^{-1}\sigma\sigma'V'^{-1}$.

The Kalman filter requires starting values for the state variable vector and its variance before it begins estimating those quantities from the data. The starting values typically used are the unconditional expectation and variance of the state equation, respectively:

$$\mathbb{E}[x(t)] = \theta \tag{3.26}$$

and

$$\text{var}[x(t)] = \int_0^\infty \exp(-\kappa u)\sigma\sigma' \exp(-\kappa' u)\, du$$
$$= V\Theta(\infty)V' \tag{3.27}$$

where

$$[\Theta(\infty)]_{ij} = \Sigma_{ij} \frac{1}{\kappa_i + \kappa_j} \tag{3.28}$$

Regarding the measurement equation, interest rates are the typical term structure data used to estimate GATSMs, so I will use interest rate expressions throughout this book (but I will also mention in section 3.3.5 how forward rates or bond prices could alternatively be used as term structure data). Hence, if K interest rates of different times to maturity τ_1 to τ_K are used to represent the yield curve at each time index t, the measurement equation for GATSMs is

$$\begin{bmatrix} R_t(\tau_1) \\ \vdots \\ R_t(\tau_K) \end{bmatrix} = \begin{bmatrix} a(\tau_1) \\ \vdots \\ a(\tau_K) \end{bmatrix} + \begin{bmatrix} [b(\tau_1)]' \\ \vdots \\ [b(\tau_K)]' \end{bmatrix} x_t + \begin{bmatrix} \eta_t(\tau_1) \\ \vdots \\ \eta_t(\tau_K) \end{bmatrix} \tag{3.29}$$

where $R_t(\tau_k)$ is the observed interest rate at time index t for the time to maturity τ_k, $a(\tau_k)$ and $b(\tau_k)$ are the GATSM interest rate functions evaluated at τ_k, and $\eta_t(\tau_k)$ is the component of $R_t(\tau_k)$ that is unexplained by the GATSM, that is, $\eta_t(\tau_k) = R_t(\tau_k) - a(\tau_k) - [b(\tau_k)]' x_t$. I will typically refer to η_t or its individual elements $\eta_t(\tau_k)$ as residuals. The time index t runs from 1 to T over the sample period with the discrete time interval Δt between observations.

Equation 3.29 may be written more conveniently in vector and matrix notation as

$$R_t = a + Hx_t + \eta_t \tag{3.30}$$

where R_t is the $K \times 1$ vector representing the yield curve data at time index t, a is a $K \times 1$ vector containing the values $a(\tau_k)$, H is a $K \times N$ matrix containing the row vectors $[b(\tau_k)]'$, and η_t is the $K \times 1$ vector of the yield curve data that is unexplained by the GATSM specification and the prevailing estimate of the state variables.

The Kalman filter also requires a specification for the variance of η_t. As standard in the literature, I specify the variance of η_t to be a diagonal matrix:

$$\Omega_\eta = \text{diag}\left[\left\{\left[\sigma_\eta(\tau_1)\right]^2, \ldots, \left[\sigma_\eta(\tau_K)\right]^2\right\}\right] \tag{3.31}$$

where Ω_η is a $K \times K$ matrix with entries $\left[\sigma_\eta(\tau_k)\right]^2$, and $\sigma_\eta(\tau_k)$ are standard deviations of $\eta_t(\tau_k)$. As also standard in the literature, I assume that the vectors η_t and ε_t are uncorrelated over time, and the covariances between η_t and ε_t are zero.

3.2.2 Partial estimation

Table 3.1 summarizes a single application of the Kalman filter algorithm to obtain a partial GATSM estimation. The example in section 3.3 provides a detailed description of each of the individual steps in Table 3.1, including precise forms for each of the vectors and matrices. At this stage I provide an overview of the flow and the essential intuition of the Kalman filter algorithm.

Note that I assume a yield curve data set will be available for the estimation, which I denote as

$$\{R_1, \ldots, R_T\} = \begin{bmatrix} R_1(\tau_1) & \cdots & R_T(\tau_1) \\ \vdots & \vdots & \vdots \\ R_1(\tau_K) & \cdots & R_T(\tau_K) \end{bmatrix}_{K \times T} \tag{3.32}$$

where $\tau_1, \ldots, \tau_K$ are the K times to maturity for the interest rate data used to represent the yield curve, $R_t(\tau_k)$ is the observed interest rate for maturity τ_k at time t, R_t is the $K \times 1$ vector of the K interest rates at time t, and $R_1, \ldots, R_T$ is the set of all yield curve observations R_t from $t = 1$ to T.

The flow of the Kalman filter is then as follows:

- **1. Setup:** F, $\Theta(\Delta t)$, a, H, and Ω_η are calculated from the relevant GATSM parameters, as detailed in section 3.2.1. These parameter vectors and matrices remain unchanged at each step of the Kalman recursion, so it is efficient to preevaluate them.
- **2. State initialization:** The starting values for the state vector and its variance, which I denote x_0^+ and P_0^+, are calculated from the relevant GATSM parameters. The starting values are the unconditional expectation and variance of the state equation, as detailed in section 3.2.1.
- **3. Kalman recursion:** I have represented the Kalman recursion as a "for/next" loop over all of the sample time steps from 1 to T. A sequence of three procedures is applied at each step of the loop.

Table 3.1 Partial GATSM estimation with Kalman filter algorithm

---

1. **Setup:**

   Calculate F, $\Theta(\Delta t)$, a, H, and Ω_η

2. **State initialization:**

   $$x_0^+ = \theta$$
   $$P_0^+ = V\Theta(\infty)V'$$

3. **Kalman recursion:**

   for $t = 1 : T$

   3.1. **Prior state estimates:**

   $$x_t^- = \theta + F\left(x_{t-1}^+ - \theta\right)$$
   $$P_t^- = FP_{t-1}^+ F' + \Theta(\Delta t)$$

   3.2. **Measurement estimates:**

   $$\eta_t = R_t - a - Hx_t^-$$
   $$M_t = HP_t^- H' + \Omega_\eta$$
   $$K_t = P_t^- H' M_t^{-1}$$

   3.3. **Posterior state estimates:**

   $$x_t^+ = x_t^- + K_t \eta_t$$
   $$P_t^+ = (I - K_t H) P_t^-$$

   next t

Notes:

x_t^-, x_t^+, and θ are $N \times 1$ vectors

η_t and a are $K \times 1$ vectors

κ_D is an $N \times N$ diagonal matrix

P_t^-, P_t^+, $\sigma\sigma'$, $\Theta(\Delta t)$, and $\Theta(\infty)$ are $N \times N$ symmetric matrices

V and F are $N \times N$ asymmetric matrices

M_t is a $K \times K$ symmetric matrix

Ω_η is a $K \times K$ diagonal matrix

K_t is an $N \times K$ matrix

H is a $K \times N$ matrix

- $t = 1$ step of the Kalman recursion:

- **3.1. Prior state estimates:** x_0^+ and P_0^+ and the state equation parameters are used to calculate the projections, or prior estimates, of the state vector and its variance for $t = 1$. I denote those prior estimates as x_1^- and P_1^-. The prior estimates are not optimal because they have only been informed by information from the previous time step.

- **3.2. Measurement estimates:** x_1^- is used along with the measurement equation parameters to provide model estimates of the yield curve at $t = 1$, and those estimates are compared to the observed yield curve data R_1. The residuals η_1 are then used to calculate the Kalman gain matrix K_1, which essentially indicates how x_1^- and P_1^- can be improved based on the $t = 1$ yield curve data.

- **3.3. Posterior state estimates:** x_1^- and P_1^- are adjusted using η_1 and K_1 to obtain improved estimates, or posterior estimates, of the state variable vector and its variance for $t = 1$. I denote those posterior estimates as x_1^+ and P_1^+. The posterior estimates are optimal (at least under the assumption that ε_t and η_t have Gaussian distributions) because they fully reflect the information from the previous time step and the conditioning provided by the yield curve data in the current time step.

- Subsequent steps of the Kalman recursion follows the sequence outlined above:

  - x_{t-1}^+ and P_{t-1}^+ are used to calculate the prior estimates x_t^- and P_t^-.
  - x_1^- and P_1^- the yield curve data R_t are used to calculate η_t and K_t.
  - η_t and K_t are used to obtain the posterior estimates x_t^+ and P_t^+. Note that using the notation x_0^+ and P_0^+ for the starting values of the Kalman recursion conveniently makes the $t = 1$ step identical to all of the other steps in the for/next loop, so there is no need to incorporate it separately.

The essential output from the Kalman filter algorithm is the estimated time series of GATSM state variable vectors $\{x_1, \ldots, x_T\}$, which will be associated with the GATSM specification, the supplied parameters, and the yield curve data used for estimation.

3.2.3 Full estimation

Table 3.2 summarizes the process for a full GATSM estimation via maximum likelihood. The example in section 3.3 details the additional steps in Table 3.2 relative to Table 3.1, but again at this stage I provide an overview of the essential intuition:

- As indicated, a full estimation requires the Kalman filter algorithm to be applied within an optimization algorithm, which I have denoted as "**A. Optimization algorithm.**" I assume the user will have such an optimization algorithm available. For example, the MatLab Optimization Toolbox has a range of optimization algorithms available, and I am aware that the freely available programming language R also has similar algorithms available.
- The objective function of the optimization algorithm is to maximize the log-likelihood function given by the expression log-$L(\{R_1, \ldots, R_T\}, \mathbb{A})$, where $\{R_1, \ldots, R_T\}$ denotes the yield curve data set for the time steps from 1 to T, and $\mathbb{A}$ denotes the full parameter set required for the Kalman filter algorithm. Note that $\mathbb{A}$ includes fixed parameters, which remain unchanged for the entire optimization, and the parameters to be estimated, which change as the optimization algorithm proceeds.

Table 3.2 Full GATSM estimation via maximum likelihood

A. Optimization algorithm

Maximize: $\log\text{-}L\left(\{R_1,\ldots,R_T\},\mathbb{A}\right)$

$$= -\tfrac{1}{2}\sum_{t=1}^{T} K\log\left(2\pi\right) + \log\left(|M_t|\right) + \eta_t' M_t^{-1}\eta_t$$

with η_t and M_t from Kalman filter algorithm.

Kalman filter algorithm

1. Setup and estimation constraints:

Calculate F, $\Theta\left(\Delta t\right)$, a, H, and Ω_η

Subject to constraints:

- $|F| < 1$
- $\sigma\sigma'$ positive definite
- Ω_η positive definite

2. State initialization:

$$x_0^+ = \theta$$
$$P_0^+ = V\Theta\left(\infty\right)V'$$

3. Recursion:

for $t = 1 : T$

    3.1. Prior state estimates:

$$x_t^- = \theta + F\left(x_{t-1}^+ - \theta\right)$$
$$P_t^- = FP_{t-1}^+ F' + \Theta\left(\Delta t\right)$$

    3.2. Measurement update:

$$\eta_t = R_t - a - Hx_t^-$$
$$M_t = HP_t^- H' + \Omega_\eta$$
$$K_t = P_t^- H' M_t^{-1}$$

    3.3. Posterior state estimates:

$$x_t^+ = x_t^- + K_t \eta_t$$
$$P_t^+ = \left(I - K_t H\right)P_t^-$$

    Record x_t^+, η_t, and M_t

next t

B. Diagnostics of estimated model

Note: See Table 3.1 for matrix dimensions.

- The yield curve data set and the parameter set $\mathbb{A}$ are passed through to the Kalman filter algorithm. The parameter set $\mathbb{A}$ is used to set up the parameter vectors and matrices for the state and measurement equations, subject to constraints to ensure that the Kalman filter algorithm always operates smoothly (i.e., without fatal or terminal errors) regardless of the values passed through by the optimization algorithm. Without such constraints, the Kalman filter algorithm could deliver infinite or imaginary values, causing it or the optimization algorithm to fail.

- The Kalman filter algorithm proceeds as in Table 3.1. I have repeated those steps in Table 3.2 for convenience.
- The time series of $\{\eta_1, \ldots, \eta_T\}$ and $\{M_1, \ldots, M_T\}$ are passed back to the optimization algorithm, and a value for $\log\text{-}L(\{R_1, \ldots, R_T\}, \mathbb{A})$ is calculated. Note that $|M_t|$ is the determinant of M_t and $\log(\cdot)$ is the natural logarithm. The optimization algorithm will contain a way of iterating to a new set of estimated parameters (e.g., using a gradient technique) to increase the value for $\log\text{-}L(\{R_1, \ldots, R_T\}, \mathbb{A})$. The entire process then repeats until convergence, which is when the iterations of the optimization algorithm can no longer obtain an increase in the value for $\log\text{-}L(\{R_1, \ldots, R_T\}, \mathbb{A})$ according to a specified tolerance.
- The final output from the maximum likelihood estimation includes the estimated GATSM parameters, the estimated series of GATSM state variable vectors $\{x_1^+, \ldots, x_T^+\}$ and their variances $\{P_1^+, \ldots, P_T^+\}$, and typically standard diagnostics associated with the optimization. Those standard diagnostics may be used to obtain estimated standard errors for the estimated GATSM parameters. Other diagnostics that are readily calculable are the goodness of fit to the data, and the confidence intervals around the estimated state variable vectors $\{x_1^+, \ldots, x_T^+\}$ derived from the variances $\{P_1^+, \ldots, P_T^+\}$. Practical diagnostics include an assessment of real-world applicability and the sensitivity of model results to different specifications.

For econometric reasons, as will I explain shortly, there is a limit on the number of parameters that can be estimated for GATSMs. The number of parameters in GATSMs, represented by a_0, b_0, κ, θ, σ, $\tilde{\theta}$, and $\tilde{\kappa}$ (or equivalently, γ and Γ could be used to define $\tilde{\theta}$ and $\tilde{\kappa}$, as in section 3.1.1), is $1 + N + N^2 + N + N^2 + N + N^2 = 1 + 3N + 3N^2$; e.g. 7 for $N = 1$, 19 for $N = 2$, or 37 for $N = 3$. However, the maximum number of parameters that can be uniquely identified with econometric estimation is $1 + 2.5N + 1.5N^2$. For example, 5 for $N = 1$, 12 for $N = 2$, or 22 for $N = 3$ (see Singleton [2006] for details). The user must choose which set of GATSM parameters to estimate, which I will denote $\mathbb{B}$, and the remainder of the GATSM parameters must be calibrated (i.e., restricted), which I will denote $\mathbb{C}$. If one attempted to estimate more parameters than the maximum possible, then the optimization algorithm would not converge to a unique set of estimated state variable and parameters. In other words, different sets of estimated state variables and parameters could provide an equivalent representation of the yield curve data, in terms of the log-likelihood value, and so the optimization algorithm would just cycle around those different results. Further parameter restrictions may also be applied, as with the ANSM(2) and ANSM(3) examples I demonstrate in sections 3.3 and 3.4. In such cases, the set of free parameters to estimate, $\mathbb{B}$, will be smaller than the maximum number of parameters that can be uniquely identified, and so convergence is again assured.

3.3 Worked example: ANSM(2)

I will use the two-factor arbitrage-free Nelson and Siegel (1987) model, hereafter ANSM(2), as a worked example throughout this book. In this chapter I use the ANSM(2) as a stand-alone model, and in subsequent chapters I will use the ANSM(2) to represent the shadow term structure in shadow/ZLB models. The ANSM(2), in its own right and later to represent the shadow term structure, is an ideal example for the following reasons:

- **The ANSM(2) is the most parsimonious GATSM with more than one state variable.** For readers wanting to learn about GATSMs, that parsimony makes the ANSM(2) very convenient for demonstrating the mathematics of GATSMs and their estimation in general, including the interrelationships between the state variables that a one-state-variable model would not contain. In particular, I have written out the vector and matrix expressions in full for the ANSM(2) and its estimation. Readers can then carry that intuition through to ANSMs and GATSMs with different specifications and more state variables.
- **The ANSM(2) produces Level and Slope components of the term structure.** These shapes are intuitively related to the primary yield curve components of long-maturity interest rates and the spread between short- and long-maturity interest rates (see Diebold and Rudebusch [2013] for further discussion). Alternatively, the Level and Slope components of the term structure may be viewed as a proxy for the first two principal components of yield curve data, which explain 99.9 percent of the variation in the yield curve data that I will later describe.
- **The ANSM(2) provides a realistic representation of the yield curve for many practical applications.** For example, in relation to macrofinance applications, the Level and Slope components of the yield curve have been shown to relate respectively to inflation and output growth (see Krippner [2008] and chapter 6 for discussion of the principles and Diebold, Rudebusch, and Aruoba [2006] for empirical evidence). For financial market applications, the Level and Slope component represents the main ways that the yield curve moves.
- **The ANSM(2) does not fit the yield curve data closely.** This feature helps to exaggerate the points I wish to make in the figures. ANSMs with three state variables are generally applied to seek a better fit to the yield curve data, and I provide the details of that model in section 3.4.1 and examples of its application in 3.5.3. However, using two state variables is preferable for some applications. For example, as I will discuss in chapter 7, shadow short rates obtained from shadow/ZLB-GATSMs with two state variables are more robust, and also have better relationships empirically with macroeconomic data, than models with three state variables.

As an additional technical point, the ANSM(2) also approximates in a well-defined sense any GATSM that could be specified. Krippner (2014d) provides the details, and I will also use the results of Krippner (2014a) to extend the nature of that approximation in chapter 6.

3.3.1 ANSM(2) Specification

As mentioned earlier, the GATSM(2) has 19 parameters, and 7 parameters are fixed to enable unique identification for econometric estimation. Following the typical specification in the literature (see Christensen and Rudebusch [2013a,b, 2014], Krippner [2013d,e], and Wu and Xia [2013, 2014], for example), I impose those restrictions with a unit b_0 vector, a lower-triangular σ matrix, a diagonal $\tilde{\kappa}$ matrix, and setting $\tilde{\theta} = 0$. The ANSM(2) imposes two more restrictions on the GATSM(2), that is, $a_0 = 0$ and $\tilde{\kappa}_1 = 0$. As I will explain further below, these additional restrictions impose a unit root process for the first state variable, which is a convenient and parsimonious representation that is generally not rejected by the data; see Krippner (2014d).

The ANSM(2) therefore has 10 free parameters to estimate, that is, $\mathbb{B} = \{\phi, \kappa_{11}, \kappa_{12}, \kappa_{21}, \kappa_{22}, \theta_1, \theta_2, \sigma_1, \sigma_2, \rho_{12}\}$. The state variables, and fixed and free parameters in their natural scalar/vector/matrix form are as follows:

$$x(t) = \begin{bmatrix} x_1(t) \\ x_2(t) \end{bmatrix}; \quad a_0 = 0; \quad b_0 = \begin{bmatrix} 1 \\ 1 \end{bmatrix}$$

$$\kappa = \begin{bmatrix} \kappa_{11} & \kappa_{12} \\ \kappa_{21} & \kappa_{22} \end{bmatrix}; \quad \theta = \begin{bmatrix} \theta_1 \\ \theta_2 \end{bmatrix}$$

$$\sigma = \begin{bmatrix} \sigma_1 & 0 \\ \rho_{12}\sigma_2 & \sigma_2\sqrt{1 - \rho_{12}^2} \end{bmatrix}$$

$$\tilde{\kappa} = \begin{bmatrix} 0 & 0 \\ 0 & \phi \end{bmatrix}; \quad \tilde{\theta} = \begin{bmatrix} 0 \\ 0 \end{bmatrix} \tag{3.33}$$

3.3.2 ANSM(2) Term structure

The ANSM(2) short rate is

$$r(t) = b_0' x(t)$$

$$= [1,1] \begin{bmatrix} x_1(t) \\ x_2(t) \end{bmatrix}$$

$$= x_1(t) + x_2(t) \tag{3.34}$$

The matrix exponential of $\tilde{\kappa}$ is the key expression required to develop the term structure and related quantities. Since $\tilde{\kappa}$ is already a diagonal matrix, the matrix exponential is simply the scalar exponential of the diagonal elements:

$$\exp\left(-\tilde{\kappa}\tau\right) = \exp\left(-\begin{bmatrix} 0 & 0 \\ 0 & \phi \end{bmatrix}\tau\right)$$

$$= \begin{bmatrix} 1 & 0 \\ 0 & \exp\left(-\phi\tau\right) \end{bmatrix} \tag{3.35}$$

Hence, under the $\mathbb{Q}$ measure, $x_1(t)$ evolves as a random walk, while $x_2(t)$ evolves as a mean-reverting process, that is,

$$\begin{bmatrix} x_1(t+\Delta t) \\ x_2(t+\Delta t) \end{bmatrix} = \begin{bmatrix} 1 & 0 \\ 0 & \exp\left(-\phi\tau\right) \end{bmatrix} \begin{bmatrix} x_1(t) \\ x_2(t) \end{bmatrix} + \begin{bmatrix} \varepsilon_1(t+\Delta t) \\ \varepsilon_2(t+\Delta t) \end{bmatrix}$$

$$= \begin{bmatrix} x_1(t) \\ x_2(t)\cdot\exp\left(-\phi\tau\right) \end{bmatrix} + \begin{bmatrix} \varepsilon_1(t+\Delta t) \\ \varepsilon_2(t+\Delta t) \end{bmatrix} \tag{3.36}$$

With that process for the state variables, the expected path of the short rate under the $\mathbb{Q}$ measure is therefore

$$\tilde{\mathbb{E}}_t\left[r(t+\tau)|x(t)\right] = a_0 + b_0'\left\{\tilde{\theta} + \exp\left(-\tilde{\kappa}\tau\right)\left[x(t) - \tilde{\theta}\right]\right\}$$

$$= [1,1]\begin{bmatrix} 1 & 0 \\ 0 & \exp\left(-\phi\tau\right) \end{bmatrix}\begin{bmatrix} x_1(t) \\ x_2(t) \end{bmatrix}$$

$$= [1,\exp\left(-\phi\tau\right)]\begin{bmatrix} x_1(t) \\ x_2(t) \end{bmatrix}$$

$$= x_1(t)\cdot 1 + x_2(t)\cdot\exp\left(-\phi\tau\right) \tag{3.37}$$

Note that the vector

$$[1,\exp\left(-\phi\tau\right)] = b_0'\exp\left(-\tilde{\kappa}\tau\right) \tag{3.38}$$

contains the factor loadings (i.e., the functions of horizon/time to maturity τ) that are applied to the state variables $x_1(t)$ and $x_2(t)$ to obtain the expected path of the short rate $\tilde{\mathbb{E}}_t\left[r(t+\tau)|x(t)\right]$ as at time t. The factor loadings for the ANSM(2) are respectively the constant 1, which arises from the random walk process for $x_1(t)$, and an exponential decay by horizon/time to maturity τ, which arises from the mean-reverting process for $x_2(t)$. As illustrated in panel 1 of Figure 3.1, those functions carry directly through to the forward rate factor loadings. The interest rate factor loadings in panel 2 are similarly shaped functions. Hence it is intuitive to call the functions Level and Slope factor loadings, and the associated state variables $x_1(t)$ and $x_2(t)$ the Level and Slope state variables. Indeed, from chapter 6 onward, I will adopt the notation $L(t)$ and $S(t)$ for the ANSM(2) state variables, but I maintain the generic GATSM notation $x_1(t)$ and $x_2(t)$ until then.

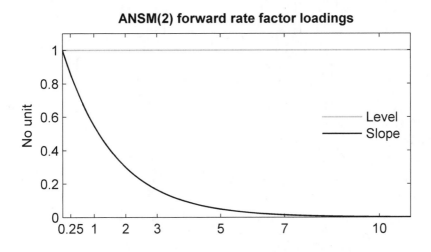

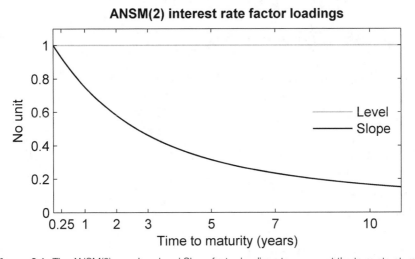

Figure 3.1 The ANSM(2) uses Level and Slope factor loadings to represent the term structure.

Forward rates for the ANSM(2) are given by equation 3.19:

$$f(t, \tau) = \tilde{\mathbb{E}}_t \left[r(t + \tau) | x(t) \right] - VE(\tau)$$

$$= \left[1, \exp(-\phi\tau) \right] \begin{bmatrix} x_1(t) \\ x_2(t) \end{bmatrix} - VE(\tau)$$

$$= -VE(\tau) + x_1(t) + x_2(t) \cdot \exp(-\phi\tau) \tag{3.39}$$

where the volatility effect may be calculated using the Heath, Jarrow, and Morton (1992) double integral as:

$$VE(\tau) = \int_0^\tau \exp(-\tilde{\kappa}\{\tau - s\}) \sigma \left[\int_s^\tau \sigma' \exp(-\tilde{\kappa}'\{u - s\}) \, du \right] ds$$

$$= \int_0^\tau \left\{ [1,1] \begin{bmatrix} 1 & 0 \\ 0 & \exp(-\phi[\tau-s]) \end{bmatrix} \begin{bmatrix} \sigma_1^2 & \rho_{12}\sigma_1\sigma_2 \\ \rho_{12}\sigma_1\sigma_2 & \sigma_2^2 \end{bmatrix} \right.$$

$$\left. \times \left[\int_s^\tau \begin{bmatrix} 1 & 0 \\ 0 & \exp(-\phi[u-s]) \end{bmatrix} \begin{bmatrix} 1 \\ 1 \end{bmatrix} du \right] ds \right\}$$

$$= \sigma_1^2 \cdot L/L + \sigma_2^2 \cdot S/S + \rho_{12}\sigma_1\sigma_2 \cdot (L/S + S/L) \tag{3.40}$$

with

$$L/L = \int_0^\tau 1 \left(\int_s^\tau 1 \, du \right) ds \tag{3.41a}$$

$$S/S = \int_0^\tau \exp(-\phi[\tau-s]) \left(\int_s^\tau \exp(-\phi[u-s]) \, du \right) ds \tag{3.41b}$$

$$L/S = \int_0^\tau 1 \left(\int_s^\tau \exp(-\phi[u-s]) \, du \right) ds \tag{3.41c}$$

$$S/L = \int_0^\tau \exp(-\phi[\tau-s]) \left(\int_s^\tau 1 \, du \right) ds \tag{3.41d}$$

From Krippner (2013e, pp. 55–58), the results are

$$L/L = \frac{1}{2}\tau^2 \tag{3.42a}$$

$$S/S = \frac{1}{2}[G(\phi,\tau)]^2 \tag{3.42b}$$

$$L/S + S/L = \tau G(\phi,\tau) \tag{3.42c}$$

where

$$G(\phi,\tau) = \frac{1}{\phi}[1 - \exp(-\phi\tau)] \tag{3.43}$$

The final result for the volatility effect is therefore

$$VE(\tau) = \sigma_1^2 \cdot \frac{1}{2}\tau^2 + \sigma_2^2 \cdot \frac{1}{2}[G(\phi,\tau)]^2 + \rho_{12}\sigma_1\sigma_2 \cdot \tau G(\phi,\tau) \tag{3.44}$$

As an aside, I also demonstrate the simpler alternative of calculating $VE(\tau)$ using the matrix product of single integrals in equation 3.18. Hence, I first calculate the single integral:

$$\int_0^\tau b_0' \exp(-\tilde{\kappa} u) \, ds = \int_0^\tau [1,1] \begin{bmatrix} 1 & 0 \\ 0 & \exp(-\phi u) \end{bmatrix} du$$

$$= \int_0^\tau [1, \exp(-\phi u)] \, du$$

$$= [\tau, G(\phi,\tau)] \tag{3.45}$$

and then substitute that result into equation 3.18 to obtain

$$\text{VE}(\tau) = \frac{1}{2}[\tau, G(\phi, \tau)] \begin{bmatrix} \sigma_1^2 & \rho_{12}\sigma_1\sigma_2 \\ \rho_{12}\sigma_1\sigma_2 & \sigma_2^2 \end{bmatrix} \begin{bmatrix} \tau \\ G(\phi, \tau) \end{bmatrix}$$

$$= \sigma_1^2 \cdot \frac{1}{2}\tau^2 + \sigma_2^2 \cdot \frac{1}{2}[G(\phi, \tau)]^2 + \rho_{12}\sigma_1\sigma_2 \cdot \tau G(\phi, \tau) \qquad (3.46)$$

Interest rates for the ANSM(2) are given by equation 3.20:

$$R(t, \tau) = -\frac{1}{\tau}\int_0^\tau \text{VE}(\tau) + \frac{1}{\tau}\int_0^\tau \tilde{\mathbb{E}}_t\left[r(t+u)\,|\,x(t)\right]du$$

$$= -\frac{1}{\tau}\int_0^\tau \text{VE}(\tau) + \frac{1}{\tau}\int_0^\tau [1, \exp(-\phi u)]\begin{bmatrix} x_1(t) \\ x_2(t) \end{bmatrix}du$$

$$= a(\tau) + [b(\tau)]'\begin{bmatrix} x_1(t) \\ x_2(t) \end{bmatrix} \qquad (3.47)$$

where

$$a(\tau) = -\frac{1}{\tau}\int_0^\tau \sigma_1^2 \cdot \frac{1}{2}\tau^2 + \sigma_2^2 \cdot \frac{1}{2}[G(\phi, \tau)]^2 + \rho_{12}\sigma_1\sigma_2 \cdot \tau G(\phi, \tau)$$

$$= -\sigma_1^2 \cdot \frac{1}{6}\tau^2 - \sigma_2^2 \cdot \frac{1}{2\phi^2}\left[1 - \frac{1}{\tau}G(\phi, \tau) - \frac{1}{2\tau}\phi[G(\phi, \tau)]^2\right]$$

$$- \rho\sigma_1\sigma_2 \cdot \frac{1}{\phi^2}\left[1 - \frac{1}{\tau}G(\phi, \tau) + \frac{1}{2}\phi\tau - \phi G(\phi, \tau)\right] \qquad (3.48)$$

and the interest rate factor loadings $[b(\tau)]'$ are

$$[b(\tau)]' = \left[\frac{1}{\tau}\int_0^\tau 1\,du, \frac{1}{\tau}\int_0^\tau \exp(-\phi\tau)\,du\right]$$

$$= \left[1, \frac{1}{\tau}G(\phi, \tau)\right] \qquad (3.49)$$

As a somewhat technical aside, note that the $-\sigma_1^2 \cdot \frac{1}{6}\tau^2$ term in $a(\tau)$ implies negative interest rates for extremely long times to maturity (all of the other functions are convergent). This is a general property for ANSMs, and it arises from the unit root process assumed for the Level state variable. There are pragmatic ways around this issue if it becomes binding in practice, for example, by imposing an appropriate near unit root process in a model like that in subsection 3.4.5. Even stationary GATSMs with highly persistent dynamics can produce negative interest rates. Fortunately, it turns out the shadow/ZLB framework provides a direct resolution, which I will return to in subsection 4.1.4.

3.3.3 Partial ANSM(2) estimation with the Kalman filter

Given a suitable set of ANSM parameters and Kalman filter parameters $\sigma_\eta(\tau_1), \ldots, \sigma_\eta(\tau_K)$, the Kalman filter algorithm can be applied to a given set of yield curve data $\{R_1, \ldots, R_T\}$ to obtain a time series of the state variables. I will fully describe in section 3.5 the yield curve data set I use for my estimations in this book. For this worked example, the key points are that the yield curve data are for the end of the month, so the time step parameter is $\Delta t = 1/12$, and there are nine different maturities for each yield curve observation, so $K = 9$. The values for τ_k range from $\tau_1 = 0.25$ years to $\tau_9 = 30$ years. Hence, the collection of all the required parameters for the Kalman filter algorithm into the parameter set $\mathbb{A}$ is as follows:

- Time step: $\Delta t = 1/12$.
- Times to maturity: $\{\tau_1, \tau_2, \tau_3, \tau_4, \tau_5, \tau_6, \tau_7, \tau_8, \tau_9\}$.
- Free ANSM(2) parameters: $\mathbb{B} = \{\phi, \kappa_{11}, \kappa_{12}, \kappa_{21}, \kappa_{22}, \theta_1, \theta_2, \sigma_1, \sigma_2, \rho_{12}\}$.
- Fixed ANSM(2) parameters: $\mathbb{C} = \{a_0 = 0, b_0 = [1, 1]', \tilde{\theta} = [0, 0]'\}$.
- Measurement equation standard deviations: $\{\sigma_\eta(\tau_1), \sigma_\eta(\tau_2), \sigma_\eta(\tau_3), \sigma_\eta(\tau_4),$ $\sigma_\eta(\tau_5), \sigma_\eta(\tau_6), \sigma_\eta(\tau_7), \sigma_\eta(\tau_8), \sigma_\eta(\tau_9)\}$.

The following subsections detail each of step of the Kalman filter algorithm outlined in Table 3.1 as applied to the ANSM(2).

1. Setup

a. Calculate F:

As outlined in section 3.2.1, first undertake the eigensystem decomposition of κ to obtain the eigenvalues κ_1 and κ_2, and the eigenvector matrix V:

$$V \kappa_D V^{-1} = \kappa$$

$$\begin{bmatrix} V_{11} & V_{12} \\ V_{21} & V_{22} \end{bmatrix} \begin{bmatrix} \kappa_1 & 0 \\ 0 & \kappa_2 \end{bmatrix} \begin{bmatrix} V_{11} & V_{12} \\ V_{21} & V_{22} \end{bmatrix}^{-1} = \begin{bmatrix} \kappa_{11} & \kappa_{12} \\ \kappa_{21} & \kappa_{22} \end{bmatrix} \tag{3.50}$$

The state equation coefficient matrix F is then

$$F = V \exp(-\kappa_D \Delta t) V^{-1}$$

$$\begin{bmatrix} F_{11} & F_{12} \\ F_{21} & F_{22} \end{bmatrix} = V \begin{bmatrix} \exp(-\kappa_1 \Delta t) & 0 \\ 0 & \exp(-\kappa_2 \Delta t) \end{bmatrix} V^{-1} \tag{3.51}$$

b. Calculate $\Theta(\Delta t)$:

Begin by calculating the matrix $\sigma \sigma'$:

$$\sigma \sigma' = \begin{bmatrix} \sigma_1 & 0 \\ \rho_{12} \sigma_2 & \sigma_2 \sqrt{1 - \rho_{12}^2} \end{bmatrix} \begin{bmatrix} \sigma_1 & \rho_{12} \sigma_2 \\ 0 & \sigma_2 \sqrt{1 - \rho_{12}^2} \end{bmatrix}$$

$$= \begin{bmatrix} \sigma_1^2 & \sigma_1\sigma_2\rho_{12} \\ \sigma_1\sigma_2\rho_{12} & \sigma_2^2 \end{bmatrix} \tag{3.52}$$

and then Σ is calculated from V and $\sigma\sigma'$

$$\Sigma = V^{-1}\sigma\sigma'V'^{-1}$$

$$= \begin{bmatrix} \Sigma_{11} & \Sigma_{12} \\ \Sigma_{12} & \Sigma_{22} \end{bmatrix} \tag{3.53}$$

From section 3.2.1, $\Theta(\Delta t)$ is defined as

$$[\Theta(\Delta t)]_{ij} = \Sigma_{ij}\frac{1}{\kappa_i+\kappa_j}\left[1-\exp\left(-\left\{\kappa_i+\kappa_j\right\}\Delta t\right)\right]$$

$$= \Sigma_{ij}G\left(\kappa_i+\kappa_j,\Delta t\right) \tag{3.54}$$

and therefore

$$\Theta(\Delta t) = \begin{bmatrix} \Theta_{11}(\Delta t) & \Theta_{12}(\Delta t) \\ \Theta_{12}(\Delta t) & \Theta_{22}(\Delta t) \end{bmatrix}$$

$$= \begin{bmatrix} \Sigma_{11}G(2\kappa_1,\Delta t) & \Sigma_{12}G(\kappa_1+\kappa_2,\Delta t) \\ \Sigma_{12}G(\kappa_1+\kappa_2,\Delta t) & \Sigma_{22}G(2\kappa_2,\Delta t) \end{bmatrix} \tag{3.55}$$

c. Calculate a and H:

The vector a and matrix H are populated by evaluating the functions $a(\tau_k)$ and $b(\tau_k)$ at each time to maturity τ_k using equations 3.48 and 3.49 with k ranging from 1 to $K=9$. That is,

$$a = \begin{bmatrix} a(\tau_1) \\ \vdots \\ a(\tau_9) \end{bmatrix}_{9\times 1} \tag{3.56}$$

where

$$a(\tau_k) = -\sigma_1^2\cdot\frac{1}{6}\tau_k^2 - \sigma_2^2\cdot\frac{1}{2\phi^2}\left[1-\frac{1}{\tau_k}G(\phi,\tau_k)-\frac{1}{2\tau_k}\phi\left[G(\phi,\tau_k)\right]^2\right]$$

$$-\rho\sigma_1\sigma_2\cdot\frac{1}{\phi^2}\left[1-\frac{1}{\tau_k}G(\phi,\tau_k)+\frac{1}{2}\phi\tau_k-\phi G(\phi,\tau_k)\right] \tag{3.57}$$

and

$$H = \begin{bmatrix} [b(\tau_1)]'_{1\times 2} \\ \vdots \\ [b(\tau_K)]'_{1\times 2} \end{bmatrix} = \begin{bmatrix} 1 & \frac{1}{\tau_1}G(\phi,\tau_1) \\ \vdots & \vdots \\ 1 & \frac{1}{\tau_9}G(\phi,\tau_9) \end{bmatrix}_{9\times 2} \tag{3.58}$$

where

$$G(\phi, \tau_k) = \frac{1}{\phi} \left[1 - \exp(-\phi \tau_k) \right]$$

d. Calculate Ω_η:

$$\Omega_\eta = \begin{bmatrix} \left[\sigma_\eta(\tau_1) \right]^2 & 0 & \cdots & & 0 \\ 0 & \ddots & \ddots & & \vdots \\ \vdots & & \ddots & \ddots & 0 \\ 0 & & \cdots & 0 & \left[\sigma_\eta(\tau_9) \right]^2 \end{bmatrix}_{9 \times 9} \tag{3.59}$$

2. State initialization:

The initial state vector x_0^+ is

$$x_0^+ = \begin{bmatrix} x_{1,0}^+ \\ x_{2,0}^+ \end{bmatrix} = \begin{bmatrix} \theta_1 \\ \theta_2 \end{bmatrix} \tag{3.60}$$

To calculate the initial variance matrix P_0^+, first calculate $\Theta(\infty)$, which is $\Theta(\Delta t)$ evaluated with $\Delta t = \infty$. Given that $\exp\left(- \left\{ \kappa_i + \kappa_j \right\} \cdot \infty \right) = 0$,

$$[\Theta(\infty)]_{ij} = \Sigma_{ij} \frac{1}{\kappa_i + \kappa_j} \tag{3.61}$$

and therefore

$$\Theta(\infty) = \begin{bmatrix} \Sigma_{11} \frac{1}{2\kappa_1} & \Sigma_{12} \frac{1}{\kappa_1 + \kappa_2} \\ \Sigma_{12} \frac{1}{\kappa_1 + \kappa_2} & \Sigma_{22} \frac{1}{2\kappa_2} \end{bmatrix} \tag{3.62}$$

The final result is

$$P_0^+ = \begin{bmatrix} P_{11,0}^+ & P_{12,0}^+ \\ P_{12,0}^+ & P_{22,0}^+ \end{bmatrix} = V\Theta(\infty) V'$$

$$= V \begin{bmatrix} \Sigma_{11} \frac{1}{2\kappa_1} & \Sigma_{12} \frac{1}{\kappa_1 + \kappa_2} \\ \Sigma_{12} \frac{1}{\kappa_1 + \kappa_2} & \Sigma_{22} \frac{1}{2\kappa_2} \end{bmatrix} V' \tag{3.63}$$

3. Kalman recursion:

3.1. Prior state estimates: The prior estimate of the state variable vector and its variance at time t, x_t^- and P_1^-, are calculated from the respective posterior estimates at time $t - 1$:

$$\begin{bmatrix} x_{1,t}^- \\ x_{2,t}^- \end{bmatrix} = \begin{bmatrix} \theta_1 \\ \theta_2 \end{bmatrix} + \begin{bmatrix} F_{11} & F_{12} \\ F_{21} & F_{22} \end{bmatrix} \left(\begin{bmatrix} x_{1,t-1}^+ \\ x_{2,t-1}^+ \end{bmatrix} - \begin{bmatrix} \theta_1 \\ \theta_2 \end{bmatrix} \right) \tag{3.64}$$

and

$$\begin{bmatrix} P_{11,t}^- & P_{12,t}^- \\ P_{12,t}^- & P_{22,t}^- \end{bmatrix} = F \begin{bmatrix} P_{11,t-1}^+ & P_{12,t-1}^+ \\ P_{12,t-1}^+ & P_{22,t-1}^+ \end{bmatrix} F' + \begin{bmatrix} \Theta_{11}(\Delta t) & \Theta_{12}(\Delta t) \\ \Theta_{12}(\Delta t) & \Theta_{22}(\Delta t) \end{bmatrix} \tag{3.65}$$

3.2. Measurement update: The unexplained component of the yield curve data at time t relative to the ANSM(2) model with the prior state variables x_t^- is obtained using the measurement equation:

$$\begin{bmatrix} \eta_t(\tau_1) \\ \vdots \\ \eta_t(\tau_9) \end{bmatrix} = \begin{bmatrix} R_t(\tau_1) \\ \vdots \\ R_t(\tau_9) \end{bmatrix} - \begin{bmatrix} a(\tau_1) \\ \vdots \\ a(\tau_9) \end{bmatrix} + \begin{bmatrix} 1 & \frac{1}{\tau_1}G(\phi,\tau_1) \\ \vdots & \vdots \\ 1 & \frac{1}{\tau_9}G(\phi,\tau_9) \end{bmatrix} \begin{bmatrix} x_{1,t}^- \\ x_{2,t}^- \end{bmatrix} \tag{3.66}$$

M_t is evaluated from the prior variance matrix P_t^- and the H and Ω_η matrices as

$$M_t = \begin{bmatrix} M_{t,11} & \cdots & M_{t,19} \\ \vdots & \ddots & \vdots \\ M_{t,19} & \cdots & M_{t,99} \end{bmatrix}_{9 \times 9}$$
$$= H P_t^- H' + \Omega_\eta, \tag{3.67}$$

and the Kalman gain matrix K_t is evaluated as

$$K_t = \begin{bmatrix} K_{11,t} & \cdots & K_{19,t} \\ K_{21,t} & \cdots & K_{29,t} \end{bmatrix}_{2 \times 9}$$
$$= P_t^- H' M_t^{-1} \tag{3.68}$$

3.3 Posterior state estimates and recording: All of the quantities required for the posterior estimates of the state variable vector and its variance are now available, and they are respectively evaluated as follows:

$$x_t^+ = \begin{bmatrix} x_{1,t}^+ \\ x_{2,t}^+ \end{bmatrix} = x_t^- + K_t \eta_t \tag{3.69}$$

and

$$P_t^+ = \begin{bmatrix} P_{11,t}^+ & P_{12,t}^+ \\ P_{12,t}^+ & P_{22,t}^+ \end{bmatrix} = (I - K_t H) P_t^- \tag{3.70}$$

The posterior estimates x_t^+ and P_t^+ are used in step 3.1 to start the next recursion, and the recursions run for all values of t from 1 to T. The final result from the Kalman filter algorithm is the time series of posterior estimates of the state variable vector $\{x_1^+, \ldots, x_T^+\}$, where each x_1^+ is a 2×1 vector. The results expressed in full are therefore a $2 \times T$ matrix:

$$\{x_1^+, \ldots, x_T^+\} = \begin{bmatrix} x_{1,1}^+ & \cdots & x_{T,1}^+ \\ x_{1,2}^+ & \cdots & x_{T,2}^+ \end{bmatrix}_{2 \times T} \tag{3.71}$$

3.3.4 Full ANSM(2) estimation with the Kalman filter

As discussed in section 3.2.3, the maximum likelihood estimation of the ANSM(2) requires the Kalman filter algorithm detailed in the previous section to be applied many times within an optimization algorithm. The optimization algorithm I use is the Nelder-Mead algorithm within the "fminsearch" function in the MatLab Optimization Toolbox. The Nelder-Mead algorithm is a derivative-free optimization algorithm, and I have found it more reliable than the quasi-derivative methods contained in the MatLab Optimization Toolbox (i.e., the "fminunc" and "fmincon" functions). The freely available programming language R also has versions of the same optimization algorithms available within the General-purpose Optimization function. For details, see http://stat.ethz.ch/R-manual/R-patched/library/stats/html/optim.html.

As also discussed in section 3.2.3, constraints on F, σ, and Ω_η are required to ensure that the Kalman filter will always deliver a finite and real numerical value back to the optimization algorithm. There are various ways to impose such constraints. I will shortly detail the standard methods I use that have worked without any issues for all of the estimations I have undertaken and for those I illustrate in this book. However, I am aware of improvements that could be made, both for extra robustness and to accommodate alternative specifications of κ. For example, I will introduce a restricted specification of κ in subsection 6.2.7 of chapter 6. Hence, the precise methods for appropriately constraining F will be subject to change.

A. Optimization algorithm

The objective of the optimization algorithm when applied to a full estimation of the ANSM(2) and the data set with 9 times to maturity is to find the set of 19 parameters

$\mathbb{A} = \{\mathbb{B}, \mathbb{C}, \mathbb{D}, \sigma_\eta(\tau_1), \ldots, \sigma_\eta(\tau_9)\}$, which I will detail below, that maximizes the following numerical calculation:

$$\text{log-}L(\{R_1, \ldots, R_T\}, \mathbb{A}) = -\frac{1}{2} \sum_{t=1}^{T} 9 \cdot \log(2\pi) + \log(|M_t|) + \eta_t' M_t^{-1} \eta_t \qquad (3.72)$$

where $\{\eta_1, \ldots, \eta_T\}$ and $\{M_1, \ldots, M_T\}$ are the time series of the 9×1 vectors η_t and the 9×9 matrices M_t obtained at each time step of the Kalman filter algorithm.

Therefore, to obtain $\{\eta_1, \ldots, \eta_T\}$ and $\{M_1, \ldots, M_T\}$ for a given set of those 19 parameters $\{\mathbb{B}, \mathbb{C}, \mathbb{D}, \sigma_\eta(\tau_1), \ldots, \sigma_\eta(\tau_9)\}$, the optimization algorithm needs to pass them along with any required fixed parameters into the Kalman filter algorithm and then receive the $\{\eta_1, \ldots, \eta_T\}$ and $\{M_1, \ldots, M_T\}$ results back.

As noted above, I again denote the entire set of parameters passed from the optimization algorithm to the Kalman filter algorithm as the parameter set $\mathbb{A}$, and it is as follows:

- Time step: $\Delta t = 1/12$.
- Set of times to maturity: $\{\tau_1, \ldots, \tau_9\}$.
- Free ANSM(2) parameters: $\mathbb{B} = \{\phi, \kappa_{11}, \kappa_{12}, \kappa_{21}, \kappa_{22}, \theta_1, \theta_2\}$.
- Fixed ANSM(2) parameters: $\mathbb{C} = \{a_0 = 0, b_0 = [1,1]', \tilde{\theta} = [0,0]'\}$.
- Proxy ANSM(2) parameters: $\mathbb{D} = \{\sigma_1^*, \sigma_2^*, \rho_{12}^*\}$.
- Measurement equation standard deviations: $\sigma_\eta(\tau_1), \ldots, \sigma_\eta(\tau_K)$.

I detail in the following subsection how those parameters are used within the Kalman filter algorithm outlined in Table 3.2 as applied to the ANSM(2). After the Kalman filter algorithm has finished for the given set of parameters, the results $\{\eta_1, \ldots, \eta_T\}$ and $\{M_1, \ldots, M_T\}$ are passed back to the optimization algorithm to evaluate the log-likelihood function for that set of parameters. The optimization algorithm will iterate to a new set of 19 parameters $\{\mathbb{B}, \mathbb{C}, \mathbb{D}, \sigma_\eta(\tau_1), \ldots, \sigma_\eta(\tau_9)\}$ and then repeat the process of passing that new iteration within the parameter set $\mathbb{A}$ into the Kalman filter algorithm again to obtain a new log-likelihood result. The entire process then repeats until the user-specified conditions of convergence. For example, I use a change of less than 10^{-2} in $\text{log-}L(\{R_1, \ldots, R_T\}, \mathbb{A})$ from the previous iteration as the indicator of convergence to the maximum likelihood value.

Once the optimization algorithm has converged, the prevailing 19 parameters $\{\mathbb{B}, \mathbb{C}, \mathbb{D}, \sigma_\eta(\tau_1), \ldots, \sigma_\eta(\tau_9)\}$ are the final parameters estimates. However, they will include the proxy parameters σ_1^*, σ_2^*, and ρ_{12}^*, and potentially negative estimated values of the parameters $\sigma_\eta(\tau_1), \ldots, \sigma_\eta(\tau_9)$. These need to be converted into σ_1, σ_2, and ρ_{12}, as noted in the following subsection, and using $\sigma_\eta(\tau_k) = \sqrt{[\sigma_\eta(\tau_k)]^2}$. The other parameter estimates do not need any adjustments.

Kalman filter algorithm

Only the setup step in the Kalman filter algorithm changes when it is used for a full estimation, that is, to the "**1. Setup and estimation constraints**" in Table 3.2. Therefore, I discuss only that step from Table 3.2 here.

a. Calculate *F*:

As detailed in section 3.3.3, first undertake the eigensystem decomposition of κ to obtain the eigenvalues κ_1 and κ_2, and the eigenvector matrix V:

$$V \kappa_D V^{-1} = \kappa$$

$$\begin{bmatrix} V_{11} & V_{12} \\ V_{21} & V_{22} \end{bmatrix} \begin{bmatrix} \kappa_1 & 0 \\ 0 & \kappa_2 \end{bmatrix} \begin{bmatrix} V_{11} & V_{12} \\ V_{21} & V_{22} \end{bmatrix}^{-1} = \begin{bmatrix} \kappa_{11} & \kappa_{12} \\ \kappa_{21} & \kappa_{22} \end{bmatrix} \tag{3.73}$$

To ensure $|F| < 1$ at all times during estimation, the real parts of κ_1 and κ_2 need to remain positive. If $\text{Real}(\kappa_n) < 0$ then $|F| > 1$, and therefore explosive dynamics would occur. That result would be unsatisfactory from an economic perspective, because interest rates do not exhibit that property, and it could potentially result in infinite values that would cause the Kalman filter algorithm to fail. Following the suggestion in Christensen, Diebold, and Rudebusch (2011) footnote 15, I therefore apply a direct constraint to ensure $\text{Real}(\kappa_n) < 0$. Specifically, the constraint I use is to set the real part of any eigenvalue of κ that is less than 10^{-6} to 10^{-6} without any change to the imaginary part, that is, if $\text{Real}(\kappa_1) < 10^{-6}$, then $\kappa_1 = 10^{-6} + i\text{Imag}(\kappa_1)$, and if $\text{Real}(\kappa_2) < 0$, then $\kappa_2 = 10^{-6} + i\text{Imag}(\kappa_2)$. The state equation coefficient matrix F is then

$$\begin{bmatrix} F_{11} & F_{12} \\ F_{21} & F_{22} \end{bmatrix} = V \begin{bmatrix} \exp(-\kappa_1 \Delta t) & 0 \\ 0 & \exp(-\kappa_2 \Delta t) \end{bmatrix} V^{-1} \tag{3.74}$$

Ideally, this constraint should only bind during the estimation process. Obtaining a final estimate of κ with eigenvalues that match the constraint would mean that the constraint rather than the data is effectively determining at least some of the parameters in κ.

b. Calculate $\Theta(\Delta t)$:

The matrix $\sigma\sigma'$ that begins the calculation of $\Theta(\Delta t)$ is the same as in section 3.3.3:

$$\sigma\sigma' = \begin{bmatrix} \sigma_1^2 & \sigma_1\sigma_2\rho_{12} \\ \sigma_1\sigma_2\rho_{12} & \sigma_2^2 \end{bmatrix}$$

but the parameters σ_1, σ_2, and ρ_{12} require an estimation constraint to ensure that $\sigma\sigma'$ is always positive definite, which is a property I will explain shortly below. Following Hamilton (1994, pp. 146–47),[4] I ensure that σ_1 and σ_2 are positive by using the proxy parameters σ_1^* and σ_2^* and the mechanism:

$$\sigma_1 = \sqrt{\sigma_1^{*2}} > 0 \tag{3.75a}$$

$$\sigma_2 = \sqrt{\sigma_2^{*2}} > 0 \tag{3.75b}$$

and that the correlation parameter ρ_{12} remains between -1 and 1 using the proxy parameter ρ_{12}^* and the mechanism:

$$-1 < \rho_{12} = \frac{\rho_{12}^*}{1 + |\rho_{12}^*|} < 1 \tag{3.76}$$

The proxy parameters being estimated by the optimization algorithm can therefore freely adopt any values, while their derived quantities σ_1, σ_2, and ρ_{12} in the Kalman filter algorithm will ensure that $\sigma \sigma'$ is positive definite. Note that I use this method because I find the specification of σ in terms of standard deviations and correlation coefficients intuitive. However, an alternative but equivalent method suggested in Hamilton (1994) and used by Christensen, Diebold, and Rudebusch (2011) is to specify σ as

$$\sigma = \begin{bmatrix} \sigma_{11} & 0 \\ \sigma_{12} & \sigma_{22} \end{bmatrix} \tag{3.77}$$

and therefore

$$\begin{bmatrix} \sigma_{11} & 0 \\ \sigma_{12} & \sigma_{22} \end{bmatrix} \begin{bmatrix} \sigma_{11} & \sigma_{12} \\ 0 & \sigma_{22} \end{bmatrix} = \begin{bmatrix} \sigma_{11}^2 & \sigma_{11}\sigma_{12} \\ \sigma_{11}\sigma_{12} & \sigma_{12}^2 + \sigma_{22}^2 \end{bmatrix} \tag{3.78}$$

will be positive definite.

Regarding the property of positive definiteness for matrices, it is essentially the analogue of ensuring a scalar number is positive. Subsections A.7.1 and A.7.4 contain further details on positive definite matrices. Without ensuring that property for $\sigma \sigma'$, the variance-related calculations in the Kalman filter algorithm, that is, Σ, P_t^-, M_t, and P_t^+ could become negative, which would be nonsensical statistically (i.e., it would imply imaginary standard deviations for the state variables and the unexplained component of the yield curve data η_t). For the optimization algorithm, a negative variance-related calculation in the Kalman filter algorithm would lead the determinants of at least some matrices M_t to be negative, that is, $|M_t| < 0$, and therefore $\log(|M_t|)$ would have imaginary components. Such an outcome would be terminal for the optimization algorithm. That is, it would cause a failure if imaginary numbers could not be accommodated, or the optimization itself would become infeasible because complex numbers cannot be subjected to maximization like real numbers.

c. Calculate a **and** H:

There is no constraint required, so the calculations are identical to those in sub-section 3.3.3. Note that, in principle, ϕ should be constrained to be a positive value. In practice, iterations of ϕ never approach negative values.

d. Calculate Ω_η:

An estimation constraint is also required to ensure the variance matrix Ω_η (and therefore M_t) remains positive definite. This occurs naturally in my setup because Ω_η is already defined using standard deviation parameters $\sigma_\eta(\tau_k)$ passed from the optimization algorithm. That is,

$$\Omega_\eta = \begin{bmatrix} \left[\sigma_\eta(\tau_1)\right]^2 & 0 & \cdots & & 0 \\ 0 & \ddots & \ddots & & \vdots \\ \vdots & & \ddots & \ddots & 0 \\ 0 & & \cdots & 0 & \left[\sigma_\eta(\tau_9)\right]^2 \end{bmatrix}_{9\times9} \tag{3.79}$$

and so each element $\left[\sigma_\eta(\tau_k)\right]^2$ will be positive regardless of the value $\sigma_\eta(\tau_k)$.

B. Diagnostics

I obtain estimated standard errors for the estimated parameters by evaluating a Hessian numerically around final parameter estimates. Hamilton (1994) pp. 388-89 provides details on the calculation of standard errors using a Hessian (along with other methods), and numerical Hessians are obtainable in practice from the optimization algorithm or by passing the estimated parameters into an optimization algorithm that uses quasi-derivative methods. For example, the "fminunc" and "fmincon" functions in the MatLab Optimization Toolbox calculate numerical Hessians, and the General-purpose Optimization function in R also includes a numerical Hessian option for its optimization algorithms.

The important point for this worked example is that the Hessian needs to be calculated for the entire set of the final 19 estimated parameters in their natural form, that is, $\mathbb{B} = \{\phi, \kappa_{11}, \kappa_{12}, \kappa_{21}, \kappa_{22}, \theta_1, \theta_2, \sigma_1, \sigma_2, \rho_{12}, \sigma_\eta(\tau_1), \ldots, \sigma_\eta(\tau_9)\}$, rather than using the estimated proxy parameters σ_1^*, σ_2^*, and ρ_{12}^* that the optimization algorithm works with during the estimation. The Hessian will be a 19×19 matrix, which I will denote $\mathbb{H}$, and the estimated standard errors of the parameters are obtained from the following calculation:

$$\text{Parameter } i \text{ std err.} = \sqrt{\left[\frac{1}{T}\mathbb{H}^{-1}\right]_{i,i}}$$

where $\mathbb{H}^{-1}$ is the matrix inverse of $\mathbb{H}$, T is the sample size, i, i denotes the diagonal elements of the matrix calculation, and taking the square root of each diagonal elements gives the 19 estimated parameter standard errors. For example the estimated standard errors for ϕ, κ_{11}, and $\sigma_\eta(\tau_9)$ will respectively be $\left[\frac{1}{T}\mathbb{H}^{-1}\right]_{1,1}$, $\left[\frac{1}{T}\mathbb{H}^{-1}\right]_{2,2}$, and $\left[\frac{1}{T}\mathbb{H}^{-1}\right]_{19,19}$.

The estimated standard deviation parameters $\sigma_\eta(\tau_1),\ldots,\sigma_\eta(\tau_9)$ provide one measure of the goodness of fit that the ANSM(2) has to the yield curve data. That is, a smaller standard deviation $\sigma_\eta(\tau_k)$ indicates a closer fit of the ANSM(2) to the interest rate of maturity τ_k. Two other common summary goodness-of-fit measures are the root mean squared error (RMSE) and the mean absolute error (MAE). The measures are respectively defined as

$$\text{RMSE}\left[\eta(\tau_k)\right] = \frac{1}{T}\sum_{t=1}^{T}[\eta_t(\tau_k)]^2$$

and

$$\text{MAE}\left[\eta(\tau_k)\right] = \frac{1}{T}\sum_{t=1}^{T}|\eta_t(\tau_k)|$$

where $\eta_t(\tau_k)$ are the unexplained components for the yield curve data for maturity τ_k at time t. Other summary measures such as means, medians, percentiles, minimums, maximums, and so forth can also be useful. Plotting a time series of the residuals $\eta_t(\tau_k)$ is often worthwhile to check for any systematic patterns in the residuals over different periods of the sample. Ideally, the residuals should be symmetrically centered around zero, and not have any substantially long and systematic periods of being entirely positive or negative that might indicate model misspecification. Some serial correlation will be present, indeed it is often noted in the literature, but that does not present any material issues.

3.4 Other GATSMs

In this section I first provide the details required for specifying and estimating the ANSM(3). The ANSM(3) is the second model that I will use throughout this book, in its own right and to represent the shadow term structure in shadow/ZLB-ANSMs. I have found the ANSM(2) and ANSM(3) to be very suitable empirically for all of the applications in this book, and I will detail in chapter 6 from a theoretical perspective why I also prefer those models and the ANSM class in general. Moreover, ANSMs may be arbitrarily extended if more flexible ANSMs and shadow/ZLB-ANSMs are required for particular applications. I provide an overview of the key results required to obtain and estimate higher-order ANSMs in section 3.4.2.

However, I also realize that some users prefer full, or stationary, GATSM specifications, that is, without the additional restrictions to create the ANSM subclass, and are therefore likely to prefer shadow/ZLB-GATSMs. Therefore, in section 3.4.3, I provide an overview of the key results required to obtain and estimate full GATSMs of any order. In section 3.4.4, I note a partially constrained GATSM with an ANSM component.

3.4.1 ANSM(3)

Specification

The ANSM(3) is detailed in Christensen, Diebold, and Rudebusch (2011), Diebold and Rudebusch (2013), and Krippner (2006, 2013d,e).[5] It is defined with three state variables, 19 free parameters, and 18 fixed parameters. I present those here in their scalar/vector/matrix form and with the typical restrictions imposed:

$$x(t) = \begin{bmatrix} x_1(t) \\ x_2(t) \\ x_3(t) \end{bmatrix}; \quad a_0 = 0; \quad b_0 = \begin{bmatrix} 1 \\ 1 \\ 0 \end{bmatrix}$$

$$\kappa = \begin{bmatrix} \kappa_{11} & \kappa_{12} & \kappa_{12} \\ \kappa_{21} & \kappa_{22} & \kappa_{23} \\ \kappa_{31} & \kappa_{32} & \kappa_{33} \end{bmatrix}; \quad \theta = \begin{bmatrix} \theta_1 \\ \theta_2 \\ \theta_3 \end{bmatrix}$$

$$\sigma = \begin{bmatrix} \sigma_1 & 0 & 0 \\ \sigma_2 \rho_{12} & \sigma_2 \sqrt{1-\rho_{12}^2} & 0 \\ \sigma_3 \rho_{13} & \sigma_3 \frac{\rho_{23}-\rho_{12}\rho_{13}}{\sqrt{1-\rho_{12}^2}} & \sigma_3 \sqrt{1-\rho_{13}^2 - \frac{(\rho_{23}-\rho_{12}\rho_{13})^2}{1-\rho_{12}^2}} \end{bmatrix}$$

$$\tilde{\kappa} = \begin{bmatrix} 0 & 0 & 0 \\ 0 & \phi & -\phi \\ 0 & 0 & \phi \end{bmatrix}; \quad \tilde{\theta} = \begin{bmatrix} 0 \\ 0 \\ 0 \end{bmatrix} \qquad (3.80)$$

The free parameter set is therefore $\mathbb{B} = \{\phi, \kappa_{11}, \kappa_{12}, \kappa_{13}, \kappa_{21}, \kappa_{22}, \kappa_{23}, \kappa_{31}, \kappa_{32}, \kappa_{33}, \theta_1, \theta_2, \theta_3, \sigma_1, \sigma_2, \sigma_3, \rho_{12}, \rho_{13}, \rho_{23}\}$.

Term structure

The ANSM(3) short rate is

$$r(t) = [1, 1, 0] \begin{bmatrix} x_1(t) \\ x_2(t) \\ x_3(t) \end{bmatrix}$$

$$= x_1(t) + x_2(t) \qquad (3.81)$$

As for the ANSM(2), the matrix exponential $\tilde{\kappa}$ is the key expression required to develop the term structure and related quantities. However, $\tilde{\kappa}$ is no longer a diagonal matrix and it has a repeated eigenvalue ϕ, so its calculation is more involved.

For example, Krippner (2013d,e) uses a Jordan decomposition, which is essentially a more general form of an eigensystem decomposition (sections A.7 and A.8 contain further details on the Jordan decomposition and its uses). The result is

$$\exp(-\tilde{\kappa}\tau) = \begin{bmatrix} 1 & 0 & 0 \\ 0 & \exp(-\phi\tau) & \phi\tau\exp(-\phi\tau) \\ 0 & 0 & \exp(-\phi\tau) \end{bmatrix} \tag{3.82}$$

The factor loadings for the expected path of the short rate $\tilde{\mathbb{E}}_t[r(t+\tau)|x(t)]$ and forward rates are therefore

$$b_0\exp(-\tilde{\kappa}\tau) = [1,1,0] \begin{bmatrix} 1 & 0 & 0 \\ 0 & \exp(-\phi\tau) & \phi\tau\exp(-\phi\tau) \\ 0 & 0 & \exp(-\phi\tau) \end{bmatrix}$$

$$= \left[1, \exp(-\phi\tau), \phi\tau\exp(-\phi\tau)\right] \tag{3.83}$$

Figure 3.2 illustrates the third forward rate factor loading for the ANSM(3), that is, the function $\phi\tau\exp(-\phi\tau)$. In light of its shape, I adopt the Krippner (2006) terminology "Bow" to describe this factor and its associated state variable $x_3(t)$.[6] Figure 3.2 also plots the third interest rate factor loading for the ANSM(3), which is a bow-shaped function of time to maturity.

Using the factor loadings $b_0\exp(-\tilde{\kappa}\tau)$, the expected path of the short rate $\tilde{\mathbb{E}}_t[r(t+\tau)|x(t)]$ for the ANSM(3) is therefore

$$\tilde{\mathbb{E}}_t[r(t+\tau)|x(t)] = \left[1, \exp(-\phi\tau), \phi\tau\exp(-\phi\tau)\right] \begin{bmatrix} x_1(t) \\ x_2(t) \\ x_3(t) \end{bmatrix}$$

$$= x_1(t) + x_2(t)\cdot\exp(-\phi\tau)$$

$$+ x_3(t)\cdot\phi\tau\exp(-\phi\tau) \tag{3.84}$$

Forward rates for the ANSM(3) are then

$$f(t,\tau) = \left[1, \exp(-\phi\tau), \phi\tau\exp(-\phi\tau)\right] \begin{bmatrix} x_1(t) \\ x_2(t) \\ x_3(t) \end{bmatrix} - VE(\tau) \tag{3.85}$$

where the volatility effect may be calculated as (see Krippner [2013d,e] for details)

$$VE(\tau) = \sigma_1^2\cdot\frac{1}{2}\tau^2 + \sigma_2^2\cdot\frac{1}{2}[G(\phi,\tau)]^2 + \sigma_3^2\cdot\frac{1}{2}[F(\phi,\tau)]^2$$

$$+ \rho_{12}\sigma_1\sigma_2\cdot\tau G(\phi,\tau) + \rho_{13}\sigma_1\sigma_3\cdot\tau F(\phi,\tau)$$

$$+ \rho_{23}\sigma_2\sigma_3\cdot G(\phi,\tau)F(\phi,\tau) \tag{3.86}$$

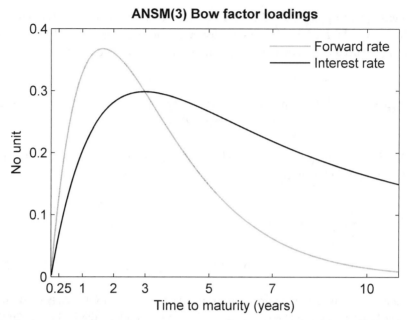

Figure 3.2 To represent the term structure, the ANSM(3) uses the Level and Slope factor loadings for forward rates and interest rates from Figure 3.1, and the Bow forward rate and interest rate factor loadings illustrated here.

where

$$F(\phi,\tau) = \frac{1}{\phi}\left[1 - \exp(-\phi\tau)\right] - \tau\exp(-\phi\tau)$$

$$= G(\phi,\tau) - \tau\exp(-\phi\tau) \qquad (3.87)$$

As for the ANSM(2), interest rates for the ANSM(3) are again calculated by integrating the forward rate expression. The result is

$$R(t,\tau) = a(\tau) + [b(\tau)]'\begin{bmatrix} x_1(t) \\ x_2(t) \\ x_3(t) \end{bmatrix}$$

where $a(\tau)$ takes the (relatively complicated, but nevertheless closed-form analytic) form

$$a(\tau) = -\sigma_1^2 \cdot \frac{1}{6}\tau^2 - \sigma_2^2 \cdot \frac{1}{2\phi^2}\left[1 - \frac{1}{\tau}G(\phi,\tau) - \frac{1}{2\tau}\phi\,[G(\phi,\tau)]^2\right]$$

$$-\rho_{12}\sigma_1\sigma_2 \cdot \frac{1}{\phi^2}\left[1 - \frac{1}{\tau}G(\phi,\tau) + \frac{1}{2}\phi\tau - \phi G(\phi,\tau)\right]$$

$$-\sigma_3^2 \cdot \frac{1}{8\phi^3\tau}\exp(-2\phi\tau)\left[-5 - 2\phi\tau\,(3 + \phi\tau)\right]$$

$$-\sigma_3^2 \cdot \frac{1}{8\phi^3 \tau} \left[8\exp\left(-\phi\tau\right)\left(2+\phi\tau\right) - 11 + 4\phi\tau \right]$$

$$-\rho_{13}\sigma_1\sigma_3 \cdot \frac{1}{2\phi^3\tau} \exp\left(-\phi\tau\right)\left[6 + 2\phi\tau\left(3+\phi\tau\right)\right]$$

$$-\rho_{13}\sigma_1\sigma_3 \cdot \frac{1}{2\phi^3\tau}\left(-6 + \phi^2\tau^2\right)$$

$$-\rho_{23}\sigma_2\sigma_3 \cdot \frac{1}{4\phi^3\tau} \exp\left(-2\phi\tau\right)\left[-3 - 2\phi\tau\right]$$

$$-\rho_{23}\sigma_2\sigma_3 \cdot \frac{1}{4\phi^3\tau}\left[4\exp\left(-\phi\tau\right)\left(3+\phi\tau\right) - 9 + 4\phi\tau\right] \tag{3.88}$$

and:

$$[b(\tau)]' = \left[1, \frac{1}{\tau}G(\phi,\tau), \frac{1}{\tau}F(\phi,\tau) \right] \tag{3.89}$$

Note that Christensen, Diebold, and Rudebusch (2011) present an equivalent calculation of $a(\tau)$, but based on a different way of specifying the variance and covariance parameters rather than my preferred expression in terms of standard deviation and correlation coefficient parameters.

Partial estimation using the Kalman filter

The partial estimation of the ANSM(3) proceeds as for the ANSM(2), except with the allowance for the extra state variable. I provide a summary of each of the steps below, but I use some of the summary expressions from Table 3.1, rather than complete expressions for every quantity as with the ANSM(2) worked example. I have also assumed $K = 9$.

1. Setup: **a. Calculate F:**

$$F = V \exp\left(-\kappa_D \Delta t\right) V^{-1}$$

$$= V \begin{bmatrix} \exp\left(-\kappa_1 \Delta t\right) & 0 & 0 \\ 0 & \exp\left(-\kappa_2 \Delta t\right) & 0 \\ 0 & 0 & \exp\left(-\kappa_3 \Delta t\right) \end{bmatrix} V^{-1} \tag{3.90}$$

where V is the 3×3 matrix of eigenvectors in columns.
b. Calculate $\Theta\left(\Delta t\right)$:

$$\sigma\sigma' = \begin{bmatrix} \sigma_1^2 & \sigma_1\sigma_2\rho_{12} & \sigma_1\sigma_3\rho_{13} \\ \sigma_1\sigma_2\rho_{12} & \sigma_2^2 & \sigma_2\sigma_3\rho_{23} \\ \sigma_1\sigma_3\rho_{13} & \sigma_2\sigma_3\rho_{23} & \sigma_3^2 \end{bmatrix} \tag{3.91}$$

$$\Sigma = V^{-1}\sigma\sigma'V'^{-1}$$

$$\Theta\left(\Delta t\right)=\begin{bmatrix} \Sigma_{11}G(2\kappa_1,\Delta t) & \Sigma_{12}G(\kappa_1+\kappa_2,\Delta t) & \Sigma_{13}G(\kappa_1+\kappa_3,\Delta t) \\ \Sigma_{12}G(\kappa_1+\kappa_2,\Delta t) & \Sigma_{22}G(2\kappa_2,\Delta t) & \Sigma_{23}G(\kappa_2+\kappa_3,\Delta t) \\ \Sigma_{13}G(\kappa_1+\kappa_3,\Delta t) & \Sigma_{23}G(\kappa_2+\kappa_3,\Delta t) & \Sigma_{33}G(2\kappa_3,\Delta t) \end{bmatrix}$$

$$(3.92)$$

c. Calculate a and H:

$$a=\begin{bmatrix} a\left(\tau_1\right) \\ \vdots \\ a\left(\tau_9\right) \end{bmatrix}_{1\times 9}$$

$$(3.93)$$

$$H=\begin{bmatrix} [b(\tau_1)]'_{1\times 3} \\ \vdots \\ [b(\tau_9)]'_{1\times 3} \end{bmatrix}=\begin{bmatrix} 1 & \frac{1}{\tau_1}G(\phi,\tau_1) & \frac{1}{\tau_1}F(\phi,\tau_1) \\ \vdots & \vdots & \vdots \\ 1 & \frac{1}{\tau_9}G(\phi,\tau_9) & \frac{1}{\tau_9}F(\phi,\tau_9) \end{bmatrix}_{9\times 3}$$

$$(3.94)$$

d. Calculate Ω_η:

$$\Omega_\eta=\begin{bmatrix} \left[\sigma_\eta\left(\tau_1\right)\right]^2 & 0 & \cdots & 0 \\ 0 & \ddots & \ddots & \vdots \\ \vdots & \ddots & \ddots & 0 \\ 0 & \cdots & 0 & \left[\sigma_\eta\left(\tau_9\right)\right]^2 \end{bmatrix}_{9\times 9}$$

$$(3.95)$$

2. State initialization:

$$\begin{bmatrix} x^+_{1,0} \\ x^+_{2,0} \\ x^+_{3,0} \end{bmatrix}=\begin{bmatrix} \theta_1 \\ \theta_2 \\ \theta_3 \end{bmatrix}$$

$$(3.96)$$

$$P^-_t=V\begin{bmatrix} \Sigma_{11}\frac{1}{2\kappa_1} & \Sigma_{12}\frac{1}{\kappa_1+\kappa_2} & \Sigma_{13}\frac{1}{\kappa_1+\kappa_2} \\ \Sigma_{12}\frac{1}{\kappa_1+\kappa_2} & \Sigma_{22}\frac{1}{2\kappa_2} & \Sigma_{23}\frac{1}{\kappa_1+\kappa_2} \\ \Sigma_{13}\frac{1}{\kappa_1+\kappa_2} & \Sigma_{23}\frac{1}{\kappa_1+\kappa_2} & \Sigma_{33}\frac{1}{\kappa_1+\kappa_2} \end{bmatrix}V'$$

$$(3.97)$$

3.1 Prior state update:

$$\begin{bmatrix} x^-_{1,t} \\ x^-_{2,t} \\ x^-_{3,t} \end{bmatrix}=\begin{bmatrix} \theta_1 \\ \theta_2 \\ \theta_3 \end{bmatrix}+F\left(\begin{bmatrix} x^+_{1,t-1} \\ x^+_{2,t-1} \\ x^+_{3,t-1} \end{bmatrix}-\begin{bmatrix} \theta_1 \\ \theta_2 \\ \theta_3 \end{bmatrix}\right)$$

$$(3.98)$$

$$P^-_t=FP^+_{t-1}F'+\Theta\left(\Delta t\right)$$

$$(3.99)$$

3.2 Measurement estimates:

$$
\begin{bmatrix} \eta_t(\tau_1) \\ \vdots \\ \eta_t(\tau_9) \end{bmatrix} = \begin{bmatrix} R_t(\tau_1) \\ \vdots \\ R_t(\tau_9) \end{bmatrix} - \begin{bmatrix} a(\tau_1) \\ \vdots \\ a(\tau_9) \end{bmatrix}
$$

$$
- \begin{bmatrix} 1 & \frac{1}{\tau_1}G(\phi,\tau_1) & \frac{1}{\tau_1}F(\phi,\tau_1) \\ \vdots & \vdots & \vdots \\ 1 & \frac{1}{\tau_K}G(\phi,\tau_K) & \frac{1}{\tau_K}F(\phi,\tau_K) \end{bmatrix} \begin{bmatrix} x_{1,t}^- \\ x_{2,t}^- \\ x_{3,t}^- \end{bmatrix} \tag{3.100}
$$

$$
M_t = HP_t^- H' + \Omega_\eta \tag{3.101}
$$

$$
K_t = P_t^- H' M_t^{-1} \tag{3.102}
$$

3.3. Posterior state estimates:

$$
x_t^+ = x_t^- + K_t \eta_t \tag{3.103}
$$

$$
P_t^+ = (I - K_t H) P_t^- \tag{3.104}
$$

Full estimation using the Kalman filter

The eigenvalue restrictions for F in the ANSM(3) are analogous to the ANSM(2), that is, if $\text{Real}(\kappa_n) < 0$, then $\kappa_n = 10^{-6} + i\,\text{Imag}(\kappa_n)$.

To obtain a positive definite matrix $\sigma\sigma'$, the ANSM(3) requires six proxy parameters $\{\sigma_1^*, \sigma_2^*, \sigma_3^*, \rho_{12}^*, \rho_{13}^*, \rho_{23}^*\}$ and the following transformations within the Kalman filter algorithm:

$$
\sigma_i = \sqrt{\sigma_i^{*2}} > 0 \tag{3.105}
$$

and

$$
-1 < \rho_{ij} = \frac{\rho_{ij}^*}{1 + \left|\rho_{ij}^*\right|} < 1 \tag{3.106}
$$

3.4.2 Higher-order ANSMs

The ANSM class of models can be extended arbitrarily, which I expect will prove useful to allow more flexibility than the ANSM(3), or the shadow/ZLB-ANSM(3) in the following chapters. In particular, even the residuals from the ANSM(3) and shadow/ZLB-ANSM(3) estimations presented in this book are sometimes larger than would be desirable or acceptable for financial market purposes. One solution would be reduce the number of securities/maturities used to define the term structure, but the alternative of extending model to four or five state variables is likely to prove more useful for some applications. Indeed, one extreme possibility from the perspective of adding further state variables would be to create term structure models with equilibrium foundations (see chapter 6) that are arbitrage free with respect to the data (i.e., they fit the observed yield curve data precisely, or to within market-quoted bid-ask spreads).[7]

Note that the higher-order ANSMs I propose in this section are distinctly different from the way the ANSM(3) is extended in Christensen, Diebold, and Rudebusch (2009). Specifically, the Christensen et al. (2009) model has two Slope and Curvature components, with each Slope and Curvature pair based on a different decay parameter, that is, ϕ_1 and ϕ_2. It also has the Level component, thereby giving a model with five state variables.

The alternative I propose continues to use a single decay parameter ϕ and extends the specifications of b_0 and $\tilde{\kappa}$ in ANSM form to create the higher-order ANSM functions. In chapter 6, I will provide a theoretical justification for my proposed extensions, but here I just state the mechanical mathematical results. Hence, the ANSM(4) is based on

$$
b_0 = \begin{bmatrix} 1 \\ 1 \\ 0 \\ 0 \end{bmatrix}; \quad \tilde{\kappa} = \begin{bmatrix} 0 & 0 & 0 & 0 \\ 0 & \phi & -\phi & 0 \\ 0 & 0 & \phi & -\phi \\ 0 & 0 & 0 & \phi \end{bmatrix}
\tag{3.107}
$$

which produces the $\tilde{\mathbb{E}}_t\left[r(t+\tau)|x(t)\right]$ and $f(t,\tau)$ factor loadings:

$$
\exp\left(-\tilde{\kappa}'\tau\right)b_0 = \begin{bmatrix} 1 \\ \exp(-\phi\tau) \\ \phi\tau\exp(-\phi\tau) \\ \frac{1}{2}(\phi\tau)^2\exp(-\phi\tau) \end{bmatrix}
\tag{3.108}
$$

The ANSM(5) is based on

$$
b_0 = \begin{bmatrix} 1 \\ 1 \\ 0 \\ 0 \\ 0 \end{bmatrix}; \quad \tilde{\kappa} = \begin{bmatrix} 0 & 0 & 0 & 0 & 0 \\ 0 & \phi & -\phi & 0 & 0 \\ 0 & 0 & \phi & -\phi & 0 \\ 0 & 0 & 0 & \phi & -\phi \\ 0 & 0 & 0 & 0 & \phi \end{bmatrix}
\tag{3.109}
$$

which produces the $\tilde{\mathbb{E}}_t\left[r(t+\tau)|x(t)\right]$ and $f(t,\tau)$ factor loadings:

$$
\exp\left(-\tilde{\kappa}'\tau\right)b_0 = \begin{bmatrix} 1 \\ \exp(-\phi\tau) \\ \phi\tau\exp(-\phi\tau) \\ \frac{1}{2}(\phi\tau)^2\exp(-\phi\tau) \\ \frac{1}{6}(\phi\tau)^3\exp(-\phi\tau) \end{bmatrix}
\tag{3.110}
$$

In general, the ANSM(N) is based on

$$b_0 = \begin{bmatrix} 1 \\ 1 \\ 0_{(N-2)\times 1} \end{bmatrix}; \quad \tilde{\kappa} = 0_{N\times N} + \Phi \tag{3.111}$$

where Φ has the following diagonal and one-off super-diagonal entries:

$$\Phi_{11} = 0$$
$$\Phi_{nn} = \phi \text{ for } n = 2 \text{ to } N$$
$$\Phi_{n,n+1} = -\phi \text{ for } n = 2 \text{ to } N-1 \tag{3.112}$$

which will produce the $\tilde{\mathbb{E}}_t \left[r(t+\tau) \,|\, x(t) \right]$ and $f(t,\tau)$ factor loadings:

$$\exp\left(-\tilde{\kappa}'\tau\right) b_0 = \begin{bmatrix} 1 \\ \exp(-\phi\tau) \\ \phi\tau \exp(-\phi\tau) \\ \frac{1}{(n-2)!}(\phi\tau)^{n-2}\exp(-\phi\tau) \\ \vdots \\ \frac{1}{(N-2)!}(\phi\tau)^{N-2}\exp(-\phi\tau) \end{bmatrix} \tag{3.113}$$

The last factor loadings for the ANSM(4), ANSM(5), and ANSM(6) are illustrated in Figure 3.3. Once those functions are converted into interest rate factor loadings, they will provide increasingly better fits to the interest rates for maturities between the shortest and longest maturity of the yield curve data. (Each additional factor loading also allows an additional local peak or trough, compared to the single stationary point for the ANSM(3), but more than one stationary point is not typical for yield curve data in practice.)

Without any further restrictions, the state variables and remaining parameters for an ANSM(N) are as for the ANSM(2) and ANSM(3) already provided, that is, full $N \times 1$ vectors for $x(t)$ and θ, a full $N \times N$ matrix for κ, an $N \times 1$ vector of zeros for $\tilde{\theta}$, and a lower diagonal $N \times N$ matrix for σ. The parameters $\sigma_1, \ldots, \sigma_N$, and ρ_{ij} for σ are most conveniently represented in the covariance expression:

$$\sigma\sigma' = \begin{bmatrix} \sigma_1^2 & \sigma_1\sigma_2\rho_{12} & \cdots & \sigma_1\sigma_N\rho_{1N} \\ \sigma_1\sigma_2\rho_{12} & \ddots & \ddots & \vdots \\ \vdots & \ddots & \ddots & \sigma_1\sigma_N\rho_{NN-1} \\ \sigma_1\sigma_N\rho_{1N} & \cdots & \sigma_1\sigma_N\rho_{N-1,N} & \sigma_N^2 \end{bmatrix} \tag{3.114}$$

and the standard deviation matrix σ can be obtained by taking the lower Cholesky decomposition:

$$\sigma = \text{Chol}\left[\sigma\sigma'\right] \tag{3.115}$$

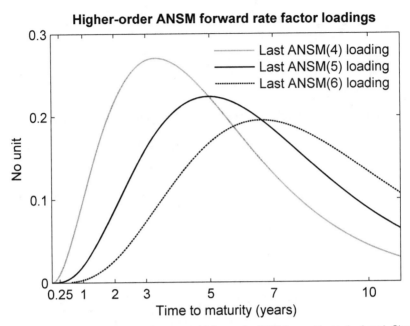

Figure 3.3 To represent the term structure, higher-order ANSMs would use the Level, Slope, and Bow factor loadings from Figures 3.1 and 3.2, plus progressively adding factor loadings from the continuation of the ANSM function series.

Section A.7.1 contains further discussion on Cholesky decompositions, and the function in MatLab is chol($\cdot$, 'lower').

The expressions for $\tilde{\mathbb{E}}_t\left[r(t+\tau)\,|\,x(t)\right]$, $\mathrm{VE}(\tau)$, forward rates, interest rates, the state equation, and the measurement equation are relatively straightforward extensions of the ANSM(2) and ANSM(3), although some of the expressions become progressively more complex. Nevertheless, I have found it straightforward to calculate the relevant expressions for the higher-order models in Mathematica, and transfer the resulting code directly to MatLab. Therefore, I have created higher-order ANSMs for practical use, as may be required. Alternatively, I have also found it straightforward to calculate succinct forms of the expressions by progressively applying integration by parts to exponential polynomial functions $(\phi\tau)^{n-2}\exp(-\phi\tau)$.

The estimation of higher-order ANSMs proceeds as for the ANSM(2) and ANSM(3), except using the relevant expressions noted in the previous paragraph.

3.4.3 Non-arbitrage-free ANSMs

Non-arbitrage-free Nelson and Siegel (1987) models, or NSMs, are simply the ANSMs already provided, but without the volatility adjustment term (i.e., setting the standard deviation parameters σ_n to zero). NSMs therefore implicitly equate

$\tilde{\mathbb{E}}_t \left[\mathrm{r}(t+\tau) | x(t) \right]$ and $\mathrm{f}(t,\tau)$. For example, the original NSM forward rate is the ANSM(3) forward rate expression outlined above without the volatility effect term.

As discussed in Krippner (2006), ignoring the volatility term is the root of the theoretical inconsistency of NSMs compared to ANSMs. Specifically, NSMs allow the estimated state variables to vary with a stochastic component between each yield curve observation, implicitly or explicitly as with dynamic NSMs applied in a time-series context, but they do not explicitly allow for the effect of that volatility in the model's yield curve expression.

Nevertheless, as discussed in Krippner (2014d), an NSM will adequately reflect the time series dynamics of the associated ANSM that could otherwise have been applied, even though the NSM is technically misspecified. The reason is that the volatility effect is time-invariant, being a function of time to maturity only. In addition, the volatility effect is relatively small compared to the typical dynamics of the yield curve data and the estimated state variables. Therefore, while not theoretically ideal, using NSMs in a time-series context is often an acceptable simplification for practical applications, and there are many examples of their successful use in this regard (e.g., see Diebold and Rudebusch [2013] for further discussion, and Diebold, Rudebusch, and Aruoba [2006] and Diebold, Li, and Yue [2008] for specific examples).

NSMs are typically estimated by directly fitting the NSM components to the yield curve data at each point in time. Specifically, setting $a(\tau) = 0$ in the ANSM measurement equation gives the interest rate as a function of the state variables and the single parameter ϕ. For example, the NSM with two state variables, which I will denote as the NSM(2), would be

$$
\begin{bmatrix} \eta_t(\tau_1) \\ \vdots \\ \eta_t(\tau_9) \end{bmatrix} = \begin{bmatrix} R_t(\tau_1) \\ \vdots \\ R_t(\tau_9) \end{bmatrix} - \begin{bmatrix} 1 & \frac{1}{\tau_1} G(\phi,\tau_1) \\ \vdots & \vdots \\ 1 & \frac{1}{\tau_9} G(\phi,\tau_9) \end{bmatrix} \begin{bmatrix} x_{1,t} \\ x_{2,t} \end{bmatrix} \tag{3.116}
$$

and the state variables may be estimated by ordinary least squares regression (OLS) given a suitable value of ϕ. Alternatively, ϕ could be estimated by using the full ANSM estimation process with the Kalman filter algorithm, but with $a(\tau)$ set to zero in the measurement equation. A related but pragmatic method that I have found to be quick, easy, reliable, and useful is to directly optimize ϕ using a standard univariate optimization algorithm (e.g., a bisection search) where the objective function is to minimize the sum of all squared residuals from the NSM estimated on each yield curve observation over the entire sample.

Finally, note that if one wants the estimated state variables to reflect the ANSM state variables, then ϕ needs be estimated as a fixed parameter, consistent with the fixed mean-reversion parameter ϕ in the ANSM. Allowing ϕ to change for each yield curve estimation, which is sometimes done for extra flexibility to fit coupon-bearing yield curve data to obtain zero-coupon yield curve data, breaks the connection between the ANSM and its associated NSM, so the resulting NS state variables would no longer adequately represent the ANSM state variables.

3.4.4 Stationary GATSMs

Fully specified GATSMs have stationary time-series dynamics, because all of the state variables follow a mean-reverting process. That is, the most persistent state variable is not constrained to be a unit root process as for ANSMs. Hence there will be no Level component (i.e., a constant by time to maturity), but rather a slow decay as a function of time to maturity as the first yield curve component. The remaining state variables also have unique rates of mean-reversion rather than the constraint of equal eigenvalues as for ANSMs.

Hereafter, I will refer to GATSMs with these characteristics as stationary GATSMs. I will provide the details for the maximally flexible three state variable GATSM, or GATSM(3), at the same time as noting the ready extension of those expressions to the maximally GATSM with N state variables, or GATSM(N). For the GATSM(1) or GATSM(2), the vectors are simply the first or first two rows from the GATSM(3), and the matrices are simply the first element or the upper-left 2×2 matrices from the GATSM(3).

Stationary GATSM specification The maximally flexible GATSM(3) has three state variables, 22 free parameters, and 15 fixed parameters. The state variables, and fixed and free parameters in their scalar/vector/matrix form are:

$$x(t) = \begin{bmatrix} x_1(t) \\ x_2(t) \\ x_3(t) \end{bmatrix}; \quad a_0; \quad b_0 = \begin{bmatrix} 1 \\ 1 \\ 1 \end{bmatrix}$$

$$\kappa = \begin{bmatrix} \kappa_{11} & \kappa_{12} & \kappa_{12} \\ \kappa_{21} & \kappa_{22} & \kappa_{23} \\ \kappa_{31} & \kappa_{32} & \kappa_{33} \end{bmatrix}; \quad \theta = \begin{bmatrix} \theta_1 \\ \theta_2 \\ \theta_3 \end{bmatrix}$$

$$\sigma = \begin{bmatrix} \sigma_1 & 0 & 0 \\ \sigma_2 \rho_{12} & \sigma_2 \sqrt{1 - \rho_{12}^2} & 0 \\ \sigma_3 \rho_{13} & \sigma_3 \frac{\rho_{23} - \rho_{12}\rho_{13}}{\sqrt{1 - \rho_{12}^2}} & \sigma_3 \sqrt{1 - \rho_{13}^2 - \frac{(\rho_{23} - \rho_{12}\rho_{13})^2}{1 - \rho_{12}^2}} \end{bmatrix}$$

$$\tilde{\kappa} = \begin{bmatrix} \tilde{\kappa}_1 & 0 & 0 \\ 0 & \tilde{\kappa}_2 & 0 \\ 0 & 0 & \tilde{\kappa}_3 \end{bmatrix}; \quad \tilde{\theta} = \begin{bmatrix} 0 \\ 0 \\ 0 \end{bmatrix} \tag{3.117}$$

The free parameter set is therefore $\mathbb{B} = \{a_0, \tilde{\kappa}_1, \tilde{\kappa}_2, \tilde{\kappa}_3, \kappa_{11}, \kappa_{12}, \kappa_{13}, \kappa_{21}, \kappa_{22}, \kappa_{23}, \kappa_{31}, \kappa_{32}, \kappa_{33}, \theta_1, \theta_2, \theta_3, \sigma_1, \sigma_2, \sigma_3, \rho_{12}, \rho_{13}, \rho_{23}\}$.

For the GATSM(N):

$$x(t) = \begin{bmatrix} x_1(t) \\ \vdots \\ x_N(t) \end{bmatrix}; \quad a_0; \quad b_0 = \begin{bmatrix} 1 \\ \vdots \\ 1 \end{bmatrix}_{N \times 1}$$

$$\kappa = \begin{bmatrix} \kappa_{11} & \cdots & \kappa_{1N} \\ \vdots & \ddots & \vdots \\ \kappa_{N1} & \cdots & \kappa_{NN} \end{bmatrix}; \quad \theta = \begin{bmatrix} \theta_1 \\ \vdots \\ \theta_N \end{bmatrix}$$

$$\tilde{\kappa} = \begin{bmatrix} \tilde{\kappa}_1 & 0 & 0 \\ 0 & \ddots & 0 \\ 0 & 0 & \tilde{\kappa}_N \end{bmatrix}; \quad \tilde{\theta} = \begin{bmatrix} 0 \\ \vdots \\ 0 \end{bmatrix}_{N \times 1} \tag{3.118}$$

and σ may be obtained as already discussed for higher-order ANSMs in sub-section 3.4.2.

Term structure

The GATSM(3) short rate is

$$r(t) = [1,1,1] \begin{bmatrix} x_1(t) \\ x_2(t) \\ x_3(t) \end{bmatrix}$$
$$= x_1(t) + x_2(t) + x_3(t) \tag{3.119}$$

and the GATSM(N) short rate is

$$r(t) = [1,\ldots,1] \begin{bmatrix} x_1(t) \\ \vdots \\ x_N(t) \end{bmatrix}$$
$$= x_1(t) + \ldots + x_N(t) \tag{3.120}$$

The matrix exponential $\tilde{\kappa}$ is again the key expression required to develop the term structure and related quantities. For the GATSM(3) the result is

$$\exp(-\tilde{\kappa}\tau) = \begin{bmatrix} \exp(-\tilde{\kappa}_1\tau) & 0 & 0 \\ 0 & \exp(-\tilde{\kappa}_2\tau) & 0 \\ 0 & 0 & \exp(-\tilde{\kappa}_3\tau) \end{bmatrix} \tag{3.121}$$

and for the GATSM(N):

$$\exp(-\tilde{\kappa}\tau) = \begin{bmatrix} \exp(-\tilde{\kappa}_1\tau) & 0 & 0 \\ 0 & \ddots & 0 \\ 0 & 0 & \exp(-\tilde{\kappa}_N\tau) \end{bmatrix} \tag{3.122}$$

The factor loadings for the expected path of the short rate $\tilde{\mathbb{E}}_t\left[r(t+\tau)|x(t)\right]$ and the forward rates of the GATSM(3) are

$$b_0 \exp(-\tilde{\kappa}\tau) = \left[\exp(-\tilde{\kappa}_1\tau), \exp(-\tilde{\kappa}_2\tau), \exp(-\tilde{\kappa}_3\tau)\right] \qquad (3.123)$$

and for the GATSM(N)

$$b_0 \exp(-\tilde{\kappa}\tau) = \left[\exp(-\tilde{\kappa}_1\tau), \ldots, \exp(-\tilde{\kappa}_N\tau)\right] \qquad (3.124)$$

The expected path of the short rate $\tilde{\mathbb{E}}_t\left[r(t+\tau)|x(t)\right]$ for the GATSM(3) is therefore

$$\tilde{\mathbb{E}}_t\left[r(t+\tau)|x(t)\right] = \left[\exp(-\tilde{\kappa}_1\tau), \exp(-\tilde{\kappa}_2\tau), \exp(-\tilde{\kappa}_3\tau)\right] \begin{bmatrix} x_1(t) \\ x_2(t) \\ x_3(t) \end{bmatrix}$$

$$= x_1(t) \cdot \exp(-\tilde{\kappa}_1\tau) + x_2(t) \cdot \exp(-\tilde{\kappa}_2\tau)$$

$$+ x_3(t) \cdot \exp(-\tilde{\kappa}_3\tau) \qquad (3.125)$$

and for the GATSM(N)

$$\tilde{\mathbb{E}}_t\left[r(t+\tau)|x(t)\right] = \left[\exp(-\tilde{\kappa}_1\tau), \ldots, \exp(-\tilde{\kappa}_N\tau)\right] \begin{bmatrix} x_1(t) \\ \vdots \\ x_N(t) \end{bmatrix}$$

$$= x_1(t) \cdot \exp(-\tilde{\kappa}_1\tau) + \ldots$$

$$+ x_N(t) \cdot \exp(-\tilde{\kappa}_N\tau) \qquad (3.126)$$

Forward rates for the GATSM(3) are

$$f(t,\tau) = \left[\exp(-\tilde{\kappa}_1\tau), \exp(-\tilde{\kappa}_2\tau), \exp(-\tilde{\kappa}_3\tau)\right] \begin{bmatrix} x_1(t) \\ x_2(t) \\ x_3(t) \end{bmatrix} - VE(\tau) \qquad (3.127)$$

where the volatility effect $VE(\tau)$ is

$$VE(\tau) = \sigma_1^2 \cdot \frac{1}{2}\left[G(\tilde{\kappa}_1,\tau)\right]^2 + \sigma_2^2 \cdot \frac{1}{2}\left[G(\tilde{\kappa}_2,\tau)\right]^2 + \sigma_3^2 \cdot \frac{1}{2}\left[G(\tilde{\kappa}_3,\tau)\right]^2$$

$$+ \rho_{12}\sigma_1\sigma_2 \cdot G(\tilde{\kappa}_1,\tau)\,G(\tilde{\kappa}_2,\tau) + \rho_{13}\sigma_1\sigma_3 \cdot G(\tilde{\kappa}_1,\tau)\,G(\tilde{\kappa}_3,\tau)$$

$$+ \rho_{23}\sigma_2\sigma_3 \cdot G(\tilde{\kappa}_2,\tau)\,G(\tilde{\kappa}_3,\tau) \qquad (3.128)$$

Forward rates for the GATSM(N) are

$$f(t,\tau) = \left[\exp(-\tilde{\kappa}_1\tau), \ldots, \exp(-\tilde{\kappa}_N\tau)\right] \begin{bmatrix} x_1(t) \\ \vdots \\ x_N(t) \end{bmatrix} - VE(\tau) \qquad (3.129)$$

and the volatility effect $VE(\tau)$ is most conveniently expressed as a summation:

$$VE(\tau) = \sum_{n=1}^{N} \sigma_n^2 \cdot \frac{1}{2} [G(\tilde{\kappa}_n, \tau)]^2$$

$$+ \sum_{n=1}^{N} \sum_{m=n+1}^{N} \rho_{mn} \sigma_m \sigma_n \cdot G(\tilde{\kappa}_m, \tau) G(\tilde{\kappa}_n, \tau) \qquad (3.130)$$

Interest rates for the GATSM(3) are calculated by integrating the forward rate expression. The result is

$$R(t, \tau) = a(\tau) + [b(\tau)]' \begin{bmatrix} x_1(t) \\ x_2(t) \\ x_3(t) \end{bmatrix} \qquad (3.131)$$

where $a(\tau)$ is most conveniently expressed as a summation for $N = 3$:

$$a(\tau) = -\sum_{n=1}^{N} \sigma_n^2 \cdot \frac{1}{2\tilde{\kappa}_n^2 \tau} \left[\tau - G(\tilde{\kappa}_n, \tau) - \frac{1}{2}\tilde{\kappa}_n [G(\tilde{\kappa}_n, \tau)]^2 \right]$$

$$- \sum_{n=1}^{N} \sum_{m=n+1}^{N} \rho_{mn} \sigma_m \sigma_n \cdot \frac{1}{(\tilde{\kappa}_m + \tilde{\kappa}_n)} \left[\frac{1}{\tilde{\kappa}_m} - \frac{1}{\tilde{\kappa}_m \tau} G(\tilde{\kappa}_m, \tau) \right.$$

$$+ \frac{1}{\tilde{\kappa}_n} - \frac{1}{\tilde{\kappa}_n \tau} G(\tilde{\kappa}_n, \tau)$$

$$\left. - \frac{1}{\tilde{\kappa}_m \tilde{\kappa}_n \tau} G(\tilde{\kappa}_m, \tau) G(\tilde{\kappa}_n, \tau) \right] \qquad (3.132)$$

and

$$[b(\tau)]' = \left[\frac{1}{\tau} G(\tilde{\kappa}_1, \tau), \frac{1}{\tau} G(\tilde{\kappa}_2, \tau), \frac{1}{\tau} G(\tilde{\kappa}_3, \tau) \right] \qquad (3.133)$$

The interest rate expression for the GATSM(N) is

$$R(t, \tau) = a(\tau) + [b(\tau)]' \begin{bmatrix} x_1(t) \\ \vdots \\ x_N(t) \end{bmatrix} \qquad (3.134)$$

where $a(\tau)$ is as above and

$$[b(\tau)]' = \left[\frac{1}{\tau} G(\tilde{\kappa}_1, \tau), \dots, \frac{1}{\tau} G(\tilde{\kappa}_N, \tau) \right] \qquad (3.135)$$

GATSM estimation

Full and partial estimations of the GATSM(3) proceed exactly as for the ANSM(3), except using the GATSM(3) $a(\tau)$ and $b(\tau)$ functions outlined in the previous subsection to create a and H for the measurement equation. Specifically, H for the GATSM(3) measurement equation is

$$
H = \begin{bmatrix} \frac{1}{\tau_1} G(\tilde{\kappa}_1, \tau_1) & \frac{1}{\tau} G(\tilde{\kappa}_2, \tau_1) & \frac{1}{\tau} G(\tilde{\kappa}_3, \tau_1) \\ \vdots & \vdots & \vdots \\ \frac{1}{\tau_K} G(\tilde{\kappa}_1, \tau_K) & \frac{1}{\tau_K} G(\tilde{\kappa}_2, \tau_K) & \frac{1}{\tau_K} G(\tilde{\kappa}_3, \tau_K) \end{bmatrix}_{K \times 3}
\tag{3.136}
$$

Full and partial estimations of the GATSM(N) are analogous to the GATSM(3) but with the following expression for H in the measurement equation:

$$
H = \begin{bmatrix} \frac{1}{\tau_1} G(\tilde{\kappa}_1, \tau_1) & \cdots & \frac{1}{\tau} G(\tilde{\kappa}_N, \tau_1) \\ \vdots & \vdots & \vdots \\ \frac{1}{\tau_K} G(\tilde{\kappa}_1, \tau_K) & \cdots & \frac{1}{\tau_K} G(\tilde{\kappa}_N, \tau_K) \end{bmatrix}_{K \times 3}
\tag{3.137}
$$

The state equation expressions for the GATSM(N) are straightforward extensions of the ANSM(2) and ANSM(3) state equation vectors and matrices to a larger value of N, as already discussed for higher-order ANSMs in subsection 3.4.2.

3.4.5 Stationary GATSMs with repeated eigenvalues

GATSMs can also be specified with repeated eigenvalues. In this case the GATSM is very similar to an ANSM, but with a stationary persistent process for the first state variable rather than the unit root specification inherent in ANSMs. For example, Wu and Xia (2013, 2014) specify a GATSM(3) with a repeated eigenvalue, although in a discrete-time GATSM. The equivalent model in continuous time would be specified as follows:

$$
b_0 = \begin{bmatrix} 1 \\ 1 \\ 0 \end{bmatrix}; \quad \tilde{\kappa} = \begin{bmatrix} \tilde{\kappa}_1 & 0 & 0 \\ 0 & \phi & -\phi \\ 0 & 0 & \phi \end{bmatrix}
\tag{3.138}
$$

The short rate is therefore

$$
r(t) = [1, 1, 0] \begin{bmatrix} x_1(t) \\ x_2(t) \\ x_3(t) \end{bmatrix},
$$

$$
= x_1(t) + x_2(t)
\tag{3.139}
$$

and $\exp(-\tilde{\kappa}\tau)$ is:

$$\exp(-\tilde{\kappa}\tau) = \begin{bmatrix} \exp(-\tilde{\kappa}_1\tau) & 0 & 0 \\ 0 & \exp(-\phi\tau) & \phi\tau\exp(-\phi\tau) \\ 0 & 0 & \exp(-\phi\tau) \end{bmatrix} \tag{3.140}$$

The $\tilde{\mathbb{E}}_t[\mathrm{r}(t+\tau)|x(t)]$ and $\mathrm{f}(t,\tau)$ factor loadings are therefore

$$b_0\exp(-\tilde{\kappa}\tau) = [1,1,0]\begin{bmatrix} \exp(-\tilde{\kappa}_1\tau) & 0 & 0 \\ 0 & \exp(-\phi\tau) & \phi\tau\exp(-\phi\tau) \\ 0 & 0 & \exp(-\phi\tau) \end{bmatrix}$$

$$= \begin{bmatrix} \exp(-\tilde{\kappa}_1\tau), \exp(-\phi\tau), \phi\tau\exp(-\phi\tau) \end{bmatrix} \tag{3.141}$$

Hence, the Wu and Xia (2013, 2014) GATSM(3) in continuous time is very similar to an ANSM(3), except the ANSM(3) forward rate Level component with a constant factor loading of 1 is replaced with $\exp(-\tilde{\kappa}_1\tau)$, and the ANSM(3) interest rate factor loading of 1 is replaced with $G(\tilde{\kappa}_1,\tau)$. These are elementary adjustments to the results already presented for the ANSM(3), so I will not specify stationary GATSMs with repeated eigenvalues separately in subsequent chapters, but they could be used to represent the shadow term structure for the shadow/ZLB GATSMs outlined in chapters 4 and 5. In any case, chapters 6 to 8 will outline why I prefer using ANSMs to represent the shadow term structure.

3.5 Empirical applications

3.5.1 Yield curve data set

The main data set that I use to illustrate the applications of the models in this book are zero-coupon interest rates derived from US overnight indexed swap (OIS) rates, supplemented with zero-coupon interest rates derived from US government bonds. Regarding the OIS rates, these are arguably the most relevant yield curve data for policymakers because they reflect the implicit market expectations for the effective federal funds rate (FFR) out to long horizons.[8] At the same time, OIS rates are also highly relevant to financial market participants, again for the policy rate expectations they imply but also because they are heavily traded in financial markets for hedging and speculative purposes.

To briefly provide the relevant background, an OIS contract is a derivative for a notional face value over a specified period. One counterparty pays the other the compounded FFR over the lifetime of the contract, while the other counterparty pays a fixed rate agreed at the inception of the contract. The payments are based on the notional face value for the OIS contract, and are exchanged at regular periods and/or at the end of the contract period depending on standard market arrangements. Arbitrage principles mean that the fixed rates for OIS contracts should closely reflect expectations on how the FFR will evolve over the lifetime of the OIS contract; otherwise, one counterparty would stand to profit easily at the expense of the other. The fixed rates for OIS contracts are quoted in financial markets as OIS rates and a yield curve of quoted OIS rates (i.e., OIS rates for different maturities) therefore provides implicit expectations of the path of the FFR due to arbitrage principles noted previously.

Indeed, the yield curve of OIS rates is almost entirely governed by market expectations of the FFR (and risks around how the path of expectations might change), because the influences of credit risk, liquidity risks, and so forth, that often influence other yield curve data are minimal. Specifically, credit risk is greatly mitigated because OIS contracts are subject to collateral exchange agreements on their mark-to-market value.[9] Therefore, any potential loss by one counterparty if the other counterparty defaulted with a mark-to-market value owing on the OIS contract is minimal. Similarly, liquidity risk is inherently very small because the OIS market is heavily traded. For example, tables in Fleming, Jackson, Li, Sarkar, and Zobel (2012) show that daily transactions of OIS contracts as at mid-2010 were $2.0 trillion (and the closely related, via arbitrage principles, forward rate agreement and interest rate swaps transactions were respectively $1.8 and $5.6 trillion).

Unfortunately, a full yield curve of consistently estimated zero-coupon OIS yield curve data is only available from Bloomberg for the United States from January 2006 (code S0042Z), which is not a sufficiently long sample for reliably estimating term structure models in general, including the models in this book. Therefore, I have taken a pragmatic decision to splice the available OIS yield curve data onto a longer sample of government yield curve data. The government yield curve data is from November 1985 to December 2005, and is described in Gürkaynak, Sack, and Wright (2007). The data set is regularly updated and available from http://www.federalreserve.gov/pubs/feds/2006/200628/200628abs.html.

The spliced data set therefore covers a long period of history and at least allows the OIS data to be used when it is most relevant, that is, from slightly before the GFC and the period when the FFR became constrained by the ZLB. For the years prior to 2006, I am essentially using the government bond data as a proxy for the OIS data, which is reasonable because government interest rates are generally viewed in conventional monetary policy environments as mainly reflecting interest rate expectations with little credit and liquidity risk. An alternative would be to estimate the model completely on the government yield curve data, but it would not be as relevant to FFR expectations in the environment of a ZLB constraint on monetary policy that has prevailed since December 2008, particularly given the influences of asset purchase programs involving government bonds. Similarly, bank-risk yield curve data (such as London interbank offered rates, LIBOR, and interest rate swap rates) could be used, but they would also not be as relevant as OIS data, particularly given the credit and liquidity risk influences from the GFC period. A more ideal approach would be to jointly model the government, bank-risk, and OIS yield curve data with formal allowances for missing data (as allowed for in the Kalman filter). However, while straightforward in principle, the exercise would be more involved in practice and so would likely detract from exposition of the GATSM framework itself. Hence, I have leave this as a project for future research.

The maturities I include from both the OIS and Gürkaynak, Sack, and Wright (2007) data sets are 0.25, 0.5, 1, 2, 3, 5, 7, 10, and 30 years, which are standard benchmarks for the United States. Note that using 30-year data provides a good "anchor" for estimating the long-horizon expectations of the short rate, which become more relevant in light of the EMS measure introduced in chapter 2, and which I will discuss further in chapters 6 and 7. Trading in OIS contracts and government bond securities beyond 10 years to maturity is not typically as heavy as for maturities up to 10 years (e.g., see Fleming, Jackson, Li, Sarkar, and Zobel [2012] for maturity profiles and discussion). However, the heavy trading in closely related markets, such as interest rate swaps and bond futures, means the 30-year data should still be consistent with the other data (the Bloomberg OIS data makes use of interest rate swap data, with appropriate spreads, to create the full OIS yield curve). I include the 0.25-, 0.5-, and 1-year data to provide information more directly on short-horizon expectations about the policy rate, which is one of the points of focus for the models in this book. However, that choice does deteriorate the fit of the longer-maturity interest rates somewhat, particularly the 30-year time to maturity. Excluding the shorter-maturity interest rates may be more appropriate for some applications. Alternatively, Knez, Litterman, and Sheinkman (1994) find that money-market interest rates have additional market influences relative to bond rates, so adding more state variables, as discussed in subsection 3.4.2, would be another potential resolution.

Figure 3.4 plots 0.25-, 5-, and 30-year rates from my data set to illustrate the characteristics of the data set in general. I have also indicated the splice point of January 2006 to illustrate that the government and OIS yield curve data sets coincide well.

3.5.2 ANSM(2) results

Tables 3.3 and 3.4 contain the parameters of the ANSM(2) estimated over the entire sample via maximum likelihood. The parameters in Table 3.3 are those that were used to obtain Figures 2.3 to 2.5 in chapter 2. Note that I have expressed θ_1, θ_2, σ_1, and σ_2 in units of percentage points (i.e., the estimates from the optimization have been multiplied by 100). All of the other parameters in Table 3.3 are the original estimates. The remaining Kalman filter parameter estimates, $\sigma_\eta(\tau_1), \ldots, \sigma_\eta(\tau_K)$, and their standard errors are in Table 3.4, and they are all expressed in basis points (i.e., the estimates from the optimization have been multiplied by 10000). Table 3.4 contains a selection of statistical summaries of the residuals, that is, the unexplained component of the yield curve data relative to the model, again expressed

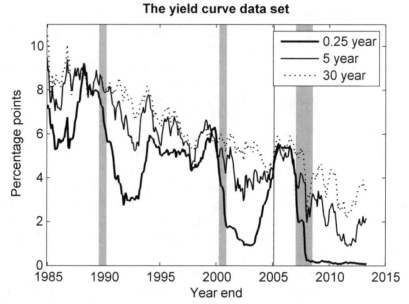

Figure 3.4 Selected interest rates from the yield curve data set used for estimations. The data are government interest rates spliced with overnight indexed swap (OIS) rates from January 2006.

Table 3.3 ANSM(2) time-series parameters and related results

Param.	Estim.	Std err.	Param.	Estim.	Std err.
ϕ	0.2239	0.0043	θ_1 (1)	−63.195	15.091
κ_{11}	0.0001	0.0001	θ_2 (1)	−2.755	0.164
κ_{12}	−0.0005	0.0012	σ_1 (1)	0.870	0.025
κ_{21}	0.0025	0.0015	σ_2 (1)	1.357	0.062
κ_{22}	0.0769	0.0581	ρ_{12}	−0.5953	0.0227

Log-likelihood: 14405.61

$\kappa_1 = 0.001$, $\kappa_2 = 0.0768$

$\lim_{\tau \to \infty} \mathbb{E}_t [r(t+\tau)] = -65.950$ pps (1)

Note: (1) These values are expressed in percentage points (pps).

in basis points. Table 3.5 contains the same statistical summaries of the residuals, but applied separately to the non-ZLB and ZLB periods.

The points to note for the ANSM(2) are as follows:

- The large and negative estimate of the parameter θ_1 in Table 3.3 is unusual. Specifically, $\theta_1 + \theta_2$ is the expected value to which the short rate $r(t)$ should converge over long horizons, according to the model. However, the large negative value of θ_1 makes that long-horizon expectation very negative, that is, $\lim_{\tau \to \infty} \mathbb{E}_t [r(t+\tau)] = -65.950\%$, which lacks economic meaning.

Table 3.4 ANSM(2) goodness-of-fit results [1]

Mat.	$\sigma_\eta\left(\tau_k\right)$	Std err.	Mean	Std dev.	RMSE	MAE
0.25	54.9	1.7	−3.7	54.5	54.5	44.5
0.5	41.4	0.1	−2.7	40.4	40.4	33.4
1	21.1	2.4	3.1	19.9	20.1	15.8
2	5.4	1.7	0.8	3.6	3.7	2.9
3	6.6	0.8	-0.5	6.0	6.0	4.6
5	6.7	1.1	-0.9	6.3	6.4	4.9
7	2.8	0.7	-0.2	1.2	1.2	0.9
10	11.5	0.6	1.6	11.0	11.2	8.8
30	64.0	3.2	35.6	52.9	63.8	54.8

Note: (1) All values are expressed in basis points (bps).

Table 3.5 ANSM(2) subsample goodness-of-fit results [1]

Mat.	Dec-1994 to Nov-2008				Dec-2008 to Jan-2014			
	Mean	Stdev	RMSE	MAE	Mean	Stdev	RMSE	MAE
0.25	−17.7	49.6	52.6	41.6	57.2	24.3	62.1	57.2
0.5	−13.6	35.3	37.8	30.7	44.5	23.7	50.3	45.2
1	−1.8	16.6	16.7	13.0	24.1	19.4	30.9	27.7
2	0.8	3.1	3.1	2.5	0.9	5.3	5.3	4.6
3	1.0	4.5	4.7	3.7	−7.1	6.8	9.8	8.6
5	−0.0	4.9	4.9	3.8	−4.6	9.7	10.6	9.7
7	−0.4	1.0	1.1	0.8	0.8	1.3	1.5	1.2
10	1.1	9.6	9.7	7.6	3.8	15.8	16.1	14.1
30	36.7	50.9	62.7	54.5	30.9	61.2	68.1	55.7

Note: (1) All values are expressed in basis points (bps).

- The fit to the data is not very close, particularly for the very short and very long times to maturity. That result is not surprising from a two-state-variable model. The extra state variable in the ANSM(3) below makes a lot of difference in that regard.
- Figure 3.5 shows that the ANSM(2) produces negative short rates even though none of the interest rate data goes negative. Panel 1 of Figure 2.5 from chapter 2 has already illustrated this result for the July 2012 yield curve observation, and also shows that the ANSM(2) produces negative estimates of shorter-maturity interest rates. As indicated in Figure 3.6 and Table 3.5, those negative model interest rates produce persistently positive residuals in the ZLB period. That is, the means for the 0.25-, 0.5-, and 1-year rates are respectively 57.2, 44.5, and 24.1 bps.

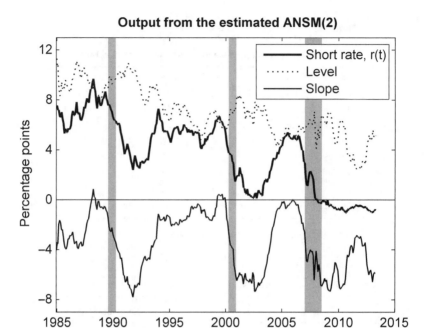

Figure 3.5 Estimated ANSM(2) Level and Slope state variables and the associated short rate.

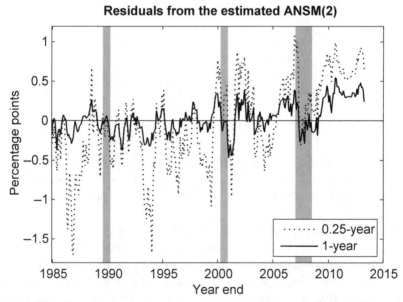

Figure 3.6 Residuals (observed data less model estimate) for the estimated ANSM(2).

- Panels 2 and 3 of Figure 2.5 from chapter 2 have already shown how the ANSM(2) produces projected short rates and interest rates with very material probabilities of being negative, even though the interest rate data has never adopted negative values.

To summarize, the ANSM(2) does not fit the data particularly well, with particular issues in the ZLB environment. Specifically, it clearly produces both model estimates and projected estimates of negative interest rates that are inconsistent with the interest rate data and the ZLB constraint.

3.5.3   ANSM(3) results

Tables 3.6 and 3.7 contain the analogous results to those previously described for the ANSM(2), but for the ANSM(3). Many of the anomalies previously noted for the ANSM(2) have now been resolved, at least superficially. That is,

- The estimate of the parameters θ_1, θ_2, and θ_3 in Table 3.6 are all plausible, and together they produce an economically meaningful estimate of long-horizon expectation of the short rate, that is, $\lim_{\tau \to \infty} \mathbb{E}_t \left[r \left(t + \tau \right) \right] = 4.669\%$.
- Tables 3.7 and 3.8 show that the fit to the data is much closer for all maturities, albeit still relatively imprecise for the 30-year maturity. The log-likelihood improvement is $15889.89 - 14405.61 = 1484.28$, which is extremely statistically significant given the 99 percent critical value $\chi^{-1} \left(0.99, 9 \right) = 21.666$ (or the 99.99 percent critical value $\chi^{-1} \left(0.9999, 9 \right) = 33.720$, where 9 is the degrees of freedom, or the difference in the number of parameters, between the ANSM(2) and ANSM(3) specifications).
- Figure 3.7 shows that the ANSM(3) produces only mildly negative short rates for a brief period following the onset of the ZLB environment.

On the face of it, the ANSM(3) seems to provide a reasonable representation of the yield curve data. However, the issue that remains with the ANSM(3) is that it still produces projected short rate and interest rate distributions with very material probabilities of negative values. Figure 3.9 illustrates this for the yield curve data for July 2012. Note also that the ANSM(3) fits the short-maturity interest rate data with an unusual shape in that region. In particular, the Bow component of the ANSM(3) produces a short rate estimate that is above all of the interest rate data out to three years.

Figure 3.10 shows that the projected probabilities of negative projected short rates and interest rates feature generally across the ZLB environment. For example, panel 1 shows that the projected probability of negative short rates in five years' time has been around 0.3 to 0.4 since late 2008. Similarly, panel 2 shows that the projected probability of the 1-year interest rate being negative in one years' time has been material since late 2008, and particularly so since mid-2010. Similarly, the projected

Table 3.6 ANSM(3) time-series parameters and related results

Param.	Estim.	Std err.	Param.	Estim.	Std err.
ϕ	0.5166	0.0077	$\theta_1^{(1)}$	7.497	2.732
κ_{11}	0.1688	0.0823	$\theta_2^{(1)}$	−2.828	2.067
κ_{12}	0.0076	0.1485	$\theta_3^{(1)}$	−0.388	1.919
κ_{13}	−0.1756	0.0884	$\sigma_1^{(1)}$	0.597	0.029
κ_{21}	0.3724	0.1371	$\sigma_2^{(1)}$	1.049	0.042
κ_{22}	0.5072	0.2291	$\sigma_3^{(1)}$	3.163	0.164
κ_{23}	−0.4654	0.1567	ρ_{12}	−0.5617	0.0373
κ_{31}	−0.6262	0.3931	ρ_{13}	−0.2693	0.0520
κ_{32}	−0.1804	0.6497	ρ_{23}	−0.0044	0.0647
κ_{33}	0.8912	0.3875			

Log-likelihood : 15889.89

$\kappa_1 = 0.0417$, $\kappa_2 = 0.3702$, $\kappa_3 = 1.1552$

$\lim_{\tau \to \infty} \mathbb{E}_t \left[r(t + \tau) \right] = 4.669$ pps $^{(1)}$

Note: (1) These values are expressed in percentage points (pps).

Table 3.7 ANSM(3) goodness-of-fit results

Maturity	$\sigma_\eta(\tau_k)$	Std err.	Mean	Stdev	RMSE	MAE
0.25	12.5	0.6	−1.9	12.4	12.5	9.3
0.5	0.6	1.0	−0.0	0.1	0.1	0.0
1	12.4	0.6	6.4	10.7	12.4	9.8
2	6.6	0.4	3.1	5.8	6.6	5.4
3	0.5	0.4	−0.0	0.1	0.1	0.0
5	4.9	0.7	−2.4	4.0	4.7	3.9
7	4.0	0.8	−0.8	2.6	2.7	2.0
10	10.6	0.7	5.1	8.1	9.6	7.9
30	45.9	3.5	29.3	34.3	45.1	37.5

Note: (1) All values are expressed in basis points (bps).

probability of a negative 5-year interest rate in one years' time has also been material since mid-2010.

To summarize, the ANSM(3) fits the data much better than the ANSM(2), even in the ZLB environment (although mildly negative estimates of the short rate and interest rates still occur, which is inconsistent with the data). However, the better fit is simply due to the mechanical flexibility offered by the third state variable, the Bow, rather than addressing the fundamental flaw of GATSMs when interest rates are near the ZLB. Specifically, the ANSM(3) still produces very material projected probabilities of negative interest rates, and that property is inconsistent with the observed interest rate data and the principle of the ZLB constraint. These properties inherent in the ANSM(3) obviously make it very unsuitable for applying to typical

Table 3.8 ANSM(3) subsample goodness-of-fit results

Mat.	Dec-1994 to Nov-2008				Dec-2008 to Jan-2014			
	Mean	Stdev	RMSE	MAE	Mean	Stdev	RMSE	MAE
0.25	−1.9	13.3	13.4	9.8	−2.0	7.8	8.0	7.3
0.5	−0.0	0.1	0.1	0.1	0.0	0.0	0.0	0.0
1	7.5	10.8	13.2	10.4	1.5	8.3	8.3	7.6
2	3.6	5.4	6.5	5.2	0.9	6.7	6.7	6.1
3	−0.0	0.0	0.0	0.0	−0.0	0.1	0.1	0.1
5	−3.1	3.3	4.5	3.7	0.3	5.5	5.4	4.7
7	−1.0	2.3	2.5	1.9	0.3	3.4	3.4	2.6
10	6.4	7.3	9.7	7.9	−0.6	9.1	9.0	7.7
30	34.2	32.6	47.3	40.2	8.2	33.7	34.4	26.1

Note: (1) All values are expressed in basis points (bps).

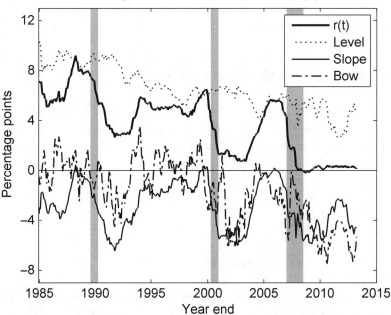

Figure 3.7 Estimated Level, Slope, and Bow state variables and the associated short rate for the ANSM(3).

tasks, such as yield curve forecasting, assessing risks for fixed interest portfolio management, pricing options on interest rate securities, and extracting estimates of risk premiums from yield curve data. The same observations would hold for higher-order ANSMs, that is, increasingly better mechanical fits to the data, but without resolving the fundamental flaw of projected interest rates with high probabilities of negative values.

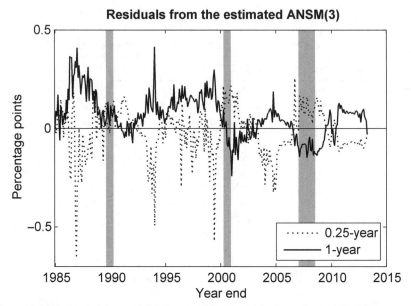

Figure 3.8 Residuals (observed data less model estimate) for the estimated ANSM(3).

3.6 Alternative estimation methods

This section is not strictly necessary from the perspective of estimating GATSMs, because using forward rates or bond prices would not typically offer any net advantages relative to using interest rate data. However, I have included this brief section in anticipation of the forthcoming discussion in section 4.6, in which I note that using forward rate or bond price data may offer net advantages, under some circumstances, for estimating Krippner (2011, 2012b,c, and 2013d,e) shadow/ZLB-GATSMs.

3.6.1 Estimation using forward rates

As mentioned earlier, interest rates are typically the form of term structure data used to estimate GATSMs. However, if available, a data set of forward rates or bond prices could be used. The estimation using forward rates requires only a very straightforward adjustment to the Kalman filter measurement equation. That is,

$$
\begin{bmatrix} f_t(\tau_1) \\ \vdots \\ f_t(\tau_K) \end{bmatrix} = \begin{bmatrix} -\text{VE}(\tau_1) \\ \vdots \\ -\text{VE}(\tau_K) \end{bmatrix} + \begin{bmatrix} b'_0 \exp(-\tilde{\kappa}\tau_1) \\ \vdots \\ b'_0 \exp(-\tilde{\kappa}\tau_K) \end{bmatrix} x_t + \begin{bmatrix} \eta_{f,t}(\tau_1) \\ \vdots \\ \eta_{f,t}(\tau_K) \end{bmatrix}
$$

$$(3.142)$$

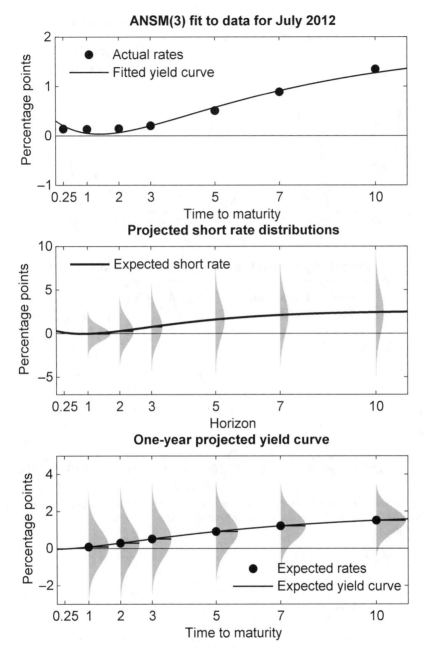

Figure 3.9 The ANSM(3) yield curve with state variables estimated from data observed in a ZLB environment (panel 1) implies very material projected probabilities of future negative short rates (panel 2) and interest rates (panel 3).

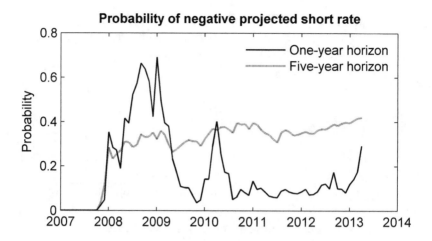

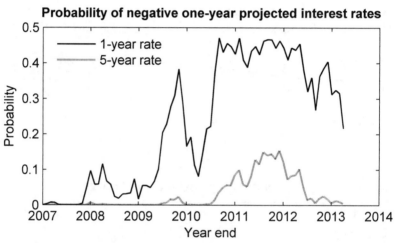

Figure 3.10 Projected ANSM(3) short rates (panel 1) and interest rates (panel 2) have very material probabilities of future negative values during the ZLB environment.

which may be written as

$$f_t = a_f + H_f x_t + \eta_{f,t} \tag{3.143}$$

For example, the forward rate measurement equation for the ANSM(2) would be

$$H_f x_t = \begin{bmatrix} 1 & \exp\left(-\phi \tau_1\right) \\ \vdots & \vdots \\ 1 & \exp\left(-\phi \tau_K\right) \end{bmatrix} \begin{bmatrix} x_1\left(t\right) \\ x_2\left(t\right) \end{bmatrix} \tag{3.144}$$

3.6.2 Estimation using bond prices

Bond prices involve the exponential of interest rates, and so the measurement equation is no longer a linear function of the state variables. For example, even for the simplest case of using zero-coupon bond prices, the measurement equation would be based on the following nonlinear function of x_t:

$$
\begin{bmatrix} P_t(\tau_1) \\ \vdots \\ P_t(\tau_K) \end{bmatrix} = \begin{bmatrix} \exp\left[-\tau_1\left\{a(\tau_1) + [b(\tau_1)]'x_t\right\}\right] \\ \vdots \\ \exp\left[-\tau_K\left\{a(\tau_K) + [b(\tau_1)]'x_K\right\}\right] \end{bmatrix} + \begin{bmatrix} \eta_{P,t}(\tau_1) \\ \vdots \\ \eta_{P,t}(\tau_K) \end{bmatrix}
$$

$$(3.145)$$

Estimation would then require a nonlinear technique, such as those I introduce in section 4.2 of the following chapter. Using the prices of coupon-bearing bonds requires accounting for multiple cashflows for each bond, which I will discuss in subsection 4.6.2.

3.7 Summary

- In this chapter I have provided a detailed exposition of how GATSMs are specified, derived, and estimated. GATSMs have proven very popular because they produce closed-form analytic solutions for all representations of the term structure (i.e., forward rates, interest rates, and bond prices), and the linear form of the interest rate function with respect to the state variables means that GATSMs can be estimated with the Kalman filter.
- GATSMs include the arbitrage-free Nelson and Siegel (1987) models (ANSMs) as a subclass. Relative to stationary (or fully mean-reverting) GATSMs, ANSMs constrain the most persistent state variable to be a random walk process, which results in a Level component for the yield curve. The mean-reversion matrix for the remaining state variables is constrained to have equal eigenvalues. Additional state variables therefore produce the Slope and Bow components of the yield curve, and adding further state variables would produce higher-order Bow-shaped yield curve functions.
- I have provided a fully worked example for the ANSM with two state variables, or the ANSM(2), and the results from a full estimation using a US yield curve data set. I have also provided the key expressions and the estimation results for the ANSM with three state variables, or the ANSM(3).
- The results for both models illustrate the fundamental deficiencies of GATSMs in general. First, I demonstrate that the estimated ANSM(2) and ANSM(3) both produce some fitted interest rates that are negative, even though none of the yield curve data is negative. More seriously, I show that both the ANSM(2)

and ANSM(3 allow high probabilities of materially negative future interest rates, which is not something observed in the historical data or consistent with the "real world" ZLB constraint due to the availability of physical currency.

- However, GATSMs and ANSMs may be used to represent the shadow term structure in shadow/ZLB-GATSMs. I detail how that is done in the following chapter.

4 | Krippner Framework for ZLB Term Structure Modeling

In this chapter, I develop a tractable ZLB term structure model based on the generic continuous-time GATSM outlined in chapter 3. This shadow/ZLB-GATSM framework first appeared in Krippner (2011), then Krippner (2012b,c, 2013d,e), and has been referred to in Christensen and Rudebusch (2013a,b, 2014) and Carriero, Mouabbi, and Vangelista (2014) as the Krippner framework. Hence, in this book I will use the name "Krippner affine Gaussian model framework," abbreviated to K-AGM framework, both for brevity and to clearly distinguish the framework from the Black (1995) shadow/ZLB-GATSM framework that will be the subject of chapter 5.

I begin in section 4.1 with an exposition of the K-AGM framework. In section 4.2, I provide an overview of the estimation method for models within the K-AGM framework. In section 4.3, I provide a fully worked example to show how the material in sections 4.1 and 4.2 is applied in practice to create and estimate a K-AGM with two state variables. Section 4.4 provides the key results for using GATSMs generally within the K-AGM framework. In section 4.5, I present results from K-AGM estimations to show that the K-AGM resolves the issues presented for the GATSMs in chapter 3. I will discuss empirical applications of the K-AGM framework more extensively in chapters 7 and 8. Section 4.6 discusses alternative ways of estimating K-AGMs.

Note that the K-AGM framework uses GATSMs to represent the shadow term structure. Therefore I will frequently refer to the exposition of the GATSM framework and examples from chapter 3 to facilitate the K-AGM exposition and examples in this chapter. In particular, it should be apparent that specifying and implementing models within the K-AGM framework is a straightforward and intuitive modification to the GATSM framework. Note also that I will use an underscore to denote any term structure expressions that are subject to the ZLB, and I will omit the underscore to denote shadow term structure expressions.

4.1 K-AGM exposition

In this section, I first provide the intuition on the foundations of the K-AGM framework and how it results in expressions that are relatively straightforward modifications to the GATSM framework. In section 4.1.2, I detail how to calculate the forward rate option effect, which is the key to allowing for the effect that the availability of physical currency has on the term structure. In section 4.1.3, I add that forward rate option effect to shadow forward rates in order to obtain the K-AGM ZLB forward rate expression. After I make some related observations on K-AGM ZLB forward rates in sections 4.1.4 and 4.1.5, I show in section 4.1.6 how the K-AGM forward rate expression is used to obtain interest rates and bond prices.

4.1.1 K-AGM Intuition

The K-AGM is based on the Black (1995) mechanism for imposing a ZLB:

$$\underline{r}(t) = \max\{0, r(t)\} \tag{4.1}$$

where $\underline{r}(t)$ is the actual short rate at time t, which is subject to the ZLB constraint, and $r(t)$ is the shadow short rate. $r(t)$ may be viewed as the short rate that would prevail in the absence of a ZLB for nominal interest rates, which in turn would be a world without the availability of physical currency. The justification offered in Black (1995) for the proposed ZLB mechanism is that the availability of physical currency offers economic agents a choice on whether or not to invest surplus funds at the prevailing level of the shadow short rate, and the choice will depend on $r(t)$:

- if $r(t) \geq 0$, the economic agent will invest at the instantaneous annualized rate of $r(t)$; and
- if $r(t) < 0$, the economic agent will hold physical currency to effectively obtain a zero instantaneous annualized rate of return.

As already noted in chapter 2, equation 4.1 may be reexpressed as

$$\underline{r}(t) = r(t) + \max\{-r(t), 0\} \tag{4.2}$$

where $r(t)$ is the shadow short rate, and $\max\{-r(t), 0\}$ is the payoff for an instantaneous call option on the shadow short rate. The intuition now is that the economic agents invest their surplus funds at the shadow short rate $r(t)$ regardless of its level, and the availability of physical currency is represented as an option that will compensate the investor with the payoff $-r(t) = |r(t)|$ whenever $r(t)$ is negative.

A simple demonstration illustrates the two mechanisms and confirms they are identical. That is, if $r(t) < 0$, then $\underline{r}(t) = \max\{0, r(t)\} = 0$, or $\underline{r}(t) = -r(t) + \max\{-[-r(t)], 0\} = -r(t) + r(t) = 0$. If $r(t) \geq 0$, then $\underline{r}(t) = \max\{0, r(t)\} = r(t)$, or $\underline{r}(t) = r(t) + \max\{-r(t), 0\} = r(t) + 0 = r(t)$.

Analogous to GATSM forward rates $f(t, \tau)$ in chapter 3, K-AGM forward rates $\underline{f}(t, \tau)$ are obtained by calculating the expected compounding return from investing in $\underline{r}(t + \tau)$ under the risk-adjusted $\mathbb{Q}$ measure. For the K-AGM, $\underline{r}(t + \tau) =$

$r(t+\tau)+\max\{-r(t+\tau),0\}$. Because the K-AGM framework uses the GATSM specification for shadow short rates, the expressions for the dynamics of $r(t+\tau)$ in terms of the state variables $x(t)$ and their associated parameters are already available. The dynamics for $r(t+\tau)$ also define the dynamics for $\max\{-r(t+\tau),0\}$, and therefore the distributions of both components required to calculate K-AGM forward rates are available. As I will detail in the following subsection, it is more convenient to undertake the required calculations using the forward $\mathbb{Q}$ measure. In summary,

$$
\begin{aligned}
\underline{f}(t,\tau) &= \tilde{\mathbb{E}}_{t+\tau}\left[r(t+\tau)\,|\,x(t)\right]+\tilde{\mathbb{E}}_{t+\tau}\left[\max\{-r(t+\tau),0\}\,|\,x(t)\right] \\
&= f(t,\tau)+z(t,\tau)
\end{aligned}
\tag{4.3}
$$

where $\tilde{\mathbb{E}}_{t+\tau}\left[\cdot\right]$ denotes expectations under the forward $\mathbb{Q}$ measure, $f(t,\tau)$ is shadow forward rate, and $z(t,\tau)$ is the K-AGM forward rate option effect. Closed-form analytic expressions for $f(t,\tau)$ are already available from chapter 3, again because the K-AGM framework uses the GATSM specification to represent the shadow term structure. I will detail how $z(t,\tau)$ is calculated in the following subsection, but the key point to note for now is that $z(t,\tau)$ turns out to be a closed-form analytic expression, which makes K-AGMs very tractable. However, I also note here that the K-AGM tractability arises from a different implicit assumption relative to the Black (1995) shadow/ZLB-GATSM framework. I will provide full details on this point in chapters 5 and 6.

Analogous to GATSM interest rates $R(t,\tau)$ in chapter 3, K-AGM interest rates $\underline{R}(t,\tau)$ are obtained by integrating K-AGM forward rates $\underline{f}(t,\tau)$. Therefore, $\underline{R}(t,\tau)$ will also consist of a shadow component, that is, GATSM interest rates $R(t,\tau)$, and an option effect component, which I denote as $Z(t,\tau)$.

Finally, and again as analogous to the GATSM, K-AGM bond prices $\underline{P}(t,\tau)$ are obtained by taking the exponential of K-AGM interest rates $\underline{R}(t,\tau)$. That transformation results in the GATSM bond price expression $P(t,\tau)$ being multiplied by a bond price option effect that I denote as $Z_{\mathrm{P}}(t,\tau)$.

Table 4.1 summarizes the discussion above. In particular, each representation of the K-AGM term structure may be envisaged as being composed of a shadow component with a GATSM form and an option effect component. Each of those components in turn relates directly back to the GATSM state variables $x(t)$ and their associated parameters that are used to specify the shadow term structure.

4.1.2 K-AGM option effect

Deriving the closed-form analytic expression for the forward rate option effect $z(t,\tau)$ is the key to the K-AGM framework. The derivation of the K-AGM option effect $z(t,\tau)$ in this section follows that of Krippner (2013d,e).[1] It proceeds essentially by calculating the distribution of future shadow rates $r(t+\tau)$ conditional on the prevailing state variables $x(t)$, and then taking expectations of that distribution

Table 4.1 K-AGM term structure components

		Shadow component (GATSM)		Option component (GATSM bond option)
Short rate:				
$\underline{r}(t)$	$=$	$r(t)$	$+$	$\max\{-r(t),0\}$
	$=$	$a_0 + b_0 x(t)$	$+$	$\max\{-[a_0 + b_0 x(t)],0\}$
Forward rates:				
$\underline{f}(t,\tau)$	$=$	$f(t,\tau)$	$+$	$z(t,\tau)$
	$=$	$\tilde{\mathbb{E}}_{t+\tau}[r(t+\tau)|x(t)]$	$+$	$\tilde{\mathbb{E}}_{t+\tau}[\max\{-r(t+\tau),0\}|x(t)]$
Interest rates:				
$\underline{R}(t,\tau)$	$=$	$R(t,\tau)$	$+$	$Z(t,\tau)$
	$=$	$\frac{1}{\tau}\int_0^\tau f(t,u)\,du$	$+$	$\frac{1}{\tau}\int_0^\tau z(t,u)\,du$
Bond prices:				
$\underline{P}(t,\tau)$	$=$	$P(t,\tau)$	$\times$	$Z_P(t,\tau)$
	$=$	$\exp[-\tau\cdot R(t,\tau)]$	$\times$	$\exp[-\tau\cdot Z(t,\tau)]$

with the truncation $\max\{-r(t+\tau),0\}$. The expression $\max\{-r(t+\tau),0\}$ represents an option payoff at time $t+\tau$, as I will detail in chapter 5. Hence, as with option calculations in general, representing $\max\{-r(t+\tau),0\}$ within an appropriate forward probability measure greatly simplifies the mathematics required to obtain the relevant pricing expressions.

In this particular case, the $t+\tau$ forward $\mathbb{Q}$ measure is applicable because the option payoff is at time $t+\tau$. Under this measure, economic agents effectively assess all cashflows and their probabilities using the $P(t,\tau)$ bond as the numeriare. Those results can be then discounted back to the current time t using $P(t,\tau)$. By comparison, the $\mathbb{Q}$ measure uses what is often called a money-market or an accumulator account as the numeriare, which directly obtains results at the current time t. Such calculations are straightforward for fixed future cashflows, but the calculations become complex for contingent future cashflows. James and Webber (2000) chapter 4 and Filipović (2009) chapter 7 contain further discussion on these issues.

Under the $t+\tau$ forward $\mathbb{Q}$ measure, the distribution of short rates for the generic shadow-GATSM is the following normal distribution:

$$r(t+\tau)|x(t) \sim N\{f(t,\tau),[\omega(\tau)]^2\} \tag{4.4}$$

where $f(t,\tau)$ and $[\omega(\tau)]^2$ are the GATSM expressions from equations 3.19 and 3.16 in chapter 3. The result for the mean of the distribution $f(t,\tau)$ arises from a standard term structure relationship that holds for any term structure model:[2]

$$\tilde{\mathbb{E}}_{t+\tau}[r(t+\tau)|x(t)] = f(t,\tau) \tag{4.5}$$

where $\tilde{\mathbb{E}}_{t+\tau}$ represents the risk-adjusted expectation under the $t + \tau$ forward $\mathbb{Q}$ measure, and $x(t)$ represents the information set available at time t. The result for the variance of the distribution arises from the definition $[\omega(\tau)]^2 = \widetilde{\text{var}}_t\,[r(t+\tau)\,|x(t)]$ provided for GATSMs in subsection 3.1.2, and the fact that the $[\omega(\tau)]^2$ is time-invariant. Therefore,

$$\widetilde{\text{var}}_{t+\tau}\,[r(t+\tau)\,|x(t)] = \widetilde{\text{var}}_t\,[r(t+\tau)\,|x(t)]$$

$$= [\omega(\tau)]^2 \qquad (4.6)$$

Given its normal distribution, the probability density function (hereafter pdf) for $r(t+\tau)\,|x(t)$ under the forward measure is

$$\text{pdf}[r(t+\tau)\,|x(t)] = \frac{1}{\omega(\tau)} \cdot \frac{1}{\sqrt{2\pi}}\exp\left(-\frac{1}{2}\left[\frac{r(t+\tau) - f(t,\tau)}{\omega(\tau)}\right]^2\right)$$

$$= \frac{1}{\omega(\tau)} \cdot \phi\left[\frac{r(t+\tau) - f(t,\tau)}{\omega(\tau)}\right] \qquad (4.7)$$

where $\phi[\cdot]$ is the standard notation for the unit normal pdf. Note that ϕ also appears in this book as a model parameter, but the use of $\phi[\cdot]$ as the unit normal pdf will present no confusion because in that context it will always be shown to be operating on the object inside the brackets. Note also that I often use expressions like $\phi[\cdot]$ for notional brevity where the value on which the function operates is apparent from the context of the preceding equation.

The $t + \tau$ forward $\mathbb{Q}$ measure relationship in equation 4.5 applied to K-AGM forward rates and ZLB short rates is

$$\underline{f}(t,\tau) = \tilde{\mathbb{E}}_{t+\tau}\,[\underline{r}(t+\tau)\,|x(t)] \qquad (4.8)$$

The K-AGM forward rate $\underline{f}(t,\tau)$ is therefore obtained by calculating the expectation of short rates $\underline{r}(t+\tau)$ under the $t + \tau$ forward $\mathbb{Q}$ measure. Figure 4.1 illustrates the distribution of short rates $\underline{r}(t+\tau)$ as the positive part of the shadow short rate distribution (heavier shading). Alternatively, expressing $\underline{r}(t+\tau)$ as the sum of shadow short rates $r(t+\tau)$ and the option effect $\max\{0,r(t+\tau)\}$, means that $\underline{f}(t,\tau)$ can be calculated as the sum of the expectations of $r(t+\tau)$ and $\max\{-r(t+\tau),0\}$ under the $t + \tau$ forward $\mathbb{Q}$ measure. Figure 4.1 illustrates the distribution of $\max\{-r(t+\tau),0\}$ as the negative part of the shadow short rate distribution (lighter shading).

Before proceeding to calculate the expectations of $\max\{-r(t+\tau),0\}$, I will first generalize the ZLB mechanism to allow for a non-zero lower bound r_L:

$$\underline{r}(t+\tau) = \max\{r_L, r(t+\tau)\}$$

$$= r(t+\tau) + \max\{r_L - r(t+\tau), 0\} \qquad (4.9)$$

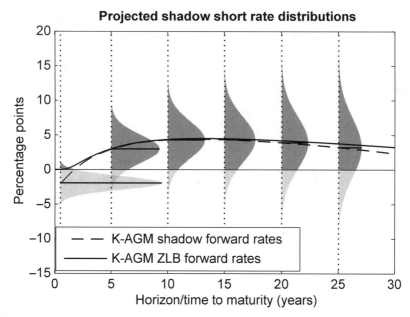

Figure 4.1 Projected distributions of shadow short rates from a GATSM specification of the shadow term structure. Realizations of future negative values in the light-shaded areas are ruled out by the ZLB mechanism, which in turn represents the option value of physical currency.

Note, however, that I will generally continue to use the generic terminology "ZLB model" for any model with an explicit lower bound, even if r_L is non-zero.

Generalizing the ZLB mechanism allows for situations in which the interest rate settings of the central bank transmitted into money-like deposits available to economic agents might provide the effective alternative investment to the shadow short rate, rather than physical currency itself. As already noted in chapter 1, central banks have generally tended to adopt policy arrangements that result in slightly positive overnight wholesale interest rates in practice, hence suggesting $r_L \gtrsim 0$. Conversely, if the central bank attempted to drive overnight wholesale interest rates below zero, economic agents would likely accept some opportunity cost for the convenience and safety of money-like deposits relative to physical currency. In that case, $r_L \lesssim 0$ would be appropriate.

With the modified ZLB mechanism, the K-AGM forward rate expression in equation 4.8 becomes

$$\underline{f}(t,\tau) = \tilde{\mathbb{E}}_{t+\tau}\left[\underline{r}(t+\tau)\,|\,x(t)\right]$$
$$= \tilde{\mathbb{E}}_{t+\tau}\left[r(t+\tau)\,|\,x(t)\right] + \tilde{\mathbb{E}}_{t+\tau}\left[\max\{r_L - r(t+\tau),0\}\,|\,x(t)\right]$$
$$= f(t,\tau) + z(t,\tau) \qquad (4.10)$$

where $f(t,\tau) = \tilde{\mathbb{E}}_{t+\tau}\left[r(t+\tau)|x(t)\right]$ is obtained from equation 4.5. The forward rate option effect, $z(t,\tau)$, is obtained by directly evaluating the given expectation:

$$
\begin{aligned}
z(t,\tau) &= \tilde{\mathbb{E}}_{t+\tau}\left[\max\{r_L - r(t+\tau),0\}|x(t)\right] \\
&= \int_{-\infty}^{\infty} \max\{r_L - r(t+\tau),0\} \cdot \text{pdf}[r(t+\tau)]\,dr(t+\tau) \\
&= \int_{-\infty}^{0} [r_L - r(t+\tau)] \cdot \text{pdf}[r(t+\tau)]\,dr(t+\tau) \\
&\quad + \int_{0}^{\infty} 0 \cdot \text{pdf}[r(t+\tau)]\,dr(t+\tau) \\
&= \int_{-\infty}^{0} [r_L - r(t+\tau)] \\
&\quad \times \frac{1}{\omega(\tau)} \cdot \frac{1}{\sqrt{2\pi}} \exp\left(-\frac{1}{2}\left[\frac{r(t+\tau)-f(t,\tau)}{\omega(\tau)}\right]^2\right) dr(t+\tau) \\
&= [r_L - f(t,\tau)] \cdot \left(1 - \Phi\left[\frac{f(t,\tau)-r_L}{\omega(\tau)}\right]\right) \\
&\quad + \omega(\tau) \cdot \phi\left[\frac{f(t,\tau)-r_L}{\omega(\tau)}\right]
\end{aligned}
\tag{4.11}
$$

where $\Phi[\cdot]$ is the standard notation for the cumulative unit normal density function.

Equation 4.11 is a closed-form analytic expression, which is the key to the tractability of the K-AGM framework. Specifically, generic closed-form analytic expressions are already available for $f(t,\tau)$ and $\omega(\tau)$ for any shadow-GATSM specification, respectively, in equations 3.19 and 3.16. Therefore, $z(t,\tau)$, and in turn $\underline{f}(t,\tau) = f(t,\tau) + z(t,\tau)$ in the following section, will also have closed-form analytic expressions for any shadow-GATSM specification.[3]

4.1.3 K-AGM forward rates

Substituting the result for $z(t,\tau)$ from equation 4.11 into equation 4.3 gives the generic K-AGM forward rate expression in terms of the shadow forward rate and the option effect:

$$
\begin{aligned}
\underline{f}(t,\tau) &= f(t,\tau) + z(t,\tau) \\
&= r_L + [f(t,\tau) - r_L] \cdot \Phi\left[\frac{f(t,\tau)-r_L}{\omega(\tau)}\right] \\
&\quad + \omega(\tau) \cdot \phi\left[\frac{f(t,\tau)-r_L}{\omega(\tau)}\right]
\end{aligned}
\tag{4.12}
$$

Note that setting $r_L = 0$ gives the results from Krippner (2011, 2012a,b):

$$\underline{f}(t,\tau) = f(t,\tau) \cdot \Phi \left[\frac{f(t,\tau)}{\omega(\tau)}\right] + \omega(\tau) \cdot \frac{1}{\sqrt{2\pi}} \exp\left(-\frac{1}{2}\left[\frac{f(t,\tau)}{\omega(\tau)}\right]^2\right) \qquad (4.13)$$

The K-AGM forward rate expression $\underline{f}(t,\tau)$ could equivalently be calculated as the expected value of $\underline{r}(t+\tau) = \max\{r_L, r(t+\tau)\}$, and Priebsch (2013) details such a derivation. Specifically, the calculation is

$$\underline{f}(t,\tau) = \tilde{\mathbb{E}}_{t+\tau}\left[\underline{r}(t+\tau)\,|\,x(t)\right]$$

$$= r_L \cdot \int_{-\infty}^{r_L} \frac{1}{\omega(\tau)} \cdot \frac{1}{\sqrt{2\pi}} \exp\left(-\frac{1}{2}\left[\frac{r(t+\tau) - f(t,\tau)}{\omega(\tau)}\right]^2\right) dr(t+\tau)$$

$$+ \int_{r_L}^{\infty} r(t+\tau) \cdot \frac{1}{\omega(\tau)}$$

$$\times \frac{1}{\sqrt{2\pi}} \exp\left(-\frac{1}{2}\left[\frac{r(t+\tau) - f(t,\tau)}{\omega(\tau)}\right]^2\right) dr(t+\tau) \qquad (4.14)$$

where the first integral captures the probability mass associated with the constant $r_L = \max\{r_L, r(t+\tau)\}$ when $r(t+\tau) < r_L$. The result is identical to equation 4.12.

To obtain an expression for $\underline{f}(t,\tau)$, only a calculation of $\omega(\tau)$ is required relative to the GATSMs already presented in chapter 3. From sub-section 3.1.2 or Krippner (2013d,e), the generic expression for $\omega(\tau)$ is

$$[\omega(\tau)]^2 = \int_0^{\tau} b_0' \exp(-\tilde{\kappa}u)\,\sigma\sigma' \exp(-\tilde{\kappa}'u)\,b_0\,du \qquad (4.15)$$

and Priebsch (2013) derives an equivalent expression. I will demonstrate how to undertake specific calculations for $[\omega(\tau)]^2$ in section 4.3 with my fully worked example.

4.1.4 Observations on the K-AGM framework

One advantage of developing the K-AGM framework based on a generic GATSM specification for the shadow term structure is that my comments below will apply to any K-AGM specification, irrespective of the number of factors and factor inter-relationships. Bearing that generality in mind, I make several observations about the K-AGM framework:

- The K-AGM framework preserves the complete flexibility that exists for the GATSM class of models. Specifically, the K-AGM framework uses a GATSM to specify the shadow term structure, and the K-AGM option effect used to modify the GATSM term structure is a simple function of the GATSM state variables and parameters.

- The K-AGM forward rate curve will always be a simple closed-form analytic expression. That is evident from the generic K-AGM being itself composed of simple closed-form analytic expressions, specifically:

  - the forward rates $f(t, \tau)$, which are defined by the state variable vector $x(t)$ and scalar exponential functions of time to maturity τ;
  - the shadow short rate standard deviations $\omega(\tau)$, which are defined by state variable innovation variances and covariances and scalar exponential functions of τ;
  - the cumulative unit normal function $\Phi\left[\{f(t, \tau) - r_L\}/\omega(\tau)\right]$; and
  - the unit normal function $\phi\left[\{f(t, \tau) - r_L\}/\omega(\tau)\right]$, which is just the scalar exponential function $\exp\left(-\frac{1}{2}\left[\{f(t, \tau) - r_L\}/\omega(\tau)\right]^2\right)$.

- K-AGM forward rates converge to r_L when the K-AGM shadow forward rates $f(t, \tau)$ are sufficiently negative relative to term structure volatility. Specifically, with $\omega(\tau)$ being time-invariant,

$$\lim_{f(t,\tau) \to -\infty} \Phi\left[\{f(t, \tau) - r_L\}/\omega(\tau)\right] = 0$$

$$\lim_{f(t,\tau) \to -\infty} \phi\left[\{f(t, \tau) - r_L\}/\omega(\tau)\right] = 0$$

$$\text{hence} \lim_{f(t,\tau) \to -\infty} \underline{f}(t, \tau) = r_L$$

Note that this property of K-AGMs also resolves the somewhat technical issue of potential negative interest rates in GATSMs for extremely long times to maturity, as mentioned at the end of subsection 3.3.2. That is, $f(t, \tau)$, and therefore the shadow rate $R(t, \tau)$, can adopt any negative value, but $\underline{f}(t, \tau)$ and $\underline{R}(t, \tau)$, which I will define in subsection 4.16, have a lower bound of r_L. As a related aside, any positive value of r_L will ensure that the associated discount factor has an asymptotic value of zero.

- K-AGM forward rates converge to K-AGM shadow forward rates $f(t, \tau)$ when the latter are sufficiently positive relative to term structure volatility. Specifically, with $\omega(\tau)$ being time-invariant,

$$\lim_{f(t,\tau) \to \infty} \Phi\left[\{f(t, \tau) - r_L\}/\omega(\tau)\right] = 1$$

$$\lim_{f(t,\tau) \to \infty} \phi\left[\{f(t, \tau) - r_L\}/\omega(\tau)\right] = 0$$

$$\text{hence} \lim_{f(t,\tau) \to \infty} \underline{f}(t, \tau) = f(t, \tau)$$

- K-AGM interest rates $\underline{R}(t, \tau)$ and bond prices $\underline{P}(t, \tau)$ can be calculated from K-AGM forward rates, as I will detail in sections 4.2 and 4.3. They will therefore respectively converge to r_L and $\exp(-r_L \tau)$ when shadow forward rates are sufficiently negative relative to term structure volatility. Similarly K-AGM interest rates and bond prices will converge to their shadow counterparts when the ZLB constraint becomes immaterial.

4.1.5 Comparison with related results in the literature

I believe the derivation in the previous section presents the most straightforward and intuitive derivation of the K-AGM forward rate expression. However, there are alternative ways of calculating the same result that have been presented in the literature, and I briefly note them here for comparison.

Krippner (2011, 2012b,c) derived $z(t,\tau)$ by modeling the availability of physical currency over finite future time steps $t + \tau + \delta$ as call options, with a strike price of 1 and an expiry of $t + \tau$, on the bond $P(t+\tau,\delta)$. I will present an analogous setup for the Black (1995) shadow/ZLB-GATSM framework in chapter 5. Denoting the price of that option as $C(t,\tau,\delta,1)$, Krippner (2011, 2012b,c) then showed that the continuous-time forward rate option effect is obtainable as the following limit:

$$z(t,\tau) = \lim_{\delta \to 0} \left\{ \frac{\mathrm{d}}{\mathrm{d}\delta} \left[\frac{C(t,\tau,\delta,1)}{P(t,\tau)} \right] \right\} \qquad (4.16)$$

For any GATSM specification, $C(t,\tau,\delta,1)$ and $P(t,\tau)$ are known to be closed-form analytic expressions (e.g., see Filipović (2009), p. 109). Therefore, substituting those expressions into equation 4.16 and evaluating the results provides a generic closed-form analytic expression for $z(t,\tau)$. Using that option/limit approach, Krippner (2011, 2012b,c) derived $\underline{f}(t,\tau)$ for GATSMs with distinct and non-zero eigenvalues for $\tilde{\kappa}$. Christensen and Rudebusch (2013a,b, 2014) applied the Krippner (2011, 2012b,c) method to obtain $\underline{f}(t,\tau)$ for the three-state-variable arbitrage-free Nelson and Siegel (1987) model, directly deriving the option price and taking the limit. Krippner (2013d,e) provides more a much more succinct derivation of $\underline{f}(t,\tau)$ for GATSMs and the ANSM(3) by directly calculating $\omega(\tau)$, which I will summarize in subsection 4.4.1.

Wu and Xia (2013, 2014) derives the discrete-time analogue of the K-AGM framework from a discrete-time GATSM. Their approach is to calculate approximate discrete-time ZLB forward rates using the first difference in the logarithm of the total expected compounded return from investing in a discrete-time short rate process that follows a truncated normal distribution. The equivalence of their results to the K-AGM framework (up to the discrete-time versus continuous-time property) is readily demonstrated using their key expressions.

Using their notation, Wu and Xia (2013, 2014) discrete-time GATSM forward rates $f^{GA}_{n,n+1,t}$ are

$$f^{GA}_{n,n+1,t} = a_n + b'_n X_t$$

where n is an integer index for finite-sized horizon/time-to-maturity increments (monthly in their application), the subscript $n, n+1, t$ for $f^{GA}_{n,n+1,t}$ represents the finite-step ZLB forward rate at time t over the horizon/time-to-maturity increment n to $n+1$, a_n is a scaler calculated via iterative difference equations, b_n is an $N \times 1$ vector of factor loadings calculated via iterative difference equations, and X_t is an $N \times 1$ vector of state variables. Note that $f^{GA}_{n,n+1,t}$, a_n, and b_n are the discrete time analogues of my continuous-time expressions for the forward rate $f(t,\tau)$, the volatility effect $-VE(\tau)$, and the factor loadings $\exp(-\tilde{\kappa}'\tau)b_0$.

Wu and Xia (2013, 2014) discrete-time ZLB GATSM forward rates $f^{SRTSM}_{n,n+1,t}$ are

$$f^{SRTSM}_{n,n+1,t} = \underline{r} + \sigma^Q_n \cdot g\left(\frac{a_n + b'_n X_t - \underline{r}}{\sigma^Q_n}\right)$$

where $\underline{r}$ is the non-zero lower bound, $\left(\sigma^Q_n\right)^2 = \text{var}^Q(r_{t+n})$, and $g(z) = z \cdot \Phi(z) + \phi(z)$, with $\Phi(z)$ and $\phi(z)$ are respectively the cumulative and probability function of a standard normal distribution.

Setting $\underline{r} = r_L$ gives $z = \left(a_n + b'_n X_t - r_L\right)/\sigma^Q_n = \left(f_{n,n+1,t} - r_L\right)/\sigma^Q_n$, and writing $g(z)$ out explicitly gives the following:

$$f^{SRTSM}_{n,n+1,t} = r_L + \sigma^Q_n \cdot \left[\frac{f_{n,n+1,t} - r_L}{\sigma^Q_n} \cdot \Phi(z) + \phi(z)\right]$$

$$= r_L + \left[f_{n,n+1,t} - r_L\right] \cdot \Phi\left[\frac{f_{n,n+1,t} - r_L}{\sigma^Q_n}\right]$$

$$+ \phi\left[\frac{f_{n,n+1,t} - r_L}{\sigma^Q_n}\right] \tag{4.17}$$

which is precisely the discrete-time analogue of equation 4.12. That is, the only difference is that the shadow forward rates and the shadow short rate volatilities are expressed in discrete time.

4.1.6 K-AGM interest rates and bond prices

The K-AGM expressions for $\underline{R}(t,\tau)$ and $\underline{P}(t,\tau)$ are not closed-form analytic, for reasons I explain below, and must be obtained via numerical integration. However, the number of numerical evaluations required for such integrals remains invariant to the specification of the K-AGM because $\underline{f}(t,\tau)$ is always a closed-form analytic expression. Therefore, the evaluation of $\underline{R}(t,\tau)$ is always an elementary univariate numerical integral of $\underline{f}(t,\tau)$ with respect to τ, regardless of the shadow-GATSM used in the K-AGM. This tractability along with the multivariate normal distributions for the K-AGM state variables means that K-AGMs retain a large degree of the GATSM-class tractability for implementation and estimation.

In notation, K-AGM interest rates $\underset{\sim}{R}(t,\tau)$ are calculated from K-AGM forward rates using the standard term structure relationship:

$$\underset{\sim}{R}(t,\tau) = \frac{1}{\tau}\int_0^\tau \underset{\sim}{f}(t,u)\,du \tag{4.18}$$

The integral does not have a closed-form analytic solution, because $\underset{\sim}{f}(t,u)$ contains the cumulative Gaussian distribution, but univariate numerical integration of $f(t,u)$ over time to maturity τ may be used to calculate the integral to arbitrary precision.

A convenient and intuitive form of numerical integration is rectangular increments with constant time-to-maturity increments $\Delta\tau$ and end-increment function values $\underset{\sim}{f}(t,j\Delta\tau)$. The numerical expression for $\underset{\sim}{R}(t,\tau)$ then simplifies to the mean of the elements of the sequence $\underset{\sim}{f}(t,\Delta\tau), \underset{\sim}{f}(t,2\Delta\tau), \dots, \underset{\sim}{f}(t,[J-1]\Delta\tau), \underset{\sim}{f}(t,J\Delta\tau)$:

$$\frac{1}{\tau}\int_0^\tau \underset{\sim}{f}(t,u)\,du \simeq \frac{1}{\tau}\left(\sum_{j=1}^{J}\underset{\sim}{f}(t,j\Delta\tau)\,\Delta\tau\right) \tag{4.19}$$

where $J = \tau/\Delta\tau$, and

$$\frac{1}{\tau}\left(\sum_{j=1}^{J}\underset{\sim}{f}(\cdot)\,\Delta\tau\right) = \frac{1}{\tau}\Delta\tau\sum_{j=1}^{J}\underset{\sim}{f}(t,j\Delta\tau)$$

$$= \frac{1}{\tau}\frac{\tau}{J}\sum_{j=1}^{J}\underset{\sim}{f}(t,j\Delta\tau)$$

$$= \frac{1}{J}\sum_{j=1}^{J}\underset{\sim}{f}(t,j\Delta\tau)$$

$$= \text{mean}\{\underset{\sim}{f}(t,\Delta\tau),\dots,\underset{\sim}{f}(t,J\Delta\tau)\} \tag{4.20}$$

Therefore:

$$\underset{\sim}{R}(t,\tau) \simeq \text{mean}\{\underset{\sim}{f}(t,\Delta\tau),\dots,\underset{\sim}{f}(t,J\Delta\tau)\} \tag{4.21}$$

If K-AGM bond prices $\underset{\sim}{P}(t,\tau)$ are required, they can be calculated via the interest rates $\underset{\sim}{R}(t,\tau)$, that is,

$$\underset{\sim}{P}(t,\tau) = \exp[-\tau\cdot\underset{\sim}{R}(t,\tau)]$$

$$\simeq \exp[-\tau\cdot\text{mean}\{\underset{\sim}{f}(t,\Delta\tau),\dots,\underset{\sim}{f}(t,J\Delta\tau)\}] \tag{4.22}$$

Note that other numerical integration methods could also be used, and may prove more suitable in practice. Also, it would be straightforward to develop a hybrid framework in which the closed-form analytic solutions for GATSM interest rates are used when the ZLB constraint is immaterial (based on some threshold appropriate to the application) and the K-AGM is used otherwise.

4.2 K-AGM estimation

In this section, I provide an overview of how K-AGMs may be estimated. Like the K-AGM term structure expressions themselves, the method for estimating K-AGMs is also essentially a relatively straightforward and intuitive modification to the method for estimating GATSMs. A modification is required because the interest rate expression for the K-AGM involves nonlinear functions of the state variables $x(t)$, via the unit normal functions $\Phi[\cdot]$ and $\phi[\cdot]$ in the K-AGM forward rate expression, rather than the linear functions that arose for the GATSM. Therefore, a nonlinear filtering technique is required to accommodate the nonlinearity of the measurement equation for interest rates when estimating K-AGMs.

I will discuss in subsection 4.2.1 a range of nonlinear Kalman filters that could be applied to estimating K-AGMs, but I will explain why my preference is to use the iterated extended Kalman filter. In subsection 4.2.2, I provide an overview and then the details for a partial K-AGM estimation, that is, how to obtain estimates of the K-AGM state variables from the data given a suitable set of parameters. In section 4.2.3, I provide an overview for full K-AGM estimations, that is, how to obtain estimates of the K-AGM parameters and state variables from the data using maximum likelihood estimation.

4.2.1 K-AGMs and nonlinear Kalman filters

Estimating K-AGMs requires a nonlinear Kalman filter due to their nonlinear measurement equations, and I will discuss a range of such filters shortly. However, most of the K-AGM estimation framework is identical to applying the Kalman filter to GATSMs. Specifically, because K-AGMs use a GATSM to represent the shadow term structure, the shadow-GATSM specification contains the state variables and the parameters for the K-AGM. Therefore the K-AGM state equation and all of its related expressions are simply obtained from the GATSM expressions already derived and discussed in section 3.2.1.

The allowance for nonlinearity is therefore only required for the measurement equation, as I will detail in the following subsection. One very straightforward nonlinear Kalman filter that could be applied to K-AGM estimations is the extended Kalman filter (hereafter EKF). The EKF has been used by Christensen and Rudebusch (2013a,b, 2014) and Wu and Xia (2013, 2014), and I will mention several further applications in chapter 7 that have used the EKF.

I prefer to use the more general iterated extended Kalman filter (hereafter IEKF) because I have found in practice that it provides much more reliable and accurate maximum likelihood estimations from different starting points. Specifically, using the EKF within an optimization algorithm often results in a likelihood value and parameter estimates that can be greatly improved on by using the IEKF within the same optimization algorithm. The IEKF-based optimization obtains a materially higher value of the likelihood function along with materially different parameter estimates than the EKF-based optimization. Indeed, in my investigations so far, I have only been able to replicate the IEKF-based parameter estimates with the EKF-based optimization by using the IEKF-based parameter estimates themselves as the starting values in the EKF-based optimization. Another issue I noticed during early testing with the EKF is that it produced substantially different estimates of the state variables depending on the frequency of the data used (e.g., daily, weekly, or monthly), which is why I originally turned to the IEKF. The IEKF produces state variables estimates that are very close to each other regardless of the frequency of the data.

The IEKF is covered in textbooks such as Simon (2006) pp. 410-12 and Grewal and Andrews (2008, pp. 312–13) and it includes the EKF as a special case. Another relatively straightforward nonlinear filtering technique that could potentially be applied is the unscented Kalman filter, which is employed in Kim and Priebsch (2013) for estimating a Black (1995) GATSM. However, Grewal and Andrews (2008) p. 312 cites Lefebvre, Bruyninckx, and De Schutter (2004) to note that the IEKF outperforms the unscented Kalman filter (and the EKF), and I also show later that using the IEKF for K-AGM estimations requires fewer computations than the unscented Kalman filter. Christensen and Rudebusch (2014) also compare the unscented Kalman filter to the EKF for estimating the K-AGM and find little difference, so presumably the IEKF will outperform the unscented Kalman filter for K-AGM estimation. A more advanced nonlinear filtering technique is the particle filter, which is covered in textbooks such as Simon (2006) and Durbin and Koopman (2012). Employing the particle filter would be much more involved than the IEKF, in terms of complexity and the computations involved, and I expect it would provide little practical benefit given that the nonlinearity of K-AGMs appears only in the measurement equation.

4.2.2 Partial estimation

Overview

Table 4.2 summarizes a single application of the IEKF algorithm to obtain a partial K-AGM estimation. The first point to note is that Table 4.2 is almost identical to Table 3.1 for the partial estimation of GATSMs, with the main exception being the step "**3.2: Measurement estimates**," which is replaced with "**3.2. Measurement/posterior state iterations**." Therefore, my overview of the intuition and flow in Table 4.2 will often refer to the overview already provided for Table 3.1 in section 3.2.2.

Note that I assume a yield curve data set $\{R_1,\ldots,R_T\}$ and a parameter set $\mathbb{A}$ are available, as discussed in section 3.2 for partial estimations of GATSMs. However, two minor differences for the partial K-AGM estimation relative to the partial GATSM estimation are:

- I have now denoted the observations of yield curve data as R_t with an underscore rather than R_t for the GATSM. The data are the same, of course, but the notation R_t emphasizes that they are subject to the ZLB.
- The parameter set $\mathbb{A}$ includes r_L, either as a fixed parameter or a free parameter to be estimated, and a parameter for the constant time-to-maturity increments $\Delta\tau$ used for the numerical integration of $f(t,\tau)$ to obtain $R(t,\tau)$. Note that $\Delta\tau$ is a distinctly different concept than the time step Δt used in the state equation expressions. The latter represents the discrete observation times of yield curve data. (e.g., daily, weekly, monthly, etc.). In general, $\Delta\tau$ will be much smaller than Δt. For example, I use $\Delta t = 1/12$ to represent monthly observations and $\Delta\tau = 0.01$ to provide 100 increments per year of maturity for numerical integration.

Once a suitable set of yield curve data $\{R_1,\ldots,R_T\}$ and a parameter set $\mathbb{A}$ are passed into the IEKF, the process proceeds as follows:

- **1. Setup:** F, $\Theta(\Delta t)$, and Ω_η are calculated from the relevant K-AGM shadow yield curve parameters, the same as they were calculated for the GATSM parameters in Table 3.1. The values a and H are not calculated for the IEKF for reasons I discuss in step 3 below. All of the expressions underlying the calculations in Table 4.2 are contained in subsection 3.2.1, but I briefly repeat them here for convenience.

$$V\kappa_D V^{-1} = \kappa \tag{4.23a}$$

$$F = V\exp\left(-\kappa_D\Delta t\right)V^{-1} \tag{4.23b}$$

$$[\Theta(\Delta t)]_{ij} = \Sigma_{ij}\frac{1}{\kappa_i + \kappa_j}\left[1 - \exp\left(-\{\kappa_i + \kappa_j\}\Delta t\right)\right] \tag{4.23c}$$

$$\Sigma = V^{-1}\sigma\sigma'V'^{-1} \tag{4.23d}$$

$$\Omega_\eta = \mathrm{diag}\left[\left\{\left[\sigma_\eta(\tau_1)\right]^2,\ldots,\left[\sigma_\eta(\tau_K)\right]^2\right\}\right] \tag{4.23e}$$

- **2. State initialization:** This step is identical to Table 3.1. From subsection 3.2.1, the additional expression $\Theta(\infty)$ required for P_t^- in Table 4.2 is

$$[\Theta(\infty)]_{ij} = \Sigma_{ij}\frac{1}{\kappa_i + \kappa_j} \tag{4.24}$$

- **3. Recursion:** I have represented the recursion identically to Table 3.1, and the following steps will apply to all observed yield curve data from $t=1$ to $t=T$.

- **3.1. Prior state estimates:** This step is identical to Table 3.1.
- **3.2. Measurement/posterior state iterations:** This step is like a combination of the "**3.2 Measurement estimate**" and "**3.3 Posterior state estimates**" steps from Table 3.1. The two key differences are the iterations and how the residual vector η_t is obtained. The residual vector η_t for the GATSM is obtained from the linear interest rate function $R(x_t, \mathbb{A}) = a + Hx_t$ and the prior state variable vector x_t^-, i.e. $\eta_t = R_t - a - Hx_t^-$. The nonlinearity of the K-AGM interest rate function requires the IEKF to calculate $\underline{R}(x_t, \mathbb{A})$ using a first-order Taylor approximation of the K-AGM interest rate function around the best available estimate of the state variable vector x_t. The initial best estimate of x_t when step 3.2 is reached is the prior state estimate x_t^-, which is denoted $x_{t,0}^+$. However, a posterior estimate can be undertaken within step 3.2 to provide an improved estimate of x_t, which will be denoted $x_{t,1}^+$. The first-order Taylor approximation can then be repeated with the new state estimate $x_{t,1}^+$, which can be used obtain a new posterior update $x_{t,2}^+$, and so on. The process can be iterated several times or to a convergence condition.
- **3.3. Posterior state estimates:** This step is similar to Table 3.2 except the posterior estimate of x_t^+ is already available as the last value of $x_{t,i+1}^+$ from step 3.2. The posterior estimate of the variance of the state variable vector P_t^+ is calculated using its prior estimate P_t^- and the last values of the matrices $K_{t,i}$ and $H_{t,i}$ from step 3.2. Note that $K_{t,i}$ and $H_{t,i}$ are the values used to calculate $x_{t,i+1}^+$ in step 3.2, which is recorded as x_t^+ in step 3.3. Therefore x_t^+ and P_t^+ are consistently based on values from the same iteration.

- x_t^+ and P_t^+ are then used as the starting values for the next recursion. The process is repeated for each yield curve observation to obtain the entire times series of state variable vectors $\{x_1^+, \ldots, x_T^+\}$ corresponding to the given parameters and yield curve data set.

The essential output from the IEKF filter algorithm is the estimated time series of K-AGM state variable vectors $\{x_1, \ldots, x_T\} = \{x_1^+, \ldots, x_T^+\}$, which is specific to the K-AGM specification, the supplied parameters, and the yield curve data used for estimation.

I now proceed with a more detailed overview of each of the steps in 3.2 and 3.3 when applied in general to K-AGMs. However, many of these expressions are best illustrated in the worked example in the following section. I also provide further comment on the EKF versus the IEKF.

Details on steps 3.2 and 3.3

Set $x_{t,0}^+ = x_t^-$:
Making this initial setting is for convenience. It means that the iteration process applies for the initial step and for subsequent iterations.

Table 4.2 Partial K-AGM estimation via IEKF

1. Setup and estimation constraints:

Calculate F, $\Theta(\Delta t)$, and Ω_η

2. State initialization:

$x_0^+ = \theta$

$P_0^+ = V\Theta(\infty)V'$

3. Recursion:

for $t = 1 : T$

3.1. Prior state estimates:

$x_t^- = \theta + F\left(x_{t-1}^+ - \theta\right)$

$P_t^- = FP_{t-1}^+ F' + \Theta(\Delta t)$

3.2. Measurement/posterior state iterations:

Set : $x_{t,0}^+ = x_t^-$; $H_{t,0} = 0$

ITERATE : from $i = 0$

$\eta_{t,i} = \underline{R}_t - \underline{R}\left(x_{t,i}^+, \mathbb{A}\right) - H_{t,i}\left(x_t^- - x_{t,i}^+\right)$

$H_{t,i} = \frac{\partial}{\partial x(t)}\underline{R}[x(t), \mathbb{A}]\Big|_{x(t)=x_{t,i}^+}$

$M_{t,i} = H_{t,i}P_t^- H_{t,i}' + \Omega_\eta$

$K_{t,i} = P_t^- H_{t,i}' M_{t,i}^{-1}$

$x_{t,i+1}^+ = x_{t,i}^+ + K_{t,i}\eta_{t,i}$

EXIT : at max (i) or $\left|x_{t,i+1}^+ - x_{t,i}^+\right|$ tolerance

3.3. Posterior state estimates:

$x_t^+ = x_{t,i+1}^+$, $\eta_t = \eta_{t,i}$, and $M_t = M_{t,i}$

$P_t^+ = \left(I - K_{t,i}H_{t,i}\right)P_t^-$

Record x_t^+, η_t, and M_t

next t

Notes:

x_t^-, x_t^+, $x_{t,i}^+$, and θ are $N \times 1$ vectors

$\eta_{t,i}$ and η_t are $K \times 1$ vectors

κ_D is an $N \times N$ diagonal matrix

P_t^-, P_t^+, $\sigma\sigma'$, $\Theta(\Delta t)$, and $\Theta(\infty)$ are $N \times N$ symmetric matrices

V and F are $N \times N$ asymmetric matrices

$M_{t,i}$ and M_t is a $K \times K$ symmetric matrix

Ω_η is a $K \times K$ diagonal matrix

$K_{t,i}$ is an $N \times K$ matrix

$H_{t,i}$ is a $K \times N$ matrix

Calculate the residual vector $\eta_{t,i}$ for iteration i:

Calculating $\eta_{t,i}$ requires the K-AGM estimate of the $K \times 1$ $\underline{R}(x_t, \mathbb{A})$ for comparison to the yield curve data $\underline{R}_t$. The nonlinearity of the K-AGM interest rate function means that the best estimate of $\underline{R}(x_t, \mathbb{A})$ is obtained as a first-order Taylor approximation of the K-AGM interest rate function around the best available estimate of the state variable vector x_t, which is $\underline{R}\left(x_{t,i}^+, \mathbb{A}\right) - H_{t,i}\left(x_t^- - x_{t,i}^+\right)$.

I will discuss the calculation of $H_{t,i}$ below, but note that $H_{t,i}\left(x_t^- - x_{t,i}^+\right) = 0$ for the initial step $i = 0$, because in that case, $x_t^- - x_{t,0}^+ = 0$ given $x_{t,0}^+ = x_t^-$. $H_{t,0}$ can therefore be set to an arbitrary value, say a matrix of zeros. For subsequent iterations, $H_{t,i}$ will be available, $x_t^- - x_{t,i}^+$ will be non-zero, and $H_{t,i}\left(x_t^- - x_{t,i}^+\right)$ ensures that the first-order Taylor expansion to approximate $R(x_t, \mathbb{A})$ is always around the latest (i.e., best) estimated state vector $x_{t,i}^+$.

Regarding the $K \times 1$ vector $\underline{R}\left(x_{t,i}^+, \mathbb{A}\right)$, each iteration i and time step t requires the calculation of $\underline{R}\left(x_{t,i}^+, \mathbb{A}, \tau_k\right)$ for all maturities τ_k that have an associated interest rate observation. From equation 4.21, $\underline{R}\left(x_{t,i}^+, \mathbb{A}, \tau_k\right)$ is calculated as the mean of the sequence of K-AGM forward rates $\underline{f}\left(x_{t,i}^+, \mathbb{A}, j\Delta\tau\right)$ from $j = 1$ to $J_k = \tau_k/\Delta\tau$.

I have found it most efficient to calculate a single sequence of forward rates $\underline{f}\left(x_{t,i}^+, \mathbb{A}, j\Delta\tau\right)$ out to the longest maturity $J_K \Delta\tau = \tau_K$, and then take the relevant means up to $J_1 = \tau_1/\Delta\tau$, $J_2 = \tau_2/\Delta\tau$, ..., $J_{K-1} = \tau_{K-1}/\Delta\tau$, $J_K = \tau_K/\Delta\tau$ to obtain the results for all elements of $\underline{R}\left(x_{t,i}^+, \mathbb{A}\right)$ at once:

$$
\underline{R}\left(x_{t,i}^+, \mathbb{A}\right) = \left[
\begin{array}{c}
\text{mean}\left\{\underline{f}\left(x_{t,i}^+, \Delta\tau\right), \dots, \underline{f}\left(x_{t,i}^+, J_1\Delta\tau\right)\right\} \\
\vdots \\
\text{mean}\left\{\underline{f}\left(x_{t,i}^+, \Delta\tau\right), \dots, \underline{f}\left(x_{t,i}^+, J_K\Delta\tau\right)\right\}
\end{array}
\right]_{K \times 1}
\tag{4.25}
$$

where $\underline{f}\left(x_{t,i}^+, \mathbb{A}, \Delta\tau\right)$, ..., $\underline{f}\left(x_{t,i}^+, \mathbb{A}, J_K\Delta\tau\right)$ is the sequence of K-AGM forward rates by time-to-maturity increments $j\Delta\tau$ out to the longest time to maturity $J_K\Delta\tau = \tau_K$. Note that the index $j = 1$ to J_K, and so the length of that sequence is therefore $J_K = \tau_K/\Delta\tau$. The K-AGM interest rates for the shorter maturities τ_k are calculated as the means up to $J_k = \tau_k/\Delta\tau$. For example, $\underline{R}_1\left(x_{t,i}^+, \tau_1\right) = \text{mean}\{\underline{f}\left(x_{t,i}^+, \mathbb{A}, \Delta\tau\right), \dots, \underline{f}\left(x_{t,i}^+, \mathbb{A}, J_1\Delta\tau\right)\}$, and so forth.

The sequence $\underline{f}\left(x_{t,i}^+, \mathbb{A}, j\Delta\tau\right)$ is obtained element-by-element from the K-AGM forward rate equation:

$$
\underline{f}\left(x_{t,i}^+, \mathbb{A}, j\Delta\tau\right) = r_L + \left[f\left(x_{t,i}^+, j\Delta\tau\right) - r_L\right] \cdot \Phi\left[\frac{f\left(x_{t,i}^+, j\Delta\tau\right) - r_L}{\omega\left(j\Delta\tau\right)}\right]
$$
$$
+ \omega\left(j\Delta\tau\right) \cdot \phi\left[\frac{f\left(x_{t,i}^+, j\Delta\tau\right) - r_L}{\omega\left(j\Delta\tau\right)}\right]
\tag{4.26}
$$

Note that, for notational convenience and brevity, I have suppressed the dependence of the functions on the parameter set $\mathbb{A}$, where that dependence is apparent from the left-hand side of the equation, and I will often do so in what follows.

The sequences $f\left(x_{t,i}^+, \mathbb{A}, j\Delta\tau\right)$ and $\omega\left(j\Delta\tau, \mathbb{A}\right)$ used to calculate $\underline{f}\left(x_{t,i}^+, \mathbb{A}, j\Delta\tau\right)$ are themselves calculated from the GATSM expressions in section 3.1, as I will demonstrate in the worked example of section 4.3.

Calculate the Jacobian matrix vector $H_{t,i}$ for iteration i:

Calculating the $K \times N$ Jacobian matrix $H_{t,i}$ at each iteration i and time step t requires the partial derivatives of each element of $\underline{R}[x(t), \mathbb{A}]$ with respect to $x(t)$ evaluated at $x_{t,i}^+$. Appendix E.2.3 from Krippner (2013d,e) explicitly calculates that expression for K-AGMs in general to show that evaluating $H_{t,i}$ for each measurement/posterior iteration requires no more numerical evaluations than are already required to obtain $\underline{R}(x_{t,i}^+, \mathbb{A})$. In summary, beginning with the definition of the Jacobian for a given time to maturity τ_k:

$$H_{t,i,k} = \left. \frac{\partial}{\partial x(t)} \underline{R}[x(t), \mathbb{A}, \tau_k] \right|_{x(t)=x_{t,i}^+} \tag{4.27}$$

and noting that $\underline{R}[x(t), \mathbb{A}, \tau_k]$ is defined as

$$\underline{R}[x(t), \mathbb{A}, \tau_k] = \frac{1}{\tau_k} \int_0^{\tau_k} b_0' \exp\left(-\tilde{\kappa}' u\right) \cdot \Phi\left[\frac{f[x(t), u] - r_L}{\omega(u)}\right] du \tag{4.28}$$

obtains the following expression:

$$H_{t,i,k} = \frac{1}{\tau_k} \int_0^{\tau_k} b_0' \exp\left(-\tilde{\kappa}' u\right) \cdot \Phi\left[\frac{f\left(x_{t,i}^+, \mathbb{A}, u\right) - r_L}{\omega(u)}\right] du \tag{4.29}$$

$H_{t,i,k}$ is a $1 \times N$ vector associated with τ_k, and stacking the $H_{t,i,k}$ vectors for each time to maturity from τ_1 to τ_K gives the $K \times N$ matrix $H_{t,i}$. Analogous to $\underline{R}(x_{t,i}^+, \mathbb{A}, \tau_k)$, $H_{t,i,k}$ does not have a closed form analytic solution. However, once again, a result to arbitrary precision may be obtained via univariate numerical integration over time to maturity τ, and regularly spaced rectangular increments conveniently produces a mean expression:

$$H_{t,i,k} = \text{mean}\left\{ h\left(x_{t,i}^+, \mathbb{A}, j\Delta\tau\right), \ldots, h\left(x_{t,i}^+, \mathbb{A}, J_K \Delta\tau\right) \right\} \tag{4.30}$$

where

$$h\left(x_{t,i}^+, \mathbb{A}, j\Delta\tau\right) = b_0' \exp\left(-\tilde{\kappa} j\Delta\tau\right) \cdot \Phi\left[\frac{f\left(x_{t,i}^+, j\Delta\tau\right) - r_L}{\omega(j\Delta\tau)}\right] \tag{4.31}$$

Note that each $h\left(x_{t,i}^+, \mathbb{A}, j\Delta\tau\right)$ is a $1 \times N$ vector of shadow forward rate factor loadings multiplied by the scalar result $\Phi[\cdot]$. $H_{t,i,k}$ is the mean of that sequence of vectors, and so it is also a $1 \times N$ vector.

As with the calculation of $\underline{R}(x_{t,i}^+, \mathbb{A})$, I have found it most efficient to use a single sequence of $h\left(x_{t,i}^+, \mathbb{A}, \Delta\tau\right), \ldots, h\left(x_{t,i}^+, \mathbb{A}, J_K \Delta\tau\right)$ vectors out to the longest maturity

τ_K, and then take the relevant means up to $J_1 = \tau_1/\Delta\tau$, $J_2 = \tau_2/\Delta\tau$, ..., $J_{K-1} = \tau_{K-1}/\Delta\tau$, $J_K = \tau_K/\Delta\tau$ to obtain the results for all elements of $H_{t,i}$ at once:

$$H_{t,i} = \begin{bmatrix} \text{mean}\{h(x_{t,i}^+, \mathbb{A}, \Delta\tau), \ldots, h(x_{t,i}^+, \mathbb{A}, J_1\Delta\tau)\} \\ \vdots \\ \text{mean}\{h(x_{t,i}^+, \mathbb{A}, \Delta\tau), \ldots, h(x_{t,i}^+, \mathbb{A}, J_K\Delta\tau)\} \end{bmatrix}_{K\times N} \quad (4.32)$$

As mentioned earlier, all of the calculations required for $h(x_{t,i}^+, \mathbb{A}, j\Delta\tau)$, $\exp(-\tilde{\kappa}j\Delta\tau)$ and $\Phi[\cdot]$, are already available from the calculations of $R(x_{t,i}^+, \mathbb{A})$. Therefore, evaluating the Jacobian comes at no expense in terms of requiring further numerical calculations. This result confers a computational and/or accuracy advantage relative to the unscented Kalman filter estimation and numerical calculations of the Jacobian, which is important in the context of full K-AGM estimations.

Specifically, estimation using the unscented Kalman filter would require at least $2N$ additional evaluations of $R(x_t^+, \mathbb{A}, \tau_k)$ around the central state variable vector x_t^+. The IEKF could instead undertake $2N$ iterations (e.g., four or six iterations respectively for a two- or three-state-variable model) in the same time, and it would typically converge before then. Jacobians could be approximated by numerical derivatives, as in the estimations from Christensen and Rudebusch (2013a,b, 2014), but that would be less accurate and computationally inefficient. For example, N additional evaluations of $R(x_t^+, \mathbb{A}, \tau_k)$ around the central state variable vector x_t^+ would be required for a numerical derivative using forward differences, or $2N$ evaluations would be required for a numerical derivative using central differences.

Calculate $M_{t,i}$ and $K_{t,i}$:
The matrices $M_{t,i}$ and $K_{t,i}$ are recalculated for each iteration using the current Jacobian $H_{t,i}$.

Calculate $x_{t,i+1}^+$:
An updated estimate of x_t^+, $x_{t,i+1}^+$, is now calculated. The estimate $x_{t,i+1}^+$ will be more optimal than the previous estimate $x_{t,i}^+$ because $x_{t,i+1}^+$ has been conditioned on the yield curve data and the improved estimate of the Jacobian matrix $H_{t,i}$. That conditioning can be repeated to continually provide improved estimates of $x_{t,i+1}^+$ given $x_{t,i}^+$. Note that no calculations of P_t^+ are required within the iterations.

Exit iterations:
My preferred method is to iterate until all elements of $\left| x_{t,i+1}^+ - x_{t,i+1} \right|$ are less than a given tolerance at each time index t, rather than using a fixed number of iterations. Doing so ensures that the accuracy of the estimates of the state variables is consistent across the sample. A tolerance is also computationally efficient, because fewer IEKF iterations will be undertaken at times when the data is immaterially constrained by the ZLB (i.e., when the K-AGM is essentially linear or only mildly nonlinear) and

more iterations will be undertaken when the ZLB constraint becomes more material (i.e., the nonlinearity of the K-AGM becomes more pronounced).

EKF versus IEKF

Using the notation introduced for the IEKF, the EKF is the special case of the IEKF with just the initial step $i = 0$ and no subsequent iterations, that is, max $(i) = 1$. The initial step of "**3.2. Measurement/posterior state iterations**" sets $x_{t,0}^{+}$ equal to x_t^{-}, but retaining the notation x_t^{-}, the residuals $\eta_{t,0}$ are

$$\eta_{t,0} = \underline{R}_t - \underline{R}\left(x_t^{-}, \mathbb{A}\right) \tag{4.33}$$

where the term $H_{t,0}\left(x_t^{-} - x_{t,0}^{+}\right) = 0$ because $x_{t,0}^{+} = x_t^{-}$.

The initial Jacobian $H_{t,0}$ is evaluated with x_t^{-} as

$$H_{t,0} = \begin{bmatrix} H_{t,0,1} \\ \vdots \\ H_{t,0,K} \end{bmatrix}_{K \times N} \tag{4.34}$$

where

$$H_{t,0,k} = \text{mean}\left\{h\left(x_t^{-}, \mathbb{A}, j\Delta\tau\right), \ldots, h\left(x_t^{-}, \mathbb{A}, J_K\Delta\tau\right)\right\} \tag{4.35}$$

and

$$h\left(x_t^{-}, \mathbb{A}, j\Delta\tau\right) = b_0' \exp\left(-\tilde{\kappa}j\Delta\tau\right) \cdot \Phi\left[\frac{f\left(x_t^{-}, j\Delta\tau\right) - r_L}{\omega\left(j\Delta\tau\right)}\right] \tag{4.36}$$

That initial Jacobian $H_{t,0}$ is used to obtain $M_{t,0}$ and $K_{t,0}$, and the single posterior update $x_{t,1}^{+}$ is $x_{t,1}^{+} = x_t^{-} + K_t\eta_{t,0}$.

The posterior update $x_{t,1}^{+}$ is passed to step "**3.3. Posterior state estimates,**" where it is recorded, and the posterior estimate of the state vector variance is calculated using the initial calculations of the Jacobian $H_{t,0}$ and the Kalman gain matrix $K_{t,0}$, i.e., $P_t^{+} = \left(I - K_{t,0}H_{t,0}\right)P_t^{-}$.

The estimates from the EKF for each time step t will therefore not be as accurate as the IEKF because the EKF results are based on less accurate estimates of the state vector at each time t than the IEKF. Furthermore, using the less accurate estimates of x_t^{+} and P_t^{+} as starting values for the next recursion means any inaccuracies can potentially propagate into the time step $t + 1$.

4.2.3 Full estimation

Table 4.3 summarizes the process for a full estimation of the K-AGM via maximum likelihood by using the IEKF algorithm within an optimization algorithm. Table 4.3

is almost identical to Table 3.2 for the full estimation of GATSMs, and the main exceptions in steps 3.2 and 3.3 have already been discussed in the previous subsection. Therefore, my overview of the intuition and flow in Table 4.3 mainly refers to the overview already provided for Table 3.2 in section 3.2.3.

- The "**A. Optimization algorithm**" denotes the optimization algorithm employed by the user, as already discussed in section 3.2.3.
- The objective function of the optimization algorithm is to maximize the log-likelihood function given by the expression $\log\text{-}L\left(\left\{\underset{\sim}{R}_1,\ldots,\underset{\sim}{R}_T\right\},\mathbb{A}\right)$, where $\left\{\underset{\sim}{R}_1,\ldots,\underset{\sim}{R}_T\right\}$ is the yield curve data set and $\mathbb{A}$ is the set of parameters required for the IEKF, and the fixed and free K-AGM parameters to be estimated. Note that $\mathbb{A}$ can include a non-zero value of r_L as an additional fixed parameter or as a parameter to be estimated.
- As discussed in section 3.2.3, the yield curve data set and the parameter set $\mathbb{A}$ are passed through to the IEKF algorithm. The same constraints as discussed in section 3.2.3 are applied to ensure the smooth operation of the IEKF algorithm for any parameter set $\mathbb{A}$.
- The IEKF algorithm proceeds as already discussed in subsection 4.2.2.
- As discussed in section 3.2.3, the time series of $\{\eta_1,\ldots,\eta_T\}$ and $\{M_1,\ldots,M_T\}$ from the IEKF algorithm are passed back to the optimization algorithm, a value for $\log\text{-}L(\{R_1,\ldots,R_T\},\mathbb{A})$ is calculated, and the optimization algorithm iterates until a user-defined convergence condition.
- The final output is the same as discussed in section 3.2.3, which I repeat here for convenience: the estimated GATSM parameters; the estimated series of GATSM state variable vectors $\left\{x_1^+,\ldots,x_T^+\right\}$ and their variances $\left\{P_1^+,\ldots,P_T^+\right\}$; and typically standard diagnostics associated with the optimization. As discussed in section 3.2.3 and detailed in section 3.3.4, the final output is used to assess whether or not the K-AGM provides an appropriate representation of the yield curve data.

4.3 Worked example: K-ANSM(2)

In this section, I provide a fully worked example for the K-AGM framework. Specifically, I use the ANSM(2) detailed in section 3.3 to represent the shadow term structure in the K-AGM framework, and so I will call the resulting shadow/ZLB-GATSM the K-ANSM(2).

4.3.1 K-ANSM(2) specification

The specification for the K-ANSM(2) shadow term structure is the ANSM(2) specification in section 3.3.1, and the K-ANSM(2) may also allow for a non-zero

Table 4.3 Full K-AGM estimation via maximum likelihood

A. Optimization algorithm

Maximize: $\log\text{-}L\left(\left\{\underline{R}_1,\ldots,\underline{R}_T\right\},\mathbb{A}\right)$

$= -\frac{1}{2}\sum_{t=1}^{T} K\log(2\pi) + \log(|M_t|) + \eta_t' M_t^{-1}\eta_t$

with η_t and M_t from IEKF algorithm.

IEKF (iterated extended Kalman filter) algorithm

1. Setup and estimation constraints:

Calculate F, $\Theta(\Delta t)$, and Ω_η

Subject to constraints:

- $|F| < 1$

- $\sigma\sigma'$ and Ω_η positive definite

2. State initialization:

$x_0^+ = \theta$

$P_0^+ = V\Theta(\infty)V'$

3. Recursion:

for $t = 1 : T$

    3.1. Prior state estimates:

    $x_t^- = \theta + F\left(x_{t-1}^+ - \theta\right)$

    $P_t^- = FP_{t-1}^+ F' + \Theta(\Delta t)$

    3.2. Measurement/posterior state iterations:

    Set : $x_{t,0}^+ = x_t^-$; $H_{t,0} = 0$

    ITERATE : from $i = 0$

    $\eta_{t,i} = \underline{R}_t - \underline{R}\left(x_{t,i}^+,\mathbb{A}\right) - H_{t,i}\left(x_t^- - x_{t,i}^+\right)$

    $H_{t,i} = \left.\frac{\partial}{\partial x(t)}\underline{R}\left[x(t),\mathbb{A}\right]\right|_{x(t)=x_{t,i}^+}$

    $M_{t,i} = H_{t,i}P_t^- H_{t,i}' + \Omega_\eta$

    $K_{t,i} = P_t^- H_{t,i}' M_{t,i}^{-1}$

    $x_{t,i+1}^+ = x_{t,i}^+ + K_{t,i}\eta_{t,i}$

    EXIT : at $\max(i)$ or $\left|x_{t,i+1}^+ - x_{t,i}^+\right|$ tolerance

    3.3. Posterior state estimates:

    $x_t^+ = x_{t,i+1}^+$, $\eta_t = \eta_{t,i}$, and $M_t = M_{t,i}$

    $P_t^+ = \left(I - K_{t,i}H_{t,i}\right)P_t^-$

    Record x_t^+, η_t, and M_t

next t

B. Diagnostics of estimated K-AGM

Note: See Table 4.2 for matrix dimensions.

lower bound parameter r_L. The K-ANSM(2) state variables, and the fixed and free parameters in their natural scalar/vector/matrix form are therefore as follows:

$$x(t) = \begin{bmatrix} x_1(t) \\ x_2(t) \end{bmatrix} ; \quad r_L ; \quad a_0 = 0 ; \quad b_0 = \begin{bmatrix} 1 \\ 1 \end{bmatrix}$$

$$\kappa = \begin{bmatrix} \kappa_{11} & \kappa_{12} \\ \kappa_{21} & \kappa_{22} \end{bmatrix}; \quad \theta = \begin{bmatrix} \theta_1 \\ \theta_2 \end{bmatrix}$$

$$\sigma = \begin{bmatrix} \sigma_1 & 0 \\ \rho_{12}\sigma_2 & \sigma_2\sqrt{1-\rho_{12}^2} \end{bmatrix}$$

$$\tilde{\kappa} = \begin{bmatrix} 0 & 0 \\ 0 & \phi \end{bmatrix}; \quad \tilde{\theta} = \begin{bmatrix} 0 \\ 0 \end{bmatrix} \tag{4.37}$$

If r_L is fixed to zero, then the K-ANSM(2) specification of the state variables and parameters are the same as the ANSM(2), but the estimates of the K-ANSM(2) state variables and parameters will of course be different.

4.3.2 K-ANSM(2) shadow term structure

The K-ANSM(2) shadow term structure has the same expressions as the ANSM(2). I repeat the key expressions here for convenience. Hence, K-ANSM(2) shadow short rates are

$$r(t) = x_1(t) + x_2(t) \tag{4.38}$$

and K-ANSM(2) shadow forward rates are

$$f(t,\tau) = x_1(t) + x_2(t) \cdot \exp(-\phi\tau)$$
$$-\sigma_1^2 \cdot \frac{1}{2}\tau^2 - \sigma_2^2 \cdot \frac{1}{2}[G(\phi,\tau)]^2 - \rho_{12}\sigma_1\sigma_2 \cdot \tau G(\phi,\tau) \tag{4.39}$$

where:

$$G(\phi,\tau) = \frac{1}{\phi}\left[1 - \exp(-\phi\tau)\right] \tag{4.40}$$

K-ANSM(2) shadow interest rates are

$$R(t,\tau) = a(\tau) + [b(\tau)]' \begin{bmatrix} x_1(t) \\ x_2(t) \end{bmatrix} \tag{4.41}$$

where

$$a(\tau) = -\sigma_1^2 \cdot \frac{1}{6}\tau^2 - \sigma_2^2 \cdot \frac{1}{2\phi^2}\left[1 - \frac{1}{\tau}G(\phi,\tau) - \frac{1}{2\tau}\phi[G(\phi,\tau)]^2\right]$$
$$-\rho\sigma_1\sigma_2 \cdot \frac{1}{\phi^2}\left[1 - \frac{1}{\tau}G(\phi,\tau) + \frac{1}{2}\phi\tau - \phi G(\phi,\tau)\right] \tag{4.42}$$

and

$$[b(\tau)]' = \left[1, \frac{1}{\tau}G(\phi,\tau)\right] \tag{4.43}$$

4.3.3 K-ANSM(2) ZLB term structure

K-ANSM(2) ZLB short rates are obtained using K-ANSM(2) shadow short rates and the ZLB mechanism:

$$\underline{r}(t) = \max\{r_L, x_1(t) + x_2(t)\} \tag{4.44}$$

K-ANSM(2) forward rates are obtained using the generic K-AGM forward rate expression:

$$\underline{f}(t,\tau) = r_L + [f(t,\tau) - r_L] \cdot f(t,\tau) \cdot \Phi\left[\frac{f(t,\tau) - r_L}{\omega(\tau)}\right]$$

$$+ \omega(\tau) \cdot \frac{1}{\sqrt{2\pi}} \exp\left(-\frac{1}{2}\left[\frac{f(t,\tau) - r_L}{\omega(\tau)}\right]^2\right) \tag{4.45}$$

with the K-ANSM(2) shadow forward rate expression from equation 4.39 and the appropriate calculation of the shadow short rate volatility function $\omega(\tau)$. For the K-ANSM(2), $\omega(\tau)$ may be calculated from equation 3.16 as follows:

$$[\omega(\tau)]^2 = \int_0^\tau b_0' \exp(-\tilde{\kappa} u)\, \sigma\sigma' \exp(-\tilde{\kappa}' u)\, b_0 \, du$$

$$= \int_0^\tau [1,1] \begin{bmatrix} 1 & 0 \\ 0 & \exp(-\phi u) \end{bmatrix} \begin{bmatrix} \sigma_1^2 & \rho_{12}\sigma_1\sigma_2 \\ \rho_{12}\sigma_1\sigma_2 & \sigma_2^2 \end{bmatrix}$$

$$\times \begin{bmatrix} 1 & 0 \\ 0 & \exp(-\phi u) \end{bmatrix} \begin{bmatrix} 1 \\ 1 \end{bmatrix} du$$

$$= \int_0^\tau \{\sigma_1^2 + \sigma_2^2 \cdot \exp(-2\phi u) + 2\rho_{12}\sigma_1\sigma_2 \cdot \exp(-\phi u)\}\, du$$

$$= \sigma_1^2 \cdot \tau + \sigma_2^2 \cdot G(2\phi,\tau) + 2\rho_{12}\sigma_1\sigma_2 G(\phi,\tau) \tag{4.46}$$

and hence

$$\omega(\tau) = \sqrt{\sigma_1^2 \cdot \tau + \sigma_2^2 \cdot G(2\phi,\tau) + 2\rho_{12}\sigma_1\sigma_2 G(\phi,\tau)} \tag{4.47}$$

As I will detail in the following subsection, K-ANSM(2) interest rates are then obtained as the mean of the sequence $\underline{f}(t,j\Delta\tau)$:

$$\underline{R}(t,\tau) = \frac{1}{J}\sum_{j=1}^{J} \underline{f}(t,j\Delta\tau) \tag{4.48}$$

4.3.4 K-ANSM(2) Estimation

Full or partial estimations of the K-ANSM(2) proceed precisely as for the ANSM(2), with identical vector and matrix expressions, up to the step "**3.2 Measurement estimates.**" Therefore, the following points only provide the additional details for the subsections "**3.2. Measurement/posterior state iterations**" and "**3.3. Posterior state estimates**" in Tables 4.2 and 4.3. I refer readers to section 3.3.3 for the details on the section "**A. Optimization algorithm**," and the steps "**1. Setup and estimation constraints**," "**2. State initialization**," and "**3.1. Prior state estimates**" within the IEKF algorithm.

With reference to the yield curve data set detailed in subsection 3.5.1, I will use $K = 9$ in the examples below to represent the nine different maturities. I note upfront that writing the details below was more burdensome than actually undertaking the calculations in practice, which simply requires several straightforward lines of vectorized code and some standard functions in MatLab (equivalent to a series of "for/next" loops or similar in other programming languages). Nevertheless, I hope the explicit details will provide additional clarity for the worked example.

Details for steps 3.2 and 3.3

Set $x_{t,0}^+ = x_t^-$:

$$\begin{bmatrix} x_{1,0}^+(t) \\ x_{2,0}^+(t) \end{bmatrix} = \begin{bmatrix} x_1^-(t) \\ x_2^-(t) \end{bmatrix} \tag{4.49}$$

Calculate the residual vector $\eta_{t,i}$ for iteration i:

For a given time t and iteration i of $x_{t,i}^+$, K-AGM interest rates are

$$\underline{R}\left(x_{t,i}^+, \mathbb{A}\right) = \begin{bmatrix} \underline{R}_1\left(x_{t,i}^+, \tau_1\right) \\ \vdots \\ \underline{R}_9\left(x_{t,i}^+, \tau_9\right) \end{bmatrix}_{9\times 1}$$

$$= \begin{bmatrix} \text{mean}\left\{\underline{f}\left(x_{t,i}^+, \mathbb{A}, \Delta\tau\right), \ldots, \underline{f}\left(x_{t,i}^+, \mathbb{A}, J_1\Delta\tau\right)\right\} \\ \vdots \\ \text{mean}\left\{\underline{f}\left(x_{t,i}^+, \mathbb{A}, \Delta\tau\right), \ldots, \underline{f}\left(x_{t,i}^+, \mathbb{A}, J_9\Delta\tau\right)\right\} \end{bmatrix}_{9\times 1} \tag{4.50}$$

where $\underline{f}(x_{t,i}^+, \mathbb{A}, \Delta\tau), \ldots, \underline{f}(x_{t,i}^+, \mathbb{A}, J_9\Delta\tau)$ is the sequence of K-ANSM(2) forward rates by time-to-maturity increments $j\Delta\tau$ out to the longest time to maturity $J_9\Delta\tau = \tau_9 = 30$ years. Note that $j = 1 : J_9$, and the length of that sequence is therefore $J_9 = \tau_9/\Delta\tau$, which equates to 3000, given $\tau_9 = 30$ years and $\Delta\tau = 0.01$ years. The K-AGM interest rates for the shorter maturities τ_k are calculated as the means up to $J_k = \tau_k/\Delta\tau$. For example, $\underline{R}_1\left(x_{t,i}^+, \tau_1\right) = \text{mean}\{\underline{f}(x_{t,i}^+, \mathbb{A}, \Delta\tau), \ldots, \underline{f}(x_{t,i}^+, \mathbb{A}, J_1\Delta\tau)\}$, where $J_1 = 0.25/\Delta\tau = 25$. $\underset{\sim}{R}_2\left(x_{t,i}^+, \tau_2\right)$ uses $J_2 = 0.5/\Delta\tau = 50$, and so forth, so values of J corresponding to each of the maturities in my yield curve data set are 25, 50, 100, 200, 300, 500, 700, 1000, and 3000.

Each term $\underset{\sim}{f}(x_{t,i}^+, \mathbb{A}, j\Delta\tau)$ of the sequence described above is obtained using equation 4.26 with the associated sequence of K-ANSM(2) shadow forward rates $f\left(x_{t,i}^+, \mathbb{A}, \Delta\tau\right), \ldots, f\left(x_{t,i}^+, \mathbb{A}, J_9\Delta\tau\right)$ and shadow short rate volatilities $\omega\left(\mathbb{A}, \Delta\tau\right), \ldots,$ $\omega\left(\mathbb{A}, J_9\Delta\tau\right)$. Specifically,

$$\underset{\sim}{f}\left(x_{t,i}^+, \mathbb{A}, \Delta\tau\right) = r_L + \left[f\left(t, j\Delta\tau\right) - r_L\right] \cdot f(t,\tau) \cdot \Phi\left[\frac{f\left(t, j\Delta\tau\right) - r_L}{\omega\left(j\Delta\tau\right)}\right]$$

$$+ \omega\left(j\Delta\tau\right) \cdot \frac{1}{\sqrt{2\pi}} \exp\left(-\frac{1}{2}\left[\frac{f\left(t, j\Delta\tau\right) - r_L}{\omega\left(j\Delta\tau\right)}\right]^2\right) \quad (4.51)$$

Each term of those sequences is itself obtained from the K-ANSM(2) shadow forward rate and shadow short rate volatility expressions, respectively:

$$f\left(x_{t,i}^+, \mathbb{A}, j\Delta\tau\right) = x_{1,t,i}^+ + x_{2,t,i}^+ \cdot \exp\left(-\phi j\Delta\tau\right)$$

$$- \sigma_1^2 \cdot \frac{1}{2}\left[j\Delta\tau\right]^2 - \sigma_2^2 \cdot \frac{1}{2}\left[G\left(\phi, j\Delta\tau\right)\right]^2$$

$$- \rho_{12}\sigma_1\sigma_2 \cdot \tau G\left(\phi, j\Delta\tau\right) \quad (4.52)$$

and:

$$\omega\left(\mathbb{A}, j\Delta\tau\right) = \sqrt{\sigma_1^2 \cdot j\Delta\tau + \sigma_2^2 \cdot G\left(2\phi, j\Delta\tau\right) + 2\rho_{12}\sigma_1\sigma_2 G\left(\phi, j\Delta\tau\right)} \quad (4.53)$$

The residual vector $\eta_{t,i}$ for the K-ANSM(2) is therefore

$$\eta_{t,i} = \underset{\sim}{R}_t - \underset{\sim}{R}\left(x_{t,i}^+, \mathbb{A}\right) - H_{t,i}\left(x_t^- - x_{t,i}^+\right)$$

$$\begin{bmatrix} \eta_{t,i,1} \\ \vdots \\ \eta_{t,i,9} \end{bmatrix} = \begin{bmatrix} \underset{\sim}{R}_t\left(\tau_1\right) \\ \vdots \\ \underset{\sim}{R}_t\left(\tau_9\right) \end{bmatrix} - \begin{bmatrix} \underset{\sim}{R}\left(x_{t,i}^+, \tau_1\right) \\ \vdots \\ \underset{\sim}{R}\left(x_{t,i}^+, \tau_9\right) \end{bmatrix}$$

$$- \begin{bmatrix} H_{t,i,1} \\ \vdots \\ H_{t,i,9} \end{bmatrix}\left(\begin{bmatrix} x_1^-(t) \\ x_2^-(t) \end{bmatrix} - \begin{bmatrix} x_{1,i}^+(t) \\ x_{2,i}^+(t) \end{bmatrix}\right) \quad (4.54)$$

where I will describe the calculation of $H_{t,i}$ in the next step. As mentioned in section 4.2, $H_{t,i}$ is not required for the initial calculation of the residual vector $\eta_{t,0}$ because $x_t^- - x_{t,0}^+ = 0$ given $x_{t,0}^+ = x_t^-$.

Calculate the Jacobian matrix vector $H_{t,i}$ for iteration i:

For a given time t and iteration i of $x_{t,i}^+$

$$H_{t,i} = \begin{bmatrix} H_{t,i,1} \\ \vdots \\ H_{t,i,9} \end{bmatrix}_{9 \times 2}$$

$$= \begin{bmatrix} \text{mean} \{ h(x_{t,i}^+, \mathbb{A}, \Delta\tau), \ldots, h(x_{t,i}^+, \mathbb{A}, J_1 \Delta\tau) \} \\ \vdots \\ \text{mean} \{ h(x_{t,i}^+, \mathbb{A}, \Delta\tau), \ldots, h(x_{t,i}^+, \mathbb{A}, J_9 \Delta\tau) \} \end{bmatrix}_{9 \times 2} \quad (4.55)$$

where $h(x_{t,i}^+, \Delta\tau), \ldots, h(x_{t,i}^+, \tau_9)$ is a sequence of 1×2 vectors by time-to-maturity increments $j\Delta\tau$ out to the longest time to maturity $J_9 \Delta\tau = \tau_9 = 30$ years. Again, $j = 1 : J_9$, and the length of that sequence is 3000 for my example. The mean of each sequence of 1×2 vectors to the given times to maturity τ_k in row k is itself a 1×2 vector. Stacking the resulting 9 mean vectors therefore gives the 9×2 matrix as indicated.

Each vector $h(x_{t,i}^+, \mathbb{A}, j\Delta\tau)$ of the sequence described above is obtained as

$$h(x_{t,i}^+, \mathbb{A},, j\Delta\tau) = b_0' \exp(-\tilde{\kappa} j\Delta\tau) \cdot \Phi \left[\frac{f(x_{t,i}^+, j\Delta\tau) - r_L}{\omega(j\Delta\tau)} \right]$$

$$= [1,1] \begin{bmatrix} 1 & 0 \\ 0 & \exp(-\phi j\Delta\tau) \end{bmatrix} \cdot \Phi \left[\frac{f(x_{t,i}^+, j\Delta\tau) - r_L}{\omega(j\Delta\tau)} \right]$$

$$= [1, \exp(-\phi j\Delta\tau)] \cdot \Phi \left[\frac{f(x_{t,i}^+, j\Delta\tau) - r_L}{\omega(j\Delta\tau)} \right] \quad (4.56)$$

$h(x_{t,i}^+, \mathbb{A}, j\Delta\tau)$ at each increment $j\Delta\tau$ is therefore the forward rate factor loading vector for the ANSM(2) $[1, \exp(-\phi j\Delta\tau)]$ multiplied by the scalar calculation of $\Phi[\{f(x_{t,i}^+, j\Delta\tau) - r_L\}/\omega(j\Delta\tau)]$. Note that those calculations are already available from the calculation of $R(x_{t,i}^+, \mathbb{A})$ in the previous step. Therefore, no additional numerical calculations are required to obtain $H_{t,i}$ if it is appropriately evaluated in tandem with $R(x_{t,i}^+, \mathbb{A})$.

Also note that MatLab readily accommodates the calculation of the mean of a sequence of vectors, but if one is using a programming language without that functionality, then row k of $H_{t,i}$ will be

$$H_{t,i,k} = [h_{1,k}, h_{2,k}], \quad (4.57)$$

where

$$h_{1,k} = \text{mean} \left\{ \Phi \left(\frac{f(x_{t,i}^+, j\Delta\tau)}{\omega(j\Delta\tau)} \right), \ldots, \Phi \left(\frac{f(x_{t,i}^+, J_k \Delta\tau)}{\omega(J_k \Delta\tau)} \right) \right\} \quad (4.58)$$

and

$$h_{2,k} = \text{mean} \left\{ \exp\left(-\phi j \Delta \tau\right) \cdot \Phi\left(\frac{f\left(x_{t,i}^+, j\Delta\tau\right)}{\omega\left(j\Delta\tau\right)}\right), \dots \right.$$

$$\left. \dots, \exp\left(-\phi j \Delta \tau\right) \cdot \Phi\left(\frac{f\left(x_{t,i}^+, J_k\Delta\tau\right)}{\omega\left(J_k\Delta\tau\right)}\right) \right\} \tag{4.59}$$

which are now both means of a series of scalar calculations.

Calculate $M_{t,i}$ and $K_{t,i}$:
Once $H_{t,i}$ is available, $M_{t,i}$ at iteration i is evaluated as

$$M_{t,i} = \begin{bmatrix} M_{t,i,11} & \cdots & M_{t,i,19} \\ \vdots & \ddots & \vdots \\ M_{t,i,19} & \cdots & M_{t,i,99} \end{bmatrix}_{9\times 9}$$

$$= H_{t,i} P_t^- H_{t,i}' + \Omega_\eta \tag{4.60}$$

and the Kalman gain matrix $K_{t,i}$ at iteration i is evaluated as

$$K_{t,i} = \begin{bmatrix} K_{t,i,11} & \cdots & K_{t,i,19} \\ K_{t,i,21} & \cdots & K_{t,i,29} \end{bmatrix}_{2\times 9}$$

$$= P_t^- H_{t,i}' M_t^{-1} \tag{4.61}$$

Calculate $x_{t,i+1}^+$:

$$\begin{bmatrix} x_{1,i+1}^+(t) \\ x_{2,i+1}^+(t) \end{bmatrix} = \begin{bmatrix} x_{1,i}^+(t) \\ x_{2,i}^+(t) \end{bmatrix} + K_{t,i}\eta_{t,i} \tag{4.62}$$

Exit iterations:
I iterate until both elements of the state variable vector $x_{t,i}^+$ change less than 1e-5, that is,

$$\left\| \begin{bmatrix} x_{1,i}^+(t) \\ x_{2,i}^+(t) \end{bmatrix} - \begin{bmatrix} x_{1,i-1}^+(t) \\ x_{2,i-1}^+(t) \end{bmatrix} \right\| < \begin{bmatrix} 1\text{e-5} \\ 1\text{e-5} \end{bmatrix} \tag{4.63}$$

which equates to 0.001 percentage points, or 0.1 basis points, for each of the elements of the state variable vector.

Details for "3.3. Posterior state estimates"

Final posterior estimate x_t^+:

$$\begin{bmatrix} x_1^+(t) \\ x_2^+(t) \end{bmatrix} = \begin{bmatrix} x_{1,i}^+(t) \\ x_{2,i}^+(t) \end{bmatrix} \tag{4.64}$$

Final posterior estimate P_t^+:
The final posterior estimate for the covariance matrix P_t^+ is calculated using the prevailing values of $K_{t,i}$ and $H_{t,i}$:

$$\left[\begin{array}{cc} P_{11,t}^+ & P_{12,t}^+ \\ P_{12,t}^+ & P_{22,t}^+ \end{array} \right] = \left(I - K_{t,i} H_{t,i} \right) P_t^- \tag{4.65}$$

Record η_t, and M_t and/or x_t^+:
Just the state variable vector x_t^+ is recorded for partial K-AGM estimations. For full K-AGM estimations, the most recent values of $\eta_{t,i}$ and $M_{t,i}$ are recorded as the values η_t and M_t to be used in the evaluation of the log-likelihood functions:

$$\eta_t = \left[\begin{array}{c} \eta_{t,i,1} \\ \vdots \\ \eta_{t,i,9} \end{array} \right]_{9 \times 1}$$

$$M_t = \left[\begin{array}{ccc} M_{t,i,11} & \cdots & M_{t,i,19} \\ \vdots & \ddots & \vdots \\ M_{t,i,19} & \cdots & M_{t,i,99} \end{array} \right]_{9 \times 9}$$

4.4 Other K-AGMs

Any GATSM, including the ANSM subclass of GATSMs, may be used to represent the shadow term structure within the K-AGM framework. Specifying and estimating the resulting K-AGM is then analogous to the process already described for the K-ANSM(2), except that the alternative shadow term structure expressions and the associated calculation of $\omega(\tau)$ are used.

I will first outline in subsection 4.4.1 the key points for the K-ANSM(3). The K-ANSM(3) is the K-AGM extension of the ANSM(3) detailed in subsection 3.4.1, and I will use the K-ANSM(3) extensively in the empirical applications of this and subsequent chapters. In subsection 4.4.2, I provide an overview of the key points for applying the K-AGM framework to higher-order ANSMs to create higher-order K-ANSMs. In subsection 4.4.3, I show that non-arbitrage-free versions of K-ANSMs provide a simple ZLB term structure representation akin to Nelson and Siegel (1987) models. Subsection 4.4.4 provides an overview of how the K-AGM framework may be applied to full GATSM specifications of the shadow term structure.

4.4.1 K-ANSM(3)

The K-ANSM(3) uses the ANSM(3) from section 3.4.1 to represent the shadow term structure. Therefore all the parameters are identical, except that the K-ANSM(3) may additionally allow for a non-zero lower bound parameter r_L, and the K-ANSM(3) shadow term structure has the same term structure expressions as the ANSM(3). I refer readers to sections 3.4.1 and 3.4.2 for the ANSM(3) expressions to use as the K-ANSM(3) shadow term structure.

K-ANSM(3) ZLB short rates are obtained using the ZLB mechanism:

$$\underline{r}(t) = \max\{r_L, x_1(t) + x_2(t)\} \tag{4.66}$$

K-ANSM(3) forward rates are obtained using the generic K-AGM forward rate expression in equation 4.12 with the K-ANSM(3) shadow forward rate expression from section 3.4.2 and the appropriate calculation of the shadow short rate volatility function $\omega(\tau)$. As detailed in Krippner (2013d,e), the K-ANSM(3) $\omega(\tau)$ function may be calculated from using the ANSM(3) factor loadings:

$$\exp(-\tilde{\kappa}\tau)b_0 = \left[1, \exp(-\phi\tau), \phi\tau\exp(-\phi\tau)\right] \tag{4.67}$$

and σ to evaluate equation 3.16. The result is

$$
\begin{aligned}
[\omega(\tau)]^2 = {} & \sigma_1^2 \cdot \tau + \sigma_2^2 \cdot G(2\phi, \tau) + \sigma_3^2 \cdot \frac{1}{2}\left[F(2\phi, \tau) - \phi\tau^2 \exp(-2\phi\tau)\right] \\
& + 2\rho_{12}\sigma_1\sigma_2 \cdot G(\phi, \tau) + 2\rho_{13}\sigma_1\sigma_3 \cdot F(\phi, \tau) \\
& + 2\rho_{23}\sigma_2\sigma_3 \cdot \frac{1}{2}F(2\phi, \tau)
\end{aligned}
\tag{4.68}
$$

Christensen and Rudebusch (2013a,b, 2014) obtained the equivalent result as above, but expressed in terms of covariance matrix parameters rather than standard deviations and correlation parameters. The Krippner (2013d,e) derivation using the generic expression for $[\omega(\tau)]^2$ is also considerably more straightforward than the lengthy derivation in Christensen and Rudebusch (2013a,b, 2014).

Partial or full estimations of the K-ANSM(3) using interest rate data proceed as summarized in Tables 4.2 and 4.3, with all of the initial steps identical to the ANSM(3). Within the measurement/posterior state iteration step, K-ANSM(3) interest rates are obtained using equation 4.25, where $\underline{f}(x_{t,i}^+, \mathbb{A}, \Delta\tau), \ldots, \underline{f}(x_{t,i}^+, \mathbb{A}, J_K\Delta\tau)$ is a sequence of K-ANSM(3) forward rates out to the longest time to maturity $J_K\Delta\tau = \tau_K$. Each term $\underline{f}(x_{t,i}^+, \mathbb{A}, j\Delta\tau)$ of that sequence is obtained using the associated sequence of K-ANSM(3) shadow forward rates $f(x_{t,i}^+, \mathbb{A}, \Delta\tau), \ldots, f(x_{t,i}^+, \mathbb{A}, J_K\Delta\tau)$ and shadow short rate volatilities $\omega(\mathbb{A}, \Delta\tau), \ldots, \omega(\mathbb{A}, J_K\Delta\tau)$. The calculations of $\underline{f}(x_{t,i}^+, \mathbb{A}, \Delta\tau)$ are obtained using the state variables $x_{t,i}^+$ and the parameters $\mathbb{A}$ in the ANSM(3) forward rate expressions

from equation 3.85 in section 3.4.1, evaluated at the times-to-maturity incre-
ments $j\Delta\tau$. The calculations of $\omega\left(\mathbb{A}, j\Delta\tau\right)$ are obtained from 4.68 evaluated at the
times-to-maturity increments $j\Delta\tau$.

The K-ANSM(3) interest rate Jacobian is equation 4.32, where $h\left(x_{t,i}^+, \Delta\tau\right)$, ...,
$h\left(x_{t,i}^+, J_K\Delta\tau\right)$ is a sequence of 1×3 vectors out to the longest time to maturity
$J_K\Delta\tau = \tau_K$. Each term of the $h\left(x_{t,i}^+, \mathbb{A}, j\Delta\tau\right)$ sequence is itself a 1×3 vector, which
is obtained as

$$h\left(x_{t,i}^+, \mathbb{A}, , j\Delta\tau\right) = \left[1, \exp\left(-\phi j\Delta\tau\right), \phi j\Delta\tau \exp\left(-\phi j\Delta\tau\right)\right]$$
$$\times \Phi \left[\frac{f\left(x_{t,i}^+, j\Delta\tau\right) - r_L}{\omega\left(j\Delta\tau\right)}\right] \qquad (4.69)$$

4.4.2 Higher-order K-ANSMs

Higher-order K-ANSMs use the ANSMs from subsection 3.4.2 to represent the
shadow term structure. ZLB short rates are always

$$\underline{r}(t) = \max\{r_L, x_1(t) + x_2(t)\} \qquad (4.70)$$

The appropriate evaluation of $\omega(\tau)$ for the given K-ANSM is obtained from
the factor loadings $\exp\left(-\tilde{\kappa}' u\right) b_0$ and the covariance expression $\sigma\sigma'$ evaluated in
equation 3.16. Similar to the calculations involved for higher-order ANSMs, these
results become progressively more complex as more state variables are added. Nevertheless, I have found it straightforward to calculate the analytic expressions for
the higher-order K-ANSMs in Mathematica and then transfer the resulting code
directly to MatLab. Therefore, I have created higher-order K-ANSMs for practical
use as may be required.

4.4.3 Non-arbitrage-free K-ANSMs

The Nelson and Siegel (1987) class of term structure models introduced in subsection 3.4.3 of chapter 3 was shown to be ANSMs with the standard deviation
parameters σ_n set to zero. Setting the standard deviation parameters σ_n to zero
for K-ANSMs therefore offers a class of non-arbitrage-free K-ANSMs, which I will
denote K-NSMs. The shadow term structure for K-NSMs will be non-arbitrage-free
ANSMs, or simply models of the Nelson and Siegel (1987) class, which I will denote
as NSMs.

As discussed in sub-section 3.4.3, NSMs have proven very popular and useful
for empirical analysis in economics and finance, despite not being arbitrage free.
K-NSMs may therefore prove just as useful in ZLB environments. Specifically, the
functional forms for K-NSM interest rates turn out to be almost as simple as for
NSM. Therefore, it appears that estimating K-NSMs from yield curve data as with

NSMs, for example, by yield curve fitting or filtering methods, would be straight-forward. My preliminary investigations with the K-NSM(2) show this to be the case.

To outline the K-NSM framework, I set all standard deviation parameters σ_n for the K-AGM framework to zero. That setting results in $\sigma = 0$, and therefore

$$[\omega(\tau)]^2 = \int_0^\tau b_0' \exp(-\tilde{\kappa} u) \sigma \sigma' \exp(-\tilde{\kappa}' u) b_0 \, du = 0 \tag{4.71}$$

With $\lim_{\omega(\tau) \to 0}$, $\{f(t,\tau) - r_L\}/\omega(\tau)$ takes the values of $\pm\infty$, and so the unit normal density becomes

$$\lim_{\omega(\tau) \to 0} \phi \left[\frac{f(t,\tau) - r_L}{\omega(\tau)} \right] = 0 \tag{4.72}$$

and the unit normal cumulative density becomes

$$\lim_{\omega(\tau) \to 0} \Phi \left[\frac{f(t,\tau) - r_L}{\omega(\tau)} \right] = \begin{cases} 0; & \text{if } f(t,\tau) - r_L < 0 \\ 1; & \text{if } f(t,\tau) - r_L \geq 0 \end{cases}$$
$$= H[f(t,\tau) - r_L] \tag{4.73}$$

where $H[\cdot]$ is the Heaviside step function.

The generic K-AGM forward rate equation 4.12 therefore becomes

$$\underline{f}(t,\tau) = r_L + [f(t,\tau) - r_L] \cdot H[f(t,\tau) - r_L] \tag{4.74}$$

Specifying $f(t,\tau)$ as an NSM will therefore create a K-NSM, that is, an NSM subject to the lower bound r_L.

As an example, the forward rate function for the two-state-variable NSM, or NSM(2), from subsection 3.4.3 is

$$f(t,\tau) = \begin{bmatrix} 1, \exp(-\phi\tau) \end{bmatrix} \begin{bmatrix} x_1(t) \\ x_2(t) \end{bmatrix}$$
$$= x_1(t) + x_2(t) \cdot \exp(-\phi\tau) \tag{4.75}$$

where $x_1(t)$ and $x_1(2)$ are respectively the Level and Slope state variables. The K-NSM(2) is therefore obtained by substituting $f(t,\tau)$ into equation 4.74:

$$\underline{f}(t,\tau) = r_L + \left[x_1(t) + x_2(t) \cdot \exp(-\phi\tau) - r_L \right]$$
$$\times H\left[x_1(t) + x_2(t) \cdot \exp(-\phi\tau) - r_L \right] \tag{4.76}$$

The K-NSM(2) interest rate expression is then

$$\underline{R}(t,\tau) = \frac{1}{\tau} \int_0^\tau \underline{f}(t,u) \, du \tag{4.77}$$

which can be simplified by finding the solution, if any, of

$$x_1(t) + x_2(t) \cdot \exp(-\phi\tau_0) - r_L = 0 \tag{4.78}$$

in the real positive domain $[0, \infty]$. The general solution for τ_0 is

$$\tau_0 = -\frac{1}{\phi} \log\left[-\frac{x_1(t) - r_L}{x_2(t)} \right] \tag{4.79}$$

If $-[x_1(t) - r_L]/x_2(t) \leq 0$, then there is no relevant solution for τ_0, and therefore $H[x_1(t) + x_2(t) \cdot \exp(-\phi\tau) - r_L] = 1$ over the entire domain $[0, \infty]$. In this case, $\underset{\sim}{R}(t, \tau)$ is the NSM(2) interest rate function:

$$\begin{aligned} \underset{\sim}{R}(t, \tau) &= \frac{1}{\tau} \int_0^\tau r_L + \left[x_1(t) + x_2(t) \cdot \exp(-\phi u) - r_L \right] du \\ &= x_1(t) + x_2(t) \cdot \frac{1}{\phi} \left[1 - \exp(-\phi\tau) \right] \end{aligned} \tag{4.80}$$

If $-[x_1(t) - r_L]/x_2(t) > 0$ then there is one relevant solution for τ_0. Therefore

$$H\left[x_1(t) + x_2(t) \cdot \exp(-\phi\tau) - r_L \right] = \begin{cases} 0; & \text{if } \tau < \tau_0 \\ 1; & \text{if } \tau \geq \tau_0 \end{cases} \tag{4.81}$$

In this case, $\underset{\sim}{R}(t, \tau)$ is

$$\begin{aligned} \underset{\sim}{R}(t, \tau) &= \frac{1}{\tau} \left[\int_0^{\tau_0} 0 \, du + \int_{\tau_0}^\tau r_L + \left[x_1(t) + x_2(t) \cdot \exp(-\phi u) - r_L \right] du \right] \\ &= \frac{1}{\tau} \left[x_1(t) \cdot u - x_2(t) \cdot \frac{1}{\phi} \exp(-\phi u) \Big|_{\tau_0}^\tau \right] \\ &= \frac{1}{\tau} \left[x_1(t) \cdot [\tau - \tau_0] + x_2(t) \cdot \frac{1}{\phi} \left[\exp(-\phi\tau_0) - \exp(-\phi\tau) \right] \right] \\ &= x_1(t) \cdot \frac{[\tau - \tau_0]}{\tau} + x_2(t) \cdot \frac{1}{\phi\tau} \left[\exp(-\phi\tau_0) - \exp(-\phi\tau) \right] \end{aligned} \tag{4.82}$$

In summary

$$\underset{\sim}{R}(t, \tau) = \begin{cases} \underset{\sim}{R}_0(t, \tau); & \text{if } f(t, \tau) - r_L < 0 \\ \underset{\sim}{R}_1(t, \tau); & \text{if } f(t, \tau) - r_L \geq 0 \end{cases} \tag{4.83}$$

where $\underset{\sim}{R}_0(t, \tau)$ is the K-NSM(2) interest rate expression in equation 4.80, and $\underset{\sim}{R}_1(t, \tau)$ is the K-NSM(2) interest rate expression in equation 4.82. Note that the shadow term structure for the K-NSM(2) is the NSM(2):

$$R(t, \tau) = x_1(t) + x_2(t) \cdot \frac{1}{\phi} \left[1 - \exp(-\phi\tau) \right] \tag{4.84}$$

and

$$f(t,\tau) = x_1(t) + x_2(t) \cdot \exp(-\phi\tau)$$
$$= \tilde{\mathbb{E}}[r(t+\tau)] = \mathbb{E}[r(t+\tau)] \tag{4.85}$$

The K-NSM(2) therefore captures the key features of the K-ANSM(2), but with a very simple functional form for $\underline{R}(t,\tau)$. Subsection 6.5.3 contains further analysis and discussion that relates to the K-NSM(2).

Similarly, a simple functional form for $\underline{R}(t,\tau)$ could be obtained for the K-NSM(3) by using equation 4.74 with the forward rate defined by the Level, Slope, and Bow state variables:

$$f(t,\tau) = x_1(t) + x_2(t) \cdot \exp(-\phi\tau) + x_3(t) \cdot \phi\tau \exp(-\phi\tau) \tag{4.86}$$

However, note that the relevant solution/s to

$$x_1(t) + x_2(t) \cdot \exp(-\phi\tau) + x_3(t) \cdot \phi\tau \exp(-\phi\tau) - r_L = 0 \tag{4.87}$$

would need to be obtained with a univariate numerical method. In addition, there could potentially be zero, one, or two relevant solutions to account for, so $\underline{R}(t,\tau)$ will generally be composed of three piecewise functions. Subsection 6.5.4 in chapter 6 contains further analysis and discussion that relates to these points.

The K-NSM(2) and K-NSM(3) models may be suitable for directly fitting independently to cross sections of yield curve data as with the NSM(2) and NSM(3), or putting into state space form for use with the IEKF if an allowance for intertemporal dependence of the state variables between the yield curve data observations is desired. These applications remain to be investigated.

4.4.4 Stationary K-AGMs

K-AGMs with stationary GATSM shadow term structures use the stationary GATSM specifications from subsection 3.4.4 to represent the shadow term structure.

To illustrate how such K-AGMs are specified and applied, I will present the key results for a K-AGM with a GATSM(3) shadow term structure, which I denote the K-AGM(3), and also a K-AGM with a GATSM(N) shadow term structure, which I denote the K-AGM(N).

The K-AGM(3) and K-AGM(N) state variables and parameters are respectively identical to those for the GATSM(3) and GATSM(N), except the K-AGM(3) and K-AGM(N) may additionally allow for a non-zero lower bound parameter r_L.

K-AGM(3) ZLB short rates are

$$\underline{r}(t) = \max\{r_L, x_1(t) + x_2(t) + x_3(t)\} \tag{4.88}$$

and K-AGM(N) ZLB short rates are

$$\underline{r}(t) = \max\{r_L, x_1(t) + \ldots + x_N(t)\} \qquad (4.89)$$

K-AGM(3) and K-AGM(N) forward rates are respectively obtained using the generic K-AGM forward rate expression with the GATSM(3) and GATSM(N) forward rate expressions from subsection 3.4.4 as the shadow forward rate $f(t,\tau)$ and the appropriate calculations of the shadow short rate volatility function $\omega(\tau)$. For the K-AGM(3), $\omega(\tau)$ may be calculated using the ANSM(3) factor loadings:

$$b_0 \exp\left(-\tilde{\kappa}'\tau\right) = \left[\exp\left(-\tilde{\kappa}_1\tau\right), \exp\left(-\tilde{\kappa}_2\tau\right), \exp\left(-\tilde{\kappa}_3\tau\right)\right] \qquad (4.90)$$

to evaluate equation 3.16. The result is

$$
\begin{aligned}
[\omega(\tau)]^2 = {} & \sigma_1^2 \cdot G(2\tilde{\kappa}_1, \tau) + \sigma_2^2 \cdot G(2\tilde{\kappa}_2, \tau) + \sigma_3^2 \cdot G(2\tilde{\kappa}_3, \tau) \\
& + 2\rho_{12}\sigma_1\sigma_2 \cdot G(\tilde{\kappa}_1 + \tilde{\kappa}_2, \tau) + 2\rho_{13}\sigma_1\sigma_3 \cdot G(\tilde{\kappa}_1 + \tilde{\kappa}_3, \tau) \\
& + 2\rho_{23}\sigma_2\sigma_3 \cdot G(\tilde{\kappa}_2 + \tilde{\kappa}_3, \tau)
\end{aligned} \qquad (4.91)
$$

For the K-AGM(N), $[\omega(\tau)]^2$ is best represented with a summation:

$$[\omega(\tau)]^2 = \sum_{n=1}^{N} \sigma_n^2 \cdot G(2\tilde{\kappa}_n, \tau) + \sum_{n=1}^{N}\sum_{m=n+1}^{N} \rho_{mn}\sigma_m\sigma_n \cdot G(\tilde{\kappa}_m + \tilde{\kappa}_n, \tau) \qquad (4.92)$$

Partial or full estimations of the K-AGM(3) proceed as summarized in Tables 4.2 or 4.3. Within the measurement iteration step, K-AGM(3), interest rates are obtained using equation 4.25, where $\underline{f}(x_{t,i}^+, \mathbb{A}, \Delta\tau), \ldots, \underline{f}(x_{t,i}^+, \mathbb{A}, J_K\Delta\tau)$ is a sequence of K-AGM(3) forward rates out to the longest time to maturity $J_K\Delta\tau = \tau_K$, and each term $\underline{f}(x_{t,i}^+, \mathbb{A}, j\Delta\tau)$ of that sequence is obtained using the associated sequence of K-AGM(3) shadow forward rates $f(x_{t,i}^+, \mathbb{A}, \Delta\tau), \ldots, f(x_{t,i}^+, \mathbb{A}, J_K\Delta\tau)$ and shadow short rate volatilities $\omega(\mathbb{A}, \Delta\tau), \ldots, \omega(\mathbb{A}, J_K\Delta\tau)$, which are in turn obtained from the K-AGM(3) shadow forward rate expressions from subsection 3.4.1 and shadow short rate volatility from equation 4.91.

The K-AGM(3) Jacobian is equation 4.32, where $h\left(x_{t,i}^+, \Delta\tau\right), \ldots, h\left(x_{t,i}^+, J_K\Delta\tau\right)$ is a sequence of 1×3 vectors out to the longest time to maturity $J_K\Delta\tau = \tau_K$. Each term of the $h\left(x_{t,i}^+, \mathbb{A}, j\Delta\tau\right)$ sequence is itself a 1×3 vector, which is obtained as

$$
\begin{aligned}
h\left(x_{t,i}^+, \mathbb{A},, j\Delta\tau\right) = {} & \left[\exp\left(-\tilde{\kappa}_1 j\Delta\tau\right), \exp\left(-\tilde{\kappa}_2 j\Delta\tau\right), \exp\left(-\tilde{\kappa}_3 j\Delta\tau\right)\right] \\
& \times \Phi\left[\frac{f\left(x_{t,i}^+, j\Delta\tau\right) - r_L}{\omega\left(j\Delta\tau\right)}\right]
\end{aligned} \qquad (4.93)
$$

where $h\left(x_{t,i}^+, \Delta\tau\right), \ldots, h\left(x_{t,i}^+, J_K\Delta\tau\right)$ is a sequence of 1×3 vectors out to the longest time to maturity $J_K\Delta\tau = \tau_K$. Each mean out to the given time to maturity τ_k in row k is a 1×3 vector.

K-AGM(N) interest rates are obtained analogous to the K-AGM(3) above, but using K-AGM(N) forward rates. The K-AGM(N) Jacobian is

$$h\left(x_{t,i}^{+}, \mathbb{A}, j\Delta\tau\right) = \left[\exp\left(-\tilde{\kappa}_1 j\Delta\tau\right), \ldots, \exp\left(-\tilde{\kappa}_N j\Delta\tau\right)\right]$$
$$\times \Phi\left[\frac{f\left(x_{t,i}^{+}, j\Delta\tau\right) - r_L}{\omega\left(j\Delta\tau\right)}\right] \qquad (4.94)$$

where $h\left(x_{t,i}^{+}, \Delta\tau\right), \ldots, h\left(x_{t,i}^{+}, \tau_K\right)$ is a sequence of $1 \times N$ vectors out to the longest time to maturity $J_K \Delta\tau = \tau_K$. Each mean out to the given time to maturity τ_k in row k is a $1 \times N$ vector.

4.5 Empirical applications

4.5.1 K-ANSM(2) results

Tables 4.4 to 4.6 and Figures 4.2 and 4.3 provide the results from estimating the K-ANSM(2) over the entire sample via maximum likelihood with $r_L = 0$. Setting $r_L = 0$ means the parameters for the K-ANSM(2) can be compared directly with those for the ANSM(2), with the only difference being the ZLB mechanism. As with the ANSM(2) in chapter 3, I have expressed θ_1, θ_2, σ_1, and σ_2 and their standard errors in units of percentage points (i.e., the estimates from the optimization have been multiplied by 100), and the remaining parameters are the original estimates. The remaining Kalman filter parameter estimates, $\sigma_\eta(\tau_1), \ldots, \sigma_\eta(\tau_K)$, and their standard errors, in Table 4.5 are expressed in basis points (i.e. the estimates from the optimization have been multiplied by 10000). The selected statistical summaries of the residuals in Tables 4.5 and 4.6 are in basis points.

Table 4.4 K-ANSM(2) time-series parameters and related results

Param.	Estim.	Std err.	Param.	Estim.	Std err.
ϕ	0.2789	0.0046	θ_1 [1]	−9.603	7.752
κ_{11}	0.0001	0.0001	θ_2 [1]	−5.057	4.252
κ_{12}	−0.0021	0.0059	σ_1 [1]	0.861	0.024
κ_{21}	−0.0020	0.0059	σ_2 [1]	1.603	0.090
κ_{22}	0.0703	0.0000	ρ_{12}	−0.5140	0.0297
Log-likelihood: 14659.52					
$\kappa_1 = 0.000, \kappa_2 = 0.0704$					
$\lim_{\tau \to \infty} \mathbb{E}_t\left[r(t+\tau)\right] = -14.660$ pps [1]					

Notes: (1) These values are expressed in percentage points (pps).

Table 4.5 K-ANSM(2) goodness-of-fit results [1]

Mat.	$\sigma_\eta\,(\tau_k)$	Std err.	Mean	Std dev.	RMSE	MAE
0.25	50.1	2.4	−7.0	49.2	49.6	37.5
0.5	36.7	2.0	−5.0	35.8	36.1	28.2
1	18.7	1.6	2.4	18.0	18.2	14.4
2	6.0	0.7	1.6	4.9	5.1	4.1
3	3.5	0.8	0.4	2.5	2.5	2.1
5	4.0	0.7	−0.7	3.9	3.9	3.2
7	0.0	0.5	0.1	0.0	0.1	0.1
10	9.1	0.6	3.1	8.6	9.1	7.6
30	55.7	3.0	37.6	41.2	55.7	47.7

Note: (1) All values are expressed in basis points (bps).

Table 4.6 K-ANSM(2) subsample goodness-of-fit results [1]

Mat.	Dec-1994 to Nov-2008				Dec-2008 to Mar-2014			
	Mean	Stdev	RMSE	MAE	Mean	Stdev	RMSE	MAE
0.25	−11.5	53.5	54.6	43.2	12.7	4.3	13.4	12.7
0.5	−8.5	38.8	39.7	32.0	10.4	6.8	12.4	11.6
1	1.4	19.3	19.3	15.2	6.6	10.2	12.1	11.3
2	1.5	4.3	4.5	3.6	1.9	6.8	7.0	6.1
3	0.5	2.6	2.6	2.1	−0.2	2.2	2.2	1.8
5	−0.9	3.7	3.8	3.0	0.3	4.6	4.6	4.0
7	0.1	0.0	0.1	0.1	0.1	0.0	0.1	0.1
10	4.7	7.9	9.2	7.5	−3.5	8.2	8.9	7.7
30	47.1	38.3	60.6	53.8	−3.3	25.6	25.6	21.1

Note: (1) All values are expressed in basis points (bps).

The parameters in Table 4.4 are those that were used to obtain Figures 2.7 to 2.14 in chapter 2. The points of note from those figures and Tables 4.4 to 4.6 are the following:

- As illustrated in Figure 2.8, the K-ANSM(2) fits the data more closely, and with a natural shape for short maturities, than the ANSM(2). In addition, as illustrated in Figure 2.9, the projected distributions of the short rate and interest rates from the K-ANSM(2) respect the ZLB, unlike the ANSM(2).
- The estimates of the parameters θ_1 and θ_2 in table 4.6, while still negative, are no longer statistically significant from zero. Therefore, the expected value to which the short rate r(t) should converge to over long horizons, that is, $\lim_{\tau \to \infty} \mathbb{E}_t\,[r\,(t+\tau)] = \theta_1 + \theta_2 = -14.660\%$ according to the model, is no longer significantly negative and lacking in economic meaning. In other words,

Table 4.7 K-ANSM(2) time-series parameters (est. lower bound)

Param.	Estim.	Std err.	Param.	Estim.	Std err.
ϕ	0.2931	0.0047	r_L	0.136	0.009
κ_{11}	0.2210	0.0770	θ_1 (1)	6.863	0.546
κ_{12}	−0.0003	0.0004	θ_2 (1)	−0.646	100.51
κ_{21}	0.0000	0.0001	σ_1 (1)	0.827	0.021
κ_{22}	0.0000	0.0001	σ_2 (1)	1.419	0.061
			ρ_{12}	−0.4480	0.0319

Log-likelihood: 15039.40

$\kappa_1 = 0.000$, $\kappa_2 = 0.2910$

$\lim_{\tau \to \infty} \mathbb{E}_t [r(t+\tau)] = 6.217$ pps (1)

Note: (1) These values are expressed in percentage points (pps).

θ_1 and θ_2 could be set to zero or slightly positive values without altering the K-ANSM(2) representation of the yield curve data in a statistically significant sense. Recall that the ANSM(2) result from Table 3.3 was $\lim_{\tau \to \infty} \mathbb{E}_t [r(t+\tau)] = -65.950\%$ and statistically significant.

- The fit to the data is much closer than for the ANSM(2), particularly for the very short times to maturity. Statistically, the K-ANSM(2) log-likelihood value is 14659.52, compared to 14405.61 for the ANSM(2). Hence, the improvement of 253.91 log-likelihood points without any change in the parameters clearly shows that the K-ANSM(2) represents the yield curve data much better than the ANSM(2).

- Panel 1 of Figure 2.8 for the July 2012 yield curve observation shows that the K-ANSM(2), unlike the ANSM(2), does not produce negative short rates. This property is guaranteed in general given the ZLB mechanism $\underline{r}(t) = \max\{r_L, x_1(t) + x_2(t)\}$ with $r_L = 0$ for this example. Figure 2.8 also shows that the K-ANSM(2) produces nonnegative estimates of shorter-maturity interest rates, which are also close to the data. Specifically, as indicated in Figure 4.3 and Table 4.6, there is no longer a persistent highly positive residual for shorter-maturity interest rates in the ZLB period. That is, the means for the 0.25-, 0.5-, and 1-year rates are respectively 12.7, 10.4, and 6.6 basis points, which compares to 57.2, 44.5, and 24.1 basis points for the ANSM(2).

Table 4.7 contains the parameter estimates for the K-ANSM(2), including an allowance for a non-zero estimated lower bound r_L. The results are very similar to those already discussed for the $r_L = 0$ estimation, except the log-likelihood value shows an improved fit to the data. Specifically, the log-likelihood difference is $15039.40 - 14659.52 = 379.88$ for the addition of a single parameter, which is extremely statistically significant given the 99 percent critical value $\chi^{-1}(0.99, 1) = 6.635$ (and the 99.99 percent critical value of 15.137).

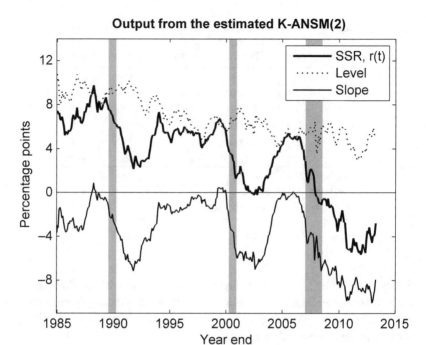

Figure 4.2 Estimated K-ANSM(2) Level and Slope state variables and the associated shadow short rate (SSR).

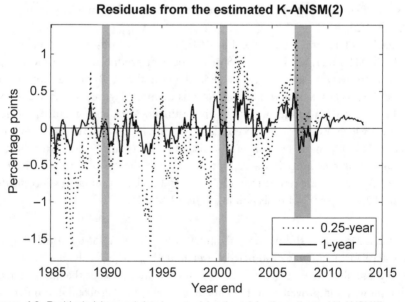

Figure 4.3 Residuals (observed data less model estimate) for the estimated K-ANSM(2).

Table 4.8 K-ANSM(2) subsample goodness-of-fit results (est. LB) [1]

Mat.	$r_L = 0\%$				$r_L = 0.14\%$ (estimated)			
	Mean	Stdev	RMSE	MAE	Mean	Stdev	RMSE	MAE
0.25	12.7	4.3	13.4	12.7	0.4	4.1	4.1	3.3
0.5	10.4	6.8	12.4	11.6	−0.6	4.2	4.2	3.3
1	6.6	10.2	12.1	11.3	−1.9	5.8	6.1	4.2
2	1.9	6.8	7.0	6.1	−1.4	3.7	3.9	3.0
3	−0.2	2.2	2.2	1.8	−0.1	2.7	2.7	2.1
5	0.3	4.6	4.6	4.0	1.6	4.0	4.3	3.4
7	0.1	0.0	0.1	0.1	0.0	0.2	0.2	0.1
10	−3.5	8.2	8.9	7.7	−5.5	6.5	8.5	7.0
30	−3.3	25.6	25.6	21.1	−8.2	20.4	21.8	17.6

Note: (1) All values are expressed in basis points (bps).

Table 4.8 shows that allowing for an estimated value of r_L greatly improves the fit of the model to the short-maturity data in the ZLB subsample, from December 2008 to March 2014. The point value of $\lim_{\tau \to \infty} \mathbb{E}_t \left[r(t + \tau) \right]$ is now also very plausible. The value of $r_L = 0.14\%$ is consistent with the US Federal Reserve persistently allowing a mildly positive Federal Funds Rate within the middle of the Federal Funds Target Rate range of 0 to 0.25 percent, and market participants allowing for that mildly positive value in their expectations.

To summarize, the K-ANSM(2) fits the data much better than the ANSM(2), and the K-ANSM(2) has no issues coping with the ZLB environment. In particular, it produces short rate and yield curve estimates along with their projected distributions that are consistent with the interest rate data and the ZLB constraint.

The K-ANSM(2) produces a series of shadow short rates that adopt negative values following the onset of the ZLB environment in December 2008 in the wake of the Global Financial Crisis. Therefore, the estimated shadow short rate series suggests itself as a quantitative measure for the stance of monetary policy during the ZLB environment. However, in chapter 7, I will show that the magnitudes of the estimated shadow short rates are different for the K-ANSM(2) depending on whether $r_L = 0$ or whether r_L is estimated. This sensitivity to model specification also shows up for the K-ANSM(3) in the following section.

4.5.2 K-ANSM(3) results

Tables 4.9 and 4.10 contain the analogous results to those previously described for the K-ANSM(2), but for the K-ANSM(3). Once again, I first present the results for the K-ANSM(3) with $r_L = 0$, so I can directly compare them with the ANSM(3) in subsection 3.5.3. I then provide results for the K-ANSM(3) with an estimated value of r_L. The main points are the following:

Table 4.9 K-ANSM(3) time-series parameters and related results

Param.	Estim.	Std err.	Param.	Estim.	Std err.
ϕ	0.5681	0.0020	$\theta_1^{(1)}$	7.313	2.927
κ_{11}	0.1909	0.1048	$\theta_2^{(1)}$	−2.601	3.281
κ_{12}	0.0004	0.1850	$\theta_3^{(1)}$	−0.240	4.962
κ_{13}	−0.1375	0.1044	$\sigma_1^{(1)}$	0.648	0.039
κ_{21}	0.1796	0.1845	$\sigma_2^{(1)}$	1.193	0.041
κ_{22}	0.3685	0.2831	$\sigma_3^{(1)}$	3.000	0.167
κ_{23}	−0.2208	0.2096	ρ_{12}	−0.6115	0.0246
κ_{31}	−0.6418	0.4319	ρ_{13}	−0.2225	0.0627
κ_{32}	0.0116	0.9254	ρ_{23}	0.1084	0.0565
κ_{33}	0.6086	0.3464			

Log-likelihood: 16039.90

$\kappa_1 = 0.0371$, $\kappa_2 = 0.3740$, $\kappa_3 = 0.7570$

$\lim_{\tau \to \infty} \mathbb{E}_t [r(t+\tau)] = 4.712$ pps $^{(1)}$

Note: (1) These values are expressed in percentage points (pps).

- The K-ANSM(3) provides a much better fit to the yield curve data than the ANSM(3). The difference is $16039.90 - 15889.89 = 150.01$. Hence, the improvement of 150.01 log-likelihood points without any change in the parametrization clearly shows that the K-ANSM(3) represents the yield curve data much better than the ANSM(3).

- The K-ANSM(3) also provides a much better fit to the yield curve data than the K-ANSM(2). Specifically, the log-likelihood difference is $16039.90 - 14659.52 = 1380.4$ with nine additional parameters, which is extremely statistically significant. The 99 percent critical value with nine degrees of freedom is 21.666, and the 99.99 percent critical value is 29.878.

- Aside from providing a very good fit to the data, Figure 4.6 shows that the K-ANSM(3) short rates, interest rates, and their projected distributions all respect the ZLB, unlike the ANSM(3).

Table 4.12 contains the K-ANSM(3) parameter estimates, including an allowance for a non-zero estimated lower bound r_L. The results are very similar to those already discussed for the $r_L = 0$ estimation, except for an improved fit to the data. In particular, the log-likelihood improvement is $16115.08 - 16039.90 = 75.18$, which is extremely statistically significant given the 99 and 99.99 percent critical values of 6.635 and 15.137.

The K-ANSM(3) with an allowance for the a non-zero estimated lower bound r_L is therefore the best model overall, at least from the perspective of fitting the yield curve data, and the ZLB mechanism means that the projected distributions of short rates and interest rates from the model respect the lower bound r_L. However, in

Table 4.10 K-ANSM(3) goodness-of-fit results [1]

Maturity	$\sigma_\eta\left(\tau_k\right)$	Std err.	Mean	Stdev	RMSE	MAE
0.25	12.2	0.6	−1.9	11.8	11.9	8.6
0.5	1.9	0.8	−0.1	0.5	0.5	0.4
1	11.8	0.6	6.0	10.2	11.8	9.0
2	5.9	0.4	2.8	5.2	5.9	4.8
3	0.8	0.4	−0.0	0.2	0.2	0.1
5	4.2	0.6	−2.1	3.3	3.9	3.3
7	3.0	0.9	−0.3	1.6	1.6	1.2
10	10.6	0.6	6.0	8.0	10.0	8.4
30	47.9	3.4	34.3	33.7	48.1	40.2

Note: (1) All values are expressed in basis points (bps).

Table 4.11 K-ANSM(3) subsample goodness-of-fit results [1]

Mat.	Dec-1994 to Nov-2008				Dec-2008 to Jan-2014			
	Mean	Stdev	RMSE	MAE	Mean	Stdev	RMSE	MAE
0.25	−2.3	12.7	12.9	9.4	0.2	5.9	5.9	5.1
0.5	−0.2	0.5	0.5	0.4	0.3	0.4	0.5	0.4
1	7.6	10.3	12.8	10.1	−1.0	5.5	5.5	4.7
2	3.7	4.9	6.2	5.0	−1.2	4.3	4.5	3.8
3	0.0	0.1	0.1	0.1	−0.1	0.2	0.3	0.2
5	−2.9	2.7	4.0	3.3	1.2	3.6	3.8	3.2
7	−0.4	1.5	1.5	1.1	0.0	2.2	2.1	1.6
10	7.9	7.0	10.5	8.9	−2.3	6.9	7.3	6.4
30	42.0	31.1	52.2	45.5	0.9	22.4	22.2	17.3

Note: (1) All values are expressed in basis points (bps).

Chapter 7, I will discuss why the best fit does not always produce the most useful output for monetary policy purposes.

4.6 Alternative estimation methods

4.6.1 Estimation using forward rates

Wu and Xia (2013, 2014) has pointed out that K-AGMs can be estimated directly from forward rates. The advantage of using forward rates as data for K-AGM estimations, as highlighted by Wu and Xia (2013, 2014), is that numerical integration is no longer required in the measurement estimate step as with K-AGM estimations

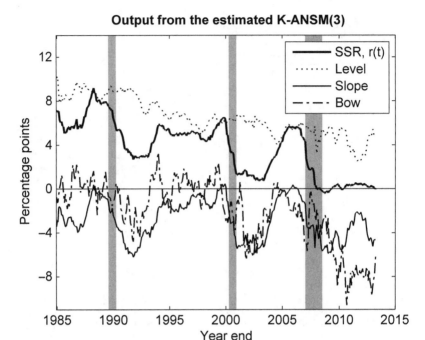

Figure 4.4 Estimated K-ANSM(3) Level, Slope, and Bow state variables and the associated shadow short rate (SSR).

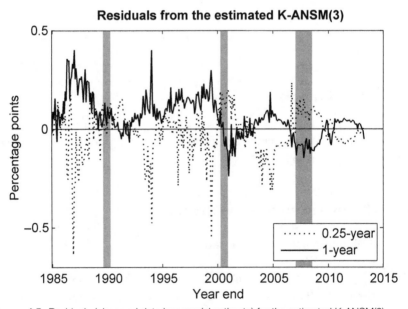

Figure 4.5 Residuals (observed data less model estimate) for the estimated K-ANSM(3).

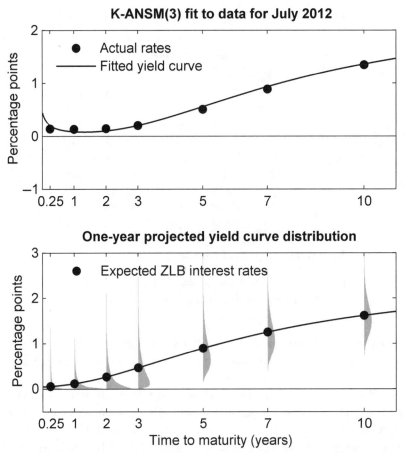

Figure 4.6 K-ANSM(3) ZLB yield curve with state variables estimated from data observed in a ZLB environment (panel 1). The ZLB yield curve and the projected ZLB interest rate distributions (panel 1) are constrained by the ZLB mechanism to be nonnegative.

using interest rate data. I will demonstrate this point shortly with a K-ANSM(2) example.

However, the disadvantage of using forward rates for K-AGM estimations is that such data are typically not readily available or obtainable from standard sources. Specifically, many yield curve data sets simply report the zero-coupon interest rates generated from the originally observed coupon-paying yield curve data without reporting either implied forward rates or the parameters from the data generation that would be required to construct forward rates. For example, the zero-coupon OIS data available on Bloomberg that I use in this book are generated using a standard method of bootstrapping (i.e., removing the estimated present value of coupon payments to create synthetic zero-coupon bonds) with piecewise linear interpolations between maturities (see Kushnir [2009] for method details, or Hull [2000] for a general description of that approach). However, the implied forward

Table 4.12 K-ANSM(3) time-series parameters (est. lower bound)

Param.	Estim.	Std err.	Param.	Estim.	Std err.
ϕ	0.5637	0.0002	r_L [1]	0.118	0.003
κ_{11}	0.1824	0.0317	θ_1 [1]	6.887	0.150
κ_{12}	−0.0023	0.0021	θ_2 [1]	−4.410	0.007
κ_{13}	−0.1322	0.0001	θ_3 [1]	−1.869	0.144
κ_{21}	0.4040	0.0175	σ_1 [1]	0.594	0.004
κ_{22}	0.3709	0.0425	σ_2 [1]	1.226	0.007
κ_{23}	−0.3602	0.0002	σ_3 [1]	2.856	0.004
κ_{31}	−1.2597	0.0232	ρ_{12}	−0.5684	0.0072
κ_{32}	−0.0993	0.3348	ρ_{13}	−0.0073	0.0126
κ_{33}	0.9949	0.0233	ρ_{23}	−0.1692	0.0309

Log-likelihood: 16115.08

$\kappa_1 = 0.0105, \kappa_2 = 0.3324, \kappa_3 = 1.2054$

$\lim_{\tau \to \infty} \mathbb{E}_t\left[r(t+\tau)\right] = 2.477$ pps [1]

Note: (1) These values are expressed in percentage points (pps).

rate data or the parameters associated with each bootstrapped yield curve are not reported. The same issue would arise generally for interest rate data generated from spline-based bootstrapping techniques.

Nevertheless, it is straightforward to construct forward rates if the relevant parameters are available or the generation method is simple enough to infer forward rates from the yield curve data. For example, Wu and Xia (2013, 2014) construct 1-month forward rates from estimated Svensson (1995)/Nelson and Siegel (1987) model parameters. Those parameters are obtained by independently fitting observations of coupon-paying yield curve data, as detailed in Gürkaynak, Sack, and Wright (2007), and the resulting set of zero-coupon data and the estimated parameters are maintained by the Federal Reserve Board. Continuous-time K-AGMs could be estimated analogously using instantaneous forward rates constructed from the same data set. Specifically, the instantaneous forward rate function $\underline{f}_{t,k}$ for the given time index t and time to maturity τ_k has the functional form:

$$\underline{f}_{t,k} = \beta_1 + \beta_2 \cdot \exp\left(-\lambda_1 \tau_k\right) + \beta_3 \cdot \lambda_1 \tau_k \exp\left(-\lambda_1 \tau_k\right)$$
$$+ \beta_4 \cdot \lambda_2 \tau_k \exp\left(-\lambda_2 \tau_k\right) \tag{4.95}$$

where β_1, β_2, β_3, β_4, λ_1, and λ_2 are the estimated Svensson (1995)/Nelson and Siegel (1987) model parameters for a given time t. Calculating $\underline{f}_{t,k}$ for all of the required times to maturity/forward horizons τ_1 to τ_K and stacking them gives the $K \times 1$ vector of constructed forward rates $\underline{f}_t$. Repeating that process for each time step over the entire sample therefore gives a time series of forward rate data $\{\underline{f}_1, \ldots, \underline{f}_T\}$ that can be used to estimate the K-AGM. Another source of implied

Table 4.13 K-AGM estimation using forward rate data

3.2. Measurement/prior estimates:

Set : $x_{t,0}^+ = x_t^-$

ITERATE : from $i = 0$

$\eta_{f,t,i} = f_t - f\left(x_{t,i}^+, \mathbb{A}\right) - H_{f,t,i}\left(x_t^- - x_{t,i}^+\right)$

$H_{f,t,i} = \left.\frac{\partial}{\partial x(t)} f[x(t), \mathbb{A}]\right|_{x(t)=x_{t,i}^+}$

$M_{f,t,i} = H_{f,t,i} P_t^- H_{f,t,i}' + \Omega_\eta$

$K_{f,t,i} = P_t^- H_{f,t,i}' M_{t,i}^{-1}$

$x_{t,i+1}^+ = x_{t,i}^+ + K_{f,t,i} \eta_{f,t,i}$

EXIT : at max (i) or $\left|x_{t,i+1}^+ - x_{t,i}^+\right|$ tolerance

---

forward rates would be from interest rate data sets generated using the Fama and Bliss (1987) method. That method is essentially based on bootstrapping with piecewise constant forward rates between maturities, and therefore, it would be straightforward to transform Fama and Bliss (1987) zero yield curve data into implied forward rates.

Assuming a data set of forward rates $\{f_1, \ldots, f_T\}$ is available, the measurement estimate step of Tables 4.2 or 4.3 would then be replaced with the steps in Table 4.13. The important point is that $\eta_{f,t,i}$ and $H_{f,t,i}$ may be obtained as closed-form analytic expressions from the forward rate specification of the K-AGM, as I will now illustrate with the K-ANSM(2) example. Note that I will continue to assume $K = 9$, and that the maturities τ_k for the forward rate data are the same as my interest rate data.

For the K-ANSM(2), the forward rate residual vector $\eta_{f,t,i}$ is

$$\eta_{f,t,i} = f_t - f\left(x_{t,i}^+, \mathbb{A}\right) - H_{t,i}\left(x_t^- - x_{t,i}^+\right)$$

$$\begin{bmatrix} \eta_{f,t,i,1} \\ \vdots \\ \eta_{f,t,i,9} \end{bmatrix} = \begin{bmatrix} f_{t,1} \\ \vdots \\ f_{t,9} \end{bmatrix} - \begin{bmatrix} f\left(x_{t,i}^+, \tau_1\right) \\ \vdots \\ f\left(x_{t,i}^+, \tau_1\right) \end{bmatrix}$$

$$- \begin{bmatrix} H_{f,t,1} \\ \vdots \\ H_{f,t,9} \end{bmatrix} \left(\begin{bmatrix} x_1^-(t) \\ x_2^-(t) \end{bmatrix} - \begin{bmatrix} x_{1,i}^+(t) \\ x_{2,i}^+(t) \end{bmatrix} \right) \qquad (4.96)$$

where each $f\left(x_{t,i}^+, \mathbb{A}, \tau_k\right)$ is obtained from the K-ANSM(2) forward rate expression in equation 4.51. The forward rate Jacobian $H_{f,t,i}$ is the 9×2 vector:

$$H_{f,t,i} = \begin{bmatrix} h\left(x_{t,i}^+, \mathbb{A}, \tau_1\right) \\ \vdots \\ h\left(x_{t,i}^+, \mathbb{A}, \tau_9\right) \end{bmatrix}_{9\times2} \qquad (4.97)$$

where each $h\left(x_{t,i}^{+}, \mathbb{A}, \tau_k\right)$ is obtained from equation 4.56. Because $\underline{f}\left(x_{t,i}^{+}, \mathbb{A}, \tau_k\right)$ and $h\left(x_{t,i}^{+}, \mathbb{A}, \tau_k\right)$ are closed-form analytic functions, calculating $\eta_{\underline{f},t,i}$ and $H_{\underline{f},t,i}$ is very straightforward.

4.6.2 Estimation using bond prices

A more general disadvantage of using either interest rates or forward rates generated from the originally observed coupon-paying yield curve data (e.g., by independent yield curve fitting or bootstrapping methods) is that the generated data will be subject to misspecification and/or any effects from ignoring estimation residuals from the generation process. Any such issues with the generated data will in turn influence the results of the term structure model being estimated with the generated data. For example, Pancost (2013) shows that the Gurkaynak, Sack, and Wright (2007) generated interest rate data sometimes deviates very materially from the original data it was derived from. Forward rate data are likely to be even more sensitive to such effects.

As discussed in chapter 3, when estimating GATSMs the distinct benefit of using generated interest rate or forward rate data is that it can be matched with the linear GATSM expressions for interest rates or forward rates. Therefore estimation may be undertaken using the Kalman filter algorithm rather than a nonlinear Kalman filter algorithm. For most applications, this relative benefit will typically more than counter any potential detrimental influence from using generated data.

However, for K-AGMs a nonlinear Kalman filter algorithm is already required for any representation of the term structure data. Therefore the relative benefit of using generated interest rate or forward rate data is no longer as distinct. In other words, if using a nonlinear Kalman filter is already required, then one might as well undertake the K-AGM estimations with the originally observed coupon-paying yield curve data to remove any potential influences from using generated interest rate or forward rate data. This would involve accounting for multiple cashflows for each observed bond price, as I will outline further below, but the logistical issues in doing so are not onerous; Krippner (2006) and Pancost (2013) are examples of estimating GATSMs directly using coupon-paying bond data.

I do not actually pursue an estimation for K-AGMs using bond prices in this book, but I intend to set up the K-AGM estimations to allow for such estimations in future research. To illustrate how this will be done, I begin with the simplest case of zero-coupon bond prices. I then generalize those results to coupon-paying bonds.

For estimations using zero-coupon bond prices, I assume a data set of such bond prices rates $\{\underline{P}_1,\ldots,\underline{P}_T\}$ is available. Otherwise, a data set can be generated readily from zero-coupon interest rate data using the relationship:

$$\underline{P}_{t,k} = \exp\left(-\tau_k \cdot \underline{R}_{t,k}\right) \tag{4.98}$$

Table 4.14 K-AGM estimation using bond price data

3.2. Measurement estimates:

Set : $x_{t,0}^{+} = x_t^{-}$

ITERATE : from $i = 0$

$\eta_{\mathbb{P},t,i} = \mathbb{P}_t - \mathbb{P}\left(x_{t,i}^{+}, \mathbb{A}\right) - H_{\underline{f},t,i}\left(x_t^{-} - x_{t,i}^{+}\right)$

$H_{\mathbb{P},t,i} = \frac{\partial}{\partial x(t)}\mathbb{P}\left[x(t), \mathbb{A}\right]\Big|_{x(t)=x_{t,i}^{+}}$

$M_{\mathbb{P},t,i} = H_{\mathbb{P},t,i}P_t^{-}H_{\mathbb{P},t,i}' + \Omega_\eta$

$K_{\mathbb{P},t,i} = P_t^{-}H_{\mathbb{P},t,i}'M_{t,i}^{-1}$

$x_{t,i+1}^{+} = x_{t,i}^{+} + K_{\mathbb{P},t,i}\,\eta_{\mathbb{P},t,i}$

EXIT : at $\max(i)$ or $\left|x_{t,i+1}^{+} - x_{t,i}^{+}\right|$ tolerance

---

The measurement estimate step of Tables 4.2 or 4.3 would then be replaced with the steps in Table 4.14. To illustrate the application of Table 4.14, I will again use my K-ANSM(2) example. Zero-coupon bond price residuals $\eta_{\mathbb{P},t,i}$ are

$$\eta_{\mathbb{P},t,i} = \mathbb{P}_t - \mathbb{P}\left(x_{t,i}^{+}, \mathbb{A}\right) - H_{\mathbb{P},t,i}\left(x_t^{-} - x_{t,i}^{+}\right)$$

$$\begin{bmatrix} \eta_{\mathbb{P},t,i,1} \\ \vdots \\ \eta_{\mathbb{P},t,i,K} \end{bmatrix} = \begin{bmatrix} \mathbb{P}_{t,1} \\ \vdots \\ \mathbb{P}_{t,9} \end{bmatrix} - \begin{bmatrix} \mathbb{P}\left(x_{t,i}^{+}, \tau_1\right) \\ \vdots \\ \mathbb{P}\left(x_{t,i}^{+}, \tau_9\right) \end{bmatrix}$$

$$- \begin{bmatrix} H_{\mathbb{P},t,1} \\ \vdots \\ H_{\mathbb{P},t,9} \end{bmatrix} \left(\begin{bmatrix} x_1^{-}(t) \\ x_2^{-}(t) \end{bmatrix} - \begin{bmatrix} x_{1,i}^{+}(t) \\ x_{2,i}^{+}(t) \end{bmatrix} \right) \qquad (4.99)$$

where each $\mathbb{P}\left(x_{t,i}^{+}, \mathbb{A}, \tau_k\right)$ is obtained from the K-ANSM(2) zero-coupon bond price expression:

$$\mathbb{P}\left(x_{t,i}^{+}, \mathbb{A}, \tau_k\right) = \exp\left[-\tau_k \cdot \underline{R}\left(x_{t,i}^{+}, \mathbb{A}, \tau_k\right)\right] \qquad (4.100)$$

with $\underline{R}\left(x_{t,i}^{+}, \mathbb{A}, \tau_k\right)$ as previously defined in section 4.3, that is,

$$\underline{R}\left(x_{t,i}^{+}, \mathbb{A}, \tau_k\right) = \mathrm{mean}\left\{\underline{f}\left(x_{t,i}^{+}, \mathbb{A}, \Delta\tau\right), \ldots, \underline{f}\left(x_{t,i}^{+}, \mathbb{A}, J_k\Delta\tau\right)\right\} \qquad (4.101)$$

The zero-coupon bond price Jacobian $H_{\mathbb{P},t,i}$ is the 9×2 vector:

$$H_{\mathbb{P},t,i} = \begin{bmatrix} H_{\mathbb{P},t,i,1} \\ \vdots \\ H_{\mathbb{P},t,i,9} \end{bmatrix}_{9 \times 2} \qquad (4.102)$$

where

$$H_{\underline{P},t,i,k} = \left. \frac{\partial}{\partial x(t)} \underline{P}\,[x(t), \mathbb{A}, \tau_k] \right|_{x(t)=x_{t,i}^+}$$

$$= \left. \frac{\partial}{\partial x(t)} \exp\left(-\tau_k \cdot \underline{R}\,[x(t), \mathbb{A}, \tau_k]\right) \right|_{x(t)=x_{t,i}^+}$$

$$= \left. -\tau_k \cdot \exp\left(-\tau_k \cdot \underline{R}\,[x(t), \mathbb{A}, \tau_k]\right) \cdot \frac{\partial}{\partial x(t)} \underline{R}\,[x(t), \mathbb{A}, \tau_k] \right|_{x(t)=x_{t,i}^+}$$

$$= -\tau_k \cdot \underline{P}\left(x_{t,i}^+, \mathbb{A}, \tau_k\right) H_{t,i,k} \tag{4.103}$$

$H_{t,i,k}$ is the expression for row k of the interest rate Jacobian $H_{t,i,k}$ previously defined in section 4.3, that is,

$$H_{t,i,k} = \text{mean}\left\{ h\left(x_{t,i}^+, \mathbb{A}, \Delta\tau\right), \ldots, h\left(x_{t,i}^+, \mathbb{A}, J_k\Delta\tau\right) \right\} \tag{4.104}$$

In summary

$$H_{\underline{P},t,i} = \begin{bmatrix} -\tau_1 \cdot \underline{P}\left(x_{t,i}^+, \mathbb{A}, \tau_1\right) H_{t,i,1} \\ \vdots \\ -\tau_9 \cdot \underline{P}\left(x_{t,i}^+, \mathbb{A}, \tau_9\right) H_{t,i,K} \end{bmatrix}_{9\times 2} \tag{4.105}$$

Therefore, both $\underline{P}\left(x_{t,i}^+, \mathbb{A}, \tau_k\right)$ and $H_{\underline{P},t,i}$ may be readily obtained from the interest rate expressions already provided in section 4.3 for the K-ANSM(2). For other K-AGMs, $\underline{P}\left(x_{t,i}^+, \mathbb{A}, \tau_k\right)$ and $H_{\underline{P},t,i}$ are obtained using the relevant K-AGM interest rate vector $\underline{R}\left(x_{t,i}^+, \mathbb{A}\right)$ and the interest rate Jacobian $H_{\underline{P},t,i}$.

The bonds and OIS contracts that actually trade in financial markets almost always bear coupons or regular fixed payments, and so the zero-coupon expressions above therefore need adjusting to allow for the intermediate cashflows between settlement and maturity. Specifically, each K-AGM bond price $\underline{P}\left(x_{t,i}^+, \mathbb{A}, \tau_k\right)$ becomes a weighted sum:

$$\underline{P}\left(x_{t,i}^+, \mathbb{A}, \tau_k\right) = \sum_{l=1}^{L(k)} C_{l,k} \cdot \exp\left[-\tau_{l,k} \cdot \underline{R}\left(x_{t,i}^+, \tau_{l,k}\right)\right] \tag{4.106}$$

where $L(k)$ is the number of cashflows for the bond k, $C_{l,k}$ is the cashflow l for bond k (specifically, the cashflows are: the negated settlement price as per the market quotation for the first cashflow; the coupon amounts or fixed payments due between settlement and maturity; and the final coupon or fixed payment plus the return of principle at maturity), and $\tau_{l,k}$ are the times of the cashflows relative to the observation.

Similarly, each row of the Jacobian $H_{\underline{P},t,i,k}$ also becomes a weighted sum, that is,

$$H_{\underline{P},t,i,k} = -\sum_{l=1}^{L(k)} \left\{ C_{l,k} \cdot \tau_{l,k} \cdot \underline{P}\left(x_{t,i}^+, \mathbb{A}, \tau_{l,k}\right) \right.$$

$$\times \left(\frac{1}{\tau_{l,k}} \int_0^{\tau_{l,k}} b_0' \exp\left(-\tilde{\kappa}'u\right) \right.$$

$$\left. \left. \times \Phi\left[\frac{f\left(x_{t,i}^+, \mathbb{A}, u\right) - r_L}{\omega(u)} \right] du \right) \right\} \qquad (4.107)$$

In summary, at the cost of a few more lines of programming, the K-ANSM IEKF estimation based on generated interest rates can readily be converted to an IEKF estimation using the interest rate security data that is actually observed in markets.

4.6.3 Iterative estimation using GATSMs

Rather than estimating K-AGMs directly via a nonlinear Kalman filter, it may be possible to base K-AGM estimations on iterations of GATSM estimations of the implied shadow term structure. I present an overview of the process for readers to consider, but I stress upfront that the procedure is just an idea and I have not yet tested it. Furthermore, even if it does work as envisaged and achieves convergence, there is no guarantee that the resulting parameter estimates will be statistically equivalent to those obtained from the IEKF estimation, so it may not be practically useful. Therefore, undertaking that testing would be required before using it in practice.

All that said, if the procedure does work as envisaged, then it may provide a ready means of converting any existing GATSM estimation framework into a K-AGM estimation framework. In particular, some fast and efficient procedures for estimating discrete-time GATSMs have recently been developed in the literature. For example, see Joslin, Singleton, and Zhu (2011), Hamilton and Wu (2012), and Adrian, Moench, and Crump (2014). Hence, being able to use those methods to estimate the shadow GATSM within a K-AGM may offer fast and efficient means for estimating K-AGMs. Discrete-time or continuous-time K-AGMs could also be estimated by using the Kalman filter to estimate the shadow GATSMs.

Table 4.15 provides the overview of the algorithm I envisage, and I explain each step below. Note that I have presented the entire process from the perspective of using interest rate data, which makes the most sense if the linearity of GATSM estimation is to be maintained. Forward rate data would also maintain that linearity, while bond price data would not, as previously discussed in subsection 4.6.2.

A brief explanation of the steps in Table 4.15 is as follows:

- Step A estimates the GATSM on the yield curve data set $\{\underline{R}_1, \ldots, \underline{R}_T\}$:

Table 4.15 Iterative K-AGM estimation

A. Estimate GATSM with $\left\{ \underset{\sim}{R}_1,\ldots,\underset{\sim}{R}_T \right\}$

$\quad \left\{ \underset{\sim}{R}_1,\ldots,\underset{\sim}{R}_T \right\} \Rightarrow \{x_1,\ldots,x_T\}_{\text{GATSM}}$ and $\mathbb{A}_{\text{GATSM}}$

$\quad \{x_1,\ldots,x_T\}_{\text{GATSM}}$ and $\mathbb{A}_{\text{GATSM}} \Rightarrow \{Z_1,\ldots,Z_T\}_0$

B. K-AGM shadow GATSM estimations:

$\quad$ **ITERATE:** from $i = 0$

$\quad\quad \{R_1,\ldots,R_T\}_i = \left\{ \underset{\sim}{R}_1,\ldots,\underset{\sim}{R}_T \right\} - \{Z_1,\ldots,Z_T\}_i$

$\quad\quad$ Estimate shadow-GATSM with $\{R_1,\ldots,R_T\}_i$

$\quad\quad \{x_1,\ldots,x_T\}_i$ and $\mathbb{A}_i \Rightarrow \{Z_1,\ldots,Z_T\}_{i+1}$

$\quad$ **EXIT:** at tolerance for changes to $\mathbb{A}_i$

$\quad\quad$ (or shadow GATSM log-likelihood value)

C. Diagnostics of estimated model

- The yield curve data is subject to the ZLB, while the GATSM allows negative interest rates. Therefore the resulting state variables $\{x_1,\ldots,x_T\}_{\text{GATSM}}$ and parameter estimates $\mathbb{A}_{\text{GATSM}}$ will not be a valid representation of the yield curve data.

- However, the results $\{x_1,\ldots,x_T\}_{\text{GATSM}}$ and $\mathbb{A}_{\text{GATSM}}$ can be used to obtain an initial estimate of the implied K-ANSM interest rate option effect $Z(t,\tau)$ for all of the yield curve observations. I have denoted these estimates as the time series $\{Z_1,\ldots,Z_T\}_0$, which is an implied interest rate option effect data set. $\{Z_1,\ldots,Z_T\}_0$ is a matrix with the same dimensions as the yield curve data set, that is, $K \times T$. Specifically, each column of $\{Z_1,\ldots,Z_T\}_0$ is the $K \times 1$ vector of interest rate option effects $Z(t,\tau)$ for each time to maturity in the data set, and there will be T columns; that is,

$$\{Z_1,\ldots,Z_T\} = \begin{bmatrix} Z_1(\tau_1) & \cdots & Z_T(\tau_1) \\ \vdots & \vdots & \vdots \\ Z_1(\tau_K) & \cdots & Z_T(\tau_K) \end{bmatrix}_{K \times T} \tag{4.108}$$

- **B. K-AGM shadow GATSM estimations:**

  - An implied shadow yield curve data set $\{R_1,\ldots,R_T\}_0$ is calculated from the ZLB yield curve data set $\left\{ \underset{\sim}{R}_1,\ldots,\underset{\sim}{R}_T \right\}$ and $\{Z_1,\ldots,Z_T\}_0$.
  - The shadow GATSM is then estimated from $\{R_1,\ldots,R_T\}_0$ to obtain state variables $\{x_1,\ldots,x_T\}_0$ and parameters $\mathbb{A}_0$.
  - The shadow GATSM results $\{x_1,\ldots,x_T\}_0$ and $\mathbb{A}_0$ are used to obtain an updated implied interest rate option effect data set $\{Z_1,\ldots,Z_T\}_1$.
  - The procedure now iterates, so a new implied shadow yield curve data set $\{R_1,\ldots,R_T\}_1$ is calculated from the ZLB yield curve data set $\left\{ \underset{\sim}{R}_1,\ldots,\underset{\sim}{R}_T \right\}$ and $\{Z_1,\ldots,Z_T\}_1$.

- The process then continues to iterate between the steps

  - Update the estimate of the shadow GATSM given the implied shadow yield curve data set $\{R_1, \ldots, R_T\}_i$.
  - Update the implied interest rate option effect data set $\{Z_1, \ldots, Z_T\}_i$ using the updated estimate of the shadow GATSM.
  - Update the implied shadow yield curve data set $\{R_1, \ldots, R_T\}_{i+1}$ using the updated implied interest rate option effect data set $\{Z_1, \ldots, Z_T\}_i$.
  - Convergence is achieved when the changes to $\mathbb{A}_i$ from the previous iteration are less than a given tolerance. Alternatively, if the shadow GATSM estimation passes a log-likelihood value, then convergence could be based on changes to those values being less than a given tolerance.

- **C. Diagnostics of estimated model**

  - The diagnostics include the estimated standard errors for the parameter estimates, goodness of fit evaluations, and so forth, as already discussed.

4.7 Summary

- In this chapter, I have developed the Krippner (2011, 2012b,c, 2013d,e) shadow/ZLB-GATSM, or K-AGM, framework as a relatively tractable modification to the GATSM class. The fundamental modification is to represent and value the availability of physical currency as an option against future realizations of negative values of the shadow short rate (or values below any specified non-zero lower bound).
- Any GATSM specification from chapter 3 can be used to represent the shadow term structure, and the K-AGM option expression leads to ZLB forward rates that are always a closed-form analytic expressions. Interest rates are therefore always straightforward to evaluate, using a univariate numerical integral over time to maturity, and they are guaranteed to be nonnegative.
- K-AGM ZLB interest rates are a nonlinear function of the state variables, so I detail how to use the iterated extended Kalman filter to allow for that nonlinearity when estimating K-AGMs. I have found the iterated extended Kalman filter to be more reliable for estimations than the extended Kalman filter.
- I have provided a fully worked example for the two-state variable K-ANSM, or K-ANSM(2), which uses the ANSM(2) from chapter 3 to represent the shadow yield curve and the K-AGM framework to impose the ZLB constraint. I have also provided the results for a full estimation of the K-ANSM(2), and the key expressions and estimation results for the K-ANSM(3).
- The results for the K-ANSM(2) and the K-ANSM(3) show substantially better fits to the yield curve data overall and in ZLB environments than their ANSM

counterparts. The K-ANSM(2) and the K-ANSM(3) also eliminate any negative fitted interest rates and probabilities of future negative interest rates. The K-ANSM(3) with an estimated non-zero bound provides the best fit to the yield curve data set overall.

5 | Black Framework for ZLB Term Structure Modeling

In this chapter, I provide an exposition of the shadow/ZLB-GATSM framework based on the approach first suggested in Black (1995) and using a GATSM to represent the shadow term structure. Hence, for brevity in the remainder of this book, I will hereafter adopt the abbreviation B-AGM (for Black affine Gaussian model) to denote the framework. The B-AGM framework is seen by many as the benchmark for shadow/ZLB-GATSMs and, as I will discuss in section 5.2, many authors have developed and applied B-AGMs using various methods. However, as I will discuss further below, there is a strong case for using the K-AGM framework as an alternative, at least from a practical perspective and potentially also on theoretical grounds. Providing a complete overview of the B-AGM framework and an explicit comparison to the K-AGM framework will best enable readers to make an informed choice about which framework they prefer to use.

I begin in section 5.1 by specifying B-AGMs in principle and using straightforward calculus to detail precisely how B-AGMs and K-AGMs are related. Section 5.2 provides an overview of the various numerical methods that have been used to implement B-AGMs in practice; that is, to generate a yield curve from a single set of B-AGM state variables and parameters. Section 5.3 contains a more in-depth discussion of Monte Carlo methods, which are generally preferred for B-AGMs with more than two state variables. Monte Carlo methods are computationally demanding, and so I also discuss in section 5.3 how standard speed-up methods can be used to reduce the computational burden.

In section 5.4, I follow up with a covariate speed-up method based on the K-AGM that greatly reduces the Monte Carlo implementations time for B-AGMs. In section 5.5, I provide an overview of how models within the B-AGM class may be estimated in principle, although I do not provide the results of any full B-AGM estimations in this book. Rather, the purpose of the overview is to illustrate why full estimations of B-AGMs are challenging in practice due simply to logistics. That is, time-consuming numerical procedures, even with speed-up methods, are required for each implementation of the B-AGM and its associated Jacobian. A full estimation requires many repeats of that core step, although I do introduce an analytic result that at least speeds up the Jacobian calculation. Combining that result with the covariate speed-up already discussed may make full estimations of B-AGMs with three or more factors practically feasible.

Having discussed the challenges of estimating B-AGMs, I then turn in section 5.6 to the alternative of explicitly using B-AGM approximations, which may provide an acceptable compromise in practice. From that perspective, if one accepts the implicit asset pricing assumptions underlying the B-AGM, which I will outline in section 5.1, then the K-AGM may be applied as a tractable B-AGM approximation. The detailed comparisons of K-AGM and B-AGM implementations in subsection 5.6.1 show that the approximation is close, and so it should be acceptable for many practical applications. Subsection 5.6.2 discusses a class of B-AGM approximations due to Priebsch (2013), which provides a very close second-order approximation to B-AGMs, albeit with a more involved process than the K-AGM. Hence, it should be applicable if one accepts the B-AGM pricing framework and requires a closer approximation than provided by the K-AGM.

There is a third alternative. If one accepts that the implicit asset pricing assumptions underlying the K-AGM are better supported by economic theory than the assumptions underlying the B-AGM, then the K-AGM would be preferred outright. In that case, the K-AGM could be applied with confidence as a ZLB term structure framework, with the added advantage that it also happens to be very tractable. In chapter 6, I will provide an economic foundation for GATSMs and K-AGMs that will help readers assess the case for using the K-AGM versus the B-AGM framework from a theoretical perspective.

5.1 The B-AGM framework principles

B-AGM bond prices may be represented generically with the following standard arbitrage pricing expression provided in many textbooks (e.g., see Filipović (2009) p. 109):

$$\underline{P}^{B}(t,\tau) = \tilde{\mathbb{E}}_{t}\left\{\exp\left(-\int_{0}^{\tau}\underline{r}(t+u)\,du\right)\cdot 1\right\} \qquad (5.1)$$

where 1 is the standard terminal cashflow for a bond (which I will typically omit in similar expressions hereafter), τ is the time to maturity, $\tilde{\mathbb{E}}_{t}$ is the risk-adjusted expectations operator based on information up to time t, and

$$\underline{r}(t+u) = \max\{0, r(t+u)\}$$

is the risk-adjusted diffusion process for the B-AGM short rate that is used to discount the terminal cashflow. The shadow short rate $r(t+u)$ is in turn defined by the GATSM specification for the shadow term structure. Note that, for notational simplicity, I will also use a lower bound of $r_L = 0$ throughout this section, which corresponds to an upper bound of 1 for B-AGM bond prices. However, $r_L = 0$ could be replaced by a non-zero lower bound r_L in any of the short rate, forward rate, or interest rate expressions, and by $\exp(-r_L \cdot \delta)$ for the appropriate time-to-maturity step δ in any of the bond price or option price expressions. Also note that I use the superscript "B" and an underscore to denote B-AGM ZLB term structure expressions, and I omit the "B" and underscore for shadow term structure expressions.

Equation 5.1 does not have a closed-form analytic solution, and therefore must be approximated with numerical methods, which I will outline in section 5.2. For this section, I will derive forward bond prices and forward rates using the generic definition of $\underline{P}^B(t,\tau)$ from equation 5.1. The objective is only to provide intuition on the B-AGM framework and to provide a transparent comparison to the K-AGM framework. To be clear, the forward bond price and forward rate expressions derived in this section do not provide any practical advantage over using $\underline{P}^B(t,\tau)$ directly, because the same numerical methods would still be required for their implementation.

B-AGM forward bond prices $\underline{P}^B(t,\tau,\delta)$ may be obtained from B-AGM bond prices using the standard term structure relationship:

$$\underline{P}^B(t,\tau,\delta) = \frac{\underline{P}^B(t,\tau+\delta)}{\underline{P}^B(t,\tau)} \tag{5.2}$$

where t is the current time, τ is the time to settlement, and δ is the time to maturity at the time of settlement. Note that τ is the time to maturity for the B-AGM bond $\underline{P}^B(t,\tau)$, and the time to maturity for the B-AGM bond $\underline{P}^B(t,\tau+\delta)$ is $\tau+\delta$. $\underline{P}^B(t,\tau+\delta)$ may be reexpressed as

$$\underline{P}^B(t,\tau+\delta) = \tilde{\mathbb{E}}_t \left\{ \exp\left(-\int_0^{\tau+\delta} \underline{r}(t+u)\, du \right) \right\}$$

$$= \tilde{\mathbb{E}}_t \left\{ \exp\left(-\int_0^{\tau} \underline{r}(t+u)\, du \right) \right.$$

$$\left. \times \exp\left(-\int_{\tau}^{\tau+\delta} \underline{r}(t+u)\, du \right) \right\} \tag{5.3}$$

and the final component of $\underline{P}^B(t,\tau+\delta)$ may be reexpressed as

$$\exp\left(-\int_{\tau}^{\tau+\delta} \underline{r}(t+u)\, du \right)$$

$$= \exp\left(-\int_{\tau}^{\tau+\delta} \max\{0, r(t+u)\}\, du \right)$$

$$= \exp\left(\int_{\tau}^{\tau+\delta} \min\{0, -r(t+u)\}\, du \right)$$

$$= \min \left\{ 1, \exp \left(-\int_\tau^{\tau+\delta} r(t+u) \, du \right) \right\}$$

$$= \min \{ 1, P(t+\tau,\delta) \}$$

$$= P(t+\tau,\delta) + \min \{ 1 - P(t+\tau,\delta), 0 \}$$

$$= P(t+\tau,\delta) - \max \{ P(t+\tau,\delta) - 1, 0 \} \tag{5.4}$$

Therefore, the B-AGM forward bond price is

$$\underline{P}^B(t,\tau,\delta) = \frac{1}{\underline{P}^B(t,\tau)} \cdot \tilde{\mathbb{E}}_t \left\{ \exp \left(-\int_0^\tau \underline{r}(t+u) \, du \right) \right.$$

$$\left. \times (P(t+\tau,\delta) - \max[P(t+\tau,\delta) - 1, 0]) \right\} \tag{5.5}$$

where $P(t+\tau,\delta) = \exp \left(-\int_\tau^{\tau+\delta} r(t+u) \right) du$ is the shadow bond price at time $t+\tau$ with a time to maturity of δ.

Hence, B-AGM forward bond prices $\underline{P}^B(t,\tau,\delta)$ are equivalent to the time $t+\tau$ cashflow of the GATSM bond price, $P(t+\tau,\delta)$, less the time $t+\tau$ cashflow of the payoff from a call option on a GATSM bond with a strike price of 1, $\max \{ P(t+\tau,\delta) - 1, 0 \}$, both discounted using B-AGM short rates $\underline{r}(t+\tau)$ under the risk-adjusted $\mathbb{Q}$ measure.

B-AGM bond prices may be obtained as the product of a sequence of B-AGM forward bond prices $\underline{P}^B(t,\tau,\delta)$. Considering B-AGM bond prices in this way offers a convenient and intuitive perspective for the discussion in the following subsection and later in chapter 6.

B-AGM forward rates are the instantaneous annualized return on B-AGM forward bond prices:

$$\underline{f}^B(t,\tau) = \lim_{\delta \to 0} \left\{ -\frac{1}{\delta} \log \left[\underline{P}^B(t,\tau,\delta) \right] \right\}$$

$$\langle \text{L'Hopital's rule} \rangle = \frac{\lim_{\delta \to 0} \left\{ -\frac{d}{d\delta} \log \left[\underline{P}^B(t,\tau,\delta) \right] \right\}}{\lim_{\delta \to 0} \left\{ \frac{d}{d\delta} \delta \right\}}$$

$$\langle \text{Chain rule} \rangle = \frac{\lim_{\delta \to 0} \left\{ -\frac{1}{\underline{P}^B(t,\tau,\delta)} \frac{d}{d\delta} \underline{P}^B(t,\tau,\delta) \right\}}{\lim_{\delta \to 0} \{ 1 \}}$$

$$\langle \text{Limit rules} \rangle = \frac{1}{\lim_{\delta \to 0} \left\{ \underline{P}^B(t,\tau,\delta) \right\}} \cdot \lim_{\delta \to 0} \left\{ -\frac{d}{d\delta} \underline{P}^B(t,\tau,\delta) \right\}$$

$$= 1 \cdot \lim_{\delta \to 0} \left\{ -\frac{d}{d\delta} \underline{P}^B(t,\tau,\delta) \right\}$$

$$= \lim_{\delta \to 0} \left[-\frac{1}{\underline{P}^B(t,\tau)} \cdot \tilde{\mathbb{E}}_t \left\{ \exp \left(-\int_0^\tau \underline{r}(t+u) \, du \right) \right. \right.$$

$$\times \frac{d}{d\delta}\left(P\left(t+\tau,\delta\right)-\max\left[-P\left(t+\tau,\delta\right)-1,0\right]\right)\Bigg\}\Bigg]$$

$$= -\frac{1}{\underline{P}^B\left(t,\tau\right)}\cdot\tilde{\mathbb{E}}_t\left\{\exp\left(-\int_0^\tau \underline{r}\left(t+u\right)du\right)\right.$$

$$\times\left(\lim_{\delta\to 0}\left\{\frac{d}{d\delta}\left(P\left(t+\tau,\delta\right)\right)\right\}\right.$$

$$\left.\left.-\lim_{\delta\to 0}\left\{\max\left[\frac{d}{d\delta}P\left(t+\tau,\delta\right),0\right]\right\}\right)\right\} \tag{5.6}$$

where the bracketed left-hand side comments refer to the standard rules of calculus applied in the derivation.

The limit of the differential of $P(t+\tau,\delta)$ with respect to δ is

$$\lim_{\delta\to 0}\left\{\frac{d}{d\delta}\left(P\left(t+\tau,\delta\right)\right)\right\} = \frac{d}{d\delta}\exp\left[-\int_\tau^{\tau+\delta} r\left(t+u\right)du\right]$$

$$\langle\text{Chain rule}\rangle = \lim_{\delta\to 0}\left\{-\exp\left[-\int_\tau^{\tau+\delta} r\left(t+u\right)du\right]\right.$$

$$\left.\times\frac{d}{d\delta}\int_\tau^{\tau+\delta} r\left(t+u\right)du\right\}$$

$$\langle\text{Calculus theorem}\rangle = \lim_{\delta\to 0}\left\{-P\left(t+\tau,\delta\right)\cdot r\left(t+\tau+\delta\right)\right\}$$

$$= -r\left(t+\tau\right) \tag{5.7}$$

where $\langle\text{Calculus theorem}\rangle$ refers to the fundamental theorem of calculus $F(x) = \int_a^x f(t)\,dt$ and $F'(x) = f(x)$.

B-AGM forward rates are therefore

$$\underline{f}^B\left(t,\tau\right) = -\frac{1}{\underline{P}^B\left(t,\tau\right)}\cdot\tilde{\mathbb{E}}_t\left\{\exp\left(-\int_0^\tau \underline{r}\left(t+u\right)du\right)\right.$$

$$\times -\left\{r\left(t+\tau\right)-\max\left[-r\left(t+\tau\right),0\right]\right\}$$

$$= \frac{1}{\underline{P}^B\left(t,\tau\right)}\cdot\tilde{\mathbb{E}}_t\left\{\exp\left(-\int_0^\tau \underline{r}\left(t+u\right)du\right)\cdot\underline{r}\left(t+\tau\right)\right\} \tag{5.8}$$

The B-AGM forward rate expression can be decomposed into a shadow forward rate expression and an option component like the K-AGM in chapter 2:

$$\underline{f}^B\left(t,\tau\right) = f(t,\tau) + z^B\left(t,\tau\right) \tag{5.9}$$

where $f(t,\tau)$ is the shadow forward rate function given by the GATSM used to represent the shadow term structure, and $z^B(t,\tau)$ is the B-AGM forward rate option effect. Therefore, all of the effects from the B-AGM ZLB term structure relative to

Table 5.1 B-AGM term structure components

		Shadow component (GATSM)		B-AGM option component
Short rate:				
$\underline{r}(t)$	$=$	$r(t)$	$+$	$\max\{-r(t),0\}$
	$=$	$a_0 + b_0 x(t)$	$+$	$\max\{-[a_0 + b_0 x(t)],0\}$
Forward rates:				
$\underline{f}^B(t,\tau)$	$=$	$f(t,\tau)$	$+$	$z^B(t,\tau)$
	$=$	$\tilde{\mathbb{E}}_{t+\tau}[r(t+\tau)|x(t)]$	$+$	$z^B(t,\tau)$
Interest rates:				
$\underline{R}^B(t,\tau)$	$=$	$R(t,\tau)$	$+$	$Z^B(t,\tau)$
	$=$	$\frac{1}{\tau}\int_0^\tau f(t,u)\,du$	$+$	$\frac{1}{\tau}\int_0^\tau z^B(t,\tau)\,du$
Bond price:				
$\underline{P}^B(t,\tau)$	$=$	$P(t,\tau)$	$\times$	$Z_P^B(t,\tau)$
	$=$	$\exp[-\tau\cdot R(t,\tau)]$	$\times$	$\exp\left[-\tau\cdot Z^B(t,\tau)\right]$

a GATSM without a ZLB have been shifted into $z^B(t,\tau)$. Defining this decomposition offers no advantage in practice, of course, because a numerical calculation of $\underline{f}^B(t,\tau)$ would first be required to obtain $z^B(t,\tau)$.

However, the decomposition does provide a direct comparison to the K-AGM framework in terms of GATSM shadow term structure expressions and associated B-AGM framework option effects. From that perspective Table 5.1 summarizes the different perspectives of the B-AGM term structure.

Therefore, just like the K-AGM framework, the B-AGM framework can be considered as a GATSM shadow term structure plus an option effect that is a function of the specified dynamics for the GATSM short rate. The difference is that the B-AGM option effect does not have a closed-form analytic solution for any of the term structure representations.

5.1.1 Initial comparison of the B-AGM and K-AGM frameworks

The K-AGM framework arises from equation 5.5 with the rate for discounting the terminal cashflows of $P(t+\tau,\delta)$ and $\max\{P(t+\tau,\delta)-1,0\}$ changed from the ZLB rate $\underline{r}(t+\tau)$ to the shadow short rate $r(t+\tau)$, and $\underline{P}^B(t,\tau) = \tilde{\mathbb{E}}_t\left\{\exp\left(-\int_0^\tau \underline{r}(t+u)\,du\right)\right\}$ replaced with $P(t,\tau) = \tilde{\mathbb{E}}_t\left\{\exp\left(-\int_0^\tau r(t+u)\,du\right)\right\}$. Specifically, equation 5.5 then becomes

$$\underline{P}(t,\tau,\delta) = \frac{1}{P(t,\tau)}\cdot\tilde{\mathbb{E}}_t\left\{\exp\left(-\int_0^\tau r(t+u)\,du\right)\cdot P(t+\tau,\delta)\right\}$$

$$-\frac{1}{P(t,\tau)}\cdot\tilde{\mathbb{E}}_t\left\{\exp\left(-\int_0^\tau r(t+u)\,du\right)\max\left[P(t+\tau,\delta)-1,0\right]\right\} \quad (5.10)$$

The K-AGM forward rate is derived from the K-AGM forward bond price following the same steps as for the B-AGM, but the final result involves the GATSM bond price and discounting the ZLB short rate with shadow short rates:

$$\underline{f}(t,\tau) = \frac{1}{P(t,\tau)}\cdot\tilde{\mathbb{E}}_t\left\{\exp\left(-\int_0^\tau r(t+u)\,du\right)\cdot\underline{r}(t+\tau)\right\}$$

$$= \tilde{\mathbb{E}}_t\left\{\frac{\exp\left(-\int_0^\tau r(t+u)\,du\right)}{P(t,\tau)}\cdot\underline{r}(t+\tau)\right\}$$

$$= \tilde{\mathbb{E}}_{t+\tau}\left[\underline{r}(t+\tau)\right]$$

$$= \tilde{\mathbb{E}}_{t+\tau}\left[r(t+\tau)\right] + \tilde{\mathbb{E}}_{t+\tau}\left[\max\{-r(t+\tau),0\}\right] \quad (5.11)$$

This result is the expression for K-AGM forward rates derived in section 4.1, using the expectations operator $\tilde{\mathbb{E}}_{t+\tau}[\cdot]$ under the $t+\tau$ forward $\mathbb{Q}$ measure.

Using the B-AGM exposition to calculate the K-AGM forward rate also provides intuition on the K-AGM foundations and an alternative expression for $\underline{f}(t,\tau)$ as derived in Krippner (2011, 2012b,c). Hence, the expectation in the first line of equation 5.10 is the GATSM bond price $P(t,\tau+\delta)$:

$$P(t,\tau+\delta) = \tilde{\mathbb{E}}_t\left\{\exp\left(-\int_0^\tau r(t+u)\,du\right)\cdot P(t+\tau,\delta)\right\} \quad (5.12)$$

The expectation in the second line of equation 5.10 is the price of a call option, with expiry $t+\tau$ and a strike price of 1, on the GATSM bond $P(t,\tau+\delta)$, which I will denote $C(t,\tau,\delta,1)$:

$$C(t,\tau,\delta,1) = \tilde{\mathbb{E}}_t\left\{\exp\left(-\int_0^\tau r(t+u)\,du\right)\cdot\max\{P(t+\tau,\delta)-1,0\}\right\} \quad (5.13)$$

$\underline{P}(t,\tau,\delta)$ may therefore be expressed directly in terms of the GATSM bond price and the call option price solutions:

$$\underline{P}(t,\tau,\delta) = \frac{P(t,\tau+\delta)}{P(t,\tau)} - \frac{C(t,\tau,\delta,1)}{P(t,\tau)} \quad (5.14)$$

Applying the derivative and limit to obtain $\underline{f}(t,\tau)$ gives

$$\underline{f}(t,\tau) = \lim_{\delta\to 0}\left\{-\frac{d}{d\delta}\underline{P}(t,\tau,\delta)\right\}$$

$$= \lim_{\delta\to 0}\left\{-\frac{d}{d\delta}\left[\frac{P(t,\tau+\delta)}{P(t,\tau)} - \frac{C(t,\tau,\delta,1)}{P(t,\tau)}\right]\right\}$$

$$= -\frac{1}{P(t,\tau)} \cdot \lim_{\delta \to 0} \left\{ \frac{d}{d\delta} P(t, \tau + \delta) \right\}$$

$$+ \lim_{\delta \to 0} \left\{ \frac{d}{d\delta} \left[\frac{C(t, \tau, \delta, 1)}{P(t, \tau)} \right] \right\} \tag{5.15}$$

and the derivative of $P(t, \tau + \delta)$ with respective to δ is

$$\frac{d}{d\delta} P(t, \tau + \delta) = \frac{d}{d\delta} \exp \left[-\int_0^{\tau+\delta} f(t, u) \, du \right]$$

$$\langle \text{Chain rule} \rangle = -\exp \left[-\int_0^{\tau+\delta} f(t, u) \, du \right]$$

$$\times \left(\frac{d}{d[\tau+\delta]} \int_0^{\tau+\delta} f(t, u) \, du \right) \cdot \frac{d[\tau+\delta]}{d\delta}$$

$$\langle \text{Calculus theorem} \rangle = -P(t, \tau + \delta) \cdot f(t, \tau + \delta) \cdot 1 \tag{5.16}$$

Therefore, the first term in the alternative expression for $\underline{f}(t, \tau)$ is

$$-\frac{1}{P(t,\tau)} \cdot \lim_{\delta \to 0} \left\{ \frac{d}{d\delta} P(t, \tau + \delta) \right\} = -\frac{1}{P(t,\tau)} [-P(t,\tau) \cdot f(t,\tau)]$$

$$= f(t, \tau) \tag{5.17}$$

and the alternative expression for K-AGM forward rates is

$$\underline{f}(t, \tau) = f(t, \tau) + z(t, \tau) \tag{5.18}$$

where

$$z(t, \tau) = \lim_{\delta \to 0} \left\{ \frac{d}{d\delta} \left[\frac{C(t, \tau, \delta, 1)}{P(t, \tau)} \right] \right\} \tag{5.19}$$

Krippner (2011, 2012b,c) calculates $z(t, \tau)$ analytically using the GATSM closed-form analytic solutions for $C(t, \tau, \delta, 1)$ and $P(t, \tau)$. Krippner (2012a, 2013c) uses a numerical calculation of the derivative for $z(t, \tau)$ from the closed-form expressions for $C(t, \tau, \delta, 1)$ and $P(t, \tau)$ and a small value of δ.

The perspective of the B-AGM and K-AGM frameworks offered above provides the initial comparison of the implicit asset pricing assumptions underlying the B-AGM and K-AGM frameworks. That is, K-AGM forward bonds $\underline{P}(t, \tau, \delta)$ and forward rates $\underline{f}(t, \tau)$ respectively result from discounting the cashflows associated with ZLB forward bonds $P(t + \tau, \delta) - \max[P(t + \tau, \delta) - 1, 0]$ and ZLB short rates $\underline{r}(t + \tau)$ with shadow short rates. Conversely, B-AGM forward bonds $\underline{P}^B(t, \tau, \delta)$ and forward rates $\underline{f}^B(t, \tau)$ discount the cashflows associated with ZLB forward bonds $P(t + \tau, \delta) - \max[P(t + \tau, \delta) - 1, 0]$ and ZLB short rates $\underline{r}(t + \tau)$ with ZLB short rates.

On the face of it, then, the B-AGM therefore suggests itself as the theoretically self-consistent framework because the discounting uses model-consistent short rates. That is, the ZLB short rates produced by the B-AGM are also used as the basis for discounting. Conversely, the K-AGM framework uses shadow short rates for discounting, which seems theoretically inconsistent. However, I will return to discuss this difference in discounting from the perspective of a simple economic model in chapter 6.

Note that Priebsch (2013) provides an alternative but equivalent way of considering the difference between the B-AGM and K-AGM frameworks. Specifically, Priebsch (2013) notes that GATSM forward rates $f(t, \tau)$ are the time t expectation of the truncated GATSM rate $r(t + \tau)$, which is my $r(t + \tau)$ conditional on $x(t)$, under the GATSM $t + \tau$ forward measure $\tilde{\mathbb{E}}_{t+\tau}[\cdot]$:

$$f(t, \tau) = \tilde{\mathbb{E}}_t \left\{ \frac{\exp\left(-\int_0^\tau r(t + u)\, du\right)}{P(t, \tau)} \cdot r(t + \tau) \right\}$$

$$= \tilde{\mathbb{E}}_{t+\tau}\left[r(t + \tau)\,|\,x(t)\right] \tag{5.20}$$

Priebsch (2013) then notes that B-AGM forward rates $\underline{f}^B(t, \tau)$ are the expectation of the B-AGM truncated GATSM rate $\max\{0, r(t + \tau)\}$ conditional on $x(t)$, calculated under the B-AGM $t + \tau$ forward measure $\tilde{\mathbb{E}}_{t+\tau}^B[\cdot]$:

$$\underline{f}^B(t, \tau) = \tilde{\mathbb{E}}_t \left\{ \frac{\exp\left(-\int_0^\tau \underline{r}(t + u)\, du\right)}{P(t, \tau)} \cdot \underline{r}(t + \tau) \right\}$$

$$= \tilde{\mathbb{E}}_{t+\tau}^B\left[\underline{r}(t + \tau)\,|\,x(t)\right] \tag{5.21}$$

$$= \tilde{\mathbb{E}}_{t+\tau}^B\left[\max\{0, r(t + \tau)\,|\,x(t)\}\right]$$

where $\tilde{\mathbb{E}}_{t+\tau}^B$ denotes that the expectations are under the risk-adjusted Black-ZLB $\mathbb{Q}$ forward measure. Denoting the latter as $\mathbb{Q}^B$, Priebsch (2013) defines $\mathbb{Q}^B$ by the Radon-Nikodym derivative:

$$\frac{d\mathbb{Q}^B}{d\mathbb{Q}} = \frac{\exp\left(-\int_0^\tau \underline{r}(t + u)\, du\right)}{\tilde{\mathbb{E}}_t\left[-\int_0^\tau \underline{r}(t + u)\, du\right]} \tag{5.22}$$

Then, as Priebsch (2013) highlights, K-AGM forward rates are obtained as a hybrid that uses the B-AGM truncated GATSM rate $\max\{0, r(t + \tau)\}$ conditional on $x(t)$, calculated under the GATSM $t + \tau$ forward measure $\tilde{\mathbb{E}}_{t+\tau}[\cdot]$:

$$\underline{f}(t, \tau) = \tilde{\mathbb{E}}_t \left\{ \frac{\exp\left(-\int_0^\tau r(t + u)\, du\right)}{P(t, \tau)} \cdot \underline{r}(t + \tau) \right\}$$

$$= \tilde{\mathbb{E}}_{t+\tau}\left[\underline{r}(t + \tau)\,|\,x(t)\right]$$

$$= \tilde{\mathbb{E}}_{t+\tau}\left[\max\{0, r(t + \tau)\,|\,x(t)\}\right] \tag{5.23}$$

5.2 B-AGM implementation

The lack of closed-form analytic solutions for any representation of the B-AGM term structure means that numerical methods are required for any implementation in practice, and such methods are generally time consuming. Note that I use the terminology "implementation" to denote the evaluation of a single set of B-AGM yields to appropriate numerical accuracy for a given set of state variables and parameters. As I will highlight in section 5.5 on estimating B-AGMs, a partial estimation using the iterated extended Kalman filter (IEKF) would require an implementation for each iteration i of the state variables for each observation of yield curve data from t. A full estimation would require many repeats of the partial estimation for each parameter set supplied by the optimization algorithm. Therefore, the feasibility of estimating a B-AGM in practice effectively condenses to the implementation speed of the particular B-AGM.

The following subsections provide an overview of all the numerical methods I have seen to implement B-AGMs, and also lists examples of their application. However, I will return to concentrate on Monte Carlo implementations in section 5.3 because they are more generally applicable to implementations of B-AGMs with more than two state variables.

5.2.1 Customized calculation methods

Gorovoi and Linetsky (2004) have developed a method for implementing a B-AGM with one state variable, that is, the Vasicek (1977) model in the Black (1995) framework. Gorovoi and Linetsky (2004) and others referencing the paper often report that the solution is closed-form analytic because it can be expressed in terms of a particular class of mathematical functions, that is, Weber-Hermite parabolic cylinder functions. However, for practical implementation, those functions themselves must be evaluated numerically and further numerical integration of those results is required. Effectively, then, the Gorovoi and Linetsky (2004) method is not really closed-form analytic, or in the words I recall from a conference participant, "it didn't look that closed-form to me."

Gorovoi and Linetsky (2004) illustrate the application of their method by fitting a single observation of Japanese government bond yield curve data with times to maturity out to 30 years to obtain the single state variable and the model parameters. Ichiue and Ueno (2006) and Ueno, Baba, and Sakurai (2006) estimate the Gorovoi and Linetsky (2004) model using Japanese government bond data with times to maturity out to 10 years.

One-factor models of the term structure are generally considered to be unrealistic, from both a cross-sectional and a time-series perspective. Unfortunately, the Gorovoi and Linetsky (2004) approach does not appear to generalize to more than one state variable (e.g., see Kim and Singleton [2012, p. 37]), and so generic numerical methods are applied to implement B-AGMs with more than one state variable.

5.2.2 Finite difference methods

Finite difference methods use a finite approximation to solve the partial differential equation, or PDE, to which an asset price must theoretically conform. James and Webber (2000) chapter 12, for example, has general background on finite difference methods applied to interest rate modeling.

As relevant background for the B-AGM, the PDE for a GATSM is the following:

$$r(t) \cdot P(t,\tau) = \frac{\partial P(t,\tau)}{\partial \tau} + \frac{\partial P(t,\tau)}{\partial x(t)} \tilde{\kappa} \left[\tilde{\theta} - x(t) \right] + \frac{1}{2} \sigma \sigma' \frac{\partial^2 P(t,\tau)}{\partial x(t) \, \partial \left[x(t) \right]'} \quad (5.24)$$

which, with the boundary condition $P(t,0) = 1$, has the closed-form analytic solution for $P(t,\tau)$ already given in section 3.1.

The PDE for a B-AGM is

$$\max \{0, r(t)\} \cdot \underline{P}^B(t,\tau) = \frac{\partial \underline{P}^B(t,\tau)}{\partial \tau} + \frac{\partial \underline{P}^B(t,\tau)}{\partial x(t)} \tilde{\kappa} \left[\tilde{\theta} - x(t) \right]$$

$$+ \frac{1}{2} \sigma \sigma' \frac{\partial^2 \underline{P}^B(t,\tau)}{\partial x(t) \, \partial \left[x(t) \right]'} \quad (5.25)$$

which, as already noted, does not have a closed-form analytic solution. However, any PDE can be solved approximately by using finite differences to represent the partial differentials. For example, the time-to-maturity derivative could be approximated with a forward difference $\partial \underline{P}^B(t,\tau)/\partial \tau \simeq \left[\underline{P}^B(t,\tau + \Delta \tau) - \underline{P}^B(t,\tau) \right]/\Delta \tau$, the first derivative of the state variable vector could be obtained similarly (although central differences are more precise in practice), and the second derivative of the state variable vector requires a difference-in-difference calculation. Discretizing time to maturity and the state variables into a grid, applying the appropriate boundary conditions, and using the finite differences around the grid points then gives all of the elements needed to approximate the PDE solution. In practice, interest rates are typically used as observables when estimating B-AGMs, and they can be obtained from the standard term structure relationship $\underline{R}(t,\tau) = -\log \left[\underline{P}(t,\tau) \right]/\tau$ once $\underline{P}(t,\tau)$ is obtained.

In general, the computing time for B-AGMs with finite difference methods will scale as the power of the number of state variables (because each state variable requires its own dimension in the grid) and linearly with the time to maturity divided by the discretization (because a longer maturity multiplies the number of points in the grid for a given discretization of time to maturity). Hence, there is a practical trade-off between computing time, model specification, and time to maturity/discretization. Regarding the latter, using a larger discretization will reduce the computing time, but at the cost of discretization errors. In principle, smaller discretizations will provide better approximations, but James and Webber (2000) note that the interplay between grid size and numerical round-off issues can become material for finite difference methods with longer times to maturity.

The application of finite difference methods to B-AGMs of which I am aware are as follows:

- Bomfim (2003) estimates the state variables for a two-factor B-AGM on US interest rate swap data out to 10 years' time to maturity. The parameters are constrained to those previously estimated from the analogous GATSM.
- Kim and Singleton (2012) undertakes a full estimation of a two-factor B-AGM on Japanese government bond rates out to 10 years' time to maturity. Note that Kim and Singleton (2012) also estimates a quadratic term structure model and a quadratic term structure model subject to the Black (1995) ZLB mechanism, and concludes that the B-AGM performs well in comparison to those models.
- Richard (2013) undertakes a full estimation of a three-factor B-AGM using US government bond rates out to 30 years' time to maturity. However, on p. 40 he notes that "it requires a long time, literally a month, on large and fast computers to estimate" (although his estimation times have subsequently been reduced to several days using parameter starting values that are closer to the global optimum, and with adjustments to the estimation techniques).

5.2.3 Lattice methods

Lattice methods in essence approximate the differential equation for the state variables under the risk-adjusted $\mathbb{Q}$ measure with a tree structure. The tree contains discrete potential values to which the state variables can evolve over each increment of time until the required time to maturity, and the probabilities of evolving to each of those values. The state variables at each node of the lattice then give the applicable discount rates, and the probability-weighted discounted value of the final cashflow can be obtained by passing it back through all nodes of the lattice. James and Webber (2000) chapter 14, for example, has general background on lattice methods applied to interest rate modeling.

For B-AGMs, the GATSM differential equation for the state variables under the $\mathbb{Q}$ measure

$$dx(t) = \tilde{\kappa} \left[\tilde{\theta} - x(t) \right] dt + \sigma d\tilde{W}(t) \tag{5.26}$$

is used to create the lattice points and probabilities. As noted in Black (1995) p. 1373 for the one-factor case that he discusses, the nodes of the lattice that produce negative short rates are then replaced with zeros. The final cashflow is 1, and the B-AGM bond prices may then be generated as the probability-weighted discounted value from the lattice and converted to interest rates using $R^B(t,\tau) = -\log\left[\underline{P}^B(t,\tau)\right]/\tau$.

In general, the computing time for B-AGMs with lattice methods scale as the power of the number of state variables (because each state variable requires its own dimension in the lattice) and linearly with the time to maturity divided by the discretization (because a longer maturity multiplies the number of points in the lattice for a given discretization of time to maturity). Hence, one is faced with similar practical trade-offs as for implementing B-AGMs with finite difference methods.

The only example of applying a lattice method to B-AGMs that I am aware of is Ichiue and Ueno (2007). In that case, the authors estimate a two-factor B-AGM on Japanese government bond rates out to 10 years' time to maturity.

5.2.4 Monte Carlo methods

As noted in James and Webber (2000), finite difference and lattice methods become prohibitive as the number of state variables is increased, so Monte Carlo methods are generally preferred for more than two and certainly for more than three state variables. Monte Carlo methods essentially approximate the standard arbitrage pricing expectation expression with the mean of asset prices results from a finite sample of simulations of discrete-time simulations of the state variable differential equation under the risk-adjusted $\mathbb{Q}$ measure. James and Webber (2000, chapter 13), for example, has general background on Monte Carlo methods applied to interest rate modeling.

As I will detail in section 5.3, the standard arbitrage pricing expression for B-AGM bond prices is

$$\underline{P}^{B}(t,\tau) = \tilde{\mathbb{E}}_t \left\{ \exp\left(-\int_0^\tau \underline{r}(t+u)\,du \right) \right\} \tag{5.27}$$

which is therefore approximated with

$$\widehat{\underline{P}}^{B}(t,\tau) = \frac{1}{J} \sum_{j=1}^{J} \exp\left[-\sum_{m=0}^{M-1} \underline{r}_{t,j,m} \cdot \Delta\tau \right] \tag{5.28}$$

where $\underline{r}_{t,j,m}$ are simulated from the discretized process for the GATSM state variables $x(t)$ under the risk adjusted $\mathbb{Q}$ measure. The estimated bond price may be converted to an estimated interest rate using the standard term structure expression:

$$\underline{R}^{B}(t,\tau) = \frac{1}{\tau} \log\left[\underline{P}^{B}(t,\tau) \right] \tag{5.29}$$

Note that both the bond prices and interest rates are values estimated from a finite sample, and so they are subject to confidence intervals or measures of accuracy relative to the true quantity they are being used to represent. An appropriate sample size is therefore required to ensure that the confidence intervals are sufficiently small for any finite sampling errors to be ignored, and that confidence interval is in turn related to how the B-AGM bond prices and interest rates will be applied. The appropriate confidence interval therefore determines the number of simulations required and hence the computing time, which I will discuss in the following section.

In general, the computing time for B-AGMs with Monte Carlo methods should scale approximately as the square of the number of factors and the square of time to maturity divided by the discretization. However, there are some nuances to which I will return in the following section.

Application of Monte Carlo methods to B-AGMs of which I am aware are as follows:

- Ueno, Baba, and Sakurai (2006) illustrates the sensitivity of the two-factor B-AGM to mean-reversion and volatility parameters.
- Bauer and Rudebusch (2013) estimates the state variables for a three-factor B-AGM on US government bond rates out to 10 years time to maturity. The parameters are constrained to those previously estimated from the analogous GATSM using data from the non-ZLB-constrained period.
- Many authors use Monte Carlo simulations to test the accuracy of their B-AGM or K-AGM results. For example, see Bomfim (2003) and Kim and Singleton (2012), as noted in subsection 5.2.2, and Christensen and Rudebusch (2013a,b, 2014), Krippner (2012a, 2013c), and Wu and Xia (2013, 2014), as noted in chapter 4.

5.3 B-AGM Monte Carlo implementations

This section provides details related to implementing B-AGMs using Monte Carlo (MC) methods. The first subsection establishes the specification and notation for implementing B-AGMs using MC methods, which I use in subsection 5.6.1 to compare B-AGM implementations with K-AGM implementations. Subsection 5.3.2 discusses how one can determine the approximate computing time for a B-AGM implementation with the required accuracy or confidence interval, which is key for considering the broad feasibility of implementing particular B-AGM specifications via MC methods for a given application (e.g., a partial or full estimation on a particular yield curve data set).

Subsection 5.3.3 discusses the antithetic sampling method for speeding up the basic Monte Carlo simulation process. Antithetic sampling is standard practice for Monte Carlo simulations. For example, James and Webber (2000) notes that "It is recommended that this technique is included as an option in any half-way serious Monte Carlo simulation." I also mention several other speed-up methods in section 5.3.4 that I think would be useful for B-AGM MC simulations.

In section 5.3.5, I provide a detailed example of how to undertake an MC simulation for a B-ANSM(2). In section 5.3.6, I also provide an overview for other B-AGMs, including the B-ANSM(3).

5.3.1 B-AGM Monte Carlo specification

It is convenient in what follows to reexpress equation 5.28 as

$$\widehat{\underline{P}}^{B}(t,\tau) = \frac{1}{J}\sum_{j=1}^{J}\underline{P}_{j}^{B}(t,\tau) \tag{5.30}$$

where the caret "^" indicates that $\widehat{\underline{P}}^{B}(t,\tau)$ is a sample estimate and J is the sample size of individual bond price simulations $\underline{P}_{j}^{B}(t,\tau)$:

$$\underline{P}_{j}^{B}(t,\tau) = \exp\left[-\sum_{m=0}^{M-1}\underline{r}_{t,j,m}\cdot\delta\right] \tag{5.31}$$

Each simulated ZLB short rate $\underline{r}_{t,j,m}$ is obtained from the ZLB mechanism:

$$\underline{r}_{t,j,m} = \max\left\{r_{L},r_{t,j,m}\right\} \tag{5.32}$$

where r_{L} allows for the lower bound to be potentially non-zero, and the simulated shadow short rate $r_{t,j,m}$ is obtained from the GATSM short rate expression:

$$r_{t,j,m} = a_{0} + b_{0}'x_{t,j,m} \tag{5.33}$$

The state variables $x_{t,j,m}$ are generated from the discretized process for the GATSM state variables $x(t)$ under the risk-adjusted $\mathbb{Q}$ measure:

$$\Delta x_{t,j,m} = \tilde{\kappa}\left(\tilde{\theta} - x_{t,j,m-1}\right)\delta + \sigma\sqrt{\delta}\epsilon_{t,j,m}$$

$$x_{t,j,m} - x_{t,j,m-1} = \tilde{\kappa}\left(\tilde{\theta} - x_{t,j,m-1}\right)\delta + \sigma\sqrt{\delta}\epsilon_{t,j,m}$$

$$x_{t,j,m} = x_{t,j,m-1} + \tilde{\kappa}\left(\tilde{\theta} - x_{t,j,m-1}\right)\delta + \sigma\sqrt{\delta}\epsilon_{t,j,m} \tag{5.34}$$

where $x_{t,j,0} = x(t)$, $\epsilon_{t,j,m}$ is an $N \times 1$ vector of independent pseudo-random draws from the unit normal distribution $\epsilon_{t,j,m} \sim N(0,1)$, and δ is the discrete time increment for the simulation, that is, $\delta = \tau/M$, with M being the number of increments from time t to time of maturity $t+\tau$. Note that I have used the notation δ for the Monte Carlo simulation time increment to clearly distinguish this parameter from the time step Δt parameter that I use to denote the time between observations in the estimation process.

Figure 5.1 provides an illustrative example of an MC valuation of a 10-year B-AGM bond. In panel 1, ZLB short rate paths have been obtained from simulating $x_{t,j,m}$ using the estimated model parameters and state variables for the

August 2008 K-ANSM(2) example with $r_L = 0$ from section 4.5 and applying $\underline{r}_{t,j,m} = \max\{0, r_{t,j,m}\}$. I have also highlighted one selected path of the ZLB short rate so its subsequent transformations can be followed, and I return to discuss the antithetic path in subsection 5.3.3. Panel 2 contains the cumulative sum for each of the sample paths, that is, $\sum_{m=0}^{M-1} \underline{r}_{t,j,m} \cdot \delta$ for each $M = \tau/\delta$ from 0 to 11 years. Note that if an MC simulation for a range of different maturities $\tau_1, \ldots, \tau_K$ is required, there is no need to undertake separate simulations; the cumulative sum of the simulations of $x_{t,j,m}$ for the shorter maturities should simply be taken from the cumulative sum of the simulation of $x_{t,j,m}$ out to the longest time to maturity τ_K. Specifically, the results for shorter times to maturity can be obtained by sampling the cumulative sum of $x_{t,j,m}$ at the points $m = M_1 = \tau_1/\delta$, $m = M_2 = \tau_2/\delta$, and so on, from the full simulation of $x_{t,j,1}, \ldots x_{t,j,M_K}$. The MC time increment δ therefore needs to be a whole-number fraction of all times to maturity $\tau_1, \ldots, \tau_K$.

Panel 3 illustrates the simulated bond prices $P_j^B(t,\tau) = \exp\left[-\sum_{m=0}^{M-1} \underline{r}_{t,j,m} \cdot \delta\right]$, and I have highlighted the individual prices for the 10-year maturity. I have also indicated the mean of those prices, which is the horizontal line with the estimated 10-year B-AGM price of approximately 0.65 for this particular simulation.

Figure 5.2 repeats the example from Figure 5.1 but for July 2012. In this case, the constraint from the ZLB on the simulated paths of the shadow short rates are more apparent, resulting in more zero values for the ZLB short rate paths in panel 1. The cumulative ZLB short rate paths in panel 2 are therefore correspondingly lower, and the simulated B-AGM bond prices and their mean value (approximately 0.87) in panel 3 are higher.

The confidence interval around the estimate $\widehat{P}^B(t,\tau)$ provides a measure of its accuracy relative to the true value, and the confidence interval is obtained from the estimated standard deviation of the mean:

$$\text{std}\left[\widehat{P}^B(t,\tau)\right] = \frac{1}{\sqrt{J}} \cdot \text{std}\left[P_j^B(t,\tau)\right] \tag{5.35}$$

For example, the two-sided 95 percent and 99 percent confidence intervals are respectively $\pm 1.96\,\text{std}[\cdot]$ and $\pm 2.58\,\text{std}[\cdot]$. Note that I have used $\sqrt{J}$ as the divisor for std$[\cdot]$, rather than $\sqrt{J-1}$, which would give the unbiased estimate of std$[\cdot]$. Using $\sqrt{J}$ is for notational and mathematical convenience, and it very closely approximates $\sqrt{J-1}$, given J is always very large for MC simulations.

In practice, interest rates are typically used as observables when estimating term structure models. The estimated bond price may be converted to an interest rate using the following standard term structure expression:

$$\widehat{R}^B(t,\tau) = -\frac{1}{\tau} \log\left[\widehat{P}^B(t,\tau)\right] \tag{5.36}$$

and the associated standard deviation may be obtained from the standard expression for the variance of the function of a random variable. That is, in generic terms,

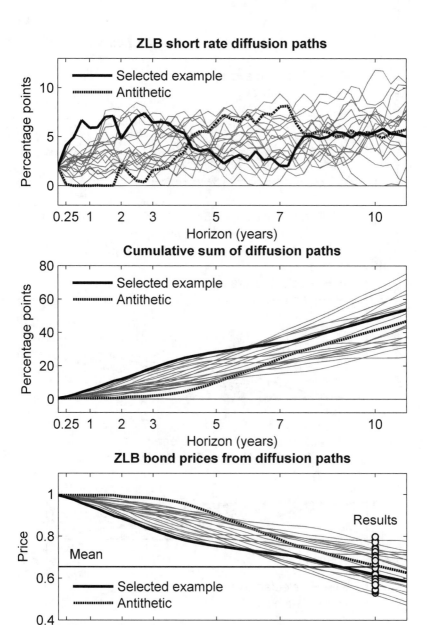

Figure 5.1 Example of a B-AGM MC simulation in a non-ZLB environment (August 2008). Each simulated diffusion path of the ZLB short rate (panel 1) is used to calculate the cumulative sum of that ZLB short rate path (panel 2) and the simulated ZLB bond price for that ZLB short rate path (panel 3). The MC result is the mean of all simulated bond prices.

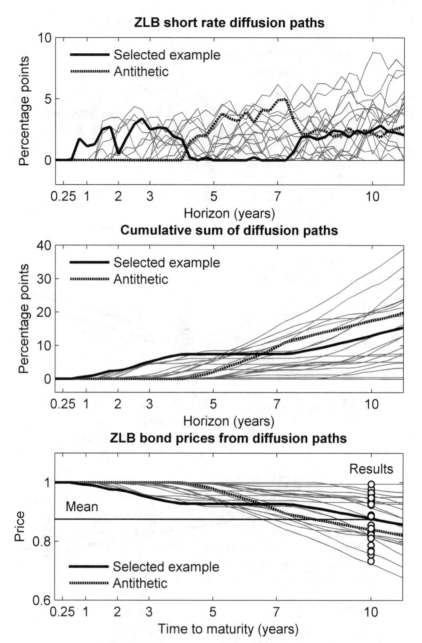

Figure 5.2 Example of a B-AGM MC simulation in a ZLB environment (July 2012). The constraint from the ZLB makes the simulated diffusion paths of the ZLB short rate and their cumulative sums (panels 1 and 2) lower than for Figure 5.1, and the simulated ZLB bond prices and their mean are therefore higher than for Figure 5.1 (panel 3).

$\mathrm{var}\left[f(X)\right] = \left[f'(\mathbb{E}[X])\right]^2 \mathrm{var}[X]$, and hence $\mathrm{std}\left[f(X)\right] = \left|f'(\mathbb{E}[X])\right| \cdot \mathrm{std}[X]$. For the B-AGM:

$$\mathrm{std}\left[f(X)\right] = \mathrm{std}\left[\widehat{\underline{R}}^{\,\mathrm{B}}(t,\tau)\right]; \quad X = \widehat{\underline{P}}^{\,\mathrm{B}}(t,\tau); \quad \mathbb{E}[X] = \underline{P}^{\mathrm{B}}(t,\tau) \tag{5.37}$$

which gives

$$\mathrm{std}\left[\widehat{\underline{R}}^{\,\mathrm{B}}(t,\tau)\right] = \left| \frac{d}{d\,\widehat{\underline{P}}^{\,\mathrm{B}}(t,\tau)} \left(\frac{1}{\tau} \log\left[\widehat{\underline{P}}^{\,\mathrm{B}}(t,\tau)\right] \right) \right| \cdot \mathrm{std}\left[\widehat{\underline{P}}^{\,\mathrm{B}}(t,\tau)\right]$$

$$= \frac{1}{\tau \cdot \widehat{\underline{P}}^{\,\mathrm{B}}(t,\tau)} \cdot \mathrm{std}\left[\widehat{\underline{P}}^{\,\mathrm{B}}(t,\tau)\right]$$

$$= \frac{1}{\tau \cdot \widehat{\underline{P}}^{\,\mathrm{B}}(t,\tau)} \cdot \frac{1}{\sqrt{J}} \cdot \mathrm{std}\left[\underline{P}_j^{\mathrm{B}}(t,\tau)\right] \tag{5.38}$$

As an aside, note that this conversion to interest rates is not equivalent to a direct calculation of interest rates for each simulation path $\underline{R}_j^{\mathrm{B}}(t,\tau) = -\log\left[\underline{P}_{-j}^{\mathrm{B}}(t,\tau)\right]/\tau$ and taking the mean. The latter expression would imply that

$$\underline{R}_{\mathrm{A}}^{\mathrm{B}}(t,\tau) = \tilde{\mathbb{E}}_t \left\{ -\frac{1}{\tau} \log\left[\exp\left(-\int_0^\tau \underline{r}(t+u)\,du \right) \right] \right\}$$

$$= \tilde{\mathbb{E}}_t \left\{ \frac{1}{\tau} \int_0^\tau \underline{r}(t+u)\,du \right\}$$

$$\neq \underline{R}^{\mathrm{B}}(t,\tau) = \tilde{\mathbb{E}}_t \left\{ \exp\left(-\int_0^\tau \underline{r}(t+u)\,du \right) \right\} \tag{5.39}$$

The difference is that $\underline{R}_{\mathrm{A}}^{\mathrm{B}}(t,\tau)$ omits the volatility effect (i.e., the Jensen's inequality term) that $\underline{R}^{\mathrm{B}}(t,\tau)$ includes to allow for the compounding return from the stochastic short rate process being lower than the compounding return from the mean short rate.

The appropriate confidence interval for interest rates will depend on the application of the B-AGM. For example, when undertaking an estimation with a two-state-variable B-AGM, one may specify that each B-AGM implementation should deliver interest rates with a 99 percent confidence interval of one basis point for all times to maturity. With reference to the K-AGM estimation and results discussed in section 4.5, numerical errors on the order of magnitude of one basis point would have little practical effect on the estimation of residuals in the IEKF. Therefore one can be reasonably assured that the parameter estimates and/or the state variables estimates along with the model specification at least provide a valid B-AGM estimation (before any diagnostic tests are undertaken to assess whether the estimated B-AGM is an appropriate representation of the data). However, a confidence interval of ten basis points would mean that the sampling error of the MC simulation would have a material effect on the B-AGM estimation. Therefore the estimation process may proceed erratically, and even if convergence is achieved, the results are likely to be invalid, or at least imprecise.

The number of simulations required to obtain sufficiently small confidence intervals is typically very large (e.g., in the order of one million as will become apparent in sections 5.4 to 5.6). In the following subsection I outline a simple method for determining the approximate number of simulations to achieve a given confidence interval.

5.3.2 Computing time for B-AGM Monte Carlo simulations

The confidence interval or level of accuracy specified by the user determines the number of simulations and therefore the computing time for a B-AGM implementation by MC methods. The computing time required to achieve a given level of accuracy for B-AGM interest rates may be determined with a trial simulation and appropriate scaling. Specifically, for a given model specification, set of parameters, set of B-AGM state variables, and the longest relevant time to maturity τ, a moderate value of $J = J_0$ (say 100 or 1000) can be used to determine an estimate of the standard deviation of the mean as

$$\text{std}\left[\widehat{R}^B(t,\tau)\right]_{J_0} = \frac{1}{\tau \cdot \widehat{P}^B_{J_0}(t,\tau)} \cdot \frac{1}{\sqrt{J_0}} \cdot \text{std}\left[\underline{P}^B_j(t,\tau)\right]_{J_0} \tag{5.40}$$

I denote the computing time required to obtain that standard deviation as $t(J_0)$.

J_0 can then be scaled to obtain the approximate number of simulations J_λ required to obtain the desired accuracy. I will denote that accuracy as a constant λ for interest rates because one would typically seek a fixed accuracy on model-generated B-AGM interest rates at each point in time. Given λ, J_λ is obtained as follows:

$$\lambda = \text{std}\left[\widehat{R}^B(t,\tau)\right]_{J_\lambda}$$
$$= \frac{1}{\tau \cdot \widehat{P}^B_{J_\lambda}(t,\tau)} \cdot \frac{1}{\sqrt{J_\lambda}} \cdot \text{std}\left[\underline{P}^B_j(t,\tau)\right]_{J_\lambda}$$
$$\simeq \frac{1}{\tau \cdot \widehat{P}^B_{J_0}(t,\tau)} \cdot \frac{1}{\sqrt{J_\lambda}} \cdot \text{std}\left[\underline{P}^B_j(t,\tau)\right]_{J_0}$$
$$= \frac{\sqrt{J_0}}{\sqrt{J_\lambda}} \frac{1}{\tau \cdot \widehat{P}^B_{J_0}(t,\tau)} \cdot \frac{1}{\sqrt{J_0}} \cdot \text{std}\left[\underline{P}^B_j(t,\tau)\right]_{J_0}$$
$$= \frac{\sqrt{J_0}}{\sqrt{J_\lambda}} \text{std}\left[\widehat{R}^B(t,\tau)\right]_{J_0} \tag{5.41}$$

and re-arranging the expression gives:

$$J_\lambda \simeq J_0 \frac{1}{\lambda^2} \left(\text{std} \left[\widehat{\underline{R}}^B (t, \tau) \right]_{J_0} \right)^2 \tag{5.42}$$

The corresponding computing time to run J_λ simulations, $t(J_\lambda)$, would be approximately

$$t(J_\lambda) \simeq t(J_0) \frac{J_\lambda}{J_0}$$

$$= t(J_0) \frac{1}{\lambda^2} \left(\text{std} \left[\widehat{\underline{R}}^B (t, \tau) \right]_{J_0} \right)^2 \tag{5.43}$$

Note that J_λ and $t(J_\lambda)$ are approximate because the sample mean and standard deviation of B-AGM MC bond prices $\underline{P}_j^B (t, \tau)$ in the trial simulation are used as proxies for the sample mean and and standard deviation in the full simulation. Given that the trial simulation J_0 uses only a relatively small number of simulations, the proxy values are only representative and not particularly good. Therefore, the actual number of simulations undertaken would typically be rounded up from the value suggested by J_λ.

The reason for using the longest time to maturity relevant to the application of the B-AGM for the trial simulation is that, for a given simulation size, the standard deviation of estimated interest rates is inevitably largest for the longest time to maturity. Figures 5.1 and 5.2 have already illustrated this result, and I will provide an explanation shortly below. Therefore, establishing the required number of simulations for a given level of accuracy λ for the longest time to maturity ensures that the accuracies for shorter times to maturity are less than λ. In principle, one could therefore undertake fewer simulations for shorter maturities, but if more simulations are required for longer maturities anyway, then improved estimates of interest rates for shorter maturities are available at no marginal computing cost.

The larger standard deviations for estimated interest rates at longer times to maturity arise from two sources:

- The diffusion process $x_{t,j,m}$ adopts more diffuse distributions as it evolves for longer times. Therefore the numerator in equation 5.38, $\text{std} \left[\underline{P}_j^B (t, \tau) \right]$, becomes larger.
- The denominator in equation 5.38, i.e. $\tau \cdot \widehat{\underline{P}}^B (t, \tau)$, becomes smaller for longer times to maturity because the exponential decrease in $\widehat{\underline{P}}^B (t, \tau)$ as a function of time to maturity outweighs the linear increase in τ.

In general, the computing time for MC simulations will scale as the square of the number of state variables (because each state variable contributes a similar amount of variance to the diffusion distributions) and as the square of the time to maturity (because the variance of the distributions rises approximately linearly over time). However, when I undertook some simulations and theoretical calculations to confirm those general principles for B-AGMs, I quickly found that very material deviations can occur depending on the precise model specification, the degree of the ZLB constraint, the longest maturity, and so forth, and even the interplays between those aspects. Therefore, using trial simulations over the potential extremes of the state variables and the model parameters is really the best and most pragmatic way to assess the appropriate number of simulations required for a given model on a given data set for a given application.

5.3.3 Antithetic sampling

Each step of each simulation for the B-AGM requires N draws from the unit normal distribution $N(0, 1)$, which is a major element of the computing time required for any MC simulation. Antithetic sampling can be used to halve the computation time for those draws, and more importantly to increase the accuracy of the MC simulation at the same time.

Essentially, antithetic sampling proceeds by drawing $\epsilon_{t,j,m}$ and then using that draw and its negated value $-\epsilon_{t,j,m}$ to run two simulations simultaneously. Specifically for the B-AGM,

$$x_{t,j,m} = x_{t,j,m-1} + \tilde{\kappa}\left(\tilde{\theta} - x_{m,j,i-1}\right)\delta + \sigma\sqrt{\delta}\epsilon_{t,j,m}$$

$$x_{t,j+1,m} = x_{t,j+1,m-1} + \tilde{\kappa}\left(\tilde{\theta} - x_{m,j,i-1}\right)\delta - \sigma\sqrt{\delta}\epsilon_{t,j+1,m} \qquad (5.44)$$

If the correlation of the simulated values $\underline{P}_j^B(t,\tau)$ and $\underline{P}_{j+1}^B(t,\tau)$ is negative, then antithetic sampling also reduces the estimate of std$\left[\widehat{P}^B(t,\tau)\right]$, and considerably if the correlation is close to -1. The latter is the case for B-AGMs that are relatively unconstrained by the ZLB, such as the example in Figure 5.1. In that case, relative to the mean of the distribution, the low bond price for the selected example is matched by a high bond price for its antithetic simulation. This symmetry occurs because the low bond price is generated by the series $\epsilon_{t,j,m}$, while the high bond price is generated by the antithetic draw $-\epsilon_{t,j,m}$. The symmetry of all the pairs of antithetic simulations around the mean bond price provides a large negative correlation and therefore offers a large decrease in the estimated standard error of the mean.

However, correlations between the results of antithetic samples will be less negative if the ZLB provides a material constraint. In this situation, the lower bond prices generated by the series $\epsilon_{t,j,m}$ are not as symmetrically matched around the mean by the higher bond prices generated by $-\epsilon_{t,j,m}$. This relative lack of symmetry arises from the ZLB constraint leaving many simulated bond prices at or close to 1. Therefore, antithetic pairs in a ZLB environment have lower negative correlations than in a non-ZLB environment, and so the number of simulations required for a given accuracy may be higher than for the relatively unconstrained example.

Using more extreme values of the state variables, consistent with material negative shadow short rates, for trial simulations would be needed to assess the likely number of simulations required.

5.3.4 Other potentially useful standard speed-up methods

Haug (2007, pp. 359–64) offers two other standard speed-up techniques for MC methods that may prove useful for B-AGM MC implementations. I mention them here for the interest of readers, but I have not yet investigated either of the techniques.

The first technique is importance sampling, which is usually applied to option pricing. The key principle is to use only simulated paths that end up in the money, and then to scale those results to allow for all the other paths that would have ended in the part of the distribution that is out of the money. The B-AGM is based on the option pricing mechanism $\underline{r}_{t,j,m} = \max\{r_L, r_{t,j,m}\}$, so paths of $r_{t,j,m} < r_L$ will be out of the money, that is, $\underline{r}_{t,j,m} = \max\{r_L, r_{t,j,m}\} = 0$. The distribution of shadow rates $r_{t,j,m}$ is known from the GATSM used to represent the shadow term structure in the B-AGM. Therefore, importance sampling on paths of $r_{t,j,m} > r_L$ suggests itself as a potential technique to speed up B-AGM MC implementations.

The second technique is to use quasi-random numbers, such as Sobel sequences, instead of pseudo-random numbers for the MC simulation. Quasi-random numbers tend to be more evenly spread out over the distributions of the state variables than pseudo-random numbers, which generally results in faster implementations (i.e., smaller confidence intervals for the same number of simulations, or a shorter time for the same confidence interval).

5.3.5 Worked example: B-ANSM(2)

In this subsection I first provide details on how to obtain a single simulated path of state variables for the B-ANSM(2), then transform that simulated state variable path into a path for shadow short rates and B-ANSM(3) short rates, and then into a simulated bond price. I also mention how the antithetic result is obtained from the same simulation.

The parameters for the risk-adjusted $\mathbb{Q}$ measure diffusion for the B-ANSM(2) are

$$a_0 = 0 \,;\, b_0 = \begin{bmatrix} 1 \\ 1 \end{bmatrix} ;\quad \tilde{\theta} = \begin{bmatrix} 0 \\ 0 \end{bmatrix} \tag{5.45}$$

$$\tilde{\kappa} = \begin{bmatrix} 0 & 0 \\ 0 & \phi \end{bmatrix} ;\quad \sigma = \begin{bmatrix} \sigma_1 & 0 \\ \rho_{12}\sigma_2 & \sigma_2\sqrt{1 - \rho_{12}^2} \end{bmatrix} \tag{5.46}$$

The simulated path of M state variable vectors is generated from the following recursion:

$$m = 1 : M$$
$$x_{t,j,m} = x_{t,j,m-1} + \tilde{\kappa}\left(\tilde{\theta} - x_{m,j,m-1}\right)\delta + \sigma\sqrt{\delta}\epsilon_{t,j,m} \tag{5.47}$$
$$\text{next } m$$

where the full vector/matrix expression for $x_{t,j,m}$ is

$$\begin{bmatrix} x_{1,t,j,m} \\ x_{2,t,j,m} \end{bmatrix} = \begin{bmatrix} x_{1,t,j,m-1} \\ x_{2,t,j,m-1} \end{bmatrix} - \begin{bmatrix} 0 & 0 \\ 0 & \phi \end{bmatrix}\begin{bmatrix} x_{1,t,j,m-1} \\ x_{2,t,j,m-1} \end{bmatrix} \times 0.01$$
$$+ \begin{bmatrix} \sigma_1 & 0 \\ \rho_{12}\sigma_2 & \sigma_2\sqrt{1-\rho_{12}^2} \end{bmatrix} + 0.1 \times \begin{bmatrix} \epsilon_{1,t,j,m} \\ \epsilon_{2,t,j,m} \end{bmatrix} \tag{5.48}$$

The initial value value for $x_{t,j,m}$ is

$$x_{t,j,0} = \begin{bmatrix} x_{1,t,j,0} \\ x_{2,t,j,0} \end{bmatrix} = \begin{bmatrix} x_1\,(t) \\ x_2\,(t) \end{bmatrix} \tag{5.49}$$

and I use $\delta = 0.01$ years, which gives $\sqrt{\delta} = 0.1$. Each $\epsilon_{t,j,m}$ draw is a 2×1 vector:

$$\epsilon_{t,j,m} = \begin{bmatrix} \epsilon_{1,t,j,m} \\ \epsilon_{2,t,j,m} \end{bmatrix} = \begin{bmatrix} N\,(0,1) \\ N\,(0,1) \end{bmatrix} \tag{5.50}$$

However, it is more efficient to create and store the entire sample of $\epsilon_{t,j,m}$ draws on the outset, so the same values can be used to create the antithetic draw. Hence, the sample of M $\epsilon_{t,j,m}$ draws would be the sequence of M 2×1 vectors:

$$\{\epsilon_{t,j,m}\} = \left\{ \begin{bmatrix} \epsilon_{1,t,j,0} \\ \epsilon_{2,t,j,0} \end{bmatrix}, \begin{bmatrix} \epsilon_{1,t,j,1} \\ \epsilon_{2,t,j,1} \end{bmatrix}, \dots, \begin{bmatrix} \epsilon_{1,t,j,M-1} \\ \epsilon_{2,t,j,M-1} \end{bmatrix}, \begin{bmatrix} \epsilon_{1,t,j,M} \\ \epsilon_{2,t,j,M} \end{bmatrix} \right\} \tag{5.51}$$

or equivalently a $2 \times M$ matrix:

$$\{\epsilon_{t,j,m}\} = \left\{ \begin{matrix} \epsilon_{1,t,j,0} & \epsilon_{1,t,j,1} & & \epsilon_{1,t,j,M-1} & \epsilon_{1,t,j,M} \\ \epsilon_{2,t,j,0} & \epsilon_{2,t,j,1} & \dots, & \epsilon_{2,t,j,M-1} & \epsilon_{2,t,j,M} \end{matrix} \right\}_{2 \times M} \tag{5.52}$$

Note that a matrix of independent $N(0,1)$ draws can be generated in MatLab using the function "randn," so $\{\epsilon_{t,j,m}\}$ above would simply be obtained as $\{\epsilon_{t,j,m}\} = \text{randn}(2, M)$.

The iterative simulation of each $x_{t,j,m}$ gives a sample $\{x_{t,j,m}\}$, which is a sequence of M 2×1 vectors:

$$\{x_{t,j,m}\} = \left\{ \begin{bmatrix} x_{1,t,j,0} \\ x_{2,t,j,0} \end{bmatrix}, \begin{bmatrix} x_{1,t,j,1} \\ x_{2,t,j,1} \end{bmatrix}, \dots, \begin{bmatrix} x_{1,t,j,M-1} \\ x_{2,t,j,M-1} \end{bmatrix}, \begin{bmatrix} x_{1,t,j,M} \\ x_{2,t,j,M} \end{bmatrix} \right\} \tag{5.53}$$

or equivalently a $2 \times M$ matrix:

$$\{x_{t,j,m}\} = \left\{ \begin{array}{ccccc} x_{1,t,j,0} & x_{1,t,j,1} & & x_{1,t,j,M-1} & x_{1,t,j,M} \\ x_{2,t,j,0} & x_{2,t,j,1} & ,\ldots, & x_{2,t,j,M-1} & x_{2,t,j,M} \end{array} \right\}_{2 \times M} \tag{5.54}$$

Shadow short rates are calculated using the simulated state variable vector at each time increment m:

$$r_{t,j,m} = a_0 + b_0' x_{t,j,m}$$

$$= [1,1] \left[\begin{array}{c} x_{1,t,j,m} \\ x_{2,t,j,m} \end{array} \right]$$

$$= x_{1,t,j,m} + x_{2,t,j,m} \tag{5.55}$$

or equivalently, the entire shadow short series can be calculated directly as a $1 \times M$ vector:

$$\{r_{t,j,m}\} = [1,1] \left\{ \begin{array}{ccccc} x_{1,t,j,0} & x_{1,t,j,1} & & x_{1,t,j,M-1} & x_{1,t,j,M} \\ x_{2,t,j,0} & x_{2,t,j,1} & ,\ldots, & x_{2,t,j,M-1} & x_{2,t,j,M} \end{array} \right\}_{2 \times M}$$

$$= \left\{ r_{t,j,0}, r_{t,j,1}, \ldots, r_{t,j,M-1}, r_{t,j,M} \right\}_{1 \times M} \tag{5.56}$$

ZLB short rates are obtained by applying the ZLB mechanism to each shadow short rate simulation:

$$\underline{r}_{t,j,m} = \max \left\{ r_L, r_{t,j,m} \right\} \tag{5.57}$$

or the entire series directly:

$$\{\underline{r}_{t,j,m}\} = \max \left\{ r_L, \{r_{t,j,m}\} \right\}$$

$$= \left\{ \underline{r}_{t,j,0}, \underline{r}_{t,j,1}, \ldots, \underline{r}_{t,j,M-1}, \underline{r}_{t,j,M} \right\} \tag{5.58}$$

The B-AGM bond price simulation is

$$\underline{P}_j^B(t,\tau) = \exp \left[-\sum_{m=0}^{M-1} \underline{r}_{t,j,m} \cdot 0.01 \right] \tag{5.59}$$

The antithetic sample for $x_{t,j+1,m}$ is calculated as for $x_{t,j,m}$ except using $-\sigma\sqrt{\delta}\epsilon_{t,j,m}$ instead of $\sigma\sqrt{\delta}\epsilon_{t,j,m}$:

$$x_{t,j+1,m} = x_{t,j+1,m-1} + \tilde{\kappa}\left(\tilde{\theta} - x_{m,j+1,m-1}\right)\delta - \sigma\sqrt{\delta}\epsilon_{t,j,m} \tag{5.60}$$

and then the simulated antithetic B-AGM bond price is

$$
\underline{P}^B_{j+1}(t,\tau) = \exp\left[-\sum_{m=0}^{M-1}\underline{r}_{t,j+1,m}\cdot 0.01\right]r_{t,j,m} \tag{5.61}
$$

where $\underline{r}_{t,j+1,m} = \max\{r_L, r_{t,j,m}\}$, with $r_{t,j,m} = a_0 + b_0'x_{t,j,m}$.

This gives two B-AGM bond price results for the sample, that is, $\underline{P}^B_j(t,\tau)$ and $\underline{P}^B_{j+1}(t,\tau)$. This step would be repeated as necessary to obtain the required sample size to provide the B-AGM bond prices estimate $\widehat{\underline{P}}^B(t,\tau)$.

5.3.6 Other B-AGMs

B-ANSM(3) and higher-order B-ANSMs

The full vector/matrix expression to simulate $x_{t,j,m}$ for the B-ANSM(3), assuming $\delta = 0.01$, is

$$
x_{t,j,m} = x_{t,j,m-1} + \tilde{\kappa}\left(\tilde{\theta} - x_{m,j,i-1}\right)\delta + \sigma\sqrt{\delta}\epsilon_{t,j,m}
$$

$$
\begin{bmatrix} x_{1,t,j,m} \\ x_{2,t,j,m} \\ x_{3,t,j,m} \end{bmatrix} = \begin{bmatrix} x_{1,t,j,m-1} \\ x_{2,t,j,m-1} \\ x_{3,t,j,m-1} \end{bmatrix} - \begin{bmatrix} 0 & 0 & 0 \\ 0 & \phi & -\phi \\ 0 & 0 & \phi \end{bmatrix} \begin{bmatrix} x_{1,t,j,m-1} \\ x_{2,t,j,m-1} \\ x_{3,t,j,m-1} \end{bmatrix} \times 0.01
$$

$$
+ \begin{bmatrix} \sigma_1 & 0 & 0 \\ \sigma_2\rho_{12} & \sigma_2\sqrt{1-\rho_{12}^2} & 0 \\ \sigma_3\rho_{13} & \sigma_3\dfrac{\rho_{23}-\rho_{12}\rho_{13}}{\sqrt{1-\rho_{12}^2}} & \sigma_3\sqrt{1-\rho_{13}^2 - \dfrac{(\rho_{23}-\rho_{12}\rho_{13})^2}{1-\rho_{12}^2}} \end{bmatrix}
$$

$$
\times 0.1 \times \begin{bmatrix} \epsilon_{1,t,j,m} \\ \epsilon_{2,t,j,m} \\ \epsilon_{3,t,j,m} \end{bmatrix} \tag{5.62}
$$

where $\tilde{\kappa}$, $\tilde{\theta}$ and σ are from the ANSM(3) specification in subsection 3.4.1. The $3 \times M$ matrix of independent $N(0,1)$ draws $\{\epsilon_{t,j,m}\}$ would simply be obtained as $\{\epsilon_{t,j,m}\} = \text{randn}(3,M)$ in MatLab.

Simulations of $x_{t,j,m}$ for higher-order B-ANSMs would be analogous to the B-ANSM(3), but with the state variable vectors, mean-reversion matrices $\tilde{\kappa}$, and volatility matrices σ as outlined in subsection 3.4.2. In particular, σ is more conveniently obtained by defining the covariance matrix $\sigma\sigma'$, and then using the lower Cholesky decomposition, $\sigma = \text{Chol}[\sigma\sigma']$.

Stationary B-AGM(3) and B-AGM(N)

The full vector/matrix expression to simulate $x_{t,j,m}$ for the B-AGM(3), assuming $\delta = 0.01$, is

$$x_{t,j,m} = x_{t,j,m-1} + \tilde{\kappa}\left(\tilde{\theta} - x_{m,j,i-1}\right)\delta + \sigma\sqrt{\delta}\epsilon_{t,j,m}$$

$$
\begin{bmatrix} x_{1,t,j,m} \\ x_{2,t,j,m} \\ x_{3,t,j,m} \end{bmatrix} = \begin{bmatrix} x_{1,t,j,m-1} \\ x_{2,t,j,m-1} \\ x_{3,t,j,m-1} \end{bmatrix} - \begin{bmatrix} \tilde{\kappa}_1 & 0 & 0 \\ 0 & \tilde{\kappa}_2 & 0 \\ 0 & 0 & \tilde{\kappa}_3 \end{bmatrix} \begin{bmatrix} x_{1,t,j,m-1} \\ x_{2,t,j,m-1} \\ x_{3,t,j,m-1} \end{bmatrix} \times 0.01
$$

$$
+ \begin{bmatrix} \sigma_1 & 0 & 0 \\ \sigma_2\rho_{12} & \sigma_2\sqrt{1-\rho_{12}^2} & 0 \\ \sigma_3\rho_{13} & \sigma_3\frac{\rho_{23}-\rho_{12}\rho_{13}}{\sqrt{1-\rho_{12}^2}} & \sigma_3\sqrt{1-\rho_{13}^2 - \frac{(\rho_{23}-\rho_{12}\rho_{13})^2}{1-\rho_{12}^2}} \end{bmatrix}
$$

$$
\times 0.1 \times \begin{bmatrix} \epsilon_{1,t,j,m} \\ \epsilon_{2,t,j,m} \\ \epsilon_{3,t,j,m} \end{bmatrix} \tag{5.63}
$$

where $\tilde{\kappa}$, $\tilde{\theta}$ and σ are from the GATSM(3) specification in section 3.4.4. The $3 \times M$ matrix of independent $N(0,1)$ draw $\{\epsilon_{t,j,m}\}$ would simply be obtained as $\{\epsilon_{t,j,m}\} =$ randn$(3,M)$ in MatLab.

Simulations of $x_{t,j,m}$ for higher-order B-AGMs would be analogous to the B-AGM(3), but with the state variable vectors, mean-reversion matrices $\tilde{\kappa}$, and volatility matrices σ as outlined in section 3.4.4. As noted for higher-order B-ANSMs in the previous subsection, σ is more conveniently obtained by defining the covariance matrix $\sigma\sigma'$, and then using the lower Cholesky decomposition, $\sigma = \text{Chol}[\sigma\sigma']$.

5.4 K-AGM as a control variate for B-AGM Monte Carlo simulations

If a suitable control variate (CV) is available for an MC simulation, which I will explain shortly, it can be used to improve the accuracy of the simulated results. In general, a CV d_j has an expected value of zero and is correlated with the j simulations being used to obtain the mean result of the MC simulation. Implicitly, d_j should also be readily calculable from the same samples as the MC simulation; otherwise, it will be of little practical use in terms of reducing computing time. With those properties, d_j can be used to reduce the estimated standard deviation of the mean from the MC simulations, and so fewer simulations are required to obtain a given accuracy. James and Webber (2000, pp. 356–59), for example, has general background on CVs for MC simulation.

Regarding B-AGM MC simulations, I will show in section 5.6.1 that K-AGM interest rates provide a very close approximation to B-AGM interest rates, and the same result will therefore hold for bond prices. Hence, the conceptual building blocks of the K-AGM framework, GATSM bond prices and portfolios of options on GATSM bonds, suggest they might provide a suitable CV for the MC simulation of B-AGM bond prices.

Krippner (2013b) has proposed such a K-AGM-based CV for B-AGM bond prices. I outline the CV proposed by Krippner (2013b) in subsection 5.4.1, and in subsection 5.4.2 provide an overview of the results from applying the CV to a one-state-variable example. In subsection 5.4.3, I provide the expressions that would be required to implement the analogous MC/CV method for B-AGMs with more than one state variable.

5.4.1 Defining the control variate

Simulated GATSM bond prices $P_j(t,\tau)$ are

$$P_j(t,\tau) = \exp\left[-\sum_{m=0}^{M-1} r_{t,j,m} \cdot \delta\right] \tag{5.64}$$

where M, δ, and the simulated shadow short rates $r_{t,j,m}$ are precisely those being used for the MC simulation of the B-AGM. That is, the shadow short rates used to simulate B-AGM bond prices are also used to simulate the control variate simultaneously. Note that antithetic sampling should be used to generate pairs of sample paths for $r_{t,j,m}$, as discussed in the previous subsection.

Krippner (2013b) defines the simulated bond price option effect $Z_j^P(t,\tau)$ as the simulated price of a portfolio of options on GATSM bonds:

$$Z_j^{PM}(t,\tau) = \sum_{m=0}^{M-1} C_j(t,m\delta,\delta,P_U) \tag{5.65}$$

where $m\delta$ is the time to expiry (i.e. $t + m\delta$ is the time of expiry), δ is the time to maturity of the underlying bond $P(m\delta,\delta)$ when the option expires, and P_U is the upper bound on the bond price, which is in turn related to the potentially non-zero lower bound r_L by:

$$P_U = \exp(-r_L \cdot \delta) \tag{5.66}$$

Note that $P_U = 1$ if $r_L = 0$, which replicates the expression in Krippner (2013b).

The simulated option prices $C_j(t,m\delta,\delta,P_U)$ used to obtain $Z_j^{PM}(t,\tau)$ are themselves obtained as

$$C_j(t,m\delta,\delta,P_U) = \exp\left[-\sum_{m=0}^{m-2} r_{t,j,m} \cdot \delta\right] \max\left\{P_j(m\delta,\delta) - P_U, 0\right\} \tag{5.67}$$

where

$$P_j(m\delta,\delta) = \exp\left[-r_{t,j,m+1} \cdot \delta\right] \tag{5.68}$$

with the shadow short rates $r_{t,j,m+1}$ already available as discussed above.

The population means of $P_j(t,\tau)$, $Z_j^{PM}(t,\tau)$, and $C_j(t,m\delta)$, which I respectively denote as $P(t,\tau)$, $Z^{PM}(t,\tau)$, and $C(t,m\delta)$, may be obtained using closed-form analytic solutions for GATSM bond and bond option prices. The bond price expressions are already available from section 3.1.3, and I will provide the expressions for the bond option prices in the following subsections.

Subtracting the population means from the sample quantities therefore produces the CV for simulated B-AGM bond prices $\underline{P}_j^B(t,\tau)$:

$$d_j(t,\tau) = \left[P_j(t,\tau) - Z_j^{PM}(t,\tau)\right] - \left[P(t,\tau) - Z^{PM}(t,\tau)\right] \tag{5.69}$$

where I use the time and time to maturity to explicitly denote that $d_j(t,\tau)$ is used as the CV for $\underline{P}_j^B(t,\tau)$. Note that, just as for simulations of $\underline{P}_j^B(t,\tau)$, the simulations for CVs of different times to maturity $\tau_1,\ldots,\tau_K$ are obtained by sampling from paths out to the longest time to maturity τ_K. The relevant population means $P(t,\tau) - Z^{PM}(t,\tau)$ are then calculated for each separate time to maturity to obtain the CVs $d_j(t,\tau_1),\ldots,d_j(t,\tau_K)$ associated with the samples for each time to maturity, i.e. $\underline{P}_j^B(t,\tau_1),\ldots,\underline{P}_j^B(t,\tau_K)$.

Being based on the K-AGM framework, $d_j(t,\tau)$ should also have a high correlation to the simulated B-AGM bond prices $\underline{P}_j^B(t,\tau)$ being used to obtain the estimate $\widehat{\underline{P}}^B(t,\tau)$. Furthermore, the CV $d_j(t,\tau)$ also has the required property of a zero mean by construction. Regarding the zero mean property, Krippner (2013b) notes that there is deliberately a subtle difference in how the proposed CV combines GATSM bond prices $P(t,\tau)$ with the bond price option effect $Z^{PM}(t,\tau)$ relative to the K-AGM treatment and its bond price option effect $Z_P(t,\tau)$. Specifically, defining the CV linearly based on simulations of $P_j(t,\tau) - Z_j^{PM}(t,\tau)$ directly matches the population mean $P(t,\tau) - Z^{PM}(t,\tau)$. Conversely, from Table 5.1, K-AGM bond prices are actually the product $P(t,\tau) \times Z_P(t,\tau)$. Due to Jensen's inequality, that product would not provide the population mean of the simulated products $P_j(t,\tau) \times Z_j^{PM}(t,\tau)$. It may be possible to analytically calculate the population mean of $P_j(t,\tau) \times Z_j^{PM}(t,\tau)$, which would be required to create the associated CV, although the calculation is likely to be relatively complex due to it being a function of the discrete time step δ used in the simulation.

The MC/CV estimate of the Black bond price, which I denote as $\underline{P}_C^B(t,\tau)$, is the estimated constant from the following ordinary least squares (OLS) regression:

$$\underline{P}_j^B(t,\tau) = \underline{P}_C^B(t,\tau) + \beta d_j(t,\tau) + v_j(t,\tau) \tag{5.70}$$

which is most clearly illustrated with an example of the data as subsequently provided in Figure 5.3. The estimated standard deviation of $\underline{P}^B_C(t,\tau)$, std$\left[\underline{P}^B_C(t,\tau)\right]$, is the standard error of the constant in the OLS regression.

There are four observations to make from the perspective of the OLS regression:

- The non-CV MC result may be viewed as an OLS regression of the simulated prices on just a constant:

$$\underline{P}^B_j(t,\tau) = \underline{P}^B(t,\tau) + \upsilon_j(t,\tau) \tag{5.71}$$

- Higher correlations between d_j and $\underline{P}_j(t,\tau)$ produce smaller standard errors for the OLS estimates, and therefore more accurate MC/CV estimates. Hence, alternative CV specifications may prove superior to the K-AGM-based CV outline here.
- More than one CV may be used, in which case $\underline{P}^B_C(t,\tau)$ is obtained as the estimated constant from a multivariate OLS regression. For example, with two CVs, $\underline{P}^B_C(t,\tau)$ and its standard error would be obtained from the following OLS regression:

$$\underline{P}^B_j(t,\tau) = \underline{P}^B_C(t,\tau) + \beta_1 d_{1,j}(t,\tau) + \beta_2 d_{2,j}(t,\tau) + \upsilon_j(t,\tau) \tag{5.72}$$

Therefore, any alternative CV would probably be best employed in addition to that already proposed by Krippner (2013b). From that perspective, if the first- and second-order B-AGM approximations due to Priebsch (2013) that I discuss in subsection 5.6.2 could both be constructed as CVs, then that may speed up MC/CV implementations considerably more.

- Allowing for the statistical properties of the residuals may improve the estimate of $\underline{P}^B_C(t,\tau)$ and its standard error. For example, Figure 5.3 in the following section shows apparent heteroskedasticity as a function of the CV, and so that could readily be allowed for using generalized least squares or other methods.

5.4.2 B-AGM(1) illustration

In this section, I outline an example from Krippner (2013b) to illustrate the concept of implementing B-AGMs with the MC/CV method using a B-AGM with one state variable, which I will call the B-AGM(1) for short. The B-AGM(1) uses the GATSM(1) to represent the shadow short rate, and therefore r(t) is the single state variable.

Krippner (2013b) uses the state variable r(t) and the parameter set from Gorovoi and Linetsky (2004) p. 71 for his example. That is, $r(t) = -0.0512$, $r_L = 0$, $\tilde{\kappa} = 0.212$, $\tilde{\theta} = 0.0354$, and $\sigma = 0.0283$ define the risk-adjusted $\mathbb{Q}$ measure process for r(t). The simulation uses antithetic draws for $\epsilon_{t,j,m}$, $\delta = 0.01$ years, and 10,000 replications. Because the shadow short rate is the only state variable in the one-factor GATSM, simulating $r_{t,j,m}$ with antithetic sampling proceeds directly as follows:

$$r_{t,j,m} = r_{t,j,m-1} + \tilde{\kappa}\left(\tilde{\theta} - r_{t,j,m-1}\right)\delta + \sigma\sqrt{\delta}\epsilon_{t,j,m}$$

$$r_{t,j+1,m} = r_{t,j+1,m} + \tilde{\kappa}\left(\tilde{\theta} - r_{t,j,m-1}\right)\delta - \sigma\sqrt{\delta}\epsilon_{t,j+1,m} \tag{5.73}$$

where $r_{t,j+1,m} = r(t)$, and $\tilde{\kappa}$, $\tilde{\theta}$, and σ are the B-AGM(1) parameters. These shadow short rates are used as I will outline below to obtain the simulated B-AGM(1) bond prices $\underline{P}_j(t,\tau)$, the simulated GATSM(1) bond prices $P_j(t,\tau)$, and the simulated option effect $Z_j^{PM}(t,\tau)$.

The population means are obtained using prices for bonds and options on bonds. Expressions for those prices are available using the respective Vasicek (1977) expressions available in the original paper and many textbooks, for example, Hull (2000), James and Webber (2000), and Haug (2007). However, for convenience and clarity, I write them here using the notation in this book. Hence, the population mean for $P_j(t,\tau)$ is

$$P(t,\tau) = \exp\left[-\tau \cdot R(t,\tau)\right] \tag{5.74}$$

where $R(t,\tau)$ are the interest rates that can be obtained from the expressions for GATSMs discussed in section subsection 3.4.4. That is, taking just the first component for the GATSM(3) or using $N = 1$ in the GATSM(N) expression gives

$$R(t,\tau) = r(t) \cdot G(\tilde{\kappa},\tau) - \sigma^2 \cdot \frac{1}{2\tilde{\kappa}^2\tau}\left[\tau - G(\tilde{\kappa},\tau) - \frac{1}{2}\tilde{\kappa}\left[G(\tilde{\kappa},\tau)\right]^2\right] \tag{5.75}$$

The population mean for $Z_j^{PM}(t,\tau)$ is

$$Z^{PM}(t,\tau) = \sum_{m=0}^{M-1} C(t,m\delta,\delta,P_U) \tag{5.76}$$

where $C(t,m\delta,\delta,P_U)$ is the B-AGM(1) option price expression. The expression for $C(t,m\delta,\delta,P_U)$ is

$$C(t,m\delta,\delta,P_U) = P(t,m\delta+\delta) \cdot \Phi\left[v_1(t,m\delta,\delta)\right]$$
$$- P_U \cdot P(t,m\delta) \cdot \Phi\left[v_2(t,m\delta,\delta)\right] \tag{5.77}$$

where $\Phi[\cdot]$ is the cumulative normal distribution function, and

$$v_{1,2}(t,\tau,\delta) = \frac{1}{\Sigma(\tau,\delta)}\log\left[\frac{P(t,\tau+\delta)}{P_U \cdot P(t,\tau)}\right] \pm \frac{1}{2}\Sigma(\tau,\delta) \tag{5.78}$$

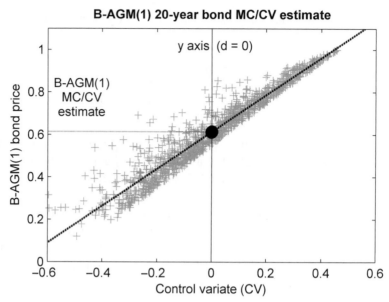

Figure 5.3 An illustration of the MC/CV data and OLS regression used to obtain the 20-year B-AGM(1) bond price (i.e., 0.6119 in Table 5.2).

where:

$$\Sigma(\tau,\delta) = \sigma \cdot G(\phi,\delta) \sqrt{G(2\phi,\tau)} \tag{5.79}$$

Note that the lower bound setting of $r_L = 0$ means that $P_U = \exp(-0 \cdot \delta) = 1$ in this example.

The simulated results $P_j(t,\tau)$ and $Z_j^{PM}(t,\tau)$ along with the population means $P(t,\tau)$ and $Z^{PM}(t,\tau)$ provide the CV $d_j(t,\tau)$ as in equation 5.69. The MC/CV B-AGM bond price results $\underline{P}_C^B(t,\tau)$ can then be evaluated using the OLS regression $\underline{P}_j^B(t,\tau) = \underline{P}_C^B(t,\tau) + \beta d_j(t,\tau) + \upsilon_j(t,\tau)$ with the $\underline{P}_j^B(t,\tau_k)$ and $d_j(t,\tau_k)$ results for each of the required times to maturity τ_k.

Figure 5.3 plots the simulated B-AGM bond prices $\underline{P}_j^B(t,\tau)$ against $d_j(t,\tau)$ for the 20-year time to maturity. Figure 5.3 also plots the OLS regression line, and therefore shows how OLS is used to obtain the MC/CV estimate of $\underline{P}_C^B(t,\tau)$ for the 20-year B-AGM bond price (i.e., 0.6119 in Table 1).

Table 5.2 shows the markedly lower estimate of std$\left[\widehat{\underline{P}_C^B}(t,\tau)\right]$ compared to the MC estimate of std$\left[\widehat{\underline{P}^B}(t,\tau)\right]$, that is, 0.0005 compared to 0.0019. The difference means that fewer simulations are required to obtain a given accuracy or confidence interval for the B-AGM bond price estimate, which therefore reduces the computing time for an implementation of the B-AGM(1). Graphically, that lower relative standard deviation std$\left[\underline{P}_C^B(t,\tau)\right]$ reflects the lower dispersion of $\underline{P}_j^B(t,\tau)$

simulations around the CV regression line, as compared to the dispersion of $P_{-j}^B (t, \tau)$ simulations against a constant (i.e., the dispersion along the y axis).

Table 5.2 also shows the calculated times it would take to generate $\text{std}\left[\widehat{R}(t, \tau)\right] = 0.3$ basis points (bps) or 0.003 percentage points (pps) for the MC and MC/CV methods given the standard deviations already achieved for the times taken to run the 10,000 simulations. The choice of 0.3 basis points is arbitrary for the illustration, but it corresponds in practice to a 99 percent confidence interval of less than one basis point around the true value (i.e., $0.3 \times \pm 2.58 = \pm 0.774$ basis points).

For example, the 20-year bond rate results obtained with the standard MC simulation are 2.46 pps with a standard deviation of 0.016 pps (to 3 decimal places). From the expression from equation 5.43 in subsection 5.3.2, a time of approximately 190 seconds (or 0.28 million simulations) would be required to reduce that standard deviation to 0.003 percentage points. That is,

$$t(J_\lambda) \simeq t(10,000) \frac{1}{\lambda^2} \left(\text{std}\left[\widehat{R}^B(t, \tau)\right]_{10,000} \right)^2$$

$$190 = 7.15 \times \frac{1}{0.003^2} \times (0.016)^2 \text{ seconds} \tag{5.80}$$

The 20-year bond rate results using the MC/CV method are an estimate of 2.46 pps with a standard deviation of 0.004 pps, and a time of 16.8 seconds would be required to reduce that standard deviation to 0.003 pps. This result represents a relative time benefit of 0.088. That is, the standard deviation of 0.3 basis points and therefore a confidence interval of ± 0.774 basis points could be obtained using the MC/CV method in less than $1/10^{\text{th}}$ of the time for the MC simulation alone.

Table 5.2 panel C includes the relative time benefits for all of the selected times to maturity. Note that each result combines the relative standard deviation benefit $\text{std}\left[\widehat{R_C^B}(t, \tau)\right] / \text{std}\left[\widehat{R^B}(t, \tau)\right]$ (e.g., 0.28 for the 20-year results), and the relatively longer time for implementing the MC/CV method (e.g., 7.85/7.15 for the 20-year results), which is due to the additional numerical and analytic evaluations required to generate the CV and the OLS regression results. While all results show a relative time benefit from using the MC/CV method, the benefit decreases by maturity, as I will explain shortly.

Figure 5.4 illustrates the reducing time benefit as a function of time to maturity, and also a tendency for the relative time benefit to worsen as the shadow short rate declines from positive values, to zero, and to negative values. Both trends are intuitive; when shadow short rates have higher probabilities of remaining or becoming negative, K-AGM-based bond price approximations that are based on shadow short rates for discounting have larger differences to B-AGM bond prices that are based on ZLB short rates for discounting. In turn, the correlation between the K-AGM-based and B-AGM bond prices will be lower, and so the effectiveness of the CV will deteriorate. I provide further discussion related to this point in section 5.6.1.

Table 5.2 B-AGM(1) MC and MC/CV simulation results

A. MC results: time 7.15 seconds for 10,000 simulations [1]

Maturity τ	1	5	10	20	30
$\widehat{P^B}(t,\tau)$	0.9998	0.9618	0.8498	0.6112	0.4307
std$\left[\widehat{P^B}(t,\tau)\right]$	0.0000	0.0005	0.0013	0.0019	0.0019
$\widehat{R^B}(t,\tau)$ pps	0.02	0.78	1.63	2.46	2.81
std$\left[\widehat{R^B}(t,\tau)\right]$	0.001	0.011	0.015	0.016	0.015
0.003 time[2]	1	87	172	190	170

B. MC/CV results: time 7.85 seconds for 10,000 simulations [1]

Maturity τ	1	5	10	20	30
$\widehat{P_C^B}(t,\tau)$	0.9998	0.9621	0.8506	0.6119	0.4306
std$\left[\widehat{P_C^B}(t,\tau)\right]$	0.0000	0.0000	0.0001	0.0005	0.0010
$\widehat{R_C^B}(t,\tau)$ pps	0.02	0.77	1.62	2.46	2.81
std$\left[\widehat{R_C^B}(t,\tau)\right]$	0.000	0.000	0.001	0.004	0.008
0.003 time[2]	0.0002	0.1	1.8	16.8	51.1

C. Relative results (i.e., MC/CV results divided by MC results)

Maturity τ	1	5	10	20	30
std[·] benefit	0.012	0.037	0.097	0.28	0.52
Time benefit	0.0002	0.0015	0.010	0.088	0.30

Notes: (1) Using Intel core i7-3770 CPU @ 3.4 GHz with 8.00 GB memory, with a 64 bit Windows 7 operating system, and a 64 bit version of MatLab without parallel processing.
(2) Estimated time to achieve interest rate std[-] of 0.003 pps.

5.4.3 Extensions to more than one state variable

The MC/CV method is extendable to B-AGMs, and therefore the B-ANSM subclass, with any number of state variables. My preliminary results using the MC/CV method on B-AGMs with up to three state variables indicate that relative time benefits and even absolute running times similar to the B-AGM(1) are attainable. One aspect behind the similar performance despite adding more state variables is that, like the K-AGM itself, the number of numerical evaluations required to generate the population mean for the K-AGM-based CV remains invariant to the B-AGM specification.

The population mean for the K-AGM-based CV requires the closed-form analytic bond price and option price expressions for the GATSM being used to represent the shadow term structure. The bond price expressions are already available in chapter 3. The option price expressions are straightforward to calculate from the generic GATSM option price expression. I provide that expression in the following subsection, and then proceed to a fully worked example using an ANSM(2) to show how to apply the expressions in practice. After that detailed example, I provide an

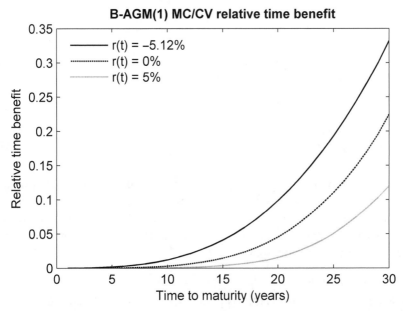

Figure 5.4 The time to achieve a given interest rate precision for the MC/CV method relative to standard MC simulation.

overview of the option price results for the ANSM(3), higher-order ANSMs, the GATSM(3), and the generic GATSM with N state variables.

In addition to the expressions for GATSM bond prices that are already available in chapter 3, the option price expressions in this subsection provide the additional building blocks that would be required to apply the Krippner (2013b) MC/CV method to implement other B-AGM specifications.

Generic GATSM option price expression

Filopović (2009, p. 109) provides the generic closed-form analytic expression for the price of call options on GATSM bonds as[1]

$$C(t,\tau,\delta,P_S) = P(t,\tau+\delta)\,\Phi\left[v_1(t,\tau,\delta)\right] - P_S \cdot P(t,\tau)\,\Phi\left[v_2(t,\tau,\delta)\right] \qquad (5.81)$$

where τ is the time to expiry (i.e., $t+\tau$ is the time of expiry), δ is the time to maturity of the underlying bond $P(t+\tau,\delta)$ when the option expires, P_S is the strike price (which would be P_U when the option price formula is used to calculate the K-AGM-based CV), $\Phi[\cdot]$ is the cumulative normal distribution function, and

$$v_{1,2}(t,\tau,\delta) = \frac{1}{\Sigma(\tau,\delta)}\log\left[\frac{P(t,\tau+\delta)}{P_S \cdot P(t,\tau)}\right] \pm \frac{1}{2}\Sigma(\tau,\delta) \qquad (5.82)$$

with

$$\Sigma(\tau,\delta) = \sqrt{\int_0^\tau \|\sigma(s,\delta)\|^2 \, ds} \tag{5.83}$$

and

$$\sigma(s,\delta) = \int_s^{s+\delta} \sigma(u) \, du \tag{5.84}$$

Note that $\Sigma(\tau,\delta)$ is the only expression required to calculate GATSM option prices in addition to the GATSM bond prices expressions $P(t,\tau+\delta)$ and $P(t,\tau)$, which are already available or readily calculable as detailed in chapter 3. Therefore, the subsections below will focus on how to calculate $\Sigma(\tau,\delta)$ and some results for particular GATSM specifications.

ANSM(2) call option prices: worked example

To obtain $\Sigma(\tau,\delta)$ for the ANSM(2) option price expression, I begin with

$$\sigma(u) = b_0' \exp(-\tilde{\kappa} u) \sigma \tag{5.85}$$

where b_0', $\tilde{\kappa}$, and σ are as previously defined in section 3.3:

$$b_0 = \begin{bmatrix} 1 \\ 1 \end{bmatrix}; \quad \tilde{\kappa} = \begin{bmatrix} 0 & 0 \\ 0 & \phi \end{bmatrix}; \quad \sigma = \begin{bmatrix} \sigma_1 & 0 \\ \rho_{12}\sigma_2 & \sigma_2\sqrt{1-\rho_{12}^2} \end{bmatrix} \tag{5.86}$$

and the relevant related results are

$$\exp(-\tilde{\kappa} u) = \begin{bmatrix} 1 & 0 \\ 0 & \exp(-\phi u) \end{bmatrix}; \quad \sigma\sigma' = \begin{bmatrix} \sigma_1^2 & \rho_{12}\sigma_1\sigma_2 \\ \rho_{12}\sigma_1\sigma_2 & \sigma_2^2 \end{bmatrix} \tag{5.87}$$

Therefore,

$$\begin{aligned}
\sigma(s,\delta) &= \int_s^{s+\delta} \sigma(u) \, du \\
&= b_0' \left(\int_s^{s+\delta} \begin{bmatrix} 1 & 0 \\ 0 & \exp(-\phi u) \end{bmatrix} du \right) \sigma \\
&= b_0' \begin{bmatrix} \delta & 0 \\ 0 & \frac{1}{\phi}\exp(-\phi s) - \frac{1}{\phi}\exp(-\phi[s+\delta]) \end{bmatrix} \sigma \\
&= b_0' \begin{bmatrix} \delta & 0 \\ 0 & \exp(-\phi s)\frac{1}{\phi}[1 - \exp(-\phi\delta)] \end{bmatrix} \sigma \\
&= b_0' \begin{bmatrix} \delta & 0 \\ 0 & \exp(-\phi s) G(\phi,\delta) \end{bmatrix} \sigma \tag{5.88}
\end{aligned}$$

and

$$\|\sigma\,(s,\delta)\|^2 = b_0' \begin{bmatrix} \delta & 0 \\ 0 & \exp\,(-\phi s)\,G\,(\phi,\delta) \end{bmatrix} \sigma\sigma'$$

$$\times \begin{bmatrix} \delta & 0 \\ 0 & \exp\,(-\phi s)\,G\,(\phi,\delta) \end{bmatrix}' b_0$$

$$= [1,1] \begin{bmatrix} \delta & 0 \\ 0 & \exp\,(-\phi s)\,G\,(\phi,\delta) \end{bmatrix} \begin{bmatrix} \sigma_1^2 & \rho_{12}\sigma_1\sigma_2 \\ \rho_{12}\sigma_1\sigma_2 & \sigma_2^2 \end{bmatrix}$$

$$\times \begin{bmatrix} \delta & 0 \\ 0 & \exp\,(-\phi s)\,G\,(\phi,\delta) \end{bmatrix} \begin{bmatrix} 1 \\ 1 \end{bmatrix}$$

$$= \sigma_1^2 \cdot \delta^2 + \sigma_2^2 \cdot [G\,(\phi,\delta)]^2 \cdot \exp\,(-2\phi s)$$

$$+ 2\rho_{12}\sigma_1\sigma_2 \cdot \delta \cdot G\,(\phi,\delta) \cdot \exp\,(-\phi s) \tag{5.89}$$

The required integrals for the relevant functions over s are

$$\int_0^\tau 1\,\mathrm{d}s = \tau \tag{5.90a}$$

$$\int_0^\tau \exp\,(-2\phi s)\,\mathrm{d}s = G\,(2\phi,\tau) \tag{5.90b}$$

$$\int_0^\tau \exp\,(-\phi s)\,\mathrm{d}s = G\,(\phi,\tau) \tag{5.90c}$$

and therefore

$$[\Sigma\,(\tau,\delta)]^2 = \int_0^\tau \|\sigma\,(s,\delta)\|^2\,\mathrm{d}s$$

$$= \sigma_1^2 \cdot \delta^2\tau + \sigma_2^2 \cdot [G\,(\phi,\delta)]^2 \cdot G\,(2\phi,\tau)$$

$$+ 2\rho_{12}\sigma_1\sigma_2 \cdot \delta \cdot G\,(\phi,\delta) \cdot G\,(\phi,\tau) \tag{5.91}$$

The ANSM(2) call option price therefore uses $\Sigma\,(\tau,\delta)$ within equations 5.81 and 5.82 along with the strike price P_S and the associated bond price expressions $P(t,\tau+\delta)$ and $P(t,\tau)$. Note that the bond prices are functions of the prevailing state variable vector $x(t)$ and the ANSM(2) parameter set. Therefore the dependence of the option price on the ANSM(2) state variables comes via the bond price expressions.

As an aside, Krippner (2011, 2012b,c) originally derived $[\omega(\tau)]^2$ for the K-ANSM(2) by deriving a generic expression for the limit of annualized volatility for GATSM options as $\delta \to 0$:

$$[\omega\,(\tau)]^2 = \frac{1}{2} \cdot \lim_{\delta \to 0} \left\{ \frac{\mathrm{d}^2}{\mathrm{d}\delta^2} [\Sigma\,(\tau,\delta)]^2 \right\} \tag{5.92}$$

and then applying that to the closed-form expression for options on ANSM(2) bonds. The relevant limit results as $\delta \to 0$ are

$$\lim_{\delta \to 0} \left\{ \frac{d^2}{d\delta^2} \delta^2 \right\} = 2$$

$$\lim_{\delta \to 0} \left\{ \frac{d^2}{d\delta^2} [G(\phi,\delta)]^2 \right\} = 2$$

$$\lim_{\delta \to 0} \left\{ \frac{d^2}{d\delta^2} [\delta \cdot G(\phi,\delta)] \right\} = 2$$

and that gives a result identical to that in subsection 4.3.3, that is,

$$[\omega(\tau)]^2 = \sigma_1^2 \cdot \tau + \sigma_2^2 \cdot G(2\phi,\tau) + 2\rho_{12}\sigma_1\sigma_2 \cdot G(\phi,\tau) \tag{5.93}$$

However, using equation 4.15 is obviously preferable if one only requires $[\omega(\tau)]^2$ and not the ANSM(2) option price expression in its own right.

ANSM(3) call option prices

Call option prices for ANSM(3) bonds require the expression for ANSM(3) bonds from section 3.4.1, and the following result for $[\Sigma(\tau,\delta)]^2$:

$$[\Sigma(\tau,\delta)]^2 = \sigma_1^2 \cdot \delta^2\tau + \sigma_2^2 \cdot [G(\phi,\delta)]^2 \cdot G(2\phi,\tau) + \sigma_3^2 \cdot \Sigma\,(\mathrm{B/B})$$

$$+2\rho_{12}\sigma_1\sigma_2 \cdot G(\phi,\tau) + \rho_{13}\sigma_1\sigma_3 \cdot \Sigma\,(\mathrm{L/B + B/L})$$

$$+\rho_{13}\sigma_1\sigma_3 \cdot \Sigma\,(\mathrm{S/B + B/S}) \tag{5.94}$$

Note that I have used the relevant results from the calculations in the previous subsection, and the remaining results required are readily obtained using the Filipović (2009) generic option price expression analogous to the calculations in the previous subsection. Hence,

$$\Sigma\,(\mathrm{B/B}) = \left\{ \frac{5}{2} [G(\phi,\delta)]^2 - 3\delta \exp(-\phi\delta)\,G(\phi,\delta) + \delta^2 \exp(-2\phi\delta) \right\} \cdot G(2\phi,\tau)$$

$$+ \left\{ -\frac{3}{2} [G(\phi,\delta)]^2 + \delta \exp(-\phi\delta)\,G(\phi,\delta) \right\} \cdot \tau \exp(-2\phi\tau)$$

$$- \frac{1}{2} [G(\phi,\delta)]^2 \cdot \phi\tau^2 \exp(-2\phi\tau) \tag{5.95}$$

$$\Sigma\,(\mathrm{L/B + B/L}) = \left[4\delta \cdot G(\phi,\delta) - 2\delta^2 \exp(-2\phi\delta) \right] \cdot G(\phi,\tau)$$

$$- 2\delta \cdot G(\phi,\delta) \cdot \tau \exp(-\phi\tau) \tag{5.96}$$

and

$$\Sigma\,(S/B+B/S) = \{3\,[G(\phi,\delta)]^2 - 2\delta\exp(-\phi\delta)\,G(\phi,\delta)\}\cdot G(2\phi,\tau)$$
$$- [G(\phi,\delta)]^2\,\tau\exp(-2\phi\tau) \tag{5.97}$$

which gives the complete expression for $[\Sigma\,(\tau,\delta)]^2$ required to calculated ANSM(3) option prices.

The equivalent result for ANSM(3) option prices first appeared in Christensen and Rudebusch (2013a), but it is defined in terms of covariances rather than my preferred notation in terms of standard deviations and correlations. Christensen and Rudebusch (2013a) also derived their result directly from the first principles of option pricing and using the ANSM(3) under the forward measure, but undertaking the calculation using the Filipović (2009) generic option price expression is much more straightforward. Furthermore, Christensen and Rudebusch (2013a) did not actually require the ANSM(3) option expression in its own right, but as the means to obtain $[\omega(\tau)]^2$ using the Krippner (2011, 2012b,c) limit expression, that is, equation 5.92. However, as already noted in subsection 4.1.5, the direct calculation of $[\omega(\tau)]^2$ using equation 4.15 is obviously preferable if one only requires $[\omega(\tau)]^2$ directly.

Stationary GATSM call option prices

Call option prices for GATSM(2) bonds are readily obtained analogously to the ANSM(2) for the worked example, but with rates of mean reversion $\tilde{\kappa}_1$ and $\tilde{\kappa}_2$ instead of 0 and ϕ. Hence,

$$\exp(-\tilde{\kappa}\,u) = \begin{bmatrix} \exp(-\tilde{\kappa}_1 u) & 0 \\ 0 & \exp(-\tilde{\kappa}_2 u) \end{bmatrix}$$

and

$$[\Sigma\,(\tau,\delta)]^2 = \sigma_1^2\cdot[G(2\tilde{\kappa}_1,\delta)]^2\cdot G(2\tilde{\kappa}_1,\tau)$$
$$+\sigma_2^2\cdot[G(2\tilde{\kappa}_2,\delta)]^2\cdot G(2\tilde{\kappa}_2,\tau)$$
$$+2\rho_{12}\sigma_1\sigma_2\cdot G(\tilde{\kappa}_1,\delta)\cdot G(\tilde{\kappa}_2,\delta)\cdot G(\tilde{\kappa}_1+\tilde{\kappa}_2,\tau) \tag{5.98}$$

Similarly, $\exp(-\tilde{\kappa}\,u)$ is always diagonal for GATSMs. Therefore, the general form of $[\Sigma\,(\tau,\delta)]^2$ for a GATSM(N) is

$$[\Sigma\,(\tau,\delta)]^2 = \sum_{n=1}^{N}\sigma_n^2\cdot[G(2\tilde{\kappa}_n,\delta)]^2\cdot G(2\tilde{\kappa}_n,\tau)$$

$$+2\sum_{n=1}^{N}\sum_{m=n+1}^{N-1}\rho_{nm}\sigma_n\sigma_m\cdot G(\tilde{\kappa}_n,\delta)\cdot G(\tilde{\kappa}_m,\delta)$$

$$\times G(\tilde{\kappa}_n+\tilde{\kappa}_m,\tau) \tag{5.99}$$

5.5 B-AGM estimation

In this section, I provide an overview of how B-AGMs may be estimated. Given the large computing time required, as I will note at the end of this section, I have not yet undertaken any full estimations of B-AGMs, and so I do not provide any results. I intend to return to that topic when my testing of the MC/CV method for speeding up the implementations of B-AGMs with more than one state variable is complete. However, the need to do so will in turn depend on the outcome of the theoretical case for K-AGMs versus B-AGMs, which I discuss in Chapter 6.

The method for estimating B-AGMs is essentially identical to the method for K-AGMs. I will therefore draw heavily from the K-AGM estimation discussion in section 4.2 of chapter 4, beginning with the comment that I think the iterated extended Kalman filter (IEKF) is likely to be the best estimation method. Specifically, a nonlinear Kalman filter is required due to the nonlinearity of the B-AGM measurement equation, and the IEKF is likely to present the most reliable means of estimation, as previously discussed for K-AGMs in subsection 4.2.1. I will therefore focus exclusively on the IEKF in this section. However, others may prefer to use the extended Kalman filter, the unscented Kalman filter, or the particle filter, as briefly introduced in subsection 4.2.1.

The crucial difference between B-AGM and K-AGM estimations is that no representation of the B-AGM term structure has closed-form analytic solutions, whereas the K-AGM has the advantage of a closed-form analytic expression for forward rates. Therefore, the calculations required for the B-AGM in the measurement step of the IEKF are necessarily based on completely numerical methods. For general B-AGM specifications, with more than two state variables, MC simulations are typically the most efficient method of the range of numerical methods presented in section 5.2. I will therefore focus exclusively on estimation via the IEKF using MC simulation.

I provide in subsection 5.5.1 an overview and then the details for a partial K-AGM estimation, that is, how to obtain estimates of the K-AGM state variables from the data given a suitable set of parameters. In subsection 5.5.2, I present an overview for full K-AGM estimations, that is, how to obtain estimates of the K-AGM parameters and state variables from the data using maximum likelihood estimation.

Note that in chapters 3 and 4, the distinction between partial and full estimations was to some extent a convenient means of splitting the details and discussion of the given Kalman filtering algorithm for a given set of parameters from the slightly more general process of using the Kalman filtering algorithm within an optimization algorithm for a full estimation. The extra effort and time to undertake the full estimation is not onerous, for example, in the order of seconds for a partial estimation and in the order of minutes or hours for a full estimation depending on the starting values. However, due to the time-consuming numerical methods required for the B-AGM implementations, the difference between a partial and full estimation of a B-AGM may well be on the order of days versus months, or even years.

5.5.1 Partial estimation

Table 5.3 summarizes a single application of the IEKF algorithm to obtain a partial B-AGM estimation. Note that Table 5.3 is identical to Table 4.2 for the partial estimation of K-AGMs, except the calculations of the residual vector $\eta_{t,i}$ and the Jacobian matrix $H_{t,i}$ in the "**3.2. Measurement/posterior state iterations**" are different. I have labeled those two steps (i) and (ii) for further discussion below. For discussion on the flow of Table 5.3, I refer readers to the K-AGM partial estimation discussion in subsection 4.2.2.

An overview of the practical difference between the K-AGM and B-AGM framework from the perspective of steps (i) and (ii) is as follows:

- A partial estimation of the K-AGM or B-AGM with the IEKF requires $\sum_{t=1}^{T} I_t$ evaluations of the residuals $\eta_{t,i}$ and the Jacobian $H_{t,i}$, where I_t represents the number of IEKF iterations $i = 0$ to I_t at each yield curve observation t, and T represents the $t = 1$ to T observations of yield curve data. As an example, by undertaking a representative K-ANSM(2) partial estimation using parameter values previously obtained from a full estimation, I found that 842 iterations were required for the 341 observations of yield curve data, or approximately 2.5 iterations per observation.
- K-AGMs have a closed-form analytic expression for forward rates. That property facilitates fast K-AGM implementations required to obtain model-implied yields, which in turn are used to obtain the residuals $\eta_{t,i}$. Note also that the results from each implementation are also used to obtain the Jacobian $H_{t,i}$, as detailed in section 4.2.2. Therefore, it only requires a small amount of computing time to undertake the $\sum_{t=1}^{T} I_t$ evaluations of the residuals $\eta_{t,i}$ and the Jacobian $H_{t,i}$ required for a partial K-AGM estimation. For example, the 842 evaluations for the representative K-ANSM(2) partial estimation mentioned above took around 0.5 seconds.
- Conversely, none of the B-AGM term structure expressions are closed-form analytic. Therefore, B-AGM implementations required to obtain model-implied yields and the residuals $\eta_{t,i}$ must in general be undertaken using time-consuming MC simulations. Consequently, it requires a larger amount of computing time to undertake the $\sum_{t=1}^{T} I_t$ evaluations of the residuals $\eta_{t,i}$ for a partial B-AGM estimation. As an example, assume $\sum_{t=1}^{T} I_t = 842$ as for the K-ANSM(2) example mentioned above, and the MC simulation time of approximately 170 seconds to achieve the 0.3 basis point standard deviation noted in panel A of Table 5.2. The total computing time would be $842 \times 170/(60 \times 60) = 39.8$ hours or 1.65 days. Even with the MC/CV speed-up method, the total computing time for estimations with data to 30 years' time to maturity would be approximately

$842 \times 51.1/(60 \times 60) = 11.9$ hours or 0.498 days, or $842 \times 16.8/(60 \times 60) = 3.93$ hours or 0.164 days with data to 10 years' time to maturity.

- Furthermore, the literature to date has relied on numerical evaluations of the Jacobian $H_{t,i}$ for B-AGM estimations, as I discuss below, which requires at least N more implementations per iteration. Therefore the computing time required for the $\sum_{t=1}^{T} I_t \times N$ implementations to obtain the Jacobians would be even more prohibitive.

- Speed-up methods for B-AGM implementations using MC methods are therefore critical to obtain timely partial B-AGM estimations in practice. These include the standard speed-up methods in subsections 5.3.3 and 5.3.4, and the B-AGM MC/CV method based on the K-AGM framework from Krippner (2013b), as presented in section 5.4. Another advance from Krippner (2013a) in terms of speeding up B-AGM estimations is to show that the Jacobian matrices $H_{t,i}$ can be obtained using just the information already available from the implementations for the residual calculation step. Therefore, the additional $\sum_{t=1}^{T} I_t \times N$ implementations to obtain the Jacobian matrices can be eliminated. I outline the details below.

Details on step "3.2 (i) B-AGM interest rates and residuals"

Calculating the $K \times 1$ vector $\underline{R}(x_{t,i}^+, \mathbb{A})$ at each iteration i and time step t requires the calculation of $\underline{R}(x_{t,i}^+, \mathbb{A}, \tau_k)$ for all maturities τ_k that have an associated interest rate observation. This calculation needs to be undertaken to the required accuracy for each iteration i and could use any of the numerical methods already outlined in section 5.2. If a Monte Carlo simulation is used, then the standard MC speed-up methods in section 5.3 and the MC/CV in section 5.4 can be used to speed up the process.

Details on step "3.2 (ii) B-AGM Jacobian"

Calculating the $K \times N$ Jacobian matrix $H_{t,i}$ at each iteration i and time step t requires the partial derivatives of each element of $\underline{R}[x(t), \mathbb{A}]$ with respect to $x(t)$ evaluated at $x_{t,i}^+$. To the best of my knowledge, those partial derivatives have typically been approximated using a numerical first-difference approximation (see the EKF estimations of Kim and Singleton [2012] and Bauer and Rudebusch [2013], for example). Specifically, the Jacobian for the time to maturity τ_k is approximated by

$$\frac{\partial}{\partial x(t)} \underline{R}[x(t), \mathbb{A}, \tau_k] \bigg|_{x(t)=x_{t,i}^+} \simeq \{\Delta\underline{R}[x_1(t), \tau_k], \ldots, \Delta\underline{R}[x_N(t), \tau_k]\}_{1 \times N}$$

(5.100)

where $\Delta\underline{R}[x_n(t), \mathbb{A}, \tau_k]$ is shorthand for a numerical first derivative. For example, the element n of the $1 \times N$ partial derivative vector (for the given time to maturity τ_k) in equation 5.100 would be

Table 5.3 Partial B-AGM estimation via IEKF

---

1. Setup and estimation constraints:

Calculate F, $\Theta(\Delta t)$, and Ω_η

2. State initialization:

$$x_0^+ = \theta$$
$$P_0^+ = V\Theta(\infty)V'$$

3. Recursion:

for $t = 1 : T$

    3.1. Prior state estimates:

$$x_t^- = \theta + F\left(x_{t-1}^+ - \theta\right)$$
$$P_t^- = FP_{t-1}^+ F' + \Theta(\Delta t)$$

    3.2. Measurement/posterior state iterations:

        Set : $x_{t,0}^+ = x_t^-$; $H_{t,0} = 0$

        ITERATE : from $i = 0$

  (i) $\eta_{t,i} = \mathbb{R}_t - \mathbb{R}\left(x_{t,i}^+, \mathbb{A}\right) - H_{t,i}\left(x_t^- - x_{t,i}^+\right)$

  (ii) $H_{t,i} = \frac{\partial}{\partial x(t)}\mathbb{R}\left[x(t), \mathbb{A}\right]\Big|_{x(t)=x_{t,i}^+}$

        $M_{t,i} = H_{t,i}P_t^- H_{t,i}' + \Omega_\eta$

        $K_{t,i} = P_t^- H_{t,i}' M_{t,i}^{-1}$

        $x_{t,i+1}^+ = x_{t,i}^+ + K_{t,i}\eta_{t,i}$

        EXIT : at $\max(i)$ or $\left|x_{t,i+1}^+ - x_{t,i}^+\right|$ tolerance

    3.3. Posterior state estimates:

$$x_t^+ = x_{t,i+1}^+, \; \eta_t = \eta_{t,i}, \text{ and } M_t = M_{t,i}$$
$$P_t^+ = \left(I - K_{t,i}H_{t,i}\right)P_t^-$$

    Record x_t^+, η_t, and M_t

next t

Notes:

x_t^-, x_t^+, $x_{t,i}^+$, and θ are $N \times 1$ vectors

$\eta_{t,i}$ and η_t are $K \times 1$ vectors

κ_D is an $N \times N$ diagonal matrix

P_t^-, P_t^+, $\sigma\sigma'$, $\Theta(\Delta t)$, and $\Theta(\infty)$ are $N \times N$
        symmetric matrices

V and F are $N \times N$ asymmetric matrices

$M_{t,i}$ and M_t is a $K \times K$ symmetric matrix

Ω_η is a $K \times K$ diagonal matrix

$K_{t,i}$ is an $N \times K$ matrix

$H_{t,i}$ is a $K \times N$ matrix

$$\Delta \underline{R}\left[x(t),\mathbb{A},\tau_k\right] = \frac{\underline{R}\left[x(t)+\Delta x_n(t),\tau_k\right]-\underline{R}\left[x(t),\tau_k\right]}{\Delta x_n(t)} \qquad (5.101)$$

and so each iteration i therefore requires N additional implementations per iteration (or $2N$ if a central difference calculation were used). Given that MC methods are time consuming, those additional implementations per iteration greatly increase the estimation time for B-AGMs.

Fortunately, Krippner (2013a) shows that the B-AGM Jacobian $H_{t,i}$ can be calculated directly from the implementation already undertaken for the central value of the state variables. In other words, the implementation already required to obtain the residual vector $\eta_{t,i}$ provides the calculations necessary for the B-AGM Jacobian $H_{t,i}$ without any additional implementations being required. This principle is similar to that already exploited for K-AGMs in chapter 4. For the B-AGM, the calculation takes advantage of the analytic properties of the B-AGM measurement equation, given the stochastic path of shadow short rates is already available from the MC simulation underlying the implementation.

To illustrate the principle, it is most convenient to undertake the relevant calculations in continuous time with the generic arbitrage expressions for the B-AGM. I then convert that final exact result into the MC basis being used to approximate the B-AGM interest rates.

Row k of the Jacobian corresponding to an interest rate $\underline{R}\left[x_{t,i}^+,\tau_k\right]$ requires the partial differential of $\underline{R}\left[x(t),\tau_k\right]$ with respect to $x(t)$. That is,

$$
\begin{aligned}
H_{t,i,k} &= \frac{\partial}{\partial x(t)}\underline{R}\left[x(t),\tau_k\right] \\[2mm]
&= \frac{\partial}{\partial x(t)}\left(-\frac{1}{\tau}\log\{\underline{P}\left[x(t),\tau_k\right]\}\right) \\[2mm]
&= -\frac{1}{\tau}\frac{\partial}{\partial x(t)}\log\{\underline{P}\left[x(t),\tau_k\right]\} \\[2mm]
\langle\text{Chain rule}\rangle &= -\frac{1}{\tau}\frac{\partial}{\partial \underline{P}\left[x(t),\tau_k\right]}\log\{\underline{P}\left[x(t),\tau_k\right]\}\cdot\frac{\partial}{\partial x(t)}\underline{P}\left[x(t),\tau_k\right] \\[2mm]
&= -\frac{1}{\tau\cdot\underline{P}\left[x(t),\tau_k\right]}\cdot\frac{\partial}{\partial x(t)}\tilde{\mathbb{E}}_t\left[\exp\left(-\int_0^{\tau_k}\underline{r}(t+u)\,du\right)\right] \\[2mm]
&= -\frac{1}{\tau\cdot\underline{P}\left[x(t),\tau_k\right]}\cdot\tilde{\mathbb{E}}_t\left\{\frac{\partial}{\partial x(t)}\exp\left(-\int_0^{\tau_k}\underline{r}(t+u)\,du\right)\right\} \\[2mm]
\langle\text{Chain rule}\rangle &= -\frac{1}{\tau\cdot\underline{P}\left[x(t),\tau_k\right]} \\[2mm]
&\quad \times\tilde{\mathbb{E}}_t\left\{\frac{\partial}{\partial y}\exp\left[y\right]\cdot\frac{\partial}{\partial x(t)}\left[-\int_0^{\tau_k}\underline{r}(t+u)\,du\right]\right\} \\[2mm]
&\left\langle y = -\int_0^{\tau}\underline{r}(t+u)\,du\,;\,\frac{\partial}{\partial y}\exp\left[y\right]=\exp\left[y\right]\right\rangle
\end{aligned}
$$

$$= -\frac{1}{\tau \cdot \underline{P}[x(t), \tau_k]} \cdot \tilde{\mathbb{E}}_t \left\{ \exp[y] \cdot \frac{\partial}{\partial x(t)} \left[-\int_0^{\tau_k} \underline{r}(t+u) \, du \right] \right\}$$

$$= -\frac{1}{\tau \cdot \underline{P}[x(t), \tau_k]}$$

$$\times \tilde{\mathbb{E}}_t \left\{ \exp[y] \cdot \left[-\int_0^{\tau_k} \frac{\partial}{\partial x(t)} \underline{r}(t+u) \, du \right] \right\} \qquad (5.102)$$

The partial differential of $\underline{r}(t+u)$ with respect to $x(t)$, which I denote as $\underline{q}(t+u)$, is

$$\frac{\partial}{\partial x(t)} \underline{r}(t+u) = \frac{\partial}{\partial x(t)} \max\{r_L, r(t+u)\}$$

$$\underline{q}(t+u) = \begin{cases} 0 & \text{if } r(t+u) \le 0 \\ \frac{\partial}{\partial x(t)} r(t+u) & \text{if } r(t+u) > 0 \end{cases} \qquad (5.103)$$

where

$$r(t+u) = a_0 + b_0' \left\{ \exp(-\tilde{\kappa}\tau) x(t) + \int_t^{t+u} \exp(-\tilde{\kappa}[u-v]) \sigma \, dW(v) \right\}$$

$$(5.104)$$

and therefore

$$\frac{\partial}{\partial x(t)} r(t+u) = b_0' \exp(-\tilde{\kappa}\tau) \qquad (5.105)$$

Substituting that result into equation 5.103 gives

$$\underline{q}(t+u) = \begin{cases} 0 & \text{if } r(t+u) < r_L \\ b_0' \exp(-\tilde{\kappa}u) & \text{if } r(t+u) \ge r_L \end{cases} \qquad (5.106)$$

which completes the partial differential calculation of $\underline{R}[x(t), \tau_k]$ with respect to $x(t)$.

The Jacobian is therefore

$$H_{t,i,k} = \frac{\partial}{\partial x(t)} \underline{R}[x(t), \tau_k] \Bigg|_{x(t)=x_{t,i}^+}$$

$$= \frac{1}{\tau_k \cdot \underline{P}[x_{t,i}^+, \tau_k]} \qquad (5.107)$$

$$\times \tilde{\mathbb{E}}_t \left\{ \exp\left(-\int_0^{\tau_k} \underline{r}(t+u) \, du \right) \cdot \int_0^{\tau_k} \underline{q}(t+u) \, du \right\} \qquad (5.108)$$

which is in continuous time. The discrete-time analogue of the continuous-time expressions within $H_{t,i,k}$ may be evaluated using the simulated shadow short rates $r_{t,j,m}$ already generated to calculate the B-AGM interest rate $\underline{R}\left[x_{t,i}^+, \tau_k\right]$ estimates:

$$H_{t,i,k} = \frac{1}{\tau_k \cdot \underline{P}_C^B\left[x_{t,i}, \tau_k\right]} \cdot \frac{1}{J} \sum_{j=1}^{J} \exp\left[-\sum_{m=0}^{M-1} r_{t,j,m} \cdot \delta\right] \cdot \sum_{m=0}^{M-1} \underline{q}_{t,j,m} \cdot \delta \qquad (5.109)$$

where

$$\underline{q}_{t,j,m} = \begin{cases} 0 & \text{if } r_{t,j,m} < r_L \\ b_0' \exp\left(-\tilde{\kappa}\tau\right) & \text{if } r_{t,j,m} \geq r_L \end{cases} \qquad (5.110)$$

The important point is that no further simulations of $r_{t,j,m}$ are required to obtain the Jacobian $H_{t,i,k}$, and the additional calculations required are elementary.

5.5.2 Full estimation

Table 5.4 summarizes the process for a full estimation of the B-AGM via maximum likelihood by using the IEKF algorithm within an optimization algorithm. Table 5.4 is identical to Table 4.3 for the full estimation of K-AGMs, except for the calculations of the residual vector $\eta_{t,i}$ and the Jacobian matrix $H_{t,i}$ in the "**3.2. Measurement/posterior state iterations,**" as already discussed in the previous subsection. I therefore refer readers to the discussion associated with Table 4.3 for comments on the flow of Table 5.4.

The point to make here is that the optimization algorithm requires many repeated partial estimations of the B-AGM to obtain the maximum likelihood estimates. I will denote this number as O_I. Therefore, it would take $O_I \times \sum_{t=1}^{T} I_t$ implementations of the B-AGM to obtain a full estimation, and O_I is typically in the order of 1000 or more, depending on the starting parameter values. Given the order of magnitude of 0.164 days for a partial estimation on data with a time to maturity out to 10 years, the full estimation is likely to take approximately 164 days, or about half a year. An estimation to the same levels of confidence on data with a time to maturity out to 30 years is likely to take 498 days, or about 1.4 years. Note that these estimated times already include the MC/CV speed-up method; otherwise, the 30-year results would be around 4.5 years.

Faced with such prohibitive times for partial and particularly full estimations on standard desk-top personal computers, there are several responses. The ideal response is to employ more computing power, first using parallel processing with all cores, multiple computers, and/or faster computers, all of which are straightforward to arrange for MC simulations. Compiling C++ of Fortran code for the simulations may also improve implementation times. A less ideal response would be to trade-off lower estimation times against aspects of the model specification, application, and the MC simulation accuracy. For example, specifying a model with fewer state variables, estimating a model using a yield curve data set with lower times to maturity,

Table 5.4 Full B-AGM estimation via maximum likelihood

A. Optimization algorithm

Maximize: $\log\text{-}L\left(\left\{\underset{\sim}{R}_1,\ldots,\underset{\sim}{R}_T\right\},\mathbb{A}\right)$

$= -\frac{1}{2}\sum_{t=1}^{T} K\log(2\pi) + \log(|M_t|) + \eta_t' M_t^{-1}\eta_t$

with η_t and M_t from IEKF algorithm.

> **IEKF (iterated extended Kalman filter) algorithm**
>
> **1. Setup and estimation constraints:**
>
> Calculate F, $\Theta(\Delta t)$, and Ω_η
>
> Subject to constraints:
>
> - $|F| < 1$
>
> - $\sigma\sigma'$ and Ω_η positive definite
>
> **2. State initialization:**
>
> $x_0^+ = \theta$
>
> $P_0^+ = V\Theta(\infty)V'$
>
> **3. Recursion:**
>
> for $t = 1 : T$
>
> > **3.1. Prior state estimates:**
> >
> > $x_t^- = \theta + F\left(x_{t-1}^+ - \theta\right)$
> >
> > $P_t^- = FP_{t-1}^+ F' + \Theta(\Delta t)$
> >
> > **3.2. Measurement/posterior state iterations:**
> >
> > > Set : $x_{t,0}^+ = x_t^-$; $H_{t,0} = 0$
> > >
> > > **ITERATE** : from $i = 0$
> >
> > (i) $\eta_{t,i} = \underset{\sim}{R}_t - \underset{\sim}{R}\left(x_{t,i}^+,\mathbb{A}\right) - H_{t,i}\left(x_t^- - x_{t,i}^+\right)$
> >
> > (ii) $H_{t,i} = \frac{\partial}{\partial x(t)}\underset{\sim}{R}[x(t),\mathbb{A}]\Big|_{x(t)=x_{t,i}^+}$
> >
> > > $M_{t,i} = H_{t,i}P_t^- H_{t,i}' + \Omega_\eta$
> > >
> > > $K_{t,i} = P_t^- H_{t,i}' M_{t,i}^{-1}$
> > >
> > > $x_{t,i+1}^+ = x_{t,i}^+ + K_{t,i}\eta_{t,i}$
> > >
> > > **EXIT** : at $\max(i)$ or $\left|x_{t,i+1}^+ - x_{t,i}^+\right|$ tolerance
> >
> > **3.3. Posterior state estimates:**
> >
> > $x_t^+ = x_{t,i+1}^+$, $\eta_t = \eta_{t,i}$, and $M_t = M_{t,i}$
> >
> > $P_t^+ = \left(I - K_{t,i}H_{t,i}\right)P_t^-$
> >
> > Record x_t^+, η_t, and M_t
>
> next t

B. Diagnostics of estimated B-AGM

Note: See Table 5.3 for matrix dimensions.

using a coarser MC time increment, and/or allowing for a wider confidence interval than approximately one basis point would all reduce the implementation time and therefore the estimation times accordingly. However, assuming that the original intention was to estimate a relatively flexible continuous-time B-AGM model that accommodates the full yield data set, then all of those trade-offs represent approximations to some degree. In addition, allowing wider confidence intervals around each implementation may affect the estimation process, its convergence, and the validity of the results if convergence can be obtained.

5.5.3 Alternative estimation methods

Subsection 4.6.1 discussed for K-AGMs using forward rates in estimations as a way to eliminate the numerical integration required for interest rates and the Jacobian in the measurement equation, albeit with the trade-offs noted in that section. The B-AGM framework does not offer any potential advantages from using forward rates as the basis for estimation. The reason is that B-AGM bond prices would still have to be generated to obtain the B-AGM forward rates.

5.6 Approximations to B-AGMs

An alternative to the trade-off for estimating B-AGMs discussed at the end of the previous section is instead to explicitly use an approximation to the B-AGM. To be clear on the thought process, assume one accepts that the implicit asset pricing assumptions underlying the B-AGM framework are correct (i.e., that ZLB forward bonds or ZLB short rates should be discounted with ZLB short rates, as discussed in section 5.1), and therefore one wants to apply a B-AGM with a particular specification. However, if estimating that particular B-AGM so that it provides a good representation of the yield curve data set is too onerous, then it may not be possible to apply it in practice. Hence, a framework that approximates the B-AGM and its key features may provide an acceptable compromise for practical use.

Therefore, in this section I provide some frameworks that can be used as approximations to the B-AGM framework, along with a discussion of their results to assess how useful the approximations are in practice. I discuss the K-AGM framework as an approximation to the B-AGM framework in subsection 5.6.1. In subsection 5.6.2, I discuss the B-AGM approximations provided in Priebsch (2013). Subsection 5.6.3 revisits non-arbitrage-free ZLB ANSM models obtained from the perspective of B-AGMs. I then follow up in section 4 with a discussion on how the B-AGM approximations may be used in practice.

5.6.1 K-AGMs as approximations to B-AGMs

In this subsection I present the K-AGM as a tractable and close approximation to the B-AGM. I have already detailed the K-AGM framework itself in chapter 4, so I simply present the empirical results in this section for comparison and discussion. Note that the context of using the K-AGM in this section is distinctly different from the third alternative already mentioned at the beginning of the chapter. Specifically, if one accepts the implicit asset pricing assumptions underlying K-AGMs (i.e., that ZLB forward bonds or ZLB short rates should be discounted with shadow short rates, as discussed in subsection 5.6.1), then one would simply use K-AGMs with confidence that they are theoretically consistent and that they also happen to be practically tractable. I will return to the theoretical case for K-AGMs in chapter 6. However, the key point for this subsection is that even if one is not convinced by the theoretical arguments for the K-AGM framework, then at least K-AGMs can be used to provide a close approximation to B-AGMs.

B-ANSM(2) versus K-ANSM(2) comparisons

In Figure 5.5, I illustrate for two selected dates the difference between the K-ANSM(2) yield curve and the B-ANSM(2) yield curve based on the same state variables and parameters. Specifically, to generate the B-ANSM(2) yield curves, I use the parameters for the K-ANSM(2) with $r_L = 0$, which are contained in Table 4.4, and the state variables for the August 2008 and July 2012 dates are respectively $x_1(t) = 5.56\%$ and $x_2(t) = -3.77\%$, and $x_1(t) = 2.62\%$ and $x_2(t) = -6.16\%$. I then use the MC simulation procedure as outlined for the B-ANSM(2) in subsection 5.3.5 and generally in section 5.3. The number of simulations in each case is one million (which takes around 1.3 hours) and this gives a 99 percent confidence interval of less than 0.5 basis points at the 30-year time to maturity. I generate the K-ANSM(2) yield curves as outlined in subsection 5.3.5, and then subtract the generated B-ANSM(2) yield curves.

Figure 5.5 shows that, for the given sets of state variables and parameters on the two dates shown, the interest rates obtained by the K-ANSM(2) moderately understate B-ANSM(2) interest rates. For example, the August 2008 K-ANSM(2) yield curve is lower than the B-ANSM(2) yield curve by fewer than 5 basis points for all maturities shown, and the July 2012 comparison is fewer than 15 basis points.

Figure 5.6 plots K-ANSM(2) less B-ANSM(2) interest rate differences for selected times to maturity, that is, 3, 10, and 30 years, over all points in the time series. The B-ANSM(2) results are generated much as described above. Specifically, I use the K-ANSM(2) state variables at each point in time and the K-ANSM(2) parameter set to generate the B-ANSM(2) results at each point in time, but using only 10,000 MC simulations. The total time taken is about 4.5 hours, given that the time required to run each simulation for the 341 monthly dates in the sample is around 47 seconds. The lower number of simulations than in Figure 5.5 is why the results appear noisier, but the key objective here is to indicate how the K-ANSM(2) yield curve compares to the B-ANSM(2) yield curve over time; Figure 5.5 has already shown that the differences are non-zero to within statistical significance of the associated B-AGM simulations.

The key results from Figures 5.5 and 5.6 are:

- The K-ANSM(2) generates lower yield curves relative to B-ANSM(2). This result is expected in general for K-AGMs versus B-AGMs because of the difference in

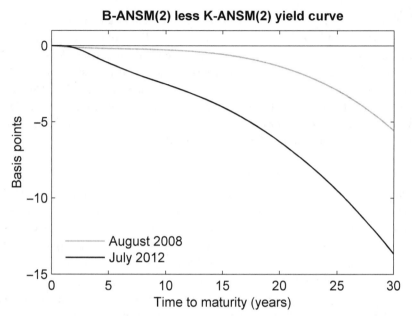

Figure 5.5 The K-ANSM(2) approximates the B-ANSM(2) to within 15 basis points even in the most constrained ZLB environment of July 2012.

discounting discussed in subsection 5.1.1. Essentially, the ZLB forward bonds that underlie K-AGM yield curves are discounted using shadow short rates, whereas the ZLB forward bonds that underlie B-AGM yield curves are discounted with ZLB short rates. Therefore, the prices of K-AGM ZLB forward bonds are higher because they are discounted with a lower average discount rate (i.e., the shadow short rate distribution includes negative rates, while the ZLB short rate distribution sets negative rates to zero). In turn, higher prices for K-AGM ZLB forward bonds will generate higher K-AGM ZLB bond prices, and higher bond prices equate to lower K-AGM ZLB interest rates.

- The K-ANSM(2) approximation to B-ANSM(2) interest rates deteriorates with longer times to maturity. This is again an expected result in general. Firstly, for short maturities, discount factors based on shadow short rates or ZLB short rates are essentially identical; discount factors are close to one for short times to maturity regardless of the interest rate. Therefore, the differences between K-AGM and B-AGM ZLB forward bonds are immaterial, and so the ZLB bond prices and ZLB interest rates from both frameworks are essentially identical. For longer times to maturity, the discount factors produced by ZLB short rates become progressively lower relative to discount factors produced by shadow short rates. In turn, that produces progressively lower ZLB forward bond prices for the B-AGM framework, progressively lower ZLB bond prices, and therefore progressively higher ZLB interest rates, all respectively relative to their K-AGM ZLB counterparts.

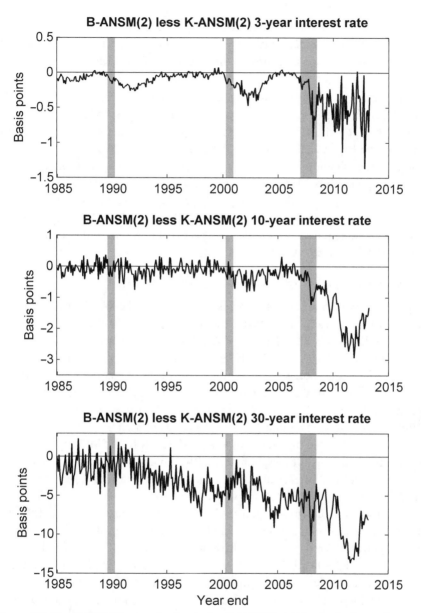

Figure 5.6 The K-ANSM(2) approximation to the B-ANSM(2) deteriorates for longer times to maturity and for larger ZLB constraints.

- The K-ANSM(2) approximation to B-ANSM(2) interest rates deteriorates as the ZLB becomes more constraining. This is also an expected result in general. Essentially, a larger ZLB constraint implies a lower mean of the shadow short rate distribution relative to the mean of the ZLB short rate distribution. That difference translates into higher discount factors for K-AGM ZLB forward bonds relative to the discount factors for B-AGM ZLB forward bonds. Therefore, K-AGM ZLB bond prices are relatively higher, and K-AGM ZLB interest rates relatively lower compared to their respective B-AGM counterparts.

In summary, if one believes the B-AGM pricing mechanism, then the K-ANSM(2) provides a reasonable approximation to the B-ANSM(2). That is, at worst, the approximation is within 15 basis points for the longest time to maturity and the largest ZLB constraint. Therefore, the K-ANSM(2) could be used for the purposes of monitoring monetary policy and providing a parsimonious tool for research applications. That said, it is well known that any term structure model with only two state variables does not typically provide a close representation of yield curve data, and so a comparison between K-AGMs and B-AGMs with three state variables is more relevant. From that perspective, I now turn to the comparison of the K-ANSM(3) and B-ANSM(3).

B-ANSM(3) versus K-ANSM(3) comparisons

Figures 5.7 and 5.8 repeat the exercises above, but for the K-ANSM(3) versus the B-ANSM(3). Figure 5.7 shows that the yields obtained by the K-ANSM(3) are even closer to the B-ANSM(3) than the K-ANSM(2) versus B-ANSM(2) comparison. For example, the August 2008 K-ANSM(3) yield curve understates the B-ANSM(3) yield curve by only 3 basis points for the 30-year time to maturity, and less than 1 basis point for the 10-year time to maturity. The July 2012 comparison has a similar profile to the August 2008 example, and the K-ANSM(3) less B-ANSM(3) 10- and 30-year differences are around 2 and 9 basis points respectively.

Figure 5.8 plots the time series of K-ANSM(3) less B-ANSM(3) differences for the 3-, 10-, and 30-year times to maturity (the standard errors of the B-ANSM are 0.68, 1.27, and 1.69 basis points). The largest gap was during the period in which the constraint from the ZLB was most extreme.

The absolute results from Figures 5.7 and 5.8 are, as already, discussed, for the K-ANSM(2) relative to B-ANSM(2), and for the same reasons. Similar results for K-AGMs with three state variables have been reported by Christensen and Rudebusch (2013a,b, 2014), Priebsch (2013), and Wu and Xia (2013, 2014), although only out to the longest time to maturity of 10 years used by those authors.

One additional point to note is that the K-ANSM(3) provides a better approximation to the B-ANSM(3) at the 30-year time to maturity, compared to the K-ANSM(2) approximation to the B-ANSM(2) at the 30-year time to maturity. Therefore, the K-ANSM(3) provides a much better fit to the yield curve data, as already detailed in section 4.5, and a better approximation to the corresponding B-AGM (i.e., the B-ANSM(3) in this case).

In summary, if one believes the B-AGM pricing mechanism, then the K-ANSM(3) provides a very close approximation to the B-ANSM(3). The approximation is certainly close enough for the purposes of providing monitoring and research information for monetary policy purposes, and it is arguably close enough

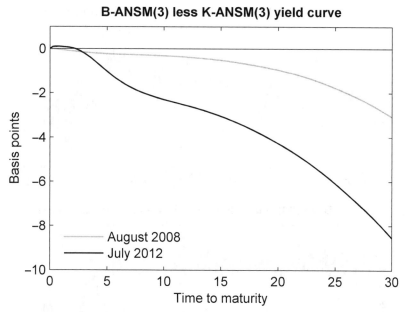

Figure 5.7 The K-ANSM(3) approximates the B-ANSM(3) to within 10 basis points even in the most constained ZLB environment of July 2012.

for most financial market purposes. That said, a pricing error of 9 basis points for a 30-year zero-coupon bond corresponds to a unit price error of approximately $\exp(-9/10000 \times 30) - 1 = -0.027$, or 27,000 per million face value, which may not be acceptable relative to the price that would have been obtained from a B-ANSM(3). Furthermore, if one is pricing options on long-maturity bonds, which I will discuss in section 8.6.3, a mispricing of 9 basis points on the underlying security would lead to even higher errors relative to the option price that would otherwise have been obtained from using a B-ANSM(3).

5.6.2 B-AGM cumulant approximations

Priebsch (2013) has introduced an alternative means of approximating B-AGMs using cumulants, which I outline shortly below. Note, however, that I have changed the notation in Priebsch (2013) to be consistent with the notation used in this book. In particular, I have replaced his time t and time-of-maturity T notation with my time t and time-to-maturity τ notation (where $\tau = T - t$). Hence, my $\underline{R}^B(t,\tau) = \underline{R}^B(t, t+\tau) = \underline{R}^B(t, T)$. I have also used bracketed values consistent with my continuous-time notation rather than subscripts, which I have reserved for discrete-time increments.

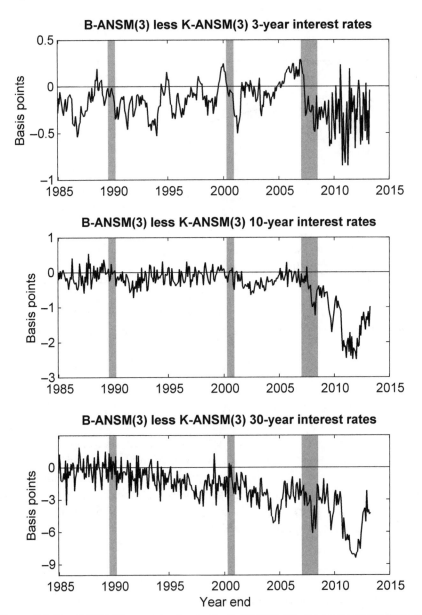

Figure 5.8 The K-ANSM(3) approximation to the B-ANSM(3) deteriorates for longer times to maturity and for larger ZLB constraints.

Priebsch (2013) expresses the logarithm of the B-AGM bond prices in terms of cumulants:

$$\log\left[\tilde{\mathbb{E}}_t\left\{\exp\left(-\int_0^\tau \underline{\mathrm{r}}(t+u)\,\mathrm{d}u\right)\right\}\right] = \sum_{j=1}^\infty (-1)^j \frac{\tilde{\underline{\xi}}_j}{j}$$

where $\tilde{\xi}_j$ is the jth cumulant of the random variable $\int_0^\tau \underline{r}(t+\tau)\,du$ under the $\mathbb{Q}$ measure. As Priebsch (2013) notes, approximations to B-AGM interest rates $\underline{R}^B(t,\tau)$ can then be computed based on a finite number of terms from this expression. I provide the details for the first-order term below to illustrate the key idea, and then provide an overview of the second-order term.

The advantage of the cumulant method is that the approximation to the B-AGM can be improved indefinitely by simply adding more terms. In practice, two terms provide a very close approximation, which is fortunate because the second-order term already comes at the cost of some additional computational burden.

First-order cumulant approximation to B-AGM

The first-order cumulant approximation to $\underline{R}^B(t,\tau)$ is

$$
\begin{aligned}
\underline{R}_1^B(t,\tau) &= \frac{1}{\tau}\tilde{\xi}_1 \\
&= \frac{1}{\tau}\tilde{\mathbb{E}}_t\left\{\int_0^\tau \underline{r}(t+u)\,du\right\} \\
&= \frac{1}{\tau}\int_0^\tau \tilde{\mathbb{E}}_t\left[\underline{r}(t+u)\right]du \\
&= \frac{1}{\tau}\left\{\int_0^\tau \tilde{\mathbb{E}}_t\left[\max\{0,r(t+u)\}\right]du\right\}
\end{aligned}
\tag{5.111}
$$

where $r(t+\tau)$ are the shadow short rates. The distribution for $r(t+\tau)$ from Priebsch (2013) is normal, that is,

$$
r(t+\tau) \sim N\left(\mu(t,\tau),[\omega(\tau)]^2\right)
\tag{5.112}
$$

where

$$
\mu(t,\tau) = \tilde{\mathbb{E}}_t\left[r(t+\tau)\right] = a_0 + b_0'x(t)
\tag{5.113}
$$

The expected value of $\underline{r}(t+\tau)$ is obtained from the truncated normal distribution $N\left(\mu(t,\tau),[\omega(\tau)]^2\right)$, with the result

$$
\tilde{\mathbb{E}}_t\left[\max\{0,r(t+\tau)\}\right] = \mu(t,\tau)\cdot\Phi\left[\frac{\mu(t,\tau)}{\omega(\tau)}\right] + \omega(\tau)\cdot\phi\left[\frac{\mu(t,\tau)}{\omega(\tau)}\right]
\tag{5.114}
$$

and therefore

$$
\underline{R}_1^B(t,\tau) = \frac{1}{\tau}\int_0^\tau \mu(t,u)\cdot\Phi\left[\frac{\mu(t,u)}{\omega(u)}\right] + \omega(u)\cdot\phi\left[\frac{\mu(t,u)}{\omega(u)}\right]du
\tag{5.115}
$$

$\underline{R}_1^B(t,\tau)$ is obtained as a numerical integral, which is very straightforward to evaluate because all of the functions in the integral are closed-form analytic expressions.

As an aside, the expression for $R_1^B(t,\tau)$ is very similar to the expression for K-AGM interest rates $R(t,\tau)$. The difference is that the mean of the shadow short rate distribution underlying $R_1^B(t,\tau)$ is $\mu(t,\tau) = \tilde{\mathbb{E}}_t[r(t+\tau)]$, or $\tilde{\mathbb{E}}_t[r(t+\tau)|x(t)]$ using my explicit notation that $r(t+\tau)$ is conditional on $x(t)$. The mean of the distribution $r(t+\tau)|x(t)$ underlying K-AGM interest rates is $f(t,\tau) = \tilde{\mathbb{E}}_t[r(t+\tau)|x(t)] - VE(\tau)$, which includes the volatility effect. The variance of both distributions is $[\omega(\tau)]^2$, and both require the same degree of numerical integration.

Priebsch (2013) tests his cumulant approximation approach by estimating a model with three state variables on a yield curve data set with maturities out to 10 years. He finds that the first-order cumulant approximation overstates the B-AGM 10-year interest rate by around 20 basis points in the non-ZLB environment and between 10 to 15 basis points in the ZLB environment.[2] By comparison, Priebsch (2013) finds that the K-AGM approximation understates the B-AGM 10-year interest rate by around one basis point or less in the non-ZLB environment and between 2 to 6 basis points in the ZLB environment. As noted above, the degree of numerical integration is identical for both approaches, so the K-AGM is preferable to the first-order cumulant approximation.

Second-order cumulant approximation to B-AGM

Priebsch (2013) gives the second-order approximation to $R^B(t,\tau)$ as

$$R_2^B(t,\tau) = \frac{1}{\tau}\tilde{\xi}_1 - \frac{1}{2\tau}\tilde{\xi}_2$$
$$= \frac{1}{\tau}\tilde{\mathbb{E}}_t\left\{\int_0^\tau r(t+u)\,du\right\}$$
$$- \frac{1}{2\tau}\widetilde{var}_t\left\{\int_0^\tau r(t+u)\,du\right\} \tag{5.116}$$

The results for the first-order component are already available, as discussed above. The evaluation of the second-order component requires a truncated bivariate normal distribution and numerical integration for the double integral. The expressions and the process required are therefore more involved than the first-order approximation, so I refer readers to the article itself for the details. Once those results are obtained, then integrating over time to maturity gives $R_2^B(t,\tau)$.

Empirically, Priebsch (2013) shows that the second-order cumulant approximation produces 10-year interest rates to within one basis point of B-AGM 10-year rates (the cumulant result is typically lower than the B-AGM result) over the entire sample period (from 1990 to 2012). As noted above, the K-AGM approximation understates the B-AGM 10-year interest rate by between 2 to 6 basis points in the ZLB environment, and therefore the second-order cumulant approximation is clearly superior (as one would expect from an additional degree of approximation).

Results out to 30 years are not available in the paper, but the author has kindly confirmed that similar relative outperformances also hold for longer times to maturity. Therefore, the choice between using the K-AGM or the second-order cumulant as an approximation to the B-AGM comes down to the trade-off between the desired degree of approximation versus the time and complexity of the two methods.

5.6.3 Non-arbitrage-free B-ANSMs

As discussed in subsection 4.4.2, setting the standard deviation parameters σ_n to zero for K-ANSMs produced non-arbitrage-free Nelson and Siegel (1987) models subject to the ZLB, or K-NSMs. Setting the standard deviation parameters σ_n in the B-ANSMs produces precisely the same framework, that is, B-NSMs are identical to K-NSMs. Specifically, the B-AGM forward rate $\underline{f}^B(t,\tau)$ is

$$\underline{f}^B(t,\tau) = \frac{1}{\underline{P}^B(t,\tau)} \cdot \tilde{\mathbb{E}}_t \left\{ \exp\left(-\int_0^\tau \underline{r}(t+u)\,du\right) \cdot \underline{r}(t+\tau) \right\} \tag{5.117}$$

and the B-AGM bond price $\underline{P}^B(t,\tau)$ is

$$\underline{P}^B(t,\tau) = \tilde{\mathbb{E}}_t \left\{ \exp\left(-\int_0^\tau \underline{r}(t+u)\,du\right) \right\}$$

Setting the standard deviation parameters σ_n in the B-AGM framework means that shadow short rate and therefore ZLB short rate evolutions become deterministic. In other words, there is no longer a probability distribution around expected future rates, and so the expectations operator simply produces the deterministic shadow short rate and ZLB short rate evolutions. Therefore

$$\begin{aligned}
\underline{f}^B(t,\tau) &= \frac{1}{\underline{P}^B(t,\tau)} \cdot \underline{P}^B(t,\tau) \cdot \underline{r}(t+\tau) \\
&= \max\{r_L, r(t+\tau)\} \\
&= r_L + \max\{0, r(t+\tau) - r_L\} \\
&= r_L + [r(t+\tau) - r_L] \cdot H[r(t+\tau) - r_L] \\
&= r_L + [f(t,\tau) - r_L] \cdot H[f(t,\tau) - r_L] \tag{5.118}
\end{aligned}$$

where the last step uses the results that $f(t,\tau) = r(t+\tau)$ if short rates are deterministic.

As discussed in section 4.4.2, K-NSMs/B-NSMs may prove useful for simple modeling in ZLB environments, just as NSMs have proven useful in non-ZLB environments. However, I have so far only tested that K-NSMs/B-NSMs are easy to estimate by fitting to yield curve data, as with NSMs. I have not yet undertaken any detailed assessment of their properties and performance.

To complete this subsection, I note that Feunou, Fontaine, and Le (2014) has recently proposed a new class of term structure models that is not strictly arbitrage free, but which produces closed-form analytic bond prices. Included in that class of models is an approximation to the Black (1995) framework based on a short rate that is a logistic function of a shadow short rate. The logistic function rules out negative short rates, and the analytic solutions for the framework delivers a tractable term structure model. I refer readers to the paper for further details.

5.6.4 Applying B-AGM approximations

Assuming one has used any of the approximations to B-AGMs discussed above for a full estimation, the results can be employed in at least three different ways. For clarity, I will assume that the user believes that the B-AGM is the correct ZLB term structure model, but has chosen the K-AGM as the B-AGM approximation and has already obtained the results of a full K-AGM estimation. The ways in which the K-AGM approximation can be used are then the following:

- The highest level of approximation is simply to use the K-AGM completely as the approximation to the B-AGM. Hence, one would assume that the estimated K-AGM state variables and parameters are those that would have been obtained from the B-AGM that could in principle have been estimated. Furthermore those state variables and parameters could be used within the K-AGM to obtain the prices for any interest rate securities with the implicit assumption that the K-AGM provides a very close approximation to the B-AGM. However, the comparisons of K-AGMs and B-AGMs in section 5.6.1 show that this approximation may not be suitable in all environments and particularly for longer maturities, so the user should keep that in mind.
- The next level of approximation is to assume that the estimated K-AGM state variables and parameters are those for the in-principle B-AGM, but then to use those state variables and parameters within the B-AGM to obtain the prices for interest rate securities. Sections 5.3 and 5.4 have already shown that a single implementation to obtain B-AGM interest rates and bond prices is not necessarily onerous, depending on the maturity and the accuracy required. This approach could therefore be employed in environments and for maturities in which the K-AGM is known not to provide a suitably close approximation to the B-AGM.
- The lowest level of approximation is to assume that the estimated K-AGM parameters are those for the in-principle B-AGM, but to undertake a partial estimation of the B-AGM with those estimated parameters. Those newly estimated B-AGM state variables can be used with the K-AGM parameters within the B-AGM to obtain the prices for interest rate securities. A partial B-AGM estimation is potentially attainable within an intra-day time span, so this approach could be

employed in environments and for maturities in which one considers it best to use B-AGM state variable estimates obtained from the data.

The "no approximation" approach is, of course, a full B-AGM estimation, in which case the estimated parameters and state variables will be consistent with the B-AGM and the data. From that perspective, the results of subsection 5.6.1 suggest that the estimated K-AGM parameters should offer good starting values for the analogous B-AGM estimation. Similarly, B-AGM trial simulations to determine the appropriate number of simulations for each implementation during the estimation could be determined using the estimated K-AGM state variables and parameters. Ideally one should use the most extreme K-AGM state variable values and appropriate confidence intervals around the estimated K-AGM parameters to ensure that the B-AGM estimation will accommodate the potential values that could arise during the estimation process.

5.7 Summary

- In this chapter, I have provided a detailed exposition of the Black (1995) shadow/ZLB-GATSM, or B-AGM, framework. To transparently compare the B-AGM framework to the K-AGM framework in chapter 4, I have shown that both frameworks effectively use ZLB forward bonds, composed of a shadow forward bond plus an option on the shadow forward bond, to represent the availability of physical currency. The B-AGM framework uses ZLB short rates to discount the cashflows of ZLB forward bonds to current time, while the K-AGM framework uses shadow rates for that discounting.
- The fundamental difference in the implicit pricing for the two frameworks means that the B-AGM framework does not have closed-form analytic expressions for any representation of the term structure, unlike the K-AGM framework. Time-consuming numerical methods must therefore be applied to implement B-AGMs (i.e., to generate a yield curve from the state variables and parameters).
- I have detailed how Monte Carlo simulations with speed-up methods can be applied to B-AGMs, including a covariate method I have proposed based on K-AGMs. However, even the estimation of just the state variables for B-AGMs given a set of parameters would be onerous, and full estimations of the state variables and parameters may not be practically feasible unless sufficient computing power and perhaps other speed-up methods are available.
- The alternative to estimating B-AGMs is to use more tractable models as an approximation. From that perspective, the K-ANSM(2) and the K-ANSM(3) respectively provide close approximations to the B-ANSM(2) and the B-ANSM(3). Therefore, K-ANSMs provide a practical compromise even if one considers B-ANSMs to be the theoretically correct shadow/ZLB framework. A

second-order method due to Priebsch (2013) provides an even closer approximation, albeit at the expense of some further numerical calculations.

- The fundamental difference in the implicit pricing for the B-AGM and the K-AGM frameworks raises the question of which is closest to economic theory. The economic framework that I develop in the following chapter helps shed some light on that question.

6 | K-ANSM Foundations and Effective Monetary Stimulus

In this chapter, I outline a generic economic framework for arbitrage-free Nelson and Siegel (1987) models, or ANSMs, based on well-accepted principles from the term structure literature. There are at least three motivations for providing this ANSM economic foundation:

- First, it provides a justification for using ANSMs generally as a parsimonious and realistic representation of the shadow term structure. In particular, I show that the ANSM Level, Slope, and Bow state variables may be explicitly interpreted as the aggregates of the state variables that represent the real production processes in a generic economy plus their associated inflation rates.
- Second, it provides a theoretical perspective for considering the pricing foundations of the K-ANSM framework, which differs from the B-ANSM framework. Specifically, section 5.1 established that the fundamental difference between the two frameworks is whether the cashflows from the series of implicit ZLB forward bonds that underlie the ZLB term structure are discounted using the ZLB short rates or shadow short rates. The economic foundation for the ANSM shadow term structure suggests that discounting with shadow short rates may be appropriate.
- Third, it helps justify the "Effective Monetary Stimulus," or EMS, summary measure for the stance of monetary policy that I introduced in section 2.4. Conceptually, the EMS summarizes current and expected ZLB short rates relative to the neutral interest rate, and the Level component of the K-ANSM is used as an estimate of the neutral interest rate. In turn, I establish that the Level component of the K-ANSM should be synonymous with long-run expectations of real output growth plus inflation, which are typically viewed as the macroeconomic determinants of the neutral interest rate.

I begin in section 6.1 by providing an overview of the key ideas and results for a generic standard classical economic model used in the term structure literature. I then provide a macroeconomic interpretation of the state variables for the generic economic model and its associated term structure. In section 6.2, I show how the state variables and factor loadings of the ANSMs can be explicitly related to the term structure for the economic model. Therefore, the macroeconomic interpretation of the economic state variables carries over to the term structure components for ANSMs. Note that these sections draw on Krippner (2008, 2012d, 2014a,d), so I will refer to those papers as required.

In section 6.3, I use the ANSM economic foundation to discuss why using ANSMs to represent the shadow term structure in shadow/ZLB term structure models is justified in principle and from a practical perspective. I then proceed to consider the difference between the B-ANSM and the K-ANSM frameworks in section 6.4. In section 6.5, I develop the EMS measure.

Before proceeding, I will mention up front that the ANSM economic foundation that I develop is useful as a tangible framework for the expositions in the remaining sections of this chapter, but those expositions are not critically dependent on the precise specification of the economic model or its reduced-form expression as an ANSM. For example, I will mention where generalizations to the economic model could be made to produce stationary GATSMs as a reduced-form expression, which would therefore incorporate K-AGMs and B-AGMs. Nevertheless, the following two chapters will demonstrate the practical advantages of using ANSMs rather than GATSMs to represent the shadow term structure. In addition, I will discuss in this chapter how ANSMs can be regarded as a reduced-form representation of any GATSM, with or without reference to an underlying economic model.

6.1 Overview of the economic model and its development

In this section, I provide an overview of the economic model, its associated term structure, and its macroeconomic interpretation that I will use subsequently in this chapter. The economic model and its term structure from Krippner (2008, 2014a) closely follow the Berardi and Esposito (1999) model, which is itself a generalization of the Cox, Ingersoll, and Ross (1985a), or CIR, framework that originally established an economic foundation for term structure models. In particular, the Berardi and Esposito (1999) model allows for multiple production processes in the economy, which therefore creates a term structure model with multiple state variables. The Berardi and Esposito (1999) model also allows for both Gaussian and square-root/Cox, Ingersoll, and Ross (1985b) dynamics in their generalization. I adopt the purely Gaussian specification, and therefore I call my framework the Gaussian-CIR economy, or GCE for short.

I will present the key elements of the GCE, its associated term structure, and its macroeconomic interpretation respectively in subsections 6.2.1 to 6.2.3. In section 6.2.4, I discuss how the relatively simple economic model could be generalized in several ways, but also how such generalizations would not alter the fundamental points I will discuss later in this chapter.

6.1.1 Establishing the GCE

The CGE is a continuous-time, closed, frictionless, production economy with identical infinitely lived and welfare-maximizing economic agents, a single representative good, and N_x production processes, where N_x is an arbitrary number. Economic agents use the instantaneous total returns from the production processes to provide instantaneous consumption based on a continually updated optimal lifetime path. The difference between total returns and consumption accumulates as wealth that is invested in the production processes. Krippner (2008, 2014a) or the references Berardi and Esposito (1999) and Cox, Ingersoll, and Ross (1985a) provide further details on the precise principles and specification of the economy. Here I concentrate on the description of the state variables for the economy and their associated parameters because those are the determinants of the term structure discussed in the following subsection.

The $N_x \times 1$ vector of short-run real state variables for the economy $x_Y(t)$ represents the instantaneous growth of the real returns on the production processes. The $N_x \times 1$ vector of short-run inflation state variables for the economy $x_\pi(t)$ represents the instantaneous inflation processes (i.e., instantaneous growth in the price levels, or deflators) for the factors of production. $x_Y(t)$ and $x_\pi(t)$ are stacked into a $2N_x \times 1$ joint vector $x(t)$ that contains all of the short-run state variables. In summary,

$$ x_Y(t) = \begin{bmatrix} x_{1,Y}(t) \\ \vdots \\ x_{N_x,Y}(t) \end{bmatrix} ; \quad x_\pi(t) = \begin{bmatrix} x_{1,\pi}(t) \\ \vdots \\ x_{N_x,\pi}(t) \end{bmatrix} ; \quad x(t) = \begin{bmatrix} x_Y(t) \\ x_\pi(t) \end{bmatrix} \quad (6.1) $$

The $N_x \times 1$ vector of long-run real state variables for the economy $\theta_Y(t)$ represents the long-horizon expectations of growth of the real returns on the production processes. The $N_x \times 1$ vector of long-run inflation state variables for the economy $\theta_\pi(t)$ represents the long-horizon expectations of the deflator/inflation processes for the factors of production. $\theta_Y(t)$ and $\theta_\pi(t)$ are stacked into a $2N_x \times 1$ joint vector $\theta(t)$ that contains all of the long-run state variables. In summary,

$$ \theta_Y(t) = \begin{bmatrix} \theta_{1,Y}(t) \\ \vdots \\ \theta_{N_x,Y}(t) \end{bmatrix} ; \quad \theta_\pi(t) = \begin{bmatrix} \theta_{1,\pi}(t) \\ \vdots \\ \theta_{N_x,\pi}(t) \end{bmatrix} ; \quad \theta(t) = \begin{bmatrix} \theta_Y(t) \\ \theta_\pi(t) \end{bmatrix} \quad (6.2) $$

The vector $x(t)$ follows a stochastic mean-reverting (i.e. Ornstein-Uhlenbeck) process to the vector of long-run levels $\theta(t)$, and the vector $\theta(t)$ itself follows a stochastic process. Krippner (2014a) assumes the process for $\theta(t)$ is a vector random walk, which is most convenient mathematically and which is also consistent with the non-stationary specification of the ANSM Level component. However,

$\theta(t)$ could also be specified to follow a persistent mean-reverting process, which would then be consistent with persistent stationary GATSM components.

The entire stochastic process for all the short-run state variables and long-run state variables in the CGE may be summarized most conveniently as an Ornstein-Uhlenbeck process for the $4N_x \times 1$ vector containing the long-run and short-run state variables:

$$d \begin{bmatrix} \theta(t) \\ x(t) \end{bmatrix} = \begin{bmatrix} 0 & 0 \\ 0 & \kappa \end{bmatrix} \left(\begin{bmatrix} 0 \\ \theta(t) \end{bmatrix} - \begin{bmatrix} \theta(t) \\ x(t) \end{bmatrix} \right) dt$$
$$+ \begin{bmatrix} \sigma_{\theta\theta} & 0 \\ \sigma_{\theta x} & \sigma_{xx} \end{bmatrix} \begin{bmatrix} dW_\theta(t) \\ dW_x(t) \end{bmatrix} \qquad (6.3)$$

where the key parameter matrix κ is a $2N_x \times 2N_x$ mean-reversion matrix:

$$\kappa = \begin{bmatrix} \kappa_{YY} & \kappa_{Y\pi} \\ \kappa_{\pi Y} & \kappa_{\pi\pi} \end{bmatrix} \qquad (6.4)$$

which determines how the short-run real and inflation state variables jointly mean revert to $\theta(t)$. The $2N_x \times 2N_x$ volatility matrices $\sigma_{\theta\theta}$, $\sigma_{\theta x}$, σ_{xx} respectively determine the covariances between the long-run state variables, the long-run and short-run state variables, and the short-run state variables.

The explicit setup from Krippner (2014a) with short-run state and long-run state variables is a convenient extension to the Berardi and Esposito (1999) model that improves the transparency and macroeconomic interpretation of the different classes of state variables and their role in shaping the term structure. The mathematically equivalent alternative to achieve the same short-run/long-run split within the Berardi and Esposito (1999) model would be to assume that some state variables follow unit root or highly persistent processes, and others are strongly mean-reverting. Either setup is consistent with the empirical evidence from GATSM and shadow/ZLB-GATSM estimations on observed term structures.

6.1.2 The nominal term structure in the GCE

The short rate is the sum of the GCE short-run state variables:

$$r_{GCE}(t) = a_0 + c_0' x_Y(t) + c_0' x_\pi(t)$$
$$= a_0 + [c_0', c_0'] \begin{bmatrix} x_Y(t) \\ x_\pi(t) \end{bmatrix}$$
$$= a_0 + d_0' x(t) \qquad (6.5)$$

where a_0 is a scalar constant, c_0 is an $N_x \times 1$ vector of ones, and d_0 is a $2N_x \times 1$ vector of ones. I will generally use notation such as $d_0' x(t)$ to conveniently express results directly as a nominal quantity, but notation in terms of $c_0' x_Y(t)$ and $c_0' x_\pi(t)$ is useful whenever the split of the nominal quantity into real and inflation state variables is helpful for the exposition, or may be of use for practical applications. In particular, the real/inflation split allows any of the ANSM term structure expressions in this book to be used as models for the real and/or inflation term structures.

The GCE expected path of the short rate under the risk-adjusted $\mathbb{Q}$ measure (conditional on the state variables $x(t)$ and $\theta(t)$, which I will omit in the notation for clarity and space considerations) is

$$\tilde{\mathbb{E}}_t \left[r_{\text{GCE}}(t+\tau) \right] = a_0 + d_0' \tilde{\theta}(t) + d_0' \exp\left(-\tilde{\kappa}\tau\right) \left[x(t) - \tilde{\theta}(t) \right] \tag{6.6}$$

where $\tilde{\theta}(t)$ is the $2N_x \times 1$ vector of long-run state variables, and $\tilde{\kappa}$ is the $2N_x \times 2N_x$ mean-reversion matrix, both under the $\mathbb{Q}$ measure. Note that, analogous to the GATSM exposition in section 3.1, $\tilde{\theta}(t)$ and $\tilde{\kappa}$ are obtained from their respective $\mathbb{P}$ measure quantities as $\tilde{\kappa} = \kappa + \Gamma$, $\tilde{\theta}(t) = \tilde{\kappa}^{-1} \left[\kappa \theta(t) - \gamma \right]$, where Γ and γ are from the market price of risk specification $\Pi(t) = \sigma_{xx}^{-1} \left[\gamma + \Gamma x(t) \right]$.

The GCE volatility effect $\text{VE}_{\text{GCE}}(\tau)$ is most conveniently split into four $2N_x \times 2N_x$ matrices, that is,

$$\text{VE}_{\text{GCE}}(\tau) = \text{VE}_{\theta\theta}(\tau) + \text{VE}_{\theta x,1}(\tau) + \text{VE}_{\theta x,2}(\tau) + \text{VE}_{xx}(\tau) \tag{6.7}$$

where $\text{VE}_{\theta\theta}(\tau)$ is the component determined by the long-run parameters only, $\text{VE}_{\theta x,1}(\tau)$ and $\text{VE}_{\theta x,2}(\tau)$ are components determined by the long-run and short-run parameters, and $\text{VE}_{xx}(\tau)$ is the component determined by the short-run parameters only. Krippner (2014a) derives these components with the following results:

$$\text{VE}_{\theta\theta}(\tau) = \frac{1}{2} d_0' \sigma_{\theta\theta} \sigma_{\theta\theta}' d_0 \cdot \tau^2 \tag{6.8}$$

$$\text{VE}_{\theta x,1}(\tau) = \frac{1}{2} d_0' G(\tilde{\kappa}, \tau) \left[\sigma_{\theta x} - \sigma_{\theta\theta} \right] \left[\sigma_{\theta x}' - \sigma_{\theta\theta}' \right] \left[G(\tilde{\kappa}, \tau) \right]' d_0 \tag{6.9}$$

where

$$G(\tilde{\kappa}, \tau) = \tilde{\kappa}^{-1} \left[I - \exp\left(-\tilde{\kappa}\tau\right) \right] \tag{6.10}$$

which is the matrix analogue of the scalar expression $G(\phi, \tau) = \frac{1}{\phi} \left[1 - \exp\left(-\phi\tau\right) \right]$,

$$\text{VE}_{\theta x,2}(\tau)$$
$$= \frac{1}{2} d_0' \sigma_{\theta\theta} \left[\sigma_{\theta x}' - \sigma_{\theta\theta}' \right] \left(\tilde{\kappa}'^{-1}\tau - \tilde{\kappa}'^{-1} \left[G(\tilde{\kappa}, \tau) \right]' \right) d_0$$
$$+ \frac{1}{2} d_0' \left[\tilde{\kappa}^{-1} G(\tilde{\kappa}, \tau) - \tilde{\kappa}^{-1}\tau \exp\left(-\tilde{\kappa}\tau\right) \right] \left[\sigma_{\theta x} - \sigma_{\theta\theta} \right] \sigma_{\theta\theta}' d_0 \tag{6.11}$$

and

$$VE_{xx}(\tau) = \frac{1}{2} d_0' G(\tilde{\kappa}, \tau) \sigma_{xx} \sigma_{xx}' [G(\tilde{\kappa}, \tau)]' d_0 \tag{6.12}$$

Analogous to the GATSM specification in section 3.1, $f_{GCE}(t, \tau)$ is the sum of the expected short rate $\tilde{\mathbb{E}}_t[r(t+\tau)]$ and the volatility effect $VE_{GCE}(t)$:

$$f_{GCE}(t, \tau) = \tilde{\mathbb{E}}_t[r_{GCE}(t+\tau)] + VE_{GCE}(\tau) \tag{6.13}$$

As discussed in section 3.1, the forward rate $f_{GCE}(t, \tau)$ equals the current expected returns, under the risk-adjusted $\mathbb{Q}$ measure, from a compounding investment in $r_{GCE}(t+\tau)$ as it mean reverts to a value determined by the long-run real and inflation state variables under the $\mathbb{Q}$ measure.

Nominal interest rates are:

$$R_{GCE}(t, \tau) = \int_0^\tau f_{GCE}(t, u) \, du \tag{6.14}$$

6.1.3 A macroeconomic interpretation of the GCE

As noted in Berardi and Esposito (1999), the real wealth of economic agents in a Cox, Ingersoll, and Ross (1985a) economy is completely invested in the production processes. The real returns on those production processes equals the real income of economic agents, and economic agents optimally allocate that income to consumption and investment.

Following Krippner (2008, 2014a), those three perspectives may be interpreted respectively as the production, income, and expenditure measures of real output. I denote instantaneous real output at time t by $Y(t)$, and instantaneous real output growth is therefore $dY(t)/dt$. Real output growth $dY(t)/dt$ is the sum of the current growth in the real returns on the production processes:

$$\frac{dY(t)}{dt} = c_0' x_Y(t) \tag{6.15}$$

where c_0 is an $N_x \times 1$ vector of ones.

Similarly, current inflation $dP(t)/dt$ is the sum of the deflator/inflation processes on the current factors of production:

$$\frac{dP(t)}{dt} = c_0' x_\pi(t) \tag{6.16}$$

and current nominal output growth $dX(t)/dt$ is real output growth plus inflation, that is,

$$\frac{dX(t)}{dt} = \frac{dY(t)}{dt} + \frac{dP(t)}{dt}$$

$$= c_0' x_Y(t) + c_0' x_\pi(t)$$
$$= d_0' x(t) \tag{6.17}$$

Comparing the relationships above to the term structure expressions in subsection 6.2.2 gives a simple yet intuitive macroeconomic interpretation of the term structure. First, the short rate in equation 6.5 is within a constant, a_0, of current nominal output growth:

$$r_{GCE}(t) = \lim_{\tau \to 0} \tilde{\mathbb{E}}_t \left[r_{GCE}(t+\tau) \right]$$
$$= a_0 + d_0' \tilde{\theta}(t) + d_0' \left[x(t) - \tilde{\theta}(t) \right]$$
$$= a_0 + d_0' x(t)$$
$$= a_0 + \frac{dX(t)}{dt} \tag{6.18}$$

The expectation of the short rate under the risk-adjusted $\mathbb{Q}$ measure in equation 6.6 is within a constant of the expectation of nominal output growth under the $\mathbb{Q}$ measure:

$$\tilde{\mathbb{E}}_t \left[r_{GCE}(t+\tau) \right] = a_0 + d_0' \tilde{\theta}(t) + d_0' \exp(-\tilde{\kappa}\tau) \left[x(t) - \tilde{\theta}(t) \right]$$
$$= a_0 + d_0' \tilde{\mathbb{E}}_t \left[x(t+\tau) \right]$$
$$= a_0 + \tilde{\mathbb{E}}_t \left[\frac{dX(t+\tau)}{dt} \right] \tag{6.19}$$

The long-horizon expectation of the short rate under the risk-adjusted $\mathbb{Q}$ measure is within a constant of the long-horizon expectation of nominal output growth under the $\mathbb{Q}$ measure. That is, from equation 6.6,

$$\lim_{\tau \to \infty} \tilde{\mathbb{E}}_t \left[r_{GCE}(t+\tau) \right] = a_0 + d_0' \tilde{\theta}(t)$$
$$= a_0 + d_0' \lim_{\tau \to \infty} \tilde{\mathbb{E}}_t \left[x(t+\tau) \right]$$
$$= a_0 + \lim_{\tau \to \infty} \tilde{\mathbb{E}}_t \left[\frac{dX(t+\tau)}{dt} \right] \tag{6.20}$$

6.1.4 GCE generalizations

The GCE as I have presented it is useful as a tangible economic framework for the expositions and their discussions in the remaining sections of this chapter. However, being a standard and generic classical model of the economy, the GCE is an oversimplification in many respects relative to the actual economy and contemporary economic models. For example, the GCE does not allow for pricing frictions,

Phillips curve relationships (i.e., output gap influences on inflation), multiple sectors of the economy (e.g., a banking sector, fiscal policy, labor markets, etc.), heterogenous economic agents, and so forth, and the monetary policy reaction function is effectively constrained to set the short-rate equal to prevailing nominal output growth. As discussed in Krippner (2014a), the GCE could in principle be generalized to include any or all of those aspects if desired. For example, Ang and Piazzesi (2003) is the seminal example that explicitly incorporates a Taylor rule policy reaction function into a (discrete-time) GATSM, and Wu (2006) shows how GATSMs can be related to Dynamic Stochastic General Equilibrium models.

Nevertheless, the remaining expositions and discussions in this chapter are not critically dependent on the precise relationships I have specified in the overview above. Specifically:

- The ANSM term structure results in subsection 6.1.2 only require that the state variables for the term structure can generally be represented with a first-order $\mathbb{Q}$ measure stochastic process. Joslin, Le, and Singleton (2013) establishes that such a result always holds in principle. In particular, if L_x lags of the $4N_x$ state variables were required for a more complex specification of the GCE, then that could be equivalently represented as a first-order $\mathbb{Q}$ measure stochastic process with $4N_x L_x$ state variables.[1] More generally, one could also abandon any explicit structural economic interpretation of the state variables and their dynamics. In this case, as in Krippner (2012d, 2014d), the ANSM results establish that any GATSM with an arbitrary specification, or what I will call a generic GATSM, can be parsimoniously represented as required by ANSMs.
- The discussion in section 6.3 on using the ANSM to represent the shadow term structure, and then in section 6.4 on the case for the K-ANSM framework only requires some acceptance that the shape of the yield curve is influenced by the current and expected growth in the real returns on the production processes in the economy, their associated deflator/inflation processes, and that long-maturity interest rates are influenced by the long-horizon expectations of those real and deflator/inflation processes. Even more comprehensive economic models would incorporate these elements.
- The discussion in section 6.5 on creating the EMS measure of the stance of monetary policy only requires an acceptance that the Level component of the term structure provides an estimate of the neutral interest rate. The Level component does not necessarily need to be justified with an economic model.

6.2 ANSMs as the reduced-form GCE term structure

In this section, I outline how ANSMs offer parsimonious reduced-form representations of the GCE term structure, and the generic GATSM. I begin in section 6.2.1 by reintroducing the ANSM(2), the ANSM(3), and higher-order ANSMs from chapter 3 in the forms and notation that will be forthcoming from manipulating the GCE term structure.

In subsections 6.2.2 to 6.2.4, I follow the principles of Krippner(2014d) and the results in Krippner (2014a) to show how the GCE short rate and its expectations under the $\mathbb{Q}$ measure relate to ANSM short rates and their expectations under the $\mathbb{Q}$ measure. In subsections 6.2.5 and 6.2.6, I follow the results in Krippner (2014a) to show how the GCE volatility effects may be related to the ANSM(2) and ANSM(3) volatility effects. These results extend those in Krippner(2014d) to show that ANSMs provide very parsimonious reduced-form representations of both the expected short rate and the volatility effect components of the GCE term structure (or the generic GATSM term structure).

In subsection 6.2.7, I outline the results from Krippner (2014a) showing that the reduced-form expression for the GCE state variables under the physical $\mathbb{P}$ measure produces a restricted form of the ANSM(2) and ANSM(3) state equations. This result creates even more parsimonious term structure models than standard ANSMs because both the $\mathbb{Q}$ and $\mathbb{P}$ measure mean-reversion matrices $\tilde{\kappa}$ and κ take the low-parametrization form implied from the original Nelson and Siegel (1987) specification.

6.2.1 ANSM specifications

I have already defined ANSMs in detail in sections 3.3 and 3.4 of chapter 3. In this section, I adopt the notation $L(t)$, $S(t)$, $B(t)$, $B_n^*(t)$ to denote the Level, Slope, Bow, and higher-order ANSM state variables, and I also adopt explicit notation for the different ANSM expressions to avoid any confusion between each ANSM and also with the GCE expressions. Specifically, I use the subscript A(2) to denote when I am specifically referring to the ANSM(2), the subscript A(3) to denote when I am referring to the ANSM(3), and the subscript A(N) to denote when I am referring to any ANSM in general.

As detailed in sections 3.3 and 3.4, ANSM forward rates are always the sum of the expected path of the short rate and the volatility effect, that is, $f_{A(N)}(t,\tau) = \tilde{\mathbb{E}}_t\left[r_{A(N)}(t+\tau)\right] - VE_{A(N)}(\tau)$, and interest rates and bond prices may be obtained from standard term structure definitions, that is $R_{A(N)}(t,\tau) = \int_0^\tau f(t,u)\,du$ and $P_{A(N)}(t,\tau) = \exp\left[-\tau \cdot R(t,\tau)\right]$. Therefore, I simply provide the expressions for $r_{A(N)}(t)$, $\tilde{\mathbb{E}}_t\left[r_{A(N)}(t+\tau)\right]$ and $VE_{A(N)}(\tau)$ for each ANSM specification without repeating the associated term structure expressions $f_{A(N)}(t,\tau)$, $R_{A(N)}(t,\tau)$, $P_{A(N)}(t,\tau)$.

ANSM(2)

The ANSM(2) is defined by the short rate:

$$r_{A(2)}(t) = [1,1]\begin{bmatrix} L(t) \\ S(t) \end{bmatrix}$$

$$= L(t) + S(t) \tag{6.21}$$

the expected path of the short rate:

$$
\tilde{\mathbb{E}}_t \left[r_{A(2)} (t + \tau) \right] = \left[1, \exp(-\phi\tau) \right] \begin{bmatrix} L(t) \\ S(t) \end{bmatrix}
$$

$$
= L(t) + S(t) \cdot \exp(-\phi\tau) \tag{6.22}
$$

and the volatility effect:

$$
\text{VE}_{A(2)} (\tau) = \sigma_L^2 \cdot \frac{1}{2}\tau^2 + \sigma_S^2 \cdot \frac{1}{2} [G(\phi,\tau)]^2
$$

$$
+ \rho_{LS}\sigma_L\sigma_S \cdot \tau G(\phi,\tau) \tag{6.23}
$$

where

$$
G(\phi,\tau) = \frac{1}{\phi} \left[1 - \exp(-\phi\tau) \right] \tag{6.24}
$$

ANSM(3)

The ANSM(3) is defined by the short rate:

$$
r_{A(3)} (t) = [1,1,0] \begin{bmatrix} L(t) \\ S(t) \\ B(t) \end{bmatrix}
$$

$$
= L(t) + S(t) \tag{6.25}
$$

the expected path of the short rate:

$$
\tilde{\mathbb{E}}_t \left[r_{A(3)} (t + \tau) \right] = \left[1, \exp(-\phi\tau), \phi\tau \exp(-\phi\tau) \right] \begin{bmatrix} L(t) \\ S(t) \\ B(t) \end{bmatrix}
$$

$$
= L(t) + S(t) \cdot \exp(-\phi\tau) + B(t) \cdot \phi\tau \exp(-\phi\tau) \tag{6.26}
$$

and the volatility effect:

$$
\text{VE}_{A(3)} (\tau) = \sigma_L^2 \cdot \frac{1}{2}\tau^2 + \sigma_S^2 \cdot \frac{1}{2} [G(\phi,\tau)]^2 + \sigma_B^2 \cdot \frac{1}{2} [F(\phi,\tau)]^2
$$

$$
+ \rho_{LS}\sigma_L\sigma_S \cdot \tau G(\phi,\tau) + \rho_{LB}\sigma_L\sigma_B \cdot \tau F(\phi,\tau)
$$

$$
+ \rho_{SB}\sigma_S\sigma_B \cdot G(\phi,\tau) F(\phi,\tau) \tag{6.27}
$$

where

$$
F(\phi,\tau) = G(\phi,\tau) - \tau \exp(-\phi\tau)
$$

Higher-order ANSMs

An ANSM with N state variables, or hereafter denoted the ANSM(N), is defined by the short rate:

$$r_{A(N)}(t) = [1,1,0,\ldots,0] \begin{bmatrix} L(t) \\ S(t) \\ B(t) \\ B_1^*(t) \\ \vdots \\ B_{N-3}^*(t) \end{bmatrix}_{N \times 1}$$

$$= L(t) + S(t) \tag{6.28}$$

the expected path of the short rate:

$$\tilde{\mathbb{E}}_t \left[r_{A(N)}(t+\tau) \right] = L(t) + S(t) \cdot \exp(-\phi\tau) + B(t) \cdot \phi\tau \exp(-\phi\tau)$$

$$+ \sum_{n=1}^{N-2} B_n^*(t) \cdot [\phi\tau]^{n+1} \exp(-\phi\tau) \tag{6.29}$$

and the volatility effect:

$$\text{VE}(\tau) = \frac{1}{2} \left[\int_0^\tau b_0' \exp(-\tilde{\kappa} u) \, du \right] \sigma \sigma' \left[\int_0^\tau \exp(-\tilde{\kappa}' u) \, b_0 \, du \right] \tag{6.30}$$

where

$$\exp(-\tilde{\kappa}' u) \, b_0 = \begin{bmatrix} 1 \\ \exp(-\phi u) \\ \phi\tau \exp(-\phi u) \\ \frac{1}{(n-2)} (\phi\tau)^{n-2} \exp(-\phi u) \\ \vdots \\ \frac{1}{(N-2)} (\phi\tau)^{N-2} \exp(-\phi u) \end{bmatrix} \tag{6.31}$$

6.2.2 GCE short rate and ANSM short rate

The GCE short rate is

$$r_{GCE}(t) = a_0 + d_0' x(t) \tag{6.32}$$

and the ANSM(N) short rate is

$$r_{A(N)}(t) = L(t) + S(t) \tag{6.33}$$

Therefore:

$$L(t) + S(t) = a_0 + d_0' x(t) \tag{6.34}$$

6.2.3 GCE and ANSM long-horizon short rate expectations

The long-horizon expectation of the GCE expected path of the short rate under the $\mathbb{Q}$ measure is obtained from equation 6.6 as

$$\lim_{\tau \to \infty} \tilde{\mathbb{E}}_t \left[r_{GCE}(t+\tau) \right] = a_0 + d_0' \tilde{\theta}(t) \tag{6.35}$$

given:

$$\lim_{\tau \to \infty} \tilde{\mathbb{E}}_t \left[\exp(-\tilde{\kappa}\tau) \right] = 0 \tag{6.36}$$

Similarly, the long-horizon expectation of the short rate for any ANSM under the $\mathbb{Q}$ measure is

$$\lim_{\tau \to \infty} \tilde{\mathbb{E}}_t \left[r(t+\tau) \right]_{A(N)} = L(t) \tag{6.37}$$

given

$$\lim_{\tau \to \infty} \left[\exp(-\phi\tau) \right] = \lim_{\tau \to \infty} \left[\phi\tau \exp(-\phi\tau) \right]$$
$$= \lim_{\tau \to \infty} \left[[\phi\tau]^{N-2} \exp(-\phi\tau) \right] = 0$$

Therefore, the Level state variable for any ANSM precisely represents the long-horizon expectation of the GCE short rate under the $\mathbb{Q}$ measure with

$$L(t) = a_0 + d_0' \tilde{\theta}(t) \tag{6.38}$$

Note that using this expression for $L(t)$ in equation 6.34 gives a direct expression for $S(t)$ in terms of GCE state variables:

$$S(t) = a_0 + d_0' x(t) - L(t)$$
$$= a_0 + d_0' x(t) - a_0 - d_0' \tilde{\theta}(t)$$
$$= d_0' \left[x(t) - \tilde{\theta}(t) \right] \tag{6.39}$$

Therefore, the Slope state variable $S(t)$ for any ANSM is the sum of the short-run GCE state variables relative to their long-run state variables.

These precise relationships follow from the unit root process inherent in the ANSM Level state variable and the unit root specification for the long-run state variable block in the GCE. The relationship would hold to a close approximation if the GCE long-run state variables under the $\mathbb{Q}$ measure were specified as a persistent stationary process.

6.2.4 GCE and ANSM short rate expectations

Eigenvalue approximation

The expectation of the GCE short rate from equation 6.6 relative to its long-horizon expectation is

$$\tilde{\mathbb{E}}_t[\mathrm{r}_{\mathrm{GCE}}(t+\tau)] - \lim_{\tau \to \infty} \tilde{\mathbb{E}}_t[\mathrm{r}_{\mathrm{GCE}}(t+\tau)]$$

$$= a_0 + d_0'\tilde{\theta}(t) + d_0'\exp(-\tilde{\kappa}\tau)\left[x(t) - \tilde{\theta}(t)\right] - \left[a_0 + d_0'\tilde{\theta}(t)\right]$$

$$= d_0'\exp(-\tilde{\kappa}\tau)\left[x(t) - \tilde{\theta}(t)\right] \tag{6.40}$$

The expression $d_0'\exp(-\tilde{\kappa}\tau)\left[x(t) - \tilde{\theta}(t)\right]$ can be explicity related to ANSMs using what Krippner (2014d) calls an eigenvalue approximation. Specifically, an eigenvalue approximation uses terms from a Taylor series expansion around the central measure of the eigenvalues for $\tilde{\kappa}$. My exposition here is equivalent to that in Krippner (2014d), but it uses the more convenient matrix notation from Krippner (2014a) rather than resorting to summations.

First, express the matrix exponential in equation 6.40 in terms of scalar exponentials using an eigensystem decomposition for the mean-reversion matrix $\tilde{\kappa}$:

$$\tilde{V}\tilde{\kappa}_D\tilde{V}^{-1} = \tilde{\kappa} \tag{6.41}$$

where $\tilde{V}$ is the $2N_x \times 2N_x$ matrix of eigenvectors in columns from the eigensystem decomposition, and $\tilde{\kappa}_D$ is the $2N_x \times 2N_x$ diagonal matrix of the $2N_x$ unique positive eigenvalues $\lambda_1, \ldots, \lambda_{2N_x}$.

Second, one can express all of the eigenvalues $\lambda_1, \ldots, \lambda_{2N_x}$ relative to a single value ϕ, which one can consider to be a central value of $\lambda_1, \ldots, \lambda_{2N_x}$, for example, $\phi = \mathrm{mean}\{\lambda_1, \ldots, \lambda_{2N_x}\}$. Therefore, each λ_n can be represented as $\phi - \phi\tilde{\delta}_{n,D}$ or $\phi\left(1 - \tilde{\delta}_{n,D}\right)$, and so the diagonal matrix $\tilde{\kappa}_D$ can be reexpressed as

$$\tilde{\kappa}_D = \begin{bmatrix} \phi\left(1 - \tilde{\delta}_{1,D}\right) & 0 & \cdots & 0 \\ 0 & \ddots & \ddots & \vdots \\ \vdots & \ddots & \ddots & 0 \\ 0 & \cdots & 0 & \phi\left(1 - \tilde{\delta}_{2N_x,D}\right) \end{bmatrix}$$

$$= \phi\begin{bmatrix} 1 - \tilde{\delta}_{1,D} & 0 & \cdots & 0 \\ 0 & \ddots & \ddots & \vdots \\ \vdots & \ddots & \ddots & 0 \\ 0 & \cdots & 0 & 1 - \tilde{\delta}_{2N_x,D} \end{bmatrix}$$

$$= \phi\left(I - \tilde{\delta}_D\right) \tag{6.42}$$

where I is the $2N_x \times 2N_x$ identity matrix, and $\tilde{\delta}_D$ is a $2N_x \times 2N_x$ diagonal matrix containing the entries $\tilde{\delta}_{1,D},\ldots,\tilde{\delta}_{2N_x,D}$. Anticipating the Taylor series expansion below, note that ϕ can always be defined to ensure that the matrix determinant $\left|\tilde{\delta}_D\right| < 1$. For example, using $\phi = \max\left\{\lambda_1,\ldots,\lambda_{2N_x}\right\}$ as an extreme value of ϕ would result in $-1 < \tilde{\delta}_{n,D} \leq 0$. In practice, ϕ is an estimated parameter.

With the eigensystem decomposition of $\tilde{\kappa}$ and the factorization of $\tilde{\kappa}_D$, the matrix exponential term in equation 6.40 then becomes

$$
\begin{aligned}
\exp\left(-\tilde{\kappa}\tau\right) &= \tilde{V} \exp\left(-\phi\left[I - \tilde{\delta}_D\right]\tau\right)\tilde{V}^{-1} \\
&= \tilde{V} \exp\left(-\phi I\tau\right)\exp\left(\phi\tilde{\delta}_D\tau\right)\tilde{V}^{-1}
\end{aligned}
\tag{6.43}
$$

The matrix exponential $\exp\left(-\phi I\tau\right)$ is a $2N_x \times 2N_x$ diagonal matrix with entries $\exp\left(-\phi\tau\right)$, which is the $2N_x \times 2N_x$ identity matrix I multiplied by the scalar exponential $\exp\left(-\phi\tau\right)$

$$
\exp\left(-\phi I\tau\right) = I\exp\left(-\phi\tau\right)
\tag{6.44}
$$

while the matrix exponential $\exp\left(\phi\tilde{\delta}_D\tau\right)$ is a $2N_x \times 2N_x$ diagonal matrix that can be represented formally as a convergent Taylor series expansion:

$$
\exp\left(\phi\tilde{\delta}_D\tau\right) = I + \phi\tilde{\delta}_D\tau + \frac{1}{2!}\left[\phi\tilde{\delta}_D\tau\right]^2 + \frac{1}{3!}\left[\phi\tilde{\delta}_D\tau\right]^3 + \ldots
\tag{6.45}
$$

Therefore $\tilde{\mathbb{E}}_t\left[r_{\text{GCE}}(t+\tau)\right] - \lim_{\tau\to\infty}\tilde{\mathbb{E}}_t\left[r_{\text{GCE}}(t+\tau)\right]$ can be approximated to arbitrary order by taking the required number of terms from the Taylor expansion.

GCE and ANSM(2) Slope component

Using just the first term of the Taylor expansion for $\exp\left(\phi\tilde{\delta}_D\tau\right)$ results in a form identical to the ANSM Slope component for the expected path of the short rate:

$$
\begin{aligned}
\exp\left(-\phi I\tau\right)\exp\left(\phi\tilde{\delta}_D\tau\right) &\simeq I\exp\left(-\phi\tau\right)I \\
&= I\exp\left(-\phi\tau\right)
\end{aligned}
\tag{6.46}
$$

Therefore,

$$
\begin{aligned}
&\tilde{\mathbb{E}}_t\left[r_{\text{GCE}}(t+\tau)\right] - \lim_{\tau\to\infty}\tilde{\mathbb{E}}_t\left[r_{\text{GCE}}(t+\tau)\right] \\
&= d_0'\exp\left(-\tilde{\kappa}\tau\right)\left[x(t) - \tilde{\theta}(t)\right] \\
&\simeq d_0'\tilde{V}I\exp\left(-\phi\tau\right)\tilde{V}^{-1}\left[x(t) - \tilde{\theta}(t)\right]
\end{aligned}
$$

$$= \exp(-\phi\tau) \cdot d_0' \tilde{V}\tilde{V}^{-1}\left[x(t) - \tilde{\theta}(t)\right]$$

$$= \exp(-\phi\tau) \cdot d_0'\left[x(t) - \tilde{\theta}(t)\right]$$

$$= S(t) \cdot \exp(-\phi\tau) \tag{6.47}$$

where

$$S(t) = d_0'\left[x(t) - \tilde{\theta}(t)\right] \tag{6.48}$$

Note that $\tilde{V}\tilde{V}^{-1} = I$ is the $2N_x \times 2N_x$ identity matrix, by definition of the eigensystem decomposition. I will frequently use the result $\tilde{V}\tilde{V}^{-1} = I$ to eliminate $\tilde{V}\tilde{V}^{-1}$ in the expositions that follow.

GCE and ANSM(3) Slope plus Bow components

Using the first two terms of the Taylor expansion for $\exp\left(\phi\tilde{\delta}_D\tau\right)$ results in a form identical to the ANSM Slope plus Bow component for the expected path of the short rate. That is, $\exp(-\phi I\tau)\exp\left(\phi\tilde{\delta}_D\tau\right)$ with two terms of the Taylor expansion is

$$\exp(-\phi I\tau)\exp\left(\phi\tilde{\delta}_D\tau\right) \simeq I\exp(-\phi\tau)\left(I + \phi\tau\tilde{\delta}_D\right)$$

$$= I\exp(-\phi\tau) + \phi\tau\exp(-\phi\tau)\tilde{\delta}_D \tag{6.49}$$

The first term may be carried through as in the preceding subsection, and the second term is

$$d_0'\tilde{V}\left[\phi\tau\exp(-\phi\tau)\tilde{\delta}_D\right]\tilde{V}^{-1}\left[x(t) - \tilde{\theta}(t)\right]$$

$$= \phi\tau\exp(-\phi\tau) \cdot d_0'\tilde{V}\tilde{\delta}_D\tilde{V}^{-1}\left[x(t) - \tilde{\theta}(t)\right] \tag{6.50}$$

Therefore,

$$\tilde{\mathbb{E}}_t[r_{\text{GCE}}(t+\tau)] - \lim_{\tau\to\infty}\tilde{\mathbb{E}}_t[r_{\text{GCE}}(t+\tau)]$$

$$= d_0'\exp(-\tilde{\kappa}\tau)\left[x(t) - \tilde{\theta}(t)\right]$$

$$\simeq S(t) \cdot \exp(-\phi\tau) + B(t) \cdot \phi\tau\exp(-\phi\tau) \tag{6.51}$$

where

$$B(t) = d_0'\tilde{V}\tilde{\delta}_D\tilde{V}^{-1}\left[x(t) - \tilde{\theta}(t)\right] \tag{6.52}$$

GCE and higher-order ANSM components

Adding successive terms in the Taylor expansion of $\exp\left(\phi\tilde{\delta}_D\tau\right)$ for the GCE results in successive higher-order ANSM representations for the expected path of the short rate relative to the Level state variable $L(t)$. For example, the ANSM(4) would result from using three terms of the Taylor expansion for $\exp\left(\phi\tilde{\delta}_D\tau\right)$:

$$\tilde{\mathbb{E}}_t\left[r_{\text{GCE}}\left(t+\tau\right)\right] - \lim_{\tau\to\infty}\tilde{\mathbb{E}}_t\left[r_{\text{GCE}}\left(t+\tau\right)\right]$$

$$= d_0'\exp\left(-\tilde{\kappa}\tau\right)\left[x(t) - \tilde{\theta}(t)\right] \tag{6.53}$$

$$\simeq S(t)\cdot\exp\left(-\phi\tau\right) + B(t)\cdot\phi\tau\exp\left(-\phi\tau\right)$$

$$+ B_1^*(t)\cdot[\phi\tau]^2\exp\left(-\phi\tau\right) \tag{6.54}$$

where

$$B_1^*(t) = d_0'\tilde{V}\frac{1}{2}\left[\tilde{\delta}_D\right]^2\tilde{V}^{-1}\left[x(t) - \tilde{\theta}(t)\right] \tag{6.55}$$

In general, an ANSM(N) would result from using $N-1$ terms of the Taylor expansion for $\exp\left(\phi\tilde{\delta}_D\tau\right)$:

$$\tilde{\mathbb{E}}_t\left[r_{\text{GCE}}\left(t+\tau\right)\right] - \lim_{\tau\to\infty}\tilde{\mathbb{E}}_t\left[r_{\text{GCE}}\left(t+\tau\right)\right]$$

$$= d_0'\exp\left(-\tilde{\kappa}\tau\right)\left[x(t) - \tilde{\theta}(t)\right]$$

$$\simeq S(t)\cdot\exp\left(-\phi\tau\right) + B(t)\cdot\phi\tau\exp\left(-\phi\tau\right)$$

$$+ \sum_{n=1}^{N-3}B_n^*(t)\cdot[\phi\tau]^{n+1}\exp\left(-\phi\tau\right) \tag{6.56}$$

where

$$B_n^*(t) = d_0'\tilde{V}\frac{1}{(n+1)!}\left[\tilde{\delta}_D\right]^{n+1}\tilde{V}^{-1}\left[x(t) - \tilde{\theta}(t)\right] \tag{6.57}$$

Therefore, the expectation of the GCE short rate relative to its long-horizon expectation can be arbitrarily approximated by $\tilde{\mathbb{E}}_t\left[r_{\text{A}(N)}(t+\tau)\right] - L(t)$. Note that $\left[\tilde{\delta}_D\right]^{n+1}$ converges to zero because $\left|\tilde{\delta}_D\right| < 0$. Smaller magnitudes of $\tilde{\delta}_D$, which in turn implies smaller differences between the non-zero eigenvalues in the GCE mean-reversion matrix $\tilde{\kappa}$, means that fewer ANSM state variables will be needed to provide a close representation of the GCE term structure (or the generic GATSM) that could otherwise be used to represent the data. In practice, the number of state variables is determined empirically, but just several state variables typically provide a good representation of the data.

6.2.5 Long-run GCE volatility effect and the ANSM Level volatility effect

The volatility effect for purely the GCE long-run state variables is

$$\text{VE}_{\theta\theta}(\tau) = \frac{1}{2} d_0' \sigma_{\theta\theta} \sigma_{\theta\theta}' d_0 \cdot \tau^2 \tag{6.58}$$

while the volatility effect purely for the Level state variable in any ANSM is

$$\text{VE}_{A(N),L}(\tau) = \sigma_L^2 \cdot \frac{1}{2} \tau^2 \tag{6.59}$$

Therefore, for any ANSM, the component of the volatility effect purely associated with the Level state variable precisely represents the volatility effect for the GCE long-run state variables:

$$\sigma_L^2 \cdot \frac{1}{2} \tau^2 = \frac{1}{2} d_0' \sigma_{\theta\theta} \sigma_{\theta\theta}' d_0 \cdot \tau^2 \tag{6.60}$$

where

$$\sigma_L^2 = d_0' \sigma_{\theta\theta} \sigma_{\theta\theta}' d_0 \tag{6.61}$$

Note again that this precise relationship follows from the unit root process inherent in the ANSM Level state variable and the unit root specification for the long-run state variable block in the GCE. The relationship would hold to a close approximation if the GCE long-run state variables under the $\mathbb{Q}$ measure were specified as a persistent stationary process.

6.2.6 Other volatility effects

Eigenvalue approximation

The expressions $\tilde{\kappa}^{-1}$, $\exp(-\tilde{\kappa}\tau)$, and $G(\tilde{\kappa}, \tau)$ that appear in the GCE volatility effect expressions $\text{VE}_{\theta x,1}(\tau)$, $\text{VE}_{\theta x,2}(\tau)$, and $\text{VE}_{xx}(\tau)$ may be reexpressed using the eigensystem decomposition $\tilde{\kappa} = \tilde{V}\tilde{\kappa}_D \tilde{V}^{-1}$, and the reexpression $\tilde{\kappa}_D = \phi\left(I - \tilde{\delta}_D\right)$ as established in subsection 6.3.4.

Therefore, the reexpression of $\tilde{\kappa}^{-1}$ is

$$\tilde{\kappa}^{-1} = \tilde{V}\tilde{\kappa}_D^{-1}\tilde{V}^{-1}$$
$$= \tilde{V}\left[\phi\left(I - \tilde{\delta}_D\right)\right]^{-1}\tilde{V}^{-1}$$
$$= \frac{1}{\phi}\tilde{V}\left(I - \tilde{\delta}_D\right)^{-1}\tilde{V}^{-1} \tag{6.62}$$

where $\left(I - \tilde{\delta}_D\right)^{-1}$ is a $2N_x \times 2N_x$ diagonal matrix that can be expressed as a Taylor series expansion:

$$\left(I - \tilde{\delta}_D\right)^{-1} = I + \tilde{\delta}_D + \tilde{\delta}_D^2 + \tilde{\delta}_D^3 + \dots \tag{6.63}$$

For convenience, I repeat the reexpression of $\exp\left(-\tilde{\kappa}\tau\right)$:

$$\exp\left(-\tilde{\kappa}\tau\right) = \tilde{V} \exp\left(-\tilde{\kappa}_D\tau\right) \tilde{V}^{-1}$$
$$= \exp\left(\phi\tau\right) \tilde{V} \exp\left(\phi\tau\tilde{\delta}_D\right) \tilde{V}^{-1} \tag{6.64}$$

and its associated Taylor series expansion:

$$\exp\left(-\phi\tau\tilde{\delta}_D\right) = I + \phi\tau\tilde{\delta}_D + \frac{1}{2!}\left[\phi\tau\tilde{\delta}_D\right]^2 + \frac{1}{3!}\left[\phi\tau\tilde{\delta}_D\right]^3 + \dots \tag{6.65}$$

Using the reexpressions for $\tilde{\kappa}^{-1}$ and $\exp\left(-\tilde{\kappa}\tau\right)$ provides a reexpression of the matrix function $G(\tilde{\kappa},\tau)$:

$$G(\tilde{\kappa},\tau) = \tilde{\kappa}^{-1}\left[I - \exp\left(-\tilde{\kappa}\tau\right)\right]$$
$$= \frac{1}{\phi}\tilde{V}\left(I - \tilde{\delta}_D\right)^{-1}\tilde{V}^{-1}$$
$$\times \left[I - \exp\left(\phi\tau\right)\tilde{V}\exp\left(\phi\tau\tilde{\delta}_D\right)\tilde{V}^{-1}\right] \tag{6.66}$$

and its Taylor expansion can be obtained using the Taylor expansions for $\left(I - \tilde{\delta}_D\right)^{-1}$ and $\exp\left(\phi\tau\tilde{\delta}_D\right)$.

Therefore, analogous to $\tilde{\mathbb{E}}_t\left[r_{GCE}\left(t+\tau\right)\right] - \lim_{\tau\to\infty}\tilde{\mathbb{E}}_t\left[r_{GCE}\left(t+\tau\right)\right]$, the GCE volatility effect expressions $VE_{\theta x,1}\left(\tau\right)$, $VE_{\theta x,2}\left(\tau\right)$, and $VE_{xx}\left(\tau\right)$ can be approximated to arbitrary order by taking the required number of terms from the two Taylor expansions. However, the calculations are more involved, so I only provide the full details for the results that relate to the ANSM(2) volatility effects. I provide the key results for the ANSM(3), but refer readers to Krippner (2014a) for the details.

GCE volatility effects and the ANSM(2) volatility effects

The first terms of the Taylor expansions for $\left(I - \tilde{\delta}_D\right)^{-1}$ and $\exp\left(\phi\tau\tilde{\delta}_D\right)$ are

$$\left(I - \tilde{\delta}_D\right)^{-1} \simeq I \tag{6.67}$$

and

$$\exp\left(\phi\tau\tilde{\delta}_D\right) \simeq I \tag{6.68}$$

Therefore,

$$\tilde{\kappa}^{-1} \simeq \frac{1}{\phi} \tilde{V} I \tilde{V}^{-1} = \frac{1}{\phi} \tilde{V} \tilde{V}^{-1} = \frac{1}{\phi} I \tag{6.69}$$

and

$$\exp(-\tilde{\kappa}\tau) \simeq \exp(\phi\tau) \tilde{V} I \tilde{V}^{-1} = \exp(\phi\tau) I \tag{6.70}$$

and so

$$
\begin{aligned}
G(\tilde{\kappa},\tau) &\simeq \frac{1}{\phi} \tilde{V} I \tilde{V}^{-1} \left[I - \exp(\phi\tau) \tilde{V} I \tilde{V}^{-1} \right] \\
&= \frac{1}{\phi} \left[I - \exp(\phi\tau) I \right] \\
&= G(\phi,\tau) I
\end{aligned}
\tag{6.71}
$$

where $\frac{1}{\phi} I$, $\exp(\phi\tau) I$, and $G(\phi,\tau) I$ are the respective scalar functions $\frac{1}{\phi}$, $\exp(\phi\tau)$, and $G(\phi,\tau) = \frac{1}{\phi} \left[1 - \exp(-\phi\tau) \right]$ multiplied by the $2N_x \times 2N_x$ identity matrix I.
Therefore $\mathrm{VE}_{xx}(\tau)$ is

$$
\begin{aligned}
\mathrm{VE}_{xx}(\tau) &= \frac{1}{2} d_0' G(\tilde{\kappa},\tau) \sigma_{xx} \sigma_{xx}' \left[G(\tilde{\kappa},\tau) \right]' d_0 \\
&\simeq \frac{1}{2} d_0' G(\phi,\tau) I \sigma_{xx} \sigma_{xx}' G(\phi,\tau) I d_0 \\
&= d_0' \sigma_{xx} \sigma_{xx}' d_0 \cdot \frac{1}{2} \left[G(\phi,\tau) \right]^2
\end{aligned}
\tag{6.72}
$$

Similarly, $\mathrm{VE}_{\theta x,1}(\tau)$ is

$$
\begin{aligned}
\mathrm{VE}_{\theta x,1}(\tau) &= \frac{1}{2} d_0' G(\tilde{\kappa},\tau) \left[\sigma_{\theta x} - \sigma_{\theta\theta} \right] \left[\sigma_{\theta x}' - \sigma_{\theta\theta}' \right] \left[G(\tilde{\kappa},\tau) \right]' d_0 \\
&\simeq \frac{1}{2} d_0' G(\phi,\tau) I \left[\sigma_{\theta x} - \sigma_{\theta\theta} \right] \left[\sigma_{\theta x}' - \sigma_{\theta\theta}' \right] G(\phi,\tau) I d_0 \\
&= d_0' \left[\sigma_{\theta x} - \sigma_{\theta\theta} \right] \left[\sigma_{\theta x}' - \sigma_{\theta\theta}' \right] d_0 \cdot \frac{1}{2} \left[G(\phi,\tau) \right]^2
\end{aligned}
\tag{6.73}
$$

and $\mathrm{VE}_{\theta x,2}(\tau)$ is

$$
\begin{aligned}
\mathrm{VE}_{\theta x,2}(\tau) &= \frac{1}{2} d_0' \sigma_{\theta\theta} \left[\sigma_{\theta x}' - \sigma_{\theta\theta}' \right] \left(\tilde{\kappa}'^{-1}\tau - \tilde{\kappa}'^{-1} \left[G(\tilde{\kappa},\tau) \right]' \right) d_0 \\
&\quad + \frac{1}{2} d_0' \left[\tilde{\kappa}^{-1} G(\tilde{\kappa},\tau) - \tilde{\kappa}^{-1}\tau \exp(-\tilde{\kappa}\tau) \right] \left[\sigma_{\theta x} - \sigma_{\theta\theta} \right] \sigma_{\theta\theta}' d_0 \\
&\simeq \frac{1}{2} d_0' \sigma_{\theta\theta} \left[\sigma_{\theta x}' - \sigma_{\theta\theta}' \right] \left(\frac{1}{\phi}\tau - \frac{1}{\phi} G(\phi,\tau) \right) d_0
\end{aligned}
$$

$$+\frac{1}{2}d_0' \left[\frac{1}{\phi}G(\phi,\tau) - \frac{1}{\phi}\tau\exp(-\tilde{\kappa}\tau)\right] [\sigma_{\theta x} - \sigma_{\theta\theta}] \sigma_{\theta\theta}' d_0$$

$$= \frac{1}{2}d_0'\sigma_{\theta\theta} \left[\sigma_{\theta x}' - \sigma_{\theta\theta}'\right] d_0 \cdot \left(\frac{1}{\phi}\tau - \frac{1}{\phi}G(\phi,\tau)\right)$$

$$+\frac{1}{2}d_0'\sigma_{\theta\theta} \left[\sigma_{\theta x}' - \sigma_{\theta\theta}'\right] d_0 \cdot \left[\frac{1}{\phi}G(\phi,\tau) - \frac{1}{\phi}\tau\exp(-\tilde{\kappa}\tau)\right]$$

$$= d_0'\sigma_{\theta\theta} \left[\sigma_{\theta x}' - \sigma_{\theta\theta}'\right] d_0 \cdot \left(\frac{1}{\phi}\tau - \frac{1}{\phi}\tau\exp(-\tilde{\kappa}\tau)\right)$$

$$= d_0'\sigma_{\theta\theta} \left[\sigma_{\theta x}' - \sigma_{\theta\theta}'\right] d_0 \cdot \tau\, G(\phi,\tau) \tag{6.74}$$

where $d_0'\sigma_{\theta\theta} \left[\sigma_{\theta x}' - \sigma_{\theta\theta}'\right] d_0 = d_0' \left[\sigma_{\theta x} - \sigma_{\theta\theta}\right]\sigma_{\theta\theta}' d_0$ because both are scalar quantities that result from the matrix multiplications, and the transpose of a scalar equals itself.

Relating $VE_{\theta x,1}(\tau)$, $VE_{\theta x,2}(\tau)$, and $VE_{xx}(\tau)$ explicitly to the ANSM(2) volatility effect expression $VE_{A(2)}(\tau)$ gives

$$VE_{xx}(\tau) + VE_{\theta x,1}(\tau)$$

$$\simeq \left(d_0'\sigma_{xx}\sigma_{xx}'d_0 + d_0' [\sigma_{\theta x} - \sigma_{\theta\theta}] \left[\sigma_{\theta x}' - \sigma_{\theta\theta}'\right] d_0\right) \cdot \frac{1}{2}[G(\phi,\tau)]^2$$

$$= \sigma_S^2 \cdot \frac{1}{2}[G(\phi,\tau)]^2 \tag{6.75}$$

where

$$\sigma_S^2 = d_0'\sigma_{xx}\sigma_{xx}'d_0 + d_0' [\sigma_{\theta x} - \sigma_{\theta\theta}] \left[\sigma_{\theta x}' - \sigma_{\theta\theta}'\right] d_0$$

$$= d_0' \left(\sigma_{xx}\sigma_{xx}' + [\sigma_{\theta x} - \sigma_{\theta\theta}] \left[\sigma_{\theta x}' - \sigma_{\theta\theta}'\right]\right) d_0 \tag{6.76}$$

and

$$VE_{\theta x,2}(\tau) \simeq \rho_{LS}\sigma_L\sigma_S \cdot \tau\, G(\phi,\tau) \tag{6.77}$$

where

$$\rho_{LS}\sigma_L\sigma_S = 2d_0'\sigma_{\theta\theta} \left[\sigma_{\theta x}' - \sigma_{\theta\theta}'\right] d_0 \tag{6.78}$$

In summary, the ANSM(2) volatility effect approximates the GCE volatility effect using the first Taylor expansion terms:

$$VE_{A(2)}(\tau) = \sigma_L^2 \cdot \frac{1}{2}\tau^2 + \sigma_S^2 \cdot \frac{1}{2}[G(\phi,\tau)]^2$$

$$+ \rho_{LS}\sigma_L\sigma_S \cdot \tau\, G(\phi,\tau)$$

$$\simeq VE_{GCE}(\tau) \tag{6.79}$$

GCE volatility effects and the ANSM(3) non-Level volatility effects

The first two of the Taylor expansions for $\left(I - \tilde{\delta}_D\right)^{-1}$ and $\exp\left(\phi\tau\tilde{\delta}_D\right)$ are

$$\left(I - \tilde{\delta}_D\right)^{-1} \simeq I + \tilde{\delta}_D \tag{6.80}$$

and

$$\exp\left(\phi\tilde{\delta}_D\tau\right) \simeq I + \phi\tau\tilde{\delta}_D \tag{6.81}$$

Therefore,

$$\tilde{\kappa}^{-1} \simeq \frac{1}{\phi}\tilde{V}\left[I + \tilde{\delta}_D\right]\tilde{V}^{-1} \tag{6.82}$$

and

$$\exp\left(-\tilde{\kappa}\tau\right) \simeq \exp\left(\phi\tau\right)\tilde{V}\left[I + \phi\tau\tilde{\delta}_D\right]\tilde{V}^{-1} \tag{6.83}$$

and so

$$\begin{aligned}
G(\tilde{\kappa},\tau) &\simeq \frac{1}{\phi}\tilde{V}\left[I + \tilde{\delta}_D\right]\tilde{V}^{-1}\left[I - \exp\left(\phi\tau\right)\tilde{V}\left[I + \phi\tau\tilde{\delta}_D\right]\tilde{V}^{-1}\right] \\
&= G(\phi,\tau)I + \left[\frac{1}{\phi} - \frac{1}{\phi}\exp\left(\phi\tau\right) - \tau\exp\left(\phi\tau\right)\right]\tilde{V}\tilde{\delta}_D\tilde{V}^{-1} \\
&= G(\phi,\tau)I + F(\phi,\tau)\tilde{V}\tilde{\delta}_D\tilde{V}^{-1}
\end{aligned} \tag{6.84}$$

where the term $-\frac{1}{\phi}\exp\left(\phi\tau\right)\tilde{V}\phi\tau\tilde{\delta}_D^2\tilde{V}^{-1}$ has been omitted in the second line because it is a second-order term in $\tilde{\delta}_D$.

Referring back to the ANSM(3) volatility effect $\text{VE}_{A(3)}(\tau)$ from sub-section 6.2.1, it is composed of the cross-products of the scalar functions τ, $G(\phi,\tau)$, and $F(\phi,\tau)$. Therefore, analogous to the fully worked example for the ANSM(2), it is apparent that $\text{VE}_{A(3)}(\tau)$ provides the GCE volatility effect using the first two Taylor expansion terms for $G(\tilde{\kappa},\tau)$. Specifically,

$$\begin{aligned}
\text{VE}_{A(3)}(\tau) = {}&\sigma_L^2 \cdot \frac{1}{2}\tau^2 + \sigma_S^2 \cdot \frac{1}{2}[G(\phi,\tau)]^2 + \sigma_B^2 \cdot \frac{1}{2}[F(\phi,\tau)]^2 \\
&+ \rho_{LS}\sigma_L\sigma_S \cdot \tau G(\phi,\tau) + \rho_{LB}\sigma_L\sigma_B \cdot \tau F(\phi,\tau) \\
&+ \rho_{SB}\sigma_S\sigma_B \cdot G(\phi,\tau)F(\phi,\tau) \\
\simeq {}&\text{VE}_{\text{GCE}}(\tau)
\end{aligned} \tag{6.85}$$

where the expressions for σ_L^2, σ_S^2, and $\rho_{LS}\sigma_L\sigma_S$ in terms of the GCE covariance matrices have already been provided, and the expressions σ_B^2, $\rho_{LB}\sigma_L\sigma_B$, and

$\rho_{SB}\sigma_S\sigma_B$ can be similarly be expressed in terms of the GCE covariance matrices. Krippner (2014a) contains the full results.

6.2.7 Parsimonious ANSM state equations

In this subsection, I provide an overview of the results from Krippner (2014a) that use the GCE to establish more parsimonious ANSM state equations than the general forms contained in sections 3.3 and 3.4. In the next two subsections, I will provide the results for the ANSM(2) and ANSM(3) as particular examples because they are the two main models developed and applied in this book. I follow those expositions with a brief comment on extensions to higher-order ANSMs and then discuss the empirical implications of having parsimonious ANSM state equations available.

GCE and ANSM(2) state equations

Section 3.3 shows that the ANSM(2) state equation is derived from the continuous-time expression

$$
\begin{bmatrix} L(t+\tau) \\ S(t+\tau) \end{bmatrix} = \exp\left(-\begin{bmatrix} \kappa_{LL} & \kappa_{LS} \\ \kappa_{SL} & \kappa_{SS} \end{bmatrix} \Delta t\right) \begin{bmatrix} L(t) \\ S(t) \end{bmatrix} + \begin{bmatrix} \varepsilon_L(t) \\ \varepsilon_S(t) \end{bmatrix} \tag{6.86}
$$

for the ANSM(2) state variables under the physical $\mathbb{P}$ measure. The value of Δt is the time step between yield curve observations. Applying the expectations operator $\mathbb{E}_t[\cdot]$ gives the more succinct expression:

$$
\mathbb{E}_t \begin{bmatrix} L(t+\tau) \\ S(t+\tau) \end{bmatrix} = \exp\left(-\begin{bmatrix} \kappa_{LL} & \kappa_{LS} \\ \kappa_{SL} & \kappa_{SS} \end{bmatrix} \Delta t\right) \begin{bmatrix} L(t) \\ S(t) \end{bmatrix} \tag{6.87}
$$

Krippner (2014a) shows that a more parsimonious form of the mean-reversion matrix in the previous two equations can be obtained by appealing to the expected path of the GCE short rate under the physical $\mathbb{P}$ measure:

$$
\mathbb{E}_t\left[r_{GCE}(t+\tau)\right] = a_0 + d_0'\theta(t) + d_0'\exp(-\kappa\tau)\left[x(t) - \theta(t)\right] \tag{6.88}
$$

Alternatively, without reference to an explicit economic model, one could simply treat $\mathbb{E}_t[r_{GCE}(t+\tau)]$ as the expected path of the short rate from a generic GATSM, either with a unit root imposed on one of the state variables, or assuming that a unit root process approximates the persistent state variable in the GATSM.

The long-horizon expectation of $r_{GCE}(t+\tau)$ can be written equivalently in two alternative ways. First, directly in terms of expected future state variables

$$
\lim_{\tau \to \infty} \mathbb{E}_t\left[r_{GCE}(t+\tau)\right] = a_0 + d_0'\mathbb{E}_t\left[\theta(t+\tau)\right]
$$

$$
= \mathbb{E}_t\left[L(t+\tau)\right] \tag{6.89}
$$

and second, in terms of current state variables:

$$\lim_{\tau \to \infty} \mathbb{E}_t \left[r_{\text{GCE}} (t + \tau) \right] = a_0 + d_0' \theta (t)$$

$$= L(t) \tag{6.90}$$

Equating the two equivalent expressions gives

$$\mathbb{E}_t \left[L(t + \tau) \right] = L(t) \tag{6.91}$$

Similarly, $\mathbb{E}_t \left[r_{\text{GCE}} (t + \tau) \right] - \lim_{\tau \to \infty} \mathbb{E}_t \left[r_{\text{GCE}} (t + \tau) \right]$ can be written equivalently in two alternative ways. First, directly in terms of terms of expected future state variables:

$$\mathbb{E}_t \left[r_{\text{GCE}} (t + \tau) \right] - \lim_{\tau \to \infty} \mathbb{E}_t \left[r_{\text{GCE}} (t + \tau) \right]$$

$$= d_0' \mathbb{E}_t \left[x(t + \tau) - \theta (t + \tau) \right]$$

$$= \mathbb{E}_t \left[S(t + \tau) \right] \tag{6.92}$$

and second, in terms of current state variables:

$$\mathbb{E}_t \left[r_{\text{GCE}} (t + \tau) \right] - \lim_{\tau \to \infty} \mathbb{E}_t \left[r_{\text{GCE}} (t + \tau) \right]$$

$$= d_0' \exp(-\kappa \tau) \left[x(t) - \theta (t) \right] \tag{6.93}$$

The eigensystem decomposition $\kappa = V \kappa_D V^{-1}$ and its reexpression using $\kappa_D = \exp(-\varphi I \tau) \exp(\varphi \delta_D \tau)$ may be applied to the mean-reversion matrix κ, as in subsection 6.2.4, but this time the notations V and φ refer to values under the $\mathbb{P}$ measure. Therefore,

$$\mathbb{E}_t \left[r_{\text{GCE}} (t + \tau) \right] - \lim_{\tau \to \infty} \mathbb{E}_t \left[r_{\text{GCE}} (t + \tau) \right]$$

$$= d_0' V \exp(-\varphi I \tau) \exp(\varphi \delta_D \tau) V^{-1} \left[x(t) - \theta (t) \right] \tag{6.94}$$

and $\exp(\varphi \delta_D \tau)$ can be written as a Taylor expansion:

$$\exp(\varphi \delta_D \tau) = I + \varphi \tau \delta_D + \frac{1}{2!} [\varphi \tau \delta_D]^2 + \frac{1}{3!} [\varphi \tau \delta_D]^3 + \dots \tag{6.95}$$

Again following subsection 6.2.4, using a single term in the Taylor expansion $\exp(\varphi \delta_D \tau) \simeq I$ gives

$$\mathbb{E}_t \left[r_{\text{GCE}} (t + \tau) \right] - \mathbb{E}_t \left[L(t + \tau) \right]$$

$$\simeq d_0' V \exp(-\varphi I \tau) V^{-1} \left[x(t) - \theta (t) \right]$$

$$= d_0' VV^{-1} [x(t) - \theta(t)] \cdot \exp(-\varphi\tau)$$
$$= d_0' [x(t) - \theta(t)] \cdot \exp(-\varphi\tau)$$
$$= S(t) \cdot \exp(-\varphi\tau) \tag{6.96}$$

Equating the two approximately equivalent expressions for $\mathbb{E}_t [r_{GCE}(t+\tau)] - \lim_{\tau\to\infty} \mathbb{E}_t [r_{GCE}(t+\tau)]$ gives

$$\mathbb{E}_t [S(t+\tau)] = S(t) \cdot \exp(-\varphi\tau) \tag{6.97}$$

The expectation of the Level state variable is independent of the Slope state variable, and the expectation of the Slope state variable is independent of the Level state variable. Therefore, the individual expectations may be combined into a two-equation expectation with a diagonal mean reversion matrix:

$$\mathbb{E}_t \begin{bmatrix} L(t+\tau) \\ S(t+\tau) \end{bmatrix} = \begin{bmatrix} 1 & 0 \\ 0 & \exp(-\varphi\tau) \end{bmatrix} \begin{bmatrix} L(t) \\ S(t) \end{bmatrix}$$
$$= \exp(-\kappa_{A(2)}\tau) \begin{bmatrix} L(t) \\ S(t) \end{bmatrix} \tag{6.98}$$

where:

$$\kappa_{A(2)} = \begin{bmatrix} 0 & 0 \\ 0 & \varphi \end{bmatrix} \tag{6.99}$$

Evaluating the expectation with $\tau = \Delta t$ provides the parsimonious ANSM(2) state equation:

$$\mathbb{E}_t \begin{bmatrix} L(t+\Delta t) \\ S(t+\Delta t) \end{bmatrix} = \begin{bmatrix} 1 & 0 \\ 0 & \exp(-\varphi\Delta t) \end{bmatrix} \begin{bmatrix} L(t) \\ S(t) \end{bmatrix} \tag{6.100}$$

GCE and ANSM(3) state equations

Establishing the intertemporal relationship with two terms in the Taylor expansion is more involved because the ANSM(3) Bow state variable $B(t)$ only arises from the GCE via the approximation of the expectations term $\mathbb{E}_t [r(t+\tau)]_{GCE}$, rather than as the precise relationships of $L(t)$ and $S(t)$ with the GCE state variables. Hence, I use the method of equating equivalent expectations from Krippner (2006).

This method equates two equivalent expressions of the expectation, both formed as at time t, of the GCE non-Level component, that is,

$$\mathbb{E}_t [r_{GCE}(t+\tau+\alpha)|x(t)] - \lim_{\tau\to\infty} \mathbb{E}_t [r_{GCE}(t+\tau+\alpha)|x(t)]$$
$$= d_0' \exp(-\kappa[\tau+\alpha])[x(t) - \theta(t)] \tag{6.101}$$

where α is an arbitrary positive increment of time, and

$$\mathbb{E}_t [r(t + \tau + \alpha) | x(t + \alpha)]_{\text{GCE}} - \mathbb{E}_t [L(t + \tau + \alpha) | x(t + \alpha)]$$
$$= d_0' \exp(-\kappa \tau) \mathbb{E}_t [x(t + \alpha) - \theta(t + \alpha)] . \quad (6.102)$$

Equating the two equivalent expressions gives

$$d_0' \exp(-\kappa \tau) \mathbb{E}_t [x(t + \alpha) - \theta(t + \alpha)] = d_0' \exp(-\kappa [\tau + \alpha]) [x(t) - \theta(t)]$$
$$(6.103)$$

and using two terms of the Taylor expansion from both sides gives the result:

$$\mathbb{E}_t [S(t + \tau)] \cdot \exp(-\varphi \alpha) + \mathbb{E}_t [B(t + \tau)] \cdot \varphi \alpha \exp(-\varphi \alpha)$$
$$= S(t) \cdot \exp(-\varphi [\tau + \alpha]) + B(t) \cdot \varphi [\tau + \alpha] \exp(-\varphi [\tau + \alpha])$$
$$= \exp(-\varphi \alpha) \cdot S(t) \cdot \exp(-\varphi \tau)$$
$$\qquad + B(t) \cdot \varphi \tau \exp(-\varphi [\tau + \alpha]) + \varphi \alpha \cdot B(t) \cdot \exp(-\varphi [\tau + \alpha])$$
$$= \exp(-\varphi \alpha) \cdot S(t) \cdot \exp(-\varphi \tau) + \exp(-\varphi \alpha) \cdot B(t) \cdot \varphi \tau \exp(-\varphi \tau)$$
$$\qquad + \varphi \alpha \exp(-\varphi \alpha) \cdot B(t) \cdot \exp(-\varphi \tau) \quad (6.104)$$

Equating the terms in $\exp(-\varphi \alpha)$ leads to

$$\mathbb{E}_t [S(t + \tau)] = S(t) \cdot \exp(-\varphi \tau) + B(t) \cdot \varphi \tau \exp(-\varphi \tau)$$
$$= [\exp(-\varphi \tau), \varphi \tau \exp(-\varphi \tau)] \begin{bmatrix} S(t) \\ B(t) \end{bmatrix} \quad (6.105)$$

and equating the terms in $\varphi \alpha \exp(-\varphi \alpha)$ leads to

$$\mathbb{E}_t [B(t + \tau)] = B(t) \cdot \exp(-\varphi \tau) \quad (6.106)$$

Therefore the expectations relationship under the $\mathbb{P}$ measure becomes:

$$\mathbb{E}_t \begin{bmatrix} L(t + \tau) \\ S(t + \tau) \\ B(t + \tau) \end{bmatrix} = \exp(-\kappa_{A(3)} \tau) \begin{bmatrix} L(t) \\ S(t) \\ B(t) \end{bmatrix} \quad (6.107)$$

where

$$\exp(-\kappa_{A(3)} \tau) = \begin{bmatrix} 1 & 0 & 0 \\ 0 & \exp(-\varphi \tau) & \varphi \tau \exp(-\varphi \tau) \\ 0 & 0 & \exp(-\varphi \tau) \end{bmatrix} \quad (6.108)$$

and

$$
\kappa_{A(3)} = \begin{bmatrix} 0 & 0 & 0 \\ 0 & \varphi & -\varphi \\ 0 & 0 & \varphi \end{bmatrix}
\tag{6.109}
$$

Evaluating the expectation with $\tau = \Delta t$ provides the parsimonious ANSM(3) state equation:

$$
\mathbb{E}_t \begin{bmatrix} L(t+\tau) \\ S(t+\tau) \\ B(t+\tau) \end{bmatrix} = \begin{bmatrix} 1 & 0 & 0 \\ 0 & \exp(-\varphi\Delta t) & \phi\tau\exp(-\varphi\Delta t) \\ 0 & 0 & \exp(-\varphi\Delta t) \end{bmatrix} \begin{bmatrix} L(t) \\ S(t) \\ B(t) \end{bmatrix}
\tag{6.110}
$$

Higher-order ANSMs

The parsimonious state equations for the ANSM(2) and ANSM(3) can be extended to higher-order ANSMs, where the generic $\mathbb{P}$-measure mean-reversion matrix $\kappa_{A(N)}$ parallels the generic $\mathbb{Q}$-measure mean-reversion matrix $\tilde{\kappa}_{A(N)}$ matrix outlined in subsection 3.4.2. For example,

$$
\kappa_{A(4)} = \begin{bmatrix} 0 & 0 & 0 & 0 \\ 0 & \varphi & -\varphi & 0 \\ 0 & 0 & \varphi & -\varphi \\ 0 & 0 & 0 & \varphi \end{bmatrix}
\tag{6.111}
$$

would be obtained with three terms of the Taylor expansion for the two sides of equation 6.104.

Discussion

Using the parsimonious state equations in conjunction with the ANSM term structure expressions offers arbitrage-free term structure frameworks with fewer parameters than ANSMs that are typically applied. For example, the ANSM(2) in section 3.3 with the state equation calculated from the parsimonious mean-reversion matrix $\kappa_{A(2)}$ rather than the general 2×2 mean-reversion matrix κ would have three fewer parameters, that is, seven instead of ten. The ANSM(3) in subsection 3.4.1 with the parsimonious mean-reversion matrix $\kappa_{A(3)}$ rather than the general 3×3 mean-reversion matrix κ would have eight less parameters, that is, 11 instead of 19.

The additional parameter restrictions effectively place a tighter constraint on the market prices of risk, as detailed in Krippner (2014a). Therefore, the validity of those additional restrictions would need to be tested with respect to the data. I have not yet fully tested the parsimonious ANSM state equations to undertake that analysis, but there are already several empirical results from one perspective that suggest the restrictions may be appropriate. Specifically, for the United States and the United Kingdom, Christensen and Rudebusch (2012, 2013b) and Carriero, Mouabbi, and Vangelista (2014) use general-to-specific methods to set statistically insignificant elements of the general ANSM(3) and/or K-ANSM(3) general 3×3 $\mathbb{P}$ measure mean-reversion matrix κ to zero. The results obtained take the form

$$\kappa_{US} = \begin{bmatrix} 10^{-7} & 0 & 0 \\ \times & \times & \times \\ 0 & 0 & \times \end{bmatrix}; \quad \kappa_{UK} = \begin{bmatrix} 10^{-7} & 0 & 0 \\ 0 & \times & \times \\ 0 & 0 & \times \end{bmatrix} \tag{6.112}$$

where "10^{-7}" represents the imposed unit root for the Level state variable under the $\mathbb{P}$ measure, and the "$\times$" entries represent the statistically significant non-zero entries. The UK matrix κ_{UK} is precisely in the form of the parsimonious $\kappa_{A(3)}$ matrix derived in Krippner (2014a), and the US matrix κ_{US} has only one entry outside the parsimonious $\kappa_{A(3)}$ matrix form.

As an alternative to the most parsimonious $\mathbb{P}$ measure mean-reversion matrices, it is easy to create parsimonious specifications of $\kappa_{A(N)}$ with more non-zero elements, while still imposing the unit root property (i.e., one zero eigenvalue) and that the other eigenvalues equal φ. I have already done so for the ANSM(2) and ANSM(3) and have estimated the associated K-ANSM(2) and K-ANSM(3) models. These specifications implicitly allow for a more flexible specification of the market prices of risk, and may prove more appropriate empirically. Once again, the models still require full empirical testing.

Finally, the top-left element could be replaced with a small positive value to provide a persistent mean-reverting process for the Level state variable under the $\mathbb{P}$ measure. However, the unit root specification is both convenient and empirically justified. That is, Bauer, Rudebusch, and Wu (2012) have shown that estimates of the most persistent component of the $\mathbb{P}$ measure mean-reversion matrix κ for GATSMs with bias adjustment to allow for small samples are typically very close to a unit root process.

6.2.8   ANSM macroeconomic interpretation

Subsection 6.2.3 provided a macroeconomic interpretation of the GCE in terms of aggregated short-run and long-run state variables, both divisible into their real and inflation components. Having now provided an explicit description of how the ANSM state variables and factor loadings relate to the GCE state variables, it is possible to provide a macroeconomic interpretation to the ANSM components directly. I will provide these only in their nominal form because I will not further develop or use the split into real and inflation components in this book. However, the macroeconomic interpretation also applies to the real and inflation components, which should prove a useful when applying ANSMs to inflation-indexed yield curve data, and implied inflation yield curves (i.e., nominal less inflation-indexed yield curve data, or data for inflation swap contracts).

The current ANSM Level state variable $L(t)$ is within a constant of the prevailing long-run expectation of risk-adjusted nominal output growth:

$$L(t) = a_0 + d_0' \theta(t)$$

$$= a_0 + \lim_{\tau \to \infty} \tilde{\mathbb{E}}_t \left[\frac{dX(t+\tau)}{dt} \right] \tag{6.113}$$

The current ANSM Slope state variable $S(t)$ equals the deviation of current nominal output growth from the current long-run expectation of risk-adjusted nominal output growth:

$$S(t) = d_0' \left[x(t) - \tilde{\theta}(t) \right]$$

$$= d_0' x(t) - d_0' \tilde{\theta}(t)$$

$$= \frac{dX(t)}{dt} - \lim_{\tau \to \infty} \tilde{\mathbb{E}}_t \left[\frac{dX(t+\tau)}{dt} \right] \tag{6.114}$$

The sum of the current non-Level ANSM components approximately equals the expected path of the deviation of risk-adjusted nominal output growth from the current long-run expectation of risk-adjusted nominal output growth. For example, the non-Level ANSM(3) components have the following relationship:

$$S(t) \cdot \exp(-\phi\tau) + B(t) \cdot \phi\tau \exp(-\phi\tau)$$

$$\simeq d_0' \exp(-\tilde{\kappa}\tau) \left[x(t) - \tilde{\theta}(t) \right]$$

$$= \tilde{\mathbb{E}}_t \left(\frac{dX(t+\tau)}{dt} - \lim_{\tau \to \infty} \tilde{\mathbb{E}}_t \left[\frac{dX(t+\tau)}{dt} \right] \right)$$

$$= \tilde{\mathbb{E}}_t \left[\frac{dX(t+\tau)}{dt} \right] - \lim_{\tau \to \infty} \tilde{\mathbb{E}}_t \left[\frac{dX(t+\tau)}{dt} \right] \tag{6.115}$$

The parsimonious $\mathbb{P}$-measure ANSM mean-reversion matrix $\kappa_{A(N)}$ creates $\mathbb{P}$-measure relationships that are identical or analogous to the $\mathbb{Q}$-measure relationships, that is:

$$L(t) = \lim_{\tau \to \infty} \mathbb{E}_t \left[\frac{dX(t+\tau)}{dt} \right] \tag{6.116}$$

$$S(t) = \frac{dX(t)}{dt} - \lim_{\tau \to \infty} \mathbb{E}_t \left[\frac{dX(t+\tau)}{dt} \right] \tag{6.117}$$

and

$$S(t) \cdot \exp(-\varphi\tau) + B(t) \cdot \varphi\tau \exp(-\varphi\tau)$$
$$\simeq \mathbb{E}_t \left[\frac{\mathrm{d}X(t+\tau)}{\mathrm{d}t} \right] - \lim_{\tau \to \infty} \mathbb{E}_t \left[\frac{\mathrm{d}X(t+\tau)}{\mathrm{d}t} \right] \tag{6.118}$$

where φ is the $\mathbb{P}$-measure mean-reversion parameter instead of the $\mathbb{Q}$-measure mean-reversion parameter ϕ. The last equation may be reexpressed as

$$\mathbb{E}_t \left[\frac{\mathrm{d}X(t+\tau)}{\mathrm{d}t} \right] \simeq \lim_{\tau \to \infty} \mathbb{E}_t \left[\frac{\mathrm{d}X(t+\tau)}{\mathrm{d}t} \right]$$
$$+ S(t) \cdot \exp(-\varphi\tau) + B(t) \cdot \varphi\tau \exp(-\varphi\tau)$$
$$= L(t) + S(t) \cdot \exp(-\varphi\tau)$$
$$+ B(t) \cdot \varphi\tau \exp(-\varphi\tau) \tag{6.119}$$

which may prove particularly useful. In short, it provides a basis for relating longer-term survey measures of nominal output growth to the state variables for ANSMs. I will not develop that idea further in this book beyond an experimental result I present in subsection 7.6.1, but it opens up a future research avenue for jointly modeling yield curve data and longer-term macroeconomic survey data. The advantage of doing so is that each data set should provide information useful to the other, and therefore the joint model can potentially provide a superior representation of both data sets than modeling each separately.

6.3 Using ANSMs to represent the shadow term structure

The discussion in the previous section indicates that KANSMs should provide a theoretically consistent and practically useful representation of the shadow term structure for shadow/ZLB term structure models. From an economic perspective, the ANSM state variables and their associated parameters provide a "natural approximation" to the aggregated GCE state variables and their associated parameters. By "natural approximation" I mean that each additional term of the Taylor expansion for the GCE corresponds precisely with each additional ANSM state variable and its parameters for the ANSM. Section 6.2 shows that the correspondence is precise for both the expected path of the short rate and the volatility effect. Therefore, one can represent the GCE term structure to an arbitrary approximation or select the parsimony versus approximation required for particular applications. Typically, three ANSM components have been sufficient for many empirical applications, but the discussion in subsection 3.4.2 shows that further extensions are very straightforward. The ANSM representation of the GCE can also be extended to parsimonious ANSM state equations so long as one is willing to accept the implicit constraint on the market price of risk specifications.

Furthermore, the GCE/ANSM correspondence provides an intuitive interpretation of the ANSM state variables (and implicitly their parameters) from a macroeconomic perspective. Using that interpretation suggests that a shadow term structure representation is consistent with the known properties of economies in practice. Specifically, from the perspective of the GCE, the ANSM Level state variable can be interpreted as a long-horizon expectation of nominal output growth. One would therefore expect that the Level state variable would remain positive, and it does empirically. The non-Level components of ANSMs correspond to the expected reversion of real output growth and/or inflation from their current values to their long-horizon expectations. Those current values and their expectations can take on negative values (e.g., recessions and deflation episodes, or expectations of those events), so one would expect them to occasionally adopt negative values.

Defining a shadow/ZLB term structure model using an ANSM to represent the shadow term structure therefore maintains the link with the macroeconomy, as just described. The ZLB overlay explicitly represents an institutional constraint, that is, the availability of physical currency, which translates the shadow term structure to the ZLB constrained nominal term structure observed in practice. Conversely, defining a ZLB nominal term structure directly, such as the models briefly introduced in section 2.5, would not necessarily have a natural correspondence to the behavior of the macroeconomy.

Establishing the ANSM correspondence to the GCE defined in very general terms also means that one can simply use the ANSM representation of the shadow term structure as the Taylor expansion of any GATSM that could otherwise be applied to represent the shadow term structure. That is, any GATSM may be parsimoniously represented with an ANSM as a reduced-form representation, just as for the GCE. Therefore, so long as one is willing to accept the (mild and typical) assumption that the dynamics of the shadow term structure may be represented in Gaussian terms, then the ANSM is guaranteed to provide a close approximation to whatever the "true" GATSM specification may be.

Nevertheless, I realize some users will prefer to use GATSMs as the shadow term structure model, so I will continue to use the more general terminologies B-AGMs and K-AGMs to emphasize that the shadow/ZLB term structure models discussed in this book apply equally to GATSMs and the ANSM subclass.

6.4   Theoretical case for the K-AGM framework

In this section, I discuss the theoretical case for the K-AGM framework. In particular, the GCE as a standard classical model of an equilibrium economy offers a useful framework for consideration, and I also draw on some fundamental principles from the finance literature.

I begin in subsection 6.4.1 by providing a reminder of the key point of difference between the B-AGM and K-AGM frameworks, and how that difference relates to standard pricing frameworks in finance. In subsections 6.4.2 to 6.4.3, I then use the GCE to outline the case for the pricing used in the K-AGM framework, first in an economy without physical currency and then in an economy that includes physical currency. Krippner (2011) contained the initial arguments along these lines.

I offer the caveat before beginning that my arguments are still in the thought-experiment/intuition stage rather than definitive, and therefore I have not even necessarily convinced myself to conventional levels of statistical significance. Not least a consideration is that the author of Black (1995) is Fischer Black, which pits my framework against a financial economist that operated at the Nobel-Prize level.

Nevertheless, raising the issues sets the stage for their ongoing consideration by myself and others via general asset pricing frameworks. The ultimate attraction is that the K-AGM framework may prove to be theoretically consistent and practically tractable. But if the theoretical-consistency component turns out not to hold up, then at least the K-AGM framework still represents one of a range of practically tractable approximations to the B-AGM framework, as already detailed in section 5.6.

6.4.1 Pricing in the B-AGM and K-AGM frameworks

As established in section 5.1, the ZLB term structure in both the K-AGM and the B-AGM frameworks may be viewed as being composed of a series of future time $t+\tau$ contingent investment cashflows $\min\{1,P(t+\tau,\delta)\}$ with a return of 1 at time $t+\tau+\delta$, where δ is a short and finite time increment. I represent those future cashflows with the ZLB finite-step bond $\underline{P}(t+\tau,\delta)=\min\{1,P(t+\tau,\delta)\}$. Note that $\underline{P}(t+\tau,\delta)$ is equivalent to the GATSM bond price and GATSM option expressions previously mentioned in section 5.1:

$$\min\{1,P(t+\tau,\delta)\} = P(t+\tau,\delta)+\min[1-P(t+\tau,\delta),0]$$
$$= P(t+\tau,\delta)-\max[P(t+\tau,\delta)-1,0] \quad (6.120)$$

but I use $\underline{P}(t+\tau,\delta)$ directly in this section for notational convenience.

The annualized return of $\underline{P}(t+\tau,\delta)$ on a continuously compounding basis over the future period $t+\tau$ to $t+\tau+\delta$ is

$$\text{Ann. Ret.} = \frac{1}{\delta}\log\left[\frac{1}{\min\{1,P(t+\tau,\delta)\}}\right]$$
$$= -\frac{1}{\delta}\log[\min\{1,P(t+\tau,\delta)\}] \quad (6.121)$$

and the annualized return in the limit of $\delta \to 0$ gives the ZLB short rate expression:

$$
\begin{aligned}
\underline{r}(t+\tau) &= \lim_{\delta \to 0} \left\{ -\frac{1}{\delta} \log \left[\min \left\{ 1, \underline{P}(t+\tau, \delta) \right\} \right] \right\} \\
&= \lim_{\delta \to 0} \left\{ \left[\max \left\{ -\frac{1}{\delta} \log [1], -\frac{1}{\delta} \log [P(t+\tau, \delta)] \right\} \right] \right\} \\
&= \max \left\{ 0, \lim_{\delta \to 0} \left(-\frac{1}{\delta} \log [P(t+\tau, \delta)] \right) \right\} \\
&= \max \left\{ 0, r(t+\tau) \right\}
\end{aligned}
\tag{6.122}
$$

As an aside for now, but related to the discussion in subsection 6.4.3, note that the expressions $\underline{P}(t+\tau, \delta) = \min\{1, P(t+\tau, \delta)\}$ or the infinitesimal equivalent $\underline{r}(t+\tau) = \max\{0, r(t+\tau)\}$ are typically justified as representing the optionality of holding physical currency with an annualized return of zero or investing in a bond if its annualized return is greater than zero. An equivalent, but perhaps more realistic way of considering the ZLB mechanism is that central banks do not set their policy lending rates below zero because doing so would open up an unlimited arbitrage opportunity for the remainder of the economy. For example, settlement banks could demand physical currency from the central bank and be paid the absolute value of the negative policy lending rate on their overdrawn settlement account balances. More generally, economic agents could borrow from the central bank at negative interest rates and use the proceeds to withdraw currency from the central bank, using the banking sector as an intermediary. Of course, these in-principle transactions leave aside the practical considerations of collateral demands from the central bank, money-market disruptions, and so forth, but it helps to establish in principle why the availability of physical currency establishes the ZLB due to the arbitrage $\underline{r}(t+\tau) = \max\{0, r(t+\tau)\}$, even without large amounts of physical currency being required to effect the arbitrage in practice.

The fundamental difference between the K-AGM and the B-AGM frameworks is how the cashflows of $\underline{P}(t+\tau, \delta)$ are discounted to present time t to provide ZLB forward bond prices, respectively to $\underline{P}(t, \tau, \delta)$ or $\underline{P}^B(t, \tau, \delta)$. The ZLB forward bond prices then establish any other representation of the observed ZLB term structure at time t.

As detailed in section 5.1, the B-AGM framework discounts the cashflows of $\underline{P}(t+\tau, \delta)$ with the expected return from ZLB short rates $\underline{r}(t+\tau) = \max\{0, r(t+\tau)\}$ under the $\mathbb{Q}$ measure:

$$
\underline{P}^B(t, \tau, \delta) = \frac{1}{\underline{P}^B(t, \tau)} \cdot \tilde{\mathbb{E}}_t \left[\exp \left(-\int_0^\tau \underline{r}(t+u)\, du \right) \min\{1, P(t+\tau, \delta)\} \right]
\tag{6.123}
$$

Therefore, the B-AGM uses model-consistent ZLB short rates to discount the cash-flows of $\underline{P}(t+\tau,\delta)$ back to $\underline{P}^B(t,\tau,\delta)$. Using ZLB short rates is also consistent with a commonly used basis for discounting cashflows in financial markets, that is, using risk-free interest rates, which are essentially the rates of return on investments with no probability of loss by default. The typical proxy for risk-free interest rates is short-maturity government or central bank interest rates and the expectations of those short-maturity rates adjusted for mark-to-market risk (i.e., revaluation fluctuations, but there is no default risk). Those actual short-maturity rates are analogous to the ZLB short rate $\underline{r}(t+\tau) = \max\{0, r(t+\tau)\}$, and the expectations are analogous to the B-AGM yield curve $\underline{R}^B(t,\tau)$, which is derived explicitly from the expectations of $\underline{r}(t+\tau)$ discounted by model-consistent ZLB short rates. There-fore, $\underline{R}^B(t,\tau)$ suggests itself as the appropriate rate for discounting the cashflows of $\underline{P}(t+\tau,\delta)$.

Conversely, the K-AGM framework discounts the cashflows of $\underline{P}(t+\tau,\delta)$ using the expected return from shadow short rates under the $\mathbb{Q}$ measure:

$$\underline{P}(t,\tau,\delta) = \frac{1}{P(t,\tau)} \cdot \tilde{\mathbb{E}}_t \left[\exp\left(- \int_0^\tau r(t+u)\, du \right) \min\{1, P(t+\tau,\delta)\} \right] \quad (6.124)$$

This treatment seems theoretically inconsistent, because the K-AGM generates ZLB short rates and interest rates $\underline{R}(t,\tau)$, but it does not use them to discount the cashflows of the future ZLB bond $\underline{P}(t+\tau,\delta)$ back to the ZLB forward bond price $\underline{P}(t,\tau,\delta)$.

The synopsis for questioning what appears to be a compelling case for the B-AGM framework is to ask the following:

- Does physical currency, or ZLB constrained money-market rates, actually rep-resent a risk-free asset that can be freely substituted for risky assets in the economy?
- If not, then what are the appropriate risk-adjusted rates for discounting the cashflows of assets generally within an economy?

This line of argument appeals to another commonly used concept for discounting in financial markets, that is, the rate of return on the market portfolio. In its most general sense, the market portfolio includes all marketable assets (e.g., claims on land, physical capital, etc.) and all nonmarketable assets (e.g., privately-held assets, human capital, etc.). There is no net holding of bonds or debt securities in the market portfolio, because the assets and liabilities that they represent to economic agents will sum to zero (I will assume some heterogeneity of agents' preferences in the economy, otherwise no lending and borrowing would be required at all). The risk-adjusted return on the market portfolio provides the appropriate rate for discounting cashflows in financial markets. This concept for discounting cashflows appears to be consistent with pricing in the K-AGM, as I will detail below.

6.4.2 The GCE market portfolio and discount rates without physical currency

To discuss the K-AGM case for discounting more fully, I first consider the GCE without physical currency (and therefore without a ZLB for the term structure). In this case, there is no question that the appropriate rate for discounting a nominal cashflow in the GCE economy is obtained from the GCE term structure. For example, an economic agent at time t wanting to value a cashflow or contigent cashflow at time $t + \tau$ would simply use the discount rate $R_{\text{GCE}}(t, \tau)$. In other words, discount rates and the GCE yield curve are fully synonomous. The discount rate can adopt negative values, which in turn can be related to the state of the macroeconomy, as I will discuss below. The GCE also provides transparency on how $R(t, \tau)$ relates back to the market portfolio and its expected rate of return, because the market portfolio in the GCE is the wealth in the economy, which is in turn the claims on all the production processes in the GCE economy. On that basis, I make the following points in turn:

- $R_{\text{GCE}}(t, \tau)$ is the mean of GCE forward rates $f_{\text{GCE}}(t, \tau)$, i.e. $R_{\text{GCE}}(t, \tau) = \frac{1}{\tau} \int_0^\tau f_{\text{GCE}}(t, u) \, du$.
- $f_{\text{GCE}}(t, \tau) = \tilde{\mathbb{E}}_t[r(t + \tau)] - VE_{\text{GCE}}(\tau)$, where $\tilde{\mathbb{E}}_t[r_{\text{GCE}}(t + \tau)]$ is the expected GCE short rate over the time period t to $t + \tau$ under the risk-adjusted $\mathbb{Q}$ measure.
- The GCE short rate $r_{\text{GCE}}(t)$ is the sum of the GCE short-run state variables $x(t)$, that is, $r_{\text{GCE}}(t) = d_0' x(t)$, and the elements contained in $x(t)$ represent the growth in the real returns on the GCE production processes, and the deflator/inflation processes for the production processes.
- $r_{\text{GCE}}(t) = d_0' x(t)$ can evolve to negative values given sufficiently negative innovations to some or all elements of $x(t)$.
- If $r_{\text{GCE}}(t)$ is negative, expectations of the risk-adjusted short rates $\tilde{\mathbb{E}}_t[r_{\text{GCE}}(t + \tau)] = a_0 + d_0' \tilde{\theta}(t) + d_0' \exp(-\tilde{\kappa}\tau)\left[x(t) - \tilde{\theta}(t)\right]$ will also be negative out to some horizon $\tau = \tau_{0,\text{r}}$. $\tilde{\mathbb{E}}_t[r_{\text{GCE}}(t + \tau)]$ being negative occurs because the GCE short-run state variables $x(t)$ follow a mean-reverting $\mathbb{Q}$ measure process back to their positive long-run state variables $\tilde{\theta}(t)$.
- If $\tilde{\mathbb{E}}_t[r_{\text{GCE}}(t + \tau)]$ is negative then $R_{\text{GCE}}(t, \tau)$ will therefore also be negative out to some horizons $\tau_{0,\text{R}}$, because $R(t, \tau) = \frac{1}{\tau} \int_0^\tau f_{\text{GCE}}(t, u) \, du = \frac{1}{\tau} \int_0^\tau \left[\tilde{\mathbb{E}}_t[r(t + u)] - VE_{\text{GCE}}(u)\right] du$.

From a macroeconomic perspective, the negative innovations to $x(t)$ would be consistent with a recession and/or a deflationary episode with no change to long-horizon expectations of output growth or inflation. Economic agents would anticipate a future return back to long-horizon output growth expectations plus long-horizon inflation expectations. Consistent with the current and expected state of the macroeconomy, the Level component of the term structure would remain steady, while the Slope state variable would decline sharply to bring $r(t)$ below zero.

6.4.3 The market portfolio and discount rates with physical currency

Now I assume that physical currency is introduced into the GCE, which I will denote as the GCE+PC. Physical currency in the GCE+PC will be a factor of production that contributes utility to economic agents equal to its convenience yield, and also a potential asset that offers a zero nominal rate of return financially. The question is, what impact will the availability of physical currency likely have on the original GCE market portfolio and therefore on the discount rates $R_{GCE}(t, \tau)$? I consider non-ZLB and ZLB environments in turn.

In a non-ZLB environment, in which $r_{GCE}(t) = d_0'x(t) > 0$, the convenience yield and the zero financial return and covariance of physical currency versus the current and expected returns on the production processes in the economy determine the holdings of physical currency. Those holdings are at the expense of some investment in the production processes, so the market portfolio in the GCE+PC therefore consists of a reduced-size GCE market portfolio plus the holdings in physical currency. However, physical currency holdings are likely to be small because they offer a zero financial return against the opportunity cost of foregone production and therefore wealth creation. Specifically, the GCE short rate $r_{GCE}(t) = d_0'x(t)$, which equals the instantaneous rate of return on the market portfolio, offers a higher rate of return than physical currency, and therefore there is little incentive to substitute away from the GCE market portfolio beyond the convenience yield of physical currency.

In a ZLB environment, $r_{GCE}(t) = d_0'x(t) < 0$. Therefore, the zero financial return on physical currency or ZLB constrained money-market rates in the GCE+PC offers a higher rate of return than the market portfolio, and hence an incentive to substitute away from the GCE market portfolio. However, the entire economy cannot make that substitution. Sales of claims on any of the production processes to invest at ZLB money-market rates need to be balanced by purchases of claims on the production processes funded by borrowing at money-market rates. In other words, net debt in the economy must sum to zero, and net assets (i.e. claims on the production processes) must remain unchanged. However, there would be no incentive for any economic agent to undertake borrowing to buy assets because the instantaneous return on the market portfolio $r_{GCE}(t) = d_0'x(t)$ is negative relative to the zero cost of borrowing. Regarding physical currency holdings, so long as the central bank does not promote large holdings of physical currency (e.g., by setting a materially negative policy rate or injecting physical currency into the economy), then the GCE+PC market portfolio remains little changed from the GCE market portfolio.

In summary, physical currency and/or ZLB constrained money-market rates will not be freely available for the economy to use as on-demand risk-free assets within the GCE+PC, in either non-ZLB or ZLB environments. The appropriate rate for discounting in the GCE+PC in both environments should therefore be similar to the GCE. Furthermore, none of the arguments for negative discount rates outlined in the previous subsection change materially. That is, the GCE short-run state variables $x(t)$ will continue to be the dominant determinant of $R_{\text{GCE+PC}}(t,\tau)$, some or all elements of GCE short-run state variables $x(t)$ can evolve to negative values, and therefore $r_{\text{GCE+PC}}(t) = d_0' x(t)$, $\tilde{\mathbb{E}}_t[r_{\text{GCE+PC}}(t+\tau)]$, and $R_{\text{GCE+PC}}(t,\tau)$ can also evolve to negative values. Therefore, the discount rate for cashflows in the GCE+PC, $R_{\text{GCE+PC}}(t,\tau)$, can/will adopt negative values if/when the growth on the returns on the production processes turn negative. Hence, the discount rate $R_{\text{GCE+PC}}(t,\tau)$ is synonymous with the concept of a shadow interest rate.

The difference in the pricing of bonds in the GCE+PC relative to the GCE arises from the difference in the cashflows that represent the forward bonds. The cashflows of the GCE are $P(t+\tau,\delta)$ and 1, where $P(t+\tau,\delta)$ is just an alternative representation of the discount rate applied to a unit face value. The cashflow of the GCE+PC are $\min\{1, P(t+\tau,\delta)\}$ and 1. As mentioned in subsection 6.4.1, these alternative cashflows arise because the central bank sets nonnegative policy lending rates due to the availability of physical currency. Note also that the cashflow $\min\{1, P(t+\tau,\delta)\}$ is no longer an alternative representation of the discount rate applied to a unit face value. In other words, the cashflows of forward bonds and the yield curve generally in the GCE+PC are no longer synonomous with the GCE+PC discount rate. The cashflows of the GCE+PC forward bonds are discounted using shadow interest rates $R_{\text{GCE+PC}}(t,\tau)$.[2]

Therefore, the K-AGM framework suggests itself as the appropriate shadow/ZLB-GATSM framework if discount rates appropriate to the market portfolio and the whole economy are adopted for all cashflows in the economy. The alternative is to have different discount rates for the contingent claim $\min\{1, P(t+\tau,\delta)\}$ and other cashflows in the economy, but that would be inconsistent with general equilibrium in the economy and no-arbitrage principles. And neither would it seem plausible for the zero financial return on physical currency to provide a floor of zero for the instantaneous risk-adjusted rates of return on all of the other assets in the market portfolio. In particular, for example, one would have to make the case that the existence of physical currency and the ZLB for interest rates somehow rules out negative expected risk-adjusted returns on equities.

6.5 The EMS measure of monetary policy

In this section, I introduce a measure from Krippner (2014b,c) called the "Effective Monetary Stimulus." The intention is primarily to deal with the principles and the mechanics of evaluating the EMS. I will discuss the EMS as a measure of monetary policy, including a comparison to the SSR, from both a cross-sectional and a time-series perspective in chapter 7.

I begin in section 6.5.1 by outlining the principles of the EMS under the risk-adjusted $\mathbb{Q}$ measure. I follow that discussion in section 6.5.2 with details on how the EMS may be calculated from K-ANSMs in general, and specifically for the

K-ANSM(2) and K-ANSM(3) that have already been estimated and used for the empirical illustrations in this book.

Before proceeding, I note that the EMS evaluation mechanics I will illustrate for K-ANSM measures equally apply to B-ANSMs, although the estimates of the shadow-GATSM parameters and state variables from the data would obviously differ. I also note that Krippner (2014b,c) discusses how the EMS can be obtained if stationary GATSMs are used in K-AGMs and B-AGMs, and also how the EMS can be calculated under the physical $\mathbb{P}$ measure. The $\mathbb{P}$-measure EMS is essentially analogous to the $\mathbb{Q}$ measure, but it is based on the K-ANSM parameters and expectations under the $\mathbb{P}$ measure. EMS estimates under both measures are likely to provide useful information for monetary policy, but I will focus on the $\mathbb{Q}$ measure to outline the framework because it generally involves simpler mathematical expressions (although the $\mathbb{P}$-measure EMS expressions with the parsimonious state equations introduced in subsection 6.2.7 are almost the same as the $\mathbb{Q}$-measure EMS expressions). Having both the $\mathbb{Q}$-measure and $\mathbb{P}$-measure estimates of the EMS available will allow the overall monetary stimulus to be divided into pure expectations about the policy rate, and risk premiums.

6.5.1 EMS Principles

Section 2.1 in chapter 1 introduced the concept that a policy rate setting below the neutral interest rate represented an easy stance of monetary policy. The EMS extends that concept by considering both the prevailing and the expected policy rates relative to a neutral rate. This concept is straightforward in a non-ZLB environment. As indicated in panel 1 of Figure 6.1, the stance of monetary policy is a positive policy rate below the neutral rate with an expectation that the policy rate will revert to the neutral rate as time evolves. The EMS is the area between the expected path of the policy rate and the neutral rate.

The EMS concept is more nuanced in a ZLB environment. As indicated in panel 2 of Figure 6.1, the stance of monetary policy is a zero policy rate with an expectation that it will become positive at some horizon in the future and then revert to the neutral rate as time evolves. The EMS is still the area between the expected path of the policy rate and the neutral rate, except that the expected path of the policy rate includes a period in which the policy rate stays at zero.

K-ANSMs and their representation of the shadow term structure with the ANSM offer a very convenient framework for estimating and justifying the EMS:

- The K-ANSM provides a mechanical representation of the shadow term structure as an ANSM, and the ANSM provides the expected path of the shadow short rates under the risk-adjusted $\mathbb{Q}$ measure, $\tilde{\mathbb{E}}_t \left[\mathrm{r}(t+\tau) \right]$.
- $\max \left\{ 0, \tilde{\mathbb{E}}_t \left[\mathrm{r}(t+\tau) \right] \right\}$ provides an expected path of the ZLB short rate. During the time when the shadow short rate is below zero, only the component of the shadow short rate between zero and the neutral rate is "effective," in the sense

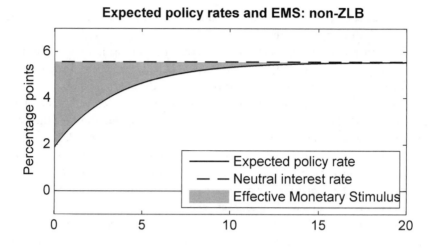

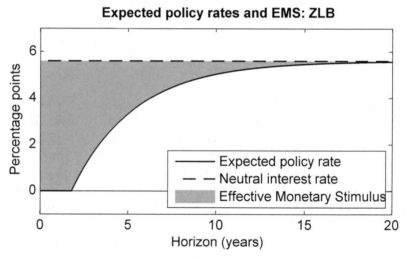

Figure 6.1 The concept of the EMS in non-ZLB environments (panel 1) and ZLB environments (panel 2).

that it can influence actual interest rates in the economy that economic agents use as the benchmarks for lending and borrowing (at appropriate margins). The remainder of the shadow short rate from its actual value at zero is "ineffective" because it cannot be transmitted to the economy.

- The K-ANSM Level state variable $L(t)$ provides the long-horizon expectation of the shadow short rate $r(t+\tau)$, $\lim_{\tau\to\infty}\tilde{\mathbb{E}}_t[r(t+\tau)] = L(t)$, and therefore the long-horizon expectation of the ZLB short rate, $\max\left\{0, \lim_{\tau\to\infty}\tilde{\mathbb{E}}_t[r(t+\tau)]\right\}$ $= \max\{0, L(t)\} = L(t)$. Therefore, $L(t)$ may be interpreted as an estimate of the time t, $\mathbb{Q}$-measure, neutral interest rate extracted from the observed yield curve data at time t using the K-ANSM. The GCE, its macroeconomic interpretation, and its reduced form as an ANSM also provide an economic intuition for using $L(t)$ as a $\mathbb{Q}$-measure neutral interest rate estimate. In particular, from section 6.2.8, $L(t)$ may be expressed in terms of long-horizon expectations of real output growth plus inflation under the risk-adjusted $\mathbb{Q}$ measure:

$$L(t) = \lim_{\tau \to \infty} \tilde{\mathbb{E}}_t \left[\frac{d}{dt} Y(t+\tau) \right] + \lim_{\tau \to \infty} \tilde{\mathbb{E}}_t \left[\frac{d}{dt} P(t+\tau) \right]$$
$$= C_0' \theta_Y(t) + C_0' \theta_\pi(t) \tag{6.125}$$

- $L(t) - \max \left\{ 0, \tilde{\mathbb{E}}_t \left[r(t+\tau) \right] \right\}$ provides an indication of the current and the expected gap between the ZLB short rate and the neutral rate under the $\mathbb{Q}$ measure. Therefore, $L(t) - \max \left\{ 0, \tilde{\mathbb{E}}_t \left[r(t+\tau) \right] \right\}$ may be interpreted to represent, as at time t, expectations of the path of the policy rate relative to the estimate of the neutral rate. Note that the policy rate/neutral rate gap $L(t) - \max \left\{ 0, \tilde{\mathbb{E}}_t \left[r(t+\tau) \right] \right\}$ can be positive or negative. A negative value would indicate a tight stance of policy, because it would mean that $\tilde{\mathbb{E}}_t \left[r(t+\tau) \right] > L(t)$, so therefore actual and expected policy rates would be above the neutral rate.
- The EMS at time t is the integral of $L(t) - \max \left\{ 0, \tilde{\mathbb{E}}_t \left[r(t+\tau) \right] \right\}$ over the future horizon τ from zero to infinity. Therefore, the EMS at time t captures the entire path of the expected path of policy rates relative to the current estimated neutral rate, under the risk-adjusted $\mathbb{Q}$ measure, in a single summary number.
- Mathematically, ANSMs are parsimonious representations of the shadow term structure with simple functional forms, so calculating and integrating $L(t) - \max \left\{ 0, \tilde{\mathbb{E}}_t \left[r(t+\tau) \right] \right\}$ for any ANSM will always be a parsimonious elementary expression. Specifically, the expression will involve just the ANSM state variables, the single parameter ϕ, and the exponential-polynomial functions $[\phi \tau]^{N-2} \exp(-\phi \tau)$ that together define $\tilde{\mathbb{E}}_t \left[r(t+\tau) \right]$ at any point in time.

Note that I have stressed above that all expectations are under the $\mathbb{Q}$ measure. The $\mathbb{Q}$-measure neutral rate and the $\mathbb{Q}$-measure EMS will therefore include the effect of risk premiums, via the risk adjustment, relative to actual expectations of $r(t+\tau)$ and the neutral rate under the physical $\mathbb{P}$ measure. Specifically regarding the $\mathbb{Q}$-measure neutral rate, the risk adjustment means it will generally differ from the $\mathbb{P}$-measure neutral rate suggested by surveyed measures of long-horizon expectations of real output growth and inflation. Section 7.6.1 will illustrate and discuss those differences further.

Note also that the concept of the EMS also applies equally to B-ANSMs and stationary B-AGMs, and K-AGMs. The key point is that, so long as the given model provides an estimate of the long-horizon expected shadow short rate that can be used mechanically as a neutral interest rate, then the expected path of the shadow short rate from the model along with the ZLB truncation can be used to calculate an EMS measure.

6.5.2 K-ANSM EMS measure

The K-ANSM framework uses an ANSM to represent the shadow term structure. Section 6.2 outlines how the state variables and factor loadings define the expected path of the short rate under the $\mathbb{Q}$ measure, which are the key elements required to calculate the EMS measure. For convenience and clarity, I repeat those elements of the ANSM specification here, but without the explicit notation for the different models as required in section 6.2, given that the context will make that apparent.

Hence, the vector of ANSM state variables is

$$x(t) = \begin{bmatrix} L(t) \\ S(t) \\ B(t) \\ B_1^*(t) \\ \vdots \\ B_{N-3}^*(t) \end{bmatrix} \tag{6.126}$$

the factor loadings are

$$\left[b_0' \exp(-\tilde{\kappa}\tau) \right]' = \begin{bmatrix} 1 \\ \exp(-\phi\tau) \\ \phi\tau \exp(-\phi\tau) \\ \frac{1}{(n-2)!}(\phi\tau)^{n-2}\exp(-\phi\tau) \\ \vdots \\ \frac{1}{(N-2)!}(\phi\tau)^{N-2}\exp(-\phi\tau) \end{bmatrix} \tag{6.127}$$

and the expected path of the short rate under the $\mathbb{Q}$ measure is

$$\tilde{\mathbb{E}}_t[r(t+\tau)] = b_0' \exp(-\tilde{\kappa}\tau)x(t)$$

Apart from the Level factor loading with a constant value of 1, all the factor loadings in ANSM are multiplied by an exponential decay term $\exp(-\phi\tau)$ with the property $\lim_{\tau\to\infty}\exp(-\phi\tau) = 0$. Hence, $L(t)$ is the only contributor to long-horizon expectations of $\tilde{\mathbb{E}}_t[r(t+\tau)]$:

$$\lim_{\tau\to\infty}\tilde{\mathbb{E}}_t[r(t+\tau)] = L(t) \tag{6.128}$$

and therefore the expected path of the short rate relative to its long-run expected value is

$$\lim_{\tau\to\infty}\tilde{\mathbb{E}}_t[r(t+\tau)] - \tilde{\mathbb{E}}_t[r(t+\tau)] = -\left[b_0'\exp(-\tilde{\kappa}\tau)\right]_{EL} x_{EL}(t) \tag{6.129}$$

where the subscript "*EL*" denotes the components of the ANSM state variable vector and the factor loadings, excluding the Level elements, respectively:

$$x_{EL}(t) = \begin{bmatrix} S(t) \\ B(t) \\ B_1^*(t) \\ \vdots \\ B_{N-3}^*(t) \end{bmatrix} \tag{6.130}$$

and:

$$\left[b_{0,EL}' \exp(-\tilde{\kappa}\tau) \right]_{EL}' = \begin{bmatrix} \exp(-\phi\tau) \\ \phi\tau \exp(-\phi\tau) \\ \frac{1}{(n-2)!}(\phi\tau)^{n-2}\exp(-\phi\tau) \\ \vdots \\ \frac{1}{(N-2)!}(\phi\tau)^{N-2}\exp(-\phi\tau) \end{bmatrix} \tag{6.131}$$

The expected path of the shadow short rate, truncated at zero if required, relative to its long-run value $L(t)$ is

$$L(t) - \max\left\{0, \tilde{\mathbb{E}}_t\left[\mathrm{r}(t+\tau)\right]\right\}$$

$$= \begin{cases} L(t) & \text{if } \tilde{\mathbb{E}}_t\left[\mathrm{r}(t+\tau)\right] < 0 \\ -\left[b_0' \exp(-\tilde{\kappa}\tau)\right]_{EL} x_{EL}(t) & \text{if } \tilde{\mathbb{E}}_t\left[\mathrm{r}(t+\tau)\right] \geq 0 \end{cases} \tag{6.132}$$

$L(t)$ and the values $\tilde{\mathbb{E}}_t\left[\mathrm{r}(t+\tau)\right]$ are readily determined from the current state variables and parameters of the K-ANSM, as I will illustrate for the K-ANSM(2) and K-ANSM(3) examples in subsections 6.5.3 and 6.5.4. The EMS is then the integral of the function $L(t) - \tilde{\mathbb{E}}_t\left[\mathrm{r}(t+\tau)\right]$ with respect to τ from zero to infinity:

$$\mathrm{EMS}(t) = \int_0^\infty L(t) - \max\left\{0, \tilde{\mathbb{E}}_t\left[\mathrm{r}(t+\tau)\right]\right\} d\tau \tag{6.133}$$

As I illustrate in subsections 6.5.3 and 6.5.4, if $\tilde{\mathbb{E}}_t\left[\mathrm{r}(t+\tau)\right]$ contains any negative values, then $L(t) - \max\left\{0, \tilde{\mathbb{E}}_t\left[\mathrm{r}(t+\tau)\right]\right\}$ is a stepwise function of τ, and therefore EMS(*t*) contains two or more components.

6.5.3 Worked example: K-ANSM(2) EMS

For the K-ANSM(2),

$$x(t) = \begin{bmatrix} L(t) \\ S(t) \end{bmatrix}; \quad b_0 = \begin{bmatrix} 1 \\ 1 \end{bmatrix}; \quad \tilde{\theta} = \begin{bmatrix} 0 \\ 0 \end{bmatrix}; \quad \tilde{\kappa} = \begin{bmatrix} 0 & 0 \\ 0 & \phi \end{bmatrix} \tag{6.134}$$

For use in the following figures, the shadow short rate is

$$r(t) = L(t) + S(t) \tag{6.135}$$

the expected path of the shadow short rate is

$$\tilde{\mathbb{E}}_t \left[r(t+\tau) \right] = L(t) + S(t) \cdot \exp(-\phi\tau) \tag{6.136}$$

where ϕ is the estimated mean-reversion parameter (0.2789 for my example below, from Table 4.4), and the long-horizon expectation of the shadow short rate is

$$\lim_{\tau \to \infty} \tilde{\mathbb{E}}_t \left[r(t+\tau) \right] = L(t) \tag{6.137}$$

Regarding the K-ANSM(2) EMS calculation,

$$x_{EL}(t) = S(t); \quad \left[b_0' \exp(-\tilde{\kappa}\tau) \right]_{EL} = \exp(-\phi\tau) \tag{6.138}$$

and equation 6.132 therefore becomes

$$L(t) - \tilde{\mathbb{E}}_t \left[r(t+\tau) \right] = \begin{cases} L(t) & \text{if } \tilde{\mathbb{E}}_t \left[r(t+\tau) \right] < 0 \\ -S(t) \cdot \exp(-\phi\tau) & \text{if } \tilde{\mathbb{E}}_t \left[r(t+\tau) \right] \geq 0 \end{cases} \tag{6.139}$$

For the integral to obtain the EMS, two cases can occur in practice for the K-ANSM(2). I provide examples first and then proceed to generate general expressions that accommodate both cases.

- **Case 1: $\tilde{\mathbb{E}}_t \left[r(t+\tau) \right]$ has no zeros.** In this case, $\tilde{\mathbb{E}}_t \left[r(t+\tau) \right] \geq 0$ for all τ over the relevant mathematical domain (i.e., from zero to infinity), as illustrated in Figure 6.2 for August 2008. In this example, the estimated K-ANMS(2) Level and Slope state variables are $L(t) = 5.55\%$ and $S(t) = -3.68\%$, giving $r(t) = 1.87\%$. The truncation $\max\left\{ 0, \tilde{\mathbb{E}}_t \left[r(t+\tau) \right] \right\}$ does not bind for any future horizons, and the EMS result is the shaded area $EMS(t) = 13.19\%$.
- **Case 2: $\tilde{\mathbb{E}}_t \left[r(t+\tau) \right]$ has one zero.** In this case, $\tilde{\mathbb{E}}_t \left[r(t+\tau) \right] < 0$ for $\tau < \tau_0$ before reaching and rising above zero for $\tau \geq \tau_0$, as illustrated in Figure 6.3 for July 2011. In this example, the estimated K-ANMS(2) Level and Slope state variables are $L(t) = 5.59\%$ and $S(t) = -9.20\%$, giving $r(t) = -3.60\%$. The truncation $\max\left\{ 0, \tilde{\mathbb{E}}_t \left[r(t+\tau) \right] \right\}$ binds for $\tau < \tau_0 = 1.78$ years, and the EMS result is the shaded area $EMS(t) = 32.97\%$.
- Note that a purely mathematical case would occur if $L(t) < 0$, but such estimates do not arise in practice. A negative neutral interest rate would also lack an economic interpretation.

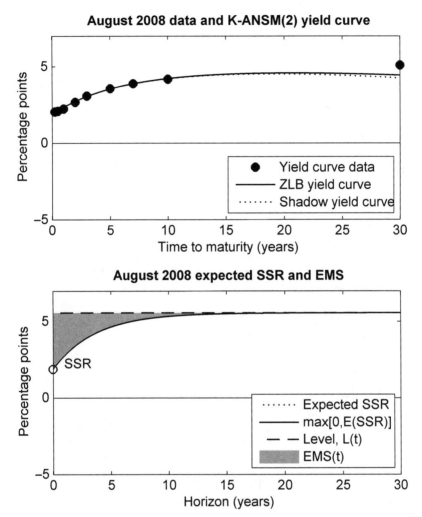

Figure 6.2 This example illustrates the case for yield curve data unconstrained by the ZLB (panel 1), and a positive K-ANSM(2) SSR (panel 2), which in turn corresponds to a non-ZLB environment.

Case 1: $\tilde{\mathbb{E}}_t [\mathrm{r}(t+\tau)]$ has no zeros:

In general, because $\tilde{\mathbb{E}}_t [\mathrm{r}(t+\tau)]$ is a monotonic function of τ for the K-ANSM(2), $\tilde{\mathbb{E}}_t [\mathrm{r}(t+\tau)] \geq 0$ will hold for all values of τ when $r(t) \geq 0$. The single component for EMS(t) is therefore

$$\mathrm{EMS}(t) = -\int_0^\infty S(t) \cdot \exp(-\phi\tau)\, d\tau$$

$$= -S(t) \cdot \frac{1}{\phi} \tag{6.140}$$

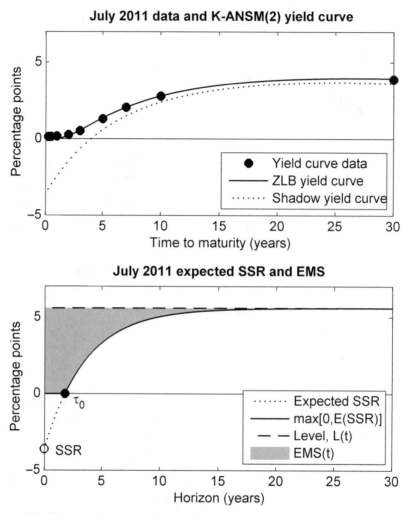

Figure 6.3 This example illustrates the case for yield curve data constrained by the ZLB (panel 1), and a negative K-ANSM(2) SSR (panel 2), which in turn corresponds to a ZLB environment.

Note that the unit is percentage points, which arises from the integral having the units of (annualized) percent per year multiplied by years, which produces the notional unit of percent. Note also that EMS(t) can and has taken on negative values (e.g., see Figures 6.4 and 6.8 subsequently), which occurs if $S(t) > 0$. That condition has an economic interpretation of a restrictive stance of monetary policy. Specifically, $S(t) > 0$ corresponds to r(t) and $\tilde{\mathbb{E}}_t\left[\mathrm{r}(t+\tau)\right] > L(t)$, that is, the current and expected path of the short rate are above the neutral interest rate.

Case 2: $\tilde{\mathbb{E}}_t\left[\mathrm{r}(t+\tau)\right]$ has one zero:

Again, because $\tilde{\mathbb{E}}_t\left[\mathrm{r}(t+\tau)\right]$ is a monotonic function of τ for the K-ANSM(2), $\tilde{\mathbb{E}}_t\left[\mathrm{r}(t+\tau)\right] < 0$ holds for values of $\tau < \tau_0$ when r(t) $= L(t) + S(t) < 0$, or

$S(t) < -L(t)$. The value of τ_0 is obtained readily for the K-ANSM(2) by setting $\tilde{\mathbb{E}}_t[r(t+\tau_0)] = L(t) + S(t) \cdot \exp(-\phi\tau_0) = 0$ and solving for τ_0. The result is

$$\tau_0 = -\frac{1}{\phi} \log\left[-\frac{L(t)}{S(t)}\right] \tag{6.141}$$

In general, EMS(t) has two components when $r(t) < 0$:

$$
\begin{aligned}
\text{EMS}(t) &= \int_0^{\tau_0} L(t)\, d\tau - \int_{\tau_0}^{\infty} S(t) \cdot \exp(-\phi\tau)\, d\tau \\
&= L(t) \cdot \tau_0 - S(t) \cdot \left[-\frac{1}{\phi} \exp(-\phi\tau) \Big|_{\tau_0}^{\infty} \right] \\
&= L(t) \cdot \tau_0 - S(t) \cdot \frac{1}{\phi} \exp(-\phi\tau_0) \tag{6.142}
\end{aligned}
$$

Combining the two K-ANSM(2) cases:

Combining the two potential cases for the K-ANSM(2) gives the general analytic expression for EMS(t) as

$$
\text{EMS}(t) =
\begin{cases}
L(t) \cdot \tau_0 - S(t) \cdot \frac{1}{\phi} \exp(-\phi\tau_0) & \text{if } r(t) < 0 \\[2mm]
-S(t) \cdot \frac{1}{\phi} & \text{if } r(t) \geq 0
\end{cases}
\tag{6.143}
$$

where τ_0 is given in equation 6.141.

Calculating EMS(t) for each yield curve observation gives the K-ANSM(2) EMS time series, which I have plotted in Figure 6.4.

6.5.4 K-ANSM(3) EMS

For the K-ANSM(3),

$$
x(t) = \begin{bmatrix} L(t) \\ S(t) \\ B(t) \end{bmatrix} ; \, b_0 = \begin{bmatrix} 1 \\ 1 \\ 0 \end{bmatrix} ; \, \tilde{\kappa} = \begin{bmatrix} 0 & 0 & 0 \\ 0 & \phi & -\phi \\ 0 & 0 & \phi \end{bmatrix} \tag{6.144}
$$

For use in the following figures, the shadow short rate is

$$r(t) = L(t) + S(t) \tag{6.145}$$

the expected path of the shadow short rate is

$$\tilde{\mathbb{E}}_t[r(t+\tau)] = L(t) + S(t) \cdot \exp(-\phi\tau) + B(t) \cdot \phi\tau \exp(-\phi\tau) \tag{6.146}$$

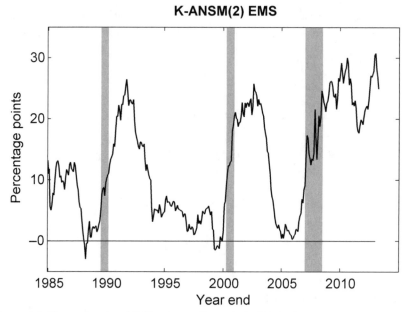

Figure 6.4 Time series plot of EMS estimates for the K-ANSM(2). Higher (lower) values reflect a more (less) stimulatory stance of monetary policy.

where ϕ is the estimated mean-reversion parameter (0.5681 for my example below, from Table 4.9), and the long-horizon expectation of the shadow short rate is

$$\lim_{\tau \to \infty} \tilde{\mathbb{E}}_t \left[\mathrm{r} \left(t + \tau \right) \right] = L \left(t \right) \tag{6.147}$$

Therefore,

$$x_{EL} \left(t \right) = \begin{bmatrix} S(t) \\ B(t) \end{bmatrix}; \quad \left[b_0' \exp \left(-\tilde{\kappa} \tau \right) \right]_{EL} = \left[\exp \left(-\phi \tau \right), \phi \tau \exp \left(-\phi \tau \right) \right] \tag{6.148}$$

and equation 6.132 becomes

$$
L \left(t \right) - \tilde{\mathbb{E}}_t \left[\mathrm{r} \left(t + \tau \right) \right]
= \begin{cases}
L \left(t \right) & \text{if } \tilde{\mathbb{E}}_t \left[\mathrm{r} \left(t + \tau \right) \right] < 0 \\[2ex]
\begin{aligned} &-S \left(t \right) \cdot \exp \left(-\phi \tau \right) \\ &-B \left(t \right) \cdot \phi \tau \exp \left(-\phi \tau \right) \end{aligned} & \text{if } \tilde{\mathbb{E}}_t \left[\mathrm{r} \left(t + \tau \right) \right] \geq 0
\end{cases}
\tag{6.149}
$$

For the integral to obtain the EMS, three cases can occur in practice for the ANSM(3), although in practice the last two are just minor variations that may result in ZLB environments due to the flexibility offered by the Bow component.

- **Case 1:** $\tilde{\mathbb{E}}_t \left[r(t + \tau) \right]$ **has no zeros.** In this case, $\tilde{\mathbb{E}}_t \left[r(t + \tau) \right] \geq 0$ for all τ over the relevant domain, as illustrated in Figure 6.5 for August 2008. In this example, the estimated K-ANSM(3) state variables are $L(t) = 5.10\%$, $S(t) = -3.25\%$, and $B(t) = -1.50\%$, giving $r(t) = 1.85\%$. The truncation $\max\left\{ 0, \tilde{\mathbb{E}}_t \left[r(t + \tau) \right] \right\}$ does not bind for any future horizons, and the EMS result is the shaded area $\text{EMS}(t) = 8.36\%$.

- **Case 2:** $\tilde{\mathbb{E}}_t \left[r(t + \tau) \right]$ **has one zero.** In this case, $\tilde{\mathbb{E}}_t \left[r(t + \tau) \right] < 0$ before reaching and rising above zero for $\tau \geq \tau_0$, as illustrated in Figure 6.6 for March 2014. In this example, the estimated K-ANSM(3) state variables are $L(t) = 4.61\%$, $S(t) = -4.68\%$, and $B(t) = -6.18\%$, giving $r(t) = -0.07\%$. The truncation $\max\left\{ 0, \tilde{\mathbb{E}}_t \left[r(t + \tau) \right] \right\}$ binds for $\tau < \tau_0 = 1.05$ years, and the EMS result is the shaded area $\text{EMS}(t) = 18.96\%$.

- **Case 3:** $\tilde{\mathbb{E}}_t \left[r(t + \tau) \right]$ **has two zeros.** In this case, $\tilde{\mathbb{E}}_t \left[r(t + \tau) \right] < 0$ for $\tau_0 < \tau < \tau_1$, which is illustrated in Figure 6.7 for July 2011. In this example, the estimated K-ANSM(3) state variables are $L(t) = 5.21\%$, $S(t) = -4.88\%$, and $B(t) = -9.55\%$, giving $r(t) = 0.34\%$. The truncation $\max\left\{ 0, \tilde{\mathbb{E}}_t \left[r(t + \tau) \right] \right\}$ binds for $0.14 < \tau < 1.86$ years, and the EMS result is the shaded area $\text{EMS}(t) = 24.67\%$.

- Again, purely mathematical cases would occur if $L(t) < 0$, but such estimates do not arise in practice, and they would lack an economic interpretation.

The expression for the K-ANSM(3) EMS is slightly more complex than for the K-ANSM(2) because it contains one extra case, and because the three different cases are not simply defined by the value of the shadow $r(t)$. The reason is that $\tilde{\mathbb{E}}_t \left[r(t + \tau) \right]$ for the K-ANSM(3) is not a monotonic function, which follows from the Bow factor loading not being monotonic.

Case 1: $\tilde{\mathbb{E}}_t \left[r(t + \tau) \right]$ **has no zeros:**
If $\tilde{\mathbb{E}}_t \left[r(t + \tau) \right] \geq 0$ for all $\tau \geq 0$, then $\text{EMS}(t)$ simply requires the addition of the Bow component integrated between zero and infinity:

$$\int_0^\infty B(t) \cdot \phi\tau \exp\left(-\phi\tau\right) d\tau$$

$$= B(t) \cdot \left[-\frac{1}{\phi} \exp\left(-\phi\tau\right) - \tau \exp\left(-\phi\tau\right) \Big|_0^\infty \right]$$

$$= B(t) \cdot \frac{1}{\phi} \tag{6.150}$$

and therefore,

$$\text{EMS}_1(t) = -S(t) \cdot \frac{1}{\phi} - B(t) \cdot \frac{1}{\phi} \tag{6.151}$$

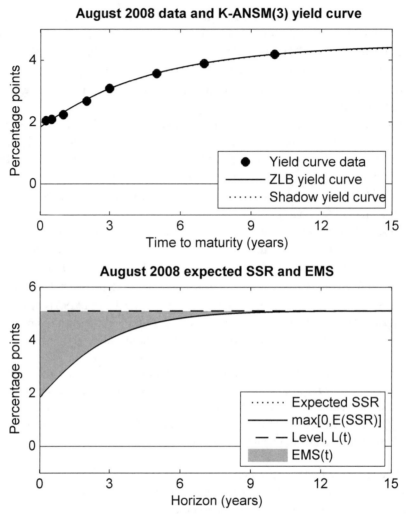

Figure 6.5 This example illustrates a non-ZLB environment for the K-ANSM(3), given that the SSR and its expectations are all above zero.

Case 2: $\tilde{\mathbb{E}}_t [r(t+\tau)]$ **has one zero:**

If $\tilde{\mathbb{E}}_t [r(t+\tau)]$ has one zero τ_0, then τ_0 is readily found numerically (e.g., using the "fzero" function in MatLab) as the solution to the univariate function $\tilde{\mathbb{E}}_t [r(t+\tau_0)] = x_1(t) + x_2(t) \cdot \exp(-\phi\tau_0) + x_3(t) \cdot \phi\tau_0 \exp(-\phi\tau_0) = 0$. The first component of the integral for $EMS_2(t)$ is $L(t) \cdot \tau_0$, as for the K-ANSM(2), and the second component is as for the K-ANSM(2), but with the addition of the Bow component integrated between τ_0 and infinity:

$$\int_{\tau_0}^{\infty} B(t) \cdot \phi\tau \exp(-\phi\tau) \, d\tau$$

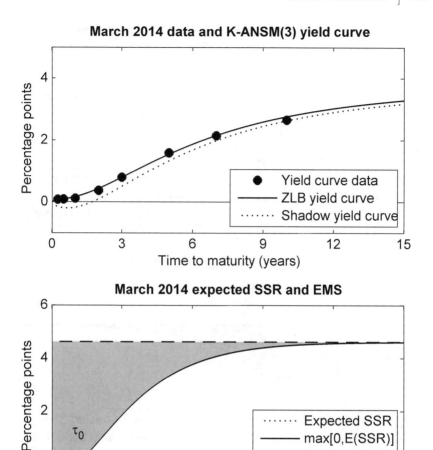

Figure 6.6 This example illustrates a ZLB environment for the K-ANSM(3), where the SSR and its expectations have one value equal to zero.

$$= B(t) \cdot \left[-\left(\frac{1}{\phi} + \tau \right) \exp(-\phi \tau) \Big|_{\tau_0}^{\infty} \right]$$

$$= B(t) \cdot \left[\frac{1}{\phi} \exp(-\phi \tau_0) + \tau_0 \exp(-\phi \tau_0) \right] \tag{6.152}$$

Collecting the two components gives

$$\text{EMS}_2(t) = L(t) \cdot \tau_0 - S(t) \cdot \frac{1}{\phi} \exp(-\phi \tau_0)$$

$$- B(t) \cdot \left[\frac{1}{\phi} \exp(-\phi \tau_0) + \tau_0 \exp(-\phi \tau_0) \right] \tag{6.153}$$

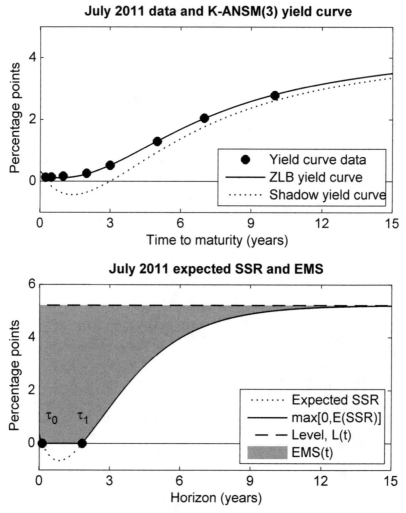

Figure 6.7 This example illustrates a ZLB environment for the K-ANSM(3), where the SSR and its expectations have two values equal to zero.

Case 3: $\tilde{\mathbb{E}}_t\left[r\left(t+\tau\right)\right]$ **has two zeros:**

If $\tilde{\mathbb{E}}_t\left[r\left(t+\tau\right)\right]$ has two zeros τ_0 and τ_1, then both need to be found numerically as solutions to $\tilde{\mathbb{E}}_t\left[r\left(t+\tau_0\right)\right]=x_1\left(t\right)+x_2\left(t\right)\cdot\exp\left(-\phi\tau_0\right)+x_3\left(t\right)\cdot\phi\tau_0\exp\left(-\phi\tau_0\right)=0$ and $\tilde{\mathbb{E}}_t\left[r\left(t+\tau\right)\right]=x_1\left(t\right)+x_2\left(t\right)\cdot\exp\left(-\phi\tau_1\right)+x_3\left(t\right)\cdot\phi\tau_1\exp\left(-\phi\tau_1\right)=0$. The first component of the integral for EMS$_3$ (t) requires the Slope and Bow components to be integrated between zero and τ_0:

$$S(t)\cdot\left[-\frac{1}{\phi}\exp\left(-\phi\tau\right)\Big|_0^{\tau_0}\right]=\frac{1}{\phi}\left[1-\exp\left(-\phi\tau_0\right)\right] \qquad (6.154)$$

$$=G\left(\phi,\tau_0\right) \qquad (6.155)$$

and,

$$B(t) \cdot \left[-\frac{1}{\phi} \exp\left(-\phi\tau\right) - \tau \exp\left(-\phi\tau\right) \Big|_0^{\tau_0} \right]$$

$$= \frac{1}{\phi} \left[1 - \exp\left(-\phi\tau_0\right) \right] - \tau_0 \exp\left(-\phi\tau_0\right)$$

$$= F(\phi, \tau_0) \tag{6.156}$$

The second component of the integral is the Level component integrated between τ_0 and τ_1:

$$\int_{\tau_0}^{\tau_1} L(t) \, d\tau = L(t) \cdot [\tau_1 - \tau_0] \tag{6.157}$$

and the third component is the Slope and Bow components integrated between τ_1 and infinity, that is:

$$S(t) \cdot \left[-\frac{1}{\phi} \exp\left(-\phi\tau\right) \Big|_{\tau_1}^{\infty} \right] = S(t) \frac{1}{\phi} \left[\exp\left(-\phi\tau_1\right) \right] \tag{6.158}$$

and therefore,

$$B(t) \cdot \left[-\left(\frac{1}{\phi} + \tau \right) \exp\left(-\phi\tau\right) \Big|_{\tau_1}^{\infty} \right]$$

$$= B(t) \cdot \left[\frac{1}{\phi} \exp\left(-\phi\tau_1\right) + \tau_1 \exp\left(-\phi\tau_1\right) \right] \tag{6.159}$$

Collecting the three components gives

$$\begin{aligned}
\text{EMS}_3(t) = & -S(t) \cdot G(\phi, \tau_0) - B(t) \cdot F(\phi, \tau_0) \\
& + L(t) \cdot [\tau_1 - \tau_0] \\
& - S(t) \frac{1}{\phi} \left[\exp\left(-\phi\tau_0\right) - \exp\left(-\phi\tau_1\right) \right] \\
& - S(t) \cdot \frac{1}{\phi} \left[\exp\left(-\phi\tau_1\right) \right] \\
& - B(t) \cdot \left[\frac{1}{\phi} \exp\left(-\phi\tau_1\right) + \tau_1 \exp\left(-\phi\tau_1\right) \right]
\end{aligned} \tag{6.160}$$

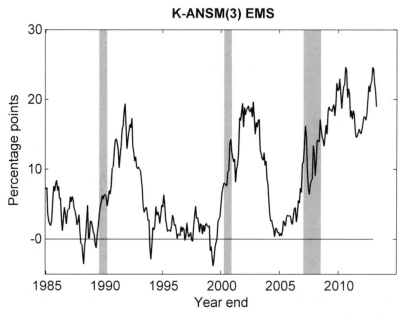

Figure 6.8 Time series plot of EMS estimates for the K-ANSM(3). Higher (lower) values reflect a more (less) stimulatory stance of monetary policy.

Combining the three potential cases for the K-ANSM(3) gives the general analytic expression for EMS(t) as

$$
\text{EMS}(t) =
\begin{cases}
\text{EMS}_1(t) & \text{if } \tilde{\mathbb{E}}_t\left[\mathrm{r}(t+\tau)\right] \text{ has no zeros} \\[2mm]
\text{EMS}_2(t) & \text{if } \tilde{\mathbb{E}}_t\left[\mathrm{r}(t+\tau)\right] \text{ has one zero} \\[2mm]
\text{EMS}_3(t) & \text{if } \tilde{\mathbb{E}}_t\left[\mathrm{r}(t+\tau)\right] \text{ has two zeros}
\end{cases}
\tag{6.161}
$$

where the zeros are obtained by numerically finding the roots of $\tilde{\mathbb{E}}_t\left[\mathrm{r}(t+\tau)\right] = x_1(t) + x_2(t) \cdot \exp(-\phi\tau) + x_3(t) \cdot \phi\tau \exp(-\phi\tau) = 0$.

Calculating EMS(t) for each yield curve observation gives the K-ANSM(3) EMS time series, which I have plotted in Figure 6.8.

6.6 Summary

- In this chapter, I have provided a theoretical justification for using ANSMs to represent the shadow term structure in shadow/ZLB-GATSMs. The first step of the theoretical justification is to specify a generic standard classical economy (the GCE) and its associated term structure, which follows well-accepted term structure modeling principles. Alternatively, one could begin from a generic

GATSM, because the term structure from an arbitrary economic model with Gaussian dynamics (which is a typical assumption) is statistically representable as a GATSM.

- The second step of the theoretical justification is to show that the GCE term structure components (or the generic GATSM components) may be aggregated into ANSM forms.
  - The aggregation is precise for the long-horizon components of the GCE term structure (or generic GATSM) and their volatility effects into the ANSM Level component and its associated volatility effect.
  - The aggregation for the short-run components of the GCE term structure (or generic GATSM) and their volatility effects proceeds as terms of a Taylor expansion around central eigenvalues of the $\mathbb{Q}$-measure, or risk-adjusted, mean-reversion matrix. The ANSM Slope component and its volatility effect represent the first term of the Taylor expansion, and the ANSM Bow component and its volatility effect represent the second term of the Taylor expansion. Higher-order ANSMs continue to add further terms of the Taylor expansion.
  - Parsimonious expressions for the $\mathbb{P}$-measure, or physical, mean-reversion matrix may also be derived from the GCE term structure (or generic GATSM) in a similar manner. Those expressions further reduce the parametrization of ANSMs, which should prove useful for estimating higher-order ANSMs.
- The GCE and/or the generic GATSM foundation for ANSMs provides a strong case for using ANSMs to represent the shadow term structure. Specifically, the GCE foundation suggests that ANSMs can be viewed as a parsimonious reflection of real output growth and inflation, along with their respective expectations. The generic GATSM foundation shows that ANSMs provide a Taylor approximation to any term structure model that would arise from an arbitrary economic model with Gaussian dynamics.
- The GCE, or any related economic model that could be specified in principle, provides a theoretical case for questioning the B-AGM framework from a general-equilibrium perspective, although this remains subject to further investigation. Specifically, the discount rates for the economy should be able to adopt negative values in line with occasional episodes of expected negative returns on the factors of production in the economy. Therefore, negative discount rates should also apply to the cashflows for ZLB forward bonds that represent physical currency in shadow/ZLB-GATSMs, which is consistent with the K-AGM framework.
- Chapter 6 also details the mechanics of calculating the "Effective Monetary Stimulus," or EMS summary measure for the stance of monetary policy from the estimated shadow term structure. I provide further discussion on the EMS, from a theoretical and empirical perspective, in the following chapter.

7 | Monetary Policy Applications

In this chapter, I discuss some of the practical applications of shadow/ZLB-GATSMs to various aspects of monetary policy. The results I present are all derived from the Krippner (2011, 2012b,c, 2013d,e) shadow/ZLB-GATSM framework using the GATSM subclass of arbitrage-free Nelson and Siegel (1987) models, or ANSMs, to represent the shadow term structure. Hence, for convenience throughout this chapter, I will typically use the abbreviation K-ANSM, in reference to Krippner ANSMs, rather than the more general shadow/ZLB-GATSM terminology introduced in chapter 2.

I begin in section 7.1 with an overview of the K-ANSM estimations used in this chapter. This overview will be essential for readers who have skipped directly to here from chapter 2 because it provides the relevant terminology and intuition for ANSMs and K-ANSMs from chapters 3 to 6 that I will continue to use throughout this chapter.

In section 7.2, I provide an overview of three different measures derived from K-ANSMs that may potentially be used as a gauge for the stance of monetary policy. I note here in advance that my preference from the three different measures is the "Effective Monetary Stimulus" (EMS), introduced at the end of section 2.4, rather than the shadow short rate (SSR). My work and that of other authors has generally found SSRs sensitive to aspects of specification and estimation, although I show that SSRs obtained from K-ANSMs with two state variables are fairly robust. In sections 7.3 to 7.5, I provide details on the three types of measures.

In section 7.6, I offer some illustrations of K-ANSM relationships with macroeconomic data, including currency rates. These illustrations are indicative only, but they suggest that ongoing research using K-ANSMs in conjunction with macroeconomic data should prove fruitful.

Before proceeding, I will make several preliminary points for readers to bear in mind. First, while I use K-ANSMs as the basis for my illustrations and discussions in this section, all of the points apply more generally to shadow/ZLB-GATSMs within the Krippner ZLB framework, as detailed in chapter 4, or within the Black (1995) framework, as detailed in chapter 5. However, the different models will obviously generate different estimates.

The second preliminary point follows immediately from the last comment. That is, estimated quantities from shadow/ZLB-GATSMs, including indicators of the stance of monetary policy, should not be quoted or interpreted independently of the model specification, the data, and the estimation method used to obtain them. Rather, the broad objective of applying shadow/ZLB-GATSMs for monetary policy purposes is to use yield curve data to obtain information that may be of use to central banks in assessing monetary conditions and understanding the macroeconomy, and that information may in turn help inform monetary policy decisions. Rigorous empirical testing of any measure, including the sensitivity of the measure itself, is of course a prerequisite to assessing its suitability against those criteria.

The third preliminary point is that, unlike policy interest rates, any measures of the stance of monetary policy obtained from a yield curve model are not under the direct control of the central bank. Specifically, any factors that influence the yield curve data will potentially change the derived measures of the monetary policy stance. The yield curve can and does change beyond the direct influence of either conventional or unconventional monetary policy actions. Therefore, measures of the stance of monetary policy outlined in this chapter should be treated as market expectation variables subject to central bank influence, rather than quantities explicitly controlled by the central bank, such as the policy interest rate or asset purchase programs.

7.1 Overview of K-ANSMs, estimation, and empirical results

K-ANSMs use ANSMs to represent the shadow term structure, and the Krippner framework to impose the lower bound constraint on nominal interest rates. Essentially, the components of K-ANSMs describe the observed yield curve data, but with an attentuation of those components based on the proximity of yield curve data to the zero lower bound (ZLB). I refer readers who want further details on ANSMs in general to chapter 3, and sections 3.3 to 3.5 in particular. I refer readers who want further details on K-ANSMs in general to chapter 4, and sections 4.3 to 4.5 in particular.

The particular K-ANSMs I will use for the illustrations in this chapter respectively use two and three components to describe the observed yield curve data, and so I call those models the K-ANSM(2) and the K-ANSM(3).

The state variables for the K-ANSM(2) are the Level $L(t)$ and Slope $S(t)$, which are applied to the Level and Slope factor loadings, as illustrated in panel 1 of Figure 7.1, to quantify the Level and Slope components in the shadow yield curve at each point in time. The Level component essentially reflects the long-maturity interest rate in the observed data, and the Slope component reflects the natural curve that typically exists between short-maturity and long-maturity interest rates. However, both components will be attenuated from the proximity of the yield curve data

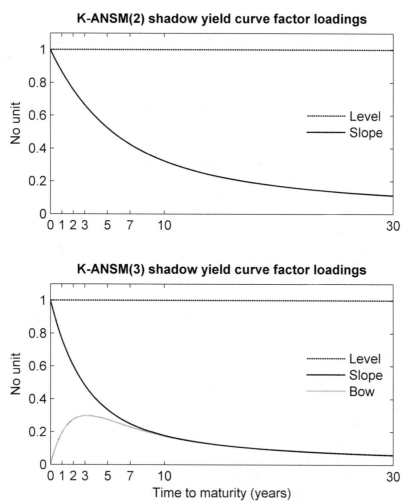

Figure 7.1 The K-ANSM(2) uses a Level factor loading and a Slope factor loading with a mean-reverion parameter ϕ (0.2943 in this example) to represent the shadow yield curve (panel 1). The K-ANSM(3) uses a Level factor loading and Slope and Bow factor loadings with a mean-reverion parameter ϕ (0.5637 in this example) to represent the shadow yield curve (panel 2).

to the ZLB, as defined in the Krippner framework. I refer readers who want further information on the K-ANSM(2) and/or the ANSM(2) used to represent the K-ANSM(2) shadow term structure to sections 4.3 and 3.3 respectively.

The state variables for the K-ANSM(3) are the Level $L(t)$, Slope $S(t)$, and Bow $B(t)$, which are applied to the Level, Slope, and Bow factor loadings, as illustrated in panel 2 of Figure 7.1, to quantify the Level, Slope, and Bow components in the shadow yield curve.[1] The Bow component essentially reflects whether mid-maturity interest rates are more elevated (or depressed) relative to the naturally curved shape already accommodated by the Slope component. Therefore, the Bow provides an extra degree of flexibility and generally a better fit to the yield curve data relative to the K-ANSM(2). I refer readers who want further information on the K-ANSM(3) and/or the ANSM(3) used to represent the K-ANSM(2) shadow term structure to sections 4.4 and 3.4 respectively.

For both the K-ANSM(2) and K-ANSM(3), I allow for three variations for the lower bound parameter r_L to further illustrate how the model specification can influence the estimated results. The variations are the following:

- An imposed lower bound of zero. I will refer to this as $r_L = 0$ percent, or 0 basis points (where 1 basis point equals 0.01 percentage points).
- An estimated lower bound. I will refer to the estimated value of r_L, respectively, $r_L = 0.14\%$ (or 14 basis points) for the K-ANSM(2) and $r_L = 0.12\%$ (or 12 basis points) for the K-ANSM(3).
- An imposed lower bound of 0.25%. This is a lower bound value proposed and used in Wu and Xia (2013, 2014). I will refer to this as $r_L = 0.25\%$, or 25 basis points.

I use end-of-month US data to estimate the K-ANSM(2) and K-ANSM(3) for each of the lower bound specifications. The following three points provide the essential description of, and justification for, the data set:

- The sample period is November 1985 to March 2014. The start of the sample is determined by the availability of 30-year interest rate data from the Gürkaynak, Sack, and Wright (2007) data set noted below, but it also coincides with a consistent macroeconomic and policy period. Specifically, the disinflation period under Chairman Volcker was completed, so inflation was already relatively low and stable, the banking sector deregulation from the early 1980s had also been completed, and the primary monetary policy lever was the Federal Funds Target Rate (FFTR) over the entire period. Note that the Federal Open Market Committee (FOMC) only began making official FFTR announcements after meetings from 1992, but market participants could infer policy changes by open market operations prior to then.
- The maturities are 0.25, 0.5, 1, 2, 3, 5, 10, and 30 years. These maturities are the standard benchmarks for Treasury notes and bonds from when the 30-year bond was first issued. I prefer to use the full maturity span of yield curve data, because the 30-year data should help provide a better estimate of the Level component of the term structure than shorter-maturity interest rates, which are subject to larger cyclical fluctuations.
- The data are government interest rates spliced with overnight indexed swap (OIS) rates. The government interest rates are from the Gürkaynak, Sack, and Wright (2007) data set, up to December 2005. I have spliced those with Bloomberg overnight indexed swap (OIS) rate data from January 2006, which is when the data set out to 30-years' time to maturity first became available. I prefer

to use OIS rates because they are directly relevant to expectations of the Federal Funds Rate. There are better, but more complex, ways of combining the government and OIS data sets, as I discuss in subsection 3.5.1. However, my pragmatic choice obtains a long time series of data with the more-relevant OIS rates over the sample period within the ZLB environment.

I use the iterated extended Kalman filter to estimate the K-ANSM(2) and K-ANSM(3) specifications from the data. I prefer to use the iterated extended Kalman filter because it is acknowledged to be more reliable than the extended Kalman filter in general, and I also found the iterated extended Kalman filter to be more reliable than the extended Kalman filter when applied to estimating K-ANSMs. I refer readers to subsection 4.2.1 for a more in-depth discussion.

The results for each K-ANSM(2) estimation are a set of parameters and a time series of Level and Slope state variables, respectively $L(t)$ and $S(t)$. As an example, the time series of $L(t)$ and $S(t)$ for the K-ANSM(2) with $r_L = 0.14$ percent are plotted in panel 1 of Figure 7.2. The parameter estimates include the key exponential decay/mean-reversion parameter $\phi = 0.2931$ that governs the shape of the Slope factor loading. The remaining parameters are available in Table 4.7 from subsection 4.5.1. The results for each K-ANSM(3) estimation are a set of parameters and a time series of Level, Slope, and Bow state variables, respectively $L(t)$, $S(t)$, and $B(t)$. As an example, the time series of $L(t)$, $S(t)$, and $B(t)$ for the K-ANSM(3) with $r_L = 0.12$ percent are plotted in panel 2 of Figure 7.2. Table 4.12 from subsection 4.5.2 contains the parameter estimates, which includes $\phi = 0.5637$ that governs the shape of the Slope and Bow factor loadings.

Note that the model specification, yield curve data, and estimation method all represent choices by the user, and those choices naturally depend on personal preferences, judgment, data availability for particular classes of yield curve data, and other aspects. Of course, different choices for any or all of these aspects will make a difference to the estimated output from the models. This is particularly the case for shadow short rates, as I will illustrate and discuss in subsection 7.3.3.

From my reading of the literature, most authors use shadow/ZLB term structure models with two or three state variables, government bond data beginning from the mid-1980s to the early 1990s with times to maturity out to 10 years, and the extended Kalman filter for estimation. That description applies to nearly all of the applications that I refer to during this chapter. Exceptions on the maturity span of the data are Richard (2013), Claus, Claus, and Krippner (2014b), and von Borstel, Eickmeier, and Krippner (2014), which use data sets with a maturity span out to 30 years, and Jackson (2014) which uses a maturity span of 5 years. Exceptions on the estimation method are Priebsch (2013, 2014) and Kim and Priebsch (2013), which use the unscented Kalman filter, and Claus, Claus, and Krippner (2014a,b) and von Borstel, Eickmeier, and Krippner (2014), which use the iterated extended Kalman filter.

One aspect that I have not yet included in my estimations is to augment them with macroeconomic data, apart from the experimental application noted in

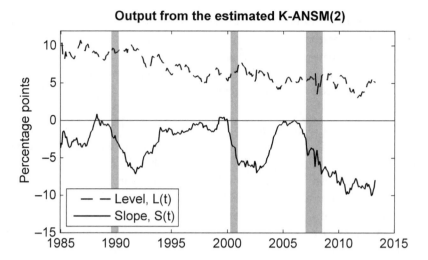

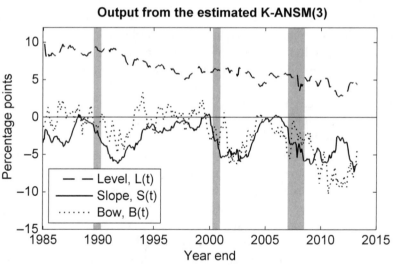

Figure 7.2 The time series of estimated K-ANSM(2) state variables (panel 1) and estimated K-ANSM(3) state variables (panel 2).

subsection 7.6.1. Bauer and Rudebusch (2013), Richard (2013), Jackson (2014), and Priebsch (2014) are examples that do so. In addition, the macroeconomic foundation for K-ANSMs from subsection 6.2.8 provides a basis for including macroeconomic survey data, as I will discuss further in subsection 7.6.1.

7.2 Measures of the stance of monetary policy

In this section, I provide an overview of three readily obtainable measures from the K-ANSM(2) and K-ANSM(3) that may potentially be used to quantify the stance of monetary policy. I include some initial empirical results for the K-ANSM(2) and K-ANSM(3) with an estimated lower bound r_L to provide the intuition for the different measures and also to allow some initial comparison between them. Subsection 7.2.2 focuses on the three measures over the ZLB environment. I have also provided a list of major easing and tightening monetary policy events over the ZLB environment, which I use as an initial means of assessing the different measures of the monetary policy stance. I provide more detail on each of the measures in sections 7.3 to 7.5.

7.2.1 Overview of three monetary policy measures

K-ANSMs, or more particularly the shadow term structure estimated for K-ANSMs, readily provide three quantitative measures that can potentially be used to gauge the stance of monetary policy. I provide an overview of those measures in this subsection along with examples for selected yield curve observations to provide intuition on the measures. The examples are for August 2008, which is a non-ZLB environment example, given that it is prior to the onset of the ZLB environment in December 2008, and July 2011 for a ZLB environment example. I provide time series of the different measures further below.

The three measures to quantify the stance of monetary policy are the following:

- **The shadow short rate (SSR)**. The SSR $r(t)$ is the shortest maturity rate from the estimated K-ANSM shadow yield curve at time t, which is $r(t) = L(t) + S(t)$ for both the K-ANSM(2) and K-ANSM(3). The SSR is essentially equal to the policy interest rate in non-ZLB environments, but it can take on negatives values in ZLB environments. As respective examples, Figure 7.3 illustrates positive estimated SSRs for the K-ANSM(2) and K-ANSM(3) in August 2008, and Figure 7.4 illustrates negative estimated SSRs for the K-ANSM(2) and K-ANSM(3) in July 2011.
- **The expected time to zero (ETZ)**. The ETZ essentially indicates the future time horizon when the expected path of the SSR will rise from zero. Specifically, when the SSR $r(t)$ and/or the expected SSR is below zero, there will be a future horizon τ_0 from time t when the expected path of the SSR will rise to zero before climbing to positive levels. The expected path of the SSR is a simple function of the estimated state variables and parameters for the K-ANSM, and so the horizon τ_0 may be readily calculated using those estimates. Note that there are no ETZ values associated with the August 2008 yield curve in Figure 7.3 because $r(t)$ and all of the expected SSRs are greater than zero.
- **The Effective Monetary Stimulus (EMS)**. The EMS summarizes the current and expected path of the ZLB-constrained short rate relative to an estimate of the neutral interest rate (where monetary policy is neither stimulatory or restrictive for output growth and inflation). Mechanically, the EMS is the total area

between the expected path of the SSR truncated at zero and the estimated neutral rate proxied by the state variable $L(t)$. For the August 2008 example in Figure 7.3 the SSR and its expected path were all positive, so no truncation at zero is required to calculate the EMS. For the July 2011 example in Figure 7.4, the SSR and its expected path are negative out to the ETZ horizon τ_0, and those values are truncated to zero to calculate the EMS. The truncation represents that only the positive part of the SSR relative to the neutral rate is effective for monetary stimulus, because the actual interest rates faced by economic agents cannot fall below zero.

Panel 1 of Figure 7.5 plots the time series Federal Funds Target Rate (FFTR) up to December 2008, when the FFTR was set to the 0 to 0.25 percent range, and then the SSR estimates obtained from the K-ANSM(2) and K-ANSM(3) thereafter. Note that the presence of positive SSRs for the K-ANSM(3) after December 2008 may be puzzling to the reader (as it initially was to the writer, for that matter), but I will explain the results fully in subsection 7.3.3.

Panel 2 of Figure 7.5 plots the ETZ for the estimated K-ANSM(2) and K-ANSM(3) specifications. Note that there are no ETZ values for the K-ANSM(2) and K-ANSM(3) prior to December 2008, given that the FFTR was positive up to that time. Panel 3 plots the EMS for the K-ANSM(2) and K-ANSM(3) over the full sample period.

7.2.2 Monetary policy measures in the ZLB environment

Figure 7.6 repeats the plots of Figure 7.5, but highlights the window from the onset of the Global Financial Crisis (GFC) during 2008 and the unconventional monetary policy period from late-2008 up to the time of writing. In the figures, I have indicated the dates of key unconventional monetary policy announcements, along with a direction on the arrow to indicate my classification of whether the event was an easing of monetary policy (a down arrow) or a tightening of monetary policy (an up arrow).

The list below summarizes the dates of the announcements indicated in the figures, along with my easing or tightening classification, and a brief description of the event itself. Note that I have also included other events that occurred during the same month as the main event, and sometimes I have combined close-by events to keep the indicators at a manageable number and distinct from each other within the figures.

1. Tuesday, December 16, 2008 (easing): The FOMC end-of-meeting statement announced a 0 to 0.25 percent range for the FFTR, from the 1 percent target rate that had prevailed since the Wednesday, October 29 statement, effectively beginning the ZLB environment. Note that this date in the figures also captures the liquidity measures put in place by the Federal Reserve prior to December 16, in

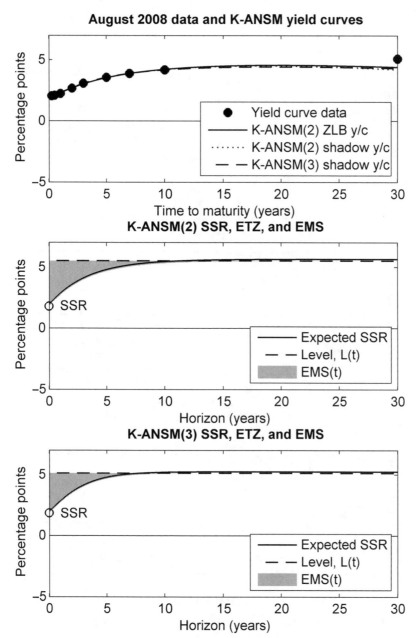

Figure 7.3 Example of the SSR and EMS obtained from the K-ANSM(2) and K-ANSM(3) shadow yield curves (y/c) in a non-ZLB environment.

particular following the Monday, September 15 Lehmans' bankruptcy. In addition, the first large-scale asset purchase program announcement, the so-called "Quantitative Easing 1," or QE1, was announced on Tuesday, November 25. QE1 amounted to purchases of $1.725 trillion of mainly asset-backed securities up to when it ended in March 2010.

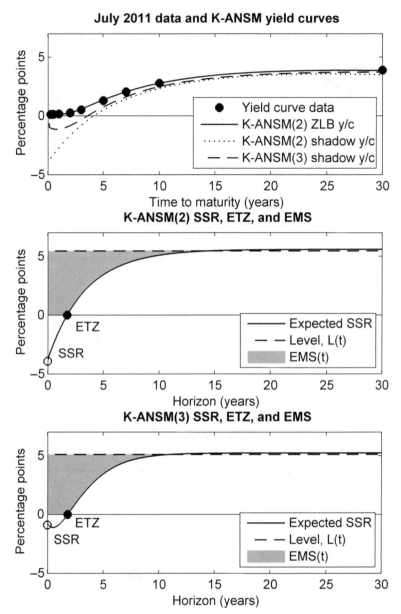

Figure 7.4 Example of the SSR, ETZ, and EMS obtained from the K-ANSM(2) and K-ANSM(3) shadow yield curves (y/c) in a ZLB environment.

2. Friday, August 27, 2010 (easing): FOMC Chairman Bernanke foreshadowed "Quantitative Easing 2," or QE2, at a speech in Jackson Hole. QE2 was subsequently introduced on Wednesday, November 3, and amounted to purchases of $0.6 trillion of US Treasuries up to when it ended in June 2011. Another

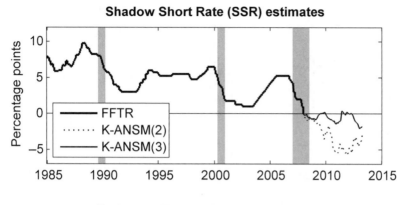

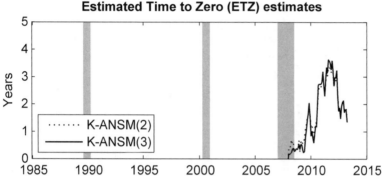

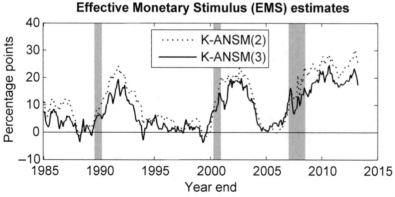

Figure 7.5 The full-sample time series of the three alternative measures of the monetary policy stance obtained from the K-ANSM(2) and K-ANSM(3) shadow term structures.

influence during this month was the Tuesday, August 10 FOMC statement that acknowledged a slowing of the economy.

3. Tuesday, August 9, 2011 (easing): The FOMC statement announced the first explicit extended calendar forward guidance for the FFTR, with a conditional expectation that it would remain near zero to mid-2013. Another influence during this month was Bernanke's announcement on Friday, August 26 that

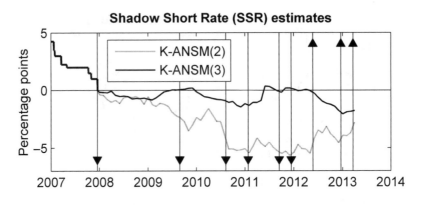

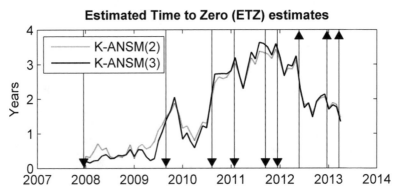

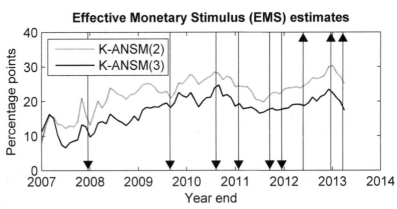

Figure 7.6 The ZLB-period time series of the three alternative measures of the monetary policy stance obtained from the K-ANSM(2) and K-ANSM(3) shadow term structures. Down (up) arrows represent monetary policy easing (tightening) events as detailed in the text.

the upcoming September 21 FOMC meeting would be extended to two days to allow a fuller discussion of the range of tools that could be used for additional monetary stimulus. I have combined this announcement indicator with an announcement in the following month:

- Wednesday, September 21, 2011 (easing): The FOMC statement announced the maturity extension program, the so-called "Operation Twist." Operation Twist was initially a $0.4 billion program to sell shorter maturity Treasury securities and buy longer-term Treasury securities, but the Wednesday, June 20, 2012 FOMC statement announced its extension, and it ultimately amounted to $0.67 trillion when it ended in late 2012.

4. Wednesday, January 25, 2012 (easing): The FOMC statement announced an extension of the calendar forward guidance to late-2014.
5. Thursday, September 13, 2012 (easing): The FOMC statement announced an extension of the calendar forward guidance to mid-2015 and the introduction of "Quantitative Easing 3," or QE3. QE3 was an open-ended program to purchase $40 billion of asset-backed securities per month.
6. Wednesday, December 12, 2012 (easing): The FOMC statement announced a change from calendar forward guidance to guidance based on an unemployment rate of 6.5 percent. At the same meeting, QE3 was increased to $85 billion purchases per month by adding $45 billion of longer-term Treasury securities.
7. Wednesday, May 22, 2013 (tightening): Chairman Bernanke foreshadowed the potential tapering of QE3 at a congressional testimony on the economic outlook. I have combined this announcement indicator with an announcement in the following month:

    - Wednesday, June 19, 2013 (tightening): Chairman Bernanke in his press conference following the FOMC meeting mentioned that 14 of 19 FOMC participants expected the first increase in the FFTR to occur in 2015.

8. Wednesday, December 18, 2013 (tightening): The FOMC statement announced the first reduction of QE3, from $85 billion to $75 billion per month.
9. Wednesday, March 19, 2014 (tightening): The FOMC statement announced the third reduction of QE3 from $65 billion to $55 billion per month, and also removed the forward guidance based on an unemployment rate of 6.5 percent in favor of a qualitative guideline of maximum employment and 2 percent inflation. The FOMC member projections for the FFTR as at year-end 2015 and year-end 2016 were revised up slightly relative to the December projections, and FOMC Chairwoman Yellen in the associated press conference mentioned the possibility of an increase in the FFTR in early 2015.

Generally, the EMS and ETZ measures, and the K-ANSM(2) SSR are consistent with the given monetary policy events. Specifically, policy easing events generally lead to rises in the EMS and ETZ measures and falls in the K-ANSM(2) SSR, while policy tightening events generally lead to falls in the EMS and ETZ measures and rises in the K-ANSM(2) SSR. The next three sections discuss each measure in more detail.

7.3 The Shadow Short Rate (SSR)

SSRs obtained from shadow/ZLB yield curve models were proposed as a measure of the stance of monetary policy in Krippner (2011, 2012b,c, 2013) as cited by Bullard (2012, 2013), and in Wu and Xia (2013, 2014) as cited by Hamilton (2013) and Higgins and Meyer (2013). The proposal has intuitive appeal because when the SSR is positive, it essentially equals the actual short rate, but the SSR is free to evolve to negative levels after the actual short rate becomes constrained by the ZLB. As already illustrated in Figures 2.12 from section 2.4 and panel 1 of Figure 7.5, negative values of the SSR may therefore be used to indicate further policy easing beyond the zero policy rate. SSRs have also been used quantitatively with some success in at least two studies. For example, when comparing the unconventional/ZLB and conventional/pre-ZLB periods for the United States, Claus, Claus, and Krippner (2014a,b) show that their estimated SSR responds to monetary policy shocks similarly to the FFR. Wu and Xia (2013, 2014) show that the effects of their estimated SSR on macroeconomic variables are similar to the FFR.

Nevertheless, using SSRs as a quantitative indicator of monetary policy has been questioned from both a theoretical and an empirical perspective. I provide an overview of the theoretical perspective first, then the empirical perspective, and will follow with some detailed examples and discussion regarding the sensitivity of SSRs depending on the model specification.

7.3.1 Theoretical overview

As discussed in Krippner (2014b,c), negative interest rates on the shadow yield curve are not actual interest rates faced by economic agents. That is, borrowers and lenders face current and expected interest rates that are based on wholesale interest rates subject to a ZLB constraint (plus appropriate margins), not negative interest rates. Therefore, the monetary stimulus from falls in the SSR when it is already negative (i.e., in a ZLB environment) is attenuated relative to the same fall in the actual policy rate/SSR when it is positive (i.e., in a non-ZLB environment). The reason is that short- and mid-maturity interest rates on the actual/ZLB yield curve have no scope or limited scope to move lower in the ZLB environment.

To highlight this point, Figure 7.7 uses a generated K-ANSM(2) example to illustrate an easing of the SSR from 5 to 0%, and then a further easing of the SSR from 0 to −5%. For this example, I use the respective values of the Slope state variable $S(t) = 0\%$, $S(t) = -5\%$, and $S(t) = -10\%$, while keeping the Level state variable unchanged at $L(t) = 5\%$, so the SSRs are r$(t) = 5\%$, r$(t) = 0\%$, and r$(t) = -5\%$ respectively.

In the first SSR easing from 5 to 0%, all interest rates on the actual yield curve move down markedly, consistent with a large monetary policy stimulus. In the second case, the ZLB constrains declines in actual short- and mid-maturity interest rates, therefore limiting the monetary policy stimulus relative to the first case.

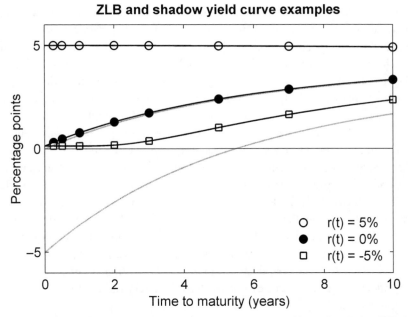

Figure 7.7 K-ANSM(2) ZLB yield curves and shadow yield curves (dotted lines below ZLB yield curves) for different values of the SSR, while keeping the long-run yields constant. The monetary stimulus from the ZLB yield curve (i.e., declines in actual interest rates) is attenuated when the SSR adopts negative values.

In other words, less of the SSR change is effective in providing additional monetary stimulus. Therefore, levels and changes in SSRs deliver different amounts of monetary stimulus to the economy depending on whether a non-ZLB or ZLB environment is prevailing. Indeed, the attenuation of falls in actual interest rates will become more pronounced as the SSR becomes more negative, because a more negative SSR indicates that interest rates for longer horizons are already subject to the ZLB constraint. More precisely, more of the expected ZLB short rates, and hence ZLB forward rates that underlie the ZLB/actual interest rates, are already subject to the ZLB constraint. I return to this point in section 7.5 when discussing the EMS.

In summary, the monetary stimulus from a change in the SSR is a nonlinear function of the level of the SSR. That nonlinearity means that the levels and changes of SSRs cannot strictly be used as a linear measure of monetary stimulus. For example, it would be incorrect to assume that the SSR levels and/or changes in ZLB environments impart similar effects to macroeconomic variables as FFTR levels and changes did in non-ZLB environments. To highlight this point, one might literally interpret the −5% SSR in Figure 7.7 as a hugely stimulatory stance of monetary policy with an effect on the macroeconomy similar to cutting the FFTR by 5 percentage points. However, the actual stimulus would be much less because actual short- and mid-maturity interest rates have not fallen in line with the SSR due to the ZLB constraint.

More formally, using the SSR without any adjustment in linear econometric applications, such as standard regression analysis and dynamic factor models, would effectively specify the relationships of SSR with the other variables to be linear. That implicit assumption of linearity would represent a model misspecification relative to the nonlinearity known to exist in the SSR as a measure of the stance of monetary policy, as already described above. Therefore, as a simple example, establishing a regression relationship over a non-ZLB and ZLB sample showing that x% easing in the SSR correlated with y% future change in real output growth would be invalid, because the future changes in real output growth should actually be larger when the SSR is positive and smaller when the SSR is negative. Indeed, Francis, Jackson, and Owyang (2014) offer empirical evidence related to this, finding that the SSR in the ZLB period does not preserve the response of macroeconomic variables to the FFTR from the non-ZLB period (although, SSRs from a model with two state variables perform better than SSRs from a model with three state variables). The results and interpretations of the Claus, Claus, and Krippner (2014a) and Wu and Xia (2013, 2014) empirical applications of SSRs mentioned earlier will be similarly affected to some extent by this nonlinearity issue, and the results should be interpreted accordingly.

7.3.2 Empirical overview

A more significant issue regarding SSRs is their sensitivity in practice to estimation choices. As highlighted in the introduction to this chapter and section 7.1, negative SSRs are necessarily estimated quantities because they are not observable, and so they vary with the practical choices underlying their estimation. I summarize the results from the literature in the categories of estimation choices already outlined in section 7.1:

- **Model specification.** Christensen and Rudebusch (2013a,b, 2014), Bauer and Rudebusch (2013), and Krippner (2013d,e) show that SSR estimates can be materially sensitive to the number of state variables. Generally, models with two state variables produce more negative SSRs than models with three state variables, which I illustrate in subsection 7.3.3 using the K-ANSM(2) and K-ANSM(3) results. Bauer and Rudebusch (2013) also shows that even small changes to the specification of the lower bound in the model can have a substantial impact on the SSR estimates. I illustrate this feature in subsection 7.3.3 and spend some time providing the intuition on why the lower bound specification leads to such sensitivity.
- **The data.** Krippner (2013d,e) provides evidence that using the maturity span of yield curve data out to 30 years delivers materially different SSRs (typically more negative) than using a maturity span of yield curve data out to 10 years.
- **The estimation method.** Krippner (2013d,e) provides evidence that using the iterated extended Kalman filter can deliver materially different SSRs (typically

more negative) than using the extended Kalman filter. As discussed in subsection 4.2.1, those results may depend on whether the starting parameters for the optimization algorithm using the extended Kalman filter were close to the globally optimal parameters.

- **Use of macroeconomic data.** Jackson (2014) and Bauer and Rudebusch (2013) show that augmenting the yield curve estimation with macroeconomic data can lead to very material differences in shadow short rates compared to just using yield curve data alone.

7.3.3 Empirical evidence

Figure 7.8 illustrates the time series of SSR estimates for the K-ANSM(2) and K-ANSM(3) with the three lower bounds for interest rates r_L as specified in section 7.1, that is, $r_L = 0\%$, $r_L = 0.25\%$, and r_L estimated as a free parameter, which results in $r_L = 0.14\%$ for the K-ANSM(2) and $r_L = 0.12\%$ for the K-ANSM(3). Note that I have only plotted the more detailed window from December 2007 onwards because the earlier data for each series are the FFTR series already plotted in Figure 7.5. I discuss each of the panels in the following two subsections.

K-ANSM(2) SSR discussion

The K-ANSM(2) SSR estimates based on the three different lower bounds show material differences in magnitudes during the period August 2011 to around June 2013. However, the profiles of all the SSR estimates are consistent, and they are also generally consistent with the key monetary policy easing and tightening announcements as indicated.

An example of the difference in the magnitudes of the SSR estimates is highlighted in Figure 7.9, where I plot the results for the three K-ANSM(2) models for July 2012. That date is the most constrained yield curve observation in the sample, given it has the lowest K-ANSM(2) SSR estimates and the 10- and 30-year interest rates were at record lows. I have included the data and ZLB yield curve results associated with Figure 7.9 in Table 7.1 to discuss the intuition underlying the different SSR estimates.

The key points to note for the K-ANSM(2) with different r_L specifications are:

- For the case $r_L = 0\%$, all of the yield curve data is above the lower bound, and so has an influence on the estimate of the K-ANSM(2) state variables. Hence, the estimate of the Slope state variable $S(t)$ has to accommodate the data across the entire yield curve, and it therefore adopts a moderately negative value to fit the short- and mid-maturity data. The estimate of the Level state variable $L(t)$ has to balance the fit of the longer-maturity interest rates, and therefore the fit to the 30-year interest rate is not particularly good.
- For the case $r_L = 0.14\%$, the estimated lower bound already fits the data well out to the 2-year interest rate, and so the estimate of $S(t)$ adopts more negative values to better fit mid- and longer-maturity interest rates. $L(t)$ can therefore

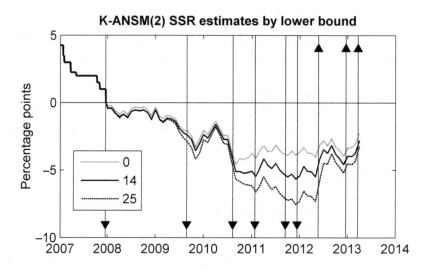

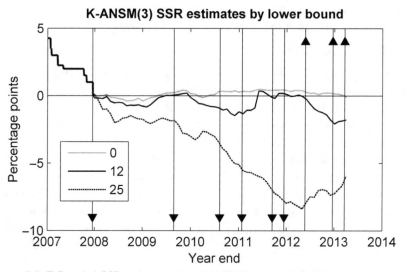

Figure 7.8 ZLB-period SSR estimates from K-ANSM(2) and K-ANSM(3) specifications with lower bounds as indicated. The flexibility of the K-ANSM(3) makes the estimated SSRs very sensitive to minor parameter differences. Note that down (up) arrows represent monetary policy easing (tightening) events as detailed in subsection 7.2.2.

better fit longer-maturity interest rates, and so the fit to the 30-year interest rate improves.

- For the case $r_L = 0.25\%$, the lower bound is already above all of the yield curve data out to $\tau = 3$ years, and so $S(t)$ is freer to adopt very negative values to better fit the mid- and longer-maturity interest rates. In particular, the 0.25-, 0.5-, and 2-year interest rate data impose no fitting penalty from the large negative value of

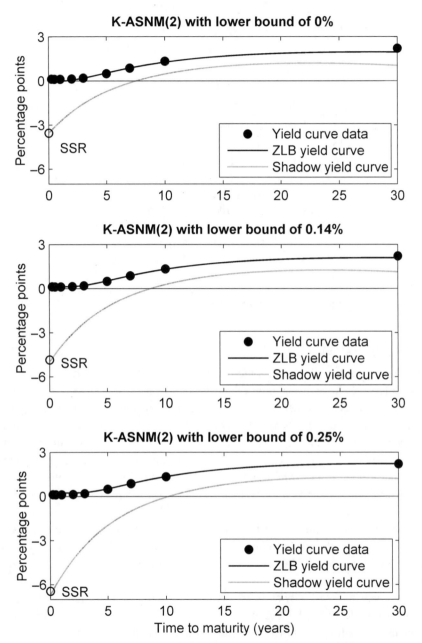

Figure 7.9 July 2012 estimated K-ANSM(2) yield curves and associated SSR estimates with lower bounds as indicated. The results illustrate the sensitivity of SSR estimates to the lower bound specification.

$S(t)$ because the ZLB mechanism means that K-ANSM(2) interest rates cannot fall below $r_L = 0.25\%$. The additional explanatory power of $S(t)$ for the mid- and longer-maturity interest rates means that $L(t)$ is left to provide a very close fit to the 30-year interest rate.

Table 7.1 July 2012 data and K-ANSM(2) results

		0%	0.12%	0.25%
r_L		0%	0.12%	0.25%
$L(t)$		2.68	2.93	3.17
$S(t)$		−6.22	−7.90	−9.87
$r(t)$		−3.54	−4.97	−6.70

τ	Data	Fit.	Res.	Fit.	Res.	Fit.	Res.
0.25	0.14	0.00	−0.14	0.14	0.00	0.25	0.11
0.50	0.13	0.00	−0.13	0.14	0.01	0.25	0.12
1	0.13	0.00	−0.13	0.14	0.01	0.25	0.12
2	0.14	0.06	−0.08	0.15	0.01	0.25	0.11
3	0.20	0.20	−0.00	0.22	0.02	0.28	0.08
5	0.51	0.55	0.04	0.53	0.03	0.53	0.02
7	0.88	0.88	0.00	0.89	0.00	0.88	−0.00
10	1.34	1.28	−0.06	1.32	−0.02	1.36	0.01
30	2.22	1.96	−0.26	2.09	−0.13	2.23	0.01

Note: All values are percentage points.

K-ANSM(3) SSR discussion

The K-ANSM(3) SSR estimates plotted in panel 2 of Figure 7.8 show very material differences in both magnitudes and profiles over the entire ZLB period. The $r_L = 0.25\%$ SSRs are generally consistent with the key monetary policy easing and tightening announcements as indicated, but the $r_L = 0\%$ and $r_L = 0.12\%$ results are very counterintuitive. In particular, those latter two SSR estimates are only mildly negative and are often positive during the ZLB environment from December 2008. In addition, from around mid-2011, those SSR estimates often rise on monetary policy easing announcements and fall on monetary policy tightening announcements.

The sensitivity of the SSR results may seem surprising, so I again use figures and a table to explain the results in full. Hence, Figure 7.10 plots the results for the three K-ANSM(3) models for July 2012, and Table 7.2 contains the associated data and results.

Essentially the sensitivity of the results arises from the same phenomenon already explained in detail for the K-ANSM(2), except the K-ANSM(3) has the Bow component as an additional function of time-to-maturity to more flexibly fit the yield curve data at each point in time. The key points to note for the K-ANSM(3) with different r_L specifications are:

- For $r_L = 0\%$ and $r_L = 0.12\%$, $B(t)$ adopts very negative values to explain the mid-maturity rates, which leaves $S(t)$ able to adopt only mildly negative values to provide a close fit to the short-maturity interest rates. However, the magnitude of $S(t)$ in both cases does not exceed $L(t)$, so $r(t) = L(t) + S(t)$ is slightly

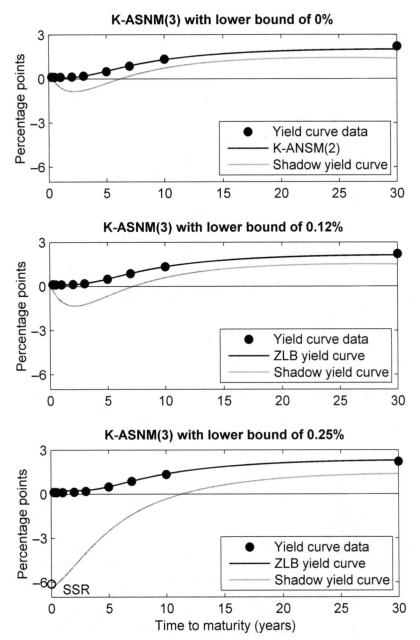

Figure 7.10 July 2012 estimated K-ANSM(3) yield curves and associated SSR estimates with lower bounds as indicated. The results illustrate that K-ANSM(3) SSR estimates can be very sensitive to the lower bound specification.

positive. The Bow component of the term structure produces materially negative values for mid-maturity interest rates, but the zero loading of the Bow factor at $\tau = 0$ means it does not appear in r(t).

Table 7.2 July 2012 data and K-ANSM(3) results

r_L			0%		0.12%		0.25%
$L(t)$			2.51		2.73		2.98
$S(t)$			−2.08		−2.59		−9.34
$B(t)$			−7.61		−9.05		−7.38
$r(t)$			0.42		0.14		−6.36

τ	Data	Fit.	Res.	Fit.	Res.	Fit.	Res.
0.25	0.14	0.20	0.06	0.14	0.00	0.25	0.11
0.50	0.13	0.13	−0.00	0.13	0.00	0.25	0.12
1	0.13	0.09	−0.04	0.13	−0.00	0.25	0.12
2	0.14	0.11	−0.04	0.14	−0.00	0.25	0.11
3	0.20	0.20	0.00	0.21	0.01	0.27	0.07
5	0.51	0.53	0.03	0.51	0.01	0.51	0.01
7	0.88	0.89	0.01	0.89	0.00	0.89	0.00
10	1.34	1.31	−0.04	1.34	0.00	1.38	0.04
30	2.22	2.01	−0.21	2.13	− 0.09	2.30	0.08

Note: All values are percentage points.

- For $r_L = 0.25\%$, $S(t)$ and $B(t)$ are both free to adopt very negative values to better fit the mid- and longer-maturity interest rates, as already explained for the K-ANSM(2) $r_L = 0.25\%$ case. The large negative value of $S(t)$ therefore leads to a large negative SSR, and it is similar in magnitude to the K-ANSM(2) $r_L = 0.25\%$ case.

7.3.4 SSR summary

In general, the results presented here, along with the results already available elsewhere, highlight the point that SSR estimates are unique to estimation choices, and they can be very sensitive to those particular choices. When combined with the theoretical issue that negative SSRs and shadow interest rates are unattainable for borrowers, that led me to search for a more theoretically appealing and empirically robust measure. I will detail the result, the EMS, in section 7.5.

However, if one prefers the concept of an SSR as a measure of the stance of monetary policy, then the discussion and results in this section suggest several take-away points:

- SSRs from K-ANSM(2) specifications are more robust than K-ANSM(3) specifications. Specifically, the Bow component of the K-ANSM(3) allows too much flexibility for short times to maturity on the model yield curve, and that leads to counterintuitive results with only minor changes to the K-ANSM(3) specification. The relative robustness of the K-ANSM(2) is due to the absence of the Bow component, but the trade-off is a poorer fit to the yield curve data. As a related point for the K-ANSM(3) and higher-order K-ANSMs, as one adds more state variables, the resulting increased model flexibility would eventually replicate the observed yield curve data. In particular, the replication would include the ZLB-constrained interest rates, but subsection 2.1.2 has already discussed that those rates lack any useful information for monetary policy. Therefore, the poor fit of the K-ANSM(2), or shadow/ZLB-GATSMs with two state variables in general, seems necessary to obtain usable SSRs for monetary policy purposes.

- K-ANSM(2) SSRs are better used as an ordinal measure. That is, lower (higher) values are generally consistent with more (less) monetary stimulus, but the attenuation effect at the ZLB means that the levels and changes in any SSR series when it is negative do not, in principle, provide a direct cardinal or linear measure of that additional (reduced) stimulus. In other words, the levels and changes of the K-ANSM(2) SSR when it is negative should not be interpreted as equivalent to FFTR levels and changes from a non-ZLB environment.

- If using K-ANSM(2) SSRs as a measure of the stance of monetary policy, at the very least the estimated SSR series should be checked for consistency with known monetary policy events. Checking for consistency with macroeconomic variables is also recommended. From that perspective, the results from Francis, Jackson, and Owyang (2014) offer support for K-ANSM(2) SSRs, rather than the Wu and Xia (2013, 2014) SSRs obtained from a model with three state variables.

7.4 The Expected Time to Zero (ETZ)

The Expected Time to Zero (ETZ) measure essentially provides an implied market-based expectation of when the actual short rate is expected to rise from zero. The ETZ is calculated from the shadow term structure estimated by the specified K-ANSM. In summary,

$$\text{ETZ}(t) = \tau_0$$

$$\tilde{\mathbb{E}}_t\left[r(t + \tau_0)\right] = 0 \tag{7.1}$$

where $\tilde{\mathbb{E}}_t\left[r(t + \tau_0)\right]$ is the expected path of the shadow short rate. As a somewhat technical point of secondary importance to the discussion here, note that $\tilde{\mathbb{E}}_t[\cdot]$ indicates the expectations are under the risk-adjusted $\mathbb{Q}$ measure, which contains risk premiums relative to actual expectations of the expected path of the shadow short rate under the physical $\mathbb{P}$ measure. Sections 3.1 and 6.5 contain further discussion on the distinction, and it will show up again in sections 7.5 and 7.6.

As detailed in section 6.5, $\tilde{\mathbb{E}}_t\left[r(t + \tau)\right]$ is a simple closed-form analytic univariate function of the horizon τ for any K-ANSM. For the K-ANSM(2), $\tilde{\mathbb{E}}_t\left[r(t + \tau)\right]$ is parametrized with the estimated state variables $L(t)$, $S(t)$, and the mean-reversion parameter ϕ, and the K-ANSM(3) adds the state variable $B(t)$. These state variables and ϕ are already available from the K-ANSM estimations. If at least some value/s of $\mathbb{E}_t[r(t+\tau)] = 0$ (or any other non-zero threshold in general) for $\tau \geq 0$, then directly calculating the root for the K-ANSM(2) or applying a root-finding technique for the K-ANSM(3) readily obtains the solution τ_0, where $\mathbb{E}_t[r(t+\tau_0)] = 0$. The K-ANSM(3) can give two solutions, in which case I use the largest value of τ_0. I refer readers to section 6.5 for the full details.

A related alternative to the ETZ is what I will call the "lift-off horizon" (LOH), which has been proposed in Bauer and Rudebusch (2013) and Wu and Xia (2013, 2014). The LOH is essentially the answer to the following question: from the current value of $r(t)$, what is the median time τ for simulated paths of future ZLB short rates $r_j(t+\tau) = \max\{0, r_j(t+\tau)\}$ to first reach 0.25 percent (or, in general, any given threshold)? In summary,

$$LOH(t) = \text{median}[\tau_j]$$
$$\max\{0, r_j(t+\tau_j)\} \geq 0.25\% \tag{7.2}$$

where $r_j(t+\tau_j)$ represents a single Monte Carlo simulation of the future SSR path, and τ_j is the horizon when 0.25% is first reached or breached by that path. τ_j is a random variable because each $r_j(t+\tau_j)$ is a randomly generated SSR path, so $LOH(t)$ is therefore the median of random variables. Bauer and Rudebusch (2013) calculates the LOH by simulation for their estimated B-AGM, and Wu and Xia (2013, 2014) has calculated an LOH by simulation for their K-AGM. Calculating LOHs for K-ANSMs by simulation would be very straightforward, following the Monte Carlo simulation principles outlined in section 5.3.

7.4.1 Theoretical overview

From a theoretical perspective, the ETZ and LOH provide indications of how long economic agents are likely to face zero policy rates. Therefore, the ETZ and LOH should in principle provide a better measure of the effective degree of monetary policy stimulus for short- and medium-term horizons than the unobtainable negative SSR.

However, the LOH and ETZ do not provide an indication of the policy rates that economic agents will face for longer horizons into the future, which should also be a relevant influence for their decisions. As a simple example, an expectation of the FFTR rising in one year's time from zero to 3% over the subsequent two years is relatively less restrictive in principle compared to an expected rise from zero to 5% over the same period. However, the LOH and ETZ would not differentiate between those two scenarios.

The biggest downside for the ETZ and LOH is that they are only available in ZLB environments because they are undefined in non-ZLB environments. For example, Figure 7.3 in subsection 7.2.1 does not contain any ETZ values τ_0 because the entire estimated K-ANSM(2) and K-ANSM(3) shadow yield curves are nonnegative. Similarly, Figure 7.11 below only plots ETZ results from December 2008 because there are no values of τ_0 for earlier yield curve observations. Therefore, the ETZ and LOH cannot be used as a stand-alone measure of the degree of monetary policy stimulus over a sample period that contains both non-ZLB and ZLB environments.

7.4.2 Empirical overview and evidence

Panel 1 of Figure 7.11 shows that ETZs from the K-ANSM(2) with different lower bound specifications have some differences in magnitude, but very similar profiles. The changes in the ETZs are generally consistent with the key monetary policy easing and tightening announcements as indicated. Panel 2 shows a similar result for the ETZs from the K-ANSM(3). Note that the ETZs are not always available in the ZLB period because the estimated expected path of the shadow short rate sometimes adopts all positive values, in which case τ_0 is undefined. Panel 3 shows that the ETZs for the K-ANSM(2) and K-ANSM(3) with estimated lower bounds are very similar in magnitude and profile, and consistent with key monetary policy announcements.

As an example of how to interpret the ETZ at any point in time, I will use the last point of the sample, March 31, 2014, as an example. The lowest ETZ was 1.30 years (for the K-ANSM(2) with $r_L = 0\%$), and the highest was 1.76 years (for the K-ANSM(3) with $r_L = 0.25\%$). Adding those respective horizons to March 31, 2014 gives a range from mid-2015 to end-2015. Hence, the OIS yield curve data for the end of March 2014 suggested a market-implied expectation for the ZLB environment to end in the second half of 2015. I have not been able to find market survey data regarding the end of the ZLB environment against which to check my estimates, but that ETZ range is broadly consistent with the guidance offered by the FOMC.

Bauer and Rudebusch (2013) has shown that the LOH is more robust than the SSR to different model specifications, and that the results are also consistent with market survey data regarding the end of the ZLB environment. Wu and Xia (2013, 2014) does not contain results of their LOH against alternative specifications, but they show that the results are consistent with known monetary policy events and with market survey data.

7.5 The Effective Monetary Stimulus (EMS)

The EMS was initially proposed as a measure of the stance of monetary policy in Krippner (2014b,c), and its calculation is detailed in section 6.5. Essentially, the EMS uses information from the entire estimated shadow term structure rather than

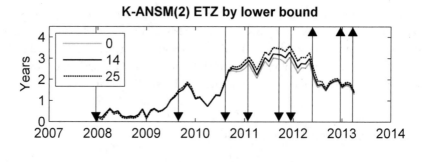

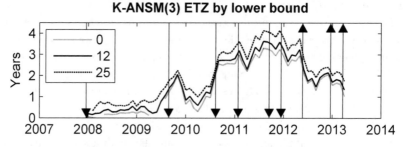

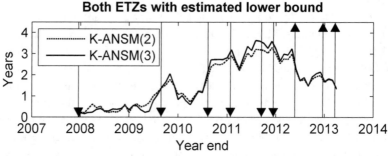

Figure 7.11 ZLB-period ETZ estimates from K-ANSM(2) and K-ANSM(3) specifications with lower bounds as indicated. Note that down (up) arrows represent monetary policy easing (tightening) events as detailed in subsection 7.2.2.

just the single points provided by the SSR and the ETZ or LOH. I provide the theoretical overview of the case for the EMS in subsection 7.5.1 and then proceed to provide empirical evidence for the EMS in subsection 7.5.2.

7.5.1 Theoretical overview

As illustrated in Figures 7.3 and 7.4 and detailed in section 6.5, the concept of the EMS is to summarize the area between the effective value of the current and expected SSR relative to an estimated neutral interest rate. As a somewhat technical point that will hopefully help to avoid any confusion on their interpretation, the estimates of the EMS presented in this book, and particularly the neutral rates (i.e., the K-ANSM Level state variables) used to obtain them, are under the risk-adjusted

$\mathbb{Q}$ measure. Therefore, the $\mathbb{Q}$-measure neutral rates include risk premiums relative to neutral rates under the physical $\mathbb{P}$ measure. The latter are the actual expectations of long-horizon interest rates held by the market, which could in turn be implied by survey measures of long-horizon output growth and inflation. Subsection 7.6.1 will make that distinction apparent graphically, and subsections 3.1.1 and 6.2.8 contain further relevant discussion. Subsection 6.5 notes that the EMS can also be obtained under the $\mathbb{P}$ measure, and that perspective is also likely to be useful for monetary policy purposes. In particular, having both the $\mathbb{Q}$-measure and $\mathbb{P}$-measure estimates of the EMS available will allow the overall monetary stimulus to be divided into pure expectations about policy rate, and risk premiums.

Regarding the "effective value" of the SSR, I mean the current and expected SSR truncated at zero, because zero is historically around the lowest interest rate at which investors have agreed to lend, and arbitrage arguments involving physical currency provide a theoretical reason why a zero lower bound should hold in principle. Specifically, if the central bank was to set a negative lending rate, then economic agents could in principle borrow from the central bank to create an income-generating liability and receive the loan proceeds as physical currency, which is a zero-return asset. Note that this arbitrage argument makes zero the best choice for calculating the EMS, even though non-zero values would be straightforward to accommodate in the EMS calculation. Hence, I use zero for my EMS calculations in all of the illustrations, even in cases in which I have specified the K-ANSM to have a non-zero lower bound.

Rather than expressing the effective part of the SSR on its own, the EMS expresses it relative to an estimate of the neutral interest rate. That specification relates back to the discussion in section 2.1 about the central bank setting policy rates below or above an estimate of the neutral interest rate to either stimulate or restrict output growth and inflation. However, the EMS includes more information than the policy interest rate versus the neutral interest rate gap alone because the EMS also accounts for market-implied expectations of where the policy interest rate/estimated neutral interest rate gap will be in the future. In principle, expectations of that gap rather than just the prevailing gap should also be an important influence on the decisions of economic agents and therefore an important component of overall monetary policy stimulus.

Regarding an estimate of the neutral interest rate, the discussion and the macroeconomic foundation provided for K-ANSMs in subsection 6.2.8 suggests using the estimated Level state variable $L(t)$ from K-ANSMs as the estimated neutral interest rate at time t. Hence, the neutral interest rate can vary, as one would expect, with changes to long-horizon expectations of real output growth and inflation, and their associated risk premiums.

The EMS is theoretically consistent over non-ZLB and ZLB environments because in both cases it measures precisely the same concept, that is, the EMS aggregates the effective component of the estimated expected SSR relative to the estimated neutral rate as proxied by the estimated Level state variable $L(t)$. In ZLB periods, as illustrated in Figure 7.4, the EMS will initially include a period of zero followed by a non-zero path that converges to the $L(t)$ from below. In non-ZLB periods, as illustrated in Figure 7.3, the expected SSR is entirely positive as it converges to the neutral rate. Figure 7.4 has already provided an example of a stimulatory stance of monetary policy in a non-ZLB environment, where the policy rate is well below the neutral rate. The expected SSR can also converge to the neutral rate from above, which would represent a very restrictive stance of monetary policy. The EMS time series plotted in Figures 7.5 and 7.12 indicates that such a situation has occurred on several occasions over the sample period.

7.5.2 Empirical overview and evidence

Figure 7.12 plots the K-ANSM(2) and K-ANSM(3) EMS results for the different lower bound specifications over the full sample. The results for both the K-ANSM(2) and K-ANSM(3) specifications have very similar profiles and magnitudes for the entire sample. However, some notable differences occur in the ZLB environment around July 2012, which I return to discuss at the end of this subsection.

To compare the two- and three-state-variable EMS estimates, panel 3 of Figure 7.12 plots the K-ANSM(2) and K-ANSM(3) EMS measures based on estimated values for r_L. There is a persistent difference in the magnitudes over the entire sample, but the profiles and ranges of the two series are very similar. Therefore, if either the K-ANSM(2) or K-ANSM(3) EMS series were used in linear econometric analysis, the results would be very similar, except for a slightly different constant.

To highlight the linear similarity of the K-ANSM(2) or K-ANSM(3) EMS series, in panel 2 of Figure 7.13 I have plotted the EMS series from panel 3 of Figure 7.12 as z-scores, that is,

$$z\text{-score} = \frac{x - \text{mean}[x]}{\text{stdev}[x]} \tag{7.3}$$

where x is the time series, mean$[x]$ is the arithmetic mean of x, and stdev$[x]$ is the (unconditional) standard deviation of x. For comparison, I have plotted in panel 1 the z-scores for the FFTR/K-ANSM(2) SSR series and the FFTR/K-ANSM(3) SSR series from the same models. Specifically, these series both use the FFTR up to November 2008, and then respectively the K-ANSM(2) or K-ANSM(3) SSR estimates from December 2008. The FFTR/SSR-based z-score series show larger deviations between the K-ANSM(2) and K-ANSM(3) compared to the EMS-based z-score series.

In Figure 7.14, I plot the data from Figures 7.12 over the window from December 2007 to highlight the EMS estimates over the ZLB environment. The expanded scale on both axes of Figure 7.13 makes the differences between the different EMS estimates over the ZLB period more apparent, but otherwise the comments already made for Figure 7.12 apply equally to Figure 7.13.

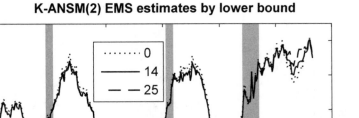

K-ANSM(2) EMS estimates by lower bound

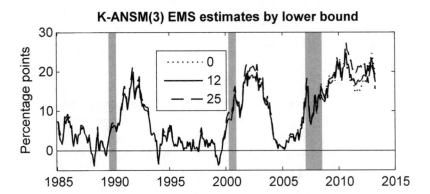

K-ANSM(3) EMS estimates by lower bound

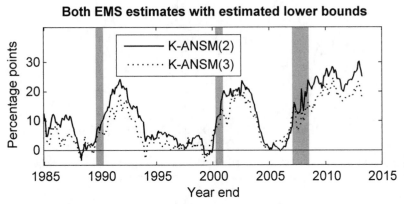

Figure 7.12 Full-sample EMS estimates from K-ANSM(2) and K-ANSM(3) specifications with lower bounds as indicated.

Figure 7.15 shows that the z-scores of the K-ANSM(2) and K-ANSM(3) EMS estimates are very similar over the ZLB environment, unlike the z-scores of the K-ANSM(2) and K-ANSM(3) SSRs.

The changes to the EMS series are typically consistent with the indicated monetary policy announcements, although there are several notable exceptions. The first

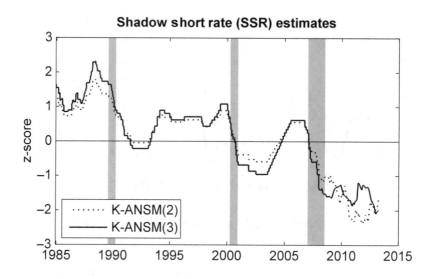

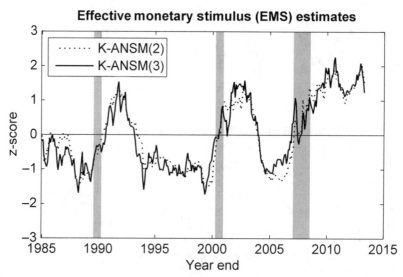

Figure 7.13 Full-sample FFTR + SSR estimates and full-sample EMS estimates from K-ANSM(2) and K-ANSM(3) specifications with estimated lower bounds, all expressed as z-scores.

two are August 2011 and January 2012, when the EMS declined following the easing announcements of calendar forward guidance, and the third is May 2013, when the EMS increased following the tightening announcements on forthcoming tapering. My preliminary investigations, which I will illustrate in section 7.6.1, suggest that these counterintuitive movements are due to long-maturity interest rates first moving well below a neutral rate suggested by macroeconomic survey data, and then moving back to a neutral rate suggested by macroeconomic survey data. For example, the 10 year rate fell by 59 basis points from July to August 2011, and declined

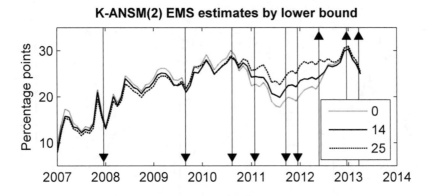

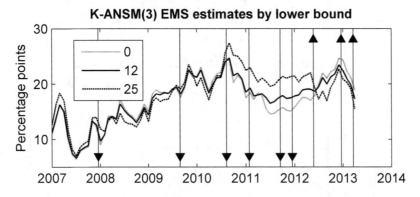

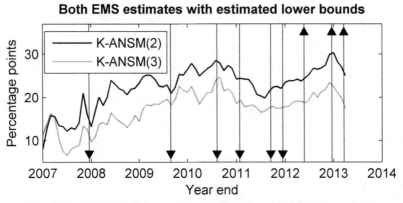

Figure 7.14 ZLB-period EMS estimates from K-ANSM(2) and K-ANSM(3) specifications with lower bounds as indicated. Note that down (up) arrows represent monetary policy easing (tightening) events as detailed in subsection 7.2.2.

by a further 84 basis points, to a low of 1.34% in July 2012. The respective changes for the 30-year interest rate over the same periods were 62 and 105 basis points to a low of 2.22%. Regarding the reversal, the 10-year rate rose by 46 basis points from April to May 2013, and rose a further 84 basis points to a local high of 2.94% in

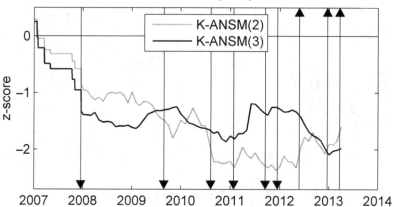

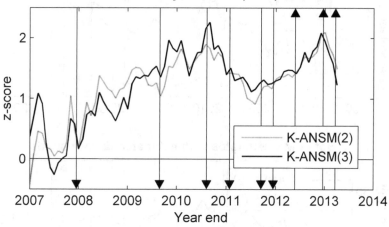

Figure 7.15 ZLB-period FFTR + SSR estimates and subsample EMS estimates from K-ANSM(2) and K-ANSM(3) specifications with lower bounds as indicated, all expressed as z-scores. Note that down (up) arrows represent monetary policy easing (tightening) events as detailed in subsection 7.2.2.

December 2013. The respective changes for the 30-year interest rate over the same periods were 42 and 74 basis points to a local high of 3.91%.

Mechanically, lower (higher) long-maturity interest rates will lead to lower (higher) K-ANSM Level state variable $L(t)$ estimates and therefore a compressed (expanded) area between the expected SSR and $L(t)$ that defines the EMS. My preliminary work from incorporating macroeconomic survey data in to the K-ANSM estimations, as I will discuss in section 7.6.1, reduces the variation in $L(t)$ and improves the estimated EMS measure. Specifically, the EMS continues to rise from August 2011, and falls from May 2013, which is a profile consistent with the easy and tightening monetary policy events mentioned above.

7.5.3 Linking the SSR and the EMS

In Figure 7.16, I provide an illustration of the nonlinear relationship between the SSR and EMS measures. This figure serves to illustrate the SSR attenuation effect that I have previously discussed in principle, but explicitly in terms of the EMS. Hence, Figure 7.16 shows for each 0.25 percentage point decrease in the SSR, the increase in the K-ANSM(2) EMS as a function of the starting values of the SSR. Working from right to left on the x axis, the figure shows the EMS change when the SSR is decreased from 10% to 9.75%, then from 9.75% to 9.50%, and so on, from 0.25% to 0%, from 0% to −0.25%, and so on, until the last movement from −9.75% to −10%. I use only the Slope state variable $S(t)$ to change the SSR, leaving the Level state variable unchanged at $L(t) = 5\%$ (hence, the neutral rate remains constant at 5%).

When the SSR is positive (i.e., a non-ZLB environment), the EMS increases by a constant value of nearly 0.8 percentage points for each 0.25 percentage point decrease in the SSR (the value will vary with the mean-reversion parameter ϕ). There are 40 0.25% decreases from 10% to 0%, which contributes $40 \times 0.8 = 32\%$ of change to the EMS. However, when the SSR moves below zero (a ZLB environment), the increase in the EMS for each further 0.25 decrease in the SSR is increasingly attenuated by the ZLB. For example, when the SSR is −5%, a decrease to −5.25% results in only about 0.4 percentage points increase in the EMS.

A decrease in the SSR when it is negative therefore still indicates more monetary stimulus, but the stimulus is increasingly attenuated in ZLB environments. That result is consistent with my suggestion that the SSR is best used as an ordinal rather than a cardinal measure. As a related aside, it would be mathematically straightforward to use the nonlinear relationship represented in Figure 7.16 to transform the SSR back into a cardinal or linear measure of monetary stimulus consistent with the FFR over the non-ZLB environment. However, such a transformation would presuppose that the EMS is the correct linear measure of monetary policy with respect to the macroeconomic data. Further empirical testing would be required to make that assessment. I include some indicative figures in the following section, but more comprehensive testing is beyond the scope of this book.

7.5.4 EMS summary

The discussion and results from this section suggest that EMS estimates from K-ANSMs should provide better measures of the stance of monetary policy than SSR estimates. From a theoretical perspective, the EMS summarizes both current and expected policy interest rates relative to an estimate of the neutral rate, and that entire gap should in principle influence the decisions of economic agents. From an empirical perspective, EMS estimates are more robust to different K-ANSM specifications than SSR estimates.

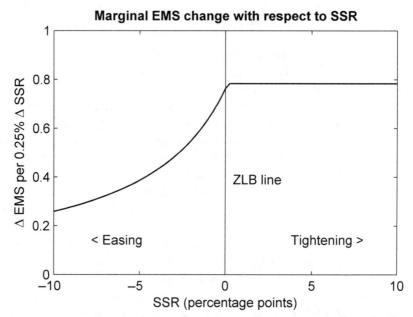

Figure 7.16 The change in the K-ANSM(2) EMS measure for 25 bp decreases in the SSR as a function of the starting values of the SSR on the x axis. The monetary stimulus from decreasing the SSR (i.e., moving from right to left on the x axis) is attenuated by the ZLB as the SSR moves through the ZLB to more negative values.

7.6 K-ANSM macrofinance relationships

In this section, I provide illustrations of relationships between estimated K-ANSM measures and macroeconomic variables, including currency rates. There are several interrelated motivations for this exercise:

- Using macroeconomic data should ultimately help improve the K-ANSM estimation and therefore the quantities derived from it. For example, Figure 7.17 indicates that surveyed long-horizon expectations of nominal output growth will provide information to improve the estimate of the K-ANSM Level state variable $L(t)$ and therefore the EMS.
- The K-ANSM quantities may help forecast macroeconomic variables. For example, Figure 7.18 indicates that relatively low levels of the EMS (i.e., indicative of restrictive monetary policy) may help forecast downturns in real output growth.
- K-ANSMs may provide a way of modeling yield curve data and macroeconomic data jointly as a parsimonious empirical macrofinance model. Such a joint model would potentially provide insights into the macroeconomy (e.g., expectations and measures of risk for macroeconomic variables such as inflation) and information on overall monetary conditions that would potentially be useful for the operation of monetary policy.

I note upfront that I intend the illustrations and discussions presented in this section to be suggestive only. I have not yet under taken any in-depth empirical analysis to fully test the ideas, but the results are encouraging enough to warrant following up in future research.

7.6.1   K-ANSM Level and long-horizon macroeconomic surveys

Panel 1 of Figure 7.17 illustrates the time series of the estimated monthly K-ANSM(2) Level state variable $L(t)$ and quarterly surveyed long-horizon expectations of nominal output growth. I have calculated the latter series using the Survey of Professional Forecasters expected average annual CPI inflation rate over the next 10 years compounded with the annual average real GDP growth rate over the next 10 years, both of which are available from December 1991.

The two series have similar levels, but there are some distinct differences between them at times, and the profile of long-horizon nominal output growth expectations is more stable than the estimate of $L(t)$. The $\mathbb{Q}$ measure, $\mathbb{P}$ measure, and risk premium discussion at the beginning of section 7.5 suggests that at least some of the differences between the two series should be explainable by time-varying risk premiums. For example, a possible explanation in term of risk premiums for the periods in which the main differences occur are as follows:

- Until around the mid-1990s, risk premiums were elevated but declining. This is consistent with markets transitioning from the 1980s, with relatively high inflation and inflation risks, into the 1980s, when inflation became relatively low and stable.
- Risk premiums dipped around the mid-2000s. This is consistent with the FOMC under Chairman Greenspan assuring markets that the tightening cycle beginning on Wednesday, June 30, 2004 (from the FFTR low of 1 percent set on Wednesday, June 25, 2003) would proceed at a measured pace.
- During the GFC, risk premiums spiked downward. This is consistent with investors' seeking the relative safety and liquidity of US Treasury securities.
- Risk premiums reduced markedly from when the FOMC first announced calendar forward guidance (the black dot), and reverted quickly to average levels after Chairman Bernanke foreshadowed the tapering of bond purchases under the QE3 program (the white dot). This is consistent with market participants first reducing their assessment of the potential for sharp unanticipated FFTR increases, and then reversing that assessment.

Panel 2 provides the results of an experimental estimation where I have also included the long-horizon macroeconomic survey data. Specifically, I have used the macroeconomic interpretation of the ANSM(2) Level and Slope state variables that I established in subsection 6.2.8 as the basis for constraining the K-ANSM(2) estimation so that the estimated state variables (under the $\mathbb{P}$ measure) are consistent

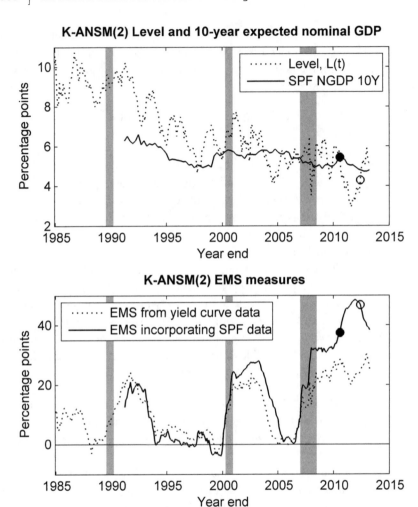

Figure 7.17 K-ANSM(3) Level state variable and long-horizon expectations of nominal output growth from the Survey of Professional Forecasters. These two series could be jointly modeled to improve the K-ANSM(3) estimates.

with the survey data, while also fitting the yield curve data (under the $\mathbb{Q}$ measure). The result is to smooth the Level state variable estimates relative to the Level estimates in panel 1, to something more similar to the survey data. The resulting EMS then adopts a more pronounced profile. In particular, the anomalies mentioned in subsection 7.5.2, where the EMS sometimes moves contrary to policy events, is resolved. Indeed, the EMS shows a further marked rise immediately after the Federal Reserve adopted calendar-based forward guidance, and a marked fall after Chairman Bernanke foreshadowed the tapering of QE3. In general, incorporating survey data, and other macroeconomic data, into a K-ANSM estimation should allow better estimates of the model and implied risk premiums.

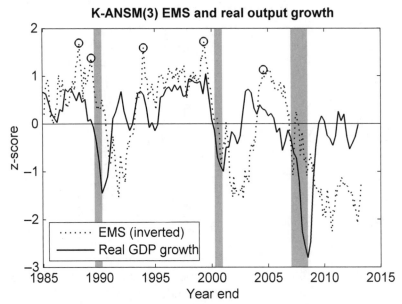

Figure 7.18 Peaks of the inverted K-ANSM(3) EMS, as indicated with white dots, indicate a restrictive stance of monetary policy. Low values of the EMS may therefore provide a useful leading indicator of downturns in real output growth.

Note that the potential analysis and discussions above are on a nominal basis, but they can all be decomposed into real and inflation components. Specifically, the survey data are already available as separate real output growth and inflation expectations, and inflation-indexed yield curve data would be required in addition to the nominal yield curve data to provide the real and inflation split for interest rates. For example, Carriero, Mouabbi, and Vangelista (2014) has already shown how to consistently model inflation-indexed and nominal yield curve data within a K-ANSM framework.

7.6.2 K-ANSM EMS and macroeconomic data

The illustrations in this and the following subsection are all based on K-ANSM(3) estimates of the EMS using the lower bound $r_L = 0.12\%$. However, the EMS estimates are very similar between all of the K-ANSM specifications discussed in section 7.1, so the results are representative for the range of different models.

Figure 7.18 illustrates the K-ANSM(3) EMS and annual real GDP growth. I have converted both series into z-scores, as I will do for all figures in this subsection, so that data series with different magnitudes are more easily comparable. I have also inverted the EMS for all figures so that higher (lower) values in the figures indicate a more restrictive (stimulatory) stance of policy.

Figure 7.18 illustrates monetary policy reactions to the real macroeconomic cycle, that is, an economic recession or downturn is followed by stimulatory monetary

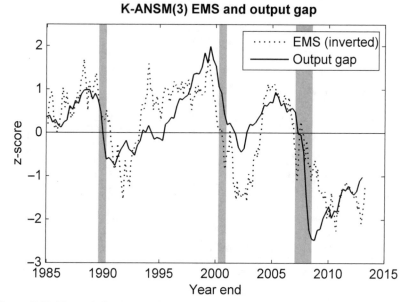

Figure 7.19 The cycle for the K-ANSM(3) EMS correlates well with the cycle for the output gap.

policy, and an economic expansion is followed by restrictive monetary policy. In addition, the peaks of the inverted EMS, which correspond to the most restrictive stances of monetary policy, appear to lead the economic recessions or downturns. This observation is consistent with a persistent empirical regularity that an inverted slope of the yield curve, often measured using the 10-year Treasury note rate less the 3-month Treasury bill rate, tends to lead recessions.

Figure 7.19 illustrates the K-ANSM(3) EMS and the output gap. This figure provides another perspective on the central bank reaction function to the real macroeconomic cycle discussed for Figure 7.18. That is, stimulatory monetary policy generally coincides with negative output gap, and restrictive monetary policy generally coincides with positive output gaps. According to the EMS, the magnitude of the stance of monetary policy over the ZLB environment seems broadly consistent with other economic cycles over the sample. The EMS did not initially fall as quickly as the output gap would suggest, but the size of the deviations appears to be typical of deviations over the earlier part of the sample.

Figure 7.20 illustrates the K-ANSM(3) EMS and annual PCE inflation (i.e., year-on-year growth in the Personal Consumption Expenditure deflator). I include this mainly for completeness. In principle, there should be some relationship between the stance of monetary policy as measured by the EMS and inflation. However, such relationships are not as apparent empirically, compared to Figures 7.18 and 7.19, partly because PCE inflation is a non-stationary series over the first part of the sample and perhaps because the influence of monetary policy on inflation is more subtle and variable than on real output growth. Nevertheless, work in progress with

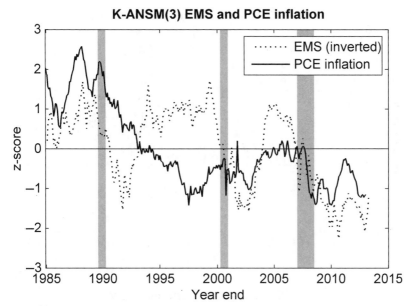

Figure 7.20 A more restrictive stance of monetary policy, as indicated by higher values of the inverted EMS, should lead to lower inflation outcomes. Work in progress at the time of writing indicates that the EMS delivers that result empirically.

a coauthor at the time of writing shows that restrictive (stimulatory) impulses to the EMS have led to statistically significant declines (increases) in future inflation. The same analysis with an FFTR/SSR series shows a typical "price puzzle" result, that is, restrictive (stimulatory) policy impulses have led to future increases (decreases) in inflation.

7.6.3 K-ANSM(3) EMS and currencies

In this subsection, I provide illustrations of how the EMS as a measure of monetary policy can potentially be applied to currency rates.

In panel 1 of each of the following figures, I have plotted EMS estimates, which I detail below, for pairs of countries, along with the difference or spread between the EMS estimates of the two countries. The EMS spread is intended to indicate the relative stance of monetary policy between the two countries. In panel 2 of each figure, I have plotted the EMS spread along with the logarithm of the nominal currency rate between the two countries.

The EMS spreads in Figures 7.21 to 7.23 are all expressed as the US EMS less the EMS in the other country. Hence, higher values of the EMS spreads indicate a more stimulatory stance of monetary policy in the United States relative to the other country. The currency levels all are expressed so that an increase corresponds to an appreciation of the currency for the given country relative to the US dollar.

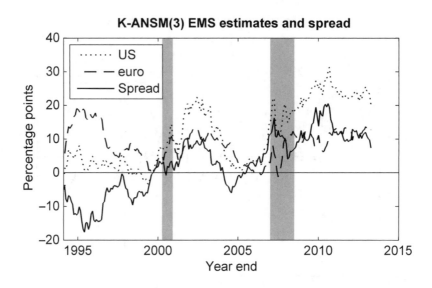

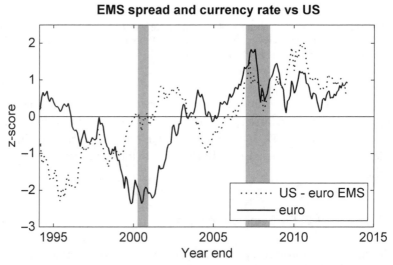

Figure 7.21 The relationship between the relative stance of monetary policy between the euro area and the United States, and the euro.

Finally, I have expressed the EMS spreads and the currency levels as a z-scores so that the relative relationships are easier to compare.

The EMS measures are obtained using the K-ANSM(3). To ensure maximum comparability for the estimations, in all cases (including the United States) I have used end-of-month Bloomberg government yield curve data over the period from January 1995 with the maturities 0.25, 0.5, 1, 2, 3, 5, 7, 10, and 30 years. The exception is the euro area, where no pan-European government bond exists. I have therefore used German government bond data until April 2008 and then euro-area

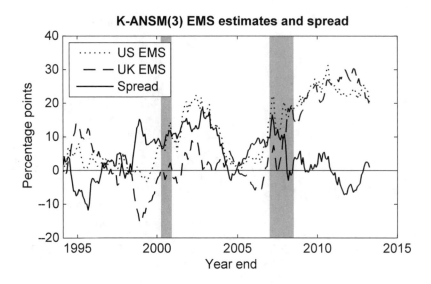

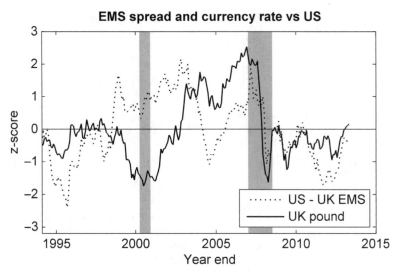

Figure 7.22 The relationship between the relative stance of monetary policy between the United Kingdom. and the United States, and the UK pound.

OIS rates from May 2008, when the full maturity span of data became available out to 30 years. The list of Bloomberg codes for the data series is F082, I0082, I018, F910, and EUSWE.

Empirically, the broad pattern for each currency is that a stronger (weaker) EMS spread relative to the long-term average correlates with a stronger (weaker) currency relative to the long-term average. That pattern is consistent with some of the stance of monetary policy in a given country being somewhat reflected in its currency. For example, the euro has remained elevated against the US dollar in the wake of the

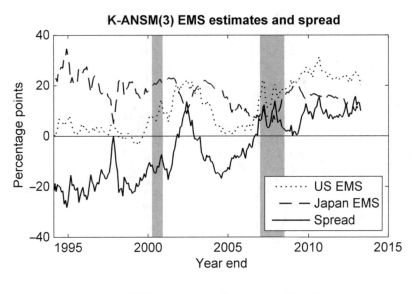

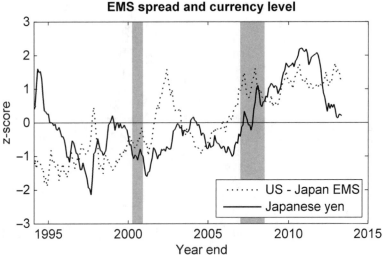

Figure 7.23 The relationship between the relative stance of monetary policy between Japan and the United States, and the Japanese yen.

GFC, consistent with the United States adopting more stimulatory monetary policy through conventional and unconventional means more quickly than Europe and retaining that relative stance since. Conversely, the UK pound has remained low against the US dollar, consistent with the relative stance of monetary policy being similar in both countries. However, the pattern obviously has substantial discrepancies in the first part of the sample for Europe and the United Kingdom, which highlights that the relative stance of monetary policy is not the singular most influential component of currency movements. For example, one influence up to the

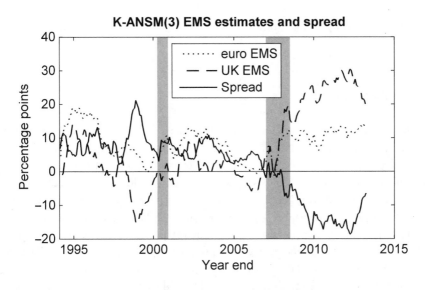

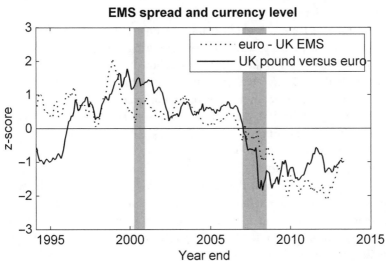

Figure 7.24 The relationship between the relative stance of monetary policy between euro area and the United Kingdom, and the UK pound versus the euro.

year 2000 was the inflow of capital to the United States during the dot-com bull market, and the US dollar also has a key role as a reserve currency. The Japanese yen will also be influenced by persistent inflation differentials against the United States.

Figure 7.24 arguably provides the cleanest cross-country comparison, because it compares the euro directly to the UK pound and therefore strips out any specific US dollar influences. Hence, the cycle in the UK pound versus the euro closely follows the cycle in the relative stance of monetary policy over the entire period. The exception is at the beginning of the sample, but that most likely reflects the legacy of the United Kingdom exiting the European Monetary System on September 16, 1992.

7.7 Summary

- In this chapter, I have undertaken a detailed assessment, from both theoretical and practical perspectives, of three different measures of the stance of monetary policy that are readily derived from estimated shadow term structures.

- The shadow short rate (SSR) is the shortest-maturity interest rate on the shadow yield curve, and so it is notionally like a central bank policy interest rate that can adopt negative values. However, negative SSRs are not theoretically compelling as a measure of the stance of monetary policy, because economic agents do not borrow and lend at negative interest rates in the "real world." Furthermore, SSR estimates are very sensitive in practice to modeling choices, including the number of state variables in the K-ANSM, the data used for estimation, and the estimation method.

- The Estimated Time to Zero (ETZ) provides an indication of how long the actual policy rate is expected to stay at zero before rising to positive levels. The ETZ is also quite robust when the model results allow it to be calculated consistently. However, the ETZ does not account for differences in the path of the actual short rate once it has become positive, and differences in the pace and ultimate expected level of the short rate should be important to the decisions of economic agents. It also does not have a value in a non-ZLB environment when the entire path of expected short rates is above zero.

- The Effective Monetary Stimulus (EMS) provides a measure of the current and the expected gap between the actual policy rate, determined as the truncated path of the expected SSR, and the estimated neutral rate. It is therefore a consistent measure over non-ZLB and ZLB environments that should be relevant to the decisions of economic agents. Empirically, EMS estimates are shown to be quite robust to modeling choices.

- I have provided illustrations of the EMS and macroeconomic variables, including currency rates. The results suggest potentially promising empirical relationships in all cases, but further work is needed to estimate and refine those relationships.

8 | Financial Market Applications

In this chapter, I discuss practical applications of shadow/ZLB-GATSMs within financial markets. In particular, I have selected two topics for which applying standard methods and GATSMs suitable for a non-ZLB environment would not be appropriate in a ZLB environment, and for which the shadow/ZLB-GATSMs can be used to bridge the gap. The first topic is the quantification of mark-to-market risk in fixed interest (or fixed income) portfolios, and the second topic is the pricing of options on bonds in a ZLB environment. Note that I mainly use K-ANSMs, that is, the Krippner (2011, 2012b,c, 2013d,e) framework with the arbitrage-free Nelson and Siegel (1987) model, to develop the frameworks in this chapter, but I will note how Black (1995) shadow/ZLB-GATSMs could generally be applied in the same context.

I begin in section 8.1 with an overview of the concepts of fixed interest portfolio risk, concentrating on risk factors or factor loadings for the yield curve and their associated factor duration measures. To provide the context of the subsequent two sections, I also introduce the difference between factor loadings and factor duration in non-ZLB and ZLB environments, notably the attenuation of the factor loadings once the ZLB becomes a constraint on the yield curve data.

In section 8.2, I develop a fixed interest portfolio risk framework applicable to non-ZLB environments based on the arbitrage-free Nelson and Siegel (1987) model, or ANSM, for the yield curve. Specifically, the ANSM Level, Slope, Bow, and higher-order components provide the factor loadings, and I show how to calculate the associated factor durations, and how to use those for fixed interest portfolio risk management. I provide a fully worked example of the framework for the ANSM with two state variables, or the ANSM(2), in section 8.3.

In section 8.4, I extend the ANSM fixed interest portfolio risk framework from section 8.2 into a framework suitable for ZLB environments using K-ANSMs. The ANSM components therefore effectively continue to provide the basis for the factor loadings and factor durations, but the Krippner framework provides the appropriate attenuation of those factor loadings and factor durations depending on the constraint from the ZLB. I provide a fully worked example of the framework for the two state variable K-ANSM, or K-ANSM(2), in section 8.5. This example will make the general points from section 8.4 clear. In particular, it shows that ignoring the ZLB is very detrimental to the standard metrics for risk measurement in fixed interest portfolios.

In section 8.6, I discuss how to price options on bonds in a ZLB environment. In particular, in subsection 8.6.1, I will first use the ANSM to illustrate that not allowing for the ZLB in the pricing model erroneously leads to positive prices for options on bonds even with a strike price of 1 or more, that is, prices generated by zero or negative interest rates. In section 8.6.2, I then show how K-ANSMs can be applied to allow for the ZLB.

8.1 Fixed interest portfolio risk

In this section, I provide an overview of the concepts of fixed interest portfolio risk to provide the context for sections 8.2 and 8.3. In particular, I begin with a brief general introduction to risk quantification in financial market portfolios and then progress in subsection 8.1.2 to fixed interest portfolio risk in non-ZLB environments from the perspective of factor loadings and factor durations. In subsection 8.1.3, I provide an initial indication of the key differences that arise for fixed interest portfolio risk in ZLB environments.

Note that my overview in this section is brief but self-contained with respect to this book, given the objective is to provide the context for the more detailed development of factor loadings and factor durations in sections 8.2 and 8.3. Of course, the overall management of fixed interest portfolios and the associated risk spans multiple topics beyond duration measures, and the associated literature is huge. I have found that the references Veronesi (2010) and Tuckman and Serrat (2012) that I occasionally cite below provide good summaries of the overall topic.

8.1.1 Security and portfolio risk

Quantifying the risk of any financial asset or security requires a measure of the potential for unanticipated changes to the mark-to-market value of that asset. By unanticipated changes I mean a probability distribution for the component of potential changes in value that is unforecastable given current information. Active managers may consider there is some forecastable component, while passive managers essentially believe there is none, although both will nevertheless agree that financial markets are dominated by unpredictable changes, at least over short and medium horizons. By mark-to-market value I mean the quoted market price of the asset if it is traded freely in financial markets and can be directly observed, or otherwise the implicit price that can be inferred from the quoted prices of comparable securities. I do not model default risk specifically, but even that aspect can be accommodated with a suitable distribution of the probability of default and the likely recovery of value from a financial asset given a default event.

Portfolio risk is in turn the sum of potential unanticipated changes in the mark-to-market value of each of the securities in the portfolio, including any diversification benefits due to imperfect correlations between the unanticipated changes to security values. Often the potential unanticipated changes for individual securities and their correlations can be adequately summarized using just several risk factors. By risk factors I mean representative variables that may influence in a systematic way the prices of all securities in the portfolio (e.g., inflation risk on equities and bonds), the prices of broad classes of securities (e.g., equity market or bond market risks), and/or the prices of subclasses of assets within a portfolio (e.g. the default risk on all the government bonds for a single country). The risk factors are typically informed by theoretical considerations and/or empirical analysis, and historical data is used gauge their probability distributions and correlations with other risk factors.

8.1.2 Fixed interest security and portfolio risk in non-ZLB environments

Within portfolios of fixed interest securities, one set of risk factors is how the interest rates of different securities change simultaneously depending on their times to maturity. In particular, the unanticipated changes to interest rates, and therefore the associated unanticipated changes to the prices of the associated interest rate securities and the value of the whole fixed interest portfolio, are typically found to be well explained empirically by three risk factors (indeed, almost entirely by two, as I discuss further below).

The most commonly used risk factor for fixed interest portfolio risk is based on the potential for equal unanticipated changes to the interest rates of all maturities. In yield curve terminology, such a change would be denoted a Level shift, or a shift in the Level component of the yield curve. Duration, or what I more precisely denote Level duration, is a commonly used measure to quantify the risk from an unanticipated Level shift to the yield curve. Level duration multiplied by a Level shift expresses the approximate change in the value of individual securities and/or the portfolio that would occur for that given Level shift. Applying the historical probability distribution of unanticipated shifts of the Level component to the Level duration will therefore provide a measure of potential unanticipated changes to the fixed interest portfolio, or in other words a measure of fixed interest portfolio risk. That risk could be expressed in many ways, but common examples are Value at Risk (VaR) or expected shortfall, in which the analysis would provide a result such as "there is a 1 percent probability of a loss of x dollars or more from an unanticipated change to the Level component of the yield curve over the next month" (or sometimes the loss would be expressed as a percentage of the portfolio value). Tracking error is a similar concept, but the VaR is relative to an index rather than absolute.

Unanticipated changes to the yield curve other than Level shifts are also common. For example, while changes to shorter-maturity interest rates are almost always in the same direction as longer-maturity interest rates, movements in short-maturity interest rates are typically larger than longer-maturity interest rates. In yield curve terminology, such a change relative to the Level shift would be denoted a Slope shift, or a shift in the Slope component of the yield curve. Similarly, sometimes mid-maturity interest rates can change by more or less than movements in the Level and Slope components would suggest, in which case that could be represented by a shift in the Bow component of the yield curve.

All of the potential Level, Slope, and Bow shifts to the yield curve are expressible as functions of time to maturity, which are known as factor loadings. Each factor loading can be used to calculate an associated duration measure, or a factor duration, which provides the approximate change in the portfolio value given a shift in that particular factor loading. Hence, the potential changes to Level, Slope, and Bow components, as discussed above, would produce Level, Slope, and Bow durations. The joint distribution of potential changes to the Level, Slope, and Bow components, including correlations, would then provide the basis for calculating risk measures for fixed interest portfolios.

I will formalize the concepts discussed above in the ANSM risk framework in section 8.2, and for the ANSM(2) as a fully worked example in section 8.3. However, it is worthwhile mentioning that the basic principles I have described may be applied in various contexts with similar results. For example, Veronesi (2010) in chapters 3 and 4 presents examples of factor loadings and factor durations based on linear functions of time to maturity obtained from representative short-, mid-, and long-maturity interest rates. Veronesi (2010) and Tuckman and Serrat (2012) also show how principle components can be used to generate yield curve factor loadings, and factor durations can be generated for each principle component.

Principal components, in brief, is a statistical technique based on an eigensystem decomposition of the covariance matrix for a time series of cross-sectional data, for example, yield curve data.[1] When applied to a yield curve data set, principal components provides functions of time to maturity that best describe the variance in the yield curve data set across time and the times to maturity in the yield curve data set. A subset of those principal components, typically the first three, essentially capture all of the empirical variation in any yield curve data set. That subset of principal components can be used as factor loadings to provide factor durations for risk management.

To illustrate an example of principal component results, Figure 8.1 provides the first three principal components for the non-ZLB part of my yield curve data set. The amounts of variance captured respectively by the first three principle components in Figure 8.1 are 92.21%, 7.16%, and 0.47%, for a total of 99.84%.

To compare the principal components to ANSM factors, Figure 8.2 provides the Level, Slope, and Bow components for the ANSM(3). While the absolute values for each component are different, the shapes are very similar. Therefore, either set of factor loadings would be essentially within a linear combination of each other.

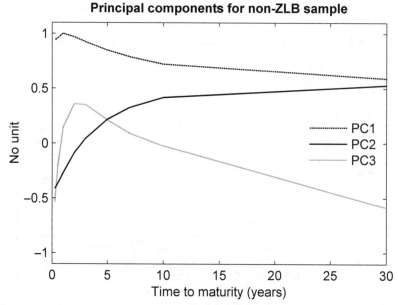

Figure 8.1 The first three principal components (PCs) for the non-ZLB part of the yield curve data set. The shapes are similar to the ANSM(3) factor loadings in Figure 8.2.

That means either principal components or the ANSM factor loadings will essentially provide the same representation of the data for fixed interest risk-management purposes, at least over non-ZLB environments.

Similarly, Diebold, Ji, and Li (2006) have proposed using Level, Slope, and Bow functions from the Nelson and Siegel (1987) model for fixed interest portfolio risk management. The Nelson and Siegel (1987) model is the non-arbitrage-free analogue to the ANSM framework that I present in section 8.2, and so the Diebold, Ji, and Li (2006) framework would be very similar to the framework I propose. Willner (1996) is a related application based on Nelson and Siegel (1987) components.

In summary, in non-ZLB environments, either principal components, the Nelson and Siegel (1987) factor loadings, or the ANSM could be used to provide very similar frameworks for fixed interest portfolio risk management.

That said, the ANSM framework has several distinct advantages over the other frameworks even in non-ZLB environments:

- Estimated ANSMs already provide the necessary factor loadings and parameters for a complete risk model:

  - The Level, Slope, and Bow factor loadings from the estimation already provide the main ways in which unanticipated changes to the yield curve can occur. Because the factor loadings are simple functions of time to maturity, the factor durations are easily calculated and are also simple functions of time to maturity.

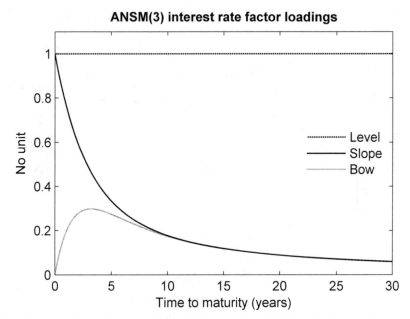

Figure 8.2 The Level, Slope, and Bow factor loadings for ANSM(3) interest rates. The shapes are similar to the first three principal components in Figure 8.1.

- The covariance matrix for the ANSM state variables from the estimation already provides the full probability distribution for translating the factor durations into an overall distribution of portfolio risk.

- ANSMs are specified in continuous time, so the factor durations can be calculated for any time to maturity. Principal components generally requires "bucketing" securities around the times to maturity from the data set used to obtain the principal components.

- The Level duration for the ANSM is precisely equivalent to the most common and popular duration calculation that is itself based on a constant shift to all interest rates. The first principal component is typically similar to a Level shift, but its origin from a statistical method means that it describes a yield curve change that is not exactly constant by time to maturity.

- ANSMs provide a consistent treatment of interest rate volatilities and risk premiums. Therefore, bond options and convexity can both be added to the ANSM framework in a model-consistent manner as required. The Nelson and Siegel (1987) model as the non-arbitrage-free analogue to the ANSM framework does not allow for bond options.

8.1.3 Fixed interest security and portfolio risk in ZLB environments

The use of factor loadings and factor durations in fixed interest portfolio risk management is implicitly based on the assumption that the factor loadings will remain approximately constant over the sample period. In other words, so long as one expects that unanticipated variations in the observed yield curve will be reasonably explained by shifts in the factor loadings being employed, then the durations for those factor loadings and the historical distributions of changes to the factor loadings can be used to provide an approximate gauge of fixed interest portfolio risk.

Unfortunately, in ZLB environments, movements in the yield curve will be constrained by the ZLB, which therefore affects how yields are likely to move as a function of time to maturity. One effect is that short-maturity and perhaps mid-maturity interest rates can only rise and not fall, and so that introduces an asymmetry of potential yield curve movements. However, a much more significant effect is the stickiness of short-maturity and mid-maturity interest rates. That stickiness arises from expectations that the short rate will stay at zero for an extended period of time. Such expectations therefore result in limited scope for any movements in short-maturity and mid-maturity interest rates in a ZLB environment relative to a non-ZLB environment, where the short rate can essentially evolve freely from its current value. The limited movement in short- and mid-maturity interest rates can also influence the movements in longer-maturity interest rates.

The change in potential movements of interest rates depending on their time to maturity in turn affects the factor loadings that are appropriate to represent potential shifts in the yield curve. For example, Figure 8.3 illustrates the first three principal components extracted from my yield curve data set over the ZLB environment, that is, December 2008 to the March 2014 end of the sample. The variances explained by these three principal components are respectively 94.08%, 5.42%, and 0.38%, for a total of 99.87%. This compares to the 99.84% for the first three principal components from Figure 8.1. However, it is clear that the ZLB principal components provide very different factor loadings relative to the non-ZLB principal components, with one notable feature being the attenuation of all the factor loadings for short maturities. In particular, the ZLB principal components are not within a linear combination of the non-ZLB principal components, so the potential yield curve shifts are very different between the non-ZLB and ZLB environments.

Therefore, the principal components obtained from historical data covering the non-ZLB period will no longer provide an adequate basis for gauging fixed interest portfolio risk. One might consider using principal components calculated from data within the ZLB environment. However, the issue is more nuanced than that simple suggestion. Specifically, the movements in the interest rates for different times to maturity in a ZLB environment are actually a function of the degree of constraint that the ZLB provides along the whole yield curve. Therefore, the principal components will change at each point of the ZLB sample period.

The K-ANSM framework provides a convenient way of illustrating how the factor loadings vary with the ZLB constraint. The ANSM representation for the shadow yield curve uses the time-invariant factor loadings already illustrated in Figure 8.2, and the Krippner framework provides a model-consistent way of attenuating the

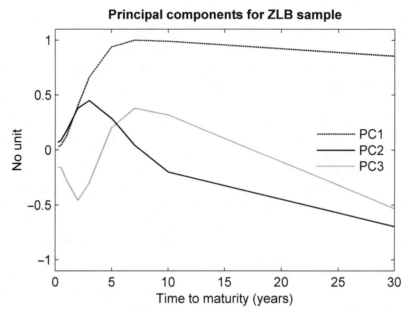

Figure 8.3 The first three principal components (PCs) for the ZLB part of the yield curve data set. The shapes are very different to the principal components and ANSM(3) factor loadings in Figures 8.1 and 8.2.

ANSM factor loadings for the constraint from the ZLB. I provide the details in section 8.4, but Figure 8.4 illustrates the idea using the K-ANSM(2) Level and Slope factor loadings for three different periods within the ZLB environment. Note that I have just used the Level and Slope factor loadings here because it relates to the fully worked examples I will develop in the remaining sections of this chapter. Using just two yield curve components is mainly for clarity in developing and illustrating the risk framework, but I also mention extensions to include the Bow component. However, the principal component results also show that two factor loadings explain more than 99% of the variance, so two yield curve components should provide a practical and parsimonious risk framework that is useful in its own right.

Compared to the non-ZLB environment example of ANSM interest rate factor loadings in Figure 8.2, all of the ZLB environment examples in Figure 8.4 show a marked attenuation of potential movements in the yield curve. In December 2008, the attenuation of both the Level and Slope factor loadings was mainly limited to shorter-maturity interest rates. By July 2011, the attenuation in both factor loadings was notable for short- and mid-maturity interest rates. By July 2012, where the ZLB constraint was largest (i.e., long-maturity interest rates were at record lows), the attenuation was very marked across all maturities. Richard (2013) provides related analysis and discussion on the variation in the Level duration and convexities based on a GATSM within a Black (1995) framework.

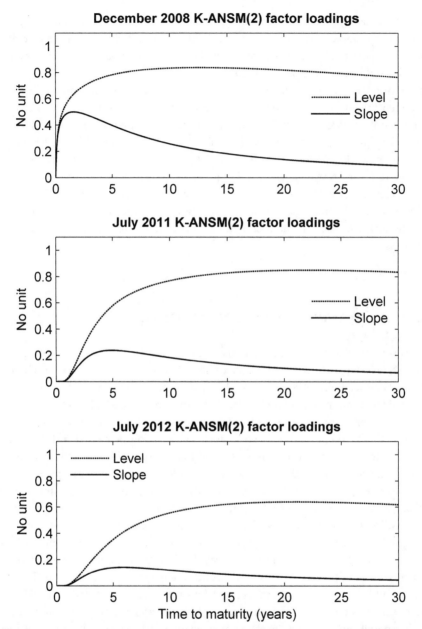

Figure 8.4 The Level and Slope factor loadings for ANSM(2) interest rates attenutated using the Krippner ZLB framework. The factor loadings change substantially depending on the degree of constraint from the ZLB.

Principal components could not be used to reliably replicate the variation in the factor loadings illustrated in Figure 8.4. Trying to do so would require using shorter subperiods within the ZLB environment to obtain principal components that relate to particular windows of time. However, because principal components are statistical estimates, shorter subperiods would leave the results subject to larger random variance. Therefore, the genuine ZLB constraint effect trying to be determined using principal components would be masked by random variance, and the result would be an unreliable risk framework.

In summary, a risk framework that applies to both non-ZLB and ZLB environments needs to accommodate how the interest rate factor loadings can change between those two environments and within the ZLB environment depending on the degree of constraint from the ZLB. The K-ANSM framework provides such a risk framework, as I discuss in sections 8.4 and 8.5. However, I first detail a risk framework for ANSMs. The exposition for ANSMs provides an illustration of standard metrics for risk in non-ZLB environments. It also enables the K-ANSM risk framework to be introduced as a straightforward modification to the ANSM risk framework, and then the non-ZLB and ZLB risk frameworks to be compared and contrasted.

8.2   A risk framework based on ANSMs

In this section, I develop a general fixed interest portfolio risk framework based on ANSMs. Subsection 8.2.1 introduces how term structure shifts are represented in an ANSM, and in subsection 8.2.2, I derive the general expression for calculating ANSM factor durations. Subsection 8.2.3 discusses how the ANSM factor durations can be used for risk measurement and management in fixed interest portfolios.

Note that throughout this chapter, I focus on duration as the first-order approximation to fixed interest portfolio risk, and I also assume instantaneous unanticipated changes to the yield curve and state variables. As detailed in Krippner (2005), it is relatively straightforward to generalize the ANSM framework to unanticipated changes that occur as time evolves, and to extend the assessment of risk and return in ANSMs to convexity, active factor duration and convexity management (i.e., targeted exposure to particular yield curve factors, if desired), fair-value mean-reversion, and portfolio optimization. While all of these topics are important in their own right, the additional notation and discussion required would be lengthy and would risk obscuring the main point I want to make about factor durations as the primary metrics for risk measurement in fixed interest portfolios. Therefore, I will generally not mention the other topics again except briefly if the context arises, and I refer readers to Krippner (2005) for further details.

The risk framework I develop for ANSMs applies equally to stationary GATSMs, which are discussed in subsection 3.3.4. The only change required is to replace the ANSM term structure expressions with the stationary GATSM term structure expressions. However, stationary GATSMs only have a persistent yield curve component with a slow decay rather than a pure Level component like ANSMs. Therefore, stationary GATSMs, like principal components, do not have a component that precisely describes a yield curve change that is constant by time to maturity, and so stationary GATSMs cannot replicate Level duration.

8.2.1 ANSM term structure shifts

From section 3.1, interest rates as a function of time to maturity in the ANSM are

$$R[x(t),\tau] = a(\tau) + [b(\tau)]' x(t) \tag{8.1}$$

where $a(\tau)$ is a scalar function, $b(\tau)$ is the $N \times 1$ vector of interest rate factor loadings, and $x(t)$ is the $N \times 1$ state variable vector. Note that I have explicitly denoted the dependence of $R[x(t),\tau]$ on the state variable vector $x(t)$ for clarity in what follows. The general expressions for $a(\tau)$ and $b(\tau)$ are contained in chapter 3.1, but are not needed for the exposition in this section. The ANSM(2) example in section 8.3 will provide an example of their form.

The first three interest rate factor loadings for ANSMs have already been illustrated in Figure 8.2, that is, the Level, Slope, and Bow, and the results in section 3.5 show that these factor loadings generally provide a good representation of any yield curve observation in non-ZLB environments. Therefore, Level, Slope, and Bow interest rate factor loadings also provide a good representation of the changes to the yield curve. Specifically, in notation, if the state variable vector $x(t)$ undergoes an arbitrary instantaneous change represented by the $N \times 1$ vector Δx, then the new yield curve will be

$$R[x(t)+\Delta x,\tau] = a(\tau) + [b(\tau)]' [x(t)+\Delta x] \tag{8.2}$$

and the change in the yield curve will be

$$R[x(t)+\Delta x,\tau] - R[x(t),\tau] = [b(\tau)]' \Delta x \tag{8.3}$$

For example, with $\Delta x = [0.50\%, 0, 0]'$ for a three-state-variable ANSM, the Level state variable would rise by 0.50 percentage points without any change to the Slope and Bow state variables. Therefore, the interest rates for all maturities would become 0.50 percentage points higher. I illustrate such a Level shift in section 8.3.1 for the ANSM(2), along with an ANSM(2) Slope shift.

8.2.2 ANSM factor durations

I will define the factor duration vector as

$$D(t,\tau) = -\frac{d}{dx(t)} P[x(t),\tau] \tag{8.4}$$

where $D(t,\tau)$ is a $N \times 1$ vector, $x(t)$ is the $N \times 1$ state variable vector, and $P[x(t),\tau]$ is the scalar ANSM bond price as a function of the state variable vector $x(t)$ and time to maturity τ. I provide the expression for $P[x(t),\tau]$ shortly below.

Equation 8.4 is equivalent to standard expressions for factor durations (e.g., see Veronesi [2010, pp. 84–5 and 132–37], but for clarity, it is worthwhile explaining several aspects. First, I use the derivative of $P[x(t),\tau]$ with respect to the state variable vector $x(t)$ to directly produce a duration vector for the different yield curve factors. The equivalent alternative would be to take the derivative of $P[x(t),\tau]$ with respect to each state variable $x_n(t)$ separately, as in Veronesi (2010), and stack those results into the duration vector. Second, my notation $D(t,\tau)$ explicitly denotes that the factor duration vector in general varies over time t and time to maturity τ, even in non-ZLB environments. Third, my definition is already expressed directly in dollar terms rather than in relative or percentage terms. Specifically, my definition is equivalent to so-called "dollar duration" in the terminology of Veronesi (2010), or equivalently the "dollar value of an 01," or DV01, in the terminology of Tuckman and Serrat (2012, chapter 4). Basis point value, or BPV, is another common term used in financial markets. Dividing by the bond price would provide the relative or percentage duration expression, $D(t,\tau)/P[x(t),\tau]$. However, I find the (dollar) factor duration expressions more convenient, not least because the total factor duration of a series of cashflows is then simply the weighted average (by face-value) of the duration vector for each individual cashflow. By contrast, relative duration measures cannot be added directly, and so are a little less easy to manipulate.

For ANSMs, the price of a zero-coupon bond $P[x(t),\tau]$ at time t with a time to maturity τ and a final payoff of 1 is

$$P[x(t),\tau] = \exp(-\tau \cdot R[x(t),\tau]) \tag{8.5}$$

where $R[x(t),\tau]$, is the interest rate at time t with a time to maturity τ, as defined in the previous subsection, and I have again explicitly denoted the dependence of $P[x(t),\tau]$ on the state variable vector $x(t)$ for clarity in what follows.

To see how the duration vector arises, consider the ANSM bond price after a yield curve shift Δx to original state variable vector $x(t)$:

$$P[x(t)+\Delta x,\tau] = \exp(-\tau \cdot R[x(t)+\Delta x,\tau])$$

The new bond price $P[x(t)+\Delta x,\tau]$ may be approximated to arbitrary precision with a Taylor expansion around $x(t)$. The duration vector is the first-order differential required for the first-order Taylor approximation:

$$P[x(t)+\Delta x,\tau] \simeq P[x(t),\tau] + \left[\frac{d}{dx(t)}P[x(t),\tau]\right]\Delta x$$
$$= \exp(-\tau \cdot R[x(t),\tau])$$
$$+ \left[\frac{d}{dx(t)}\exp(-\tau \cdot R[x(t),\tau])\right]\Delta x \tag{8.6}$$

The first-order approximation of the change in the zero-coupon bond price for the instantaneous change Δx in the state variable vector is therefore

$$P[x(t),\tau] - P[x(t)+\Delta x,\tau] \simeq -\left[\frac{d}{dx(t)}\exp(-\tau \cdot R[x(t),\tau])\right]\Delta x$$

$$= D(t,\tau)\Delta x \tag{8.7}$$

$D(t,\tau)$ is an $N \times 1$ duration vector that may be calculated explicitly as follows:

$$D(t,\tau) = -\frac{d}{dx(t)}\exp(-\tau \cdot R[x(t),\tau])$$

$$\langle \text{Chain rule} \rangle = -\frac{d}{dR[x(t),\tau]}\exp(-\tau \cdot R[x(t),\tau])\left(\frac{d}{dx(t)}R[x(t),\tau]\right)$$

$$= \tau \cdot \exp(-\tau \cdot R[x(t),\tau])\, b(\tau)$$

$$= \tau \cdot P[x(t),\tau]\, b(\tau) \tag{8.8}$$

where I have used a standard matrix differentiation result (e.g., see Greene [1997, p. 51]) to obtain the derivative of $R[x(t),\tau]$ with respect to $x(t)$, that is,

$$\frac{d}{dx(t)}R[x(t),\tau] = \frac{d}{dx(t)}a(\tau) + \frac{d}{dx(t)}[b(\tau)]'x(t)$$

$$= 0 + b(\tau) \tag{8.9}$$

The expression $D(t,\tau)$ is used to evaluate the duration vector for any single cashflow. The duration vector for multiple cashflows, such as a coupon-paying security and/or a fixed interest portfolio with multiple securities, is the weighted sum of the cashflows:

$$D_{\text{Port.}}(t) = \sum_{k=1}^{K}CF(t,\tau_k)D(t,\tau_k) \tag{8.10}$$

where $D_{\text{Port.}}(t)$ is the total duration, $CF(\tau_k)$ is the cashflow associated with the time to maturity τ_k, and $D(t,\tau_k)$ is the duration vector associated with the time to maturity τ_k.

8.2.3 ANSM fixed interest portfolio risk

Using the distribution of potential unanticipated changes in the state variable vector Δx along with the duration vector $D(t,\tau)$ provides the basis for obtaining an approximate distribution of potential unanticipated value changes. A model-consistent estimate of the distribution of Δx is already available from the ANSM model specification and estimated parameters. Specifically, from section 3.1, the instantaneous annualized variance of $x(t+\tau)$ conditional on $x(t)$ is

$$\widetilde{\mathrm{var}}_t\left[x(t+\tau)\,|\,x(t)\right] = \int_0^{\Delta t} \exp\left(-\tilde{\kappa}u\right)\sigma\sigma'\exp\left(-\tilde{\kappa}'u\right)\mathrm{d}u \tag{8.11}$$

For relatively short horizons, $\exp\left(-\tilde{\kappa}u\right) \simeq I$, the $N \times N$ identity matrix, and so $\widetilde{\mathrm{var}}_t\left[x(t+\tau)\,|\,x(t)\right]$ may be more conveniently expressed as

$$\widetilde{\mathrm{var}}_t\left[x(t+\tau)\,|\,x(t)\right] \simeq \int_0^{\Delta t} \sigma\sigma'\,\mathrm{d}u$$

$$= \sigma\sigma'\Delta t \tag{8.12}$$

The approximate distribution of unanticipated changes in the value of the portfolio, which I will call the Risk Distribution or Risk Dist., is therefore

$$\text{Risk Dist.} \simeq \mathrm{N}\left\{0,\sigma_{\mathrm{D}}^2\right\} \tag{8.13}$$

where $\mathrm{N}\{\cdot,\cdot\}$ is the normal distribution with a mean of zero, and σ_{D}^2 is the variance:

$$\sigma_{\mathrm{D}}^2 = [\mathrm{D_{Port.}}(t)]'\sigma\sigma'\mathrm{D_{Port.}}(t) \cdot \Delta t \tag{8.14}$$

The Risk Distribution can then be translated into any of the standard forms to express fixed interest portfolio risk, such as Value at Risk (VaR) or expected shortfall.

Note that there are three main sources of approximation in the Risk Distribution expression I have given. I make those approximation sources explicit here for clarity, and also to indicate how improvements could be made:

- The first-order Taylor approximation. This approximation is often sufficient for many practical applications, but it deteriorates progressively for larger potential unanticipated changes to the yield curve Δx. Larger values of Δx are in turn a function of the variance matrix $\sigma\sigma'$ (i.e., larger state variable variances produce larger potential yield curve shifts) and the time to maturity τ (i.e., the yield curve can potentially evolve to more extreme values over longer times). Using a second-order Taylor approximation (i.e., three terms of the Taylor expansion) would provide a much closer approximation. The second-order approximation is the basis for factor convexities, which would require an $N \times N$ convexity matrix for a complete treatment (see Krippner [2005] for further details).
- The matrix exponential approximation $\exp\left(-\tilde{\kappa}u\right) \simeq I$. For longer horizons, the attenuation of $\exp\left(-\tilde{\kappa}u\right)$ would need to be accounted for. At the same time, longer horizons are also subject to larger unanticipated changes to the yield

curve, and so an allowance for convexity as discussed in the previous point would likely be required.

- The normal distribution assumption. The normal distribution is consistent with the specification of the ANSM, and it is also very easy to manipulate to obtain risk expressions in practice. However, assuming a normal distribution is often inappropriate for relatively short horizons (e.g., one day, one week, or one month) because unanticipated interest rate changes generally have higher probabilities of extreme movements than implied by the normal distribution. Therefore, a better way of generating the Risk Distribution in practice is to use the actual unanticipated changes to $x(t)$, that is, the residuals ε_t from the original model estimation, and sample from those with replacement to obtain an empirical distribution for Δx (e.g., see Hull [2002, p. 356]).

These are all straightforward extensions of the basic framework and examples that I present. However, they are not central to the main points I want to make in this book, so I do not discuss them further.

8.3 Worked example: ANSM(2)

In this section, I provide a fully worked example using the ANSM(2), which will illustrate the points from the previous section. I begin with examples of how unanticipated changes to interest rates may be represented using the Level and Slope state variables and factor loadings for the ANSM(2) yield curve. In subsection 8.3.2, I detail the duration vector calculation for the ANSM(2).

In subsections 8.3.3 and 8.3.4, I provide numerical results to illustrate that the Level and Slope durations provide a close approximation to the changes in the values of the securities and the portfolio as a whole. The securities I use for this exposition are four zero-coupon bonds with times to maturity of $\tau_1 = 1$, $\tau_2 = 3$, $\tau_3 = 10$, and $\tau_4 = 30$ years, and each with a face-value of 1 (i.e., a cashflow of 1 at the time of maturity).

In subsection 8.3.5, I illustrate how the duration vector results may be combined with the variance parameters for the ANSM(2) state variables to provide an approximate distribution of unanticipated changes to portfolio value. I finish in section 8.3.6 with a brief overview of how the ANSM(2) can be extended to the ANSM(3) for duration calculations and risk management.

8.3.1 ANSM(2) yield curve shifts

The ANSM(2) uses just two components, Level and Slope, to represent the yield curve. Therefore $N = 2$, and from chapter 3 the state variable vector and the factor loading vector for the ANSM(2) are

$$x(t) = \begin{bmatrix} L(t) \\ S(t) \end{bmatrix}; \quad b(\tau) = \begin{bmatrix} 1 \\ \frac{1}{\tau} G(\phi, \tau) \end{bmatrix} \tag{8.15}$$

where

$$G(\phi, \tau) = \frac{1}{\phi} \left[1 - \exp(-\phi\tau) \right] \tag{8.16}$$

with $\phi = 0.2789$ (for my examples), which is the Slope mean-reversion parameter. ANSM(2) interest rates are therefore

$$R[x(t), \tau] = a(\tau) + [b(\tau)]' x(t)$$

$$= a(\tau) + \left[1, \frac{1}{\tau} G(\phi, \tau) \right]' \begin{bmatrix} L(t) \\ S(t) \end{bmatrix}$$

$$= a(\tau) + L(t) + S(t) \cdot \frac{1}{\tau} G(\phi, \tau) \tag{8.17}$$

where $a(\tau)$ is a scalar function of time to maturity:

$$a(\tau) = -\sigma_L^2 \cdot \frac{1}{6} \tau^2 - \sigma_S^2 \cdot \frac{1}{2\phi^2} \left[1 - \frac{1}{\tau} G(\phi, \tau) - \frac{1}{2\tau} \phi [G(\phi, \tau)]^2 \right]$$

$$- \rho \sigma_L \sigma_S \cdot \frac{1}{\phi^2} \left[1 - \frac{1}{\tau} G(\phi, \tau) + \frac{1}{2} \phi\tau - \phi G(\phi, \tau) \right] \tag{8.18}$$

with $\sigma_L = 0.8612\%$, $\sigma_S = 1.6032\%$, and $\rho_{LS} = -0.5140$, which are the state variable standard deviation and correlation parameters.

Figure 8.5 provides an example of a yield curve using the ANSM(2) functional form for $R[x(t), \tau]$ and the state variable vector:

$$x(t) = \begin{bmatrix} L(t) \\ S(t) \end{bmatrix} = \begin{bmatrix} 5.55\% \\ -3.68\% \end{bmatrix} \tag{8.19}$$

The shadow short rate is 1.87% and all interest rates are above zero, so the example is suitable for a non-ZLB illustration. In Figure 8.5, I have also indicated the ANSM(2) interest rates for the four maturities $\tau_1 = 1$, $\tau_2 = 3$, $\tau_3 = 10$, and $\tau_4 = 30$ years that I use for my numerical examples.

Shifts to the ANSM(2) yield curve, Δx, also use just two components and result in a new state variable vector $x(t) + \Delta x$. In general, simultaneous arbitrary instantaneous shift to both the Level and Slope components would be represented as an instantaneous shift Δx to the state variable vector $x(t)$:

$$x(t) + \Delta x = \begin{bmatrix} L(t) \\ S(t) \end{bmatrix} + \begin{bmatrix} \Delta L \\ \Delta S \end{bmatrix} \tag{8.20}$$

which would result in the new interest rate curve:

$$R[x(t) + \Delta x, \tau] = a(\tau) + \left[1, \frac{1}{\tau}G(\phi, \tau)\right]' \left[\begin{array}{c} L(t) + \Delta L \\ S(t) + \Delta S \end{array}\right]$$

$$= a(\tau) + [L(t) + \Delta L]$$

$$+ [S(t) + \Delta S] \cdot \frac{1}{\tau}G(\phi, \tau) \qquad (8.21)$$

Or more directly, the change in the yield curve would be

$$R[x(t) + \Delta x, \tau] - R[x(t), \tau] = \left[1, \frac{1}{\tau}G(\phi, \tau)\right]' \left[\begin{array}{c} \Delta L \\ \Delta S \end{array}\right]$$

$$= \Delta L + \Delta S \cdot \frac{1}{\tau}G(\phi, \tau) \qquad (8.22)$$

For clarity, I use separate pure Level and Slope shifts in my examples, specifically a 0.50% change to the Level state variable and a 1.50% change to the Slope state variable. In terms of Δx, these Level and Slope shifts are defined respectively as

$$\Delta x_L = \left[\begin{array}{c} 0.50\% \\ 0\% \end{array}\right]; \quad \Delta x_S = \left[\begin{array}{c} 0\% \\ 1.50\% \end{array}\right] \qquad (8.23)$$

Figure 8.5 plots the base yield curve with instantaneous shifts in the Level and Slope components. Specifically, panel 1 contains 0.50% shifts in the Level component of the base yield curve, which are obtained with the instantaneous change vector Δx_L as follows:

$$x(t) \pm \Delta x_L = \left[\begin{array}{c} 5.55\% \\ -3.68\% \end{array}\right] \pm \left[\begin{array}{c} 0.50\% \\ 0\% \end{array}\right]$$

$$= \left[\begin{array}{c} 6.05\% \\ -3.68\% \end{array}\right] \text{ and } \left[\begin{array}{c} 5.05\% \\ -3.68\% \end{array}\right]$$

Panel 2 contains 1.50% shifts in the Slope component of the base yield curve, which are obtained with the instantaneous change vector Δx_S as follows:

$$x(t) \pm \Delta x_S = \left[\begin{array}{c} 5.55\% \\ -3.68\% \end{array}\right] \pm \left[\begin{array}{c} 0\% \\ 1.50\% \end{array}\right]$$

$$= \left[\begin{array}{c} 5.55\% \\ -2.18\% \end{array}\right] \text{ and } \left[\begin{array}{c} 5.55\% \\ -5.18\% \end{array}\right]$$

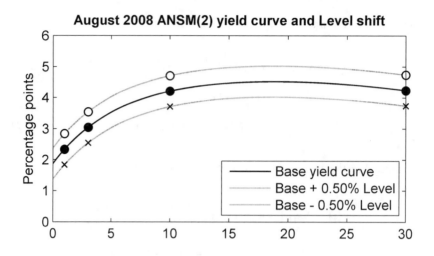

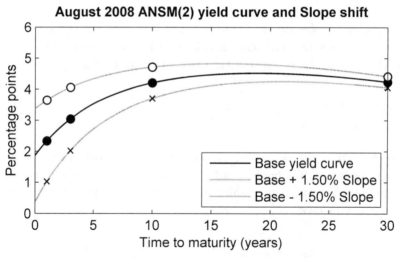

Figure 8.5 Examples of how yield curve shifts in the ANSM(2) can be represented by changes to the Level and Slope state variables.

8.3.2 ANSM(2) duration vector

From subsection 8.2.2, the general ANSM factor duration result for a zero-coupon bond with a cashflow of 1 at the time to maturity τ is

$$D(t,\tau) = \tau \cdot P[x(t),\tau] b(\tau) \tag{8.24}$$

Using the $b(\tau)$ specification for the ANSM(2) gives the duration vector as the following 2×1 vector:

$$D(t,\tau) = \tau \cdot P[x(t),\tau] \begin{bmatrix} 1 \\ \frac{1}{\tau}G(\phi,\tau) \end{bmatrix}$$

$$= \begin{bmatrix} P[x(t),\tau] \cdot \tau \\ P[x(t),\tau] \cdot G(\phi,\tau) \end{bmatrix}$$

$$= \begin{bmatrix} D_L(t,\tau) \\ D_S(t,\tau) \end{bmatrix} \qquad (8.25)$$

where

$$P[x(t),\tau] = \exp(-\tau \cdot R[x(t),\tau]) \qquad (8.26)$$

with $R[x(t),\tau]$ as defined in equation 8.17.

The interest rates, bond prices, and the duration vectors for each of the times to maturity τ_k are contained in Table 8.1. Table 8.1 also contains the portfolio value and the portfolio duration vector $D_{\text{Port.}}(t)$. They are simply the sum of the results for the individual securities because the face values are all 1:

$$D_{\text{Port.}}(t) = \sum_{k=1}^{K} CF(t,\tau_k) \, D(t,\tau_k)$$

$$= \sum_{k=1}^{K} 1 \times \begin{bmatrix} D_L(t,\tau_k) \\ D_S(t,\tau_k) \end{bmatrix} \qquad (8.27)$$

$$= \begin{bmatrix} D_L(t,1) + D_L(t,3) + D_L(t,10) + D_L(t,30) \\ D_S(t,1) + D_S(t,3) + D_S(t,10) + D_S(t,30) \end{bmatrix}$$

$$= \begin{bmatrix} D_{\text{Port.},L}(t) \\ D_{\text{Port.},S}(t) \end{bmatrix} \qquad (8.28)$$

Note that I have left the portfolio interest rate undefined, because it is not the sum or even the simple average of the underlying securities. A suitable weighted average could be defined, but it is not important to the exposition in this section, or the remainder of the chapter.

8.3.3 Level duration approximation to Level shifts

In Table 8.2, I show how the Level durations calculated in subsection 8.3.2 may be used to provide a close approximation to the actual changes in the price of the bond given a Level shift. The objective is not necessarily to convince readers of the mathematics of Level duration; I expect readers will already be very familiar (and

Table 8.1 August 2008 base yield curve summary values for ANSM(2)

Time to maturity, τ	1	3	10	30	Sum
$R[x(t),\tau]$	2.34	3.04	4.21	4.24	n/a
$P[x(t),\tau]$	0.9769	0.9128	0.6564	0.2806	2.8267
$D_L(t,\tau)$	0.98	2.74	6.56	8.42	18.70
$D_S(t,\tau)$	0.85	1.86	2.21	1.01	5.92

convinced) on that topic. Rather, the example provides intuition and results that I later use to compare and contrast with the results from the ZLB environment.

Panel 1 of Table 8.2 provides the base yield curve $R[x(t),\tau]$ and the interest rates obtained from applying positive and negative Level shifts Δx_L relative to the base yield curve. The last two lines of panel 1 are the interest rate changes given the Level shifts, that is, $R[x(t)+\Delta x_L,\tau]-R[x(t),\tau]$ and $R[x(t)-\Delta x_L,\tau]-R[x(t),\tau]$, which I have abbreviated to $\Delta R[x(t)+\Delta x_L,\tau]$ and $\Delta R[x(t)-\Delta x_L,\tau]$. As one would expect from the constant unit factor loading for the Level component of the ANSM(2), all of the interest rates change by $\pm 0.50\%$ in response to the Level shift.

Panel 2 summarizes the bond prices for the base yield curve $P[x(t),\tau]$ and the bond prices calculated from the Level-shifted interest rates in panel 1. The next two lines are the changes in the bond prices $P[x(t)+\Delta x_L,\tau]-P[x(t),\tau]$ and $P[x(t)-\Delta x_L,\tau]-P[x(t),\tau]$, abbreviated to $\Delta P[x(t)+\Delta x_L,\tau]$ and $\Delta P[x(t)-\Delta x_L,\tau]$. Note that these are the actual changes in the bond prices, which I compare to the approximation based on the Level duration. I have also summed the results to give the actual changes in the portfolio value given the Level shifts.

Panel 3 contains the approximate change in the bond prices based on the bond Level durations $D_L(t,\tau_k)$ and the Level shift of 0.50% defined in Δx_L. The last column provides the approximate change in portfolio value based on the portfolio Level duration.

The key point to note is that the Level duration calculations provide a close approximation to the changes in bond prices for upward and downward Level shifts to the yield curve. The approximation is better for shorter times to maturity and deteriorates progressively for longer maturities, as foreshadowed in subsection 8.2.3, but the results are sufficiently close for practical purposes. The Level duration calculation also holds for the portfolio as a whole. Hence, Level duration may be used for risk measurement and management in the portfolio.

8.3.4 Slope duration approximation to Slope shifts

Analogous to Table 8.2, in Table 8.3, I show how the Slope durations calculated in subsection 8.3.2 may be used to provide a close approximation to the actual changes in the price of the bond given a Slope shift.

Table 8.2 August 2008 ANSM(2) Level duration example

Time to maturity, τ	1	3	10	30	Sum
1. ANSM(2) interest rates and changes					
$R[x(t),\tau]$	2.34	3.04	4.21	4.24	n/a
$R[x(t)+\Delta x_L,\tau]$	2.84	3.54	4.71	4.74	n/a
$R[x(t)-\Delta x_L,\tau]$	1.84	2.54	3.71	3.74	n/a
$\Delta R[x(t)+\Delta x_L,\tau]$	0.50	0.50	0.50	0.50	n/a
$\Delta R[x(t)-\Delta x_L,\tau]$	-0.50	-0.50	-0.50	-0.50	n/a
2. ANSM(2) bond prices and changes					
$P[x(t),\tau_k]$	0.9769	0.9128	0.6564	0.2806	2.8267
$P[x(t)+\Delta x_L,\tau]$	0.9720	0.8992	0.6244	0.2415	2.7371
$P[x(t)-\Delta x_L,\tau]$	0.9818	0.9266	0.6901	0.3260	2.9245
$\Delta P[x(t)+\Delta x_L,\tau]$	-0.0049	-0.0136	-0.0320	-0.0391	-0.0896
$\Delta P[x(t)-\Delta x_L,\tau]$	0.0049	0.0138	0.0337	0.0454	0.0978
3. ANSM(2) Level duration approximations					
$D_L(t,\tau_k)$	0.98	2.74	6.56	8.42	18.70
$0.50\% \times D_L(t,\tau)$	0.0049	0.0137	0.0328	0.0421	0.0935

Panel 1 of Table 8.3 provides the base yield curve $R[x(t),\tau]$ and then the interest rates obtained from applying positive and negative Slope shifts Δx_S relative to the base yield curve. The last two lines of panel 1 are the interest rate changes given the Slope shifts, that is, $R[x(t)+\Delta x_S,\tau]-R[x(t),\tau]$ and $R[x(t)-\Delta x_S,\tau]-R[x(t),\tau]$, abbreviated to $\Delta R[x(t)+\Delta x_S,\tau]$ and $\Delta R[x(t)-\Delta x_S,\tau]$. The changes in interest rates are now a function of time to maturity, which reflects the factor loading for the Slope:

$$\frac{1}{\tau}G(\phi,\tau) = \frac{1}{\phi\tau}\left[1-\exp\left(-\phi\tau\right)\right] \tag{8.29}$$

Therefore, interest rates change by $\pm1.50\%$ at $\tau = 0$, by zero at $\tau = \infty$, and by $\pm1.50\% \times \frac{1}{\tau}G(\phi,\tau)$ for intermediate times to maturity.

Panel 2 summarizes the bond prices for the base yield curve $P[x(t),\tau]$ and the bond prices calculated from the Slope-shifted interest rates in panel 1. The next two lines are the changes in the bond prices $P[x(t)+\Delta x_S,\tau]-P[x(t),\tau]$ and $P[x(t)-\Delta x_S,\tau]-P[x(t),\tau]$, abbreviated to $\Delta P[x(t)+\Delta x_S,\tau]$ and $\Delta P[x(t)-\Delta x_S,\tau]$, and I have also summed the results to give the actual changes in the portfolio value given the Slope shifts.

Panel 3 contains the approximate change in the bond prices based on the bond Slope durations $D_S(t,\tau_k)$ and the Slope shift of 1.50% defined in Δx_S. The last column provides the approximate change in portfolio value based on the portfolio Slope duration.

Table 8.3 August 2008 ANSM(2) Slope duration example

Time to maturity, τ	1	3	10	30	Sum
1. ANSM(2) interest rates and changes					
$R[x(t),\tau]$	2.34	3.04	4.21	4.24	n/a
$R[x(t)+\Delta x_S,\tau]$	3.65	4.06	4.71	4.42	n/a
$R[x(t)-\Delta x_S,\tau]$	1.03	2.02	3.70	4.06	n/a
$\Delta R[x(t)+\Delta x_S,\tau]$	1.31	1.02	0.51	0.18	n/a
$\Delta R[x(t)-\Delta x_S,\tau]$	−1.31	−1.02	-0.51	−0.18	n/a
2. ANSM(2) bond prices and changes					
$P[x(t),\tau]$	0.9769	0.9128	0.6564	0.2806	2.8267
$P[x(t)+\Delta x_S,\tau]$	0.9642	0.8854	0.6241	0.2658	2.7395
$P[x(t)-\Delta x_S,\tau]$	0.9898	0.9411	0.6905	0.2961	2.9174
$\Delta P[x(t)+\Delta x_S,\tau]$	−0.0127	−0.0274	−0.0324	−0.0147	−0.0872
$\Delta P[x(t)-\Delta x_S,\tau]$	0.0129	0.0283	0.0340	0.0155	0.0907
3. ANSM(2) Slope duration approximations					
$D_S(t,\tau)$	0.85	1.86	2.21	1.01	5.92
$1.50\% \times D_S(t,\tau)$	0.0128	0.0278	0.0331	0.0151	0.0888

Analogous to the Level duration, the Slope duration calculations provide a close approximation to the changes in bond prices for upward and downward Slope shifts to the yield curve (and with less variation by time to maturity). The approximation also holds for the portfolio as a whole, and so Slope duration may be used for risk measurement and management in the portfolio.

8.3.5 ANSM(2) fixed interest portfolio risk

The general expression for the Risk Distribution in subsection 8.2.3 is

$$\text{Risk Dist.} \simeq N\left\{0,\sigma_D^2\right\} \tag{8.30}$$

where σ_D^2 is the variance:

$$\sigma_D^2 = [D_{\text{Port.}}(t)]' \sigma\sigma' D_{\text{Port.}}(t) \cdot \Delta t \tag{8.31}$$

For the ANSM(2),

$$\sigma_D^2 = \left[D_{\text{Port.},L}(t), D_{\text{Port.},S}(t)\right] \begin{bmatrix} \sigma_L^2 & \rho_{LS}\sigma_L\sigma_S \\ \rho_{LS}\sigma_L\sigma_S & \sigma_S^2 \end{bmatrix}$$

$$\times \begin{bmatrix} D_{\text{Port.},L}(t) \\ D_{\text{Port.},S}(t) \end{bmatrix} \cdot \Delta t \tag{8.32}$$

where $\sigma_L^2 = (0.8612)^2 \times \left[10^{-2}\right]^2 = 0.7417 \times 10^{-4}$, $\sigma_S^2 = (1.6032)^2 \times \left[10^{-2}\right]^2 = 2.5703 \times 10^{-4}$, and $\rho_{LS}\sigma_L\sigma_S = -0.5140 \times 0.8612 \times 1.6032 = -0.7097 \times 10^{-4}$, and I use a horizon of one month, that is, $\Delta t = 1/12$ for my example. Note that my Risk Distribution expression is based on the simplifying approximation $\exp(-\kappa u) \simeq I$ for all horizons out to Δt, and the closeness of the approximation is readily illustrated for this example. Specifically,

$$\exp(-\kappa\Delta t) = \exp\left(-\begin{bmatrix} 0 & 0 \\ 0 & \phi \end{bmatrix}\Delta t\right)$$

$$= \begin{bmatrix} 1 & 0 \\ 0 & \exp(-\phi\Delta t) \end{bmatrix} \tag{8.33}$$

and evaluating $\exp(-\kappa\Delta t)$ with the parameters $\phi = 0.2789$ and $\Delta t = 1/12$ gives

$$\begin{bmatrix} 1 & 0 \\ 0 & \exp(-\phi\Delta t) \end{bmatrix} = \begin{bmatrix} 1 & 0 \\ 0 & \exp\left(-0.2789 \times \frac{1}{12}\right) \end{bmatrix}$$

$$= \begin{bmatrix} 1 & 0 \\ 0 & 0.9770 \end{bmatrix} \simeq \begin{bmatrix} 1 & 0 \\ 0 & 1 \end{bmatrix} \tag{8.34}$$

The variance of the distribution of unanticipated changes to the value of the portfolio over a one-month horizon is approximately

$$\sigma_D^2 = [18.70, 5.92] \begin{bmatrix} 0.7417 & -0.7097 \\ -0.7097 & 2.5703 \end{bmatrix} \times 10^{-4} \times \begin{bmatrix} 18.70 \\ 5.92 \end{bmatrix} \cdot \frac{1}{12}$$

$$= 16.026 \times 10^{-4} \tag{8.35}$$

and the standard deviation is

$$\sigma_D = \sqrt{16.026} \times \sqrt{10^{-4}}$$

$$= 0.0400 \text{ dollars} \tag{8.36}$$

Therefore the ANSM(2) model-consistent estimate of unanticipated changes to the portfolio value over a one-month horizon is the following normal distribution:

Risk Dist. $\simeq N(0, 0.0400)$ dollars $\tag{8.37}$

which I have expressed with a standard deviation instead of a variance. That expression can be readily used to calculate one-month VaRs. For example, the one-month, one-percent VaR would be $-2.33 \times 0.0400 = -0.0932$ dollars, where -2.33 is the number of standard deviations to give a cumulative probability of one percent for the normal distribution. Hence, one percent of the time, unanticipated losses to the portfolio value would be 0.0932 dollars or more, over a one-month horizon.

8.3.6 Extension to ANSM(3)

From section 3.4, the factor loading vector for the ANSM(3) is the 3×1 vector:

$$
b(\tau) = \begin{bmatrix} 1 \\ \frac{1}{\tau} G(\phi, \tau) \\ \frac{1}{\tau} F(\phi, \tau) \end{bmatrix}
\tag{8.38}
$$

where

$$
G(\phi, \tau) = \frac{1}{\phi} \left[1 - \exp(-\phi\tau) \right]
\tag{8.39}
$$

and

$$
\begin{aligned}
F(\phi, \tau) &= \frac{1}{\phi} \left[1 - \exp(-\phi\tau) \right] - \tau \exp(-\phi\tau) \\
&= G(\phi, \tau) - \tau \exp(-\phi\tau)
\end{aligned}
\tag{8.40}
$$

Therefore, the ANSM(3) duration vector for a zero-coupon bond with a cashflow of 1 at the time to maturity τ is the following 3×1 vector:

$$
\begin{aligned}
D(t,\tau) &= \tau \cdot P[x(t),\tau] \begin{bmatrix} 1 \\ \frac{1}{\tau} G(\phi, \tau) \\ \frac{1}{\tau} F(\phi, \tau) \end{bmatrix} \\
&= \begin{bmatrix} P[x(t),\tau] \cdot \tau \\ P[x(t),\tau] \cdot G(\phi, \tau) \\ P[x(t),\tau] \cdot F(\phi, \tau) \end{bmatrix}
\end{aligned}
\tag{8.41}
$$

I refer readers to Krippner (2005) for complete worked examples using the ANSM(3).

8.4 A risk framework based on K-ANSMs

In this section, I develop a general fixed interest portfolio risk framework based on K-ANSMs. Because ANSMs are used to represent the shadow term structure in ANSMs, the framework is a relatively straightforward modification to the ANSM risk framework presented in section 8.2.

I introduce in subsection 8.4.1 how term structure shifts are represented in a K-ANSM, and in subsection 8.4.2, I derive the general expression for calculating K-ANSM factor durations. Subsections 8.4.3 and 8.4.4 discuss how the K-ANSM factor durations can be used for risk measurement and management in fixed interest portfolios.

Note that the risk framework I develop for K-ANSMs applies equally if a stationary GATSM term structure is used to represent the shadow yield curve. However, as noted in the introduction of section 8.2, stationary GATSMs will not have a Level component like ANSMs.

8.4.1 K-ANSM yield curve shifts

A K-ANSM yield curve shift can essentially be envisaged as an ANSM yield curve shift for the K-ANSM shadow yield curve, but with the attenuation of the ANSM yield curve shift provided by the Krippner framework. However, the actual mechanics of the calculation do not directly follow that description. It is better to consider both K-ANSM ZLB and shadow yield curve shifts directly as changes to the K-ANSM state variables.

Shifts in the K-ANSM shadow yield curve will therefore remain identical to the ANSM discussed in section 8.2.1. Specifically, shadow interest rates as a function of time to maturity have the ANSM form defined in section 8.2.1:

$$R[x(t),\tau] = a(\tau) + [b(\tau)]' x(t) \tag{8.42}$$

but the ANSM Level, Slope, and Bow interest rate factor loadings now provide the representation of the changes to the K-ANSM shadow yield curve. Specifically, an $N \times 1$ vector Δx will represent changes to the state variable vector $x(t)$, and the new shadow yield curve will be

$$R[x(t) + \Delta x, \tau] = a(\tau) + [b(\tau)]' [x(t) + \Delta x] \tag{8.43}$$

The associated shift in the K-ANSM ZLB yield curve $\underline{R}[x(t),\tau]$ is not obtained directly from the ANSM yield curve, but rather by using the initial and the new state variable vector in the expressions for K-ANSM interest rates from section 4.1. Specifically, $\underline{R}[x(t),\tau]$ is defined as

$$\underline{R}[x(t),\tau] = \frac{1}{\tau} \int_0^\tau \underline{f}[x(t),u]\, du \tag{8.44}$$

where $\underline{f}[x(t),u]$ is the K-ANSM ZLB forward rate. $\underline{f}[x(t),u]$ has the general functional form for ZLB forward rates in the K-AGM framework, that is,

$$\underline{f}[x(t),\tau] = r_L + [f[x(t),\tau] - r_L] \cdot \Phi\left[\frac{f[x(t),\tau] - r_L}{\omega(\tau)}\right]$$
$$+ \omega(\tau) \cdot \phi\left[\frac{f[x(t),\tau] - r_L}{\omega(\tau)}\right] \tag{8.45}$$

where r_L is the lower bound, $\omega(\tau)$ is the volatility of the expected path of the shadow short rate under the risk-adjusted $\mathbb{Q}$ measure, $\Phi[\cdot]$ is the cumulative unit normal density function, $\phi[\cdot]$ is the unit normal density function, and $f[x(t),\tau]$ is the shadow forward rate. $f[x(t),\tau]$ has the ANSM functional form analogous to the ANSM expression for $R[x(t),\tau]$. That is,

$$f[x(t),\tau] = -\mathrm{VE}(\tau) + b_0' \exp\left(-\tilde{\kappa}'\tau\right) x(t) \tag{8.46}$$

where the general expression for the volatility effect $\mathrm{VE}(\tau)$ is contained in subsection 3.1.2 but it is not needed for the exposition in this section, and $b_0' \exp\left(-\tilde{\kappa}'\tau\right)$ is the forward rate factor loading vector. As detailed in section 4.1 and the examples in sections 4.3 to 4.5, $f[x(t),\tau]$ is a closed-form analytic expression, but straightforward univariate numerical integration over time to maturity τ is required to evaluate $R[x(t),\tau]$.

Evaluating the ZLB yield curve shift represented by the vector Δx in the K-ANSM ZLB yield curve requires the calculation of $R[x(t),\tau]$ and $R[x(t)+\Delta x,\tau]$. The ZLB yield curve shift is then the difference $R[x(t)+\Delta x,\tau] - R[x(t),\tau]$. I illustrate a Level and Slope shift for the K-ANSM(2) in subsections 8.5.3 and 8.5.4.

8.4.2 K-ANSM factor durations

The K-ANSM factor duration vector is defined analogous to the ANSM factor duration vector:

$$D(t,\tau) = -\frac{d}{dx(t)} P[x(t),\tau] \tag{8.47}$$

where $D(t,\tau)$ is a $N \times 1$ vector, $x(t)$ is the $N \times 1$ state variable vector, and $P[x(t),\tau]$ is the scalar K-ANSM bond price as a function of the state variable vector $x(t)$ and time to maturity τ:

$$P[x(t),\tau] = \exp\left(-\tau \cdot R[x(t),\tau]\right) \tag{8.48}$$

where $R[x(t),\tau]$ is the K-ANSM interest rate defined in the previous subsection.

The K-ANSM bond price after a state variable shift Δx is

$$P[x(t)+\Delta x,\tau] = \exp\left(-\tau \cdot R[x(t)+\Delta x,\tau]\right) \tag{8.49}$$

and the new K-ANSM bond price $P[x(t)+\Delta x,\tau]$ may be approximated to arbitrary precision with a Taylor approximation around $x(t)$. The duration vector again arises as the first-order differential required for the first-order Taylor approximation:

$$P[x(t)+\Delta x,\tau] \simeq P[x(t),\tau] + \left[\frac{d}{dx(t)} P[x(t),\tau]\right] \Delta x$$
$$= \exp\left(-\tau \cdot R[x(t),\tau]\right)$$
$$+ \left[\frac{d}{dx(t)} \exp\left(-\tau \cdot R[x(t),\tau]\right)\right] \Delta x \tag{8.50}$$

and therefore the approximation of the change in the zero-coupon bond price for the instantaneous change Δx in the state variable vector is

$$\underline{P}[x(t),\tau] - \underline{P}[x(t)+\Delta x,\tau] \simeq -\left[\frac{d}{dx(t)}\exp\left(-\tau \cdot R[x(t),\tau]\right)\right]\Delta x$$
$$= \underline{D}(t,\tau)\,\Delta x \tag{8.51}$$

$\underline{D}(t,\tau)$ is an $N \times 1$ duration vector that may be calculated explicitly as follows:

$$\underline{D}(t,\tau) = -\frac{d}{dx(t)}\exp\left(-\tau \cdot R[x(t),\tau]\right)$$
$$\langle\text{Chain rule}\rangle = -\frac{d}{d\underline{R}[x(t),\tau]}\exp\left(-\tau \cdot R[x(t),\tau]\right)\left(\frac{d}{dx(t)}\underline{R}[x(t),\tau]\right)$$
$$= \tau \cdot \underline{P}[x(t),\tau]\frac{d}{dx(t)}\underline{R}[x(t),\tau] \tag{8.52}$$

The key difference between the ANSM and K-ANSM for the purposes of this section is that K-ANSM interest rates $\underline{R}[x(t),\tau]$ are a nonlinear function of the state variable vector $x(t)$ because the nonlinear functions of $x(t)$, $\Phi[\cdot]$ and $\phi[\cdot]$, appear in $\underline{f}[x(t),\tau]$. Therefore, calculating the derivative of $\underline{R}[x(t),\tau]$ with respect to $x(t)$ is more involved than for the linear function for GATSM interest rates $R[x(t),\tau] = a(\tau)+[b(\tau)]'x(t)$ in subsection 8.2.2.

Fortunately, the results are already available from the Jacobian expression used as part of the K-ANSM estimation process detailed in subsection 4.2.2. Hence,

$$\frac{d}{dx(t)}\underline{R}[x(t),\tau] = \frac{1}{\tau}\int_0^\tau \exp\left(-\tilde{\kappa}u\right)b_0\Phi\left[\frac{f[x(t),u]-r_L}{\omega(u)}\right]du \tag{8.53}$$

and therefore

$$\underline{D}(t,\tau) = \underline{P}[x(t),\tau]\int_0^\tau \exp\left(-\tilde{\kappa}u\right)b_0\Phi\left[\frac{f[x(t),u]-r_L}{\omega(u)}\right]du$$

Like $\underline{R}[x(t),\tau]$, straightforward univariate numerical integration over time to maturity τ is required to evaluate $\underline{D}(t,\tau)$. Section 4.2.2 and the examples in sections 4.3 to 4.5 contain the details.

The expression $\underline{D}(t,\tau)$ is used to evaluate the duration vector for any single cashflow, and duration vector for multiple cashflows is the cashflow- or face-value-weighted-sum:

$$\underline{D}_{\text{Port.}}(t) = \sum_{k=1}^{K}CF(t,\tau_k)\underline{D}(t,\tau_k)$$

where $\underline{D}_{\text{Port.}}(t)$ is the total duration, $CF(\tau_k)$ is the cashflow associated with the time to maturity τ_k, and $\underline{D}(t, \tau_k)$ is the duration vector associated with the time to maturity τ_k.

Before proceeding, I note here that factor durations for B-ANSMs would be calculated analogously to K-ANSMs, but using the Jacobian expressions available in subsection 5.5.1. The difference relative to the K-ANSM expressions outlined in this subsection is that the B-ANSM calculations would need to be obtained using the numerical method of Monte Carlo simulation, which is much more computationally onerous than the straightforward univariate numerical integration required for K-ANSMs. Chapter 5 contains details on Monte Carlo simulations for the Black (1995) framework. However, subsection 5.6.1 shows that K-ANSMs provide close approximations to the corresponding B-ANSM, so using K-ANSMs as the basis for a risk framework will be far preferable in practice.

8.4.3 K-ANSM fixed interest portfolio risk

Using the distribution of potential unanticipated changes in the state variable vector $x(t)$ along with the duration vector $\underline{D}(t, \tau)$ provides the basis for obtaining an approximate distribution of potential unanticipated value changes.

The dynamics for the K-ANSM state variables have the same specification as the ANSM state variables, because the ANSM is used as the shadow term structure within the K-ANSM. The distributions of unanticipated changes for the K-ANSM state variables, again with the approximation $\exp(-\tilde{\kappa}u) \simeq I$ for relatively short horizons, is therefore

$$\widetilde{\text{var}}_t\left[x(t+\tau)|x(t)\right] \simeq \int_0^{\Delta t} \sigma\sigma' \, du$$

$$= \sigma\sigma' \Delta t \tag{8.54}$$

The K-ANSM Risk Distribution is

$$\text{Risk Dist.} \simeq N\left\{0, \sigma_{\underline{D}}^2\right\} \tag{8.55}$$

where $N\{\cdot\}$ is the normal distribution with a mean of zero, and $\sigma_{\underline{D}}^2$ is the variance:

$$\sigma_{\underline{D}}^2 = \left[\underline{D}_{\text{Port.}}(t)\right]' \sigma\sigma' \underline{D}_{\text{Port.}}(t) \cdot \Delta t \tag{8.56}$$

Note that I have denoted the variance $\sigma_{\underline{D}}^2$ with the subscript $\underline{D}$ to show that it is a quantity subject to the ZLB constraint.

8.5 Worked example: K-ANSM(2)

In this section, I provide two fully worked examples using the K-ANSM(2), which will illustrate the points from the previous section. The examples use the ANSM(2) from section 8.3 to represent the shadow term structure, so all of the parameters and expressions for the ANSM(2) carry over to this section. I summarize the additional expressions required in subsections 8.5.1 and 8.5.2.

In subsection 8.5.3, I provide an example of applying the K-ANSM(2) in a non-ZLB environment. I use the same state variables, state variable shifts, and the four zero-coupon bonds for this example, so the results may be compared directly to the ANSM(2) results in section 8.3. Indeed, the ANSM(2) is the shadow yield curve for the example in subsection 8.5.3.

In subsection 8.5.4, I provide an example of applying the K-ANSM(2) in a ZLB environment. Again for comparability, I repeat the example from subsection 8.5.3, but I use state variables that imply a material constraint from the ZLB environment.

8.5.1 K-ANSM(2) term structure specification

From section 4.3 and using $r_L = 0$ to ensure comparability to the ANSM(2) example in section 8.3, the K-ANSM(2) forward rate expression is

$$\underline{f}[x(t),\tau] = f[x(t),\tau] \cdot \Phi \left[\frac{f[x(t),\tau]}{\omega(\tau)} \right] + \omega(\tau) \cdot \phi \left[\frac{f[x(t),\tau]}{\omega(\tau)} \right] \tag{8.57}$$

The K-ANSM(2) shadow forward rate expression is the ANSM(2) forward rate, which is defined by

$$x(t) = \begin{bmatrix} L(t) \\ S(t) \end{bmatrix}; \quad \exp\left(-\tilde{\kappa} u\right) b_0 = \begin{bmatrix} 1 \\ \exp\left(-\phi\tau\right) \end{bmatrix} \tag{8.58}$$

and the general ANSM(2) forward rate expression

$$f[x(t),\tau] = -VE(\tau) + b_0' \exp\left(-\tilde{\kappa}'\tau\right) x(t)$$

$$= \left[1, \exp\left(-\phi\tau\right)\right] \begin{bmatrix} L(t) \\ S(t) \end{bmatrix} - VE(\tau)$$

$$= L(t) + S(t) \cdot \exp\left(-\phi\tau\right)$$

$$-\sigma_1^2 \cdot \frac{1}{2}\tau^2 - \sigma_2^2 \cdot \frac{1}{2} [G(\phi,\tau)]^2 - \rho_{12}\sigma_1\sigma_2 \cdot \tau G(\phi,\tau) \tag{8.59}$$

The volatility function $\omega(\tau)$ is

$$\omega(\tau) = \sqrt{\sigma_1^2 \cdot \tau + \sigma_2^2 \cdot G(2\phi,\tau) + 2\rho_{12}\sigma_1\sigma_2 G(\phi,\tau)} \tag{8.60}$$

where

$$G(2\phi, \tau) = \frac{1}{2\phi} \left[1 - \exp\left(-2\phi\tau\right) \right] \tag{8.61}$$

K-ANSM(2) interest rates are

$$\underline{R}[x(t), \tau] = \frac{1}{\tau} \int_0^\tau \underline{f}[x(t), u] \, du \tag{8.62}$$

which are obtained by numerical integration, as detailed in section 4.3, and K-ANSM(2) bond prices are

$$\underline{P}[x(t), \tau] = \exp\left(-\tau \cdot \underline{R}[x(t), \tau]\right) \tag{8.63}$$

8.5.2 K-ANSM(2) duration vector

From subsection 8.4.2, the general K-ANSM factor duration result for a zero-coupon bond with a cashflow of 1 at the time to maturity τ is

$$\underline{D}(t, \tau) = \underline{P}[x(t), \tau] \int_0^\tau \exp\left(-\tilde{\kappa} u\right) b_0 \Phi \left[\frac{f[x(t), u]}{\omega(u)} \right] du \tag{8.64}$$

Using the $\exp\left(-\tilde{\kappa} u\right) b_0$ specification for the K-ANSM(2) gives the following 2×1 duration vector:

$$\underline{D}(t, \tau) = \underline{P}[x(t), \tau] \int_0^\tau \begin{bmatrix} 1 \\ \exp\left(-\phi u\right) \end{bmatrix} \Phi \left[\frac{f[x(t), u]}{\omega(u)} \right] du \tag{8.65}$$

which is obtained by straightforward univariate numerical integration, as detailed in section 4.3.

8.5.3 Non-ZLB environment

For the illustrations in this section, I will use the K-ANSM(2) state variable vector from subsection 8.3.1:

$$x(t) = \begin{bmatrix} L(t) \\ S(t) \end{bmatrix} = \begin{bmatrix} 5.55\% \\ -3.68\% \end{bmatrix} \tag{8.66}$$

The shadow short rate is 1.87%, and all shadow interest rates are above zero, so the example is suitable for a non-ZLB environment illustration.

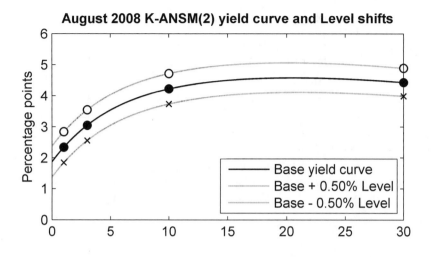

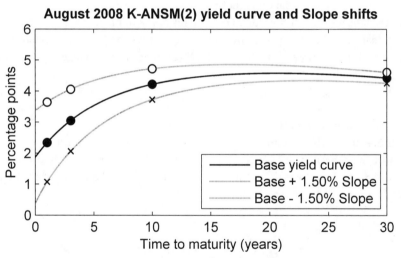

Figure 8.6 Examples of yield curve shifts in a non-ZLB environment obtained by changes to the K-ANSM(2) Level and/or Slope state variables.

K-ANSM(2) yield curve shifts

For my non-ZLB example, I use the same 0.50% Level shifts via $\pm\Delta x_L$, and the same 1.50% Slope shifts via $\pm\Delta x_S$ as already defined in subsection 8.3.1. Panel 1 of Figure 8.6 plots the K-ANSM ZLB base yield curve along with the Level shifts, and panel 2 plots the K-ANSM ZLB base yield curve along with the Slope shifts. Just to be clear, to generate the yield curve shifts in Figure 8.6, I first shift the state variable vector $x(t)$ respectively by the given amounts $\pm\Delta x_L$ and $\pm\Delta x_S$, and I then use the K-ANSM(2) framework to generate the new K-ANSM(2) ZLB yield curves.

The K-ANSM(2) shadow base yield curve and the shadow yield curve shifts associated with this present K-ANSM(2) example are in Figure 8.5. Hence, it is apparent

Table 8.4 August 2008 base yield curve summary values for K-ANSM(2)

Time to maturity, τ	1	3	10	30	Sum
1. K-ANSM(2) base yield curve evaluations					
$R[x(t),\tau]$	2.34	3.05	4.22	4.43	n/a
$P[x(t),\tau]$	0.9769	0.9127	0.6556	0.2645	2.8097
K-ANSM $D_L(t,\tau)$	0.97	2.71	6.45	7.19	17.33
K-ANSM $D_S(t,\tau)$	0.85	1.84	2.18	0.94	5.81
2. ANSM(2) duration from K-ANSM(2) bond prices					
ANSM $D_L(t,\tau)$	0.98	2.74	6.56	7.93	18.21
ANSM $D_S(t,\tau)$	0.86	1.86	2.21	0.95	5.86

that there is no substantial difference between the K-ANSM(2) shadow yield curve and the K-ANSM(2) ZLB yield curve in terms of the initial interest rate levels and their changes. This is apparent by comparing the K-ANSM(2) ZLB interest rate changes in Tables 8.5 and 8.6 to the ANSM(2) interest rate changes in Tables 8.2 and 8.3.

K-ANSM(2) duration calculation

Table 8.4 summarizes the interest rates, bond prices, and the duration vectors for each of the time to maturity τ_k. The portfolio value and the portfolio duration vector $D_{Port.}(t)$ are the sum of the results for the individual securities because the face values are all 1.

$$D_{Port.}(t) = \sum_{k=1}^{K} CF(t,\tau_k) \, D(t,\tau_k)$$

$$= \sum_{k=1}^{K} 1 \times \begin{bmatrix} D_L(t,\tau_k) \\ D_S(t,\tau_k) \end{bmatrix}$$

$$= \begin{bmatrix} D_{Port.,L}(t) \\ D_{Port.,S}(t) \end{bmatrix} \tag{8.67}$$

At the bottom of Table 8.4, I have also included the calculation of the ANSM duration vector, that is, using the ANSM factor duration expressions and the K-ANSM(2) bond prices. I use those ANSM factor durations in the following tables to indicate how much difference it makes if one applies, either naively or as an approximation, standard factor duration calculations that do not allow for the ZLB constraint to "real world" bond prices that are constrained by the ZLB.

Table 8.5 August 2008 K-ANSM(2) Level duration example

Time to maturity, τ	1	3	10	30	Sum
1. K-ANSM(2) interest rates and changes					
$R[x(t),\tau]$	2.34	3.05	4.22	4.43	n/a
$R[x(t)+\Delta x_L,\tau]$	2.84	3.54	4.72	4.89	n/a
$R[x(t)-\Delta x_L,\tau]$	1.84	2.55	3.73	3.99	n/a
$\Delta R[x(t)+\Delta x_L,\tau]$	0.50	0.50	0.49	0.46	n/a
$\Delta R[x(t)-\Delta x_L,\tau]$	−0.49	−0.49	-0.49	−0.45	n/a
2. K-ANSM(2) bond prices and changes					
$P[x(t),\tau]$	0.9769	0.9127	0.6556	0.2645	2.8097
$P[x(t)+\Delta x_L,\tau]$	0.9720	0.8992	0.6240	0.2305	2.7258
$P[x(t)-\Delta x_L,\tau]$	0.9817	0.9262	0.6885	0.3025	2.8990
$\Delta P[x(t)+\Delta x_L,\tau]$	−0.0049	−0.0135	−0.0316	−0.0340	−0.0839
$\Delta P[x(t)-\Delta x_L,\tau]$	0.0048	0.0136	0.0329	0.0380	0.0893
3. K-ANSM(2) Level duration approximations					
K-ANSM $D_L(t,\tau)$	0.97	2.71	6.45	7.19	17.33
$0.50\% \times D_L(t,\tau)$	0.0049	0.0135	0.0323	0.0360	0.0866
4. ANSM(2) Level duration approximations					
ANSM $D_L(t,\tau)$	0.98	2.74	6.56	7.93	18.21
$0.50\% \times D_L(t,\tau)$	0.0049	0.0137	0.0328	0.0397	0.0910

K-ANSM(2) Level duration and Level state variable shifts

Table 8.5 provides the results for K-ANSM(2) Level shifts and the K-ANSM Level duration calculations. The pattern of results is very similar to those already discussed for the ANSM(2) in subsection 8.3.3. That is, panel 1 shows that the Level shift still results in all interest rates moving up and down by close to 0.50%. However, there is some asymmetry for all times to maturity, which reflects the ZLB constraint restricting downward movements in interest rates. There is also some attenuation in the interest rate movements for longer times to maturity relative to the 0.50% change in the Level state variable. This attenuation arises from the option effect on interest rates for longer maturities, which in turn reflects that the widening distribution of shadow short rates for longer horizons results in larger probabilities of negative values.

The actual changes in K-ANSM bond prices are calculated using the actual interest rates contained in panel 1, and these are summed to obtain the portfolio value.

Panel 3 of Table 8.5 contains the K-ANSM Level duration calculations. These closely approximate the actual changes for the individual security prices and the portfolio total from panel 2. The K-ANSM(2) Level duration results are also very similar to the ANSM(2) Level duration results in subsection 8.3.3, for reasons I will detail in subsection 8.5.5.

The last two lines of Table 8.5 summarize the results from using ANSM Level durations to approximate the changes in K-ANSM(2) bond prices from the Level shift. While there is some difference from the fully consistent K-ANSM Level duration calculations, the results still provide an acceptable approximation.

Therefore, in a non-ZLB environment, it makes little practical difference whether one uses the fully consistent K-ANSM Level duration calculation or the inconsistent ANSM Level duration calculation to approximate the change in the bond prices and portfolio value for a Level shift. I will provide further details on this aspect in subsection 8.5.5.

K-ANSM(2) Slope duration and Slope state variable shifts

Table 8.6 provides the results for K-ANSM(2) Slope shift and the K-ANSM Slope duration calculations. The pattern of results is very similar to that already discussed for the ANSM(2) in section 8.3.4. That is, the interest rates move up and down in accordance with the shape of the Slope factor loading. However, there is some asymmetry and attenuation for the interest rate movements for all times to maturity, which again reflects the ZLB constraint.

As for Table 8.5, the K-ANSM Slope duration calculations provide close approximations to the actual changes for the individual security prices and the portfolio total, and the K-ANSM(2) results are very similar to the ANSM(2) results in section 8.3.

The extra two lines at the bottom of Table 8.6 summarize the results from using ANSM Slope durations to approximate the changes in K-ANSM(2) bond prices from the Slope shift. The differences are very minor compared to the fully consistent K-ANSM Level duration calculations, so in a non-ZLB environment it makes little practical difference which factor duration framework is applied.

K-ANSM(2) fixed interest portfolio risk

The general expression for the K-ANSM Risk Distribution in subsection 8.4.3 is

$$\text{Risk Dist.} \simeq N\left\{0, \sigma_{\underset{\sim}{D}}^2\right\} \tag{8.68}$$

where $N\{\cdot\}$ is the normal distribution with a mean of zero, and $\sigma_{\underset{\sim}{D}}^2$ is the variance:

$$\sigma_{\underset{\sim}{D}}^2 = \left[\underset{\sim}{D}_{\text{Port.}}(t)\right]' \sigma\sigma' \underset{\sim}{D}_{\text{Port.}}(t) \cdot \Delta t \tag{8.69}$$

For the K-ANSM(2)

$$\sigma_{\underset{\sim}{D}}^2 = \left[D_{\text{Port.},L}(t), D_{\text{Port.},S}(t)\right] \begin{bmatrix} \sigma_L^2 & \rho_{LS}\sigma_L\sigma_S \\ \rho_{LS}\sigma_L\sigma_S & \sigma_S^2 \end{bmatrix}$$

$$\times \begin{bmatrix} \underset{\sim}{D}_{\text{Port.},L}(t) \\ \underset{\sim}{D}_{\text{Port.},S}(t) \end{bmatrix} \cdot \Delta t \tag{8.70}$$

Table 8.6 August 2008 K-ANSM(2) Slope duration example

Time to maturity, τ	1	3	10	30	Sum
1. K-ANSM(2) interest rates and changes					
$R[x(t),\tau]$	2.34	3.05	4.22	4.43	n/a
$R[x(t)+\Delta x_S,\tau]$	3.65	4.06	4.72	4.61	n/a
$R[x(t)-\Delta x_S,\tau]$	1.07	2.06	3.73	4.26	n/a
$\Delta R[x(t)+\Delta x_S,\tau]$	1.31	1.01	0.50	0.18	n/a
$\Delta R[x(t)-\Delta x_S,\tau]$	−1.27	−0.99	-0.49	−0.17	n/a
2. K-ANSM(2) bond prices and changes					
$P[x(t),\tau]$	0.9769	0.9127	0.6556	0.2645	2.8097
$P[x(t)+\Delta x_S,\tau]$	0.9642	0.8853	0.6236	0.2508	2.7239
$P[x(t)-\Delta x_S,\tau]$	0.9893	0.9400	0.6887	0.2787	2.8967
$\Delta P[x(t)+\Delta x_S,\tau]$	−0.0127	−0.0273	−0.0321	−0.0137	−0.0858
$\Delta P[x(t)-\Delta x_S,\tau]$	0.0124	0.0274	0.0330	0.0142	0.0871
3. K-ANSM(2) Slope duration approximations					
K-ANSM $D_S(t,\tau)$	0.85	1.84	2.18	0.94	5.81
$1.50\% \times D_S(t,\tau)$	0.0127	0.0276	0.0327	0.0140	0.0871
4. ANSM(2) Slope duration approximations					
ANSM $D_S(t,\tau)$	0.86	1.86	2.21	0.95	5.86
$1.50\% \times D_S(t,\tau)$	0.0128	0.0278	0.0331	0.0142	0.0879

where the simplifying approximation $\exp(-\kappa u) \simeq I$ holds and the parameters are as outlined for the ANSM(2) example of section 8.3. I again use a horizon of one month, that is, $\Delta t = 1/12$ for this example.

The variance of the distribution of unanticipated changes to the value of the portfolio over a one-month horizon is approximately

$$\sigma_D^2 = [17.33, 5.81] \begin{bmatrix} 0.7417 & -0.7097 \\ -0.7097 & 2.5703 \end{bmatrix} \times 10^{-4} \times \begin{bmatrix} 17.33 \\ 5.81 \end{bmatrix} \cdot \frac{1}{12}$$

$$= 13.883 \times 10^{-4} \tag{8.71}$$

and the standard deviation is

$$\sigma_D = \sqrt{13.883} \times \sqrt{10^{-4}}$$

$$= 0.0373 \text{ dollars} \tag{8.72}$$

Therefore, the K-ANSM(2) model-consistent estimate of unanticipated changes to the portfolio value over a one-month horizon is the normal distribution:

$$\text{Risk Dist.} \simeq N(0, 0.0373) \text{ dollars} \tag{8.73}$$

The one-month 1% VaR would be $-2.33 \times 0.0373 = -0.0869$ dollars. Hence, 1% of the time unanticipated losses to the portfolio value would be 0.0869 dollars or more over a one-month horizon.

As a comparison, I now calculate the Risk Distribution using the ANSM(2) duration calculations for the K-ANSM(2) bond prices. Hence, the variance is

$$\sigma_D^2 = [18.21, 5.86] \begin{bmatrix} 0.7417 & -0.7097 \\ -0.7097 & 2.5703 \end{bmatrix} \times 10^{-4} \times \begin{bmatrix} 18.21 \\ 5.86 \end{bmatrix} \cdot \frac{1}{12}$$

$$= 15.229 \times 10^{-4} \tag{8.74}$$

and the standard deviation is

$$\sigma_D = \sqrt{15.229} \times \sqrt{10^{-4}}$$

$$= 0.0390 \text{ dollars} \tag{8.75}$$

Therefore the K-ANSM(2) model-consistent estimate of unanticipated changes to the portfolio value over a one-month horizon is the normal distribution:

$$\text{Risk Dist.} \simeq N(0, 0.0390) \text{ dollars}, \tag{8.76}$$

again expressed with a standard deviation instead of a variance. The one-month 1% VaR would be $-2.33 \times 0.0390 = -0.0909$ dollars, which for practical purposes is not materially different from the fully consistent K-ANSM(2) VaR calculation earlier.

8.5.4 ZLB environment

For the illustrations in this subsection, I use the K-ANSM(2) results for July 2012, which is defined with the state variables:

$$x(t) = \begin{bmatrix} 2.68\% \\ -6.22\% \end{bmatrix} \tag{8.77}$$

The shadow short rate is -3.54%, and the base yield curve in Figure 8.7 shows that shadow interest rates are negative out to approximately 8 years. Therefore, the example is suitable for a ZLB environment illustration.

K-ANSM(2) yield curve shifts

I apply the same 0.50% Level shifts via $\pm \Delta x_L$ and 1.50% Slope shifts via $\pm \Delta x_S$, as already defined in subsection 8.3.1. These respectively change the Level and Slope state variables for the K-ANSM(2) from the starting values already given above in

$x(t)$. Specifically, given the starting value of $x(t)$, the Level and Slope shifts now give

$$x(t) \pm \Delta x_L = \begin{bmatrix} 2.68\% \\ -6.22\% \end{bmatrix} \pm \begin{bmatrix} 0.50\% \\ 0\% \end{bmatrix}$$

$$= \begin{bmatrix} 2.18\% \\ -6.22\% \end{bmatrix} \text{ and } \begin{bmatrix} 3.18\% \\ -6.22\% \end{bmatrix}$$

and

$$x(t) \pm \Delta x_S = \begin{bmatrix} 2.68\% \\ -6.22\% \end{bmatrix} \pm \begin{bmatrix} 0\% \\ 1.50\% \end{bmatrix}$$

$$= \begin{bmatrix} 2.68\% \\ -4.72\% \end{bmatrix} \text{ and } \begin{bmatrix} 2.68\% \\ -7.72\% \end{bmatrix}$$

Figure 8.7 illustrates the K-ANSM(2) shadow yield curve and the effect that the Level and Slope shifts have on the K-ANSM(2) shadow yield curve. The shadow yield curve shifts are identical to those in subsection 8.3.1, which is apparent from Tables 8.8 and 8.9. The difference is that a large part of the base shadow yield curve and the shifted shadow yield curves have negative shadow interest rates. Those negative interest rates indicate that the K-ANSM(2) ZLB yield curve is materially constrained by the ZLB.

Figure 8.8 shows that the material constraint from the ZLB in this example translates into a substantial difference for the K-ANSM(2) ZLB yield curve and its changes relative to the K-ANSM(2) shadow yield curve and its changes. Panel 1 of Figure 8.8 plots the K-ANSM(2) base yield curve along with the Level shifts, and panel 2 plots the K-ANSM(2) base yield curve along with Slope shifts.

In both cases, relative to the shifts in the K-ANSM(2) shadow yield curve, the changes to the K-ANSM(2) ZLB yield curve are very attenuated, and particularly so for shorter maturities. Indeed, the 1-year ZLB interest rate hardly moves at all in response to either the Level or Slope shift, which is very different from the result in the non-ZLB environment. Also very different is that the Level shifts no longer lead to an approximately uniform shift to all interest rates along the yield curve, which is a point I return to further below.

K-ANSM(2) duration calculation
Table 8.7 summarizes the shadow interest rates, ZLB interest rates, ZLB bond prices, and the ZLB duration vectors for each of the times to maturity τ_k, and the portfolio value and the portfolio duration vector $D_{Port.}(t)$ as the sum of the results for the individual securities. I have again included the calculation of the ANSM duration vector at the bottom of the table for use in the following tables. Unlike the non-ZLB environment example, it is already clear that the K-ANSM(2) factor durations are very different from the ANSM(2) factor durations, particularly for the shorter

Table 8.7 July 2012 base yield curve summary values for K-ANSM(2)

Time to maturity, τ	1	3	10	30	Sum
1. K-ANSM(2) base yield curve evaluations					
Shadow $R[x(t),\tau]$	−2.76	−1.56	0.48	1.06	n/a
ZLB $\underline{R}[x(t),\tau]$	0.00	0.20	1.28	1.96	n/a
ZLB $\underline{P}[x(t),\tau]$	1.0000	0.9941	0.8799	0.5552	3.4292
K-ANSM $\underline{D}_L(t,\tau)$	0.0086	0.551	4.89	10.30	15.75
K-ANSM $\underline{D}_S(t,\tau)$	0.0068	0.297	1.05	0.76	2.11
2. ANSM(2) duration from K-ANSM(2) bond prices					
ANSM $D_L(t,\tau)$	1.00	2.98	8.80	16.66	29.44
ANSM $D_S(t,\tau)$	0.87	2.02	2.96	1.99	7.84

Table 8.8 July 2012 K-ANSM(2) Level duration example

Time to maturity, τ	1	3	10	30	Sum
1. K-ANSM(2) shadow interest rates and changes					
$\underline{R}[x(t),\tau]$	−2.76	−1.56	0.48	1.06	n/a
$\underline{R}[x(t)+\Delta x_L,\tau]$	−2.26	−1.06	0.98	1.56	n/a
$\underline{R}[x(t)-\Delta x_L,\tau]$	−3.26	−2.06	−0.02	0.56	n/a
$\Delta \underline{R}[x(t)+\Delta x_L,\tau]$	0.50	0.50	0.50	0.50	n/a
$\Delta \underline{R}[x(t)-\Delta x_L,\tau]$	−0.50	−0.50	−0.50	−0.50	n/a
2. K-ANSM(2) ZLB interest rates and changes					
$\underline{R}[x(t),\tau]$	0.00	0.20	1.28	1.96	n/a
$\underline{R}[x(t)+\Delta x_L,\tau]$	0.01	0.31	1.58	2.28	n/a
$\underline{R}[x(t)-\Delta x_L,\tau]$	0.00	0.12	1.02	1.67	n/a
$\Delta \underline{R}[x(t)+\Delta x_L,\tau]$	0.01	0.11	0.30	0.32	n/a
$\Delta \underline{R}[x(t)-\Delta x_L,\tau]$	−0.00	−0.08	−0.26	−0.29	n/a
3. K-ANSM(2) bond prices and changes					
$\underline{P}[x(t),\tau]$	1.0000	0.9941	0.8799	0.5552	3.4292
$\underline{P}[x(t)+\Delta x_L,\tau]$	0.9999	0.9908	0.8542	0.5039	3.3489
$\underline{P}[x(t)-\Delta x_L,\tau]$	1.0000	0.9964	0.9031	0.6066	3.5060
$\Delta \underline{P}[x(t)+\Delta x_L,\tau]$	−0.0001	−0.0033	−0.0257	−0.0513	−0.0803
$\Delta \underline{P}[x(t)-\Delta x_L,\tau]$	0.0000	0.0023	0.0231	0.0513	0.0768
4. K-ANSM(2) Level duration approximation					
K-ANSM $\underline{D}_L(t,\tau)$	0.0086	0.551	4.89	10.30	15.75
$0.50\% \times \underline{D}_L(t,\tau)$	0.0000	0.0028	0.0245	0.0515	0.0787
5. ANSM(2) Level duration approximations					
ANSM $D_L(t,\tau)$	1.00	2.98	8.80	16.66	29.44
$0.50\% \times D_L(t,\tau)$	0.0050	0.0149	0.0440	0.0833	0.1472

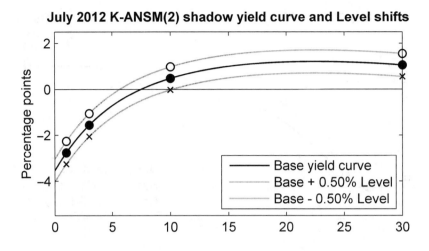

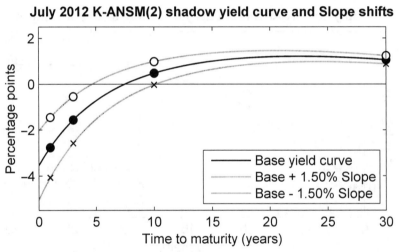

Figure 8.7 Examples of how shadow yield curve shifts in a ZLB environment can be repre-sented by changes to the K-ANSM(2) shadow Level and/or Slope state variables.

maturities. Therefore, it will make a large difference if one naively applies stan-dard factor duration calculations without allowing for the ZLB constraint on "real world" bond prices and fixed interest portfolios.

K-ANSM(2) Level duration and Level state variable shifts

Table 8.8 provides the results for the K-ANSM(2) Level shift and K-ANSM(2) Level duration calculations. Panel 1 contains the 1-, 3-, 10-, and 30-year shadow inter-est rate results for the base and the shifted K-ANSM(2) shadow yield curves. Note that the K-ANSM(2) shadow interest rate changes are identical to the interest rate changes from the ANSM(2) Level shift in subsection 8.3.3, because the state variable change vector Δx_L is identical.

July 2012 K-ANSM(2) ZLB yield curve and Level shifts

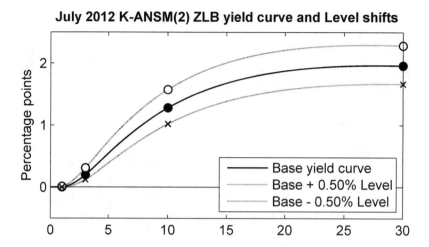

July 2012 K-ANSM(2) ZLB yield curve and Slope shifts

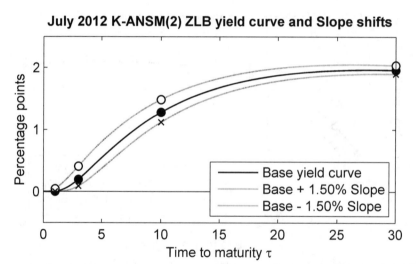

Figure 8.8 Examples of yield curve shifts in a ZLB environment respectively obtained by changes to the K-ANSM(2) Level and Slope state variables.

Panel 2 contains the K-ANSM(2) ZLB interest rate results for the base and the shifted K-ANSM(2) ZLB yield curves. As previously illustrated, the K-ANSM(2) ZLB interest rate changes are very attenuated compared to the K-ANSM(2) shadow interest rate changes. The asymmetries of the changes are also a bit more pronounced. Both of these results reflect the large constraint from the ZLB.

The actual changes in K-ANSM(2) bond prices are calculated using the K-ANSM(2) ZLB interest rates contained in panel 2, and these are summed to obtain the portfolio value. Panel 4 provides the K-ANSM(2) Level duration calculations. These results show that the fully consistent K-ANSM(2) duration calculations give the correct approximation to the actual bond price and portfolio total changes in panel 3.

Panel 5 provides the ANSM(2) Level duration calculations. These results show that it now makes a large difference if one applies standard factor duration calculations without allowing for the ZLB constraint to "real world" bond prices and fixed interest portfolios. In particular, the ANSM Level duration results greatly overstate the risk from Level shifts, very severely for shorter maturities, and approximately double for the portfolio.

K-ANSM(2) Slope duration approximation to Slope state variable shifts

Table 8.9 provides the results for the K-ANSM(2) Slope shift and K-ANSM Slope duration calculations.

The results and discussion are analogous to those already provided for the K-ANSM(2) Level duration. That is, panel 1 shows that the K-ANSM(2) shadow interest rate changes are identical to the interest rate changes from the ANSM(2) Slope shift in subsection 8.3.4, and panel 2 shows that the K-ANSM(2) ZLB interest rate changes are asymmetric and very attenuated compared to the K-ANSM(2) shadow interest rate changes.

Panel 4 shows that the fully consistent K-ANSM(2) duration calculations give the correct approximation to the actual K-ANSM(2) bond prices and portfolio value changes in panel 3.

Panel 5 again shows that it makes a large difference if one applies standard factor duration calculations without allowing for the ZLB constraint to "real world" bond prices and fixed interest portfolios that are constrained by the ZLB. In other words, using a naive calculation of ANSM(2) Slope duration for the ZLB-constrained bonds would greatly overstate the risk from Slope shifts, very severely for shorter maturities and by approximately four times for the portfolio.

K-ANSM(2) fixed interest portfolio risk

Following the variance calculation σ_D^2 for the Risk Distribution of the K-ANSM(2) in the non-ZLB environment, the result in the ZLB environment is

$$\sigma_{\underline{D}}^2 = [15.75, 2.11] \begin{bmatrix} 0.7417 & -0.7097 \\ -0.7097 & 2.5703 \end{bmatrix} \times 10^{-4} \times \begin{bmatrix} 15.75 \\ 2.11 \end{bmatrix} \cdot \frac{1}{12}$$

$$= 12.355 \times 10^{-4} \tag{8.78}$$

and the standard deviation is

$$\sigma_D = \sqrt{12.355} \times \sqrt{10^{-4}}$$

$$= 0.0352 \text{ dollars} \tag{8.79}$$

The one-month 1% VaR would be $-2.33 \times 0.0352 = -0.0819$ dollars.

Table 8.9 July 2012 K-ANSM(2) Slope duration example

Maturity, τ	1	3	10	30	Sum
1. K-ANSM(2) shadow interest rates and changes					
$\underset{\sim}{R}[x(t),\tau]$	−2.76	−1.56	0.48	1.06	n/a
$\underset{\sim}{R}[x(t)+\Delta x_S,\tau]$	−1.45	−0.54	0.98	1.24	n/a
$\underset{\sim}{R}[x(t)-\Delta x_S,\tau]$	−4.07	−2.58	−0.03	0.88	n/a
$\Delta\underset{\sim}{R}[x(t)+\Delta x_S,\tau]$	1.31	1.02	0.51	0.18	n/a
$\Delta\underset{\sim}{R}[x(t)-\Delta x_S,\tau]$	−1.31	−1.02	−0.51	−0.18	n/a
2. K-ANSM(2) ZLB interest rates and changes					
$R[x(t),\tau]$	0.00	0.20	1.28	1.96	n/a
$R[x(t)+\Delta x_S,\tau]$	0.04	0.41	1.48	2.04	n/a
$R[x(t)-\Delta x_S,\tau]$	0.00	0.09	1.12	1.90	n/a
$\Delta R[x(t)+\Delta x_S,\tau]$	0.04	0.21	0.21	0.08	n/a
$\Delta R[x(t)-\Delta x_S,\tau]$	−0.00	−0.11	−0.16	−0.06	n/a
3. K-ANSM(2) bond prices and changes					
$\underset{\sim}{P}[x(t),\tau]$	1.0000	0.9941	0.8799	0.5552	3.4292
$\underset{\sim}{P}[x(t)+\Delta x_S,\tau]$	0.9996	0.9878	0.8620	0.5426	3.3920
$\underset{\sim}{P}[x(t)-\Delta x_S,\tau]$	1.0000	0.9973	0.8941	0.5656	3.4570
$\Delta\underset{\sim}{P}[x(t)+\Delta x_S,\tau]$	−0.0004	−0.0063	−0.0179	−0.0126	−0.0373
$\Delta\underset{\sim}{P}[x(t)-\Delta x_S,\tau]$	0.0000	0.0032	0.0142	0.0103	0.0278
4. K-ANSM(2) Slope duration approximation					
K-ANSM $\underset{\sim}{D}_S(t,\tau)$	0.0068	0.297	1.05	0.76	2.11
$1.50\% \times \underset{\sim}{D}_S(t,\tau)$	0.0001	0.0045	0.0158	0.0113	0.0317
5. ANSM(2) Slope duration approximations					
ANSM $D_S(t,\tau)$	0.87	2.02	2.96	1.99	7.84
$1.50\% \times D_S(t,\tau)$	0.0131	0.0303	0.0444	0.0298	0.1177

The Risk Distribution using the ANSM(2) duration calculations for the K-ANSM(2) bond prices is

$$\sigma_D^2 = [29.44, 7.84]\begin{bmatrix} 0.7417 & -0.7097 \\ -0.7097 & 2.5703 \end{bmatrix} \times 10^{-4} \times \begin{bmatrix} 29.44 \\ 7.84 \end{bmatrix} \cdot \frac{1}{12}$$

$$= 39.435 \times 10^{-4} \tag{8.80}$$

and the standard deviation is

$$\sigma_D = \sqrt{39.435} \times \sqrt{10^{-4}}$$

$$= 0.0628 \text{ dollars} \tag{8.81}$$

Therefore, the K-ANSM(2) model-consistent estimate of unanticipated changes to the portfolio value over a one-month horizon is the normal distribution:

$$\text{Risk Dist.} \simeq N(0, 0.0628) \text{ dollars} \tag{8.82}$$

The one-month 1% VaR would be $-2.33 \times 0.0628 = -0.146$ dollars, which is substantially different from the fully consistent K-ANSM(2) VaR calculation.

8.5.5 A perspective on the K-ANSM versus ANSM factor duration results

The relatively small differences between the factor duration calculations I have presented for the non-ZLB environment are best explained by the fact that the K-ANSMs naturally revert to being ANSMs when the ZLB is an immaterial constraint. Regarding the duration, note that when $f[x(t), \tau]$ is large, the cumulative unit normal density function is approximately 1, that is,

$$\Phi \left[\frac{f[x(t), \tau] - r_L}{\omega(\tau)} \right] \simeq 1 \tag{8.83}$$

because r_L is constant and $\omega(\tau)$ is a time-invariant function of time to maturity. Therefore,

$$
\begin{aligned}
\underline{D}(t, \tau) &= \underline{P}[x(t), \tau] \int_0^\tau \left[\frac{1}{\exp(-\phi u)} \right] \Phi \left[\frac{f[x(t), u] - r_L}{\omega(u)} \right] du \\
&\simeq \underline{P}[x(t), \tau] \int_0^\tau \left[\frac{1}{\exp(-\phi u)} \right] du \\
&= \underline{P}[x(t), \tau] \left[\frac{1}{\phi}[1 - \exp(-\phi \tau)] \right] \\
&= \left[\frac{\underline{P}[x(t), \tau] \cdot \tau}{\underline{P}[x(t), \tau] \cdot \frac{1}{\phi}[1 - \exp(-\phi \tau)]} \right]
\end{aligned}
$$

Hence, in general for non-ZLB environments, the ANSM duration calculations applied to the K-ANSM bond prices provide a close approximation to the fully-consistent K-ANSM duration calculation $\underline{D}(t, \tau)$. In other words, ANSM factor durations calculated on "real world" ZLB-constrained bond prices provide a practically adequate risk framework in a non-ZLB environment.

The same comment applies generally to factor durations based on principal components or other methods. That is, it will be practically adequate to apply standard duration calculations, that is, based on models without an explicit ZLB constraint, in non-ZLB environments, even though interest rates and bond prices are known to be constrained by the ZLB. Of course, as illustrated in subsection 8.5.4, applying standard duration models in ZLB environments is not appropriate, and the results are potentially very misleading.

As an aside, note that $\underline{P}[x(t),\tau] \simeq P[x(t),\tau]$ when $f[x(t),\tau]$ is large (see subsection 4.1.4). Therefore, K-ANSM durations and ANSM durations calculated on shadow bond prices are also approximately equal in non-ZLB environments. For example, the K-ANSM(2) result would be

$$
\underline{D}(t,\tau) \simeq
\left[
\begin{array}{c}
P[x(t),\tau] \cdot \tau \\
P[x(t),\tau] \cdot \frac{1}{\phi}\left[1 - \exp(-\phi\tau)\right]
\end{array}
\right]
$$
$$
= D(t,\tau) \tag{8.84}
$$

However, shadow bond prices are not observed in practice, so the ANSM duration results with K-ANSM ZLB bond prices is the practically relevant result.

8.6 Bond option pricing

In this section, I discuss how to price options on bonds in a ZLB environment using the K-ANSM, and how that resolves issues that arise with models that do not respect the ZLB.

I begin in subsection 8.6.1 by using the ANSM(2) to illustrate how using a model that does not allow for the ZLB constraint leads to anomalous prices for call options on bonds in a ZLB environment. In particular, a strike price of 1 still produces positive prices for call options, even though the probability of exercise is zero in the "real world" because the ZLB constraint on interest rates prevents negative interest rates and therefore bond prices above 1.

In subsection 8.6.2, I show how K-ANSMs can be applied to price call options on "real world" bonds. Specifically, K-ANSM interest rates are constrained by the ZLB, therefore K-ANSM bonds are constrained by the upper bound of 1, and I show how to price options on those ZLB-constrained bonds. The K-ANSM option pricing framework therefore corrects the ANSM anomaly discussed in subsection 8.6.1.

In section 8.6.3, I provide an overview of how B-ANSMs could be applied to price call options on ZLB bonds. While the pricing could readily be undertaken by following the process I outline, my main purpose in this section is show how the process becomes more complex when the process for obtaining ZLB bond prices is not tractable.

8.6.1 ANSM option pricing

Call options on bonds within the GATSM framework may be defined with the generic arbitrage expression (e.g., see Filopović [2009, pp. 109]) as

$$C(t, \tau_1, \tau_2, P_S) = \tilde{\mathbb{E}}_t \left\{ \exp\left(-\int_0^{\tau_1} r(t+u)\, du \right) \right.$$
$$\left. \times \max\left[P(t+\tau_1, \tau_2) - P_S, 0 \right] \right\} \tag{8.85}$$

where $C(t, \tau_1, \tau_2, P_S)$ is the price of a call option, as at time t, with an expiry at time $t + \tau_1$, and a strike price P_S, where the underlying asset is a GATSM bond $P(t + \tau_1, \tau_2)$ that has a remaining time to maturity of τ_2 at time $t + \tau_1$ (or in other words, settlement at time $t + \tau_1$ with a time of maturity $t + \tau_1 + \tau_2$). $\tilde{\mathbb{E}}_t \{\cdot\}$ denotes expectations under the risk-adjusted measure. As I return to later, that expectation may essentially be viewed as the mean of many (i.e., an infinity of) Monte Carlo simulations of the expression within the curly brackets for paths of the short rate $r(t+u)$ and the prices $P(t+\tau_1, \tau_2)$ at the end of each path.

From the generic arbitrage expression, the prices of options on bonds within the GATSM framework can be derived as a closed-form analytic solution. For example, the expression for the ANSM(2) call option price that I will use for my illustrations in this section is

$$C(t, \tau_1, \tau_2, P_S) = P(t, \tau_1 + \tau_2)\, \Phi\left[v_1\, (t, \tau_1, \tau_2) \right]$$
$$- P_S \cdot P(t, \tau_1)\, \Phi\left[v_2\, (t, \tau_1, \tau_2) \right] \tag{8.86}$$

where $\Phi[\cdot]$ is the cumulative normal distribution function and

$$v_{1,2}\, (t, \tau_1, \tau_2) = \frac{1}{\Sigma\, (\tau_1, \tau_2)} \log\left[\frac{P(t, \tau_1 + \tau_2)}{P_S \cdot P(t, \tau_1)} \right] \pm \frac{1}{2} \Sigma\, (\tau_1, \tau_2) \tag{8.87}$$

with

$$[\Sigma\, (\tau_1, \tau_2)]^2 = \sigma_1^2 \cdot \tau_1 \tau_2^2 + \sigma_2^2 \cdot G(2\phi, \tau_1) \cdot [G(\phi, \tau_2)]^2$$
$$+ 2\rho_{12}\sigma_1\sigma_2 \cdot \tau_1 \cdot G(\phi, \tau_1) \cdot G(\phi, \tau_2) \tag{8.88}$$

and

$$P(t, \tau) = \exp\left(-\tau \cdot R(t, \tau) \right) \tag{8.89}$$

where

$$R(t, \tau) = a(\tau) + L(t) + S(t) \cdot \frac{1}{\tau} G(\phi, \tau) \tag{8.90}$$

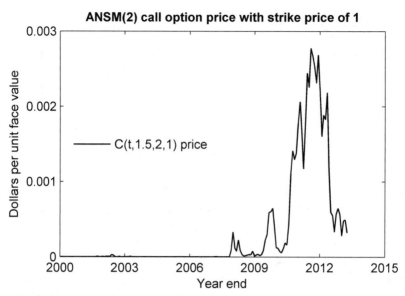

Figure 8.9 An example of positive prices for call options on bonds with a strike price of 1, which equates to an interest rate of zero.

and

$$a(\tau) = -\sigma_L^2 \cdot \frac{1}{6}\tau^2 - \sigma_S^2 \cdot \frac{1}{2\phi^2}\left[1 - \frac{1}{\tau}G(\phi,\tau) - \frac{1}{2\tau}\phi\,[G(\phi,\tau)]^2\right]$$

$$- \rho\sigma_L\sigma_S \cdot \frac{1}{\phi^2}\left[1 - \frac{1}{\tau}G(\phi,\tau) + \frac{1}{2}\phi\tau - \phi G(\phi,\tau)\right] \qquad (8.91)$$

Subsection 5.4.3 provides the general expression for GATSM bond option prices and also calculates the bond options expressions for the ANSM(2) and ANSM(3), and other GATSMs.

Using this ANSM(2) call option price expression and the estimated ANSM(2) state variables and parameters from Table 3.3 in subsection 3.5.2, I calculate the price of a call option $C(t, 1.5, 2, 1)$ with an expiry in $\tau_1 = 1.5$ years, a strike price of $P_S = 1$, and written on a bond with $\tau_2 = 2$ years to maturity on the expiry of the option. The time and strike price are arbitrary choices. Similar results hold for other choices I tried, and the key point is to illustrate the material results that can arise from using typical option pricing parameters.

Figure 8.9 plots the results and shows that the call option sometimes has a positive price, particularly following the onset of the ZLB period, but even mild instances prior. To illustrate the materiality, note that the 0.001 dollar magnitude per unit face value implies that one could sell the call option for $1,000 per million dollar face value.

If one used the non-zero prices for the ANSM(2) call options in the "real world," that would imply there is a non-zero probability of the bond price being above the strike price of 1 at the time of expiry. However, a bond price above 1 corresponds to an interest rate below zero, and such an outcome should not be possible given that the ZLB constraint prevents interest rates from evolving below zero. Indeed, the arbitrage opportunity would be to sell options with a strike at or above 1, thereby receiving the positive option price with no probability of a payout on the expiry of the option.

This example highlights one of the undesirable features of the GATSM option pricing framework in principle and in practice, that is, GATSM option prices will always include some effect from the probability of bond prices being above 1 at the time of expiry.

Discussing the GATSM option price result in principle as a Monte Carlo simulation of the generic arbitrage pricing expression provides the intuition for the results. The exposition is also very useful for comparing it to the pricing of options in the K-AGM and B-AGM frameworks that I outline in next two subsections.

For GATSM option prices, first consider that the price of the GATSM bond $P(t + \tau_1, \tau_2)$ on which the option is written is itself representable by its own generic arbitrage expression:

$$P(t + \tau_1, \tau_2) = \tilde{\mathbb{E}}_{t+\tau_1} \left\{ \exp\left(-\int_0^{\tau_2} r(t + \tau_1 + u)\, du\right) \cdot 1 \right\} \tag{8.92}$$

where 1 is the final payoff for the bond, $\tilde{\mathbb{E}}_{t+\tau_1}\{\cdot\}$ denotes expectations under the risk-adjusted measure at time $t + \tau_1$, and $r(t + \tau_1 + u)$ are the paths of the short rate up to the bond maturity τ_2. Each simulated path of the short rate $r(t + \tau_1 + u)$ begins from the value of $r(t + \tau_1)$, and each value of $r(t + \tau_1)$ is in turn obtained as the end result from simulating the path $r(t + u)$ from the starting value of $r(t)$ to $r(t + \tau_1)$.

The current and future simulated values of $r(t)$ are themselves obtained from the state variable vector $x(t)$ and its simulations from the Gaussian diffusion process. Regardless of the initial starting values of $x(t)$, the mathematically infinite domain of any Gaussian diffusion process always produces some values of $x(t + \tau_1)$ and hence paths $r(t + \tau_1 + u)$ that will result in $P(t + \tau_1, \tau_2) > P_S$. Therefore, some payoffs $\max[P(t + \tau_1, \tau_2) - P_S, 0]$ will be positive, regardless of the value of P_S, even while many payoffs may result in a zero payoff. The discounting process represented by $\exp\left(-\int_0^{\tau_1} r(t + u)\, du\right)$ will alter the present value of each payoff, but each payoff will remain either positive or zero. The expected value, or mean, of zero and positive payoffs will therefore be positive. Therefore, the call option will always have a positive value regardless of the strike price P_S. Of course, this general result is purely mathematical; the actual value is often negligible in practice, but the example already provided shows that the positive value becomes material near the ZLB.

8.6.2 K-AGM option pricing

Call options on bonds within the K-AGM framework may be defined with a modified form of the generic arbitrage expression introduced in the previous subsection. Specifically, the only adjustment necessary is to change the GATSM bond price $P(t + \tau_1, \tau_2)$ in the option payoff to the K-AGM bond price $\underline{P}(t + \tau_1, \tau_2)$:

$$\underline{C}(t, \tau_1, \tau_2, P_S) = \tilde{\mathbb{E}}_t \left\{ \exp\left(-\int_0^{\tau_1} r(t + u)\, du \right) \right.$$

$$\left. \times \max\left[\underline{P}(t + \tau_1, \tau_2) - P_S, 0 \right] \right\} \tag{8.93}$$

where all of the notation is as already presented for the GATSM framework, except $\underline{C}(t, \tau_1, \tau_2, P_S)$ denotes the price of a call option on the K-AGM bond $\underline{P}(t + \tau_1, \tau_2)$ that is subject to the ZLB constraint.

Unfortunately, I do not think that the generic arbitrage expression for $\underline{C}(t, \tau_1, \tau_2, P_S)$ is likely to have a closed-form analytic expression. As background on this point, the GATSM bond option expression essentially relies on both $r(t + u)$ and $r(t + \tau_1 + u)$ having Gaussian distributions (see Filopović [2009, pp. 109–10]). However, section 4.1 shows that $\underline{P}(t + \tau_1, \tau_2)$ arises from the truncated Gaussian distribution $\max\{0, r(t + \tau_1 + u)\}$, which is not itself a Gaussian distribution.[2]

Nevertheless, the tractable expressions for the term structure in the K-ANSM framework make the calculation of $\underline{P}(t + \tau_1, \tau_2)$ very straightforward to use as part of a Monte Carlo simulation. Essentially, one only needs to simulate the paths of the state variables $x(t + u)$ out to τ_1 and then use those results to calculate $\underline{P}(t + \tau_1, \tau_2)$ and therefore the option payoff $\max[\underline{P}(t + \tau_1, \tau_2) - P_S, 0]$. The state variables $x(t + u)$ out to τ_1 provide the shadow short rates $r(t + u)$ to discount the option payoff back to zero.[3]

Section 5.3 contains the details on Monte Carlo simulations in the context of obtaining B-AGM bond prices and the associated interest rates. A brief overview of the key points required for this section is that the Monte Carlo simulation result for $\underline{C}(t, \tau_1, \tau_2, P_S)$ is obtained as

$$\widehat{\underline{C}}(t, \tau_1, \tau_2, P_S) = \frac{1}{J} \sum_{j=1}^{J} \underline{C}_j(t, \tau_1, \tau_2, P_S) \tag{8.94}$$

where the caret "^" indicates that $\widehat{\underline{C}}(t, \tau_1, \tau_2, P_S)$ is a sample estimate and J is the sample size of individual option price simulations $\underline{C}_j(t, \tau_1, \tau_2, P_S)$. The J values of $\underline{C}_j(t, \tau_1, \tau_2, P_S)$ are each obtained as the simulations

$$\underline{C}_j(t, \tau_1, \tau_2, P_S) = \exp\left[-\sum_{m=0}^{M-1} r_{t,j,m} \cdot \delta \right] \max\left[\underline{P}_j(t + \tau_1, \tau_2) - P_S, 0 \right] \tag{8.95}$$

where the simulated shadow short rates $r_{t,j,m}$ are obtained from the shadow short rate expression:

$$r_{t,j,m} = a_0 + b_0' x_{t,j,m} \qquad (8.96)$$

and a_0 and b_0 represent fixed parameters for the GATSM specification used to represent the K-AGM shadow term structure. The sample state variables $x_{t,j,m}$ are generated from the discretized process for the GATSM state variables $x(t)$ under the risk adjusted $\mathbb{Q}$ measure:

$$x_{t,j,m} = x_{t,j,m-1} + \tilde{\kappa}\left(\tilde{\theta} - x_{t,j,i-1}\right)\delta + \sigma\sqrt{\delta}\epsilon_{t,j,m}$$

where $x_{t,j,0} = x(t)$, $\tilde{\kappa}$, $\tilde{\theta}$, and σ represent fixed GATSM parameters, δ is the simulation time increment $\delta = \tau_1/M$ with M being the number of increments from time t to the time of expiry $t + \tau_1$, and $\epsilon_{t,j,m}$ is an $N \times 1$ vector of independent pseudo-random draws from the unit normal distribution, $\epsilon_{t,j,m} \sim N(0,1)$.

For each simulation, once $x_{t,j,M}$ is obtained, I then set $x(t + \tau_1) = x_{t,j,M}$ and I calculate $P(t + \tau_1, \tau_2)$ using the methods outlined in subsection 8.5.1 or more fully in chapter 4. Next, I calculate the option payoff $\max[P(t + \tau_1, \tau_2) - P_S, 0]$, and that gives all of the elements required to calculate the simulation result $C_j(t, \tau_1, \tau_2, P_S)$. Repeating this step J times provides the sample used to obtain $\widehat{C}(t, \tau_1, \tau_2, P_S)$ as the mean of the results $C_j(t, \tau_1, \tau_2, P_S)$. I have used just 1,000 simulations for each of the points in Figure 8.10, which took about 0.3 seconds for each option price. Section 5.3 provides guidance on how to determine an appropriate value for J in practice, which I expect would be at least tens of thousands, if not more.

As a simple illustration of applying the K-AGM option pricing framework, Figure 8.10 plots the prices of call and put options on K-ANSM(2) bonds. The time to expiry is $\tau_1 = 1.5$ years, the bond maturity on expiry is $\tau_2 = 2$ years, and I have used a single strike price based on a 2 percent interest rate at the time of expiry, that is, $P_S = \exp(-2 \times 0.02) = 0.9608$. The maximum payoff for all call options on expiry is therefore $1 - P_S = 0.0392$, as indicated in Figure 8.10. The x axis is the current (i.e., time t) shadow short rate, which I vary using the Slope state variable $S(t)$ and keeping the Level state variable fixed at $L(t) = 5\%$.

As an example of interpreting Figure 8.10, consider the call option price results. The call option will have a payoff if the 2-year interest rate is below 2% at the time of expiry, which is in 1.5 years' time. The probability of that outcome increases, and therefore the call option price becomes higher, as the yield curve becomes more constrained by the ZLB. The degree of constraint is in turn indicated by more

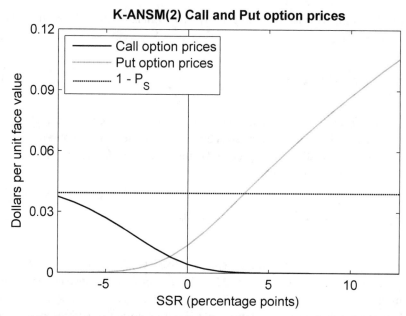

Figure 8.10 Example of call option and put option prices for the K-ANSM(2). The call option payoff (and therefore the option price) is limited by the ZLB, while the put option payoff (and therefore the option price) is unconstrained.

negative values of the shadow short rate. However, the maximum payoff at the time of expiry is 0.0392, so the price of the call option is constrained even if the shadow short rate adopts more negative values.

Conversely, the price of the put option depends on the 2-year interest rate being above 2% at the time of expiry, and the payoff is unbounded. Therefore the price of the put option continues to rise as the shadow short rate adopts more positive values.

Note that the ZLB mechanism in the K-AGM by construction eliminates the probability of bond prices being above 1. Therefore call option prices with a strike price of 1 or above have prices of zero. For a non-zero lower bound, the same principle holds, but the highest strike price will be the highest attainable bond price given the specified non-zero lower bound.

8.6.3 B-AGM option pricing

Call options on bonds within the B-AGM framework may be defined with a modified form of the generic arbitrage expression introduced for GATSMs in subsection 8.6.1. Specifically, the two adjustments are to change the GATSM short rates $r(t + u)$ to B-AGM short rates $\underline{r}(t + u) = \max[0, r(t + u)]$, and the GATSM bond price

$P(t+\tau_1,\tau_2)$ in the option payoff to the B-AGM bond price $\underline{P}^B(t+\tau_1,\tau_2)$. The resulting expression is

$$\underline{C}^B(t,\tau_1,\tau_2,P_S) = \tilde{\mathbb{E}}_t\left\{\exp\left(-\int_0^{\tau_1}\underline{r}(t+u)\,du\right)\right.$$

$$\left.\times\max\left[\underline{P}^B(t+\tau_1,\tau_2)-P_S,0\right]\right\} \tag{8.97}$$

where all of the notation is as already presented for the GATSM framework, except $\underline{C}^B(t,\tau_1,\tau_2,P_S)$ denotes the price of a call option on the B-AGM bond $\underline{P}^B(t+\tau_1,\tau_2)$ that is subject to the ZLB constraint.

As already noted in section 5.1, the generic arbitrage expression for $\underline{P}^B(t+\tau_1,\tau_2)$ does not have a closed-form analytic solution, so $\underline{C}^B(t,\tau_1,\tau_2,P_S)$ will not have a closed-form analytic solution. Monte Carlo simulation can be used to obtain solutions, but the process is more involved than for K-AGMs.

The B-AGM Monte Carlo process for a single simulation j follows the K-AGM process up to the expiry time τ_1 to obtain a simulated state variable vector $x_{t,j,M}$. The difference is that the K-AGM at that stage uses the tractable evaluation of the bond price $\underline{P}_j(t+\tau_1,\tau_2)$ with the state variable vector $x(t+\tau_1) = x_{t,j,M}$ to obtain the option payoff for that simulation. However, the B-AGM does not have tractable solutions available, so one must use again time-consuming numerical techniques to obtain the bond price for that path. In generic terms, the result required for $x(t+\tau_1) = x_{t,j,M}$ is

$$\underline{P}^B(t+\tau_1,\tau_2) = \tilde{\mathbb{E}}_{t+\tau_1}\left\{\exp\left(-\int_0^{\tau_2}\underline{r}(t+\tau_1+u)\,du\right)\cdot 1\right\} \tag{8.98}$$

where 1 is the fixed payoff for the bond at time $t+\tau$. In general, as detailed in section 5.3, calculating an estimate of $\underline{P}^B(t+\tau_1,\tau_2)$ requires a further full Monte Carlo simulation of many paths from $x(t+\tau_1) = x_{t,j,M}$. Specifically, as detailed in section 5.3, a Monte Carlo simulation of the discretized process for $\underline{r}(t+u)$ under the $\mathbb{Q}$ measure would be used to obtain a sample of values for the expression $\underline{P}^B_j(t+\tau_1,\tau_2) = \exp\left(-\int_{\tau_1}^{\tau_2}\underline{r}(t+u)\,du\right)\cdot 1$. The mean of those simulated sample values $\underline{P}^B_j(t+\tau_1,\tau_2)$ provides an estimate $\widehat{\underline{P}}^B(t+\tau_1,\tau_2)$ of $\underline{P}^B(t+\tau_1,\tau_2)$, and the standard error of the mean of that sample will give the precision of the estimate $\widehat{\underline{P}}^B(t+\tau_1,\tau_2)$ relative to the true mean.

As highlighted in section 5.3, the number of simulations required to obtain an estimate $\widehat{\underline{P}}^B(t+\tau_1,\tau_2)$ that is precise enough for practical purposes (e.g., with a 99% confidence interval of one basis point) is typically in the order of hundreds of thousands, if not millions. Those simulations would be required for each of the J simulations that are required provide the initial state variables at time $t+\tau_1$. Hence, the combination of those two requirements would make the calculation of B-AGM option prices much more computationally onerous than K-AGM option prices.

8.7 Summary

- In this chapter, I have provided two detailed frameworks for applying ANSMs and K-ANSMs to financial market topics, that is, measuring fixed interest portfolio risk and pricing options on bonds. The fully worked examples are for the ANSM(2) and K-ANSM(2), and I also show that the frameworks readily extend to the K-ANSM(3).
- The results show that using the ANSM(2) in ZLB environments is seriously deficient in both applications:
    - As a means of providing metrics for fixed interest portfolio risk, ANSM(2) Level and Slope durations seriously overstate the valuation changes for individual bonds and the portfolio total from yield curve shifts, and therefore the estimated Value at Risk (VaR) is also seriously overstated.
    - The ANSM(2) delivers materially positive prices for call options on bonds, even when the strike price is set at 1, or more. Those strike prices would suggest interest rates were at or below the ZLB. Selling such call options with no "real world" probability of a payout would represent an arbitrage opportunity.
- K-ANSMs provide straightforward and easily implemented solutions to both of those financial market applications in ZLB environments:
    - The K-ANSM framework effectively attenuates shadow yield curve shifts appropriately so that the resulting K-ANSM(2) Level and Slope durations provide good representations of the associated valuation changes for individual bonds and the portfolio. The result is therefore much-improved VaR calculations.
    - K-ANSMs eliminate the probability of negative interest rates, so the prices of call options with a strike price of 1 or more are zero. The K-ANSM(2) illustration of put and call option prices on bonds shows an asymmetry depending on the degree of the ZLB constraint. Call options have a payoff that is limited by the ZLB, while put options have potentially large payoffs because interest rates are free to evolve to positive values.
- While it would be possible to use B-ANSMs for both applications, their lack of tractability would make practical applications much more onerous.

9 | Conclusion and Future Research Directions

I have three objectives in this final chapter. The first is to briefly summarize, in section 9.1, the key points from each of the main chapters of the book.

The second objective is to provide an overview of the case for using K-ANSMs, that is, the Krippner (2011, 2012b,c, 2013,d,e) shadow/ZLB framework with arbitrage-free Nelson and Siegel (1987) models (ANSMs) to represent the shadow term structure. I mentioned in chapter 1 that I consider K-ANSMs to be the most suitable subclass of shadow/ZLB term structure models, in principle and for practical applications, so in section 9.2, I can now summarize the reasons for that preference in light of the material covered in the book.

The third objective is to provide some avenues for future research and applications related to K-ANSMs. I have already mentioned ideas at various stages in the book, but section 9.3 provides a summary and some context on priorities.

9.1 Summary

In this book, I have developed term structure frameworks and associated monetary policy measures that can accommodate the near-zero nominal interest rate environments that have prevailed in most major economies since late-2008/early-2009. The zero lower bound (ZLB) constraint for interest rates is an historically new environment, so new frameworks to apply to practical issues are needed.

In the main chapters, I have worked from an overview and motivation of the topic, through the details of term structure modeling and introducing a ZLB mechanism, to applications of the new frameworks to monetary policy and financial market topics. I summarize the key points from each of the main chapters in the order in which I introduced them in chapter 1:

- **Chapter 2: A new framework for a new environment.** This nontechnical overview discussed how operating and monitoring monetary policy using a policy interest rate, and using Gaussian affine term structure models (GATSMs) for financial market applications are no longer applicable when interest rates are at or near the ZLB. Term structure models within the shadow/ZLB-GATSM class provide a solution to the deficiencies of GATSMs in ZLB environments, and they essentially revert to being GATSMs in non-ZLB environments. The shadow yield curve also provides potentially useful information for operating and monitoring unconventional monetary policy.

- **Chapter 3: Gaussian affine term structure models.** This chapter provided the details for specifying and estimating GATSMs, and the ANSM subclass. The estimation results reinforced the point from chapter 1 that GATSMs are deficient for term structure applications in ZLB environments, because they allow high probabilities of negative interest rates which is a property that does not occur in the "real world." However, GATSMs can be used to represent the shadow term structure in shadow/ZLB-GATSMs.

- **Chapter 4: Krippner framework for ZLB term structure modeling.** This chapter showed that the Krippner shadow/ZLB-GATSM (i.e., K-AGM) framework is a relatively straightforward modification to the GATSM class, because specifying and estimating K-AGMs is largely based on GATSMs, as outlined in chapter 3. Applications of the K-AGM framework with ANSMs to represent the shadow yield curve (i.e., K-ANSMs) are shown to be tractable and to provide empirical results that respect the ZLB and are consistent with the properties of the data in ZLB environments.

- **Chapter 5: Black framework for ZLB term structure modeling.** This chapter provided an exposition of the Black (1995) shadow/ZLB-GATSM framework and showed that its implementation using numerical methods makes its practical application much less tractable than the K-AGM framework. However, K-ANSMs are shown to closely approximate B-ANSMs (i.e., the Black [1995] framework with ANSMs to represent the shadow yield curve). Therefore, K-ANSMs provide a practical compromise even if one considers B-ANSMs to be the theoretically correct shadow/ZLB framework.

- **Chapter 6: K-ANSM foundations and "Effective Monetary Stimulus."** This chapter developed a generic economic foundation for ANSMs to justify using them as a parsimonious and realistic representation of the shadow term structure. The economic foundation also provides a theoretical case for using K-ANSMs rather than B-ANSMs, independent of the practical approximation outlined in chapter 5. Chapter 6 also detailed the "Effective Monetary Stimulus," or EMS, summary measure for the stance of monetary policy.

- **Chapter 7: Monetary policy applications.** This chapter showed that negative shadow short rates (SSRs) are not a theoretically compelling measure of the stance of monetary policy, and that SSR estimates are also very sensitive to modeling choices, including the model specification, the data used for estimation, and the estimation method. Conversely the "Effective Monetary Stimulus," or EMS, measure aggregates current and expected actual policy interest rates relative to a neutral interest rate as a measure of the stance of monetary policy, and EMS estimates are shown to be quite robust to modeling choices.

- **Chapter 8: Financial market applications.** This chapter showed that using ANSMs is seriously deficient in ZLB environments when used as the basis for fixed interest portfolio risk frameworks and for pricing options on bonds. K-ANSMs provide solutions to both of those financial market applications, and the frameworks are shown to be straightforward to apply in practice. While it would be possible to use B-ANSMs for both applications, their lack of tractability would make practical applications much more onerous.

9.2 The case for K-ANSMs

To make the case for K-ANSMs, I have summarized in Table 9.1 the different classes of term structure models and a list of assessment criteria that I have introduced at various stages throughout the book. The classes of models are

- **Gaussian affine term structure model (GATSMs).** This class was detailed in chapter 3, and it includes three subcategories:
  - **Stationary GATSMs (Stat. GATSMs).** As discussed in subsection 3.3.4, all of the state variables in stationary GATSMs follow a mean-reverting process, and therefore the factor loadings of all yield curve components contain an exponential decay by horizon/time to maturity.
  - **Arbitrage-free Nelson and Siegel (1987) models (ANSMs).** The ANSM subclass of GATSMs is where the most persistent state variable is constrained to be a random walk process, and the mean-reversion matrix for the remaining state variables is constrained to have equal eigenvalues. The yield curve component associated with the random walk is a Level function (a constant by time to maturity), and the additional state variables progressively produce a Slope function, a Bow function, and then higher-order Bow functions. Sections 3.3 and 3.4 provided the details for ANSMs.
  - **Nelson and Siegel (1987) models (NSMs).** The NSM subclass of GATSMs incorporates the ANSM constraints noted above and, as discussed in subsection 3.4.3, the ANSM standard deviations for all of the state variables are also set to zero.
- **Krippner shadow/ZLB-GATSMs (K-AGMs).** As detailed in chapter 4, these models use GATSMs to represent the shadow term structure and the Krippner (2011, 2012b,c, 2013,d,e) shadow/ZLB framework to produce a term structure that is subject to the ZLB constraint. The GATSMs used to represent the shadow term structure may be any of those already noted above, so K-AGMs will include the three subcategories of stationary K-AGMs, K-ANSMs, and K-NSMs (see sections 4.4, 4.3, and 4.4, and subsection 4.4.3 respectively).
- **Black shadow/ZLB-GATSMs (B-AGMs).** As detailed in chapter 5, these models use GATSMs to represent the shadow term structure and the Black (1995) shadow/ZLB framework to produce a term structure that is subject to the ZLB

constraint. The GATSMs used to represent the shadow term structure may be any of those already noted above, so B-AGMs will include the three subcategories of stationary B-AGMs, B-ANSMs, and B-NSMs (see subsections 5.3.6, 5.3.5, and 5.3.6, and 5.3.6 respectively).

- **Alternative ZLB models.** As discussed in section 2.5, models in this class are designed to respect the ZLB, but they do so by directly specifying alternative model dynamics rather than applying a ZLB mechanism to a shadow term structure model. The three classes of models I have used as examples in section 2.5 are square-root/Cox, Ingersoll, and Ross (1985b) models, log-normal models, and quadratic Gaussian models. However, they have similar properties, so I just use one entry in Table 9.1 to represent all three alternative ZLB model classes.

The assessment criteria I use in Table 9.1 are divided into purely theoretical considerations, and aspects related to practical applications. The theoretical criteria are the following:

- **A. Arbitrage free.** This category denotes whether the model is arbitrage free with respect only to its specified or implied model dynamics. Being arbitrage free with respect to physical currency is covered in item C. As discussed in subsection 3.4.3, Nelson and Siegel (1987) models, or NSMs, are not arbitrage free because they ignore the effects of short rate volatility when calculating compounding returns.
- **B. Dynamics match data.** This category denotes whether the dynamics specified for the model are able to match the dynamics observed in the data. As discussed in chapters 2 and 3, GATSMs and alternative ZLB models produce dynamics that are inconsistent with the data when near the ZLB.
- **C. Respects ZLB.** This category denotes whether the models eliminate the probability of negative interest rates. All members of the GATSM class allow negative interest rates, so therefore they would allow arbitrage opportunities with respect to physical currency, as discussed in subsection 6.4.1, or positive prices of options for unattainable bond prices, as discussed in section 8.6.

The practical criteria for evaluating the different classes of models are the following:

- **D. Generally tractable.** This category denotes how easily the model can be applied in practice, for example, how quickly it can be used to generate model-implied yield curve and be estimated from a yield curve data set. As discussed in chapter 5, Black shadow/ZLB models are not tractable because they lack closed-form analytic expressions for any term structure perspective, and therefore they must be implemented with time-consuming numerical methods.

Table 9.1 The case for K-ANSMs

Assessment criteria	Theory			Practice				Total
	A	B	C	D	E	F	G	
GATSMs								
Stat. GATSMs	×	·	·	×	·	·	·	2
ANSMs	×	·	·	×	·	×	×	4
NSMs	·	·	·	×	·	×	·	2
Krippner shadow/ZLB-GATSMs (K-AGMs)								
Stat. K-AGMs	×	×	×	×	×	·	·	5
K-ANSMs	×	×	×	×	×	×	×	7
K-NSMs	·	×	×	×	×	×	·	5
Black shadow/ZLB-GATSMs (B-AGMs)								
Stat. B-AGMs	×	×	×	·	×	·	·	4
B-ANSMs	×	×	×	·	×	×	×	6
B-NSMs	·	×	×	×	×	×	·	5
Alternative ZLB models								
Alt. ZLB models	·	×	·	×	·	·	·	2

Criteria:

A. Arbitrage free.
B. Dynamics match data.
C. Respects ZLB.
D. Generally tractable.
E. Provides shadow information.
F. Includes Level component.
G. Representative of class.

- **E. Provides shadow information.** I include this category to indicate whether the model provides shadow yield curve information that can be used for monetary policy purposes, such as the EMS measure discussed in chapter 7. As discussed in section 2.5, alternative ZLB models do not provide shadow yield curve information.

- **F. Includes Level component.** I include this category to indicate whether the model has a component to represent longer-maturity interest rates and also provide a Level duration measure for risk management. As mentioned in section 8.2 and 8.4, stationary GATSMs do not have a Level component, so they cannot produce Level durations, and it is more difficult to represent longer-maturity interest rates.

- **G. Representative of class.** This category denotes whether the model has the capacity to represent any other model in the same class. As detailed in section 6.2, ANSMs represent any GATSM as a well-defined approximation, where the ANSM Level directly represents any GATSM state variables with unit root or persistent processes, and the ANSM non-Level variables represent terms of the Taylor expansions for all remaining GATSM state variables with a mean-reverting process. Therefore, ANSMs, K-ANSMs, and B-ANSMs may be applied to any yield curve data with the minimal (and typical) assumption that Gaussian dynamics adequately represent the underlying data-generating process.

From the perspective of this book, which was to develop models suitable for practitioners to apply in ZLB environments, the case for K-ANSMs is clear. K-ANSMs meet all of the theoretical criteria and all of the practical criteria I have listed. However, I will add one caveat on the "A. Arbitrage free" criteria when discussing future research on K-ANSMs and B-ANSMs in the following section.

B-ANSMs meet all but one of the criteria, with only "Generally tractable" missing. K-NSMs and B-NSMs (which are identical; see subsection 5.6.3) are ranked next equal, along with K-AGMs. The trade-off with K-NSMs/B-NSMs is that, while being particularly tractable, they are not arbitrage free. Nevertheless, they may prove useful as a pragmatic yield curve representation that allows for ZLB environments, just as NSMs have proven very useful in non-ZLB environments.

I will not go through the remainder of the models, but it is worthwhile highlighting the relatively poor performance of all models in the GATSM class. The clear message is that models from the GATSM class are deficient in ZLB environments. Therefore, it is preferable to apply shadow/ZLB-GATSMs that accommodate both ZLB and non-ZLB environments, and more specifically K-ANSMs if one accepts the case I have outlined.

9.3 Future research directions

I have mentioned a number of topics for future research at various points in the book. This section collects those points together and adds several others from the perspective of developing and applying K-ANSMs. I have divided the topics into those that I think are the major and/or most fruitful, and I have collected the remaining aspects into a list that would be ideal to follow up to provide a complete assessment of K-ANSMs.

The major avenues for future research are the following:

- **Theoretical foundation for K-ANSMs.** I have provided an initial theoretical case for K-ANSMs in chapter 6, and section 6.4 in particular. However, further work is required from the perspective of asset pricing theory and more comprehensive economic modeling to fully assess the theoretical foundation for K-ANSMs. As I noted in chapter 6, the ultimate attraction would be to justify the K-ANSMs as a theoretically consistent framework that also happens to be practically tractable.

- **Applications to monetary policy topics.** Chapter 7 presented a detailed assessment of the EMS as a measure of the stance of monetary policy. The illustrations in section 7.6 indicate that the EMS shows promise empirically when related to macroeconomic and currency data. However, further work will be required to confirm and refine those suggested empirical relationships (and potentially others).

- **Applications to financial market topics.** I have provided two detailed examples in chapter 8 that clearly illustrate the deficiencies of using ANSMs in non-ZLB environments, and how those deficiencies are resolved using K-ANSMs. In subsection 2.2.2, I have mentioned further examples of issues and resolutions presented by other authors. Further topics to investigate include the relative value, convexity, and active fixed interest portfolio management I mentioned in section 8.2. The application of K-ANSMs to bank-risk and corporate-risk interest rate securities would also be worthwhile investigating, because it may allow the effects of the ZLB constraint and changing risk premiums in the wake of the Global Financial Crisis to be disentangled.

- **Joint modeling of macroeconomic survey and yield curve data.** Macroeconomic survey data for long horizons provides another source of information about expectations that should influence longer-maturity interest rates. In turn, that information should help estimate implied risk premiums in the yield curve. The discussion in subsection 7.6.1 already showed promise in that regard, and the economic framework outlined in chapter 6 offers a straightforward way of incorporating both survey information and yield curve data into a joint estimation.

- **Applying K-ANSMs to other countries.** I have undertaken K-ANSM estimations for the purposes of the illustrations in chapter 7. However, all of the applications and topics mentioned in this book, including those below, are obviously repeatable for other countries.

Other issues to follow up include the following:

- Developing and adding to the speed-up methods, including additional covariates, for Monte Carlo simulation of B-ANSMs. This development will allow for timely partial estimations of B-ANSMs, and perhaps full estimations, which will be required if the theoretical work noted in the first bullet point of major research avenues determines that the Black (1995) shadow/ZLB framework is theoretically preferable to the Krippner (2011, 2012b,c, 2013d,e) shadow/ZLB framework.

- Further testing of the sensitivity of partial and full K-ANSM estimations to different filters, including the EKF, IEKF, unscented Kalman filter, and potentially the particle filter. Repeatedly simulating data from a given shadow/ZLB-specification, and then testing which estimation method best recovers the original parameters in a statistical sense would be a useful exercise in this regard.

- Operationalizing and testing the proposed iterative method for estimating K-ANSMs, as discussed in subsection 4.6.3. There may also be other econometric methods that could be applied to full estimations.
- Further empirical testing on the robustness of K-ANSM estimates and derived monetary policy indicators to the yield curve data used for estimation, including the sample period and the maximum time to maturity.
- Estimation using alternative data, particularly coupon-paying bond data. As mentioned in chapter subsection 4.6.2, using the directly observed market data rather then preprocessing it into zero-coupon interest rates or forward rates may offer more efficient estimations.
- Empirical testing of K-NSMs/B-NSMs. This analysis would test the importance of the arbitrage-free constraint on K-ANSMs. K-NSMs/B-NSMs may provide a pragmatic model for many applications.
- Empirical testing of the K-ANSM(2) and K-ANSM(3) with the parsimonious state equations introduced in subsection 6.3.7. If these are found to be acceptable relative to using full state equations, then higher-order K-ANSMs with parsimonious state equations could also be tested. Such models provide a parsimonious representation of risk premiums, which may provide insights into the variation of risk premiums over interest rate and macroeconomic cycles.

Adding the answers to these and related questions to the steadily expanding ZLB yield curve literature should ultimately help to provide general, practical, and robust frameworks that can be applied to the real world challenges faced by central bankers and financial market participants in the current ZLB environment (and any future episodes). By giving readers the background and means of developing and applying shadow/ZLB yield curve models, my hope from this book is to facilitate that progression.

Appendix A: Matrix Notation

In this appendix, I provide background information on matrices and their operations that I use in chapters 3 to 6, and 8. For further details, I refer readers to Greene (1997) chapter 2 and Moler and Van Loan (2003).

A.1 Scalars, vectors, and matrices

A scalar is simply a single number, like 2 or a, or a function that produces a single number, like $\exp(-\phi\tau)$. Hence, a scalar has a matrix dimension of 1×1.

A vector is a list of numbers or functions with an arbitrary number N elements. Hence, a vector can have matrix dimensions $1 \times N$, which is sometimes called a row vector, or $N \times 1$, which is sometimes called a column vector. The following examples are 3×1 (column) vectors:

$$b = \begin{bmatrix} 1 \\ 1 \\ 0 \end{bmatrix}; \quad x(t) = \begin{bmatrix} x_1(t) \\ x_2(t) \\ x_3(t) \end{bmatrix}; \quad y(\phi,\tau) = \begin{bmatrix} 1 \\ \exp(-\phi\tau) \\ \phi\tau\exp(-\phi\tau) \end{bmatrix} \tag{A.1}$$

and $[1,1,0]$ would be an example of a 1×3 (row) vector. I usually just provide the dimensions of the vector rather than using the names "column" and "row." Note that I have denoted $y(\phi,\tau)$ with the parameter ϕ and variable τ used in the individual functions for the elements of $y(\phi,\tau)$. It is not essential to do so, but I typically use that notation for clarity about what determines the vector (or matrix) elements.

A matrix is a rectangular array of numbers or functions, with an arbitrary number of M rows and an arbitrary number of N columns. Hence, it has matrix dimensions of $M \times N$. The following are matrix examples:

$$A = \begin{bmatrix} 1 & \frac{1}{2} \\ 1 & \frac{1}{2} \\ 0 & \frac{1}{4} \end{bmatrix}; \quad B = \begin{bmatrix} \sigma_1^2 & \rho_{12}\sigma_1\sigma_2 \\ \rho_{12}\sigma_1\sigma_2 & \sigma_2^2 \end{bmatrix}; \quad C(\phi,\tau) = \begin{bmatrix} 1 & 0 \\ 0 & \exp(-\phi\tau) \end{bmatrix}$$

$$\tag{A.2}$$

which respectively have dimensions 3×2, 2×2, and 2×2.

Because scalars and vectors are just particular cases of matrices, I will generally adopt the generic name matrices hereafter in this appendix. Note that elements of a matrix can also be defined as numbers in an array by referencing their row and column index number. For example, the matrix 3×2 A could be defined with entries A_{mn}:

$$A = A_{mn} \tag{A.3}$$

where $m = 1$ to 3 and $n = 1$ to 2. Then, for example, the $(1,2)$ element of A is $A_{12} = \frac{1}{2}$.

A.2 Matrix transpose

I denote the transpose of a matrix with the prime symbol " $'$ ", which is common in the literature. The transpose interchanges the row and column indices. For example, A' is

$$A' = \begin{bmatrix} 1 & 1 & 0 \\ \frac{1}{2} & \frac{1}{2} & \frac{1}{4} \end{bmatrix} \tag{A.4}$$

or

$$[A_{mn}]' = A_{nm} \tag{A.5}$$

and b' is:

$$b' = [1,1,0] \tag{A.6}$$

Note that the matrix transpose is sometimes denoted " ^{T} ", but I do not use that notation in this book.

A.3 Some special and useful matrices

Within the entire class of matrices, there are many subcategories that are useful or that have special roles. The following provides a brief overview of the ones I use:

- **Square matrix:** The number of rows equals the number of columns, that is, $M = N$. For example, B and $C(\phi, \tau)$ are square matrices.
- **Symmetric matrix:** The transpose of a symmetric matrix equals itself, that is, $B = B'$, or $B_{mn} = B_{nm}$. Symmetric matrices are therefore necessarily square. For example, B and $C(\phi, \tau)$ are symmetric matrices.
- **Lower-triangular matrix:** All non-zero elements are in the elements A_{mn}, where $n \leq m$, and the remaining entries A_{mn}, where $n > m$ are zero. Subsection A.7.1 contains an example of a lower-triangular matrix σ.

- **Upper-triangular matrix:** All non-zero elements are in the elements A_{mn}, where $n \geq m$, and the remaining entries A_{mn}, where $n < m$ are zero. Subsection A.7.1 contains an example of an upper-triangular matrix σ'.
- **Diagonal matrix:** All non-zero elements are in the elements where the row and column indices are equal, that is, A_{nn} where $n = 1$ to N, and the remaining entries A_{mn} with $m \neq n$ are zeros. Diagonal matrices are therefore both square and symmetric. For example, $C(\phi, \tau)$ is a diagonal matrix. Note that diagonal matrices can be written in abbreviated form $\mathrm{diag}[A_{11}, \ldots, A_{NN}]$ or $\mathrm{diag}[A_1, \ldots, A_N]$, where the N elements of the vector $A_1, \ldots, A_N$ are used as the diagonal entries of the $N \times N$ matrix. For example, $C(\phi, \tau) = \mathrm{diag}\left[1, \exp(-\phi\tau)\right]$.
- **Identity matrix:** A diagonal matrix with non-zero entries of 1. The identity matrix is denoted I. As an example, the following is the 2×2 identity matrix:

$$I = \begin{bmatrix} 1 & 0 \\ 0 & 1 \end{bmatrix} \tag{A.7}$$

If specific dimensions are not given, then the convention is to assume that I has dimensions that are conformable for addition and/or multiplication, which I discuss in sections A.4 and A.5, within the given matrix expression where I is being used. Note that I is the matrix analogue of the scalar 1, as I highlight in subsection A.5.4.

- **Zero matrix:** An arbitrary matrix with zeros in every element. A zero matrix is typically denoted as 0. As an example, the following is the 2×3 zero matrix:

$$0 = \begin{bmatrix} 0 & 0 & 0 \\ 0 & 0 & 0 \end{bmatrix} \tag{A.8}$$

If specific dimensions are not given, then the convention is to assume that the zero matrix has dimensions that are conformable for addition and/or multiplication, which I discuss in sections A.4 and A.5, within the given matrix expression where the zero matrix is being used. Note that a zero matrix is the matrix analogue of the scalar 0, as I highlight in section A.4.

- **Partitioned matrix:** A matrix can be divided into sub matrices for convenient manipulation. Alternatively, two or more matrices may be concatenated to form a partitioned matrix if the dimensions of the original matrices are conformable to do so. For example, the matrices A and B can be concatenated vertically because they have the same number of columns:

$$\begin{bmatrix} A \\ B \end{bmatrix} = \begin{bmatrix} 1 & \frac{1}{2} \\ 1 & \frac{1}{2} \\ 0 & \frac{1}{4} \\ \sigma_1^2 & \rho_{12}\sigma_1\sigma_2 \\ \rho_{12}\sigma_1\sigma_2 & \sigma_2^2 \end{bmatrix} \tag{A.9}$$

Hence, the 3×2 and 2×2 matrices are combined into a 5×2 matrix. However, A and B cannot be concatenated horizontally because they do not have the same number of rows. $[A', B]$ would be an acceptable concatenation, which produces a 2×5 matrix.

A.4 Matrix addition and subtraction

Two matrices are conformable for addition if they have the same dimensions. They can then be added element by element, and the result is a matrix with the same dimensions. For example,

$$b + x(t) = \begin{bmatrix} 1 + x_1(t) \\ 1 + x_2(t) \\ x_3(t) \end{bmatrix} \tag{A.10}$$

Subtraction is simply adding the negative of a matrix, for example,

$$b - x(t) = \begin{bmatrix} 1 - x_1(t) \\ 1 - x_2(t) \\ -x_3(t) \end{bmatrix} \tag{A.11}$$

Adding or subtracting a zero matrix to any matrix leaves the matrix unchanged, that is, $A_{mn} + 0 = A_{mn}$, which is the matrix analogue of the scalar result $a + 0 = a$.

A.5 Matrix multiplication

Two matrices are conformable for multiplication if the number of columns in the first matrix equals the number of rows in the second matrix. They can then be multiplied, and the result is a matrix with the number of rows of the first matrix and the number of columns of the second matrix. I begin with the case for two vectors and then generalize that result to matrices. The remaining subsections provide related observations.

A.5.1 Multiplying two vectors

Multiplying two conformable vectors gives a scalar result:

$$b'x(t) = [1, 1, 0] \begin{bmatrix} x_1(t) \\ x_2(t) \\ x_3(t) \end{bmatrix}$$

$$= 1 \cdot x_1(t) + 1 \cdot x_2(t) + 0 \cdot x_3(t)$$

$$= \qquad\qquad x_1(t) + x_2(t) \qquad\qquad \text{(A.12)}$$

Note that the easiest way to confirm that the vectors are conformable for multiplication is to write the dimensions of the vectors being multiplied as $[1 \times 3] \times [3 \times 1]$ and note that the inner indices of 3 (for the columns of b' and rows of $x(t)$ respectively) are adjacent. The outer indices give the dimensions of the result, that is, 1×1.

Note that $b'x(t)$ can also be expressed as summation:

$$b'x(t) = 1 \cdot x_1(t) + 1 \cdot x_2(t) + 0 \cdot x_3(t)$$

$$= \sum_{n=1}^{3} b_n x_n(t) \qquad\qquad \text{(A.13)}$$

More generally, multiplying two conformable vectors proceeds by multiplying the elements $(1, n)$ of the first vector with the elements $(n, 1)$ of the second vector, and then summing the individual results. For example, with an arbitrary number of elements N in the vectors b and $x(t)$, the result could be written as the summation:

$$b'x(t) = \sum_{n=1}^{N} b_n x_n(t) \qquad\qquad \text{(A.14)}$$

where the result is again a scalar, that is, $[1 \times N] \times [N \times 1] = 1 \times 1$.

A.5.2 Multiplying two matrices

General matrix multiplication is simply repeated operations of vector multiplications, where the row vector in each row m of the first matrix is multiplied with the columns vector of each column n of the second matrix. For example,

$$A'x(t) = \begin{bmatrix} 1 & 1 & 0 \\ \frac{1}{2} & \frac{1}{2} & \frac{1}{4} \end{bmatrix} \begin{bmatrix} x_1(t) \\ x_2(t) \\ x_3(t) \end{bmatrix}$$

$$= \begin{bmatrix} [1,1,0] \begin{bmatrix} x_1(t) \\ x_2(t) \\ x_3(t) \end{bmatrix} \\ [\frac{1}{2},\frac{1}{2},\frac{1}{4}] \begin{bmatrix} x_1(t) \\ x_2(t) \\ x_3(t) \end{bmatrix} \end{bmatrix}$$

$$= \begin{bmatrix} x_1(t) + x_2(t) \\ \frac{1}{2}x_1(t) + \frac{1}{2}x_2(t) + \frac{1}{4}x_3(t) \end{bmatrix} \qquad\qquad \text{(A.15)}$$

Note that each row m of A' is a 1×3 vector, and each column of $x(t)$ is a 3×1 vector, so each element (m, n) in the resulting $A'x(t)$ matrix is a scalar. The result is a 2×1 vector, that is, $[2 \times 3] \times [3 \times 1] = 2 \times 1$.

The following example is a $[2 \times 2] \times [2 \times 2] = 2 \times 2$ matrix multiplication:

$$
BC(\phi, \tau) = \begin{bmatrix} \sigma_1^2 & \rho_{12}\sigma_1\sigma_2 \\ \rho_{12}\sigma_1\sigma_2 & \sigma_2^2 \end{bmatrix} \begin{bmatrix} 1 & 0 \\ 0 & \exp(-\phi\tau) \end{bmatrix}
$$

$$
= \begin{bmatrix} [\sigma_1^2, \rho_{12}\sigma_1\sigma_2] \begin{bmatrix} 1 \\ 0 \end{bmatrix} & [\sigma_1^2, \rho_{12}\sigma_1\sigma_2] \begin{bmatrix} 0 \\ \exp(-\phi\tau) \end{bmatrix} \\ [\rho_{12}\sigma_1\sigma_2, \sigma_2^2] \begin{bmatrix} 1 \\ 0 \end{bmatrix} & [\rho_{12}\sigma_1\sigma_2, \sigma_2^2] \begin{bmatrix} 0 \\ \exp(-\phi\tau) \end{bmatrix} \end{bmatrix}
$$

$$
= \begin{bmatrix} \sigma_1^2 & \rho_{12}\sigma_1\sigma_2 \cdot \exp(-\phi\tau) \\ \rho_{12}\sigma_1\sigma_2 & \sigma_2^2 \cdot \exp(-\phi\tau) \end{bmatrix} \tag{A.16}
$$

A.5.3 Need for matrix notation in term structure modeling

Multiplying two matrices as in the previous subsection could be represented using summations over N within each of the resulting matrix elements:

$$
BC(\phi, \tau) = \begin{bmatrix} \sum_{n=1}^{3} B_{1,n} C_{n,1}(\phi, \tau) & \sum_{n=1}^{3} B_{1,n} C_{n,2}(\phi, \tau) \\ \sum_{n=1}^{3} B_{2,n} C_{n,1}(\phi, \tau) & \sum_{n=1}^{3} B_{2,n} C_{n,2}(\phi, \tau) \end{bmatrix} \tag{A.17}
$$

However, such notation is already awkward and lengthy.

Multiplying three or more matrices becomes notationally untenable, because double summations, triple summations, and so forth, would be required. Furthermore, expressions like $b'C(\phi, \tau)\sigma\sigma'C(\phi, \tau)b$ arise routinely when specifying and deriving term structure models. The result is actually a scalar, because $[1 \times N] \times [N \times N] \times [N \times N] \times [N \times N] \times [N \times N] \times [N \times 1] = 1 \times 1$. However, writing $b'C(\phi, \tau)\sigma\sigma'C(\phi, \tau)b$ as a quintuple summation expression would obviously be notationally prohibitive.

Therefore, matrix notation is really the only practical way of denoting the general expressions that arise in term structure modeling. However, reexpressing the results as summations can still be useful in some instances.

A.5.4 The identity matrix revisited

A matrix multiplied by an identity matrix, or vice versa, results in the original matrix. For example,

$$
A'I = \begin{bmatrix} 1 & 1 & 0 \\ \frac{1}{2} & \frac{1}{2} & \frac{1}{4} \end{bmatrix} \begin{bmatrix} 1 & 0 \\ 0 & 1 \end{bmatrix}
$$

$$
= \begin{bmatrix} 1 & 1 & 0 \\ \frac{1}{2} & \frac{1}{2} & \frac{1}{4} \end{bmatrix} = IA' \tag{A.18}
$$

This result shows that the identity matrix is the matrix analogue of the scalar result $a \times 1 = 1 \times a = a$.

A.5.5 Powers of matrices

A square matrix can be multiplied by itself indefinitely, which is represented by raising the matrix to a positive integer power. For example,

$$[C(\phi,\tau)]^P = \prod_{p=1}^{P} \begin{bmatrix} 1 & 0 \\ 0 & \exp(-\phi\tau) \end{bmatrix} \tag{A.19}$$

where $\prod_{p=1}^{P}$ indicates that $C(\phi,\tau)$ is multiplied P times. This example has a simple closed form expression, because $C(\phi,\tau)$ is diagonal, that is,

$$[C(\phi,\tau)]^P = \begin{bmatrix} 1 & 0 \\ 0 & \exp(-P\phi\tau) \end{bmatrix} \tag{A.20}$$

A.5.6 Multiplying partitioned matrices

Partitioned matrices may be multiplied analogous to standard matrix multiplication, but using the entire matrices within each partition as if they were individual elements. However, the partitioned matrices do need to be conformable with each other.

For example,

$$[A',B] \begin{bmatrix} A \\ B \end{bmatrix} = A'A + BB \tag{A.21}$$

where $A'A$ is conformable with the result having dimensions $[2 \times 3] \times [3 \times 2] = 2 \times 2$, BB is conformable with the result having dimensions 2×2, and therefore $A'A$ and BB can be added, with the result having dimensions 2×2. Note that multiplying the entire partitioned matrix directly would give the same result with the same dimensions, that is, $[2 \times 5] \times [5 \times 2] = 2 \times 2$.

A.5.7 Multiplying a matrix by a scalar

In this case, each entry of the matrix is simply multiplied by the scalar. For example,

$$\tau C(\phi,\tau) = \tau \begin{bmatrix} 1 & 0 \\ 0 & \exp(-\phi\tau) \end{bmatrix}$$

$$= \begin{bmatrix} \tau & 0 \\ 0 & \tau \cdot \exp(-\phi\tau) \end{bmatrix} \tag{A.22}$$

I have left this result to last, because it is the exception to the "conformable for multiplication" rules outlined above. That is, the matrix dimensions in the example are actually $[1 \times 1] \times [2 \times 2]$, but the result is nevertheless defined and is a 2×2 matrix.

A.6 Matrix inverse

If a matrix is square and has a non-zero determinant, where I define the determinant in subsection A.7.4, then an inverse of the matrix can be calculated. The inverse of a matrix is denoted by raising it to the power of negative 1, for example, the matrix inverse of B is B^{-1}. The matrix inverse is the matrix analogue of the scalar reciprocal $a^{-1} = 1/a$, which is only defined if $a \neq 0$.

A matrix multiplied by its inverse, or vice versa, results in the identity matrix I:

$$BB^{-1} = B^{-1}B = I \tag{A.23}$$

which is the matrix analogue of the scalar result $a^{-1}a = aa^{-1} = 1$. Also, a square matrix raised to the zeroth power is

$$BB^{-1} = B^0 = I \tag{A.24}$$

which is the matrix analogue of the scalar result $a^0 = 1$.

There is no need to explicitly calculate the inverses of any general square matrices either algebraically or numerically in this book.[1] However, the inverse of a diagonal matrix is a useful and straightforward algebraic result that I use occasionally. It is simply the reciprocal of the non-zero diagonal entries, that is $A_{nn} \rightarrow 1/A_{nn}$, where $n = 1$ to N. For example,

$$[C(\phi, \tau)]^{-1} = \begin{bmatrix} \frac{1}{1} & 0 \\ 0 & \frac{1}{\exp(-\phi\tau)} \end{bmatrix}$$

$$= \begin{bmatrix} 1 & 0 \\ 0 & \exp(\phi\tau) \end{bmatrix} \tag{A.25}$$

or

$$\left(\mathrm{diag}\left[1, \exp(-\phi\tau)\right] \right)^{-1} = \mathrm{diag}\left[1, \exp(\phi\tau)\right] . \tag{A.26}$$

The following result is useful when considering the inverse of the transpose of a matrix:

$$[D']^{-1} = [D^{-1}]'$$

and the brackets in the first expression are often removed for notational convenience, that is, $[D']^{-1} = D'^{-1}$.

A.7 Matrix decompositions

A.7.1 Cholesky decomposition

If a symmetric matrix is positive definite, which I define in subsection A.7.4, then a Cholesky decomposition may be used to represent the matrix as the product of a lower diagonal matrix and its transpose. For example, the Cholesky decomposition of the matrix B is

$$\text{Chol}(B) = \begin{bmatrix} \sigma_1 & 0 \\ \rho_{12}\sigma_2 & \sigma_2\sqrt{1-\rho_{12}^2} \end{bmatrix} \begin{bmatrix} \sigma_1 & \rho_{12}\sigma_2 \\ 0 & \sigma_2\sqrt{1-\rho_{12}^2} \end{bmatrix}$$

$$= \sigma\sigma' \tag{A.27}$$

The Cholesky decomposition is the matrix analogue of the scalar square root, and it is typically used (as in this book) to obtain a standard deviation matrix from a covariance matrix. Alternatively, one can define a covariance matrix from a standard deviation matrix with a guarantee that the covariance matrix is positive definite, for example,

$$\begin{bmatrix} \sigma_1^2 & \rho_{12}\sigma_1\sigma_2 \\ \rho_{12}\sigma_1\sigma_2 & \sigma_2^2 \end{bmatrix} = \sigma\sigma' \tag{A.28}$$

A.7.2 Eigensystem decomposition

For my discussion of eigensystem decompositions relevant to this book, I will use an $N \times N$ square matrix κ that has real entries. By real entries I mean that the values in κ are not complex (i.e., the elements have no imaginary components).

An eigensystem decomposition of κ requires the eigenvalues to be unique, by which I mean that no eigenvalues are repeated. I assume in this section that the eigenvalues of κ are unique. The criteria can be checked in practice by directly calculating the eigenvalues, either algebraically or numerically. The Jordan decomposition below is used to accommodate cases with repeated eigenvalues.

The eigensystem decomposition of κ is

$$\kappa = V\kappa_D V^{-1} \tag{A.29}$$

where V is a matrix of eigenvectors in columns and κ_D is diagonal matrix of unique eigenvalues.

As an example, assume κ_A is a general 2×2 matrix:

$$\kappa_A = \begin{bmatrix} \kappa_{11} & \kappa_{12} \\ \kappa_{21} & \kappa_{22} \end{bmatrix} \tag{A.30}$$

The eigensystem decomposition of κ_A is therefore:

$$\begin{bmatrix} \kappa_{11} & \kappa_{12} \\ \kappa_{21} & \kappa_{22} \end{bmatrix} = \begin{bmatrix} V_{11} & V_{12} \\ V_{21} & V_{22} \end{bmatrix} \begin{bmatrix} \kappa_1 & 0 \\ 0 & \kappa_2 \end{bmatrix} \begin{bmatrix} V_{11} & V_{12} \\ V_{21} & V_{22} \end{bmatrix}^{-1} \tag{A.31}$$

where the eigenvectors and their associated eigenvalues are respectively:

$$\begin{bmatrix} V_{11} \\ V_{21} \end{bmatrix} \leftrightarrow \kappa_1 \tag{A.32}$$

and:

$$\begin{bmatrix} V_{12} \\ V_{22} \end{bmatrix} \leftrightarrow \kappa_2 \tag{A.33}$$

The typical convention, which I also use, is to normalize each eigenvector to 1. Normalization is the square root of the transpose of a vector multiplied with the original vector. For example, normalizing the first eigenvector to 1 means that

$$\sqrt{[V_{11}, V_{21}] \begin{bmatrix} V_{11} \\ V_{21} \end{bmatrix}} = \sqrt{V_{11}^2 + V_{21}^2}$$

$$= 1 \, .$$

Regardless of the normalization, the following result holds by definition:

$$VV^{-1} = V^{-1}V = I \tag{A.34}$$

For non symmetric square matrices, the eigenvalues may be real or appear as pairs of complex conjugates, for example, $c + di$ and $c - di$, and the real or complex conjugate values respectively feature in the associated eigenvectors.

If a matrix is symmetric, then the eigenvalues and their eigenvectors all have real values. Furthermore, the eigenvector matrix also has the property that

$$V^{-1} = V' \tag{A.35}$$

or equivalently:

$$\kappa_A = V \kappa_D V' \tag{A.36}$$

A.7.3   Jordan decomposition

If some or all of the eigenvalues of κ are not unique, then a Jordan decomposition may be applied instead of an eigensystem decomposition. The Jordan decomposition of κ is

$$\kappa = V \kappa_J V^{-1} \tag{A.37}$$

where κ_J is a diagonal matrix of eigenvalues, but it also contains entries of 1 in some $(n, n+1)$ elements (sometimes called the off-diagonal elements) to represent repeated eigenvalues. V is a matrix of eigenvectors in columns. The eigenvectors are still normalized to 1 for the unique eigenvalues and the first occurrence of the repeated eigenvalue/s, but the eigenvectors for the repeated eigenvalues are not normalized to 1.

It is easiest to show the form of Jordan decomposition by example, and the example I will use relates specifically to the general form of the arbitrage-free Nelson and Siegel (1987), or ANSM, class of term structure models that I develop in sections 3.3 and 3.4. Hence, the following 3×3 matrix is used for the three-state-variable ANSM:

$$\tilde{\kappa}_B = \begin{bmatrix} 0 & 0 & 0 \\ 0 & \phi & -\phi \\ 0 & 0 & \phi \end{bmatrix} \tag{A.38}$$

where the tilde "~" simply replicates my notation in sections 3.3 and 3.4. $\tilde{\kappa}_B$ has a unique eigenvalue of 0 and a twice-repeated eigenvalue of ϕ. The Jordan decomposition is

$$\tilde{\kappa}_B = \tilde{V} \tilde{\kappa}_J \tilde{V}^{-1}$$

$$\begin{bmatrix} 0 & 0 & 0 \\ 0 & \phi & -\phi \\ 0 & 0 & \phi \end{bmatrix} = \begin{bmatrix} 1 & 0 & 0 \\ 0 & 1 & 0 \\ 0 & 0 & -\frac{1}{\phi} \end{bmatrix} \begin{bmatrix} 0 & 0 & 0 \\ 0 & \phi & 1 \\ 0 & 0 & \phi \end{bmatrix} \begin{bmatrix} 1 & 0 & 0 \\ 0 & 1 & 0 \\ 0 & 0 & -\phi \end{bmatrix} \tag{A.39}$$

Note the off-diagonal entry of 1 in the $(2, 3)$ element of $\tilde{\kappa}_J$, and that the third column of the eigenvector matrix $\tilde{V}$ is not normalized to 1 (i.e., the third eigenvector has a magnitude of $1/\phi$).

The extension to the 4×4 matrix for four-state-variable ANSM is

$$\tilde{\kappa}_C = \tilde{V} \tilde{\kappa}_J \tilde{V}^{-1}$$

$$\begin{bmatrix} 0 & 0 & 0 & 0 \\ 0 & \phi & -\phi & 0 \\ 0 & 0 & \phi & -\phi \\ 0 & 0 & 0 & \phi \end{bmatrix} = \begin{bmatrix} 1 & 0 & 0 & 0 \\ 0 & 1 & 0 & 0 \\ 0 & 0 & -\frac{1}{\phi} & 0 \\ 0 & 0 & 0 & \frac{1}{\phi^2} \end{bmatrix} \begin{bmatrix} 0 & 0 & 0 & 0 \\ 0 & \phi & 1 & 0 \\ 0 & 0 & \phi & 1 \\ 0 & 0 & 0 & \phi \end{bmatrix}$$

$$\times \begin{bmatrix} 1 & 0 & 0 & 0 \\ 0 & 1 & 0 & 0 \\ 0 & 0 & -\phi & 0 \\ 0 & 0 & 0 & \phi^2 \end{bmatrix} \tag{A.40}$$

The continued extensions to the matrices for higher-order ANSMs have diagonal entries of $(-\phi)^{-n}$ in the eigenvector matrix $\tilde{V}$ for $n \geq 1$, diagonal entries of ϕ in the

Jordan matrix $\tilde{\kappa}_J$ for $n \geq 1$, and entries of 1 in the $(n, n+1)$ elements of the Jordan matrix $\tilde{\kappa}_J$ for $n \geq 1$.

A.7.4 Using eigensystem and Jordan decompositions

- **Matrix determinant:** The determinant of a matrix is the product of its eigenvalues, and is denoted $|\cdot|$. For example, the determinant of the matrix κ_A in subsection A.7.2 is $|\kappa_A| = \kappa_1 \times \kappa_2$, and the determinants of all the examples of $\tilde{\kappa}$ in subsection A.7.3 are zero.
- **Positive definite matrix:** If the eigenvalues of a matrix are all real and positive, then the matrix is positive definite. Positive definiteness is the matrix analogue of a scalar being a positive number, which means that one can take its square root without the result being an imaginary number.
- **General powers of a matrix:** The eigensystem and Jordan decompositions greatly facilitate evaluations of the powers of a matrix, as I detail shortly. The concept is important for the following section on matrix exponentials.

As an example of the simplification provided by an eigensystem decomposition, here is the 2×2 matrix κ raised to the third power:

$$
\begin{aligned}
\kappa_A^3 &= \left[V \kappa_D V^{-1} \right] \left[V \kappa_D V^{-1} \right] \left[V \kappa_D V^{-1} \right] \\
&= V \kappa_D \left[V^{-1} V \right] \kappa_D \left[V^{-1} V \right] \kappa_D V^{-1} \\
&= V \kappa_D I \kappa_D I \kappa_D V^{-1} \\
&= V \kappa_D \kappa_D \kappa_D V^{-1} \\
&= V \kappa_D^3 V^{-1}
\end{aligned}
\tag{A.41}
$$

κ_D^3 is straightforward to calculate because κ_D is a diagonal matrix, $\kappa_D = \mathrm{diag}[\kappa_1, \kappa_2]$. Therefore κ_D^3 is also diagonal, with its entries being the diagonal elements of κ_D raised to third power:

$$
\kappa_D^3 = \begin{bmatrix} \kappa_1 & 0 \\ 0 & \kappa_2 \end{bmatrix}^3 = \begin{bmatrix} \kappa_1^3 & 0 \\ 0 & \kappa_2^3 \end{bmatrix},
\tag{A.42}
$$

or $\kappa_D^3 = \mathrm{diag}\left[\kappa_1^3, \kappa_2^3\right]$.

In general, an arbitrary square $N \times N$ matrix κ with unique eigenvalues raised to any non-negative power Z, including non-integer values, is

$$
\kappa^Z = V \kappa_D^Z V^{-1},
\tag{A.43}
$$

where $\kappa_D^Z = \mathrm{diag}\left[\kappa_1^Z, \ldots, \kappa_N^Z\right]$. The expression also holds for negative values of Z, so long as the determinant of κ is non-zero. A zero determinant would imply at least one zero eigenvalue, and the negative power of zero in $\kappa_D^Z = \mathrm{diag}\left[\kappa_1^Z, \ldots, \kappa_N^Z\right]$ would be undefined.

If κ has some repeated eigenvalues, then the Jordan decomposition is used with analogous results to the eigensystem decomposition:

$$\kappa^Z = V\kappa_J^Z V^{-1} \qquad (A.44)$$

However, κ_J is upper triangular rather than diagonal, so raising it to the power of Z is not quite as straightforward as for κ_D. The results are similar to those for the matrix exponential below, but the general result that $\kappa^Z = V\kappa_J^Z V^{-1}$ is sufficient for this section.

A.8 The matrix exponential

For any square $N \times N$ matrix κ, the matrix exponential is defined as

$$\exp\left(\kappa\right) = \sum_{i=0}^{\infty} \frac{\kappa^i}{i!}$$

$$= I + \kappa + \frac{\kappa^2}{2} + \frac{\kappa^3}{6} + \ldots \qquad (A.45)$$

and $\exp\left(\kappa\right)$ is also a square $N \times N$ matrix. Note that this definition is the matrix analogue of the scalar exponential:

$$\exp\left(a\right) = \sum_{i=0}^{\infty} \frac{a^i}{i!}$$

$$= 1 + a + \frac{a^2}{2} + \frac{a^3}{6} + \ldots \qquad (A.46)$$

The eigensystem decomposition greatly facilitates the calculation of the matrix exponential when the eigenvalues are unique, which in turn uses the results in the previous section for calculating the powers of a matrix. For the example I use here to illustrate, I multiply κ by the scalar $-\tau$ so that it relates directly to the matrix exponentials that I use in section 3.2.

Hence, reexpressing $\exp\left(-\kappa\tau\right)$ in terms of the eigensystem decomposition of κ gives

$$\exp\left(-\kappa\tau\right) = \sum_{i=0}^{\infty} \frac{\left[-V\kappa_D V^{-1}\tau\right]^i}{i!}$$

$$= \sum_{i=0}^{\infty} \frac{V\left[-\kappa_D\tau\right]^i V^{-1}}{i!}$$

$$= V \left[\sum_{i=0}^{\infty} \frac{[-\kappa_D \tau]^i}{i!} \right] V^{-1}$$

$$= V \exp(-\kappa_D \tau) V^{-1} \tag{A.47}$$

Calculating $\exp(-\kappa_D \tau)$ is very straightforward because the matrix exponential of a diagonal matrix is a diagonal matrix of scalar exponentials:

$$\exp(-\kappa_D \tau) = \exp\left(-\tau \operatorname{diag}[\kappa_1, \ldots, \kappa_N]\right)$$

$$= \exp\left(\operatorname{diag}[-\kappa_1 \tau, \ldots, -\kappa_N \tau]\right)$$

$$= \operatorname{diag}\left[\exp(-\kappa_1 \tau), \ldots, \exp(-\kappa_N \tau)\right] \tag{A.48}$$

See, for example, Moler and Van Loan (2003, p. 21).

Similarly, the Jordan decomposition greatly facilitates the calculation of the matrix exponential when some or all eigenvalues are repeated. Hence, reexpressing $\exp(-\tilde{\kappa} \tau)$ in terms of the Jordan decomposition of $\tilde{\kappa}$ gives

$$\exp(-\tilde{\kappa} \tau) = \sum_{i=0}^{\infty} \frac{\left[-V \kappa_J V^{-1} \tau\right]^i}{i!}$$

$$= \sum_{i=0}^{\infty} \frac{V \left[-\kappa_J \tau\right]^i V^{-1}}{i!}$$

$$= V \left[\sum_{i=0}^{\infty} \frac{\left[-\kappa_J \tau\right]^i}{i!} \right] V^{-1}$$

$$= V \exp\left(-\kappa_J \tau\right) V^{-1} \tag{A.49}$$

The exponential of a Jordan matrix is an upper triangular matrix of scalar exponentials. The exact form depends on the number of repeated eigenvalues, but the following example establishes the relevant pattern of results for the general ANSM class of term structure models that I develop in sections 3.3 and 3.4. If

$$\tilde{\kappa}_J = \begin{bmatrix} 0 & 0 & 0 & 0 & 0 \\ 0 & \phi & 1 & 0 & 0 \\ 0 & 0 & \phi & 1 & 0 \\ 0 & 0 & 0 & \phi & 1 \\ 0 & 0 & 0 & 0 & \phi \end{bmatrix} \tag{A.50}$$

then $\exp\left(-\kappa_J \tau\right)$ is the partitioned matrix:

$$\exp\left(-\kappa_J \tau\right) = \begin{bmatrix} 1 & 0 \\ 0 & \Lambda(\phi, \tau) \end{bmatrix} \tag{A.51}$$

where:

$$\Lambda(\phi,\tau) = \exp(-\phi\tau) \begin{bmatrix} 1 & -\tau & \frac{1}{2}\tau^2 & -\frac{1}{3}\tau^3 \\ 0 & 1 & -\tau & \frac{1}{2}\tau^2 \\ 0 & 0 & 1 & -\tau \\ 0 & 0 & 0 & 1 \end{bmatrix} \tag{A.52}$$

Moler and Van Loan (2003, p. 24), for example, contains the result for $\Lambda(\phi,\tau)$.

As an example, the key expression required to develop the ANSM with three state variables is

$$\exp(-\kappa_J\tau) = \begin{bmatrix} 1 & 0 & 0 \\ 0 & 1 & 0 \\ 0 & 0 & -\frac{1}{\phi} \end{bmatrix} \begin{bmatrix} 1 & 0 & 0 \\ 0 & \exp(-\phi\tau) & -\tau\exp(-\phi\tau) \\ 0 & 0 & \exp(-\phi\tau) \end{bmatrix}$$

$$\times \begin{bmatrix} 1 & 0 & 0 \\ 0 & 1 & 0 \\ 0 & 0 & -\phi \end{bmatrix}$$

$$= \begin{bmatrix} 1 & 0 & 0 \\ 0 & \exp(-\phi\tau) & \phi\tau\exp(-\phi\tau) \\ 0 & 0 & \exp(-\phi\tau) \end{bmatrix} \tag{A.53}$$

which is the result in subsection 3.4.1.

A.9 Matrix calculus

The following results cover the matrix calculus used in this book:

- **Differentiating the product of two vectors with respect to a vector.** The result is a vector, for example,

$$\frac{d}{dx(t)}\left[b'x(t)\right] = b \tag{A.54}$$

- **Differentiating the product of a matrix and a vector with respect to a vector.** The result is a matrix, for example,

$$\frac{d}{dx(t)}\left[Bx(t)\right] = B' \tag{A.55}$$

- **Differentiating the matrix exponential with respect to a scalar.** The result is the analogue of the scalar exponential differentiation, for example,

$$\frac{d}{d\tau}\exp(B\tau) = B\exp(B\tau) = \exp(B\tau)B \tag{A.56}$$

- **Integrating the matrix exponential with respect to a scalar.** The result follows from the previous point, for example,

$$\int \exp(B\tau)\, d\tau = B^{-1} \exp(B\tau) = \exp(B\tau)\, B^{-1} \tag{A.57}$$

Notes

Chapter 2   A New Framework for a New Environment

1 For in-depth treatments see, for example, Romer (2001) on macroeconomic modeling, Walsh (2003) on monetary policy, and Mishkin (2004) on monetary policy and financial markets.
2 As an additional technical point, macroeconomic data are typically based on surveys and/or partial data. Hence, they are themselves estimates provided by the relevant statistical agency rather than definitive values for the state of the economy.
3 The Lombardi and Zhu (2014) shadow short rate is not derived from a shadow/ZLB-GATSM. It uses factors extracted from interest rate, monetary aggregates, and central bank balance sheet data to produce a shadow short rate measure.
4 The ZLB mechanism would also work for non-GATSM models (e.g., models with mixed square-root and Gaussian dynamics), but the solutions and interpretation may be more complex than for GATSMs.
5 Black (1995) did not actually include the given expression, because it was a conceptual and descriptive paper. However, the applications of the Black (1995) framework referenced in chapter 5 all specify the expression, which is consistent with the description in Black (1995), while rightfully attributing it to Black (1995). The name "shadow short rate" is from Black (1995), but it does not necessarily imply a shadow price in the usual economic sense. That is, it does not appear to have been obtained as a marginal change for a given objective function with respect to a constraint, although it may be possible to do so.

Chapter 3   Gaussian Affine Term Structure Models

1 This is the "essentially affine" specification from Duffee (2002), but for a model with full Gaussian dynamics. Also see Cheridito, Filipović, and Kimmel (2007) for further discussion on market price of risk specifications.
2 Dai and Singleton (2002) p. 438 provides the same results, but with the left eigensystem decomposition $\kappa = V^{-1}\kappa_D V$. My right eigensystem decomposition is consistent with the default output from MatLab using $[V,D] = \text{eig}(\kappa)$.
3 As a simple illustration, compounding the returns from a coin flip process that gives a ±50 percent return on top of a mean 50 percent return results in a total return of $(1.5 + 0.5) \times (1.5 - 0.5) = 2$. Compounding the returns based on the mean return gives a total return of $1.5 \times 1.5 = 2.25$. Ito's lemma (e.g., see James and Webber [2000] pp. 92-93) is typically used to obtain the volatility effect by specifying bond prices as a function of the stochastic short rate under the $\mathbb{Q}$ measure.

4 Greene (1997) pp. 210-14 also provides an excellent discussion on optimization with constraints, including alternative ways that the constraints noted could be imposed (e.g. using exponentials of proxy parameters to enforce positivity, and a logistic function to respect a range).

5 Krippner (2006) presents a more restricted version of the ANSM(3) with constant risk premiums and uncorrelated state variables.

6 My preferred name, "Bow", is often referred to as "Curvature" in Diebold and Rudebusch (2013) and the related literature. However, the Slope component itself has a natural curvature, resulting from its exponential decay functional form. Hence "Bow" is an unambiguous (and syllable-saving) name for the third ANSM component.

7 Alternatively, the results from the shadow/ZLB-ANSM(2) or shadow/ZLB-ANSM(3) could be used in conjunction with the Heath, Jarrow, and Morton (1992) framework to create models that were arbitrage free with respect to the data.

8 Federal Funds futures contracts also provide implied market expectations of the Federal Funds Rate, e.g., see Gurkaynak, Sack, and Swanson (2005a,b and 2007), but they are only available for shorter horizons.

9 Collateral exchange is now more routine following the GFC, but it was available by request prior to the GFC.

Chapter 4   Krippner Framework for ZLB Term Structure Modeling

1 I acknowledge a debt of gratitude to Scott Richard for comments on truncated normal distributions that ultimately led me to the deriviation presented in those papers and this book.

2 See, for example, Filipović (2009) p. 107, James and Webber (2000) pp. 99-100, or Klebaner (2005) p. 337, which discuss the Heath, Jarrow, and Morton (1992) framework under the forward measure. These references all use time and time of maturity notation $\tilde{\mathbb{E}}_T \{r(T) | \mathcal{F}_t\} = f(t, T)$, which I express equivalently using my time and time to maturity notation. The conditionality on $|\mathcal{F}_t$, which is the information set available at time t, is more general notation for my conditioning on $|x(t)$.

3 Of course, technically $\Phi[\cdot]$ does not actually have a mathematical closed-form analytic solution, but it can be treated as having one because it is so well-tabulated or approximated by closed-form analytic functions.

Chapter 5   Black Framework for ZLB Term Structure Modeling

1 Filipović (2009) already assumes $t = 0$ (see Filipović (2009) footnote 1, p. 109) without loss of generality, so no change of variables is required to convert from time-of-maturity notation to my time-to-maturity notation. That is, T and S from Filipović (2009) are respectively equivalent to my τ and $\tau + \delta$. Chen (1995) provides the bond option expression for a two-factor GATSM, and notes that the results readily extend to N factors, but

that is only the case if $\tilde{\kappa}$ has distinct eigenvalues. The generic Filipović (2009) expression accommodates GATSMs with zero eigenvalues and repeated eigenvalues for $\tilde{\kappa}$, which accommodates the ANSM(3).

2 Priebsch (2013) also notes that the first-order approximation with the two-state-variable model is equivalent to the model proposed independently in Ichiue and Ueno (2013). However, the latter authors do not report comparisons to the associated B-AGM.

Chapter 6   K-ANSM Foundations and Effective Monetary Stimulus

1 The discrete-time result is standard in time series econometrics, for example, see Hamilton (1994) pp. 7–8 and 259. The analogue in continuous time is also a standard result. That is, an nth-order stochastic differential equation can be equivalently represented as an n-dimensional first-order stochastic differential equation. See, for example, Klebaner (2005) pp. 179–80.

2 Krippner (2011) pp. 14–15 discusses the foundation for the K-AGM framework from the perspective of the partial differential equation (PDE) for the equivalent of the GCE+PC in this book. In particular, the Krippner (2011) PDE for ZLB bonds expressed here in the form of equations 5.24 and 5.25 of this book is

$$r(t) \cdot \underline{P}(t,\tau+\delta) = \frac{\partial \underline{P}(t,\tau+\delta)}{\partial \tau} + \frac{\partial \underline{P}(t,\tau+\delta)}{\partial x(t)}\tilde{\kappa}\left[\tilde{\theta}-x(t)\right] + \frac{1}{2}\sigma\sigma'\frac{\partial^2 \underline{P}(t,\tau+\delta)}{\partial x(t)\partial[x(t)]'} \quad (1)$$

where $r(t)$ is $r_{GCE+PC}(t) = d_0'x(t)$ for the GCE+PC, and $\underline{P}(t,\tau+\delta) = P(t,\tau+\delta) - C(t,\tau,\delta,1)$, using the notation of subsection 5.1.1. Krippner (2011) uses $\underline{P}(t,\tau+\delta)$ in the limit as $\delta \to 0$ to calculate instantaneous ZLB forward rates $\underline{f}(t,\tau)$. An alternative perspective would be to apply the PDE to ZLB forward bonds $\underline{P}(t,\tau,\delta)$, as discussed in section 5.1.1, and then take the limit as $\delta \to 0$. However, in either case, the GCE+PC PDE still uses the principle that the shadow short rate $r(t)$ remains the appropriate discount rate or risk-adjusted rate of return for assets in the economy.

Chapter 7   Monetary Policy Applications

1 I prefer the name "Bow" rather than "Curvature". See pp. 77–78 and footnote 7 of Chapter 3 for further comments.

Chapter 8   Financial Market Applications

1 Litterman and Sheinkman (1991) is an early example of the application of principal components to fixed interest markets. Joliffe (2002) is a comprehensive reference for the entire topic of principal components analysis and its general applications.

2 It might be possible to use the combination of the Gaussian and truncated Gaussian distributions in an approximation method analogous to Priebsch (2013), as discussed in subsection 5.6.2. I leave this to future research.

3 The method should also be readily applicable to coupon-payng bonds. That is, a coupon-paying bond price may be evaluated from the K-AGM for each set of state variables. I thank Scott Richard for making this observation.

Appendix A   Conclusion and Future Research Directions

1 Greene (1997) chapter 2 contains a variety of algebraic results for those interested in further reading.

Bibliography

Adrian, T. and M. Fleming (2013, 5 August). The recent bond market selloff in historical perspective. URL: http://libertystreeteconomics.newyorkfed.org/2013/08/the-recent-bond-market-selloff-in-historical-perspective.html.

Adrian, T., E. Moench, and R. Crump (2014). Pricing the term structure with linear regressions. *Journal of Financial Economics 110(1)*, 110–138.

Andreasen, M. and A. Meldrum (2013). Dynamic term structure models: The best way to enforce the zero lower bound. *Presented at Term Structure Modeling at the Zero Lower Bound Workshop, Federal Reserve Bank of San Francisco, 11 October 2013.*

Ang, A. and M. Piazzesi (2003). A no-arbitrage vector autoregression of term structure dynamics with latent variables. *Journal of Monetary Economics 50(4)*, 745–787.

Backus, D., S. Foresi, and C. Telmer (2010). Discrete-time models of bond pricing. In N. Jegadeesh and B. Tuckman (Eds.), *Advanced Fixed Income Valuation Tools*. Wiley.

Bauer, M. and G. Rudebusch (2013). Monetary policy expectations at the zero lower bound. *Working Paper, Federal Reserve Bank of San Francisco 18.*

Bauer, M., G. Rudebusch, and C. Wu (2012). Correcting estimation bias in dynamic term structure models. *Journal of Business and Economic Statistics 30(3)*, 454–467.

Berardi, A. and M. Esposito (1999). A base model for multifactor specifications of the term structure. *Economic Notes 28(2)*, 145–170.

Black, F. (1995). Interest rates as options. *Journal of Finance 50(7)*, 1371–1376.

Black, F., E. Derman, and W. Toy (1990). A one-factor model of interest rates and its application to Treasury bond options. *Financial Analysts Journal January-February*, 33–39.

Black, F. and P. Karasinki (1991). Bond and option pricing when short rates are lognormal. *Financial Analysts Journal July-August*, 52–59.

Bomfim, A. (2003). 'Interest Rates as Options': assessing the markets' view of the liquidity trap. *Working Paper, Federal Reserve Board of Governors 45.*

Bullard, J. (2012). Shadow Interest Rates and the Stance of U.S. Monetary Policy. *Speech at the Annual Conference, Olin Business School, Washington University in St. Louis, 8 November 2012.* URL: http://www.stlouisfed.org/newsroom/displayNews.cfm?article=1574.

Bullard, J. (2013). Perspectives on the Current Stance of Monetary Policy. *Speech at the NYU Stern, Center for Global Economy and Business, 21 February 2013.* URL: http://www.prweb.com/releases/2013/2/prweb10455633.htm.

Carriero, A., S. Mouabbi, and E. Vangelista (2014). The UK term structure at the zero lower bound. *Manuscript.*

Chen, R. (1995). A two-factor, preference-free model for interest rate sensitive claims. *Journal of Futures Markets 15(3)*, 345–372.

Chen, R. and L. Scott (1992). Pricing interest rate options in a two-factor Cox–Ingersoll-Ross model of the term structure. *Review of Financial Studies 5(4)*, 613–636.

Cheridito, P., D. Filipović, and R. Kimmel (2007). Market price of risk specifications for affine models: theory and evidence. *Journal of Financial Economics 83(1)*, 123–170.

Christensen, J., F. Diebold, and G. Rudebusch (2009). An arbitrage-free generalized Nelson-Siegel term structure model. *Econometrics Journal 12(3)*, 33–64.

Christensen, J., F. Diebold, and G. Rudebusch (2011). The affine arbitrage-free class of Nelson-Siegel term structure models. *Journal of Econometrics 164(1)*, 4–20.

Christensen, J., J. Lopez, and G. Rudebusch (2010). Inflation expectations and risk premiums in an arbitrage-free model of nominal and real bond yields. *Journal of Money, Credit, and Banking Supplement to 42(6)*, 143–178.

Christensen, J. and G. Rudebusch (2012). The response of interest rates to US and UK quantitative easing. *Economic Journal 122(564)*, F385–F414.

Christensen, J. and G. Rudebusch (2013a). Estimating shadow-rate term structure models with near-zero yields. *Manuscript*.

Christensen, J. and G. Rudebusch (2013b). Modeling yields at the zero lower bound: are shadow rates the solution? *Working Paper, Federal Reserve Bank of San Francisco 39*.

Christensen, J. and G. Rudebusch (2014b). Estimating shadow-rate term structure models with near-zero yields. *Journal of Financial Econometrics (forthcoming)*.

Claus, E., I. Claus, and L. Krippner (2014a). Asset markets and monetary policy shocks at the zero lower bound. *Working Paper, Reserve Bank of New Zealand 2014-03*.

Claus, E., I. Claus, and L. Krippner (2014b). Asset markets and monetary policy shocks at the zero lower bound. *Discussion Paper, Centre for Applied Macreconomic Analysis 42/2014*.

Cox, J., J. Ingersoll, and S. Ross (1985a). An intertemporal general equilibrium model of asset prices. *Econometrica 53(2)*, 363–384.

Cox, J., J. Ingersoll, and S. Ross (1985b). A theory of the term structure of interest rates. *Econometrica 53(2)*, 385–407.

Dahlquist, M. and L. Svensson (1996). Estimating the term structure of interest rates for monetary policy analysis. *Scandinavian Journal of Economics 98(2)*, 163–183.

Dai, Q. and K. Singleton (2002). Expectation puzzles, time-varying risk premia, and affine models of the term structure. *Journal of Financial Economics 63*, 415–441.

Diebold, F., L. Ji, and C. Li (2006). A three-factor yield curve model: non-affine structure, systematic risk sources and generalized duration. In L. Klein (Ed.), *Macroeconomics, Finance and Econometrics: Essays in Memory of Albert Ando*, pp. 240–274. Cheltenham, U.K: Edward Elgar.

Diebold, F., C. Li, and V. Yue (2008). Global yield curve dynamics and interactions: a dynamic Nelson-Siegel approach. *Journal of Econometrics 146*, 351–363.

Diebold, F. and G. Rudebusch (2013). *Yield Curve Modeling and Forecasting: The Dynamic Nelson-Siegel Approach*. Princeton University Press.

Diebold, F., G. Rudebusch, and S. Aruoba (2006). The macroeconomy and the yield curve: a dynamic latent factor approach. *Journal of Econometrics 131(1-2)*, 309–338.

Duffee, G. (2002). Term premia and interest rate forecasts in affine models. *Journal of Finance 57(1)*, 405–443.

Durbin, J. and S. Koopman (2012). *Time Series Analysis by State Space Methods, Second Edition*. Oxford University Press.

Fama, E. and R. Bliss (1987). The information in long-maturity forward rates. *American Economic Review 77(4)*, 680–692.

Feunou, B., J. Fontaine, and A. Le (2014). Term structure modeling when monetary policy is unconventional: a new approach. *Preliminary Working Paper*.

Filipović, D. (2009). *Term-Structure Models: A Graduate Course*. Springer.

Filipović, D., M. Larsson, and A. Trolle (2013). Linear-rational term structure models. *Working Paper*.

Fleming, M., J. Jackson, A. Li, A. Sarkar, and P. Zobel (2012). An analysis of OTC interest rate derivatives transactions: Implications for public reporting. *Federal Reserve Bank of New York Staff Reports 557.*

Francis, N., L. Jackson, and M. Owyang (2014). How has empirical monetary policy analysis changed after the financial crisis? *Working Paper, Federal Reserve Bank of St. Louis 2014-19A.*

Gorovoi, V. and V. Linetsky (2004). Black's model of interest rates as options, eigenfunction expansions and Japanese interest rates. *Mathematical Finance 14(1)*, 49–78.

Greene, W. (1997). *Econometric Analysis, Third Edition.* Prentice Hall.

Grewal, M. and A. Andrews (2008). *Kalman Filtering, Third Edition.* Wiley and Sons.

Gürkaynak, R., B. Sack, and E. Swanson (2005a). Do actions speak louder than words? The response of asset prices to monetary policy actions and statements. *International Journal of Central Banking 1(1)*, 55–93.

Gürkaynak, R., B. Sack, and E. Swanson (2005b). The sensitivity of long-term interest rates to economic news: evidence and implications for macroeconomic models. *American Economic Review 95(1)*, 425–436.

Gürkaynak, R., B. Sack, and E. Swanson (2007). Market-based measures of monetary policy expectations. *Journal of Business and Economic Statistics 25(2)*, 201–212.

Gürkaynak, R., B. Sack, and J. Wright (2007). The U.S. Treasury yield curve: 1961 to the present. *Journal of Monetary Economics 54(8)*, 2291–2304.

Hamilton, J. (1994). *Time Series Analysis.* Princeton University Press.

Hamilton, J. (2013, 10 November). Summarizing monetary policy. URL: http://www.econbrowser.com/archives/2013/11/summarizing-mon.html.

Hamilton, J. and J. Wu (2012). Identification and estimation of affine-term-structure models. *Journal of Econometrics 168(2)*, 315–331.

Haug, E. (2007). *The Complete Guide to Option Pricing Formulas, Second Edition.* McGraw Hill.

Heath, D., R. Jarrow, and A. Morton (1992). Bond pricing and the term structure of interest rates: a new methodology for contingent claims valuation. *Econometrica 60(1)*, 77–106.

Higgins, P. and B. Meyer (2013, 20 November). The Shadow Knows (the Fed Funds Rate). URL: http://macroblog.typepad.com/.

Hördahl, P., O. Tristani, and D. Vestin (2008). The yield curve and macroeconomic dynamics. *Economic Journal 118*, 1937–1970.

Hull, J. (2000). *Options, Futures and Other Derivitives, Fourth Edition.* Prentice Hall.

Ichiue, H. and Y. Ueno (2006). Monetary policy and the yield curve at zero interest: the macro-finance model of interest rates as options. *Working Paper, Bank of Japan 06-E-16.*

Ichiue, H. and Y. Ueno (2007). Equilibrium interest rates and the yield curve in a low interest rate environment. *Working Paper, Bank of Japan 07-E-18.*

Ichiue, H. and Y. Ueno (2013). Estimating term premia at the zero lower bound: an analysis of Japanese, US, and UK yields. *Working Paper, Bank of Japan 13-E-8.*

Ioannides, M. (2003). A comparison of yield curve estimation techniques using UK data. *Journal of Banking and Finance 27(1)*, 1–26.

Jackson, L. (2014). Monetary policy, macro factors, and the term structure at the zero lower bound. *Preliminary and incomplete manuscript.*

James, J. and N. Webber (2000). *Interest Rate Modelling.* Wiley and Sons.

Jarrow, R. (2013). The zero-lower bound on interest rates: Myth or reality? *Finance Research Letters 10(4)*, 151–156.

Joliffe, I. (2002). *Principle Components Analysis (Second Edition).* Springer-Verlag.

Joslin, S., A. Le, and K. Singleton (2013). Gaussian macro-finance term structure models with lags. *Journal of Financial Econometrics 11(4)*, 581–609.

Joslin, S., K. Singleton, and H. Zhu (2011). A new perspective on Gaussian dynamic term structure models. *Review of Financial Studies 24(3)*, 926–970.

Kim, D. and A. Orphanides (2007). The bond market term premium: What is it, and how can we measure it? *BIS Quarterly Review June*, 27–40.

Kim, D. and M. Priebsch (2013). Estimation of multi-factor shadow rate term structure models. *Preliminary Draft*.

Kim, D. and K. Singleton (2012). Term structure models and the zero bound: an empirical investigation of Japanese yields. *Journal of Econometrics 170(1)*, 32–49.

Klebaner, F. (2005). *Introduction to Stochastic Calculus With Applications, Second Edition*. Imperial College Press.

Knez, P., R. Litterman, and J. Sheinkman (1994). Explorations into factors explaining money market returns. *Journal of Finance 49(5)*, 1861–1882.

Kozicki, S., E. Santor, and L. Surchnek (2011). Unconventional monetary policy: the international experience with central bank asset purchases. *Bank of Canada Review Spring 2011*, 13–25.

Krippner, L. (2005). Attributing returns and optimising United States swaps portfolios using an intertemporally-consistent and arbitrage-free model of the yield curve. *Working Paper, University of Waikato 05/03*.

Krippner, L. (2006). A theoretically consistent version of the Nelson and Siegel class of yield curve models. *Applied Mathematical Finance 13(1)*, 39–59.

Krippner, L. (2008). A macroeconomic foundation for the Nelson and Siegel class of yield curve models. *Research Paper, University of Technology Sydney 226*.

Krippner, L. (2011). Modifying Gaussian term structure models when interest rates are near the zero lower bound. *Discussion paper, Centre for Applied Macroeconomic Analysis 36/2011*.

Krippner, L. (2012a). Measuring the stance of monetary policy in zero lower bound environments. *Discussion Paper, Reserve Bank of New Zealand DP2012/04*.

Krippner, L. (2012b). Modifying Gaussian term structure models when interest rates are near the zero lower bound. *Discussion paper, Centre for Applied Macroeconomic Analysis 5/2012*.

Krippner, L. (2012c). Modifying Gaussian term structure models when interest rates are near the zero lower bound. *Discussion Paper, Reserve Bank of New Zealand DP2012/02*.

Krippner, L. (2012d). A theoretical foundation for the Nelson and Siegel class of yield curve models. *Discussion Paper, Centre for Applied Macreconomic Analysis 11/2012*.

Krippner, L. (2013a). Efficient Jacobian evaluations for estimating zero lower bound term structure models. *Working Paper, Centre for Applied Macroeconomic Analysis 77/2013*.

Krippner, L. (2013b). Faster solutions for Black zero lower bound term structure models. *Working Paper, Centre for Applied Macroeconomic Analyis 66/2013*.

Krippner, L. (2013c). Measuring the stance of monetary policy in zero lower bound environments. *Economics Letters 118(1)*, 135–138.

Krippner, L. (2013d). A tractable framework for zero-lower-bound Gaussian term structure models. *Discussion Paper, Centre for Applied Macreconomic Analysis 49/2013*.

Krippner, L. (2013e). A tractable framework for zero-lower-bound Gaussian term structure models. *Discussion Paper, Reserve Bank of New Zealand DP2013/02*.

Krippner, L. (2014a). A generic economic model for arbitrage-free Nelson-Siegel models. *In draft*.

Krippner, L. (2014b). Measuring the stance of monetary policy in conventional and unconventional environments. *Working Paper, Centre for Applied Macroeconomic Analysis 6/2014*.

Krippner, L. (2014c). Measuring the stance of monetary policy in conventional and unconventional environments. *Working Paper*. http://conference.nber.org/confer/2014/EASE14/Krippner.pdf.

Krippner, L. (2014d). A theoretical foundation for the Nelson-Siegel class of yield curve models. *Journal of Applied Econometrics (forthcoming)*.

Kushnir, V. (2009). Building the Bloomberg interest rate curve - definitions and methodology. *Bloomberg*.

Lefebvre, T., H. Bruyninckx, and J. De Schutter (2004). Kalman filters for nonlinear systems: A comparison of performance. *International Journal of Control 77(7)*, 639–653.

Litterman, R. and J. Sheinkman (1991). Common factors affecting bond returns. *Journal of Fixed Income 2*, 54–61.

Lombardi, M. and F. Zhu (2014). A shadow policy rate to calibrate US monetary policy at the zero lower bound. *Working Paper, Bank of International Settlements 452*.

Meucci, A. (2010). Review of statistical arbitrage, cointegration, and multivariate Ornstein-Uhlenbeck. *Working Paper, SYMMYS*.

Mishkin, F. (2004). *The Economics of Money, Banking, and Financial Markets, Seventh Edition*. Pearson.

Moler, C. and C. Van Loan (2003). Nineteen dubious ways to compute the exponential of a matrix, twenty-five years later. *SIAM Review 45(1)*, 3–48.

Monfort, A., F. Pegoraro, J. Renne, and G. Roussellet (2014). Staying at zero with affine processes: a new dynamic term structure model. *Working Paper*.

Nelson, C. and A. Siegel (1987). Parsimonious modelling of yield curves. *Journal of Business 60(4)*, 473–489.

Pancost, A. (2013). Zero-coupon yields and the cross-section of bond prices. *Working Paper, University of Chicago*.

Piazzesi, M. (2010). Affine term structure models. In L. Hansen and Y. A it-Sahalia (Eds.), *Macroeconomics, Finance and Econometrics: Essays in Memory of Albert Ando*, pp. 691–766. Elsevier.

Priebsch, M. (2013). Computing arbitrage-free yields in multi-factor Gaussian shadow-rate term structure models. *Working Paper, Federal Reserve Board 2013-63*.

Priebsch, M. (2014). (Un)Conventional monetary policy and the yield curve. *Preliminary draft*.

Renne, J. (2013). A model of the euro-area yield curve with discrete policy rates. *Working Paper*.

Richard, S. (2013). A non-linear macroeconomic term structure model. *Working Paper, University of Pennsylvania*.

Romer, D. (2001). *Advanced Macroeconomics, Second Edition*. McGraw-Hill.

Rudebusch, G. (2009). The Fed's monetary policy response to the current crisis. *Federal Reserve Bank of San Francisco Economic Letter 2009-17*.

Rudebusch, G. (2010). Macro-finance models of interest rates and the economy. *The Manchester School Supplement 2010*, 25–52.

Sercu, P. and X. Wu (1997). The information content in bond model residuals: an empirical study on the Belgian bond market. *Journal of Banking and Finance 21(5)*, 685–720.

Simon, D. (2006). *Optimal State Estimation*. Wiley and Sons.

Singleton, K. (2006). *Empirical Dynamic Asset Pricing: Model Specification and Econometric Assessment.* Princeton University Press.

Svensson, L. (1994). Estimating and interpreting forward interest rates: Sweden 1992-4. *Discussion Paper, Centre for Economic Policy Research 1051.*

Svensson, L. (1995). Estimating forward interest rates with the extended Nelson and Siegel model. *Quarterly Review, Sveriges Riksbank 1995(3),* 13–26.

Swanson, E. (2011). Lets twist again: a high-frequency event-study analysis of Operation Twist and it's implications for QE2. *Brookings Papers on Economic Activity 2011 (Spring),* 151–188.

Taylor, J. (1993). Discretion versus policy rules in practice. *Carnegie-Rochester Conference Series on Public Policy 39,* 195–214.

Taylor, J. (1999). A historical analysis of monetary policy rules. In J. Taylor (Ed.), *Monetary Policy Rules,* pp. 319–341. Chicago: University of Chicago.

Tchuindjo, L. (2008). Factor's correlation in the Heath-Jarrow-Morton interest rate model. *Applied Stochastic Models in Business and Industry 24(4),* 359–368.

Tchuindjo, L. (2009). An extended Heath-Jarrow-Morton risk-neutral drift. *Applied Mathematics Letters 22(3),* 396–400.

Tuckman, B. and A. Serrat (2012). *Fixed Income Securities: Tools for Today's Markets, Third Edition.* Wiley.

Ueno, Y., N. Baba, and Y. Sakurai (2006). The use of the Black model of interest rates as options for monitoring the JGB market expectations. *Working Paper, Bank of Japan 06-E-15.*

Vasicek, O. (1977). An equilibrium characterisation of the term structure. *Journal of Financial Economics 5(2),* 177–188.

Veronesi, C. (2010). *Fixed Income Securities: Valuation, Risk, and Risk Management.* Wiley.

von Borstel, J., S. Eickmeier, and L. Krippner (2014). The interest rate pass-through in the euro area before and during the sovereign debt crisis. *Preliminary Working Paper.*

Walsh, C. (2003). *Monetary Theory and Policy, Second Edition.* MIT Press.

Williams, J. (2011). Unconventional monetary policy: lessons from the past three years. *Federal Reserve Bank of San Francisco Economic Letter 2011-31.*

Willner, R. (1996). A new tool for portfolio managers: level, slope, and curvature durations. *Journal of Fixed Income 6(1),* 48–59.

Woodford, M. (2012). Methods of policy accommodation at the interest-rate lower bound. *Speech at Jackson Hole Symposium, 20 August 2012.* URL: www.kc.frb.org/publicat/sympos/2012/mw.pdf.

Wu, J. and F. Xia (2013). Measuring the macroeconomic impact of monetary policy at the zero lower bound. *Working Paper.*

Wu, J. and F. Xia (2014). Measuring the macroeconomic impact of monetary policy at the zero lower bound. *Working Paper, National Bureau of Economic Research 20117.*

Wu, T. (2006). Macro factors and the affine term structure of interest rates. *Journal of Money, Credit and Banking 38(7),* 1847–1875.

Zumbrun, J. (2014, 1 February). Bernanke secret sauce drops Fed rate as QE quantified. URL: http://www.bloomberg.com/news/2014-01-31/bernanke-secret-sauce-drops-effective-fed-rate-as-qe-quantified.html.

Index